Negotiation Theory and Practice

Negotiation
Theory
and
Practice

Edited by

J. William Breslin
and Jeffrey Z. Rubin

**The Program on Negotiation
at Harvard Law School
Cambridge, Massachusetts**

Program on Negotiation Books

Published by the
Program on Negotiation
at Harvard Law School
513 Pound Hall
Harvard Law School
Cambridge, Mass. 02138

First published in 1991. Third printing published in 1995.

Library of Congress Cataloging-in-Publication Data

Negotiation theory and practice / edited by J. William Breslin and Jeffrey Z. Rubin.
  p. cm.
  Includes bibliographical references and indexes.

  ISBN 1-880711-00-1 : $20.00

  1. Negotiation in business. 2 Negotiation. 3. Conflict management.

  I. Breslin, J. William (John William), 1948-. II. Rubin, Jeffrey Z. III. Harvard Law School. Program on Negotiation.

HD58.6.N465   1993
658.4—dc20   93-27057
                                                                            CIP

We dedicate this book
to our Mothers,
Marguerite H. Breslin and Frances Rubin,
who have given us many valuable lessons
in the art of settling conflict through negotiation.

Contents

Section IV: The Negotiations Proper

Section V: The Negotiation Context

Section VI: Culture, Race, Gender, and Style

Section VII: Follow-up and Implementation

Section VIII: Multilateral Negotiation

Section IX: Third Party Intervention

Preface

The past several years have witnessed a dramatic increase in the study and practice of negotiation. Through our association with *Negotiation Journal* and the Program on Negotiation at Harvard Law School, we have been privileged to witness, and be part of, this growth process. The collection of edited articles presented here, though by no means exhaustive, reflects the increasing interest in the field and, we hope, serves as a useful "source book" on critical issues in contemporary negotiation scholarship and practice.

Negotiation Theory and Practice has been published for two primary reasons: First, as the editors responsible for the first seven years of *Negotiation Journal*, we believe that a periodic assessment of the field, as seen through the pages of our journal and other publications, is appropriate. The articles presented in this book of readings, in many ways, serve as a barometer of the concerns and challenges of the field. Secondly, the Program on Negotiation has been developing a draft *Curriculum for Negotiation and Conflict Management* for the last several years. The *Curriculum* consists of nine modules, each of which is meant to be a free-standing listing of teaching ideas, negotiation exercises, and suggested readings. This book of readings is organized along the same nine topic areas of the *Curriculum*, and may be used as a supplement to that publication.

Our audience here is much the same as it is for readers of *Negotiation Journal*—scholars and practitioners working in realms as diverse as international relations, labor-management relations, family mediation, the law, psychology, anthropology, the corporate world, government and public policy, and numerous other fields. All of these very diverse contexts are linked by the pivotal practice of negotiation, the way in which people and organizations work to resolve conflict, plan the future, or set policy. Authors of work in this book are known as negotiation scholars and practitioners, and most of them are known as both. In parallel fashion, we believe that the articles presented here will be of interest to both scholar and practitioner. *Negotiation Journal* has had a long-standing commitment to publishing articles that, by developing lessons of sufficient generalizability, are useful to scholars, researchers, teachers, and practitioners. It will therefore come as no surprise that we hope to reach very much the same broad range of readership through the pages of this book.

Many of the articles printed here originally appeared in the pages of *Negotiation Journal*, which is published by Plenum Publishing Corp. of New York, in cooperation with the Program on Negotiation, an inter-university applied research center based at the Harvard Law School. Two articles previously appeared in the *Journal of Social Issues*, published by Plenum and the Society for the Psychological Study of Social Issues; several articles originally appeared in a special issue of *American Behavioral Scientist*, published by Sage Publications; and one article is an adaptation of work that originally appeared in *Getting Disputes Resolved*, a book published by Jossey-Bass Inc. We are most grateful to Plenum, the Society for the Psychological Study of Social Issues, Sage Publications, and Jossey-Bass Inc. for their permission to reprint this copyrighted material. In particular, we would like to express our appreciation for the support and advice given to us on this project and over the years by several Plenum officials: Eliot L. Werner, executive editor, Carol L. Bischoff, associate vice president for journals, and Thomas Mulak, associate vice president for circulation and distribution. We also would like to acknowledge the courtesy and assistance of Mary Gallagher of Sage Publications and Alice S. Morrow of Jossey-Bass Inc.

Deborah Kolb, Executive Director of the Program on Negotiation, and Elaine Landry, Program on Negotiation Associate, are (with Jeffrey Rubin) the authors of the *Curriculum on Negotiation and Conflict Resolution*. The work on both this book and the curriculum project frequently overlapped, and it has been a pleasure to be involved with both projects.

Elaine Potter of Puritan Press Inc. and Peter Amirault of Desktop Publishing Services provided invaluable assistance in the typesetting and production of this book. We are also indebted to Betsy Goldberg, Jack Sarkissian, Carol Kaito, and Tom Pixton of the Office of the University Publisher, Harvard University, for their assistance with the first edition; and to Heather Pabrezis and Jennipher Ray of the Program on Negotiation staff, for their help in proofreading and other areas.

Most importantly, and most sincerely, we thank the authors of work in this book. Their ideas, analyses, reports, and criticism provide a rich source of information on negotiation and conflict resolution. We have greatly enjoyed working with all of these authors; their well-written, thought-provoking essays should provide many hours of reading pleasure and intellectual stimulation for anyone interested in this fascinating field.

J. William Breslin
Jeffrey Z. Rubin
Cambridge, Massachusetts
June, 1991

Acknowledgments

The following essays (listed by author name in alphabetical order) originally appeared in *Negotiation Journal*, published by Plenum Publishing Corp., 233 Spring St., New York, N.Y. 10013. They are reprinted here with permission of the publisher and copyright holder.

Aurisch, Klaus L. The Art of Preparing a Multilateral Conference, vol. 5, no. 3, pp. 279-288.

Bazerman, Max H., Russ, Lee E., and Yakura, Elaine. Post-Settlement Settlements in Two-Party Negotiations, vol. 3, no. 3, pp. 283-292.

Breslin, J. William. Breaking Away from Subtle Biases, vol. 5, no. 3, pp. 219-222.

Davis, Albie M. An Interview with Mary Parker Follett, vol. 5, no. 3, pp. 223-235.

Fisher, Roger. Negotiating Inside Out: What are the Best Ways to Relate Internal Negotiations with External Ones?, vol. 5, no. 1, pp. 33-41.

Fisher, Roger. Beyond *YES*, vol. 1, no. 1, pp. 67-70.

Gilkey, Roderick and Greenhalgh, Leonard. The Role of Personality in Successful Negotiating, vol. 2, no. 3, pp. 245-256.

Goldberg, Stephen B., Green, Eric D. and Sander, Frank E. A. Saying You're Sorry, vol. 3, no. 3, pp. 221-224.

Heckscher, Charles. Multilateral Negotiation and the Future of American Labor, vol. 2, no. 2, pp. 141-154.

Honeyman, Christopher. Bias and Mediators' Ethics, vol. 2, no. 2, pp. 175-178.

Janosik, Robert J. Rethinking the Culture-Negotiation Link, vol. 3, no. 4, pp. 385-395.

Kolb, Deborah M. and Silbey, Susan S. Enhancing the Capacity of Organizations to Deal with Disputes, vol. 6, no. 4, pp. 297-304.

Kremenyuk, Victor A. The Emerging System of International Negotiations, vol. 4, no. 3, pp. 211-218.

Kriesberg, Louis. Timing and the Initiation of De-Escalation Moves, vol. 3, no. 4, pp. 375-384.

Lax, David A. and Sebenius, James K. The Power of Alternatives or the Limits to Negotiation, vol. 1, no. 2, pp. 163-179.

Lax, David A. and Sebenius, James K. Interests: The Measure of Negotiation, vol. 2, no. 1, pp. 73-92.

McCarthy, William. The Role of Power and Principle in *Getting to YES*, vol. 1, no. 1, pp. 59-66.

McKersie, Robert B. The Eastern Airlines Saga: Grounded by a Contest of Wills, vol. 5, no. 3, pp. 213-218.

Nyerges, Janos. Ten Commandments for a Negotiator, vol. 3, no. 1, pp. 21-27.

Raiffa, Howard. Post-Settlement Settlements, vol. 1, no. 1, pp. 9-12.

Raiffa, Howard. Mock Pseudo-Negotiations with Surrogate Disputants, vol. 1, no. 2, pp. 111-115.

Roth, Alvin E. Some Additional Thoughts on Post-Settlement Settlements, vol. 1, no. 3, pp. 245-247.

Rowe, Mary P. The Corporate Ombudsman: An Overview and Analysis, vol. 3, no. 2, pp. 127-140.

Rubin, Jeffrey Z. and Sander, Frank E. A. When Should We Use Agents? Direct vs. Representative Negotiation, vol. 4, no. 4, pp. 395-401.

Salacuse, Jeswald W. Your Draft or Mine?, vol. 5, no. 4, pp. 337-341.

Salacuse, Jeswald W. Making Deals in Strange Places: A Beginner's Guide to International Business Negotiations, vol. 4, no. 1, pp. 5-13.

Salacuse, Jeswald W. Renegotiations in International Business, vol. 4, no. 4, pp. 347-354.

Saunders, Harold H. We Need a Larger Theory of Negotiation: The Importance of Pre-Negotiating Phases, vol. 1, no. 3, pp. 249-265.

Schelling, Thomas C. Strategy and Self-Command, vol. 5, no. 4, pp. 343-347.

Smith, William P. Effectiveness of the Biased Mediator, vol. 1, no. 4, pp. 363-372.

Touval, Saadia. Multilateral Negotiation: An Analytic Approach, vol. 5, no. 2, pp. 159-173.

Ury, William L. and Smoke, Richard. Anatomy of a Crisis, vol. 1, no. 1, pp. 93-100.

Zartman, I. William. Common Elements in the Analysis of the Negotiation Process, vol. 4, no. 1, pp. 31-43.

*   *   *

Section 1

The Nature of Conflict and Negotiation

Conflict is at least as old as Cain and Abel. Negotiation has an even longer history, going back to one of the world's first Great Deals, when the Serpent tempted Eve, who then proceeded to make an offer to Adam that he just couldn't refuse.

Almost as old as conflict and negotiation is human interest in understanding how to get one's way. Far more recent, however, is the systematic exploration of the theoretical underpinnings of conflict and negotiation. It has really only been within the last several decades of this century that scholars and practitioners (outside of the diplomatic community) have come to recognize these areas as comprising a distinct field of study.

While this field is still young, it is already highly complex. This complexity stems not only from the mix of research and practice, theory and application, but also from the variety of intellectual disciplines that have focused attention on conflict and negotiation. For example, the essays in this first section feature the work of authors whose primary fields of study are anthropology, political science, social psychology, and international relations. It is precisely because of the rich array of disciplines that comprise conflict and negotiation studies that it has proven so very difficult to distill their common elements. As a result, the challenge of identifying the boundaries of our developing field remains.

Each of the four papers comprising Section I attempts in its own way to address the problems of boundary and overlap. Thus, Jeffrey Z. Rubin's essay ("Some Wise and Mistaken Assumptions about Conflict and Negotiation") places negotiation within the broader context of approaches to the settlement of conflict. He distinguishes conflict *resolution* from conflict *settlement*, arguing that negotiation is primarily the province of settlement. Rarely, if ever, can negotiation be appropriately used to bring about the fundamental change in individuals or organizations that is implied by the term "resolution." The essay outlines a set of general considerations, each of which has implications for a more complete understanding of both conflict and negotiation.

Mary Parker Follett, whose writings are the subject of the second essay, worked in the early twentieth century and is known as one of the founders of the organizational behavior studies field. Follett's approach to management in organizational settings is as pertinent today as it was when her ideas first appeared nearly a century ago. Of particular relevance to this book are her writings as one of the earliest proponents of the "collaborative problem solving" or "integrative approach" to negotiation. In her creative essay, Albie M. Davis ("An Interview with Mary Parker Follett") uses an "interview" with the long-deceased Mary Parker Follett to present an important sampling of the writings of this influential thinker.

The third essay ("Strategic Choice in Negotiation"), by Dean G. Pruitt, extends Follett's analysis by outlining four major strategic choices that are available to negotiators: *problem solving*, which involves developing mutually acceptable alternatives; *contending*, or forcing one's own will on another; *yielding*, an approach that entails lowering one's expectations or goals; and *inaction*, or purposefully introducing the passage of time. Pruitt's essay moves from this helpful typology to prescriptive advice about the circumstances under which one strategic choice is preferable to another.

Finally, William L. Ury and Richard Smoke's article ("Anatomy of a Crisis") places the work on conflict and negotiation in a highly specific, but extremely important context: a crisis. The authors introduce four factors, each of which is particularly prominent in crisis situations, and which interact with one another: *high stakes, little time, high uncertainty*, and *a sense of narrowing options*. These factors, of course, can be found not only in crises, but in *any* instance of conflict, to a greater or lesser degree.

Some Wise and Mistaken Assumptions About Conflict and Negotiation

Jeffrey Z. Rubin

For many years the attention of conflict researchers and theorists was directed to the laudable objective of conflict *resolution*. This term denotes as an outcome a state of attitude change that effectively brings an end to the conflict in question. In contrast, conflict *settlement* denotes outcomes in which the overt conflict has been brought to an end, even though the underlying bases may or may not have been addressed. The difference here is akin to Herbert Kelman's (1958) useful distinction among the three consequences of social influence: compliance, identification, and internalization. If conflict settlement implies the consequence of compliance (a change in behavior), then conflict resolution instead implies internalization (a more profound change, of underlying attitudes as well as behavior). The third consequence, *identification*, denotes a change in behavior that is based on the target of influence valuing his or her relationship with the source, and it serves as a bridge between behavior change and attitude change.

In keeping with the flourishing research in the 1950s on attitudes and attitude change, social psychological research on conflict in the 1950s and 1960s focused on conflict *resolution*. Only recently has there been a subtle shift in focus from attitude change to behavior change. Underlying this shift is the view that, while it is necessary that attitudes change if conflict is to be eliminated, such elimination is often simply not possible. Merely getting Iran and Iraq, Turkish and Greek Cypriots, Contras and Sandinistas to lay down their weapons — even temporarily — is a great accomplishment in its own right, even if the parties continue to hate each other. And this simple act of cessation, when coupled with other such acts, may eventually generate the momentum necessary to move antagonists out of stalemate toward a settlement of their differences. Just as "stateways" can change "folkways" (Deutsch and Collins, 1951), so too can a string of behavioral changes produce the basis for subsequent attitude change.

The gradual shift over the last years from a focus on resolution to a focus on settlement has had an important implication for the conflict field: It has increased the importance of understanding *negotiation* — which, after all, is a method of settling conflict rather than resolving it. The focus of negotiation is not attitude change per se, but an agreement to change behavior in ways that make settlement possible. Two people with underlying differences of beliefs or values (for example, over the issue of a woman's right to abortion or the existence of a higher deity) may come to change their views through

Jeffrey Z. Rubin is Professor of Psychology at Tufts University, Medford, Mass. and a Senior Fellow of the Program on Negotiation at Harvard Law School.

discussion and an exchange of views, but it would be inappropriate and inaccurate to describe such an exchange as "negotiation."

Similarly, the shift from resolution to settlement of conflict has also increased the attention directed to the role of *third parties* in the conflict settlement process — individuals who are in some way external to a dispute and who, through identification of issues and judicious intervention, attempt to make it more likely that a conflict can be moved to settlement.

Finally, the shift in favor of techniques of conflict settlement has piqued the interest and attention of practitioners in a great many fields, ranging from divorce mediators and couples' counselors to negotiators operating in environmental, business, labor, community, or international disputes. Attitude change may not be possible in these settings, but behavior change — as the result of skillful negotiation or third-party intervention — is something else entirely. Witness the effective mediation by the Algerians during the so-called Iranian hostage crisis in the late 1970s; as a result of Algerian intervention, the Iranian government came to dislike the American Satan no less than before, but the basis for a *quid pro quo* had been worked out.

Cooperation, Competition, and Enlightened Self-Interest

Required for effective conflict settlement is neither cooperation nor competition, but what may be referred to as "enlightened self-interest." By this I simply mean a variation on what several conflict theorists have previously described as an "individualistic orientation" (Deutsch, 1960) — an outlook in which the disputant is simply interested in doing well for himself or herself, without regard for anyone else, out neither to help nor hinder the other's efforts to obtain his or her goal. The added word "enlightened" refers to the acknowledgment by each side that the other is also likely to be pursuing a path of self-interest — and that it may be possible for *both* to do well in the exchange. If there are ways in which I can move toward my objective in negotiation, while at the same time making it possible for you to approach your goal, then why not behave in ways that make both possible?

Notice that what I am describing here is neither pure individualism (where one side does not care at all about how the other is doing) nor pure cooperation (where each side cares deeply about helping the other to do well, likes and values the other side, etc.) — but an amalgam of the two.

Trivial though this distinction may seem, it has made it possible in recent years for work to develop that, paradoxically, creates a pattern of *inter*dependence out of the assumption of *in*dependence. Earlier work, focusing as it did on the perils of competition and the virtues of cooperation, made an important contribution to the field of conflict studies. However, in doing so, it also shifted attention away from the path of individualism — a path that is likely to provide a way out of stalemate and toward a settlement of differences. I do not have to like or trust you in order to negotiate wisely with you. Nor do I have to be driven by the passion of a competitive desire to beat you. All that is necessary is for me to find some way of getting what I want — perhaps even *more* than I considered possible — by leaving the door open for you too to do well. "Trust" and "trustworthiness," concepts central to the development of cooperation, are no longer necessary — only the understanding of what the other person may want or need.

A number of anecdotes have emerged to make this point; perhaps the most popular is the tale of two sisters who argue over the division of an orange between them (Fisher and Ury, 1981; Follett, 1940). Each would like the entire orange, and only reluctantly do the sisters move from extreme demands to a 50-50 split. While such a solution is eminently fair, it is not necessarily wise: one sister proceeds to peel the orange, discard the peel, and eat her half of the fruit; the other peels the orange, discards the fruit, and uses her 50% of the peel to bake a cake! If only the two sisters had understood what each wanted the orange for — not each side's "position," but rather each side's underlying "interest" — an agreement would have been possible that would have allowed each to get everything that she wanted.

Similarly, Jack Sprat and his wife — one preferring lean, the other fat — can lick the platter clean if they understand their respective interests. The interesting thing about this conjugal pair is that, married though they may be, when it comes to dining preferences they are hardly interdependent at all. For Jack and his wife to "lick the platter clean" requires neither that the two love each other nor care about helping each other in every way possible; nor does it require that each be determined to get more of the platter's contents than the other. Instead, it is enlightened self-interest that makes possible an optimal solution to the problem of resource distribution.

The lesson for international relations is instructive. For the United States and the Soviet Union, Israel and its Arab neighbors, Iran and Iraq, the Soviet Union and Afghanistan, the United States and Nicaragua to do well, neither cooperation nor competition is required, but rather an arrangement that acknowledges the possibility of a more complex mixture of these two motivational states — enlightened individualism. While the United States and Soviet Union will continue to have many arenas of conflict in which their interests are clearly and directly opposed, and will also continue to find new opportunities for cooperation (as in the management of nuclear proliferation, hazardous waste disposal, or international political terrorism), there are also arenas in which each side is not at all as dependent on the other for obtaining what it wants (e.g., the formulation of domestic economic or political policy). The world is a very big place; the pie is big enough for both of us, and for many others, (as my grandmother might have said) to live and be well![1]

A Common Process Substrate

It has been fashionable for several years now to observe that conflicts are fundamentally alike, whether they take place between individuals, within or between groups, communities, or nations. Nevertheless, conflict analysts in each of these domains have tended not to listen closely to one another, and have largely proceeded as if international conflict, labor disputes, and family spats are distinct and unrelated phenomena.

Within the last decade or so, with the advent of conflict and negotiation programs around the United States, a different point of view has begun to emerge: one that argues for a common set of processes that underlie all forms of conflict and their settlement.[2] Third-party intervention — whether in divorce, international business and trade negotiations, a labor dispute, a conflict over nuclear siting or hazardous waste disposal, or an international border dispute — follows certain principles that dictate its likely effectiveness. Similarly, the principles of negotiation apply with equal vigor to conflicts at all levels of complexity, whether two or more than two parties are involved, negotiating one issue or many issues, with problems varying in difficulty, etc.

Acceptance of this bit of ideology has had an extremely important effect on the field of conflict studies, for it has made it possible for conversations to take place among theorists and practitioners, at work in an extraordinarily rich and varied set of fields. Anthropologists, sociologists, lawyers, psychologists, economists, business men and women, community activists, labor experts, to name but a few, have now started to come together to exchange ideas, to map areas of overlap and divergence. This, in turn, has made it possible for the development of conflict theory and practice to take shape under a larger umbrella than ever before. In fact, the symbolic location of these conversations is more like a circus tent than an umbrella, with beasts of different stripe, size, and coloring all finding a place under the big top.

Most recently, yet another twist has appeared. Having emerged in fruitful preliminary conversations about the nature of conflict and negotiation in their respective fields and disciplines, scholars and practitioners are now turning to areas of *divergence* rather than *similarity*. Instead of homogenizing theory and practice in the different social sciences, analysts are now beginning to look beyond the areas of process similarity to the distinguishing features that characterize dispute management in different arenas.

At another but related level, conflict analysts are at last beginning to acknowledge that our pet formulations have been devised by, and are directed to, a community that is predominantly white, Western, male, and upper middle class. Now that fruitful conversations have begun to take place among members of our own intellectual community, it is becoming clear that some of our most cherished ideas may be limited in their applicability and generalizability. Other societies — indeed, other people within our own society — may not always "play the conflict game" by the set of rules that scholars and researchers have deduced on the basis of American paradigms.

As one example of what I mean, "face saving" has been an extremely important element of most conflict/negotiation formulations: the idea that people in conflict will go out of their way to avoid being made to look weak or foolish in the eyes of others and themselves. While face saving seems important in the United States and in countries such as Japan or Korea, less obvious is the extent to which this issue is of *universal* significance. Do Pacific Islanders, Native Americans, or South Asians experience "face," and therefore the possibility of "loss of face?" It is not clear. Do women experience face saving and face loss, or is this a phenomenon that is largely restricted to the XY genetic portion of the population?

Similarly, what does it mean to set a "time limit" in negotiations in different cultures? Do other cultures measure a successful negotiation outcome the same way we tend to in this country? Are coalitions considered equally acceptable, and are they likely to form in much the same way, from one country to the next? Do different countries structure the negotiating environment — everything from the shape of the negotiating table to the presence of observing audiences and various constituencies — in the same way? The answers to questions such as these are not yet in, and we must therefore learn to be cautious in our propensity to advance a set of "universal" principles.

The Importance of "Relationship" in Negotiation

Much of the negotiation analysis that has taken place over the last 25 years has focused on the "bottom line": who gets how much once an agreement has been reached. The emphasis has thus largely been an *economic* one, and this emphasis has been strengthened by the significant role of game theory and other mathematical or economic formulations.

This economic focus is being supplanted by a richer, and more accurate, portrayal of negotiation in terms not only of economic, but also of relational, considerations. As any visitor to the Turkish Bazaar in Istanbul will tell you, the purchase of an oriental carpet involves a great deal more than the exchange of money for an old rug. The emerging relationship between shop-keeper and customer is far more significant, weaving ever so naturally into the economic aspects of the transaction. An initial conversation about the selling price of some item is quickly transformed into an exchange of a more personal nature: Who one is, where one is from, stories about one's family and friends, impressions of the host country, and lots more. When my wife and I purchased several rugs in Turkey some years ago, we spent three days in conversation with the merchant — not because that is how long it took to "cut the best deal," but because we were clearly having a fine time getting to know one another over Turkish coffee, Turkish delight, and Turkish taffy. When, at the end of our three-day marathon transaction, the shopkeeper invited us to consider opening a carpet store in Boston that could be used to distribute his wares, I was convinced that this invitation was extended primarily to sustain an emerging relationship — rather than to make a financial "killing" in the United States.

Psychologists, sociologists, and anthropologists have long understood the importance of "relationship" in any interpersonal transaction, but only recently have conflict analysts begun to take this as seriously as it deserves. Although it seems convenient to distinguish negotiation in one-time-only exchanges (ones where you have no history of contact with the other party, come together for a "quickie," and then expect never to see the other again) from negotiation in ongoing relationships, this distinction is more illusory than real. Rarely does one negotiate in the absence of future consequences. Even if you and I meet once and once only, our reputations have a way of surviving the exchange, coloring the expectations that others will have of us in the future.

Negotiation in a Temporal Context

For too long, analysts have considered only the negotiations proper, rather than the sequence of events preceding negotiation and the events that must transpire if a concluded agreement is to be implemented successfully. Only recently, as analysts have become more confident in their appraisal of the factors that influence effective negotiation, has attention been directed to the past and future, as anchors of the negotiating present.

Analysts of international negotiation (e.g., Saunders, 1985) have observed that some of the most important work takes place *before the parties ever come to the table*. Indeed, once they get to the table, all that typically remains is a matter of crossing the *t*'s and dotting the *i*'s in an agreement hammered out beforehand. It is during *prenegotiation* that the pertinent parties to the conflict are identified and invited to participate, that a listing of issues is developed and prioritized as an agenda, and that the formula by which a general agreement is to be reached is first outlined. Without such a set of preliminary understandings, international negotiators may well refuse to sit down at the same table with one another.

Prenegotiation is important in other contexts as well, something I discovered in conversation with a successful Thai businessman. He observed that Thais are extremely reluctant to confront an adversary in negotiation, or to show any sign whatsoever of disagreement, let alone conflict. Yet many Thais have succeeded admirably in negotiating agreements that are to their advantage. The key to their success is prenegotiation, making sure beforehand that there really *is* an agreement before labeling the process "negotiation," before ever sitting down with that other person. In effect, they use prenegotiation to arrange matters to their own advantage, and they do so without ever identifying the relationship with the other party as conflictual, or signaling in any way that concessions or demands are being made.

At the other end of the temporal continuum lies the matter of follow-up and implementation. To reach an agreement through negotiation is not enough. Those parties who are in a position to sabotage this agreement, unless their advice is solicited and incorporated, must be taken into account if a negotiated agreement is to succeed. (Witness the failure of the Michael Dukakis campaign to consult sufficiently with Jesse Jackson and his supporters, prior to the 1988 Democratic Party convention in Atlanta.) Note the trade-off here: The greater number of parties to a negotiation, the more difficult it will be to reach any agreement at all. But only if the relevant parties and interests are included in the negotiations is the agreement reached likely to "stick."

As negotiation analysts have broadened the temporal spectrum to include pre- and post-negotiation processes, more work has been done toward devising creative options for improving upon the proceedings. To cite but one example, Howard Raiffa (1985) has proposed a procedure known as "post-settlement settlement," by which parties who have already concluded an agreement are given an opportunity — with the assistance of a third party — to improve upon their agreement. The third party examines the facts and figures that each side has used in reaching a settlement; based on this information, which is kept in strict confidence, the third party proposes a settlement that improves upon the agreement reached. Either side can veto this post-settlement settlement, in which case the *status quo ante* remains in effect. However, if both sides endorse the proposed improvement on the existing contract, then each stands to benefit from this proposal — and the third party, in turn, is guaranteed a percentage of the "added value" of the contract.

Negotiating from the Inside Out

Conventional wisdom regarding effective negotiation calls for the parties to start by making extreme opening offers, then conceding stepwise until an agreement is reached. If you want to sell a used car, purchase a rug, secure a new wage package or settle a territorial dispute with a neighboring country, you begin by asking for more than you expect to settle for, then gradually move inward until you and the other side overlap; at that point you have got a negotiated settlement.

A large body of negotiation analysis has proceeded in accordance with this conventional wisdom. Moreover, this way of negotiating "from the outside in" makes good sense for several reasons: It allows each negotiator to explore various possible agreements before settling, to obtain as much information as possible about the other negotiator and his or her preferences, before closing off discussion (Kelley, 1966). It also allows each party to give its respective constituency some sense of the degree to which the other side has already been "moved," thereby maintaining constituency support for the positions taken in negotiation.

On the other hand, this "traditional" way of conducting the business of negotiation ignores an important and creative alternative: working "from the inside out." Instead of beginning with extreme opening offers, then moving slowly and inexorably from this stance until agreement is reached, it often makes sense to start with an exchange of views about underlying needs and interests — and on the basis of such an exchange, to build an agreement that both parties find acceptable. The key to such an approach is, as negotiation analysts have observed (e.g., Fisher and Ury, 1981), to work at the level of interests rather than positions —what one really needs and wants (and why), rather than what one states that one would like to have.

This was precisely what happened in October of 1978 at Camp David where, with the mediation of President Jimmy Carter and his subordinates, President Anwar Sadat of Egypt and Prime Minister Menachem Begin of Israel were able to settle the disposition of the Sinai Peninsula. The Sinai had been taken by the Israelis in 1967, and its complete and immediate return had been demanded by the Egyptians ever since. Had the discussions about the fate of the Sinai been conducted solely at the level of positions — with each side demanding total control of the land in question, then making step-wise concessions from these extreme opening offers — *no* agreement would have been possible. Instead, with assistance from President Carter, the Egyptians and Israelis identified their own respective underlying interests — and were able to move to an agreement that allowed the Israelis to obtain the security they required, while the Egyptians obtained the territory they required. "Security in exchange for territory" was the formula used here, and it was a formula devised not by moving from the outside in, but by building up an agreement from the inside out.

A useful variation on this inside-out idea is the "one-text" negotiation procedures (Fisher, 1981), whereby a mediator develops a single negotiating text that is critiqued and improved by each side until a final draft is developed for approval by the interested parties. Instead of starting with demands that are gradually abandoned, the negotiators criticize a single document that is rewritten to take these criticisms into account, and eventually —through this sort of inside-out procedure — a proposal is developed for which both sides have some sense of ownership.

The Role of "Ripeness"

Although it is comforting to assume people can start negotiating any time they want, such is not the case. First of all, just as it takes two hands to clap, it takes two to negotiate. *You* may be ready to come to the table for serious discussion, but your counterpart may not. Unless you are both at the table (or connected by a telephone line or cable link), no agreement is possible.

Second, even if both of you are present at the same place, at the same time, one or both of you may not be sufficiently motivated to take the conflict seriously. It is tempting to sit back, do nothing, and hope that the mere passage of time will turn events to your advantage. People typically do not sit down to negotiate unless and until they have reached a point of "stalemate," where each no longer believes it possible to obtain what he or she wants through efforts at domination or coercion (Kriesberg, 1987). It is only at this point, when the two sides grudgingly acknowledge the need for joint work if any agreement is to be reached, that negotiation can take place.

By "ripeness," then, I mean a stage of conflict in which all parties are ready to take their conflict seriously, and are willing to do whatever may be necessary to bring the conflict to a close. To pluck fruit from a tree before it is ripe is as problematic as waiting too long. There is a *right* time to negotiate, and the wise negotiator will attempt to seek out this point.

It is also possible, of course, to help "create" such a right time. One way of doing so entails the use of threat and coercion, as the two sides (either with or without the assistance of an outside intervenor) walk (or are led) to the edge of "lover's leap," stare into the abyss below, and contemplate the consequences of failing to reach an agreement. The farther the drop — that is, the more terrible the consequences of failing to settle — the greater the pressure on each side to take the conflict seriously. There are at least two serious problems with such "coercive" means of creating a ripe conflict: First, as can be seen in the history of the arms race between the United States and the Soviet Union, it encourages further conflict escalation, as each side tries to "motivate" the other to settle by upping the ante a little bit at a time. Second, such escalatory moves invite a game of "chicken," in which each hopes that the other will be the first to succumb to coercion.

There is a second — and far *better* — way to create a situation that is ripe for settlement: namely, through the introduction of new opportunities for joint gain. If each side can be persuaded that there is more to gain than to lose through collaboration — that by working jointly, rewards can be harvested that stand to advance each side's respective agenda — then a basis for agreement can be established. In the era of *glasnost*, the United States and Soviet Union are currently learning this lesson — namely, that by working together they can better address problems of joint interest, the solution of which advances their respective self-interest. Arms control stands to save billions of dollars and rubles in the strained budgets of both nations, while advancing the credibility of each country in the eyes of the larger world community. The same is true of joint efforts to slow the consequences of the "greenhouse effect" on the atmosphere, to explore outer space, and to preserve and protect our precious natural resources in the seas.

A "Residue" that Changes Things

It is tempting for parties to a conflict to begin by experimenting with a set of adversarial, confrontational moves in the hope that these will work. Why not give hard bargaining a try at first, since if moves such as threat, bluff, or intimidation work as intended, the other side may give up without much of a fight? Moreover, even if such tactics fail, one can always shift to a more benign stance. The problem with such a sticks-to-carrots approach is that once one has left the path of joint problem solving, it may be very difficult to return again. It takes two people to cooperate, but only one person is usually required to make a mess of a relationship. The two extremes of cooperation and competition, collaboration and confrontation, are thus *not* equally balanced; it is far easier to move from cooperation to competition than the other way around.

In the course of hard bargaining, things are often said and done that change the climate of relations in ways that do not easily allow for a return to a less confrontational stance. A "residue" is left behind (Pruitt and Rubin, 1986), in the form of words spoken or acts committed, which cannot be denied and which may well change the relationship. The words, "I've never really liked or respected you," spoken in the throes of an angry exchange, may linger like a bad taste in the mouth, even when the conflict has apparently been settled. Similarly, a brandished fist or some other threatening gesture may leave scars that long outlive the heat of the moment. Thus, the escalation of conflict often carries with it moves and maneuvers that alter a relationship in ways that the parties do not anticipate.

The implication of this point for conflict and negotiation studies is clear: Insufficient attention has been directed to the lasting consequences of confrontational tactics. Too often scholars, researchers, and practitioners have assumed cooperation and competition are equally weighted, when in fact cooperation is a slippery slope; once left, the path leading to return is difficult indeed. Required for such a return journey is a combination of cooperation and persistence — the willingness to make a unilateral collaborative overture, and then to couple this with the tenacity necessary to persuade the other side that this collaborative overture is to be taken seriously (Axelrod, 1984; Fisher and Brown, 1988).

NOTES

1. Two recent books (Lax and Sebenius, 1986; Susskind and Cruickshank, 1987) treat rather extensively the topic of enlightened self-interest, pointing out the ways of expanding the resource pie, or finding uses for it that satisfy the interest of each side.

2. See, for example, the draft curriculum developed in cooperation with the Program on Negotiation for use in universities outside the United States.

REFERENCES

Axelrod, R. (1984). *The evolution of cooperation*. New York: Basic Books.

Deutsch, M. (1960). "The effect of motivational orientation upon trust and suspicion." *Human Relations* 13:123-139.

———. and **Collins, M. E.** (1951). *Interracial housing: A psychological evaluation of a social experiment*. Minneapolis: University of Minnesota Press.

Fisher, R. (1981). "Playing the wrong game?" In J. Z. Rubin (ed.), *Dynamics of third party intervention: Kissinger in the Middle East*. New York: Praeger.

———. and **Ury, W. L.** (1981). *Getting to YES: Negotiating agreement without giving in*. Boston: Houghton Mifflin.

Follett, M. P. (1940). "Constructive conflict." In H.C. Metcalf and L. Urwick (eds.), *Dynamic administration: The collected papers of Mary Parker Follett*. New York: Harper.

Kelley, H. H. (1966). "A classroom study of the dilemmas in interpersonal negotiations." In K. Archibald (ed.), *Strategic interaction and conflict: Original papers and discussion*. Berkeley, Calif.: Institute of International Studies.

Kelman, H. C. (1958). "Compliance, identification, and internalization: Three processes of attitude change." *Journal of Conflict Resolution* 2:51-60.

Kriesberg, L. (1987). "Timing and the initiation of de-escalation moves." *Negotiation Journal* 3:375-384

Lax, D. A., and **Sebenius, J.** (1986). *The manager as negotiator*. New York: Free Press.

Pruitt, D. G., and **Rubin J. Z.** (1986). *Social conflict: Escalation, stalemate, and settlement*. New York: Random House.

Raiffa, H. (1985). "Post-settlement settlements." *Negotiation Journal* 1:9-12.

Russell, R. W. (ed.). (1961). "Psychology and policy in a nuclear age." *Journal of Social Issues* 17 (3).

Saunders, H. H. (1985). "We need a larger theory of negotiation: The importance of prenegotiating phases." *Negotiation Journal* 2:249-262.

Susskind, L., and **Cruickshank, J.** (1987). *Breaking the Impasse*. New York: Basic Books.

An Interview with Mary Parker Follett

Albie M. Davis

In the early 1900s, long before contemporary authors on the subject, Mary Parker Follett was an advocate for creative and constructive approaches toward conflict resolution. Yet today, few of us know her name or have read her work. Why did Follett fade from our view? One reason, given by an admirer of hers, Elliot M. Fox, appeared in a 1968 publication honoring what would have been her 100th birthday: "She almost always expressed herself in simple, fairly commonplace terms. Perhaps she would be more carefully studied if she had developed a jargon that invited periodic efforts at interpretation. As it is, her phraseology was so ordinary that few feel the need to explain it" (Fox, 1968). Undoubtedly there are additional explanations why she did not maintain her reputation as a pioneer, and it would be interesting to explore them. For the time being, however, the most important task is to bring Follett's ideas back into our line of vision. We have much to learn and she has much to teach us. I have designed this article to encourage that process.

Far ahead of her times, Follett moved easily between the worlds of theory and practice, between interpersonal examples and international ones, between speculation and assurance. Her writing remains fresh, nondogmatic, experimental, and inspiring. To paraphrase her would be to do her a disservice. For that reason, I use the device of an imaginary interview. The questions are mine and, I hope, yours. Follett's responses are entirely in her own words as recorded in three books: *The New State* (1918) and *The Creative Experience* (1924), which she authored, and *Dynamic Administration* (1942), a collection of her papers. Citations are provided at the end of each answer and will appear as follows: *The New State*, (NS); *The Creative Experience*, (CE); and *Dynamic Administration*, (DA). Full information on each citation is available in the accompanying reference section.

The brief second section of the article begins to answer the question, "Who was Mary Parker Follett?" and to explore the significance of her ideas and possible reasons why her work has not received wider recognition from the conflict resolution movement.

I regret that after a decade of activity in this field, I did not become acquainted with Follett until early this year. Now that I am familiar with her writing, I see Follett as must reading. Therefore, I have included a list of her works and publications about her as an appendix. Ideally, some day soon, all of her books will be reprinted and widely distributed. At present, however,

---

Albie M. Davis is Director of the Massachusetts District Court Mediation Program, Holyoke Square, Salem, Mass. She is also currently working on a book-length manuscript on the life and work of Mary Parker Follett.

many of these publications are out of print, so some detective work will be necessary on the part of readers. Enjoy the search. You will be rewarded!

The Interview

Davis: *Thank you for agreeing to this interview. I find your ideas so stimulating and significant, it is difficult to know where to begin. As a starting point, however, could you share your thoughts on the nature of conflict?*

Follett: As conflict — difference — is here in the world, as we cannot avoid it, we should, I think, use it. Instead of condemning it, we should set it to work for us. Why not? What does the mechanical engineer do with friction? Of course his chief job is to eliminate friction, but it is true that he also capitalizes friction. The transmission of power by belts depends on friction between the belt and the pulley. The friction between the driving wheel of the locomotive and the track is necessary to haul the train. All polishing is done by friction. The music of the violin we get by friction. We left the savage state when we discovered fire by friction. We talk of the friction of mind on mind as a good thing. So in business, too, we have to know when to try to eliminate friction and when to try to capitalize it, when to see what work we can make it do (DA, p. 30-31)

Davis: *What method of dealing with conflict do you recommend?*

Follett: There are three main ways of dealing with conflict: domination, compromise, and integration. Domination, obviously, is a victory of one side over the other. This is the easiest way of dealing with conflict, the easiest for the moment but not usually successful in the long run. . .

The second way of dealing with conflict, that of compromise, we understand well, for it is the way we settle most of our controversies; each side gives up a little in order to have peace, or, to speak more accurately, in order that the activity which has been interrupted by the conflict may go on. Compromise is the basis of trade union tactics. In collective bargaining, the trade unionist asks for more than he expects to get, allows for what is going to be lopped off in the conference. Thus we often do not know what he really thinks he should have, and this ignorance is a great barrier to dealing with conflict fruitfully.

But I certainly ought not to imply that compromise is peculiarly a trade union method. It is the accepted, the approved, way of ending controversy. Yet no one really wants to compromise, because that means a giving up of something. Is there, then, any other method of ending conflict?

There is a way beginning now to be recognized at least, and even occasionally followed: when two desires are *integrated*, that means that a solution has been found in which both desires have found a place, that neither side has had to sacrifice anything.

Let us take a very simple illustration. In the Harvard Library one day, in one of the smaller rooms, someone wanted the window open, I wanted it shut. We opened the window in the next room, where no one was sitting. This was not a compromise, because there was no curtailing of desire; we both got what we really wanted. For I did not want a closed room, I simply did not want the north wind to blow directly on me; likewise the other occupant did not want that particular window open, he merely wanted more air in the room.

I have already given this illustration in print. I repeat it here because this instance, from its lack of any complications, shows my point at once I think. (DA, p. 32)

Davis: *I agree. Its simplicity is its virtue. You'll be pleased to know the story has lasted over time. Fisher and Ury use it in* **Getting to YES** *(1981, p. 41) to illustrate the concept of focusing on interests, not positions. They mention your name in their foreword. What advice do you give to the person wishing to try your integrative approach toward negotiation?*

Follett: If we do not think that differing necessarily means fighting, even when two desires both claim right of way, if we think that integration is more profitable than conquering or compromising, the first step toward this consummation is to *bring the differences into the open*. We cannot hope to integrate our differences unless we know what they are. The first rule, then, for obtaining integration is to put your cards on the table, face the real issue, uncover the conflict, bring the whole thing into the open. (DA, p. 36)

Davis: *"The whole thing?" What do you mean by that?*

Follett: The highest lights in a situation are not always those which are most indicative of the real issues involved. Many situations are decidedly complex, involve numerous and varied activities, overlapping activities. There is too great a tendency (perhaps encouraged by popular journalism) to deal with the dramatic moments, forgetting that these are not always the most significant moments. . . .*To find the significant rather than the dramatic features* of industrial controversy, of a disagreement in regard to policy on boards of directors or between managers, is essential to integrative business policies. (DA, p. 40)

Davis: *After determining the significant rather than the dramatic features of a controversy, what next?*

Follett: Take the demands of both sides and break them up into their constituent parts. Contemporary psychology shows how fatal it is to try to deal with conglomerates. I know a boy who wanted a college education. His father died and he had to go to work at once to support his mother. Had he then to give up his desire? No, for on analysis he found that what he wanted was not a college education, but an education, and there were still ways of getting that. You remember the southern girl who said, "Why, I always thought 'damned Yankee' was one word until I came north." (DA, p. 40)

Davis: *Can you further illustrate this concept of breaking up demands into their constituent parts?*

Follett: You will notice that to break up a problem into its various parts involves the *examination of symbols*, involves, that is, the careful scrutiny of the language used to see what it really means. A friend of mine wanted to go to Europe, but also she did not want to spend the money it would cost. Was there any integration? Yes, she found one. In order to understand it, let us use the method I am advocating; let us ask, what did "going to Europe" symbolize to her? In order to do that, we have to break up this whole, "going to Europe."

What does "going to Europe" stand for to different people? A sea voyage, seeing beautiful places, meeting new people, a rest or change from daily duties, a dozen other things. Now, this woman had taught for a few years after leaving college an then had gone away and led a somewhat secluded life for a good many years. "Going to Europe" was to her a symbol not of snow mountains, or cathedrals, or pictures, but of meeting people — that was what she wanted. When she was asked to teach in a summer school of young men and women where she would meet a rather interesting staff of teachers and a rather interesting group of students, she immediately accepted. This was her integration. This was not a substitution for her wish, it was her real wish fulfilled. (DA, p. 43)

Davis: *What do you see as the obstacles to the integrative approach to conflict?*

Follett: It requires a high order of intelligence, keen perception and discrimination, more than all, a brilliant inventiveness; it is easier for the trade union to fight than to suggest a better way of running the factory.

Another obstacle to integration is that the matter in dispute is often theorized over instead of being taken up as a proposed activity. I have been interested to watch how often disagreement disappears when theorizing ends and the question is of some definite activity to be undertaken.

A serious obstacle to integration. . .is the language used . . . I think that the "grievance committees" which exist in most factories are a mistake. I do not like the "trouble specialists" of the Ford plant. I wish it were not so often stated that shop or department committees were formed to "settle disputes."

I have left untouched one of the chief obstacles to integration — namely, the undue influence of leaders — the manipulation of the unscrupulous on the one hand, and the suggestibility of the crowd on the other. Moreover, even when the power of suggestion is not used deliberately, it exists in all meetings between people; the whole emotional field of human intercourse has to be taken fully into account in dealing with methods of reconciliation. (DA, p. 45-48)

Davis: *I find myself attracted to your notion of solving problems by working together to solve them, rather than theorizing about how they might be solved. Could you expand on this idea?*

Follett: Through our observation of human relations, through the teachings of psychology, we learn that from our concrete activities spring both the power and the guide for those activities. Experience is the dynamo station; here are generated will and purpose. Further, and of the utmost importance, here too arise the standard with which to judge that same will and purpose. Men used to say that they relied on their wives' intuitions, but wives today are more apt to be out viewing facts for themselves than staying at home intuiting. (CE, p. 85)

Davis: *How do you incorporate your activity-oriented approach toward problem-solving into your ideas about integrative negotiations?*

Follett: To put this still another way: integration, the resolution of conflict, the harmonizing of difference, must take place on the motor level, not on the intellectual level. We cannot get genuine agreement by mere discussion in conference. As our responses are governed by past habits, by what has been incorporated in the organism, the only way of getting other responses is by getting other things incorporated in the organism.

We have not understood this: a man goes home from an international conference and wonders why he cannot carry his people with him in regard to what has there been agreed on. We assign a number of reasons for this; the real reason is that agreement has to come from and through what is going on every day in that nation. To persuade his people into verbal acceptance means only a pseudoagreement, and the underlying dissent will only crop up again in some other form. . .Genuine integration occurs in the sphere of activities, and not of ideas or wills. Hence the present aim of our international conferences is wrong; the aim should be not intellectual agreement alone, but to provide opportunities for actual agreement through the activities of the nations involved. (CE, p. 150)

Davis: *So, you see your ideas having application to both interpersonal and international affairs!*

Follett: The only thing that will help toward any genuine solution of our world problems today are methods which will open the way for those responses which will help to create a different situation. Concepts can never be presented to me merely, they must be knitted into the structure of my being, and this can be done only through my own activity. (CE, p. 151)

Davis: *But, don't your concepts for constructive conflict require a world where people share the same values?*

Follett: What people often mean by getting rid of conflict is getting rid of diversity, and it is of the utmost importance that these should not be considered the same. We may wish to abolish conflict, but we cannot get rid of diversity. We must face life as it is and understand that diversity is its most essential feature . . . Fear of difference is dread of life itself. It is possible to conceive conflict as not necessarily a wasteful outbreak of incompatibilities, but a *normal* process by which socially valuable differences register themselves for the enrichment of all concerned. (CE, p. 300)

Davis: *What would you recommend we do to increase the use of the integrative approach?*

Follett: Perhaps the greatest of all obstacles to integration is our lack of training for it. In our college debates we try always to beat the other side. In the circular announcing the courses to be given at the Bryn Mawr Summer School for Workers, I find: "English Composition and Public Speaking: to develop the art of oral and written expression." I think that in addition to this, there should be classes in discussion which should aim to teach the "art" of cooperative thinking. (DA, p. 48)

Davis: *The integrative approach toward conflict that you recommend — some critics today would say it is naive, wishful thinking. An integrative negotiator won't stand a chance against a combative one. How would you respond to them?*

Follett: Some people tell me that they like what I have written on integration, but say that I am talking of what ought to be instead of what is. But indeed I am not; I am talking neither of what is, to any great extent, or of what ought to be merely, but of what perhaps may be. This we can discover only by experiment. That is all I am urging, that we try experiments in methods of resolving differences; differences on the board of directors, with fellow managers or heads of departments, with employees, or in other relations. If we do this, we may take a different attitude toward conflict. (DA, p. 34)

Davis: *By seeking to understand the desires of the other person, doesn't the integrative negotiator risk giving in to those who would dominate?*

Follett: A friend of mine said to me, "Open-mindedness is the whole thing, isn't it?" No, it isn't; it (negotiation) needs just as great a respect for your own view as for that of others, and a firm upholding of it until you are convinced. Mushy people are no more good at this than stubborn people. (DA, p. 48)

Davis: *Thomas Colosi teaches that "the creation and maintenance of doubts about the consequences of nonagreement (or one decision versus another) is central to inducing skeptics to settle" (Colosi, 1985, p. 234). What do you see as central to settlement?*

Follett: One of the most important reasons for bringing the desire of each side to a place where they can be clearly examined and valued is that evaluation often leads to revaluation. We progress by a revaluation of desire, but usually we do not stop to examine a desire until another is disputing right of way with it. Watch the evolution of your desires from childhood through youth, etc. The baby has many infantile desires which are not compatible with his wish for approbation; therefore he revalues his desires. We see this all through our life. We want to do so-and-so, but we do not estimate how much this really means to us until it comes into conflict with another desire. Revaluation is the flower of comparison. This conception of the revaluation of desire is necessary to keep in the foreground of our thinking in dealing with conflict, for neither side ever "gives in" really, it is hopeless to expect it, but there often comes a moment when there is a simultaneous revaluation of interests on both sides and unity precipitates itself. . .Integration is often more a spontaneous flowing together of desire than one might think from what I have said; the revaluing of interests on both sides may lead the interests to fit into each other, so that all find some place in the final solution. (DA, p. 39-40)

Davis: *In* **Getting to YES** *(1981, p. 118), Fisher and Ury recommend the "one-text procedure," that is, drawing out the interests of both sides and using that combined information to build a solution. What are your thoughts on this concept?*

Follett: *The field of desire* is an important psychological and sociological conception; many conflicts could, I believe, be prevented from ending disastrously by getting the desires of each side into one field of vision where they could be viewed together and compared. We all believe to a certain extent in Freud's "sublimation," but I believe still more that various desires get orientated toward one another and take on different values in the process of orientation. (DA, p. 39)

Davis: *In* **Disputes and Negotiations: A Cross-Cultural Perspective** *(1979), Philip H. Gulliver speaks of the two principal general processes in negotiation — the cyclical and the developmental. He describes various* *phases which move toward agreement while shifting between moods of antagonism or coordination. Do you see conflict as having a cyclical nature?*

Follett: The conception of circular behavior throws much light on conflict, for I now realize that I can never fight you, I am always fighting you plus me. I have put it this way: that response is always to a relation. I respond, not only to you, but to the relation between you and me. Employees do not respond only to their employers, but to the relation between themselves and their employers . . . Circular behavior as the basis of integration gives us the key to constructive conflict. (DA, p. 45)

Davis: *I am reminded of the challenge to the orthodox scientific method presented by James Gleick in* **Chaos: Making a New Science** *(1987). He notes that "tiny differences in input could quickly become overwhelming differences in output," thus leading to the notion of the "butterfly effect," that is, a "butterfly stirring the air today in Peking can transform storm systems next month in New York." You seem to have anticipated the butterfly effect in relation to problem-solving.*

Follett: We can never understand the total situation without taking into account the evolving situation. And when a situation changes, we have not a new variation under the old fact, but new fact. . .A professor of philosophy told me that it made him dizzy to talk with me because, he says, he wishes always to compare varying things with something stationary. (CE, p. 69)

Davis: *I'd like to shift to another topic. Today experiments with mediation, arbitration and various dispute resolution hybrids are taking place in every nook and cranny of society. Arbitration and conciliation or mediation are undoubtedly the most commonly used processes; in fact, the two words are often used interchangeably. What do you see as the primary features of each process?*

Follett: In regard to the difference between conciliation and arbitration, while in practice it is often difficult to draw the line, in theory the two are wholly different. The principle of arbitration is that of an adjudicated dispute; the arbitrator. . .hears both sides and gives the decision. In cases of conciliation, an attempt is made to bring the two sides to agreement. It is encouraging that conciliation is pretty generally recognized to be a more satisfactory way of settling industrial disputes than arbitration. In many cases arbitration is resorted to only when conciliation fails. (DA, p. 230)

Davis: *Do you favor one process over the other?*

Follett: In pure arbitration the only task recognized is that of deciding between, not of bringing the two parties *together*. The conciliator or mediator, on the other hand, tries to energize the two parties to the controversy to reach their own decision. Unless both sides are satisfied, the struggle will go on, underneath if not openly.

If I have seemed to speak against arbitration as a method of settling industrial disputes, it must be understood that I believe in it unless a better way can be made to work, as I am entirely in favor of it for international disputes — until we find a better way. (DA, p. 238)

Davis: *You use the expression "pure arbitration." What do you mean by that?*

Follett: I had to do that because we have so many different methods followed in arbitration. . .I think we may say that the most successful arbitrator is one who does not "arbitrate," but who gets the parties in the controversy face to face and helps them to work out the decision for themselves, helps them to larger understandings, to reciprocal modifyings and adjustments. (DA, p. 237-238)

Davis: *"Make the forum fit the fuss!" That's a contemporary expression in the dispute resolution field to capture the notion that the process used to settle a conflict should be in some way tailored to the particular situation. Do you have any recommendations about appropriateness?*

Follett: The search in the settling of disputes should always be for the best future activities of the parties concerned. This very fundamental psychological principle is accepted by most conciliators. An impartial chairman in the clothing industry said to me, "The courts are concerned with what has happened; our problem is always what is going to happen afterwards." Another man said to me, "Arbitration looks to the past, conciliation to the future." (DA, p. 238)

Davis: *Let's look to the future of the world as a whole. Are you hopeful? Will those of us who seek a path to peace find a way?*

Follett: In making a plea for some experiment in international cooperation, I remember, with humiliation, that we have fought because it is the easy way. Fighting solves no problems. The problems which brought on. . .war will all be there to be settled when the war ends. But we have war as the line of least resistance. We have war when the mind gives up its job of agreeing as too difficult. It is often stated that conflict is a necessity of the human soul, and that if conflict should ever disappear from among us, individuals would deteriorate and society collapse. But the effort of agreeing is so much more strenuous than the comparatively easy stunt of fighting that we can harden our spiritual muscles much more effectively on the former than the latter.

Suppose I disagree with you in a discussion and we make no effort to join our ideas, but "fight it out." I hammer away with my idea, I try to find all the weakest parts of yours, I refuse to see anything good in what you think. That is not nearly so difficult as trying to recognize all the possible subtle interweavings of thought, how one part of your thought, or even one aspect of one part, may unite with one part or one aspect of one part of mine. Likewise with cooperation and competition in business: cooperation is going to prove so much more difficult than competition that there is not the slightest danger of any one getting soft under it. (NS, p. 357)

Davis: *Are you saying, then, that facing conflict constructively is hard work, but it must be done?*

Follett: We have thought of peace as the passive and war as the active way of living. The opposite is true. War is not the most strenuous life. It is a kind of rest-cure compared to the task of reconciling our differences . . . From war to peace is not from the strenuous to the easy existence; it is from the futile to the effective, from the stagnant to the active, from the destructive to the creative way of life . . . We may be angry and fight, we may feel kindly and want peace — it is all about the same. The world will be regenerated by the people who rise above both these passive ways and heroically seek, by whatever hardship, by whatever toil, the methods by which people can agree. (NS, p. 358-359)

Davis: *Thank you! You've given me much to think about and a new respect for the value of my own experience.*

Follett: Experience may be hard but we claim its gifts because they are real, even though our feet bleed on its stones. (CE, p. 302)

About Mary Parker Follett

To read Mary Parker Follett's fresh and original work, knowing it was written or spoken so many years ago, is to wonder: Who was she? How did she develop her visionary ideas? And, why haven't I heard of her earlier?

To the extent that she is known today, it is usually in the field of business administration, for her that is where she focused much of her thought during the last ten years of her life. After her death, the talks she gave to business administrators were collected together into *Dynamic Administration* (1942), which, for a time, was highly influential in the field of business management. Today, there is a movement in the business world to revive and revisit Follett. Her work is popular in Japan, where her ideas about leadership and management are highly valued, and in Britain, where she lived and lectured during the last years of her life. Yet, to call her "the first management consultant" or an "organizational consultant," as is often done, is equivalent to describing Leonardo da Vinci as a "graphic artist." Her interests are much deeper and broader.

For a time, Follett was acknowledged for her contributions to the field of integrative negotiation. In one of the most frequently cited books in our field, *A Behavioral Theory of Labor Negotiation: An Analysis of a Social Interaction System* (Walton and McKersie, 1965), the authors investigate the concepts of integrative and distributive bargaining. They duly credit Follett several times, noting that "in a pioneering and impressionistic statement about administration, Mary Parker Follett discusses the concept of integrative bargaining." Walton and McKersie's 1965 credits seem to be Follett's Waterloo in the field of negotiation and conflict resolution. From that time on, with few exceptions, when integrative bargaining is discussed, it is generally they who are cited. Follett falls through the cracks, so to speak, to resurface some 15 years later in the acknowledgement section of Fisher and Ury's bestseller, *Getting to YES.* A very few of the older members of our field are familiar with her work, but she is unknown to the great majority.

No full biography of Follett exists and the available information about her is both skimpy and contradictory. The good news, however, is that since 1981 Joan C. Tonn, a professor at the University of Massachusetts/Boston, has been working on a biography. The book, which a small but growing number of Follett's fans eagerly await, will be published by Oxford University Press late in 1990 or early in 1991.

When I told Tonn that I was writing an article about Follett's ideas and wanted to include background information, she cautioned me, noting, "Much of what is written is wrong, including what Follett said about herself." Rather than a complete chronological accounting, then, I will paint a more impressionistic picture of Follett. While many facets of her life remain a mystery, one thing is clear: she evoked a passionate response in those who knew her personally, and she continues to do so in those who meet her for the first time through the written word.

Tonn agrees it is safe to say that Follett was born in Quincy, Massachusetts, a suburb of Boston, in 1868 and that she died in 1933 at the age of 65 in Boston.

Follett displayed her quick mind at an early age, graduated from lower school early and entered the prestigious Thayer Academy in South Braintree, a suburb adjacent to Quincy, when she was eleven or twelve. Anne Boynton Thompson, herself a brilliant scholar, taught Follett during her teenage years at Thayer, and remained a friend and strong influence throughout her life. In 1885, both Follett's father and her maternal grandfather died, leaving her an inheritance of sufficient size to permit her to live independently for the remainder of her life. Follett's freedom from financial pressures undoubtedly allowed her to follow her fertile mind wherever it took her, and it took her many places.

In 1888, at the age of 20, she enrolled in the Society for the Collegiate Instruction of Women by Professors and Other Instructors at Harvard, or "The Annexe," which had been organized about ten years earlier to allow women to enjoy the benefits of Harvard College. During Follett's student days, the Annexe became Radcliffe College. The impressive faculty at Harvard included George Santayana and William James, the latter of whom appeared to have a strong influence upon Follett's thinking. The person at Radcliffe who had the greatest influence, however, was Professor Albert Bushnell Hart, from whom she took the equivalent of ten semesters of history. Hart pushed his students to produce original research and to draw original conclusions.

A major clue to Follett's unique abilities is found in her first book, *The Speaker of the House*, which was started originally in 1889-90 as a required thesis for a two-semester history course with Professor Hart. Follett was a tireless researcher of the past, and was fearless about obtaining first-hand information. She examined every possible historical document available and conducted interviews with current and retired speakers as well as other members of Congress. At 23, while studying at Newnham College in England, she presented a paper on the topic before the Historical Society. She continued her research when she returned to Radcliffe, and the book was published in 1896, when she was but 28. *The Speaker* was immediately recognized as a significant contribution to the field of political science and brought Follett a degree of prominence unusual for someone her age and even more unusual for one of her gender. Teddy Roosevelt gave the book high marks and indicated that he thought Follett "understood the operation of Congress a great deal better than Woodrow Wilson," whose *Congressional Government* had appeared the previous year (Roosevelt, p. 177).

When *The Speaker* so clearly demonstrated Follett's scholarly talents, friends expected her to pursue an academic career. She surprised them by plunging into what then was called social work, but which might more appropriately be called community organizing today. These activities provided her with direct experience in managing hundreds of people and in balancing the interests of many groups.

The most notable of her achievements centered around the public schools, an interest which she shared with Isobel Briggs, her companion of 30 years and Ella Cabot Lyman, a best friend who remained a devoted supporter of Follett throughout her life. Follett saw that school buildings were empty in the afternoon and evenings, and that neighborhoods needed community centers to provide recreation and services such as job placement. She started the community schools program in Boston and helped it become a national movement, working hand-in-hand with people from all backgrounds. All the while, she kept detailed notes about her activities and the consequences of them. After a dozen or more years of effective work at the community level, she began to write the story of the extended school movement. In time, she realized that her interests went far beyond one successful community-based enterprise to the whole notion of the role of groups in assuring democracy. Her second book, *The New State: Group Organization The Solution of Popular Government*, was published in 1918 and, once again, she received positive reviews. In a prophetic convergence of the thinking of two people who would ultimately have great impact of the field of dispute resolution, Follett asked Roscoe Pound, Dean of Harvard Law School, to review her manuscript (*The New State*, p. 15).

By now Follett had become both a public figure in Massachusetts and a nationally-known author. She was invited to sit on boards that set minimum wages, on arbitration panels, and on various committees which further convinced her that adversarial notions of conflict interfered with the ability of groups to come up with creative solutions. These experience led her to write her third successful book, *The Creative Experience* (1926).

Ever the learner, the analyst, the synthesizer, the philosopher, she moved boldly into the world of business while in her fifties. "I have been asked several times why I am studying business management," Follett wrote. "I will try to tell you. Free to choose between different paths of study, I have chosen this for a number of reasons. First of all, it is among business men (not all, but a few) that I find the greatest vitality of thinking today, and I like to do my thinking where it is most alive. . .Here the ideal and the practical have joined hands. That is why I am working at business management, because, while I care for the ideal, it is only because I want to help bring it into our everyday affairs." (*Dynamic Administration*, p. 17).

She liked the willingness of business people to experiment. She talked of the contrast between economists and politicians, whose discussions seemed to go nowhere, and of businessmen who "where not theorizing or dogmatizing," but "were thinking of what they had actually done and. . .were willing to try new ways the next morning, so to speak." Business responded with equal enthusiasm to Follett. From 1924 on, she became a featured speaker at the most important business conferences held in the United States and in England. In the last years of her life, she made her home with Dame Katherine Furse in Chelsea, England, and lectured at various British institutions, including the London School of Economics.

In the fall of 1933, Follett took a trip to Boston to ascertain the impact of the Depression upon her investments and to check into her health, which had been a cause of concern. She underwent an operation, perhaps for a goiter, and it was found that she had invasive cancer. She died two days after the operation at the Deaconess Hospital in Boston, on December 18, 1933. Shortly after Follett's death, Dame Furse summed up her special skill of communication in a letter to their mutual friend, Ella Lyman Cabot: "What I miss most now is Mary's power of expression," wrote Furse, "She knew how to find words for all that is finest and best, never elaborate tiresome words, but the right words every time" (Furse, 1934).

Conclusion

There are several reasons why it is important for the field of dispute resolution to become reacquainted with Mary Parker Follett. First of all, her ideas remain fresh and visionary —she is *still* ahead of her times. We need her creative flexible thinking to help us dust the cobwebs from our theory and practice. Secondly, her ideas deserve to be read in full. When her concepts are taken out of context, something essential is lost, for thinking is holistic. As Pauline Graham observes in the introduction to *Dynamic Managing: The Follett Way*, "Some of the spokes of her wheel have been reinvented since then. . .but not all" (Graham, 1987, p. 4).

Lastly, both women and men in the profession should take pride in the fact that a woman originally articulated the integrative approach to negotiation. Our field, which is increasingly being stratified by gender, with women at the lower-paid and less prestigious end of the evolving hierarchy, is at risk. We must do everything we can to encourage the original and invaluable contributions of women. Follett provides us with a strong role model.

NOTE

I am indebted to the following people for inspiration and assistance on this article: John Chandler, Margaret Shaw, Carol Davis Pino, Janet Rifkin and Matthew Davis, for sharing my obsession to learn more about Follett and for helping me find sources of information; Linda L. Putnam, Department of Communication, Purdue University, for sending me her own and other contemporary articles on or about Follett; Claudia Morner, friend, neighbor and Boston College librarian, for her imaginative investigation; Jane Knowles, archivist, and the many staff members of the Schlesinger Library at Radcliffe College who gave so freely of their expertise and resources; and J. William Breslin, Managing Editor of *Negotiation Journal* for editorial assistance "above and beyond the call of duty."

REFERENCES

Colosi, T. (1983). "Negotiation in the public and private sectors: A core model." *American Behavioral Scientist*, 27: 229-253.

Fisher, R. and Ury, W. L. (1981). *Getting to YES: Negotiating agreement without giving in.* Boston: Houghton Mifflin.

Follett, M. P. (1896). *The Speaker of the House of Representatives.* Cambridge, Mass.: Radcliffe College Monographs. No. 5.

———. (1918). *The new state: Group organization the solution of popular government.* New York: Longmans, Green and Co.

———. (1924). *Creative experience.* New York: Longmans, Green.

———. (1942), *Dynamic administration: The collected papers of Mary Parker Follett,* ed. H. C. Metcalf and L. Urwick. New York: Harper.

Fox, E. M. (1968). "Mary Parker Follett: The enduring contribution." *Public Administration Review* 28 (reprint).

Furse, K. (1934). Letter to Ella Cabot Lyman. Schlesinger Library, Radcliffe College, Cambridge, Mass.

Gleick, J. (1987). *Chaos: The making of a new science.* New York. Penguin Books.

Graham, P. (1987). *Dynamic managing: The Follett way.* London. Professional Publishing Limited.

Gulliver, P.H. (1979). *Disputes and negotiations: A cross-cultural perspective.* New York: Academic Press.

Roosevelt, T. (1896). *American Historical Review* 2: 177.

Walton, R.E. and McKersie, R.B. (1965). *A behavioral theory of labor negotiation.* New York: McGraw-Hill.

APPENDIX I

A Brief Bibliography of Books and Articles about Mary Parker Follett

Cabot, R. C. (1934). "Mary Parker Follett: An appreciation." Radcliffe Quarterly, p. 80-82.
Follett, M. P. (1896). *The Speaker of the House of Representatives*. Cambridge, Mass.: Radcliffe College Monographs. No. 5.
———. (1918). *The New State: Group organization the solution of popular government*. New York: Longmans, Green and Co.
———. (1924). *Creative experience* New York: Longmans, Green.
———. (1924). *Creative experience*. Reprint. New York: Peter Smith, 1951.
———. (1942). *Dynamic administration: the collected papers of Mary Parker Follett*, ed. H.C. Metcalf and L. Urwick. New York: Harper.
———. (1978). "The giving of orders." *Classics of Organization Theory*, ed. J. M. Shafritz and P. H. Whitbeck. Oak Park, Ill.: Moore Publishing.
———. (1987). *Freedom and Co-ordination: Lectures in business organization*. Reprint. New York Garland Publishing, Inc.
Fox, E. M. (1968). "Mary Parker Follett: The enduring contribution." *Public Administration Review* 28 (reprint).
Graham, P. (1987). *Dynamic managing: The Follett way*. London. Professional Publishing Limited.
Hata, S. (1983). "Mary Parker Follett: The Boston environment and other influences." Presented at 43rd Annual Meeting, Academy of Management, Dallas, Texas, August 16, 1983.
Linderman, E. C. (1934). "Outline of Mary Follett's contributions to modern thought." *Survey Graphic* 23: 86.
Lyons, N. (1988). "Negotiating conflict: Rediscovering the art of Mary Parker Follett." *Institute for the Management of Lifelong Education Bulletin* 1: 8-9.
Parker, L. E. (1984). "Control in organization life: The contribution of Mary Parker Follett." *Academy of Management of* Review 9: 736-745.
Putnam, L. L. (1987). "Reframing integrative and distributive bargaining: An interaction perspective." Presented at the Conference on Research on Negotiation in Organizations, Mt. Sterling, Ohio, April 24-26, 1987.
Stever, J. A. (1986). "Mary Parker Follett and the quest for pragmatic administration." *Administration and Society* 18: 159-177.
Urwick, L. (1935). "The problem of organization: A study of the work of Mary Parker Follett." *Bulletin of the Taylor Society* 1: 163-169.
Wood, A. E. (1926). "The social philosophy of Mary Parker Follett." *Social Forces* 4: 759-769.

Strategic Choice in Negotiation

Dean G. Pruitt

Four basic strategies are available to negotiators: (a) *problem solving*, which involves an effort to find an alternative that is acceptable to both parties; (b) *contending*, which involves an effort to force one's will on the other party; (c) *yielding*, which involves a reduction in one's basic aspirations; and (d) *inaction*, which involves doing as little as possible in the negotiation. The first three of these can be called *coping strategies* because they seek to move the process toward agreement. A fifth strategy, withdrawal, is also available but will not be covered in this article.

These strategies are somewhat incompatible because they require different psychological orientations and tend to send out contradictory signals to the other party. Hence, they are usually adopted one at a time. Nevertheless, combinations are possible, especially when two strategies can be insulated from one another, as when contentious tactics are employed in the formal sessions while informal problem solving goes on in secret.

Though a negotiator can persist in a particular strategy for a period of time, these strategies should not be confused with hard-and-fast orientations. Indeed, they often succeed one another at a fairly rapid pace.

The bulk of this article deals with the forms taken by these strategies, the outcomes they encourage, and the determinants of their use. After this is a brief discussion of the vigor with which these strategies are enacted. A final section will examine how negotiators can influence their opponents' strategic choice.

The Strategies and their Outcomes

Problem Solving

Problem solving involves pursuit of a formula for reconciling the two parties' aspirations. Various types of formulae are available for this purpose, including the following: expanding the pie, in which a way is found to increase resources that have been in short supply; cost cutting, in which one party gets what it wants while cutting the other's cost of conceding, logrolling, in which each party concedes on issues of low priority to itself; and bridging, in which a totally new option is developed that satisfies both parties major aims.

A number of possible tactics is available to implement the strategy of problem solving. These can be classified in terms of the risk involved to the user (Pruitt, 1981). Examples of riskier tactics are conceding with the expectation of receiving a return concession; mentioning possible compromises as

---

Dean G. Pruitt is Professor of Psychology at the State University of New York in Buffalo, N.Y.

talking points; and revealing one's interests (i.e. one's goals and values) to the other party. The risk inheres in the fact that the other party may misinterpret or take advantage of these tactics, if his or her basic approach is contentious: for example, by concluding that one is weak, treating one's talking points as firm proposals, failing to reciprocate one's concessions, or constructing threats based on knowledge of one's interests. Examples of more cautious problem-solving tactics are hinting at possible compromises, sending disavowable intermediates, talking in back channels, and communicating through a mediator. Such indirect tactics are less likely to backfire in the face of a contentious other.

So far, problem solving has been described as an individual activity, but it can also be a joint enterprise. In joint problem solving, the parties exchange accurate information about their underlying interests, collectively identify new issues in light of this information, brainstorm to locate alternative ways of dealing with these issues, and (sometimes) work together to evaluate these alternatives. Joint problem solving is an excellent way to locate mutually acceptable solutions. But it is sometimes not practical because one party is not ready for it or the parties do not trust each other.

The outcome of problem solving is often of great benefit to both parties. This is especially true under the following two conditions:

(1) *When there is high integrative potential* (Walton & McKersie, 1965). That is, a strong possibility of expanding the pie, cost cutting, compensation, logrolling, or bridging. Not all situations have high integrative potential. For example, when a tourist and a merchant are dickering about the price of a rug in a Middle Eastern bazaar, it may only be possible to find a simple compromise (i.e., a middle alternative on some obvious dimension). But most situations have far more integrative potential than meets the eye.

(2) *When both parties maintain high (but not too high) aspirations.* (Pruitt, 1981). High aspirations provide a challenge to the parties, stretching creativity to the limits of the integrative potential. However, aspirations should not be so high that agreement is impossible. Another way of putting this is that problem solvers should be firm but not bull-headed about their basic interests.

The latter point needs qualification. Firmness with respect to basic interests should not extend to the proposals that express these interests. Indeed, problem solvers should be flexible about their proposals so as to locate an agreement that will serve both parties' interests. The two points together suggest that high joint benefit is achieved by adopting a policy of *firm flexibility*[1] (Pruitt, 1983). This involves a stance of being unwilling to compromise on ends, unless they are clearly unobtainable, yet being open-minded and innovative with respect to the means of these ends, so as to encourage the development of jointly acceptable alternatives.

There are a number of reasons for being interested in the antecedents of high joint benefit and hence in the conditions that encourage problem-solving. Agreements involving high joint benefit are more likely to endure, to enhance the relationship between the parties, and to contribute to the welfare of overarching social entities that include both parties (such as a firm in which the parties are departments). Furthermore, there are many circumstances in which individuals cannot prosper unless the group as a whole is successful. This is true for tasks requiring teamwork, such as winning a basketball game or a political campaign. It is also true when aspirations are so high that the obvious alternatives are unacceptable to one or both sides.

Contending

Contending (or contentious behavior) involves trying to persuade the other party to accept alternatives that favor one's own interests. Another name for this is "positional bargaining" (Fisher and Ury, 1981). Efforts are made to dominate the other party by means of pressure tactics such as the following: demands that far exceed what is actually acceptable; commitments to "unalterable" positions; persuasive arguments aimed at convincing the other that concessions are in his or her own best interest; threats, for example to withdraw from the negotiation or punish the other for failing to make concessions; demonstrations that there is more time pressure on the other than on oneself. While seeking information about the other party's goals and fall-back positions, contenders try to conceal information about their own so that the other cannot use it against them.

Past theorists (e.g., Deutsch, 1973) and researchers (e.g., Pruitt and Carnevale, 1982) have generally painted a grim picture of the outcomes resulting from contentious behavior. When both parties contend, agreement often will not be reached because the parties become rigid in their demands. If agreement is reached, it is likely to be much delayed and to take the form of a last-minute, low-level compromise because the parties have not been able to do any creative thinking. Worse yet, a dangerous escalative process may set in, with each party reacting harshly to the other's harsh reactions. When only one party contends, he or she can sometimes outpoint the other and reap high individual benefit. But such behavior is more likely to summon the same response from the other, producing the bilateral case.

While supported by certain lines of evidence, this indictment of contentious behavior seems overdrawn. Negotiations that reach reasonable agreements often go through an initial contentious stage followed by a later stage of joint problem solving (Morley and Stephenson, 1977). Furthermore, it can be argued that contending is often a necessary precursor to successful problem solving. Negotiators commonly start out with aspirations that greatly outstrip the integrative potential. In other words, their aspirations are so high that no degree of problem solving can yield a solution (Bazerman and Neale, 1983). Under such conditions, they are likely to engage in initial contentious behavior. During this stage, however, both parties often become more realistic about what aspirations can be sustained. If their actions have not produced too much antagonism, they can then enter a stage of joint problem solving that has prospects of yielding agreement because of their reduced aspirations.

Yielding

Yielding involves reductions in the underlying goals and values sought rather than in overt demands. However, it often shows its face in the form of reduced demands.

Yielding is a straightforward operation. Hence a negotiator who chooses this strategy is not faced with a subset of possible tactics as in the case of problem solving and contending.

Yielding is sometimes advantageous. Heavy yielding is a good way to end negotiation quickly, which may be desirable when issues are unimportant and time pressure is high. As mentioned above, lighter yielding often makes problem solving more effective by bringing aspirations into the range allowed by the integrative potential.

However, there is a danger in yielding too far. This point is obvious when one of the parties yields and the other does not, because the latter is likely to win the lion's share of the outcome. But the point also applies to yielding by both parties. Take for example the case of newly formed romantic couples or other groups that are highly cohesive but whose members lack faith in their status in the group. Out of a fear of conflict or of failure to reach agreement, they may both yield so far that they are not challenged to be creative. The result will be lower joint benefit than would otherwise be available. As evidence of this process, Fry, Firestone, and Williams (1979) have found that newly formed romantic couples achieve lower joint benefit in negotiation than male-female stranger dyads.

The ideal is for parties to yield to a point that is compatible with the integrative potential and then hold firm while engaging in flexible problem solving. But how can this be accomplished? If they can assess the integrative potential (as when they have had past experience with similar situations), they may be able to gauge how far to yield. Otherwise a sequential trial-and-error procedure makes the most sense. They should start with high aspirations and engage in problem solving. If no agreement is reached, they should lower their aspirations and try more problem solving, repeating the same steps over and over until agreement is reached. Kelly and Schenitzki (1972) and more recently Pruitt and Carnevale (1982) have demonstrated the value of such a trial-and-error procedure for generating agreements involving high joint benefits.

Inaction
Inaction wastes time and sometimes even temporarily suspends the negotiation. This, of course, tends to delay agreement and can even contribute to a breakdown in the negotiation if it leads the other party to become discourage and break off.

Choosing a Strategy
Two main theories about the determinants of choice among the four strategies will now be presented. The first, which is called the dual concern model, traces a negotiator's choice to the relative strength of concern about own and the other party's outcomes. The second, which in no way contradicts the first, explains this choice by the perceived feasibility and cost of enacting the various strategies.

The Dual Concern Model
The dual concern model is shown in Figure 1. It makes the following predictions about the antecedents of the four strategies: concern about both own and other party's outcomes encourages a problem-solving strategy; concern about only one's own outcomes encourages contending; concern about only the other party's outcomes encourages yielding; concern about neither party's outcomes encourages inaction.

Figure 1

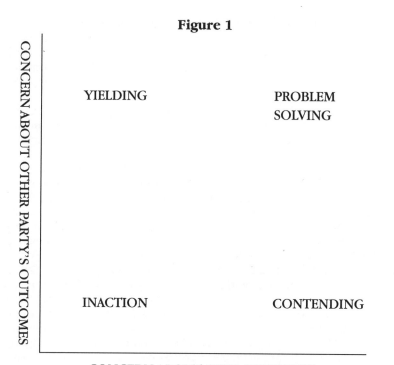

CONCERN ABOUT OTHER PARTY'S OUTCOMES

YIELDING

PROBLEM
SOLVING

INACTION

CONTENDING

CONCERN ABOUT OWN OUTCOMES

The dual concern model has its origins in Blake and Mouton's (1964) Managerial Grid and has been adapted to the analysis of conflict by various authors (Filley, 1975; Gladwin and Walter, 1980; Rahim, 1983; Ruble and Thomas, 1976; Thomas, 1976). Other labels are sometimes given to the dimensions in this model. For example, concern about own outcomes is sometimes called "assertiveness," and concern about other's outcomes is sometimes called "cooperativeness."

Other versions of the dual concern model postulate a fifth strategy called "compromising," which is ordinarily shown in the middle of the graph because it is viewed as due to a moderate concern about self and other. This approach is not taken in the present article because compromises are seen as arising from lazy problem solving involving a half-hearted attempt to satisfy both parties' interests. In other words, it seems unnecessary to postulate a separate strategy to explain the development of compromises.

Thomas (1976) notes that the two concerns in the dual concern model are often erroneously reduced to a single dimension. Concern about the other's outcomes is assumed to be the opposite of concern about one's own outcomes — that is cooperativeness is assumed to be the opposite of selfishness. By postulating dual concerns, we are forced to distinguish between two forms of cooperativeness, yielding and problem solving. We are also forced to distinguish between two ways of advancing one's own interests, contending and problem solving.

Determinants of Concern about Own Outcomes

Concern about own outcomes is partly a function of the importance of the issues under consideration — what Gladwin and Walter (1980) call a party's "stakes." When the issues are important, one is more likely to pursue one's interests by contentious or problem-solving tactics and less likely to yield or remain inactive.

Concern about own outcomes is much the same thing as resistance to yielding, which is manifested by slow concession-making in negotiation. Hence determinants of concession rate can be viewed as antecedents of this concern.

Research on concession rate (Kelley et al., 1967) suggests that resistance to yielding is greater, and hence concern about own outcomes is larger, the closer one's aspirations are to one's limit (i.e., one's ultimate fallback position). This has several implications. One is that a higher limit will encourage greater use of both contentious and problem-solving strategies, a conclusion supported by research (Kimmel et al., 1980; Ben-Yoav and Pruitt). Another, which follows from the first, is that these strategies are more likely to be used by parties who have a favorable alternative to agreement or a high zero-point of utility.

Resistance to yielding, and hence concern about own outcomes, diminishes when one is afraid of conflict. This fear is found when one is attracted toward or dependent on the other but distrustful of the other's opinion of oneself. Such sentiments, which have been termed "false cohesiveness" (Longley and Pruitt, 1980), are especially common at the beginning of a relationship when people are feeling each other out. Research suggests that such sentiments can block all forms of assertiveness, including problem solving (Fry, et al., 1979).

The forces mentioned so far affect individuals negotiating on their own behalf, but the negotiating parties are often groups. Enhanced concern about certain of one's outcomes frequently develops in cohesive groups of people with similar life situations who discuss their common fate with one another. This is especially likely when the members of such groups regard themselves as part of a broader social movement, making common cause with similar groups in other locations (Kriesberg, 1973). Political controversy within a group can also enhance dedication to own side's outcomes by making its leaders reluctant to seem less concerned about the group welfare than are their rivals.

When the parties are groups or organizations, actual negotiation is usually carried out by representatives. Research (e.g., Benton and Druckman, 1973) suggests that representatives are ordinarily more resistant to yielding than are individuals bargaining on their own behalf. This is because they are trying to please their constituents and usually view them as nonconciliatory (Benton and Druckman, 1974). Other studies suggest that representatives are especially reluctant to yield under conditions that make them anxious to please their constituents, such as when they have low status in their groups (Kogan, et al., 1972), are distrusted by their constituents (Wall, 1975), wish to continue their association with their constituents (Klimoski, 1972), or are negotiating on behalf of women as opposed to men (Forcey, et al., 1983). These conditions can be viewed as enhancing concern about own side's outcomes.

Research suggests that accountability to constituents has much the same effect (e.g., Klimoski and Ash, 1974). Accountable representatives therefore should be especially prone to engage in contentious and problem-solving behavior, a generalization that has received support in a study by Ben-Yoav and Pruitt (forthcoming).

Determinants of Concern about the Other Party's Outcomes

Concern about the other party's outcomes takes two basic forms. The first is genuine concern, aimed at helping the other because one has an intrinsic interest in the other's welfare. The second is strategic concern, aimed at helping the other in order to advance one's own interests; for example, to ingratiate oneself with the other or move the negotiation toward agreement.

There is an important difference between these two forms of concern. Since strategic concern is aimed at impressing the other, it is stronger to the extent that the other is more concerned about his or her own outcomes. By contrast, genuine concern aims at serving the other regardless of the other's self-concern.

Genuine concern about the other party's outcomes can be enhanced by such factors as interpersonal attraction (Clark and Mills, 1979), common group identity (Hatton, 1967), and positive mood (Isen and Levin, 1972).

Strategic concern about the other's outcomes is common whenever one sees oneself as dependent on the other party — when the other seems able to provide rewards and penalties. An example would be the expectation of further negotiation in the future. Dependence leads to the conclusion that it is desirable to build a relationship with the other now. Hence, one tries to impress the other with one's concern about his or her welfare.

Dependence is by no means a one-way street. Mutual dependence is quite common and can encourage either mutual yielding or mutual problem solving. The impact on mutual problem solving is illustrated by a case study of mediation between two managers in the same company, Mack and Sy (Walton, 1969). It was not until both men became aware that they could be hurt by one another that they began trying to solve the problems they were having with each other.

Antagonism Toward the Other. Concern about the other party's outcomes ranges from neutral to strongly positive in the dual concern model. Missing from this model are antagonistic concerns, resulting from anger, hostility, negative attitudes, ethnocentrism, and the like. (To show these concerns in Figure 1 would require extending the ordinate downward below the abscissa.) Antagonism presumably encourages contentious behavior, regardless of the degree of self-concern.

Predictions from the Model

We have recently completed three studies that tested precise derivations from the dual concern model. All three were successful, suggesting that the model has value for predicting process and outcome in negotiation. These studies employed a research task in which two subjects play the roles of buyer and seller in a wholesale market. The task has hidden integrative potential of the logrolling type, in the sense that it is possible to achieve high joint profit by agreeing to a low price on one item and a high price on the other. All studies employed a 2 X 2 design involving a manipulation of the two kinds of concern. Both subjects in a dyad always received the same treatment.

In the first two studies, concern about own outcomes was manipulated by means of instructions about limit. High concern was produced by telling both subjects privately that they had to reach an agreement involving a large total profit; low concern, by telling them nothing about a lower limit on profit.

The first study (Pruitt et al., 1983) involved a manipulation of genuine concern about the other's outcomes. High concern was produced by putting the subjects in a good mood, which has been shown to induce a desire to be helpful (Isen and Levin, 1972). Just before the beginning of the negotiation, both subjects received gifts from a confederate of the experimenter. No gifts were given in the low concern condition. The second study (Ben-Yoav and Pruitt, forthcoming) involved a manipulation of strategic concern. High concern was produced by giving the subjects an expectation of cooperative future interaction. They were told that they would have to work together toward a common goal on a task following the negotiation. The aim of this instruction was to make them feel dependent on each other and hence desirous of developing a working relationship. In the low concern condition, they were told that they would be working alone on a subsequent task.

In both studies, a combination of high concern about own outcomes and high concern about the other's outcomes produced especially high joint benefit (measured as the sum of the two parties' profits). This is evidence of active problem-solving behavior, as predicted by the dual concern model. Other evidence of problem solving in this condition is the fact that the negotiators were especially likely to provide each other information about the entries in their profit schedules. A combination of high concern about own outcomes and low concern about the other's outcomes produced moderately low joint benefit. Contentious statements such as persuasive arguments and threats were especially common in this condition, again supporting the dual concern model. A combination of low concern about own outcomes and high concern about the other's outcomes produced the lowest joint benefit of all, suggesting the yielding (i.e., aspiration collapse) predicted by the dual concern model.

The results of these studies indicate that concern about the other's outcomes is a two-edged sword. In conjunction with concern about own outcomes, it leads to problem solving and (when the two concerns are shared by both parties) especially high joint benefit. But when concern about own outcomes is weak, it produces yielding and especially low joint benefit.

In the third study, concern about the other party's outcomes was again manipulated by the presence versus absence of an expectation of cooperative future interaction. Concern about own outcomes was manipulated by means of high versus low accountability to constituents. Under high accountability, the constituents (who were confederates) were able to divide the money earned in the negotiation and write and evaluation of the outcomes achieved by their negotiators. Under low accountability, the negotiators divided the money and no evaluations were written.

As predicted by the model, high accountability in the absence of an expectation of cooperative future interaction encouraged heavy contentious verbalizations and low joint benefit. The impact of accountability, however, was completely reversed when there was an expectation of future interaction. This condition encouraged especially high joint benefit presumably because it fostered heavy joint problem solving. The nature of this problem solving is not clear at this time, but it is hard to imagine any process other than problem solving that could have generated this level of joint benefit.

These results suggest that accountability is also a two-edged sword. Under normal conditions, it fosters contentious behavior and low joint benefit. But under conditions that encourage good relations between the opposing negotiators, it fosters problem solving and high joint benefit.

Perceived Feasibility and Cost

Choice among the strategies is also a matter of perceived feasibility and cost. The notion of perceived feasibility requires explanation. A strategy is seen as feasible to the extent that it seems capable of achieving the concerns that give rise to it.

Feasibility is only in doubt for the strategies of contending and problem solving, because these strategies seek responses from the other party, which party is seldom under one's control. Yielding and inaction are always feasible (though by no means always costless) because then success relies only on the negotiator's own behavior.

Considerations of feasibility and cost supplement those specified by the dual concern model. The latter model indicates the strategies preferred under different combinations of concern about own and other's outcomes. But for a strategy actually to be chosen, it also must be seen as minimally feasible and without undue cost. If not, another strategy will be chosen, even if it is less consistent with the current combination of concerns.

Take for example, negotiators who are concerned about both their own and the other's outcomes. Problem solving is their preferred strategy. But if this seems infeasible or too risky, they are likely to shift to yielding or contending, their next best alternatives. Which of these is chosen will be determined by the relative strength of the two concerns and by considerations of feasibility and cost. If they are more concerned about the other's outcomes than their own, they will take a yielding approach, provided that it is not too costly. If they are more concerned about their own outcomes than the other's, they will shift to contentious behavior, provided that it seems reasonably feasible and costless.

Another example would be negotiators who are concerned mainly with their own outcomes. Contending is their preferred strategy because it holds the promise of getting something for nothing. But problem solving is a close second if problems of feasibility or cost are associated with contending. Indeed, problem solving often seems to be the most feasible way of pursuing one's own interests.

Feasibility and Cost of Problem Solving

Perceived Common Ground. Problem solving seems more feasible the greater the *perceived common ground* (PCG) is. PCG is a party's assessment of the likelihood of finding a mutually acceptable alternative. PCG becomes greater

(a) the lower the party's own aspirations, (b) the lower the other's perceived aspirations, and (c) the greater the party's faith in the possibility of devising alternatives that are favorable to both parties.

The last theme needs further elaboration. At any given point in negotiation, some alternatives are known and the availability of others is suspected. PCG is maximal when a known alternative is believed to satisfy both parties' aspirations. It is moderately high when a suspected alternative has these characteristics — the more definite the existence of the alternative, the higher the PCG. It is minimal when there appears to be no way of satisfying both sets of aspirations.

Greater clarity about the concept of PCG is provided by the graphs in Figure 2. The abscissa in these graphs maps the negotiator's own benefits; the ordinate, his or her perception of the other party's benefits. The heavy points in these graphs refer to known alternatives, the medium points to alternatives that seem potentially discoverable, and the light points to long shots. The location of a point in the space shows the perceived value of that alternative to the two parties. The vertical lines in these graphs refer to own aspirations and the horizontal lines to the other's perceived aspirations.

PCG is greater when more points are to the northeast of the intersection of these lines and the points are darker. PCG is greater in Figure 2B than 2A because own aspirations are lower. It is greater in 2C than 2B because other's perceived aspirations are lower. It is greater in 2D than 2C because of the greater perceived likelihood that mutually beneficial alternatives can be developed (as shown by the fact that the darker points are farther from the origin in the northeast direction).

The ideas just presented suggest that problem solving is more likely to occur under conditions that diminish own and other's perceived levels of aspiration and enhance the perceived likelihood of developing mutually beneficial alternatives.

A number of conditions contribute to the choice of problem solving by enhancing the perceived likelihood of developing mutually beneficial alternatives. These include the following:

(1) *Faith in own problem-solving ability.* Some people are good communicators and/or understand well how to devise mutually beneficial alternatives. Hence, their experience will lead them to see considerable common ground in the present situation. Others less well-endowed are likely to view conflicts as more intractable, and to adopt strategies of yielding or contending rather than problem solving.

(2) *Momentum.* Momentum refers to prior success at reaching agreement in the current negotiation. The more frequent and recent such successes have been, the greater will be one's faith that they can be reproduced in the future, and hence one's conviction that problem solving is worthwhile. Momentum can sometimes be encouraged by placing easier issues earlier in a negotiation agenda, so that a solid experience of success is established by the time more difficult issues are encountered (Pruitt and Syna, 1983).

(3) *Availability of a Mediator.* Mediators often serve as communication links between the parties, coordinating movement toward compromise or helping to develop integrative solutions. Hence their availability should make problem solving seem more likely to be successful.

Figure 2

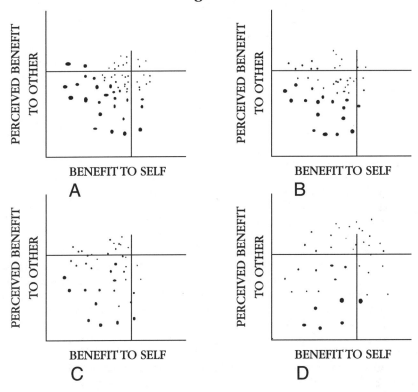

An example of the latter mechanism can be seen in the British reaction to the Argentine occupation of the Falkland Islands in 1982. Yielding was ruled out on the grounds of cost to the British image. Inaction seemed inadvisable since every day of the occupation enhanced the legitimacy of the Argentine action. In short, the choice was between contending and problem solving. At first it appeared that there might be common ground since American Secretary of State Alexander Haig was trying to mediate the crisis. Hence the British adopted a problem-solving strategy — working with Haig while defending their basic interests by moving their fleet slowly toward South America. However, PCG disappeared with the failure of Haig's mission, making problem solving seem quite infeasible. As a result, the British adopted an exclusively contentious approach — an all out invasion of the islands.

(4) *Trust.* Problem solving seems more feasible and less costly if one trusts the other party. The term "trust" has at least two meanings. In some contexts, it means a belief in the truthfulness of what the other says. In other contexts, it means a belief that the other party is concerned about our interests and hence is ready to yield or engage in problem solving. The latter meaning is the one employed here. It is not necessary that the other party's concern be seen as genuine or long lasting. A party whose concern is motivated by temporary strategic considerations can be trusted up to a point.

Trust contributes to the perceived feasibility of problem solving by making it seem more likely that mutually beneficial alternatives can be found. This is because a trusted other can be expected to help search for good solutions. Trust also cuts costs by diminishing certain risks associated with problem solving. These are the risk of (a) image loss — a perception by the other that one is willing to yield further than was previously thought (such perceptions encourage stonewalling by the other); (b) position loss — a perception by the other that one has conceded from a previously enunciated demand (such perceptions can be hard to undo); and (c) information loss — insight by the other into how far one can be pushed and what sorts of incentives are likely to make one concede. These three kinds of loss are most likely to occur if one employs direct, risky problem-solving tactics, such as discussing possible new alternatives or providing information about one's interests. Hence moderate distrust is likely to inhibit the use of such tactics. Profound distrust can even inhibit cautious, indirect approaches, such as hinting at possible compromises or cooperating with a mediator. Hence all forms of problem solving become infeasible when trust is very low.

The effect of trust on strategic choice can be seen in a study by Kimmel, Pruitt, Magenau, Konar-Goldband, and Carnevale (1980). The method used was the same as described earlier. Some subjects were given high limits so that they could not easily yield. They were also instructed to take a problem-solving approach. When trust was high, they followed these instructions, providing each other considerable information about their profit schedules. But when trust was low, they tended instead to employ persuasive arguments, threats and positional commitments — forms of contentious behavior.

While the existence of trust allows problem-solving behavior, it is no guarantee that this strategy will be employed. Indeed, trust can sometimes have quite the opposite effect, encouraging high, inflexible aspirations defended by contentious behavior.

A major key to whether trust will encourage problem solving or contending lies in the other party's perceived resistance to yielding; that is, the apparent firmness of the other's aspirations. A trusted other whose aspirations do not seem firm will be expected to give in to our demands. Hence, contentious behavior seems especially feasible. If the other's aspirations seem firm, however, trust implies instead that the other will cooperate if, and only if, we cooperate. This encourages problem solving.

Evidence that problem solving is encouraged by a combination of trust and perceived firmness comes from several studies. All examined bargainer response to helpful actions from the other party (which presumably engendered trust). When the other party had been helpful, bargainers were more willing to cooperate if the other also (a) had high threat capacity (Michener, et al., 1975); (b) had a tough constituent (Wall, 1977); (c) had been unyielding or competitive in the past (Deutsch, 1973); and (d) had been unwilling to make unilateral concessions in the past (McGillicuddy, et al., 1983). These findings suggest that trust encourages problem solving when there is reason to believe that the other has firm aspirations.

Trust develops in a number of ways. It is encouraged by a perception that the other party has a positive attitude toward us, is similar to us, or is dependent on us. As an example of the latter point, Solomon (1960) has shown that trust is greater when one sees oneself as having a capacity to punish the other for failing to cooperate. Trust also tends to develop when one has helped another party, since one assumes that the other will reciprocate one's helpful behavior.

Trust is an especially common response when the other's helpful behavior is seen as voluntary and not a product of environmental forces. Thus, we tend to trust others whose helpful behavior is not required by their role or seems to be costly to them. These points can be derived from attribution theory (Kelley, 1971).

Feasibility and Cost of Contending

Perceived Feasibility. Contending seems more feasible when the other's resistance to yielding seems lower. There is not much point in putting pressure on a party who has extremely strong feelings, or has powerful and resolute constituents, or has already yielded to the bare bone of need. Hence tactics other than contending are likely to be adopted.

The points just made imply that contentious behavior will often be self-liquidating, a victim of both failure and success. If it fails, this indicates that the other's resistance is greater than originally thought. Hence the tactic will tend to be abandoned. If it succeeds and the other yields, the other's resistance to further yielding is likely to grow because the other will come closer to his or her limit. Hence again, the tactic is likely to be abandoned.

The feasibility of contending is also a function of one's apparent capacity to employ contentious tactics and the other's apparent capacity to counter these tactics. Does one have good arguments? Does the other have counter-arguments? Is one adept at arguing one's case? How effective is the other as a debater? Can one reward or punish the other? How good are the other's defenses against such tactics? Does one have ways to commit oneself credibly? Is the other capable of undoing these commitments? Such capacities are sometimes called "power" and "counterpower." But these terms are so broad and diffuse that it seems better not to use them.

In a stable, long-term relationship, each party's capacity to employ contentious tactics tends to be matched by the other's level of resistance, so that there is relatively little advantage to either party in employing contentious tactics. Hence, on important issues where parties cannot easily yield, joint problem solving is the most likely strategic choice. This is even true when threat capacity greatly favors one side, as in a relationship between master and slave. Joint problem solving is not uncommon in such relationships, though the outcome is likely to benefit the master far more than the slave. The slave's situation produces aspirations that are so low that his or her resistance to further yielding is strong enough to balance the master's superior threat capacity.

Perceived Cost. Contentious behavior, particularly in its more severe forms, runs the risk of alienating the other party and starting a conflict spiral. There is also some danger of third-party censure for use of contentious tactics. Such considerations can deter contentious behavior, particularly when one is dependent on the other party or on watchful third parties.

Costs are also associated with constituent surveillance. Negotiators who are being observed by their constituents usually fear getting out of line with these constituents' expectations. If they believe the constituents favor toughness, they will tend to adopt contentious behavior. If they see them as conciliatory, they will avoid contending. These points are supported by a study of the joint effect of surveillance and sex of constituent (Forcey, Van Slyck, Carnevale and Pruitt, 1983) on strategic choice. Surveillance by male constituents was found to enhance negotiator contentiousness, while surveillance by female constituents was found to have the opposite effect. This makes sense if we assume that the subjects subscribed to the usual stereotype that men favor a tough approach and women a soft approach to interpersonal relations.

Time Pressure as a Cost of Inaction

Inaction is obviously the greatest time waster of the strategies. Hence time pressure should discourage use of this strategy and encourage the three coping strategies.

Time pressure can be due to the cost of continued negotiations, for example, time lost from other pursuits, the expense of maintaining negotiators in the field, or rapid deterioration of the object under dispute (e.g., fruits and vegetables). It can also result from closeness to a deadline, such as the point at which a labor contract expires.

An example of the impact of time pressure on strategic choice can be seen in the 1968 student rebellion in Mexico City, which occurred just before the Olympic Games in that city. As the opening of the games approached, the Mexican government became increasingly concerned about the continuing student disorder. In effect, deadline pressures were increasing, and the existing impasse with the students seemed less and less viable. All three of the coping strategies were employed in quick succession. First, the government yielded to a few of the students' demands and then entered into unfruitful problem-solving discussions. Finding the latter unsuccessful, the government then took the contentious (!) approach of shooting hundreds of students at a rally.

While all three coping strategies are possible in the face of time pressure, research (Carnevale et al., 1979) suggests that the favorite strategy is yielding. This is presumably because yielding is the fastest way to move toward agreement. It follows that contending and problem solving will be adopted in the face of time pressure only if there is heavy resistance to yielding.

The Vigor of Strategic Behavior

The three coping strategies can be implemented more or less vigorously. In the case of contentious behavior, vigor refers to the heaviness of the actions taken. Shouts are more vigorous than persuasive communications, blows more vigorous than shouts, shots more vigorous than blows. In the case of problem solving, vigor refers to the creativity of the problem-solving effort. At the low end of vigor would be a simple, dull effort to coordinate concession-making toward an obvious compromise. At the high end would be an active effort to understand the other's interests and thoughtful search for a way to reconcile these interests with one's own. In the case of yielding, vigor refers simply to how far down one moves one's aspirations. Vigor has no meaning with respect to the strategy of inaction.

It is common for negotiators who have adopted a copy strategy to start less vigorously and move toward greater vigor if earlier efforts do not achieve agreement. Such gradualism ensures that no greater costs will be incurred than are necessary to achieve their goals. This point is most obvious in the realm of contentious behavior. Like the United States in the Vietnam War, parties commonly begin cautiously and only escalate if unsuccessful.

An exception to this generalization can be seen in certain cases of contentious behavior. The gradualist approach to contending is defective in that the adversary is unlikely to be surprised when the heavier tactics are unveiled. Hence, he or she may have become quite prepared to resist these tactics. As a result, parties sometimes decide to employ heavily contentious tactics immediately so as to take advantage of the element of surprise. An example would be the Japanese attack on Pearl Harbor in 1941. Anticipating that lower-level action would encourage the United States to scatter its Pacific fleet, Japan went directly from the negotiation table to an all-out assault.

The vigor of two of the coping strategies is, paradoxically, a function of some of the conditions that discourage these strategies.

One of these strategies is contending. As mentioned earlier, the expectation of resistance from the other party discourages contentious behavior. But suppose that other conditions (e.g., hostility toward the other party) predispose a negotiator to contending. What is the effect of expected resistance then? Our hypothesis is that heavier contentious tactics will be used. If the other looks like a pushover, it should be easy to get a concession by simple stonewalling or persuasive argumentation. But if the other's position seems engraved in stone, heavier guns will be needed, in the form of threats or other coercive actions.

Problem solving is the other strategy with this paradoxical feature. Low PCG discourages problem solving. But it also encourages a creative form of problem solving if this strategy is adopted for other reasons. Suppose, for example, that there is a complete stalemate — both parties are totally unwilling to yield and contentious tactics seem useless. If inaction is also unattractive (e.g., because of time pressure), problem solving is the only possible approach. To the extent that PCG is low — whether because of high aspirations, a perception that the other party has high aspirations, or lack of obvious alternatives — will seem necessary to employ a more creative effort in order to reach agreement.

The latter point can be illustrated by reference to Figure 2. PCG is lower in case A than in any of the other three cases in this figure. Hence there is a reduced likelihood of problem solving. But suppose that problem solving must be employed despite its infeasibility. Then a greater creative effort would be needed in case A, because the viable options seem more remote.

Conclusion: Influencing
the Other Party's Strategic Choice

The theory presented in this article can provide guidance for influencing the other party's strategic choice. It is often desirable to try to wean one's adversary away from contentious behavior and toward a strategy of problem solving. Our theory helps understand how this can be accomplished.

The dual concern model suggests one approach, which is to try to encourage the other party to become concerned about one's outcomes. Favors can be done for the other, an effort can be made to dramatize one's similarity to the other, the other can be made dependent on oneself, the other can be put in a good mood.

Feasibility considerations suggest another approach. This is to adopt an explicit problem-solving strategy toward the other — one that is clearly understood as such by the other party. Like the bumper sticker that says "Courtesy is catching," we argue that "Problem solving is catching."

The essence of problem solving is firm flexibility within the framework of an effort to be responsive to the other party's interests. One is firm with respect to basic interests but flexible about one's proposals so as to accommodate the other's needs and values. While unwilling to compromise on ends unless they are clearly unobtainable, one is emphatic and pliable with respect to the means for accomplishing these ends. Fisher and Ury refer to this approach when they say, "It may not be wise to commit yourself to your position but it is wise to commit yourself to your interests. This is the place in negotiation to spend your aggressive energies" (1981: 55).

What are we arguing now is that a problem-solving strategy, if clearly telegraphed to the other party, will encourage that party to adopt a similar strategy. In other words, the other party is especially likely to adopt a problem-solving strategy if a manifest firmness on fundamentals is coupled with a clear flexibility on concrete details and an enthusiasm for seeking jointly beneficial options.

Our reasoning is as follows: the firm part of this strategy should convince the other that contentious behavior is infeasible, that one will never give in under pressure. The conciliatory and flexible parts should produce enough PCG and trust that the other will see problem solving as thoroughly feasible.

An example of explicit problem solving can be seen in statements and actions taken by American president John F. Kennedy in 1961 during the Second Berlin Crisis. The Russians, under Premier Nikita Khrushchev, had been trying to end American occupation of West Berlin by threatening to sign a separate peace treaty with East Germany and buzzing planes in the Berlin Corridor. Recognizing that some concessions had to be made, Kennedy "decided to be firm on essentials but negotiate on non-essentials" (Snyder and Diesing, 1977: 566). In a speech on July 25, he announced three fundamental principles that ensured the integrity and continued American occupation of West Berlin. The firmness of these principles was underscored by a pledge to defend them by force and a concomitant military buildup. Yet he also indicated flexibility and a concern about Russian sensitivities by calling for negotiations to remove "actual irritants" to the Soviet Union and its allies. Two results were achieved: the building of the Berlin wall, which (though regrettably odious to the population of Berlin) can be viewed as a bridging solution that solved the problem of population loss from East Germany without disturbing American rights in West Berlin, and eventual negotiations, which put these rights clearly in writing.

Alternatives to Explicit Problem Solving

There are three alternatives to explicit problem solving. Each is a variation of the firm flexibility theme.

One involves "firm firmness," that is, stonewalling with respect to both interests and proposals. This approach is useful when the other is weak, under severe time pressure, or has low stakes in the matter under discussion; but it is by no means a universal remedy. In most circumstances, it simply calls out a similar response from the other party so that an eventual shift to problem solving is necessary if agreement is to be reached.

The second consists of "flexible flexibility." One is willing to compromise both interests and proposals. If clearly telegraphed, this encourages stonewalling by the other party, which can harm one's interests and (if one is unwilling to capitulate) lead to failure to reach agreement.

The third alternative, "flexible firmness," would appear to be the worst of all. This entails an unyielding position at the bargaining table combined with signs of lack of commitment to the interests underlying this position. The impact of this strategy on the other party is to discourage problem solving, since it appears that nothing can be accomplished by talk, but to encourage the use of heavy contentious tactics designed to probe one's underlying flexibility.

A possible example of this approach can be seen in British behavior prior to the Argentine takeover of the Falkland Islands. According to Freedman (1982), Britain was being extremely intransigent at the negotiation table, offering little to the Argentines other than the status quo. At the same time Britain was sending out signals of a lack of commitment to the islands and their inhabitants. Certain rights of citizenship were removed from the inhabitants, the islands were made dependent on Argentina for communication with the outside world and finally a decision was made to remove the only remaining naval vessel from the South Atlantic. It appears that the Argentines received the message that there was no way to resolve the status of the islands by diplomacy but that the British would not fight.

Signaling Firmness

One element of explicit problem solving is to signal a firm commitment to one's basic interests. Our analysis suggests several ways in which this can be done. One is to make a vigorous verbal defense of these interests. A second is to be unwilling to make unilateral concessions. A third is to encourage tough statements from one's constituents, who must pass on the final acceptability of the agreement.

It may sometimes also be necessary to employ contentious tactics in order to underscore firmness with respect to basic principles. This can be particularly important when one has recently yielded ground. Otherwise, the other party may interpret one's flexibility as a sign of weakness, maintain or raise its aspirations and redouble its dedication to a contentious approach. Kennedy's performance is again a good example. His pledge to defend western rights in Berlin by force and the contemporary troop movements had this function.

The problem with contentious tactics is that they can easily militate against problem solving by rigidifying the user and alienating the adversary. In short, contentious tactics have the capacity of both contributing to and detracting from the development of integrative agreements. How can the advantages of these tactics be achieved while avoiding the pitfalls?

There are at least four answers to this question:

(1) Use contentious tactics to defend basic interests rather than a particular solution to the controversy.

(2) Send signals of flexibility and concern about the other party's interests in conjunction with contentious displays. Such maneuvers are designed to make the integrative potential seem large enough to the other party that problem solving seems warranted.

(3) Insulate contentious behavior from problem-solving behavior so that neither undermines the other. The most common form of insulation is the "black-hat/white-hat" routine, in which contentious behavior is assigned to one team member (the black hat) and problem-solving behavior to another (the white hat). In the context of the black hat's threats, the white hat's offer of cooperation is more likely to be reciprocated by the target. In the context of the white hat's blandishments, the black hat's escalation is less likely to produce a reciprocal escalation by the target. An example would be an agent who indicates to a laggard creditor that his or her principal will sue unless the two of them can reach a mutually acceptable agreement.

(4) Employ deterrent rather than compellent threats (see Schelling, 1966). Deterrent threats indicate that a particular option favored by the other is intolerable but do not speak to the adequacy of other options. Compellent threats require that a particular option be adopted. In other words, deterrent threats involve saying "no" to the other party without demanding that the other say "yes."

Signaling Flexibility and Concern
The other element of explicit problem solving is to signal flexibility about the shape of the final agreement and concern about the other's outcomes. Tactics available for this purpose include:

(1) Openly express concern with the other's welfare, in other words, "acknowledge their interests as part of the problem" (Fisher and Ury, 1981: 55).

(2) Indicate a willingness to change one's proposals if a way can be found to bridge the two parties' interests.

(3) Demonstrate problem-solving capacity, for example, by developing an expert negotiation team so that it is obvious to the other that the team has the capacity to develop useful new ideas.

(4) Maintain open communication channels to show the other party that one is ready to work with them.

(5) Reexamine any elements of one's supposed interests that are clearly unacceptable to the other party to be sure that they are essential to one's welfare. If such elements turn out to be low in priority to oneself, it may be possible to drop them. If high in priority, it may be possible to discover interests underlying these interests (Pruitt, 1983) that are not compatible with the other party's stance.

In summary, the theory presented in this article has implications for influencing the adversary's strategic choice. A reasonable goal is to try to win the adversary away from contending and toward problem solving. One possible approach is to encourage the other to become concerned about one's outcomes. Another is to engage in explicit problem-solving behavior oneself, thereby diminishing the perceived feasibility of contentious behavior for the other party and enhancing the perceived feasibility of problem solving.

NOTE

1. Firm flexibility was called "flexible rigidity" in an earlier publication (Pruitt, 1981).

REFERENCES

Bazerman, M. H. and Neale, M. A. (1983). "Heuristics in negotiation: limitation to dispute resolution effectiveness." In M. H. Bazerman and R. J. Lewicki (eds.) *Negotiations in Organizations* Beverly Hills, Calif.: Sage.

Benton, A. A. and Druckman, D. (1973). "Salient solutions and the bargaining behavior of representatives and nonrepresentatives." *International Journal of Group Tensions* 3: 28-29.

——— and Druckman, D. (1974). "Constituent's bargaining orientation and intergroup negotiations." *Journal of Applied Social Psychology* 4: 141-150.

Ben-Yoav, O. and Pruitt, D. G. (forthcoming a) "Resistance to yielding and the expectation of cooperative future interaction in negotiation." *Journal of Experimental Social Psychology*.

——— and Pruitt, D. G. (forthcoming b) "Accountability to constituents: a two edged sword." Organization Behavior and Human Performance.

Blake, R. R. and Mouton, J. A. (1964). *The managerial grid*. Houston: Gulf.

Carnevale, P. J. D., Sherer, D. and Pruitt, D. G. (1979). "Some determinants of concession rate and distributive tactics in negotiation." Presented at the annual meeting of the American Psychological Association, New York.

Clark, M. S. and Mills, J. (1979). "Interpersonal attraction in exchange and communal relationships." *Journal of Personality and Social Psychology* 37: 12-24.

Deutsch, M. (1973). *The resolution of conflict: Constructive and destructive processes*. New Haven, Conn.: Yale Univ. Press.

Filley, A. C. (1975). *Interpersonal conflict resolution*. Glenview, Ill.: Scott, Foresman.

Fisher, R. and Ury, W. (1981). *Getting to YES: Negotiation agreement without giving in*. Boston: Houghton-Mifflin.

Forcey, B., Van Slyck, M. R., Carnevale, P. J. D. and Pruitt, D. G. (1983). "Looking strong: gender differences in negotiation behavior under constituent surveillance." Presented at the annual meeting of the American Psychological Association, Los Angeles.

Freedman, L. (1982). "The war of the Falkland Islands, 1982." *Foreign Affairs* 61: 196-210.

Fry, W. R., Firestone, I. J. and Williams, D. (1979). "Bargaining process in mixed-singles dyads: loving and losing." Presented at the annual meeting of the Eastern Psychological Association, Philadelphia.

Gladwin, T. N. and Walter, I. (1980). *Multinationals under fire: Lessons in the management of conflict*. New York: John Wiley.

Hatton, J. M. (1967). "Reactions of negroes in a biracial bargaining situation." *Journal of Personality and Social Psychology* 7: 301-306.

Isen, A. M. and Levin, P. E. (1972). "Effect of feeling good on helping: cookies and kindness." *Journal of Personality and Social Psychology* 21: 384-388.

Kelley, H. H. (1971). *Attribution in social interaction*. Morristown, N.J.: General Learning Press.

——— and Schenitzki, D. P. (1972). "Bargaining." In C. G. McClintock (ed.) *Experimental social psychology*. New York: Holt, Rinehart and Winston.

———, Beckman, J. J. and Fischer, C. S. (1967). "Negotiating the division of reward under incomplete information." *Journal of Experimental Social Psychology* 3: 361-398.

———, Pruitt, D. G., Magenau, J. M., Konar-Goldband, E. and Carnevale, P. J. D. (1980). "Effects of trust aspiration and gender on negotiation tactics." *Journal of Personality and Social Psychology* 38: 9-23.

Klimoski, R. J. (1972). "The effects of intragroup forces on intergroup conflict resolution." *Org. Behavior and Human Performance* 8: 363-383.

——— and Ash, R. A. (1974). "Accountability and negotiation behavior." *Organizational Behavior and Human Performance* II: 409-425.

Kogan, N., Lamm, H. and Trommsdorff, G. (1972). "Negotiation constraints in the risk-taking domain: effects of being observed by partners of higher or lower status." *Journal of Personality and Social Psychology* 23: 143-156.

Kriesberg, L. (1973). *The sociology of social conflict*. Englewood Cliffs, N. J.: Prentice-Hall.

Longley, J. and Pruitt, D. G. (1980). "A critique of Janis's theory of groupthink." In L. Wheeler (ed.) *Review of personality and social psychology*, Vol. 1. Beverly Hills, Calif.: Sage.

McGillicuddy, N. B., **Pruitt, D. G.**, and **Syna, H.** (1983). "Perceptions of firmness and cooperativeness in negotiation." Presented at the annual meeting of the Eastern Psychological Association, Philadelphia.

Michener, H. A., **Vaske, J. J.**, **Schleifer, S. L.**, **Plazewski, J. G.** and **Chapman, L. J.** (1975). "Factors affecting concession rate and threat usage in bilateral conflict." *Sociometry* 38: 62-80.

Morley, I. E. and **Stephenson, J. M.** (1977) *The social psychology of bargaining*. London: Allen & Unwin.

Pruitt, D. G. (1983). "Achieving integrative agreements." In M. H. Bazermand and R. J. Lewicki (eds.) *Negotiations in organizations*. Beverly Hills, Calif.: Sage.

———, (1981). *Negotiation behavior*. New York: Academic.

——— and **Carnevale, P. J. D.** (1982). "The development of integrative agreements." In V. J. Derlega and J. Grzelak (eds.) *Cooperation and helping behavior*. New York: Academic.

——— and **Syna, H.** (1983). "Successful problem solving." In D. Tjosvold and D. W. Johnson (eds.) *Productive conflict management*. New York: Irvington.

———, **Carnevale, P. J. D.**, **Ben-Yoav, O.**, **Nochajski, T. H.** and **Van Slyck, M. R.** (1983). "incentives for cooperation in integrative bargaining." In R. Tietz (ed.) *Aspiration levels in bargaining and economic decision making*. Berlin: Springer.

Rahim, M. A. (1983). "A measure of styles of handling interpersonal conflict." *Academy of Management Journal* 26: 268-276.

Ruble, T. L. and **Thomas, K. W.** (1976). "Support for a two-dimensional model of conflict behavior." *Organizational Behavior and Human Performance* 16: 143-155.

Schelling, T. C. (1966). *Arms and influence*. New Haven, Conn.: Yale Univ. Press.

Snyder, G. H. and **Diesing, P.** (1977). *Conflict among nations*. princeton, N. J.: Princeton University Press.

Solomong, L. (1960). "The influence of some types of power relationships and game strategies upon the development of interpersonal trust." *Journal of Abnormal and Social Psychology* 61: 223-230.

Thomas, K. W. (1976). "Conflict and conflict management." In M. D. Dunnette (ed.) *Handbook of industrial and organizational psychology*. Chicago: Rand McNally.

Wall, J. A., Jr. (1977). "Intergroup bargaining: effects of opposing constituent's stance, opposing representative's bargaining, and representative's locus of control." *Journal of Conflict Resolution* 21: 459-474.

———, (1975). "Effects of constituent trust and representative bargaining orientation on intergroup bargaining." *Journal of Personality and Social Psychology* 31: 1004-1012.

Walton, R. E. (1969). *Interpersonal peacemaking: Confrontations and third party consultation*. Reading, Mass.: Addison-Wesley.

——— and **McKersie, R. B.** (1965). *A behavioral theory of labor negotiations*. New York: McGraw-Hill.

Anatomy of a Crisis

William L. Ury and Richard Smoke

Crises abound in and around our lives. One spouse discovers the other's infidelity and threatens a divorce unless the illicit liaison is broken off immediately. A union is on the verge of declaring a strike. Congress, about to adjourn, has failed to agree on a budget, preventing the government from paying its bills. A Third World country, unable to meet its debt payments to foreign banks, is about to be declared in default. The Soviet Union sends nuclear missiles to Cuba and the president of the United States goes on television to demand their immediate withdrawal and to announce a naval blockade of the island.

In each of these cases, a negotiation may take place to try to avert an impending major loss. Times of crisis call for a special kind of negotiation. There is no time for drawn-out discussion or the usual diplomatic dance, and typically the negotiators are under considerable stress. Nowhere is the critical role of negotiation so clear as in crisis, for here it can make the difference between peace and war, metaphorically and sometimes literally.

Richard Lebow points out that if the Cuban Missile Crisis of 1962 had developed into a cataclysmic war, historians would have had little trouble explaining why this war was inevitable, arising as it did from the deep-seated geopolitical and ideological conflict between the superpowers, the spiraling arms race, and the heightened tension of the Cold War.[1]

This paper seeks to understand the dynamics of the decision-making process in crises. What makes a crisis a crisis? What are key variables which, if manipulated in one direction, intensify the crisis, or if manipulated the other way, tend to diffuse it? Where can the decision-making process fail? We do not offer here a summary of the valuable and extensive literature which analyzes crises, but rather to attempt to distill a simple conceptual framework for understanding a crisis that a practitioner could use. Our immediate concern is not the question of how to control a crisis, but how one might usefully think about a crisis as a first step toward controlling it.

This discussion is based on two chapters in a study recently completed by the Nuclear Negotiation Project at Harvard for the United States Arms

William L. Ury is Associate Director of the Program on Negotiation at Harvard Law School, Cambridge, Mass. and Director of the Negotiation Network. **Richard Smoke** is Professor of Political Science at Brown University, Providence, R.I.

Control and Disarmament Agency. The concern of that study is how best to control a crisis between the United States and the Soviet Union to avert a nuclear war. Thus our examples are drawn from international crises.

Despite the many obvious differences between crises of this type and those between labor and management, marital partners, businesses, and governmental bureaucracies, the basic conceptual framework offered here may be of use to practitioners in all these domains.

Four Factors in a Crisis

Among the many factors that interact in a crisis, four are particularly prominent. First, *high stakes* are involved. Second, *little time* is available for making crucial decisions, and there is a felt urgency to act. Moreover, critical information is often lacking, leading to *high uncertainty* about both what is happening and how to respond. Finally, there is often a sense of *narrowing options* for coping with crisis.[2]

Each factor — stakes, time, uncertainty, and options — is more subjective than objective. What counts is not how much time there actually is, but rather the *perceived* scarcity of time. Crisis exists ultimately in people's heads.

We will discuss each of these key factors in turn, with illustrations from international crises, and suggest a few ways in which decision-makers can fail to cope adequately with each factor, either by underestimating its effect or by overreacting in ways that exacerbate the crisis to the detriment of both sides.

High Stakes

A crisis is distinguished from the normal flow of decision-making (which often included short deadlines and a feeling of urgency) by the expectation of severe losses — in other words, high stakes.

From the Western point of view, the Berlin crises of 1958 and 1961 were critical, not so much because half a city might have been lost, but because it was feared that the German alliance would unravel and, with it, NATO. If the stakes are not high, decision-makers may see themselves as "putting out fires," but not as dealing with a genuine crisis.

An inadequate grasp of the long-term stakes in a crisis can sometimes lead decision-makers to raise the stakes deliberately in the short term, in ways that they later regret. World War I provides a good example. In 1914, when Kaiser Franz Josef of the Austro-Hungarian Empire delivered an ultimatum to Serbia, in reaction to the assassination of Archduke Franz Ferdinand one month earlier, he never dreamt that he was initiating a chain of events that within a month would involve all of Europe and much of the rest of the world in a catastrophic war, and that within four years would result in the destruction of the empire he and his ancestors had ruled for centuries. Nor when Czar Nicholas II responded to the ultimatum by mobilizing the huge Russian armies along the Austrian border did he foresee a bloody, four-year war which in the end would cost him his throne and his life.

Each of these actions represents a failure to anticipate adequately a possible sequence of escalation in a crisis. Each exemplifies the difficulty, when immersed in a crisis and under great stress, of properly gauging the potential consequences of one's own actions. In focusing so narrowly on getting the adversary to concede, one can easily neglect other effects of one's actions or the chain of reactions that can ensue and end in war. All too often parties calculate potential short-term gains without adequately appreciating possible long-term losses. Failing to realize fully the ultimate stakes in the crisis, one party or both boldly raises the immediate stakes.

The 1967 Middle East War illustrates another kind of failure to control the stakes: mutual reinforcement of hostile expectations. In 1967, in response to reports that the Israelis were about to attack Syria, President Nasser of Egypt ordered U.N. peacekeeping forces out of the Sinai and closed the Gulf of Aqaba to Israeli shipping. Fearing an imminent attack, Israel decided to launch a preemptive war.

Each side misread the other's moves, which were essentially reactive and defensive, as offensive. The mutual reinforcement of hostile expectations thus helped provoke an unnecessary war. This failure to control the perceived stakes is particularly relevant in the nuclear age. For while each superpower has a strong incentive not to strike as long as war seems unlikely, each side may have an incentive to strike first if it believes war is imminent. Mutual, self-reinforcing expectations of hostile action by the other side could trigger a nuclear war.

Little Time
In the Spring of 1958, Premier Khrushchev threatened to take unilateral action in Berlin unless the issue of its status was resolved by the end of December. As the date drew near, the sense of crisis mounted in the West. Early in December, however, when reporters questioned Khrushchev about whether and when the Soviets would act, he is said to have responded, "Well, if not *this* December, then *some* December." Needless to say, government officials in the West slept more peacefully that night.

True or not, this story illustrates that however grave the issues at stake, an event is usually not thought of as a crisis if plenty of time is available.

Little available time to decide is a fundamental aspect of crises. The 1973 Middle East War became an acute superpower crisis when the Israelis encircled the Egyptian Third Army and threatened to capture it, which would have been a grave humiliation for Egypt and her Soviet patron. In the Cuban Missile Crisis of 1962, President Kennedy sought to move the naval blockade from eight hundred miles to five hundred miles away from Cuba, precisely to give Premier Khrushchev more time to think, to consult with his advisers, and to negotiate.

Decision-makers may fail to appreciate the value of time in a crisis or potential crisis, thereby unintentionally allowing the crisis to grow worse. A failure to gain potential time is illustrated by the Sinai crisis of 1967. When President Nasser asked the U.N. peacekeeping force to leave the Sinai, Secretary General U Thant complied within two days. Although he had serious misgivings about responding immediately, he believed he could not refuse without questioning Egypt's sovereign authority. But if instead he had told Nasser that the matter needed to be raised first in the Security Council, he might have bought precious time for mediation efforts to reassure all sides that none contemplated an attack. In fact, none did, originally. But Nasser's action led almost directly to the Israeli preemptive strike that touched off another Middle East War.

Sometimes decision-makers will deliberately reduce the time available for decision as a way of escalating crisis. One classic method is the ultimatum, which by definition includes a tight deadline.

The ultimatum Kaiser Franz Josef gave Serbia in July 1914 presented the following terms: surrender the archduke's murderer and make certain concessions within forty-eight hours or expect military action. Allowing only forty-eight hours for a response hardly gave the Serbians' patron, Russia, time to deliberate wisely. The czar refused, and the escalation sequence leading to World War I continued swiftly: within days Germany had issued a twenty-four-hour ultimatum to Russia and an eighteen-hour ultimatum to France. There was little time for cool heads to prevail.

Not every ultimatum, of course, is so ill-advised; some may be appropriate. But many, like Franz Josef's, so constrict the time available for deciding that wise decisions in the interests of both sides become difficult or impossible.

High Uncertainty

Decision-makers often report that one major feature of the crisis experience is a sense of great uncertainty. Not enough clear information is available, and they feel that they are groping in a fog.

Three kinds of uncertainty should be distinguished. The simplest is a lack of critical *information* about what is going on. To what degree are the opponent's forces mobilized? Where are they deployed? What exactly is occurring? Factual data generally are incomplete.

Almost always there is great uncertainty about the other side's *intentions*. During the 1973 Middle East War, for instance, American intelligence discovered that the Soviets were shipping nuclear material through Bosporus. Did this mean that they were about to introduce nuclear weapons to the war? Or threaten to do so?

Closely related to uncertainty about the opponent's intentions is great uncertainty about the *escalation* sequences that could result from the current situation. In the Cuban Missile Crisis, the American leaders worried that Khrushchev might suddenly move against Berlin or take another drastic action. If so, the West would have to respond, of course, which might well provoke a Soviet counter-response, and so on. Who knew where it might end?

A considerable amount of uncertainty is intrinsic in crises. But sometimes the uncertainties are increased unnecessarily, either because one party fails to communicate its intentions and interests, or because decision-makers fail to take seriously the communications they do receive.

A classic example of the former preceded the crisis over Korea in 1950. In a famous speech, Secretary of State Acheson described the perimeter of American vital interests. His exclusion of South Korea from this defense zone is widely considered to have encouraged the North Koreans, with Soviet assent and backing, to invade the south. They apparently did not expect the massive American military intervention that followed. A failure by the U.S. to communicate and by the Communists to understand American intentions thus may well have contributed to the outbreak of the Korean War.

Sometimes serious warnings are given but go unheeded. The Cuban Missile Crisis might have been averted if Premier Khrushchev had believed American warnings that the U.S. would not tolerate missiles in Cuba. If he had known President Kennedy would establish a naval blockade around Cuba and issue an ultimatum, it is doubtful he would have ordered the missiles sent to Cuba. The Soviets did receive strong American warnings on several occasions during the summer and early fall of 1962. The failure was thus not one of communication but of credibility: Khrushchev did not take the warnings seriously — or seriously enough.

Narrowing Options

Even with short time, high stakes, and high uncertainty, a crisis may not seem severe as long as decision-makers feel they have usable options available. In a mounting crisis, decision-makers typically see their options as narrowing. As this process continues, the options often lie at the extremes of escalating or backing down, with each approach carrying a high risk; options in the middle are lacking. In Roberta Wohlstetter's phrase, options in a crisis are "sliced thick" compared to normal times when more differentiated or "fine tuned" options are available or can be developed. During the first few days of the Cuban Missile Crisis, for instance, only two options were really discussed: doing nothing in response, or carrying out an air strike that could easily have triggered a war.

When options do exist, or could be invented, that might help resolve a crisis, decision-makers sometimes reduce their flexibility unnecessarily. They may fail to generate a larger range of options; or, on occasion, they may shrink their range of options deliberately.

A good example of the former is provided by the Bay of Pigs episode which occurred early in the Kennedy administration. A secret operation to invade Cuba and overthrow Fidel Castro with Cuban emigres was hatched by the CIA during the Eisenhower administration and presented to President Kennedy for decision. As Kennedy neither requested nor was offered any credible alternatives, he was faced with choosing between executing a risky plan or incurring heavy bureaucratic and political costs for not acting at all. The ill-conceived venture which resulted proved a fiasco. The failure can be attributed to many mistakes, but surely one of the most significant was the lack of options from which to choose at the time of decision.

Failure to generate additional options is one thing; foreclosing deliberately on options that could defuse a crisis is quite another. This strategy, known as a "commitment strategy" and resembling the game of chicken, is graphically illustrated by Thomas Schelling's anecdote of two dynamite trucks barreling toward each other on a single-lane road. The question is which truck will go off the road to avoid a collision. As the trucks near each other, one driver, in full view of the other, pulls off his steering wheel and throws it out the window. Seeing this, the other driver can only choose between a crash and driving his truck off the road into a ditch.

International affairs rarely present choices this stark, but nations often do visibly increase their commitment to some course of action. This strategy may strengthen one's bargaining position but, when indulged in by both sides during a crisis, may leave no other option except war. Such was the case, for example, in the conflict between the British and French in North America in the mid-eighteenth century. The actions each side took to demonstrate its own resolve did not have a demonstrative effect but instead progressively narrowed the other side's expectations about likely futures. The two sides came to perceive each other no longer as limited adversaries but as implacable enemies.[3] The result was a bloody seven-year worldwide war which neither the British nor the French had originally intended.

The Trajectory of Crises

As a crisis intensifies, decision-makers typically sense that all four factors are becoming more serious. The press of time becomes more noticeable. The stakes rise; and partly because, as they do, they bring new considerations into play about which little is known, the uncertainties also increase. As a crisis mounts, decision-makers often have the sense that they are rapidly approaching the point where they will have only a few and extreme options left. This sense of constricting possibilities is one of the psychologically distinctive features of the crisis experience. In the various Berlin crises, for instance, Western decision-makers sometimes found themselves only a couple of steps away from the point where they would have to order a major military action, which might well have provoked a European war. At points in the 1973 Middle East Crisis, U.S. officials felt they were only a few steps from an intense East-West confrontation.

An intensifying crisis compels decision-makers to consider and make tradeoffs among values, tradeoffs that they rarely have to make otherwise. Typically they may face a greater risk of major war, and an increased chance of a major politico-diplomatic (and perhaps military) victory, as well as other risks and gains. Not only must they judge the risks as well as they can, but they must make uncomfortable choices. In the Cuban Missile Crisis, for instance, Soviet leaders ultimately were faced with the uncomfortable choice between appearing to back down before American threats and demands, and running a serious risk of global nuclear war. In normal times leaders can try to pursue multiple goals in parallel, but the constricted possibilities inherent in crises force leaders to assign weights to different goals.

The possibility of a serious defeat or war (i.e., the rising stakes) also tends to increase decision-makers' sense of hostility toward the other side, and expectations of hostility from the other side. Short time, the uncertainties, the difficult value tradeoffs, and the sense of constricting possibilities exacerbate the hostility felt and expected. As it increases, decision-makers naturally become less sensitive to indications that the other side may not be entirely hostile. Tentative feelers toward finding some kind of resolution may be dismissed or downgraded. Genuine opportunities to defuse the crisis may be missed.

Crises in Their Context

Up to this point, we have discussed the dynamics of crises independent of their causes: the known motivations which create and sustain them. Anatomy is different from etiology but eventually must be related to it.

The four crisis factors just described are like levers people may pull, mostly by intention, sometimes not. Crises rarely just occur; they occur (at least up to a point) because people want them to occur. Policy-makers seek objectives which they often hope will be achievable without a crisis. But if they are eager enough to attain these objectives, they will be willing to assume some risk of precipitating a crisis in the process. Nations have vital interests that they will try to satisfy at almost any cost, and they often go beyond vital interests to try to satisfy aspirations as well.

Once a crisis is on, decision-makers face a crucial dilemma: how to avoid the great losses that may be incurred in escalating to war while still furthering vital interests. Even where the interest in avoiding war outweighs other interests — as in cases where there is a danger of nuclear war — attempts to defuse the crisis pose a profound problem. If one backs down in order to preserve peace, may one thereby encourage the other side to press its advantage — immediately or later — and provoke another, perhaps even more dangerous, crisis?

Even if a crisis begins with cool calculation, it can end with runaway escalation. Crises sometimes escape the control of the decision-makers on both sides and end in outcomes unfavorable to both. At the height of the Cuban Missile Crisis, Premier Khrushchev vividly expressed this dual quality of deliberateness and inadvertence in a letter to President Kennedy:

> If you have not lost your self-control and sensibly conceive what this might lead to, then, Mr. President, we and you ought not to pull on the ends of the rope in which you have tied the knot of war, because the more the two of us pull. the tighter the knot will be tied. And a moment may come when the knot will be tied so tight that not even he who tied it will...have the strength to untie it, and then it will be necessary to cut that knot, and what that would mean is not for me to explain to you, because you yourself understand perfectly of what terrible forces our countries dispose.[4]

Conclusions

While people may pull the four crisis levers for many reasons, the levers themselves are neutral. To the extent one has an interest in escalating a crisis, one can do so by raising the perceived stakes, reducing the perceived time, increasing the perceived uncertainty, and decreasing the perceived available options. To the extent, however, that one wants to defuse the crisis, one wants to foster on both sides a high-quality decision-making process that tries to:

1. control the perceived stakes
2. insure adequate time for each side to consult and to decide
3. insure a flow of accurate, credible information about the situation and the other side's intentions (thereby helping to reduce uncertainty)
4. maintain enough flexibility of action (i.e., enough options) for both sides to be able to defuse the crisis.

In 1914, just after the Austro-Hungarian crisis had turned into a general European war, Prince Bernhard von Bülow, ex-Chancellor of Germany, is reputed to have asked his successor, " How did it all happen?" "If only we knew," came the answer. In this discussion, we have attempted to provide a rudimentary conceptual framework for understanding the dynamics of crises that might make for a more intellectually satisfying answer. Even better, it might contribute to a greater understanding of crises among those who are trying to make sure von Bülow's question need never be asked in the first place.

NOTES

1. See Richard N. Lebow, *Between Peace and War* (Baltimore: Johns Hopkins University Press, 1981), p. 3.

2. We are indebted to Roger Fisher for his characteristically elegant summation of a crisis as a situation with high stakes, short time, and high uncertainty. To his list we have added a fourth element: narrowing options.

3. See Richard Smoke, *War: Controlling Escalation* (Cambridge, Mass.: Harvard University Press, 1077), p. 236.

4. Khrushchev to Kennedy, 26 October 1962, cited in Graham T. Allison, *Essence of Decision: Explaining the Cuban Missile Crisis* (Boston: Little, Brown, 1971), pp. 222-23. Allison reconstructs the letter, which is still classified, from public sources.

Section II

Organizing Your Team

Before coming to the negotiating table, two forms of pre-negotiation are critical to the success of the ensuing exchange. First, *internal agreement* is necessary among the individuals whose interests should be represented; this is the subject of the present section. And second, it is important for negotiators to *come to the table prepared*, either through individual or joint work; this is the focus of Section III.

Effective pre-negotiation requires that the members of each negotiating side or team agree among themselves about various substantive and procedural matters. Negotiations within an organization or team are often just as important as the negotiations involving the other parties — and sometimes internal negotiations are even more important than the external. Despite this fact, internal negotiations are too often overlooked in favor of the transactions that subsequently take place at the table itself. Effective internal preparation accomplishes several objectives: it makes less likely the possibility of encountering a nasty surprise later on, and it does this by making sure that possible conflicting interests have been taken into account; second, it provides an often much-needed "dress rehearsal" for the subsequent proceedings.

Each of the four selections in Section II points to one or more of the kinds of preparatory work that can — and should — take place before coming to the table. Harold H. Saunders' essay ("We Need a Larger Theory of Negotiation: The Importance of Pre-negotiating Phases") develops the view that it is the obstacles *to* negotiation (rather than the hurdles *in* negotiation) that often make it impossible for successful negotiation to occur. Using the ongoing conflict in the Middle East as a case in point, he outlines five stages that are found in all negotiations, arguing for the pre-negotiation importance of three of these in particular: defining the problem in a way that leads itself to solution through negotiation; producing a prior commitment to a negotiated settlement; and third, anticipating the arrangement details of an upcoming negotiation.

Roger Fisher's article ("Negotiating Inside Out: What are the Best Ways to Relate Internal Negotiations with External Ones?") begins by analyzing several sources of difficulty that may influence the effectiveness of internal negotiations. He then provides a draft set of guidelines that he believes should be followed in preparing one's side to negotiate.

The third selection ("When Should We Use Agents? Direct vs. Representative Negotiation") outlines the tradeoffs involved in choosing between negotiating through agents or direct exchanges. This is obviously a matter of paramount concern during the internal negotiations that precede getting to the table, since the ensuing process may go rather differently when disputants are engaged directly, rather than approaching each other through representatives as intermediaries. As described by Jeffrey Z. Rubin and Frank E. A. Sander, agents can be used (or anticipated) in negotiation as a way of providing greater expertise on substance and/or process; as a buffer between disputants who may be so angry that direct exchange is likely to prove harmful; and to give the principals an additional decision-making opportunity to reject whatever agreement the agents tentatively reach. On the other hand, the use of agents introduces the possibility of incompetence (on the part of these representatives) and increases the chances that the presence of additional "moving parts" will complicate or delay reaching a mutually acceptable agreement.

In the concluding essay of this section ("Mock Pseudo-Negotiations with Surrogate Disputants"), Howard Raiffa outlines a creative approach to evaluating the suitability and likely outcome of negotiation — before ever coming to the table. According to the Raiffa proposal, an "analytical intervenor" (AI) could be used to develop a likely negotiating scenario based on the existing data about a conflict. Based on the intervenor's assessment, the disputants could better evaluate the results that are likely to occur in an actual negotiation, and could develop a greater sense of motivation to negotiate (or not), as the case may be.

We Need a Larger Theory of Negotiation: The Importance of Pre-Negotiating Phases

Harold H. Saunders

The Larger Negotiating Process

Crucial as it is, around-the-table negotiation is only a later part of a larger process needed to resolve conflicts by peaceful means. In many cases, persuading parties to a conflict to commit to a negotiated settlement is even more complicated, time-consuming, and difficult than reaching agreement once negotiations have begun. Those who try to resolve conflict peacefully need to think in terms of a process that deals with the obstacles *to* negotiation as well as the hurdles *in* negotiation. Unless we enlarge our scope to understand why parties to a conflict will not talk, we are not constructing a theory of negotiation most likely to give negotiation a chance.

This article is written from the perspective of someone who spent much of two decades dealing with the Arab-Israeli-Palestinian conflict, where most of the parties refuse to talk or even to recognize each other. In my opinion, negotiating theory that concentrates only on what happens around the negotiating table does not provide the President and Secretary of State with as useful a theory of negotiation as they need to conduct the nation's foreign policy. My views developed mainly from experience in foreign affairs — particularly the efforts to join a negotiation among the parties to the conflict after the 1967 Arab-Israeli war, the Kissinger shuttles, Camp David, the negotiation of the Egyptian-Israeli peace treaty, and the probes and negotiations on the release of the American hostages in Tehran.

I believe these observations are just as applicable to other fields of negotiation. I would suggest that the marriage counsellor's main task is to probe how a couple can be persuaded to talk seriously, for when the couple reaches the negotiating table with lawyers, the marriage is probably over. The litigator may often serve a client best when he or she avoids the confrontation of a trial and finds a way to establish communication and negotiation out of court. The employer may serve his or her institution best by finding mechanisms for resolving employee concerns before a costly strike and prolonged negotiation or arbitration. In short, we would all profit from paying as much attention to persuading parties to talk before a confrontation as we do to advising them on how to handle themselves once they are negotiating their way out of a confrontation. Breaking the pre-negotiating impasse in any field may depend as much on the insight of the psychiatrist, the social psychologist, or the cultural anthropologist as on the practitioner in around-the-table

Harold H. Saunders, Director of International Affairs for the Kettering Foundation in Washington, D.C., served as U.S. Assistant Secretary of State for Near Eastern and South Asian Affairs from 1978 to 1981.

negotiation. It is a question ripe for those who are willing to try distilling general observations about it from an interdisciplinary base.

In urging that we think in terms of a larger negotiating process, I recognize that I may be walking into that academic buzzsaw called a "definitional problem." When are we talking about negotiation, and when are we talking about the general conduct of human relations or international relations? William Zartman and Maureen Berman say, "Long before the first formal session opens, the negotiation process begins with the decision made by each party to explore the possibility of negotiating." My next question is: What do we do before that decision is made? Zartman and Berman usefully present a three-stage model that begins with what they call the "diagnostic phase" in which efforts are made to bring about negotiations.[1] I suggest that we must reach back even further and more extensively into the period before that decision to negotiate is made, and analyze what can be done to help parties reach that decision.

Concentrating on the field of foreign affairs, I have two major reasons to persist in suggesting a larger negotiating process as the framework for teaching and research in this field. They are:

1. Many of the world's most intractable conflicts at home and abroad force us to spend much of our effort in the pre-negotiation period before a decision to negotiate has been made. We need to know a lot more about how to produce that decision. We need to analyze more thoroughly why parties stop short of that decision. What would persuade some parties not talking at all, like Israelis and Palestinians, to negotiate seriously? What would persuade others who often engage only in a show of negotiation to commit themselves to a negotiated agreement? One could find this question at the heart of decisions on how to conduct the critical relationship between the United States and the Soviet Union. It is in these stages before formal negotiation that the decision is most likely to be made to pursue or avoid conflict. It is at this point that nations decide whether they must go to war to change the balance for an ultimate negotiation.

2. Analyzing the pre-negotiation phase of a conflict more fully may enable us to establish useful reciprocal links between negotiation theory, the psychology of interpersonal or cross-cultural relations, and the conduct of diplomacy and foreign policy. Students of negotiation itself have written about using the insights of psychology, anthropology, sociology, group dynamics, problem solving and other disciplines in the negotiating room. That is important, but it may be even more important to world peace to redouble efforts to apply those insights to the moments in which decisions on confrontation versus negotiation are made. In the field of foreign affairs, an enlarged theory of the negotiating process can provide a framework for analyzing the status of potentially confrontational relationships like the U.S.-Soviet relationship. It could help in developing a strategy for conducting the relationship while protecting individual interests, building on common interests, and avoiding conflict. And, in addition, focusing on different parts of the negotiating process will help us to use the tools best-suited for the job at any particular point in that process.

My examples are drawn from experience in what we have called the Middle East "peace process." My purpose is not, at this stage, to provide detailed analysis of the pre-negotiation phase, but rather to see whether we can frame a perspective that is useful. Such a framework could provide pegs on which to hang specific analyses of various elements of the negotiating process so as to help differentiate what are appropriate actions in each of them. For those in the field of foreign affairs, this approach may suggest ways of thinking about strategies for crisis prevention and management, peacemaking, and negotiation that may themselves become the essence of policy.

The Middle East 'Peace Process'

I want to set the stage by talking about the Middle East "peace process" because it is the route by which I have arrived at this larger view of the negotiating process. After leaving government, I was asked to speak about negotiation alongside someone who was explaining the techniques of around-the-table negotiation. It occurred to me that I had worked on the Arab-Israeli conflict for seven years before I saw any direct contact between parties, and for five more before I saw an agreement mediated. By that time the conflict was already entering its third decade. For me the problem was how to persuade the parties to negotiate, not how they would negotiate. That problem lay in a larger field of negotiation theory than any I had read. It required us to ask: *Why don't people negotiate?*

I recognize that the phrase, "peace process," has little standing in academic literature, but something like it was needed. In the 1970s, those of us working with the Arab-Israeli-Palestinian conflict coined the phrase to fill a gap in the vocabulary of diplomacy and negotiating theory. There were no words that we knew to describe what we were engaged in.

Much of the theory of negotiation seemed inadequate to deal with the fact that parties to this intractable conflict would not recognize each other, would not talk with each other, would not commit themselves to a negotiated settlement, and would not negotiate. In the wake of the 1973 war, we were mediating interim agreements between the parties that committed them to negotiate a larger settlement. During the Kissinger shuttles, the United States gained Saudi agreement to lift the oil embargo; resumed diplomatic relations with three Arab governments that had been broken in 1967; established joint economic commissions with four governments; and facilitated the reorientation of Egypt's primary external political, economic, and military relationships from the Soviet Union to the West. The "process" was a complicated mix of diplomacy, negotiation, and economic, political, and military decisions with each step reinforcing others and, in turn, making new relationships possible. In short, the negotiating process was an inseparable part of a larger diplomatic process designed in part to help build a political environment that would make the next round of negotiation more possible.

We needed a shorthand way of describing the total effort in which we were engaged to manage crisis, to produce negotiation, and to use negotiation to improve the climate for further negotiation. While the term "shuttle negotiations" generally made the headlines, to those of us involved from the President and Secretary of State down, this process was a coherent effort to move toward peace negotiations and settlements through a series of interrelated steps, programs and agreements. It was an effort at the same time to build broad political support for those who were negotiating. Thus, the phrase "peace process" was intended to provide a framework which could be useful in discussing an approach to international conflict that may include but goes well beyond negotiation.

Even if one returns from such wide horizons more concretely to the field of theories about negotiation itself, there is one important reason for thinking in terms of a process larger than what happens around the negotiating table: If we do not understand where we are in the negotiating process, we may use the wrong instruments in trying to move the process forward.

By the end of the 1970s, for instance, many Americans came to think of the Arab-Israeli negotiations in terms of the familiar pictures of Egyptians and Israelis sitting across the table from each other — with lawyers exchanging texts, military men exchanging maps and timetables, political leaders meeting to sign agreements. Most Americans forgot the nearly thirty years of terrorist and retaliatory attacks and the five armed conflicts that preceded those around-the-table negotiations. We were driving in fourth gear, but we forgot those years when one side would not even talk of peace with the other, when face-to-face negotiations were impossible.

After 1979, when we moved beyond the Egyptian-Israeli peace treaty to face the Israeli-Palestinian problem we had to shift back to first gear. Once again, we were in the early stages of the peace process — where people neither recognize nor talk to each other, and where neither side is committed to a fairly negotiated settlement with the other. The techniques of around-the-table negotiation may help, but they may not be adequate by themselves. Other techniques of political process such as the use of force, appeal to political constituencies, or shifts in the balance between potential negotiating parties may come into play more decisively.

Anyone coping with the Arab-Israeli-Palestinian problem is aware that negotiation is only one element needed to resolve conflict. In fact, getting to negotiation may be much more complex than working toward agreement once actual negotiation begins. Moreover, if we try now to use only the techniques of the negotiating table in this phase, we may well overlook the instruments of influence that could make a difference.

Some theorists define negotiation broadly enough to say that every human exchange is a negotiation of sorts and that the elements of negotiation are involved even when people are not sitting around the table with each other. I accept the point but do not believe it is a solution to the problem being discussed. I am afraid that it will narrow our perspective and leave out too many of the instruments important in bringing parties to negotiation.

Look at some of the steps that led to negotiation of the Egypt-Israel peace treaty or which now block Israeli-Palestinian negotiations. They make clear that instruments removing obstacles to negotiation have sometimes been those not normally considered techniques common in around-the-table negotiation:

- Egyptian President Nasser used to ask: "How can I negotiate when I'm flat on my back with a sword at my throat?" President Sadat knew that he had to erase the humiliation of the Arab defeat in the 1967 war before he could negotiate. He went to war in 1973, regained some territory east of the Suez Canal, and agreed to a ceasefire while Israeli forces were pouring across the Canal and encircling the Egyptian Third Army. Without reference to the military situation on the ground, he declared victory and his readiness to negotiate from a new position of dignity. He used the war to remove a psychological obstacle to negotiating peace.

• Saudi Arabia used the "oil weapon" to reinforce Sadat's other purpose in going to war: to put the weight of the United States back on the side of a fairly negotiated peace, partially offsetting Israel's continuing military superiority. The Arab oil-producers made the point that they could no longer live comfortably with the United States' seemingly unqualified support for Israel's retention of territories occupied in the 1967 war. The long lines at the gas pumps in the U.S. — by Saudi design or not — forced the American people to realize there was an Arab side to the Middle East story, and that events in the Middle East affect American lives and pocketbooks.

• On his historic visit to Jerusalem in 1977, President Sadat took with him a negotiating position unacceptable to Israelis: withdrawal to the 1967 borders, an independent Palestinian state, and restoration of Arab sovereignty in East Jerusalem. Why did Israel respond so warmly and eventually agree to give back the Sinai and its precious oil fields? Because Sadat's very presence brought a message that was more important: Egypt recognizes Israel, Egypt will commit itself to "no more war," Egypt will make peace with Israel, Egypt will accept Israel as a Jewish state in the Middle East, Egypt will enter into normal relations with Israel. No other negotiating formula or technique could have removed the main obstacle to negotiation so decisively or have set the stage for Sadat to achieve important objectives once negotiations began.

• Today, neither Palestinians nor Israelis are committed to peace with each other. In the early 1970s, Prime Minister Golda Meir said that Egypt's closing of the Suez Canal reminded her of a sign on a door in the small Russian town where she lived as a child which read "No Jews." The shutdown of the Canal was the sign of Arab refusal to accept and recognize Israel. Early in 1983, Abu Iyad, one of the Palestine Liberation Organization's top officials, said: "....if the Reagan plan is improved by adding one word — self determination — things would change completely."[2] From the Palestinian viewpoint, the sign hanging on the door today reads "No Palestinians." The President of the United States has called for resolving the Palestinian problem "in association with Jordan" — not by treating the Palestinians as a people entitled to separate political expression of their own identity. The Government of Israel will not sit with the PLO and has stated its policy of encouraging Palestinians to live as an ethnic minority in other states.

Removing the obstacles to negotiation is the critical first task in the process of moving toward negotiated agreements. These examples are but a few suggesting that removing obstacles to negotiation may require approaches and instruments different from those required at the negotiating table. At issue is whether or not there is a framework within which to identify precisely and to examine why parties to a conflict will not negotiate, and what changes in the situation might enable them to do so. The remainder of this article addresses these issues as two questions: (1) Can the parties organize themselves to make the decisions necessary for negotiation? (2) What in their analysis of the situation stands against a decision to negotiate? In responding to these questions, I will suggest that we think more intensively about those parts of the negotiating process which take place before around-the-table negotiation begins.

Are They Organized to Negotiate?

Before probing the substantive reasons why either side may be reluctant to negotiate, we must understand how decisions are made on both sides. One of the principal obstacles to negotiation sometimes is inability on one or both sides to organize for negotiation. Related is the absence on one side or the other of representatives with a clear mandate to speak for their side.

Both Israelis and Palestinians have problems of this kind. The problem on the Palestinian side has long been how fully Chairman Yasir Arafat is supported by his own organization in developing a common negotiating position with King Hussein of Jordan. Palestinian leaders in the territories occupied by Israel, who could be invited to join negotiations to set up a Palestinian self-governing authority in the West Bank and Gaza, see no way to put together a mandate for themselves to speak for the entire Palestinian movement in such negotiations. Israel, on the other hand, has a well-tested system for choosing leaders and giving them a mandate, but Israel is deeply divided over how to settle with the Palestinians. Both political parties in Israel represent divergent schools of thought in the Zionist movement; any government knows it could face strong and possibly violent opposition to some kinds of settlement. The prospect of internal division could paralyze Israeli decision making on this issue.

Whatever the substance of efforts to break the impasse, progress toward negotiation in this case requires working with the politics of decision making on each side. Where states or liberation organizations are involved, tactics not excluding war and other forms of violence have to be taken into account.

Identifying the Substantive Obstacles:
A Five-Part Process

Does the experience of the Middle East "peace process" offer a useful framework for analyzing substantive obstacles to negotiation? What are its elements? Let me lay out for discussion what I would describe as the five parts of the negotiating process as we have experienced it. The three parts before actual negotiation begins are my main interest here.

I must underscore that, while I might speak interchangeably in terms of "parts" or "stages" of the negotiating process, I do *not* think in terms of a succession of discrete stages where one is complete before the next begins. There is a chronological element, but my experience in decision making, diplomacy, and negotiation suggests that important issues are rarely completely resolved. A President of the United States will normally make policy decisions that do not close the door on later mid-course corrections as he works his way through political minefields. In international relations one agreement is often the prelude to others rather than the end of a problem. Therefore, to speak of "parts" or "stages" is to speak of groups of judgments that need to be made in logical progression. That progression cannot be rigid. It must allow for constant review. Each judgment will be tentative because later judgments based on new experience may cause a party to go back and rethink. Despite this fluidity, it is worth reflecting on the questions, decisions and activities which are most likely to appear in each of these five areas in the course of the negotiating process:

1. *Defining the Problem*

In policymaking, how one defines a problem begins to determine what he or she will do about it. The definition of the problem begins to determine policy. In negotiation theory, the recognition of a common problem that two sides share an interest in solving is almost a prerequisite to negotiation. In fact, negotiation is sometimes defined as a shared effort to solve a problem. Determining how each side defines the problem and whether or not their definitions overlap may be a first step in isolating some of the reasons why parties negotiate or fail to negotiate.

The definition of interests and objectives is a profoundly political act and not just an abstract academic exercise. Prolonged national debates take place over these issues. Bringing a nation to consensus or majority opinion on the shape of the problem and national objectives is a necessary prelude to serious negotiation. One can legitimately argue that this subject belongs in a study of national decision making and not in a discussion about negotiation. Perhaps so, but for the diplomat negotiating resolution of a conflict, the two are not separable. Trying to negotiate before the parties share some common definition of the problem leads to failure.

Let me again use the Arab-Israeli-Palestinian conflict as an example of how a problem has been differently defined over three and a half decades and how the shifting perspective on the problem has dictated different policies toward it:

- Before 1948, the problem was clearly defined in Washington in terms of a contest between the rising number of Jewish immigrants coming to Palestine and the Palestinian Arabs already living there, with each party claiming the same land west of the Jordan River. It was a problem of two peoples — two nationalist movements — pursuing the right of self-determination in land that each claimed. The problem, rooted deep in religion and history, also had overtones as fresh as the experience of decolonization and growing nationalism that intensified in the postwar period.

- After the state of Israel was established as an independent state, however, all of those involved came to think of the conflict as the Arab-Israeli conflict — a conflict among states. The Palestinian people, who had been the other half of the equation in the 1940s, were left as refugees or as second-class citizens. The Arab states assumed the role of the Palestinian Arabs in Palestine. The Israelis viewed the Palestinians as refugees or as an ethnic minority within established states.

- Only in the late 1960s and 1970s did the Palestinians reassert their claim to separate national identity, and it was not until 1974 that the Arab states proclaimed that the Palestine Liberation Organization would speak for the Palestinian people. At Camp David in 1978, the governments of Egypt, Israel, and the United States declared, in effect, that there could be no solution to the Arab-Israeli state-to-state conflict without a resolution of the problem of the Palestinian people as well.

Despite the agreement at Camp David, a common definition of the problem still does not exist on all sides. The philosophy of the coalition that governed Israel under Prime Ministers Menachem Begin and Yitzhak Shamir defines the primary problems as consolidating and securing greater Israel in all the land west of the Jordan River. For mainstream Palestinians today, the problem seems to have become how to gain recognition of their right as a people to exercise self-determination in some part of that land from which Israel would withdraw in a peace settlement. For the United States, the problem remains how two peoples — Israelis and Palestinians — can live together in peace and dignity within the framework of peace between Israel and the established Arab states. There are Israelis and Palestinians who would define the problem in more or less the same way as the United States, but they have not in recent years been able to commit their respective bodies politic to act from that position.

Today, even in Israel and in the United States, there is not full agreement on the nature of the problem. One of the most politically contentious issues since the early 1970s has been whether the Palestinian problem is absorbed in the state-to-state conflict or whether the Palestinian problem remains, in significant part, a conflict between two peoples with claims to the same land. In some quarters it is still seen as a state-to-state conflict between Israel and neighboring states with the Palestinians not recognized as a separate people but simply as "Arabs" who can be absorbed as ethnic minorities in existing Arab states. Others believe that there will be no resolution of the state-to-state Arab-Israeli conflict until the Palestinian people are recognized as a people with a separate identity in their own right and have the opportunity for full political expression in the land of their fathers.

Efforts to deal constructively with the problem must begin with efforts to establish a shared or complementary definition of the problem to assure that parties to a negotiation would at least address the same issues. If this seems abstract, remember the numerous acts of terrorism in the past decade designed to demonstrate that the Palestinians are a people capable of political action in their own name. Remember persistent PLO refusal to say simply and authoritatively that they would make peace with Israel. Remember political efforts at the United Nations and other international organizations to establish observer status for the PLO, or to produce diplomatic recognition for the PLO by most of the world's governments. Remember Israel's efforts to prevent these moves and its refusal to sit with the PLO. And remember that, in the summer of 1982, Israel went to war in Lebanon to destroy the organized Palestinian movement which Israel's government regarded as a potential threat — not to the physical integrity of the state of Israel but to Israel's exclusive claim to all the land west of the Jordan river.

Unless these different pictures of the problem come closer and begin to overlap, negotiations are unlikely to begin. If negotiations do begin, those holding widely different definitions of the problem will use delaying tactics in the negotiation as another instrument for blocking movement. Political leaders will be distracted from taking the steps they need to take to change public perceptions of the problem. Defining the problem — even as a base for U.S. policymaking — is not an abstract exercise. It is the highly political task on which negotiating depends. Breaking the impasse to negotiation between Israelis and Palestinians may require leaders on both sides — and in Washington — to define the problem courageously as one that the two peoples share. Leaders' definition of a problem is the vehicle for marshalling political support behind the course of action which flows from that definition. In this case that course of action would be negotiation. How policymakers define a problem and talk about it will color what they decide to do about it.

Heads of government formulate policy judgments with an eye to winning public support for them.

2. *Producing A Commitment to a Negotiated Settlement*

Before leaders will negotiate, they have to judge whether a negotiated solution would be better than continuing the present situation, whether a fair settlement could be fashioned, whether the other side could accept, and whether the balance of forces would permit agreement on such a settlement. This phase — producing a commitment to a negotiated settlement — is the most complex of all because it involves a series of interrelated judgments. For the sake of discussion, let us look at four of these:

First is a judgment that the present situation no longer serves a party's interests. To put it the other way around, in analyzing why a party refuses to negotiate, we must determine why that party believes that perpetuating the present situation serves its interests. We must understand why one side may judge that the possible outcomes from negotiation are less attractive than the alternatives to negotiation. From that analysis we may understand what might change such an assessment.

In the Israeli-Palestinian case, neither party has believed that the passage of time without negotiation would irretrievably hurt its cause. Israel under the Begin-Shamir leadership judged that negotiating would create a situation from which the only outcome could be some Israeli withdrawal from territories occupied in 1967. Israel's stated policy was to use time to establish its irreversible presence in territories that would otherwise be lost in negotiation. The Palestinians and other Arabs in the past seem to have judged that time was on their side — that over time they would accumulate the military power to force Israel to some kind of accommodation. Many Arabs, such as King Hussein, seem to recognize that Israel's actions in the territories may leave little to negotiate in the foreseeable future. However, they may know it took centuries to drive the crusaders out and, over the longer term, Israel too can be pressed to withdraw from the territories it occupied in 1967.

Breaking the impasse would require persuading leaders on both sides who want to negotiate to address directly the consequences of passing time. Israeli leaders might, for instance, discuss openly the consequences of creating a forty percent Arab minority in the Jewish state by perpetuating control over all the land west of the Jordan River. Palestinian leaders might consider publicly the consequences of passing up an opportunity to begin putting together a government of their own in the West Bank and Gaza. In the United States leaders might acknowledge that Israel is debating the future character of the Zionist state and say straightforwardly that the unchanging commitment of the United States for almost forty years has been to a settlement in which the land west of the Jordan River is fairly shared. An American president might also reflect on the consequences for the United States and its friends of either a negotiated settlement or of one imposed over time by force from one side or the other.

Second is a judgment that the substance of a fair settlement is available. Leaders on each side must be able to see the shape of an agreeable settlement that might come out of negotiation. This judgment, of course, depends on whether the alternatives to a negotiated settlement may be better than any foreseeable settlement. This is the definition of the settlement against which the alternative of maintaining the present situation is measured.

To illustrate what I mean by being able to see the shape of a settlement that could be politically defensible, let me recall an incident from one of the Kissinger shuttles. More than a week into the thirty-five day shuttle that produced the Israeli-Syrian disengagement agreement of May 1974, reporters in the back of Kissinger's airplane asked him what he was then discussing. He responded that he was talking about the principles of settlement. The reporters asked how he could possibly be discussing something so general as principles after some ten days of intense shuttling. The point was that Kissinger knew it was essential to draw the parties toward a common view of a settlement before committing anything to paper. How big a pullback of troops? What kinds of buffer zones? Would there be an international observer force? If drafting began before there was a common picture of the answers to these questions, arguments over words would begin to hide arguments over substantive issues. He preferred to talk about the main elements of an agreement, to reach a verbal understanding of the outlines of an agreement before putting anything on paper.

To use another example, what made possible President Sadat's visit to Jerusalem and the eventual agreement at Camp David was an understanding of the principle that if Egypt offered full peace to Israel, Egypt could get back all of its territory that Israel had occupied in the 1967 war. It is this understanding of the outlines — the main elements in a deal — that I am talking about when I discuss the shape of a settlement.

In the contemporary Israeli-Palestinian situation, each side has been internally divided over the shape of possible solutions. In some ways, the kind of settlement each envisions relates to the basic view of the problem, but it includes in addition some thought about the key elements in a settlement and the relative importance of each.

Israel is divided between those who give priority to control over all the land west of the Jordan River, and those whose primary concerns are security and the somewhat related question of protecting the integrity of the Jewish state from dilution by incorporating a large non-Jewish population. For those who want to control all the land, compromise focuses on finding ways to provide some autonomy for the non-Jewish population. Those concerned with security focus on military and political means of protecting Israel from invasion and terror. The Palestinians are divided between those who still refuse to accept the partition of Palestine and hold out for one secular state and those who recognize that Israel is here to stay and seek a Palestinian state in the land from which Israel withdraws.

A central element in the judgment that a fair settlement is possible is the realization that each side's ideal solution is not attainable. If Israelis concluded that their security needs and access to the historic sites of Biblical Israel could be achieved without total control over the territory, the door to negotiation might open a bit wider. If Palestinians concluded that their right of self-determination could be achieved — while still negotiating common security arrangements with Israel and rights for both Israelis and Palestinians to live, work, and do business in each other's territory — they might be more prepared to negotiate.

For the United States, a past and potential future mediator, the task is not just to urge each side to come to the negotiating table. The task includes addressing the key interests of both sides intensively to help them understand both the consequences of extreme solutions and the possibility of meeting basic objectives — such as security and self-determination — through a variety of possible arrangements. The present impasse remains unbroken because neither side has come to grips within its own body politic with the fit among basic objectives and possible settlements.

Third, leaders on each side will make their own estimates of whether the other side would accept a negotiated solution and is willing to reach a compromise. One side may be ready to negotiate but refuse to do so because it does not want the humiliation of offering to negotiate with an adversary who does not take the process seriously. Related to this judgment are thoughts on whether the two sides could overcome suspicion and mistrust enough to work together. The psychological obstacles to negotiation may be greater than the substantive.

Even if there is a common view of the shape of a settlement, two sides may be divided by such suspicion and mistrust that they will conclude that the other side is not committed to successful negotiation. Neither Palestinians nor Israelis believe the other would settle for any but extreme solutions. In the case of Egypt and Israel — though emissaries of Sadat and Begin had secretly given each other reason to believe that total Israeli withdrawal from the Sinai could lead to full peace between the two nations — it was not until Sadat's visit to Jerusalem that peace seemed possible. Much of the negotiating position that Sadat outlined to the Israeli parliament was not acceptable to the Israeli government. However, Sadat's very presence, as well as his words, brought an even more important message: Egypt accepts Israel as a state in the Middle East and is prepared to live in peace and normal relations with no more war between them. The fact that he came to Jerusalem underscored that his message was different.

As Sadat said in his speech to the Israeli Knesset in Jerusalem after outlining the differences in substantive positions: "Yet there remains another wall. This wall constitutes a psychological barrier between us, a barrier of suspicion, a barrier of rejection; a barrier of fear, of deception, a barrier of hallucination without any action, deed or decision. . . .A barrier of distorted and eroded interpretation of every event and statement. It is this psychological barrier which I described in official statements as constituting 70% of the whole problem."[3]

In the context of overcoming the psychological barriers to negotiation, we occasionally find a particular situation where one side may feel committed as a matter of principle not to negotiate with an adversary. Khomeini refused to negotiate directly with the "Great Satan" during the hostage crisis. President-elect Reagan said at that time, "We don't negotiate with terrorists." The PLO refuses to negotiate with Israel until it recognizes the Palestinians' rights as a people. Israel refuses to talk with the PLO. It is always difficult to know when principle is being invoked to cover other purposes. And when it is invoked, it is important to ask where the real obstacle lies.

A fourth factor contributing to commitment to a negotiated settlement is a judgment that the balance of forces will permit a fair settlement. The

Arabs have normally seen Israeli military power as precluding a fair negotiation. Syria's President Assad is quite open in saying that the Arabs cannot negotiate a settlement of their conflict with Israel until they are Israel's military equal. President Sadat recognized that it would be a long time before the Arabs would achieve military parity with Israel, so he went to war for the limited purpose of drawing the United States and the Soviet Union into more active diplomatic efforts to negotiate a settlement. He sought to put big power political weight on the scale alongside the limited Arab military power that had demonstrated its capacity at least to inflict on Israel a serious psychological shock and significant war losses. The question is how the balance of forces can be structured to produce a realistic hope of a fair negotiation.

A specific obstacle to an Israeli-Palestinian negotiation has been Arab concern that Israel, with its superior military power, would not feel compelled to negotiate all outstanding issues fairly. Palestinians particularly cite Israel's policy of expropriating land in the West Bank and Gaza for settlement and security purposes as evidence that Israel is resolving the key issue of control over land unilaterally outside negotiation. Israelis, on the other hand, have accused the Arabs of not being willing to negotiate at all, and of wanting the United States to do their work for them by pressuring Israel.

Powers outside the region, especially the United States, have played a critical role in the balance of forces that affect negotiation. Increasingly in the 1980s, Arab parties have not seen the United States as able or willing to assure a fair negotiation of all outstanding issues against Israeli opposition. Israelis in the Begin and Shamir governments knew that the United States in a negotiation would press for some withdrawal and have not wanted to put themselves in the way of sharp difference with Washington. Re-establishing the credibility of a mediator or third "full partner" to assure a fair negotiation could be a factor in the balance of forces that might encourage parties to test perceptions of whether the substance of a possible compromise exists.

All of these points — judging whether the situation continues to serve one's interests, seeing the shape of a politically defensible settlement, believing that the other side could accept, or judging that the balance of forces will permit a fair settlement — are elements in deciding on a commitment to a negotiated settlement. We need to understand a lot more fully how to analyze the substantive and psychological obstacles to that commitment and how they can be removed. This is the work of the second part of the negotiating process.

3. Arranging Negotiations
Whereas the commitment to negotiate is a political decision that can be made known in a variety of general ways, the effort to arrange a specific negotiation tends to focus on the general approach and on more detailed terms of reference. In a sense, this may be a mini-negotiation about how to negotiate. This has two aspects:

One is to define the objective of the negotiation in a way that provides agreement on the principles that will guide drafting of a settlement. Underlying this will also be some understanding of the strategy for putting a settlement together. For instance, will it provide a comprehensive settlement of all outstanding issues? Or will it attempt to resolve them incrementally through a series of agreements?

The other aspect is to deal with those physical arrangements that may have political implications. This can involve issues such as what roles the supporters may play or whether the Palestine Liberation Organization will have a place at the table. Or it can concern who will sit next to whom at the table. Large or small, these practical questions are politically symbolic and can become significant obstacles to negotiation.

This part of the negotiating process, along with the actual negotiation, has received far more attention elsewhere and requires less attention here. Suffice it to say that the central aim in this part of the process is to reach agreement on the objectives and procedures for negotiation. This can involve doctrinal debates involving a dictionary of diplomatic code words as well as arguments over the "shape of the table." One can experience this phase for months and even years.

These three stages complete the pre-negotiation phases on which this paper concentrates. Two further phases need only be mentioned briefly to round out a complete picture of the negotiating process. Because they have received so much attention already, I will do no more than put them in place here. However, they must be established in any analytical framework both because they are the objective of what goes before *and* because they may well become elements in the pre-negotiating phases of a later negotiation. Negotiations must be conducted with their role in the larger process in mind.

4. The Actual Negotiation
The most visible stage of the "peace process" is the negotiation itself. Here I only wish to underscore that negotiation lies only at a later part of a prolonged political process. The pre-negotiation phases may take much more time and effort than the negotiation itself, and pre-negotiation must be conducted with a view to the situation that will be created.

5. Implementation
It is also important to note for the sake of completeness that implementation of any agreement is an important part of the negotiating process. This is true for the obvious reason that negotiation has not succeeded unless it has produced an agreement that the negotiating parties have a stake in implementing. It is also true in diplomacy, as in some other relationships, that careful implementation of one agreement may be the jumping-off place for the next negotiation. The key element in the step-by-step diplomacy of the Kissinger shuttles was the view that one agreement — negotiated and scrupulously implemented — would begin to change the political atmosphere and make possible tomorrow what seemed impossible yesterday. No one would have thought in 1973 that an Egyptian-Israeli peace treaty would be signed a scant six years later.

In laying out the elements in this five-part negotiating process, I have used the Middle East for my analysis. But one might, I think, analyze the development of U.S.-Soviet relations and negotiations in the 1970s within a similar framework. If we were to attempt that analysis, we would find that the two superpowers in that period were engaged on several negotiating tracks at the same time, and that progress on one could make progress on another more likely. More important, we might analyze U.S.-Soviet relations in the early 1980s to determine how to return them to some norm.

Concluding Words

I have written this paper with several purposes in mind:

First, to encourage specialists from several disciplines to contribute to understanding better what keeps people and nations from negotiating. Our political leaders in a nuclear world are in desperate need of this help. The future of arms control as well as avoiding nuclear conflict may lie more in their hands than in the hands of arms control specialists.

Second, the paper suggests a way of stepping back from a regional impasse like that in the Arab-Israeli-Palestinian conflict and re-focusing efforts to remove some of the obstacles to negotiation. The problem today is how to precipitate a commitment to negotiate, not how to negotiate.

Third, it assumes that insights developed from study of this problem may enhance understanding of how to manage or conduct important relationships — whether across international borders, across the management-employee gulf, or across the breakfast table. Conducting relationships may seem a far cry from negotiating theory; however, the purpose of managing relationships instead of letting them drift is to prevent blockages from hardening or, at least, to keep the parties always within negotiating range so that if trouble comes, peaceful remedies are at hand.

Above all, it records two convictions strongly held: (1) Peacemakers at home and abroad will find the pre-negotiation fields the most fruitful in which to work; and (2) the world's future depends on their success.

NOTES

This article was developed from a much briefer one prepared for the Center for the Study of Foreign Affairs in the Foreign Service Institute of the U.S. Department of State, Washington, D.C., in June, 1983. That paper appears in the proceedings of the conference published by the Center as *International Negotiation: Art and Science*, ed. Diane B. Bendahmane and John W. McDonald, Jr., 1984. It also reflects suggestions made during a February, 1984 discussion at Harvard University in an evening session of the Program on Negotiation. The analytical approach was first applied to the Arab-Israeli impasse in *Perspective on the Middle East 1983: Proceedings of a Conference*, published jointly by the Fletcher School of Law and Diplomacy at Tufts University and the Middle East Institute in Washington, D.C. and then, tentatively in the present organization, in an oral presentation at a conference, also in February, 1984, at the Center for International Affairs at Harvard University.

1. See I. William Zartman and Maureen R. Berman, *The Practical Negotiator* (New York and London: Yale University Press, 1982), pp. 9, 42.

2. *Christian Science Monitor* 23 February 1983, p. 1.

3. Address of Anwar Sadat to Israeli Knesset, 20 November, 1977, *New York Times*, 21 November 1977, p.18.

Negotiating Inside Out

What Are the Best Ways to Relate Internal Negotiations with External Ones?

Roger Fisher

In every negotiation involving an organization, internal negotiations have a major impact on external ones. When a union, a corporation, a government, or even a family is about to engage in negotiations, discussions and decisions among the "insiders" are likely to make it difficult for that body — as an entity — to conduct ideal problem-solving negotiations with others. No matter how creative and flexible the internal process may be, it is likely to result in instructions that unduly tie the hands of a negotiator acting on behalf of an institution.

An institution is not a single rational actor, nor does it behave like one. Within a government, for example, individuals pursue their own careers and seek to advance the interests of their own particular office or agency as well as seek to advance the cumulative interests of the government as a whole. Another complicating factor concerns the role negotiators believe they play in the process. Many negotiators view themselves as someone who "represents" the institution and defends its position; they do not perceive themselves as persons hired to work out an optimal solution. But how should a government, a corporation, or other institution relate its internal negotiations to those it has with outsiders?

Suppose high officials of two corporations are contemplating the possibility of negotiating a complex agreement. What is the best advice that experts could give them on how to structure those negotiations to maximize the chance that they would not only reach an agreement, but also would reach an optimal one — an agreement that could not be better for one corporation without being worse for the other? Having formulated the best advice that we could give the two together, would our advice to one alone be significantly different?

Consider, for instance, the case of a diplomat who will be negotiating under instructions from his government. Both he and the government are likely to see the problem in terms of discretion: either the negotiator will believe that he has too little freedom of action or the government will believe that he has too much. Instructions are likely to be written before government officials have done much hard thinking about the interests of the other government or much creative thinking about possible ways of reconciling the differing interests of the two governments.

When discussions take place within a government in advance of an international negotiation, participants are likely to assume that their task is to

Roger Fisher is Williston Professor of Law, *emeritus*, at Harvard Law School and Director of the Harvard Negotiation Project, 523 Pound Hall, Harvard Law School, Cambridge, Mass. 02138.

reach internal agreement on something. Traditionally, that "something" is a position — a statement of what the negotiator will demand or the minimum that he or she has authority to accept. Frequently, such a position reflects an odd kind of compromise — one that adds up the desires of the different parts of a government. In advance of U.S.-Soviet arms control negotiations, for example, the Air Force is likely to agree that the Navy can keep its new submarines so long as the Air Force can keep its new missiles. The Army and the Navy are each likely to take a similar stance in the internal negotiations. Each will agree to a position *only if* the interests of its department or agency are fully met. The result is likely to be a minimum position or "floor" that is floating far above the real world.

An alternative symptom, equally unsatisfying to governments, is to leave a negotiator with enormous discretion. A negotiator typically sees her job as reaching an international agreement consistent with her instructions. Of course, the more favorable to her government an agreement may be, the better the government will like it. But reaching any agreement — even a poor one — within instructions is likely to be considered a success, whereas failure to reach an agreement would be considered a failure. Further, a negotiator armed only with positions and arguments is unlikely to appreciate the interests of different elements of the bureaucracy. In these circumstances, there is a high risk that the goal of reaching agreement will cause a diplomat to settle for an outcome that is substantially short of the best that might have been attained. Giving a negotiator wide discretion thus runs the risk of making it too easy to reach agreement — so easy, in fact, that an agreement does not serve a government's interests as well as it might.

Faced with this choice, a government tends to limit discretion. Our hypothetical negotiator will find her hands safely tied. If she later wants to make a concession, she can ask authority to do so, and the government can later decide if that concession is justified. The result is that international negotiations often involve three layers of positional bargaining:

- one among the different interests groups within each government;
- one between each negotiator and his or her own government; and
- one between the two negotiators acting on behalf of their respective governments.

Such a process is hardly conducive to wise joint problem solving. Analytically, what is wrong with the process? How might it be improved?

Analysis: Four Possible Causes of Difficulty

To reduce the destructive impact that internal negotiations have on external ones, we will need some hypotheses about what is going wrong. Let me advance four. It appears that the possibility of reaching a good outcome in external negotiations is handicapped to the extent that:

(1) Throughout the process, the focus is on the single element of commitment;

(2) The perceived function of the external negotiator remains fixed over time;

(3) Internal and external negotiations are compartmentalized — they are viewed as separate and distinct functions; and

(4) Negotiators see their role as simply being partisans.

Each of these hypotheses deserves analysis. Each also suggests a proposition about what might be done to improve the process.

Focus Negotiations on More Elements than Commitment

The first hypothesis is that there is an undue focus on the single element of commitment. At the Harvard Negotiation Project, we organize much of our thinking on negotiation around seven elements:

1. The INTERESTS of the parties — their needs, wants, hopes, fears and concerns of all kinds such as for security, profit, recognition, or status.

2. The LEGITIMACY of an agreed outcome as measured by precedent, law, practice, or other external criteria of fairness that are persuasive to one or both parties.

3. The RELATIONSHIP that exists between the parties and between their negotiators. The better the working relationship, the easier it will be to produce an outcome that well serves the interests of all.

4. The BATNAs. The Best Alternative To a Negotiated Agreement that each party has. (What is the best each can do by walking away?)

5. The OPTIONS on which they might agree, some of which, it is hoped, will be better for each party than its BATNA.

6. The COMMITMENTS of the parties — statements of what they will or won't do, made during a negotiation or embodied in an agreement.

7. The COMMUNICATION between the parties. The more effective that communication, the more efficient the negotiating process is likely to be.

In general, in most interactions between internal and external negotiators, too much attention is paid to the single element of the commitments to be made and the authority to make them, and too little attention is paid to what the negotiators could be doing with respect to each of the other six elements. A suggested approach to deal with this problem would be for those within a government — or any other organization — to develop instructions that say something about all seven elements.

Good outcomes tend to be more likely when negotiators fully understand a problem before committing themselves or their organizations to a particular solution. This means that better results will usually be achieved if the making of commitments is postponed until after the negotiators:

• have established a good personal working relationship;

• have developed easy and effective communication;

• have come to understand the interests of both parties;

• have explored precedents and other possible criteria of fairness that might be persuasive to one government or the other;

• have fully understood their own alternatives to a negotiated agreement and have estimated those of the other side; and

• have considered a range of possible options that might form a basis for agreement.

To the extent that this premise is correct, instructions from an organization to a negotiator should reflect the fact that much work should be done *before* either of them decides on the commitments that ought to be made.

During the early stages of a significant negotiation, communication between a government and its negotiator should be concerned with interests, options, and criteria of fairness. Beyond standard instructions regarding establishing effective communication and a good working relationship, a government would be well advised to instruct its negotiator about the interests at stake in the negotiation, the government's current thinking about the relative priority of those interests, and possible tradeoffs among them. Internal negotiations might also produce a number of options that the negotiator could explore with the negotiator from the other side. Further, early internal negotiations might be directed toward finding and evaluating precedents and other external standards of fairness that would be both highly satisfactory to "our" government and persuasive to the other side.

This means that, instead of establishing "demands" or "positions," early instructions should limit the authority to commit. There is an ironic contrast between power and authority. The more power that a diplomat has to make commitments, the more tightly a government is likely to confine the exercise of that power — and the less practical ability that diplomat is likely to have to engage in constructive work. An ambassador is typically "plenipotentiary." Vis-à-vis another government, an ambassador has full power. Under international law, any commitment that an ambassador makes is binding on his or her government. Even an oral statement by someone with full powers can have serious consequences. In 1933, for instance, the World Court held that when the Norwegian Minister of Foreign Affairs had said that his government "would not make any difficulties" in the settlement of the Greenland question, it placed Norway "under an obligation to refrain from contesting sovereignty over Greenland as a whole."

Because of this extraordinary power, governments typically give an ambassador instructions that set firm limits on what the ambassador is allowed to do. For fear that something a diplomat might say would constitute a commitment, the dipolmat is instructed not to discuss any issue on which the government does not wish to be committed. Such instructions preclude a diplomatic negotiator from engaging in the kind of exploration of interests, options, and criteria of fairness that are useful, and will sometimes be essential, to reaching a sensible agreement.

This suggests that, in addition to requesting an external negotiator to explore those elements, it might be well — during the early stages of a negotiation — to make clear to one's own representative, to the representative of the other side, and perhaps to the press and public, that the representative has no authority whatsoever to make a substantive commitment. He or she has full authority to *discuss* anything, can make personal commitments, and can commit the government to procedural issues like agreeing on an agenda or a date for the next meeting, but may not make any substantive concession or commitment until different instructions have been received and explained to the other side.

The Functions of a Negotiator
Should Change as a Negotiation Proceeds

Traditionally, each round of talks in a negotiation is seen as having essentially the same task — to deal with positions. A government beginning a major negotiation that will continue over a period of months or years is aware that the instructions it gives a diplomat will be changed over time. At the outset, they may authorize an extreme opening position, designed to provide plenty of "negotiating room." Later, that position may be changed. Nonetheless, it seems to be true that the successive instructions tend to cover the same ground, authorizing a negotiator to advance, defend, or revise proposed commitments in an ongoing game of positional bargaining.

Yet the role of negotiator should not be treated like that of a dog on a leash, with the length of the leash being gradually extended. Rather a negotiator should be treated more like a handyman who is asked to undertake different tasks at different times. As a negotiation progresses, the work to be done changes, and so should the instructions.

Both internal and external negotiations will be more effective if there is an ongoing interaction between them with respect to understanding each other's interests, generating a wide range of options, evaluating them in the light of persuasive criteria, and the making of commitments. The character of the instructions should be expected to change during the course of a negotiation, focusing at first on interests and options and later exchanging views on possible commitments.

This does not mean that each side should disclose its innermost secrets to the other. A corporation, for example, may rightfully fear the consequences of disclosing business secrets. It may also fear that if it discloses how keenly it wants some particular thing it may be forced to pay a lot for it. Further, it may not wish to disclose how desperately it wants to reach agreement in view of the absence of any attractive alternative.

It is difficult to solve a problem unless the negotiators understand what that problem is. It is also difficult to reconcile interests if they remain unknown. However, it is possible to disclose the nature of one's interests without disclosing the intensity of one's feeling about them.

Internal and External Negotiations
Should Become an Interactive Process

People tend to see internal negotiations as a process that is wholly distinct and separate from the external negotiations that may be taking place on the same subject. In a typical big negotiation, a large number of people with different perspectives, differing interests, and different talents will be involved. Some of these people will be working within one organization, some within another, and some will be the negotiators themselves or their staffs. Outside experts and people from other organizations or governments might also have a contribution to make. One who will be conducting external negotiations will often participate in the internal discussions as well. In fact, negotiators often play a significant role in the drafting of their own instructions. But the internal negotiations on each side are likely to be compartmentalized and kept quite apart from the external negotiations.

A highly structured division between internal and external negotiations tends to restrict the contribution of knowledgeable people to what each can do within a carefully prescribed role. If an all-knowing God were considering an international problem in which, say, 22 people were involved, each of whom knew different things and represented a particular point of view, and if His objective were to produce an optimal outcome — one that could not be better for one country without being worse for the other — it is unlikely that He would design the current model. He would not put ten people in one room and ten people in another, each group to issue positional instructions to its diplomat, the two of whom would then meet and bargain. Even without divine guidance, we should be able to design a process that will do better. Such a rigid and adversarial structure is unlikely to be the best way of engaging multiple parties with diverse interests and skills in successful joint problem solving. We will want to use a process that permits people to build on each other's knowledge and skills.

The talents of all of those involved, whether a member of an "internal" team or a "negotiator" — whether within one government or another — should be orchestrated to produce the best possible outcome. This means that the structure of the negotiations should be flexible and open, with substantial use of prenegotiating sessions and nongovernmental experts. Contacts among all of them should probably be planned and encouraged rather than discouraged. Subcommittees, joint fact-finding teams, brainstorming sessions, and small working groups of specialists from both sides (such as military officers, lawyers, or technical experts) should be put to good use.

Every Negotiator Has a Dual Role: Both Partisan Advocate and Co-Mediator

A negotiator may understandably have a bias in favor of his own side. In fact, a diplomat may correctly perceive his mandate to behave as a zealous advocate of his nation's interests. But arguing in favor of one set of interests is less than half his job. Two diplomats negotiating on behalf of their respective countries also have the joint task of efficiently producing a workable agreement that reconciles as well as can be the interests of the two governments in a manner that is acceptable to both. Although each negotiator's task can thus be seen as that of a co-mediator, the normal relationship between internal and external negotiations does not make it possible for two negotiators to use the tools and techniques that a skilled mediator might employ. Instructions to negotiators should maximize the chance that they can function effectively together and jointly develop a solution that will be acceptable to their two governments. One particular tool that they should be able to use is the "One-Text-Procedure," based on the concept of a single negotiating text.

When using such a text, two negotiators, without seeking or obtaining commitments from anyone, jointly prepare a rough draft of a possible agreement and then, in the light of comments from knowledgeable people in both governments, revise and refine successive versions of that draft until they can make it no better. At that time, they jointly recommend the draft as a proposal to their two governments.

A Way to Begin

A useful way to think clearly about how best to relate internal negotiations to external ones is to try to draft some standard clauses for instructions that might be given to all international negotiators. Despite the magnitude of the task — in fact, because of it — it may be worthwhile to get started. Here is a first attempt:

Some Possible Standard Instructions:
An Illustrative Draft

1. Unclassified. Although you will also receive some confidential instructions, this part of your instructions is open. You are free to show these instructions to the other side, and are encouraged to do so. Thereafter they may be made public.

2. Authority. You have full authority to discuss any issue relevant to the subject matter of these negotiations about which either you or the negotiator with whom you are dealing wishes to talk.

You also have authority to make procedural commitments with respect to agenda, the time and place of meetings, etc.

Further, you may make personal commitments of substantive recommendations that you will make to your government, but are encouraged to be cautious in doing so. You should emphasize that such statements are your recommendation to the government, not necessarily the action the government will take.

You will be given explicit authority to make substantive commitments at an appropriate time. If at any time you believe that such authority would be helpful to you, please request it. In the meantime, knowing that what you say will not commit the government gives you great freedom to pursue the tasks necessary to generate an agreement that will well serve the interests of this government as well as serving the legitimate interests of others involved.

3. National Interests. You are negotiating in order to advance the national interests of your government broadly conceived. These interests, in their normal order of priority, are as follows:

(a) *Building and maintaining a good working relationship with all other governments*. Our security is enhanced to the extent that problems and incidents that involve other governments and peoples can be solved acceptably at a professional level without the risk of escalating into political or military crises. The contrast between war and peace lies in how governments deal with their differences. The more serious our differences, the more important it is that we deal with them in a practical, businesslike way.

(b) *An orderly international regime based on respect for international law and for our rights under international law. In general,* the way we reconcile our many substantive interests with our interest in peace is to pursue our substantive interests within a framework of international law and order.

(c) *The prestige and reputation of our government.* We want to be widely regarded as a good government with high ideals and values, one that is honest and reliable. Honesty does not require full disclosure, but what you state as fact should be so. Consistent with that reputation, we would also like to be respected as a strong government, one that will listen to reason and be open to persuasion, but also as one that will not back down to threats or pay blackmail.

(d) *Particular interests.* Your confidential instructions for each negotiation will more particularly spell out the relative priority of particular concerns of the government and the tradeoffs among them.

4. Personal Working Relationships. You should seek to establish a problem-solving climate in which you and the negotiator from the other government see each other not as adversaries come to do battle, but rather as professional colleagues working side-by-side to deal with a practical situation in which your two governments have differences.

5. Effective Communication. The better the communication between two negotiators, the greater will be their joint ability to deal well with international differences. You may not disclose classified information to the other negotiator as a means of building personal confidence in yourself. On the other hand, within your discretion you may respect confidences and need not report to the government everything that you have been told.

6. Functions. Before committing yourself or your government to any particular solution to the problem about which you are negotiating, you should do your best to satisfy yourself that you fully understand that problem. This means that you should:

(a) understand in some detail the interests and concerns of the other government, as they perceive them to be, and demonstrate to the other negotiator that you do understand them;

(b) explain our basic interests honestly, and make sure that the other negotiator understands them (Do not disclose secret information nor should you disclose the value we place on some particular interest if that will make us vulnerable.);

(c) tentatively establish a proposed scope for a substantive agreement that lists the subjects and issues to be covered;

(d) generate a range of options that might conceivably be acceptable to both governments and might meet their interests as well as they can be reconciled;

(e) identify different standards of fairness, equality, or reciprocity that might provide a sound basis for satisfying the leaders and constituents of each country that they are being fairly treated in an agreement; and

(f) revise and improve those options that either negotiator believes hold promise of meeting the legitimate concerns of both governments.

7. Structure of Meetings. You should feel free to design your own negotiating session in a variety of ways: sometimes formal, sometimes informal; sometimes in a private meeting and sometimes with others invited to join you; sometimes in "brainstorming" sessions designed to generate fresh ideas, and sometimes in sessions designed to evaluate and improve ideas that have been generated. You should feel free to invite people from either government and nongovernmental experts to join you as you and your fellow negotiator may decide.

8. Subcommittees, Consultants, and Facilitators. You and your fellow negotiator may find it useful to ask specialists on each side to form a subcommittee for the purpose of gathering information, developing new options, or studying and refining some proposal. If a part of the negotiation involves secret information that one side or both is reluctant to disclose, you may find it helpful to obtain the assistance of a trusted neutral who could speak with each side in confidence and recommend ways to proceed. Such a neutral third party might also play a useful role in facilitating meetings where progress is otherwise difficult.

9. Propose Work for the Government. The work that you are doing with the other negotiator and the internal work being done by your government constitute a single, ongoing, and interactive process. Whenever you would like help in clarifying interests, generating options, gathering data, suggesting appropriate criteria, or performing any other function that might lead to a good agreement, please inform the government.

10. Request Revised Instructions. As the negotiations proceed, we will all learn more about the problem and about possible solutions. The government expects to revise your instructions from time to time as we move from the exploratory and creative phases of the negotiation toward the commitment stage. One of your responsibilities is to do your best to see to it that the government has the full benefit of your experience, wisdom, and judgment not only in implementing instructions but in improving them. As time and circumstances permit, please propose additions or revisions in your instructions.

When Should We Use Agents? Direct vs. Representative Negotiation

Jeffrey Z. Rubin and Frank E. A. Sander

Although we typically conceive of negotiations occurring directly between two or more principals, often neglected in a thoughtful analysis are the many situations where negotiations take place indirectly, through the use of representatives or surrogates of the principals. A father who speaks to his child's teacher (at the child's request), two lawyers meeting on behalf of their respective clients, the foreign service officers of different nations meeting to negotiate the settlement of a border dispute, a real estate agent informing would-be buyers of the seller's latest offer — each is an instance of negotiation through representatives.

In this brief essay, we wish to build on previous analyses of representative negotiation[1] to consider several key distinctions between direct and representative negotiations, and to indicate the circumstances under which we believe negotiators should go out of their way either to choose or to avoid negotiation through agents.

The most obvious effect of using agents — an effect that must be kept in mind in any analysis of representative negotiation — is complication of the transaction. As indicated in Figure 1, (page 82), if we begin with a straightforward negotiation between two individuals, then the addition of two agents transforms this simple one-on-one deal into a complex matrix involving at least four primary negotiations, as well as two subsidiary ones (represented by the dotted lines in Figure 1). In addition, either of the agents may readily serve as a mediator between the client and the other agent or principal. Or the two agents might act as co-mediators between the principals. At a minimum, such a complex structure necessitates effective coordination. Beyond that, this structural complexity has implications — both positive and negative — for representative negotiation in general. Let us now review these respective benefits and liabilities in turn.

Expertise

One of the primary reasons that principals choose to negotiate through agents is that the latter possess expertise that makes agreement — particularly favorable agreement — more likely. This expertise is likely to be of three different stripes:

Substantive knowledge. A tax attorney or accountant knows things about the current tax code that make it more likely that negotiations with an

Jeffrey Z. Rubin is Professor of Psychology at Tufts University in Medford, Mass. **Frank E. A. Sander** is the Bussey Professor of Law at Harvard Law School, Cambridge,Mass.

Figure 1

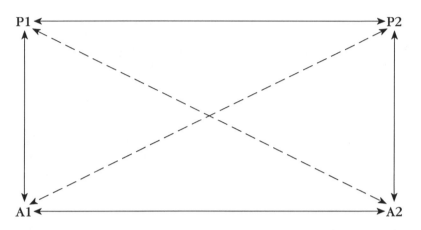

Possible relations among two principals (P1 and P2) and their respective agents (A1 and A2). A solid line denotes an actual relation, a dotted line a potential one.

IRS auditor will benefit the client as much as possible. Similarly, a divorce lawyer, an engineering consultant, and a real estate agent may have substantive knowledge in a rather narrow domain of expertise, and this expertise may redound to the client's benefit.

Process expertise. Quite apart from the specific expertise they may have in particular content areas, agents may have skill at the negotiation process, per se, thereby enhancing the prospects of a favorable agreement. A skillful negotiator — someone who understands how to obtain and reveal information about preferences, who is inventive, resourceful, firm on goals but flexible on means, etc. — is a valuable resource. Wise principals would do well to utilize the services of such skilled negotiators, unless they can find ways of developing such process skills themselves.

Special influence. A Washington lobbyist is paid to know the "right" people, to have access to the "corridors of power" that the principals themselves are unlikely to possess. Such "pull" can certainly help immensely, and is yet another form of expertise that agents may possess, although the lure of this "access" often outweighs in promise the special benefits that are confirmed in reality.

Note that the line separating these three forms of expertise is often a thin one, as in the case of a supplier who wishes to negotiate a sales contract with a prospective purchaser, and employs a former employee of the purchaser to handle the transaction; the former employee, as agent, may be a source of both substantive expertise and influence.

Note also that principals may not always know what expertise they need. Thus, a person who has a dispute that seems headed for the courts may automatically seek out a litigator, not realizing that the vast preponderance of cases are settled by negotiation, requiring very different skills that the litigator may not possess. So, although agents do indeed possess different forms of expertise that may enhance the prospects of a favorable settlement, clients do not necessarily know what they need; it's a bit like the problem of looking up the proper spelling of a word in the dictionary when you haven't got a clue about how to spell the word in question.

Detachment

Another important reason for using an agent to do the actual negotiation is that the principals may be too emotionally entangled in the subject of the dispute. A classic example is divorce. A husband and wife, caught in the throes of a bitter fight over the end of their marriage, may benefit from the "buffering" that agents can provide. Rather than confront each other with the depth of their anger and bitterness, the principals (P1 and P2 in Figure 1) may do far better by communicating only indirectly, via their respective representatives, A1 and A2. Stated most generally, when the negotiating climate is adversarial — when the disputants are confrontational rather than collaborative — it may be wiser to manage the conflict through intermediaries than run the risk of an impasse or explosion resulting from direct exchange.

Sometimes, however, it is the agents who are too intensely entangled. What is needed then is the detachment and rationality that only the principals can bring to the exchange. For example, lawyers may get too caught up in the adversary game and lose sight of the underlying problem that is dividing the principals (e.g., how to resolve a dispute about the quality of goods delivered as part of a long-term supply contract). The lawyers may be more concerned about who would win in court, while the clients simply want to get their derailed relationship back on track. Hence the thrust of some modern dispute resolution mechanisms (such as the minitrial) is precisely to take the dispute out of the hands of the technicians and give it back to the primary parties.[2]

Note, however, that the very "detachment" we are touting as a virtue of negotiation through agents can also be a liability. For example, in some interpersonal negotiations, apology and reconciliation may be an important ingredient of any resolution (see, e.g., Goldberg, Green, and Sander, 1987). Surrogates who are primarily technicians may not be able to bring to bear these emphatic qualities.

Tactical Flexibility

The use of agents allows various gambits to be played out by the principals, in an effort to ratchet as much as possible from the other side. For example, if a seller asserts that the bottom line is $100,000, the buyer can try to haggle, albeit at the risk of losing the deal. If the buyer employs an agent, however, the agent can profess willingness to pay that sum but plead lack of authority, thereby gaining valuable time and opportunity for fuller consideration of the situation together with the principal. Or an agent for the seller who senses that the buyer may be especially eager to buy the property can claim that it is necessary to go back to the seller for ratification of the deal, only to return and up the price, profusely apologizing all the while for the behavior of an "unreasonable" client. The client and agent can thus together play the hard-hearted partner game.

Conversely, an agent may be used in order to push the other side in tough, even obnoxious, fashion, making it possible — in the best tradition of the "good cop/bad cop" ploy — for the client to intercede at last, and seem the essence of sweet reason in comparison with the agent. Or the agent may be used as a "stalking horse," to gather as much information about the adversary as possible, opening the way to proposals by the client that exploit the intelligence gathered.

Note that the tactical flexibility conferred by representative negotiations presupposes a competitive negotiating climate, a zero-sum contest in which each negotiator wishes to outsmart the other. It is the stuff of traditional statecraft, and the interested reader can do no better than study the writings of Schelling (1960) and Potter (1948), as well as Lax and Sebenius (1986). To repeat, the assumption behind this line of analysis is that effective negotiation requires some measure of artifice and duplicity, and that this is often best accomplished through the use of some sort of foil or alter ego — in the form of the agent. But the converse is not necessarily true: Where the negotiation is conducted in a problem-solving manner (cf., Fisher and Ury, 1981), agents may still be helpful, not because they resort to strategic ruses, but because they can help articulate interests, options, and alternatives. Four heads are clearly better than two, for example, when it comes to brainstorming about possible ways of reconciling the parties' interests.

Offsetting — indeed, typically *more* than offsetting — the three above apparent virtues of representative negotiation are several sources of difficulty. Each is sufficiently important and potentially problematic that we believe caution is necessary before entering into negotiation through agents.

Extra "Moving Parts"

As indicated in Figure 1, representative negotiations entail greater structural complexity, additional moving parts in the negotiation machinery that — given a need for expertise, detachment, or tactical flexibility — can help move parties toward a favorable agreement. Additional moving parts, however, can also mean additional expense, in the form of the time required in the finding, evaluating, and engaging of agents, as well as the financial cost of retaining their services. And it can mean additional problems, more things that can go wrong. For instance, a message intended by a client may not be the message transmitted by that client's agent to the other party. Or the message received by that agent from the other party may be very different from the one that that agent (either deliberately or inadvertently) manages to convey to his or her client.

At one level, then, the introduction of additional links in the communication system increases the risk of distortion in the information conveyed back and forth between the principals. Beyond that lies a second difficulty: the possibility that eventually the principals will come to rely so extensively on their respective agents that they no longer communicate directly — even though they could, and even though they might well benefit from doing so. In effect (see Figure 1), P1, in order to reach P2, now invariably goes through the A1-A2 chain, even though such maneuvering is no longer warranted. Consider, for example, the case of a divorcing couple who, in explicit compliance with the advice of their adversary lawyers, have avoided any direct contact with each other during the divorce proceedings. Once the divorce has been obtained, will the parties' ability to communicate effectively with each other (e.g., over support and custody issues) be adversely affected by their excessive prior reliance on their attorneys?

Yet another potentially problematic implication of this increasingly complex social machinery is that unwanted coalitions may arise that apply undue pressure on individual negotiators. Thus A2, in performing a mediatory function between P2 and the other side (P1 and A1) may be prone to become allied with the opposing team — or at least to be so viewed by P2. Greater number does not necessarily mean greater wisdom, however, and the pressures toward uniformity of opinion that result from coalition formation may adversely affect the quality of the decisions reached.

In sum, the introduction of agents increases the complexity of the social apparatus of negotiation, and in so doing increases the chances of unwanted side effects. A related problem should be briefly noted here: the difficulty of asymmetry, as when an agent negotiates not with another agent but directly with the other principal. In effect, this was the case in 1978 when Egypt's Sadat negotiated with Israel's Begin at Camp David. Sadat considered himself empowered to make binding decisions for Egypt, while — at least partly for tactical purposes — Begin represented himself as ultimately accountable to his cabinet and to the Israeli parliament. While this "mismatched" negotiation between a principal (Sadat) and an agent (Begin) *did* result in agreement (thanks in good measure to President Carter's intercession as a mediator), it was not easy. The asymmetry of role meant that the two sides differed in their readiness to move forward toward an agreement, their ability to be shielded by a representative, and their willingness/ability to guarantee that any agreement reached would "stick."[3]

Different dynamics will characterize the negotiation depending on whether it is between clients, between lawyers, or with both present. If just the clients are there, the dealings will be more direct and forthright, and issues of authority and ratification disappear. With just the lawyers present, there may be less direct factual information, but concomitantly more candor about delicate topics. Suppose, for example, that an aging soprano seeks to persuade an opera company to sign her for the lead role in an upcoming opera. If she is not present, the opera's agent may try to lower the price, contending that the singer is past her prime. Such candor is not recommended if the singer is present at the negotiation!

Problems of "Ownership" and Conflicting Interests

In theory, it is clear that the principal calls the shots. Imagine, however, an agent who is intent on applying the *Getting to YES* (Fisher and Ury, 1981) approach by searching for objective criteria and a fair outcome. Suppose the client simply wants the best possible outcome, perhaps because it is a one-shot deal not involving a future relationship with the other party. What if the agent (a lawyer, perhaps) *does* care about his future relationship with the other *agent*, and wants to be remembered as a fair and scrupulous bargainer? How *should* this conflict get resolved and how, in the absence of explicit discussion, *will* it be resolved, if at all? Conversely, the client, because of a valuable long-term relationship, may want to maintain good relations with the other side. But if the client simply looks for an agent who is renowned for an ability to pull out all the stops, the client's overall objectives may suffer as the result of an overzealous advocate.

This issue may arise in a number of contexts. Suppose that, in the course of a dispute settlement negotiation,[4] a lawyer who is intent on getting the best possible deal for a client turns down an offer that was within the client's acceptable range. Is this proper behavior by the agent? The Model Rules of Professional Conduct for attorneys explicitly requires (see paragraphs 1.2(s), 1.4) that every offer must be communicated to the principal, and perhaps a failure to do so might lead to a successful malpractice action against the attorney if the deal finally fell through.

Another illustration involves the situation where the agent and principal have divergent ethical norms. Suppose that a seller of a house has just learned that the dwelling is infested with termites, but instructs the agent not to reveal this fact, even in response to specific inquiry from the buyer. How should these tensions be fairly resolved, keeping in mind the fact that the agent may be subject to a professional code of conduct that gives directions that may conflict with the ethical values of the client?[5] There may, of course, be artful ways of dealing with such dilemmas, as, for example, slyly deflecting any relevant inquiry by the buyer. But preferably these problems should be explicitly addressed in the course of the initial discussion between agent and principal. To some extent, the problem may be resolved by the principal's tendency to pick an agent who is congenial and compatible. But, as we pointed out before, principals are not always aware of and knowledgeable about the relevant considerations that go into the choice of an agent. Hence, if these issues are not addressed explicitly at the outset, termination of the relationship midstream in egregious cases may be the only alternative.

Differing goals and standards of agent and principal may create conflicting pulls. For example, the buyer's agent may be compensated as a percentage of the purchase price, thus creating an incentive to have the price as high as possible. The buyer, of course, wants the lowest possible price. Similarly, where a lawyer is paid by the hour, there may be an incentive to draw out the negotiation, whereas the client prefers an expeditious negotiation at the lowest possible cost.

While these are not insoluble problems, to be sure, they do constitute yet another example of the difficulties that may arise as one moves to representative negotiations. Although in theory the principals are in command, once agents have been introduced the chemistry changes, and new actors — with agenda, incentives, and constraints of their own — are part of the scene. Short of an abrupt firing of the agents, principals may find themselves less in control of the situation once agents have come on the scene.

Encouragement of Artifice and Duplicity

Finally, as already noted, the introduction of agents often seems to invite clients to devise stratagems (with or without these agents) to outwit the other side. Admittedly, there is nothing intrinsic to the presence of representatives that dictates a move in this direction; still, perhaps because of the additional expense incurred, the seductive lure of a "killing" with the help of one's "hired gun," or the introduction of new, sometimes perverse incentives, representative negotiations often seem to instill (or reflect) a more adversarial climate.

Conclusion

It follows from the preceding analysis that, ordinarily, negotiations conducted directly between the principals are preferable to negotiation through representatives. When the principals' relationship is fundamentally cooperative or informed by enlightened self-interest, agents may often be unnecessary; since there is little or no antagonism in the relationship, there is no need for the buffering detachment afforded by agents. Moreover, by negotiating directly, there is reduced risk of miscoordination, misrepresentation, and miscommunication.

On the other hand, representative negotiation *does* have an important and necessary place. When special expertise is required, when tactical flexibility is deemed important and — most importantly — when direct contact is likely to produce confrontation rather than collaboration, agents *can* render an important service.

Above all, the choice of whether to negotiate directly or through surrogates is an important one, with significant ramifications. It therefore should be addressed explicitly by weighing some of the considerations advanced above. And if an agent is selected, careful advance canvassing of issues such as those discussed here (e.g., authority and ethical standards) is essential.

NOTES

We thank Michael Wheeler for the many constructive comments, suggestions, and conversations that preceded this article; and we gratefully acknowledge the helpful comments of Stephen B. Goldberg on an earlier draft of this manuscript.

1. See, in particular, the concise and insightful discussion by Lax and Sebenius (1986) in Chapter 15 of their *The Manager as Negotiator*.

2. Compare in this connection the unfortunate recent decision of the United States Court of Appeals for the Seventh District to the effect that a federal district court judge has no power to compel principals with settlement authority to attend a settlement conference. *G. Heileman Brewing Co. v. Joseph Oat Corp.*, 848 F 2d 1415 (7th Circuit 1988).

3. Compare in this connection Section 4.2 of the American Bar Association's Model Rules of Professional Conduct, which prohibits a lawyer from dealing directly with the opposing principal, if that principal is represented by an attorney.

4. See Sander and Rubin (1988) for a discussion of the differences between dealmaking and dispute settlement negotiation.

5. See, for example, the ABA's Model Rules of Professional Conduct, Section 4.1, prohibiting attorneys from making materially false statements.

REFERENCES

Fisher, R. and Ury, W.L. (1981) *Getting to YES: Negotiating agreement without giving in*. Boston: Houghton Mifflin.
Goldberg, S. Green, E. and Sander, F.E.A. (1987). "Saying you're sorry." *Negotiation Journal* 3: 221-224.
Lax, D.A. and Sebenius, J.K. (1986) *The manager as negotiator*. New York: The Free Press.
Potter, S. (1948). *The theory and practice of gamesmanship: The art of winning games without actually cheating*. New York: Holt.
Sander, F.E.A. and Rubin, J.Z. (1988). "The Janus quality of negotiation: Dealmaking and dispute settlement." *Negotiation Journal* 4: 109-113.
Schelling, T. (1960). *The strategy of conflict*. Cambridge, Mass.: Harvard University Press.

Mock Pseudo-Negotiations With Surrogate Disputants

Howard Raiffa

Some heated disputes are never negotiated and never resolved — they just roll along. It is my contention that individuals, corporations and nations involved in such disputes often settle for outcomes that are far from efficient,[1] and that includes maintenance of the status quo. Why else do we currently have 40 or so small "hot" wars and a potential massive one looming on the horizon?

Disputants often do not try to negotiate themselves out of undesirable situations because they can easily imagine their plight becoming even worse than it is. They cannot conceive of a brighter world for themselves that would also be acceptable to the "other sides."

It may be possible, however, for an outside intervenor to demonstrate the value of negotiations to immovable disputants by developing a mock negotiation scenario involving situations not unlike those found in the real dispute. The outside intervenor I have in mind would be an analyst who is knowledgeable about negotiation and conflict resolution —possibly an academic researcher or a doctoral student. The intervenor would contribute to the resolution of the dispute by writing a highly structured report on mock, pseudo-negotiations involving surrogate disputants that is designed to influence the subsequent behavior of the real disputants. The five-part structure I propose for such a report is as follows:

Part 1: History of the Dispute

The analytical intervenor (the AI, henceforth) will attempt to describe past facts in a way that portrays the history of the dispute as neutrally as possible. The AI will obtain the facts from published documents and from interviews with experts unofficially representing each side. A preliminary copy of the AI's historical report will be discussed with representatives of each side and their comments and reservations will be duly recorded for all to peruse.

A real mediator or arbitrator might attempt to ferret out the facts of a case in a similar manner. However, in real negotiations, the intervenor would have access to the principals and would not usually codify his or her understanding of the facts in a document that the principals could critique. Furthermore, in real disputes, the fact finder will often obtain strategically biased accounts of the past history. And, since these are not reviewed formally by the other side(s), egregious misperception might persist. There is no guarantee that this will not happen in Part I of the AI's report, but the dis-

Howard Raiffa is Frank Plumpton Ramsey Professor of Managerial Economics at the Harvard Business School and the John F. Kennedy School of Government, Harvard University.

torting tendencies will be less. Of course, this may not be to the liking of the real disputants.

Part 2: Analysis of the Interests of the Disputing Parties

The AI will first identify the relevant parties to the dispute. If a major disputant represents disparate factions, it may be necessary to identify sub-parties of that party. Parties should be identified who, in the opinion of the intervenor, would ideally be included in normal, collegial negotiations if only they could be conducted — which we are assuming is not the case.

Part 2 is then divided into several sections, one for each identifiable disputant. Each section will map the underlying interests of one of the disputants. It may not be sufficient merely to identify what these interests are; it may be necessary to examine, in a quantitative sense, various tradeoffs, such as: "How much would you be willing to give up of attribute number six for an increase of one unit of attribute number two?" In short, a multiple-attribute utility analysis will be constructed to represent the values of that disputant as gleaned by the analytical intervenor from published sources and from extensive interviews with the disputant or, more likely, a surrogate or proxy representative. If the disputant is an elected official, the surrogate may be a person who formerly might have held a similar position. At other times, the surrogate might consist of a panel whose members will be asked to provide information collectively about their perceptions of the disputant's values.[2]

In real negotiations, collegially-inclined, nonadversarial protagonists may divulge some of their interests to each other in an attempt to solve a mutual problem together. However, they seldom divulge to the other side(s) their own underlying interests that involve intricate, multiple tradeoffs and attitudes towards risks. In fact, they rarely articulate these values and beliefs to themselves. This task usually requires professional help.

Part 3: Analysis of the No-Agreement State

This section of the proposed report may prove difficult to complete. And, although not critical to the exercise, it would be instructive to attempt to do.

For each disputant, what would the future be like with no agreement? What is his or her utility evaluation for the best alternative to no agreement? A ballpark figure for each disputant would be helpful to have in order to assess potential improvements.

Part 4: Devising Efficient Contracts

The AI, with advice from a panel of surrogate disputants and other devisers, should generate a host of creative alternatives. Many of these alternatives will involve dynamic strategies that exploit the role of time. What is needed are creative ideas without commitments. In real integrative negotiation situations there is a tension between creating and claiming. By using surrogates in brainstorming sessions it may be possible for the discussants to create without the burden of staking out claims.

After devising an appropriate set of potential contracts, the problem can then be formulated as a complex mathematical programming problem: given utility functions for the surrogate disputants and given the set of alternative contracts, the task is to identify and characterize a set of efficient contracts (i.e., contracts that do not leave potentiality for joint gains on the table). In order to be efficient, contracts must exploit differences among the negotiating parties — differences in probabilistic perceptions and beliefs about future events, in attitudes towards risk, in temporal tradeoffs (e.g., discount rates), in needs for symbolic achievements and, most importantly, in tradeoffs among diverse attributes.

Efficient contracts can be generated for a very simple class of negotiations where multiple-attribute utility functions are additive and where the contract outcomes are themselves the attributes of concern.[3] In more complicated cases the mathematical programming problem for generating efficient contracts, though considerably more complex, is still manageable with the aid of modern analytical programming techniques and the use of modern computers.

A display of several efficient contracts should act as a lure to entice real disputants to engage in real negotiations. At least, that's the hope!

Part 5: The Creation of Single Negotiating Texts
The set of efficient contracts using the utility functions of the surrogate disputants may not be quite appropriate for the real world of the real disputants. The assessed utility functions might be distorted and some promising compromises may not actually be feasible. In addition, other possible types of contracts may have been overlooked by the AI and the panel of devisers. The real players, once they become involved, may be even more creative. So the generation of efficient contracts signifies only a suggestion of what might be possible rather than an accurate representation of what is actually achievable.

Part 5 of the AI's report is designed to help a real mediator in possible real negotiations with the real disputants. It develops one (or more) single negotiating texts (SNTs) that could be used as starting points in those subsequent negotiations.[4]

Part 5 (or Part 6) would conclude with helpful suggestions about possible first steps that could be taken to bring the disputants to the negotiating table.

*   *   *

Why go through all the effort involved in doing an in-depth analysis of mock pseudo-negotiation with surrogate disputants? The analytical intervenor may be motivated by two different types of reasons: to do right by the world and to do challenging, methodological (and publishable!) analyses.

Let's consider the second reason first. Valuable information and techniques about real interventions might be learned from analyses of mock pseudo-negotiations. The state of the science of intervention might be advanced by the vicarious experience we could gain from mock pseudo-negotiations. Such analyses might be fascinating not only as methodological challenges but also because they might elucidate substance: they might reveal the essence of a given dispute.

Now for the main reason for such an activity: to do right by the world. In some circumstances, compromise solutions that would be jointly acceptable might not exist; in this case, mock pseudo-negotiations might only help to clarify this negative conclusion. Even that might be a help. But other times, jointly acceptable solutions might exist but not be imaginable; other times they might be imaginable but not politically attainable; other times they might be foreseeable as being politically feasible but other, less desirable outcomes might also be feasible and the risk may not be worth taking; other times acceptable compromises might be seen as achievable but it might require too high a level of entrepreneurship to sell to others; other times one side might be convinced, "but it takes two to thaw." In all those "other times," mock pseudo-negotiations might be of positive benefit.

A completed study of mock pseudo-negotiation might raise aspirations, might convince skeptics, might undercut the power of blocking coalitions. If real negotiations were to start with a single negotiating text that initially was better than the alternative of no agreement for each disputant, then the parties might at least feel obligated to try to see if they could do better.

Now for a bit of reality on the negative side: The research task for an AI might be formidable and time consuming. Who is to support such analytical interventions and how should these AIs be selected? An AI might be biased but still do a professionally neutral and honest job. After all, the product of the research is to be exhibited for all sides to see and criticize. But still, a disputant might be suspicious that the activity is merely a propaganda ploy of the other side and the report may be read with a jaundiced eye. The biggest deficiency of the procedure, however, is lack of commitment. The report is based on someone else's ideas; it also did not build up any commitment from the disputants that stems from their active participation in the process of discovery. As the saying goes, "The disputants don't *own* the solution."

Analysis of pseudo-negotiations by surrogate disputants has drawbacks. It may not be as good as the real thing but it may be an alternative if the real thing is not possible.

There is also the possibility of mixtures between reality and fiction. For example, the real disputants might commission, or at least be kept abreast of, the analytical intervenor's report of the pseudo-negotiations. And, unofficially and at-arms-length, they may peruse the report as it unfolds. The real disputants might then help to coach their surrogates and, if things work out well, they can take credit for contributing to the product.

All the preceding is intended only as a suggested agenda for practical research. What is desperately needed are a few success stories of analytical interventions in some not-too-horrendous conflicts.

NOTES

1. An outcome is "efficient" only if there does not exist an alternate outcome that is preferred by each disputant. An "inefficient" outcome can be improved upon in a way that gives each disputant more satisfaction; an inefficient outcome leaves potential joint gains for all on the table.

2. For an extensive discussion of the techniques of Multiple Attitude Utility Theory (MAUT), see Ralph Keeney and Howard Raiffa, *Decisions with Multiple Objectives: Preferences and Value Tradeoffs* (New York: John Wiley, 1976).

3. See Raiffa, *The Art and Science of Negotiation* (Cambridge, Mass.: Harvard University Press, 1982), esp. pp. 251-255.

4. See Raiffa, *The Art and Science of Negotiation* and Roger Fisher and William Ury, *Getting to YES* (Boston: Houghton Mifflin, 1981) for an explanation of the rationale for the use of SNTs — Single Negotiating Texts.

Section III

Getting to the Table Prepared

If, as described in the preceding section, a first aspect of pre-negotiation calls for the resolution of as many internal differences as possible, then the second prerequisite entails adequate preparation for the negotiations themselves. Such preparation includes, among other things, attempting to evaluate one's own power and one's alternatives to negotiated settlement — as well as the power and alternatives of the other side. As the selections in Section III make clear, the relationship between power and alternatives is a close one; indeed, one reasonable way of beginning to define one's negotiating power is by examining exactly how dependent one is on the other for an agreement. The greater one's dependence, the less one's negotiating power; conversely, the better one's alternatives away from the negotiating table, the more powerful the negotiator is apt to be.

As a case in point, the first essay, by David A. Lax and James K. Sebenius ("The Power of Alternatives or the Limits to Negotiation") develops the view that power in negotiation is largely determined by one's alternatives away from the table (what Roger Fisher and William Ury [1981] refer to as BATNA, or best alternative to negotiated agreement). The better one's alternatives away from the table, the less dependent one will be on whatever proposals the other side happens to toss one's way, and the better able one will be to choose wisely between the advantages conferred by negotiated agreement and the outcomes that can be obtained unilaterally. Lax and Sebenius offer several helpful prescriptions in their essay, including the observation that one's alternatives away from the table are typically far more important in determining negotiating power than such things as tactical skill, the ability to make commitments or inflict harm, and one's willingness to take risks or incur costs.

Perhaps the most influential of all the books on negotiation within the last 10-15 years is the highly readable *Getting to YES* by Roger Fisher and

William Ury (1981). Translated into many languages, and having sold more than one million copies, the book has found widespread use as a tool of preparation for negotiation. The formulation described in *Getting to YES*, however, is not without its critics. In an insightful and provocative contribution, Lord William McCarthy ("The Role of Power and Principle in *Getting to YES*"), while agreeing with many key tenets of the Fisher and Ury book, also raises several serious challenges. Among these is his assertion that *Getting to YES* is only or especially valuable for those parties to a negotiation who are in positions of low power. If one sits "upstream" in a river dispute, argues McCarthy, one need not negotiate with the "downstream" interest at all, since one can dam, pollute, or otherwise manipulate the water exactly as one pleases.

In an equally provocative response to the McCarthy essay, Roger Fisher ("Beyond YES") accepts the validity of several questions raised by the critic, then proceeds to move beyond the scope of his book with Ury to develop a more general theory of power. In this essay, as well as the fourth essay of the section ("Negotiating Power: Getting and Using Influence"), Roger Fisher argues that power is determined less by the tangible resources in one's possession than by one's ability to negotiate effectively. In particular, Fisher develops the view that power in negotiation can derive from such things as a negotiator's skill and knowledge, the ability to make a commitment, the legitimacy of one's arguments, the elegance of solutions proposed, one's ability to develop a good relationship, and (as also observed in the selection by Lax and Sebenius) the attractiveness of one's alternatives to negotiating.

The fifth and final essay ("Saying You're Sorry") brings a different slant to the business of preparation for negotiation. While the other essays of this section, in one way or another, focus on alternatives to negotiation and power issues, this selection (written by Stephen B. Goldberg, Eric D. Green, and Frank E. A. Sander) argues that one can often avoid the kind of confrontation that makes negotiation difficult or impossible through the timely use of an apology. What an apology may do, in effect, is make less appealing to the other side various alternatives away from the table, and make more attractive the possibility of exchange represented by the negotiation process.

The Power of Alternatives or the Limits to Negotiation

David A. Lax and James K. Sebenius

People faced with upcoming negotiations often seek advice. Invariably, many if not most of their questions have a tactical slant: How much should I find out about the other side's psyche and past? Should I make the first contact? By phone, in person, by mail, or through a third party? Wear a dark suit and meet in an expensive restaurant near my office? Order them strong drinks? Sit with my back to the wall and the sun in their eyes? Make the first offer? Start high? Concede slowly? Settle the easy issues first? Act conciliatory, tough, threatening, or as a joint problem-solver? Arrange for a "hard-hearted" partner? Look for self-serving rationales or objective principles? And so forth.

Such tactical concerns have often occupied the attention of negotiation analysts and practitioners. Yet practical and theoretical responses to these concerns often share an important implicit premise. By attempting to influence or predict the outcome of a negotiation *within* a given range of possible agreements, the responses generally take this range as unchanging. By contrast, in this article we investigate a complementary set of questions about the factors and moves that *determine* and may alter the range of possible agreements.

If one characterizes negotiation as an interactive process by which two or more people seek jointly or cooperatively to do better than they could otherwise, then the "otherwise" becomes crucial. The parties' best alternatives without agreement imply the *limits* to any agreement. For each side, the basic test of any proposed joint agreement is whether it offers higher subjective worth than that side's best course of action absent agreement. Thus, moves "away from the table" to shape the parties' alternatives to agreement may be as or more important than tactics employed "at the table." Actions of the first type delimit the range of possible agreements; those of the second type influence which point in the range may be chosen. The strategic arsenal from which moves of the second type are drawn includes actions that improve alternatives to the negotiation at hand: for example, searching for a better price or another supplier, cultivating a friendly merger partner in response to hostile takeover negotiations, or preparing an invasion should talks fail to yield a preferable outcome.

David A. Lax is managing director and general partner in ECO Management, New York City. **James K. Sebenius** is Professor of Management at the Harvard Business School. They are the co-authors of *The Manager as Negotiator* (New York: The Free Press, 1986).

By stressing that the desirability of negotiated agreement derives from its possible superiority to individual action, we emphasize our view that negotiation is a *means* of doing better cooperatively than would be possible otherwise.[1]

As such, potential negotiated agreements should be evaluated as competitors to other possibilities for furthering desired ends. This focus helps determine whether to negotiate at all, whether to continue the process, whether to accept a proposal, and whether an agreement, once reached, will be secure.

1. Alternatives in Theory

Many theorists take for granted that if bargaining is inconclusive, the parties fall back to their best alternatives. For example, game theorists (e.g., Roth, 1979) routinely include disagreement possibilities in their specification of bargaining situations. Other formal treatments and conventional accounts of bargaining implicitly incorporate the potential for improved alternatives into the evaluation of a failure to agree. Yet relatively little attention is given to the strategic aspects of alternatives or to negotiators' complex moves to shape, protect, and improve them. Generally, analysts take the strategy (*including* any search for better alternatives) to be employed in case of no agreement as a given or a sort of benchmark for the study of subsequent bargaining. This approach often carries the implication that the alternatives, like the parties or the issues, form an unchangeable part of a bargain's specification. By this reasoning, admitting moves that affect alternatives and then discovering that the negotiation changes amounts to analytic sleight of hand.

Many circumstances, however, can justify treating alternatives as subject to change during the negotiation, thereby overcoming the theorist's potential objection. Improving alternatives can take time, and searches begun prior to a negotiation may run concurrently with it. Generating new alternatives can be costly, and only a limited search may be optimal at the outset. Especially in complex, protracted negotiations, new information and interpretations may become available about the external environment and about the bargaining situation itself (the real interests, aspirations, and tactics of other participants; subjective probabilities of reaching different outcomes; as well as the likely costs in money, energy, and time required for a settlement). Thus decisions on the extent and intensity of moves to affect alternatives should be conditioned by current assessments of the bargaining's future course. At the same time, the results of such moves can affect the nature of the bargaining and the tactics employed in it. In view of this dynamic relationship between bargaining "inside" and searching "outside," fully rational participants may continually contemplate altering their choice of tactics, including the possibility of a reactivated or intensified search for better alternatives. In general, resources such as effort, time, or money should go toward affecting alternatives or generating new ones until the expected improvement in the value of the negotiated outcome from expending additional resources just equals the cost of doing so.[2]

Like the commitment, the threat, and the promise, the alternative can fundamentally affect the bargaining process. Highlighting it as such, however, risks a negative emphasis, for in concentrating on the *limits* of negotiation, the *potential* is ignored. Many techniques and principles exist to help invent and improve joint arrangements that each side would value more than its best alternative. After all, the main point of negotiating lies in the possibility of gains from cooperation. But alternatives — by implying the limits, reservation prices, or bottom lines — provide the standards against which to measure potential agreements.

Alternatives can be as varied as the negotiating situations they circumscribe. They may be certain and have a single attribute: an ironclad competing price quote for an identical new car. They may be contingent and multi-attributed: going to court rather than accepting a negotiated settlement can involve uncertainties, trial anxieties, legal fees, time costs, and precedents that contrast with the certain, solely monetary nature of a pretrial accord. Alternatives may change over time with new information, interpretations, competitive moves, or opportunities. In case of no agreement, the *status quo ante* may be superseded by something much worse for one side: a now neutral island nation may intend to lease its naval base to one superpower if current negotiations fall through with the other. In multiparty and organizational negotiations, one side's alternatives may be the set of agreements that could be reached by potential opposing coalitions. Outright threats by one party to change the no-agreement alternatives of another are commonly made: the godfather's "offer you can't refuse." Or, the best alternative to the negotiated agreement may be to keep negotiating: in arms control, organizational deliberations, or minor marital disputes, failure to agree may involve worse relations, forgone benefit, and altered settlement possibilities, but in any case the necessity remains of continued dealings among the same parties. In all these disparate situations, the central analytical feature of alternatives flows from the bargainer's evaluation of no agreement compared with that of agreement. There is a strategic commonality regardless of whether the alternatives are certain or uncertain, have one, many, or different attributes, are static or dynamic, or depend or do not depend on other bargaining parties.

A variety of well-developed techniques exist to help understand and evaluate many of these types of alternatives to negotiated agreement. The subjective expected utility of the best alternative provides a strict lower bound for the minimum worth required of any acceptable settlement. One's "reservation price" (bottom line, threat- or resistance-point) is any settlement that gives exactly this minimum expected utility. When alternatives are uncertain or change over time, decision analysis can provide a systematic guide to action (Raiffa, 1968). Multi-attribute value and utility theory can clarify the outcomes when they have many attributes; even when the features of the alternatives differ from those of the agreements (Keeney and Raiffa, 1976; Barclay and Peterson, 1976). In certain cases, there are many possible alternatives to negotiation, each with associated uncertainties and costs of discovery. In such cases, optimal search theory can provide strategies for searching efficiently among the alternatives and valuing the expected findings from such a search (Lax, forthcoming). Where the parties' alternatives to agreement are interdependent, concepts from game theory — including the dynamics of threats and counterthreats as well as the many variants of coalition analysis — can help bargainers understand their alternatives and, in so doing, better understand the rationale for bargaining (Luce and Raiffa, 1957; Raiffa, 1982).

In certain ritualized or institutionalized negotiations, such as collective bargaining or the purchase of expensive items, alternatives to agreement (strikes, lockouts, other price quotes) are obvious, well defined, and tactically prominent. In other situations, alternatives can be subtler and can play less straightforward roles. Many bargainers tend to focus on tactics and the process itself, effectively assuming that a deal will result and trying to improve it as much as possible. In such situations, alternatives may function more as last resorts or afterthoughts than as primary influences on the negotiation.

2. Prescriptions and Propositions

To counter this common tendency, we have argued that analysts and practitioners should complement their customary focus on the bargaining process with scrutiny of moves intended favorably to alter the bargaining range itself. Lurking barely below the surface of the preceding discussion has been a general prescription that can be easily summarized: Realize the potential of alternatives to agreement.

To develop those ideas in more depth and to enhance their value in application, we offer a series of related propositions and prescriptions. Our first prescription is minimal but often honored only in the breach. A negotiator should evaluate all parties' alternatives, consider enhancing them, and be prepared to take his or her no-agreement alternative when it dominates negotiable possibilities. Second, evaluation of alternatives is inherently subjective and, thus, depends on perceptions. Experimental evidence suggests that negotiators tend to have inconsistently optimistic perceptions of their own alternatives. They should anticipate such systematic biases. Third, because improved alternatives generally yield better bargaining positions, it should not be surprising that notions of bargaining "power" are bound up with alternatives. A clearer understanding of this link can improve strategic and tactical choices. Fourth, the importance of alternatives does not end once agreement is reached. The enforceability and sustainability of many agreements depend on each party's alternatives to continued adherence. Agreements can be secured by ensuring that each party perceives continued compliance as superior to its alternatives. Finally, the preceding advice extends beyond face-to-face encounters to influencing decentralized bargains. Managers, policymakers, and legislators can affect far-flung negotiations by their ability to change negotiators' perceptions of their alternatives to agreement.

A. Evaluate Alternatives to Agreement

Obviously negotiators should *evaluate* what the alternative actions are likely to be for all sides. Sometimes it is appropriate for this evaluation to make use of sophisticated technical tools, such as those mentioned earlier; at other times careful thought will suffice. An intergovernmental example illustrates the point.

Over a number of years, states spent large amounts of money on certain types of social services, partially in the expectation of federal reimbursement. The circumstances were murky, the amounts of money ran into the billions, and it was not clear whether this was good public policy or merely a loophole in laws and regulations. For several years, however, these state claims against the federal government had been a considerable thorn in the side of federal-state relations. A new administration came into office and placed improved intergovernmental relations high on its priority list. Still, finances were tight and budgets were under close scrutiny. Early in the new administration's tenure, negotiations over these social service claims resumed in earnest. The federal official in charge of these talks thought very hard about tactics and approaches within the negotiations themselves but he also focused a great deal of attention on the parties' best alternatives to a negotiated agreement.

If the parties did not reach agreement voluntarily, they would go to court. In fact, in previous suits over these claims, the two sides had already seen each other in court. The federal government had demonstrated its commitment to a legal battle by appealing to earlier adverse decisions on rather narrow grounds. Yet for all sides the prospect of continued legal battles was unappealing: the outcomes were uncertain, many resources would be expended, and the opportunity for an improved relationship could be lost in the ensuing adversarial process. In fact, the hoped-for value of voluntary agreement impelled both sides toward a solution. If they settled this long-standing problem between themselves, it could set an excellent procedural precedent and have benefits in many other areas.

Yet, in preparing, the federal official thought hard about the role of time and realized that in at least four distinctive ways it worked strongly against the state's alternatives to a negotiated agreement with the federal government. First, inflation was eating away at any possible settlement. The administration could credibly threaten to tie up the claims in court for many more years. Beyond economic costs to the states from a failure to agree, he realized, and probably much more important, political factors rendered a settlement much less valuable to the states if delayed beyond gubernatorial elections. The money spent on social services had been expended years ago; for the states it was a sunk cost. Any state administration receiving reimbursement in effect would get a windfall which could be crucial toward, say, balancing a current state budget or funding a favorite program. State governors' terms were all shorter than or equal to the tenure of the new federal administration. The credible federal threat to drag out the settlement process could thus deny the governors great political credit. A third factor working against certain states was the frequent turnover in their personnel who would be able to back up their cases in court. In effect, as their ability to substantiate their legal claims eroded, the quality of those states' best alternatives declined over time relative to that of the federal government.

Finally, the federal official portrayed administration eagerness to settle this issue as a sort of "fading opportunity" for the states. Settlement of this divisive issue briefly held a cabinet secretary's attention. Yet the secretary's alternative to any sort of agreement on claim settlement was simply to ignore the dispute. The claims would move off his priority list and would be handled at the same low bureaucratic echelons where they had been inconclusively mired for years.

Thus, the worsening of their alternatives over time pushed the states toward early settlement for a variety of reasons. Each of these factors, of course, had exactly the opposite effect on the federal government's alternatives to a negotiated agreement. Any claims settled in the future would be paid with cheaper dollars and, critically, as a budget liability to a later — not the current — administration. Relative to many states, the federal ability to uphold its legal case would not erode. Moreover, the alternative to secretarial resolution of this issue was a host of other important, pressing issues.

These factors heavily influenced state (and federal) perceptions of the zone of possible agreement. Within a clearer range, it was then possible to search for appropriate principles to govern a negotiated settlement. The sides did reach an agreement far below the states' original claims but one that was realistic given the sides' alternatives. The result did, however, have a strong benefit of improving intergovernmental relations across a variety of issues.

If careful evaluation of the sides' alternatives is the first part of realizing their potential, a good negotiator will often consider improving his or her alternatives. The 1971 Maltese-British negotiations over renewed base rights provide an instructive example (Wriggens, 1976). Britain had enjoyed the use of a Maltese naval base and had extended its use to other NATO countries. Nevertheless, advances in ship design and warfare methods rendered the Maltese bases of considerably less importance than in earlier years. To obtain much-improved base rental terms, however, the Maltese made highly visible overtures to the Soviet Union about locating one of their bases in Malta. They also approached Libya and other Arab states for large assistance payments in return for Malta's neutrality. At a simple level, this increased the attractiveness of Malta's alternatives to negotiated agreement with the British. But the same moves made Britain's alternatives to agreement with Malta considerably worse. As *The Times* of London noted, "What is important . . . is not that [the facilities] are badly needed in an age of nuclear war but that they should not on the other hand be possessed by Russia." Not only did these actions put pressure directly on Britain, but NATO anxiety, which the Maltese carefully cultivated, served indirectly to increase the pressure. Beyond vastly increased base rentals from Britain, other NATO members ultimately agreed to provide supplemental aid to Malta. Without passing judgment on the questionable prudential or moral implications of such tactics, especially in the longer run, it is worth highlighting the fact that the Maltese actions to improve their own alternatives and worsen those of their negotiating counterparts considerably improved their bargaining position.

When preparing for a future negotiation, one side may change the expected nature of this encounter by taking steps to affect the other side's alternatives to an agreement favorable to the first side. For example, in the early 1960s, Chilean expropriation of Kennecott Copper's El Teniente mine seemed increasingly likely (Smith and Wells, 1975). In preparing to negotiate the terms of expropriation, such as the timing, compensation, and any continued management involvement with the mine, Kennecott sought early on to involve a variety of other parties to change the nature of Chile's alternatives to agreement on Kennecott's preferred terms. Somewhat surprisingly, the company offered to sell a majority interest in the mine to Chile. Kennecott then turned to the Export-Import Bank and the proceeds of this sale of equity to finance expansion of the mine. The Chilean government guaranteed this loan and made it subject to New York State law. The company then insured as much as possible of its assets under a U.S. guarantee against expropriation. The mine's output was to be sold under long-term contracts with Asian and European customers, and the collection rights for these contracts were sold to a consortium of European banks and Japanese institutions.

The result was that customers, governments, and creditors shared Kennecott's concern about future changes in Chile. Moreover, the guarantee and insurance improved Kennecott's alternatives if no deal could be worked out with the host country. When no agreement could be reached and Chile acted to expropriate the operation, Kennecott was able to call this host of parties in on its side. Though the mine was ultimately nationalized, Chile's worsened alternatives to Kennecott's preferred outcome gave the firm a better position in the dealings than those of similar companies who did not take such actions.

If negotiation is seen as a *means* of doing better by joint action than would be possible otherwise, it should not be surprising that non-negotiation courses of action will sometimes prove to be the superior means. A clear-headed focus on the alternatives may help clarify this judgment. For example, the mentor of a very ambitious young man in an investment management company found himself trying to renegotiate the terms of the young man's association with the firm. The young man had made a great deal of money for the firm but had done so in a direction contrary to the strategy agreed to by the firm's principals. Moreover, the young man had gone "outside normal procedures" in furthering his aims. His mentor, the firm's president, could envision many possible joint arrangements that might be better from the firm's point of view. But, ultimately, any set of terms agreeable to the firm seemed worse to the young man than separation (and vice versa). Carefully focusing both sides' attention on the unilateral alternative clarified the ultimate resolution — the young man left — which, though it may be regarded as a failed negotiation, was probably a superior outcome for both sides.

In a more strident vein, President Reagan's early dealings with professional air traffic controllers over their contract was resolved when the president fired them all and activated a contingency plan to run the nation's air traffic control system. From Reagan's perspective, decisive, non-cooperative action not only settled the air traffic situation but sent strong signals for moderation to other public employee unions and enhanced the president's reputation for toughness. Again, this case suggests a "failure" of negotiation that at least for one participant offered a superior alternative to any negotiable agreement.

Our first prescription, therefore, is to evaluate all sides' alternatives, to consider steps to improve them, and, when negotiated possibilities are distinctly inferior — having carefully accounted for effects on relationships and future linked dealings — to take the best alternative course of action.

B. Anticipate Inflated Perceptions of Alternatives
A negotiator's evaluation of alternatives is inherently subjective and, thus, depends on perceptions. Analysts and practitioners should, therefore, be sensitive to different possible perceptions of the same alternative. In an experi-

ment at Harvard, the findings of which have been replicated in many contexts with students and executives, players were given detailed information about the history of an out-of-court negotiation over insurance claims arising from a personal injury case (Raiffa, 1982). They were not told whether the negotiators settled or if the case went into court. Each player was assigned to the role of either the insurance company or the defendant. After reading the case file, the players were privately asked to give their true probability estimates that the plaintiff would win the case and, given a win, the expected amount of the ultimate judgment. Systematically, those assigned the role of the plaintiff estimated the chances of winning and the expected amount of winning as much higher than those assigned the role of the insurance company defendant. Players who were not assigned a role prior to reading the case gave private estimates that generally fell between those of the advocates for each position. Similar results have been found in cases involving the worth of a company that is up for sale. Even given identical business information, balance sheets, income statements, and the like, those assigned to buy the company typically rate its true value as low, while those assigned to sell it give much higher best estimates. Neutral observers ranked the potential someplace in between.

These results, in combination with many other negotiation experiences, suggest that advocates tend to overestimate the attractiveness of their alternatives to negotiated agreement. If each side has an inflated expectation of its alternatives, no zone of possible agreement for negotiation may exist. Awareness of this common bias dictates a conscious attempt to be more realistic about one's own case, not to "believe one's own line" too much, and to be aware and seek to alter counterparts' estimates of their alternatives. A number of tactics can help deflate unrealistic perceptions. At a minimum one may seek advice from uninvolved parties whose estimates are not colored by their roles. So-called mini-trials can bring executives of opposing sides together to hear each other's arguments presented in a mock courtroom setting. Firsthand exposure to the other side's point of view may alter executives' estimates of the court alternatives which were principally derived from overly optimistic corporate counsel. Roger Fisher (1983) even suggests establishing *settlement* divisions of law firms or general counsel's offices (whose lawyers would not be involved in the court "alternative"), separate from *litigation* departments whose lawyers would prepare cases for trial. The optimistic biases of such lawyers might even make them more effective advocates if no settlement could be achieved.

One often hears that a particular dispute is not "ripe" or "mature" for negotiation or resolution. This state of affairs often arises when the sides have inconsistently optimistic estimates of their noncooperative alternatives. For example, a consortium of Midwestern power companies proposed to build a dam to bring electricity at lower rates to the area's customers. Environmentalists opposed this plan, claiming that it would damage the downstream habitat of the endangered whooping crane. Farm groups lined up against the project, fearing that the dam would reduce water flow in the area. Though the sides tried early on to negotiate, each believed its alternatives to agreement to be quite favorable. Negotiations sputtered until the environmentalists and farmers won a substantial court victory (quite unexpected by the power companies) and, in their turn, the power companies got strong indications of favorable congressional action. With each side's perception of its alternatives to a negotiated agreement considerably less optimistic than at the outset, the stage was set for more realistic negotiation, which ultimately resulted in a creative agreement for a smaller dam, stream flow guarantees, and a trust fund for preserving the habitats of endangered species.

Many other examples could present themselves of disputes that are not "ripe" for negotiation given the parties' inconsistently optimistic perceptions of their alternatives. If this is the diagnosis, however, getting people in a room together and employing all sorts of careful procedural means to foster negotiation will likely be to no avail. The basic condition for a negotiated agreement will not be met, since possible agreements will appear inferior to at least one side in comparison with its unilateral alternatives. When this is the case, strategy should focus *not* on the negotiation process but instead on actions away from the table that can reshape perceptions in a manner that generates a zone of possible agreement.

In each of these cases, then, negotiators should anticipate inflated perceptions of alternatives. The implied prescriptions are (1) be aware of and seek to counteract the biases of one's own role, and (2) where the sides have inconsistent perceptions of the attractiveness of alternatives, focus negotiating strategy on altering those perceptions so that joint action will appear preferable by comparison.

C. Understand the Link between Alternatives and So-Called "Power"

Because improvement in perceptions of one's alternatives implies a favorable change in the bargaining range, the ability to affect alternatives — and perceptions of them — lies at the root of many conceptions of bargaining "power." The tight complimentarity of alternatives and the negotiation process as well as the relation of alternatives to concepts of power are perfectly clear in a variety of settings. Suppose the boss orders an ethically questionable action. Contrast the resulting situation of the employee who can generate a good outside job offer with that of the one who cannot. Consider how the presence of marketable skills can likewise change a wife's approach to negotiating the end of a bad marriage. What comes of the onerous claims of the neighborhood bully when his reliably protective older brother is drafted?

In an economic setting, one can say equivalently that monopoly power in a product market results either from a single seller or from buyers without alternatives. Labor unions may favor high minimum wage laws in part to limit the attractiveness of employers' alternatives to the union scale. Of course, negotiation over product or labor prices is wholly driven out by pure competition in which everyone's alternative to a proposed higher price is the going market rate.

These straightforward examples suggest the intuitive proposition that an increase in the desirability of one's alternatives increases one's "power," whether the increase is from more highly valued attributes, less risk, less aversion to risk, earlier receipt of the alternative's benefits, or later payment of its costs. A long line of observers has noted a connection between alternatives and "power."[3] Sketchy but very suggestive experimental evidence seems to confirm that, other things being equal, improvement in a bargainer's alternative improves the distribution of his or her negotiated outcomes. This connection can be clarified by reference to conceptions of bargaining strength in which bargaining strength derives from tactical skills, how much each side "cares" about the issues at stake, ability to inflict harm, dependence of one party on the other, or willingness to take risks and incur costs. The next sections explore the intimate relationships between these antecedents of bargaining strength and negotiators' alternatives to agreement. For ease of exposition, we consider a series of simple negotiations with potential ranges of mutually beneficial agreements and the possibility of credible, binding commitments. (The strong assumption that commitments can succeed facilitates analysis and highlights the distinctive role of alternatives.)

Tactical Skill. Bargaining tactics are often held to be potent. As noted above, however, the best alternative decisively limits the *range* in which they are applicable. The would-be house buyer who psychoanalyzes the seller, details the dwelling's flaws, and makes a low offer is wasting time if the seller can elicit a better price elsewhere.

This simple observation circumscribes the claims that high-priced consultants, true believers, and prescriptive theorists of negotiation can legitimately assert. Although the title, for example, of Cohen's 1980 best-seller, *You Can Negotiate Anything*, caters to widespread popular notions of the limitless power of bargaining skill, an academic version of the same book might gracelessly add: "With Some Probability, Provided Your Counterpart Finds It Better than His or Her Alternatives."

Intensity of Preference. Suppose that Sarah desperately wants a Mercedes but is negotiating with a salesman who, having exceeded his annual quota, now seems fairly unexcited at the prospect of another sale. Or say that neighborhood pools legally must be lifeguarded and that a pool's owners are trying to allocate this time-consuming responsibility among themselves. What is the relative position of the parent in the group whose child will swim most frequently? And who has the "power" in the discussion between the supervisor of many employees and a particular employee who asks for a raise? It is commonly asserted that the party who "cares more" about the issues at stake in a negotiation is at a disadvantage and that this "greater" interest can be exploited.

As Thomas Schelling has implied, however, once the bargaining range is correctly specified (with all relevant attributes factored in, from the immediate issue at hand to potential anger, altruism, spite, precedent, the relationship, and so forth), it is not relative "intensity of preference" that influences the outcome. Instead, the bargain is "won" by the side that is first to commit credibly and irreversibly to a preferred point — provided that point is the slightest bit better for the other side than its best alternative. The uncommitted side has lost; it faces a simple choice between the commitment point and the inferior alternative. If Sarah knows the salesman's true minimum, she can credibly commit to a slightly higher price. If there are six other pool owners, each known to have two days a week potentially free for lifeguarding, the parent-owner whose child swims the most could prevail by committing to equal sharing or nothing. If the supervisor, figuring the employee's productivity and the precedent set for other workers, were ultimately willing to offer up to an x percent raise, then the employee's commitment to getting an x minus ¼ percent raise or else to resign would be successful. (Again, the exposition — but not the underlying point — relies on perfect commitment possibilities. See Schelling [1960] for a splendid discussion of the art of commitment.)

The strategic situation, of course, is completely symmetric when the range is known and each side can successfully commit. If the salesman divines Sarah's maximum and first commits to a slightly lower figure, he has won. If the five other pool owners initially band together and irrevocably demand that the intensive swimmer's parent either drop out or guard for two days a week, while they each take one day, their demand will succeed. And similarly with the supervisor. In situations of pure bargaining, the first commitment within a mutually acceptable range prevails.

Better alternatives enter this strategic picture in two ways. First, though a prior binding commitment is invulnerable to other commitments or threats, a newfound better alternative dominates such a prior commitment. If, in the face of the Mercedes dealer's irrevocable commitment to a price just below Sarah's maximum, another dealer offers her a better price, the first dealer has lost. If, on confronting the larger group's two-day demand, the intensive swimmer's parent locates a different pool that requires only a half-day per week of parental guard duties, the group has lost. A new job paying more than the wage committed to by the supervisor allows the worker to "beat" the commitment.

Notice, second, that if "intensity of preference" has any meaning at all, it is only with respect to the differences of preference for possible agreements and that for available alternatives. Sarah may live for the possibility of owning a Mercedes, but a firm offer by another dealer close to the prices under discussion with the first salesman renders uninteresting the judgment that Sarah may "care more." Thus preference strength, high or low with respect to available alternatives, is tactically unimportant in the presence of credible commitment possibilities, which in turn are vulnerable to better alternatives.

The Ability to Commit. Schelling's analysis closely identifies "power" with the ability to commit to a position from which one cannot be expected to recede. One commits to a point in the bargaining range by imposing large costs upon oneself for accepting settlements less attractive than the specified point. If these conditional costs render lesser settlements unacceptable relative to one's current alternatives, one's counterpart faces a preordained choice between accepting either the point in the bargaining range or a less desirable alternative. A commitment, therefore, functions by restricting the bargaining range in a way that favors the committing party.

There is a complementarity between strategic moves to commit and strategic moves to improve one's alternative. Improving one's alternative also restricts the bargaining range in a favorable way, but by a different mechanism: it changes the standard of acceptability to which possible settlements are compared. Committing, by contrast, changes the agreement possibilities relative to a fixed standard of acceptability. To accept less than one's improved alternative is to forgo an attainable benefit. To accept less than the point to which one has committed is to incur a self-imposed cost.

Notice that both committing and improving alternatives may add new elements to an already specified bargaining game. Committing invokes the latent ability to incur conditional costs by contracting with third parties, staking one's reputation with others, and using a host of other ploys involving new attributes, issues, and participants. Similarly, improving alternatives by searching for better outside terms, soliciting another offer, forging a new alliance, hiring better counsel, or building up military might can all be seen as tactics that alter the original game.

Commitments and strategic improvements in alternatives are thus somewhat complementary tactics. Bargainers must expend resources to employ either. But successful commitments are risky because they are difficult to make credible, binding, visible, and irreversible. Negotiators often do not know the limits of the mutually acceptable bargaining range. Thus a commitment to a favorable point involves the additional risk of falling outside the true range. A better alternative, however, does not incur this liability. Moreover, one's commitment is vulnerable both to the other side's prior commitment and to an improvement in its alternative. An improvement in one's alternative, though, cannot be superseded by prior or subsequent commitments. A threat, of course, may hold the possibility of degrading the opponent's original or even improved alternatives. A negotiator's choice among tactics should reflect these considerations.

Ability to Inflict Harm. The ability to inflict harm or withhold benefits is a classical bargaining lever. Of course, "the offer that can't be refused" and a nation's threat of economic or military sanctions can both be understood as functioning through alternatives to agreement, specifically, worsening those of the other side if acquiescence is not forthcoming.

The ability to change another's alternative conceptually differs from the ability to improve one's own. Roger Fisher nicely illustrates this point by contrasting the distinct sorts of "power" possessed by the job interviewee whose back pocket holds either a gun or an attractive competing offer.

The threat to inflict harm unless some action is taken can be understood as a conditional commitment. Prior commitments therefore can neutralize subsequent threats: if the job interviewer has dropped an irrevocable "do not hire" judgment into the pneumatic tube, the applicant's drawn gun can exact revenge but cannot win the job.

The firm facing an unfriendly takeover can attempt to deter it by threatening huge legal costs. The threat fails if the bidder has committed to bear all acquisition costs, no matter how large. If, however, the target company finds a "white knight" firm, it can prevent the unfriendly takeover or compel better terms. Such improvement in the alternative can negate the aggressor's commitment where ability to impose costs cannot. The threat of harm, therefore, can be understood as conditionally changing a counterpart's alternatives; it is conceptually distinct from improving one's own.

Dependence on the Other Party. A dependent relationship, such as that of child and parents, of worker and boss, or of colony and colonial power, is often thought to imply the bargaining weakness of the dependent party. Dependence increases as agreement (which *depends* on the other side) yields greater benefits relative to the value of independent alternatives.

A superpower can seek favorable terms by threatening to impose costs on or withhold benefits from a satellite country. A colony is dependent on the colonial power that is the sole buyer of its only product. Along with overtones of differing preference intensities (considered above), "power" in dependent relationships thus can be understood as a variable combination of two key elements also earlier analyzed: the ability to change another's alternatives and the attractiveness of one's own competing alternatives. Notions of power derived from dependence are thus driven by the negotiators' alternatives.

As analysis of these elements implies, attributing "power" in dependent relationships is often trickier than it may first appear. The country in danger of default as well as the borrower who owes the bank $50,000, is six payments behind on his car, and has a sick wife may each think they have problems; instead, it could well be their bankers who are in trouble.

Willingness to Take Risks or Incur Costs. These qualities, often loudly proclaimed, can be directly translated into the language of alternatives. The more risk-prone and cost-insensitive a bargainer is, the more attractive a risky, costly alternative to a proffered deal becomes. The subjective utility of no agreement is key to the role of alternatives. Risk and cost attitudes are merely part of the utility yardstick by which a bargainer evaluates potential outcomes and portrays them to the other negotiators.

"Power" is a notoriously slippery concept. Yet a number of common notions of bargaining power — tactical skill, intensity of preference, ability to commit, dependence, and risk-proneness — are all intimately related to alternatives. When ambiguous statements about power can be reduced to precise statements about alternatives, we prefer to speak directly in terms of alternatives. A bargainer's quest for power should often start with alternatives.

D. Focus on Alternatives to Continuing Agreement

Thus far, advice has concerned alternatives to negotiated agreement before and during the negotiation. Quite frequently, however, once an agreement is hammered out, its terms may not be secure. One or the other party may renege on or demand a revision of the terms. Sometimes such a demand is quite predictable. Consider the case of a multinational mining company negotiating with a country over digging a mine. Before the project has commenced, the company's alternative to agreement with the host is to take its business elsewhere. The country may have only a limited number of weaker contenders for the deposit. Yet once terms are agreed upon and the company has sunk hundreds of millions of dollars into the mine, its alternative to continuing agreement is to leave, now an expensive and losing proposition. With the construction of the mine, however, the country's alternatives to continuing the agreement may have shifted dramatically. Pressure for renegotiation may be expected to mount.

In fact, the structure of this situation is so common that Raymond Vernon has dubbed such mineral agreements "obsolescing bargains," and other analysts (Raiffa, 1982; Lax and Sebenius, 1981) have investigated the general properties of these so-called insecure contracts. An insecure contract is an agreement in which one party's incentives to abide by the terms are reduced after the other party has made an irrevocable first move in accord with the agreement. Equivalently, each party's alternative to negotiated agreement changes in a predictable way over the life of the contract.

A generic solution to the insecure contracts problem involves carefully tracing each side's alternatives to *continued* agreement and taking steps to make agreement superior to the alternatives at each stage. In the preceding Kennecott-Chile example, the company sought, with only partial success, to change Chile's alternatives to continuing with the original agreement. Kennecott sought to change Chile's alternatives to ousting the company, which appeared as a one-shot, bilateral encounter, to a longer term, multi-lateral encounter involving many other entities that Chile would have to deal with and rely on across a range of other issues. Many modern mineral contracts design their financial structures to accomplish exactly this same end, that is, to worsen the host's perceptions of the consequences of not staying with the original contract (Fruhan, 1979).

In a related example, the new head of the Brazilian subsidiary of a British multinational company persuaded his parent board of directors to centralize all South American operations and to move away from the previous strategy of customized products to a mass standardized approach. Selling his strategy had been a long battle, and he had made numerous enemies at British corporate headquarters in London. Though he was the nominal head of the new South American organization, he had only limited authority over certain key decisions. Many of the formerly autonomous country managers resented his new status. The sales force preferred the old customer relationships and higher quality image. The company's South American engineers liked their prerogatives of individual design. Though the new South American manager took some steps toward implementing this strategy, he needed to obtain the more wholehearted cooperation of key South American players to act in accord with his chosen strategy.

At the outset of his new venture, he was only able to tempt each critical South American group into "agreement" with him by holding out the lure of joint gain from the new strategy. He offered a certain new status to country managers, he offered higher volume and profits to the sales force, and he challenged the company's engineers with new design problems. But at the early stages of the new strategy, each South American group's alternative to "agreeing" to act in accord with the new strategic vision was simply to ignore the new head or make end runs around him to the British headquarters. London had simply not given the new manager the tools to force compliance. However, the new South American manager's strategy was designed in such a way that, once embarked on, it involved the entire South American group in a price war with competitors and destruction of old ways of doing business. In short, the South Americans' alternative to continued agreement, once the strategy was under way, was a very much worse situation than had earlier prevailed. This kept the entire group on board and worked against the incentives and opportunities to resist, not to go along, or to defect. As it happened, the strategy was exceedingly successful, and all parties in South America as well as Britain shared in enormous profits. But the new South American manager had carefully designed his strategy such that, once implemented, the alternative to continued agreement with him always appeared worse for the parties than the cooperation he sought to obtain. This accords with the general prescription to focus on alternatives to continued agreement.

E. Manipulate Alternatives to Influence Decentralized Bargaining

Our final proposition concerns the role of alternatives in shaping a network of negotiations to be carried on by others. Quite frequently the rules or structures imposed by others will heavily condition decentralized bargaining. For example, in professional sports a large number of individual negotiations take place between players and teams. Under some league-players' union contracts, players are bound to one team and may not negotiate with others; thus, a player has *no* alternatives (except for nonsports occupations). Predictably, this "reserve clause" system tilts the balance in favor of teams. At the other end of the rules spectrum, players may have the right to negotiate with *all* teams and play for the highest bidder. Under this "free agency" rule, the players have *many* alternatives and, not surprisingly, player salaries tend to be much higher. Between free agency and the reserve clause lie many intermediate options that specify the player's alternatives in more balanced ways. For example, one rule would specify that, if agreement is not reached with a designated team, the player must sit out for a year, without salary or experience, before entering unrestricted free agent status. Another set of rules might allow the player free negotiations but with a limited number of teams. The important point in this example is that the structure of rules governing a large number of decentralized bargains affects those bargains directly through the alternatives available to the parties.

The budgeting procedures of a well-known computer company illustrate this point. In this very successful firm, budgets are constructed by negotiation among all interested divisions and departments. Each division or department has the option of concurring or not concurring with proposals of the others. If nonconcurrences cannot be resolved by negotiation, they escalate through corporate ranks and finally reach a central management committee that renders a decision. Top management in this firm wishes to stimulate a variety of constructive negotiations among the people in the company who are closest to the problems and who have the most expertise. High-level "arbitration" functions as the ultimate alternative to negotiated agreement among people throughout the company. Beyond resolving individual disputes, top management wishes to affect perceptions in two ways by its pattern of decisions. First, by affecting employees' perceptions of the costs of disagreement, top management hopes to stimulate a large number of lower-level agreements. Second, by the pattern of its choices, this body wishes to affect the *content* of lower-level agreements in ways that accord with certain corporate objectives and policies. They wish to make recourse to the central management committee a desirable alternative for those whose lower-level disagreement is for reasons in accord with preferred company strategy. Similarly, top management wishes to make the escalation alternative unpleasant and very costly for those who disagree for reasons that are out of line with preferred policies. By carefully manipulating perceptions of alternatives to lower-level agreement, this corporate management has effectively influenced a large number of negotiations that are carried out throughout the company. Managers in many settings enjoy analogous possibilities.

3. Conclusions

Throughout this article, we have treated negotiation as a means, albeit an important and promising one, to further desired ends. As such, what goes on "away from the table" may compete in importance with what goes on "at the table." Generally one is in a better negotiating position when one's alternatives improve and one's counterpart's alternatives erode. Bargainers employ a variety of tactics to create the impression that this in fact is happening. Before and during a negotiation, we counsel participants to evaluate alternatives to agreement. They should routinely anticipate inflated perceptions and seek to counter them. A diagnosis that a dispute is not "ripe" for settlement may derive from inconsistently optimistic perceptions of alternatives; where this is the case, strategy should focus on altering those perceptions. We have also suggested several ways in which, as the negotiating process unfolds, the quest for "power" is bound up with alternatives. Even afterward, a key to securing agreements lies in reshaping subsequent alternatives so they remain inferior to continued agreement. This advice generalizes from conventional, face-to-face encounters to decentralized bargains that one wishes to influence. Across these points, the broader prescription is obvious: Realize the potential of alternatives to agreement. The challenge that this advice poses for negotiators, of course, is to find ways of cooperating to do even better.

NOTES

1. Roger Fisher and William Ury (1981) have christened the BATNA (Best Alternative to Negotiated Agreement) as a useful acronym for the economist's bland "no-trade" point or the game theorist's ominous "threat-point." See note 3 below for elaboration of the history of this idea in relation to bargaining "power."

2. More precisely, taking simultaneous account of other tactical possibilities, one should expend resources to enhance alternatives or generate new ones if the subjective probability distribution of negotiated outcomes thereby improves sufficiently to offset the expenditure. Optimal search theory shows that, to set a reservation price for the negotiation, one need not actually expend resources to search when the distribution of possible negotiated outcomes would not thereby be changed. In such a case, one merely needs to take such prospects into account when calculating the reservation price. When the search for alternatives can change the distribution of negotiation outcomes, one may well search less promising distributions of alternatives if actually finding a better alternative would sufficiently improve the outcome distribution. Lax (1983) discusses these issues in more detail.

3. For example, in an economic context, Jan Pen (1952) wrote: "When are the foundations of power economic in character? The answer is simple . . . . If . . . goods are in the hands of a seller who cannot be perfectly substituted by another seller, the buyer becomes dependent on the seller. The seller can exercise economic power by threatening to withhold the goods" (p. 32). By implication, if the buyer could better substitute for the seller (develop more attractive alternatives), he could lessen the seller's power and improve his own. In his classic *Exchange and Power in Social Life*, Peter Blau (1964) noted that "Generally, the greater the difference between the benefits an individual supplies to others and those they can obtain elsewhere, the greater is his power over them likely to be" (p. 120). In summarizing the work of several authors on the "bases of power" and applying these ideas to business strategy formulation, Ian MacMillan (1978) stated, "The structures of alternatives available to an organization and its opponents are important determinants of power" (p. 20). In *Power and Politics in Organizations*, Samuel Bacharach and Edward Lawler (1980) considered the position of "an organizational subgroup embedded in a network of relationships with other subgroups" and noted that "the power of the subgroup in any one relation is determined partially by the nature and level of outcomes available from the other relationships" (p. 20). Though these and other students of bargaining have noted and elaborated the relationship between alternatives and "power," Fisher and Ury made a key contribution to

prescriptive approaches by making the conscious development of alternatives a basic tenet of their advice: "What if they are more powerful? Develop your BATNA." While they emphasize this as a strategy for increasing the weaker party's "power," the concept applies to all parties. See also Dunlop (1950), Chamberlain (1951), and Emerson (1962).

4. See Bacharach and Lawler (1981). In a number of unpublished experiments, we have observed similar phenomena.

REFERENCES

Bacharach, S. B. and Lawler, E. J. (1980). *Power and politics in organizations: The social psychology of conflict, coalitions, and bargaining*. San Francisco: Jossey-Bass.

———. and ———. (1981). *Bargaining: Power, tactics, and outcomes*. San Francisco: Jossey-Bass.

Barclay, S. and Peterson, C. (1976). "Multi-attribute utility models for negotiations." Technical Report 76-1. McLean, Va.: Decisions and Designs, Inc.

Blau, P. M. (1964). *Exchange and power in social life*. New York: John Wiley & Sons

Chamberlain, N. W. (1951). *Collective bargaining*. New York: McGraw-Hill.

Cohen, H. (1980). *You can negotiate anything*. Secaucus, N.J.: Lyle Stuart.

Dunlop, J. T. (1950). *Wage determination under trade unions*. New York: Augustus M. Kelley.

Emerson, R. M. (1962). "Power-dependence relations." *American Sociological Review* 27: 31-40.

Fisher, R. (1983). "What about negotiation as a specialty?" *American Bar Association Journal* 69: 1221-24.

Fisher, R., and Ury, W. L. (1981). *Getting to YES: Negotiating agreement without giving in*. Boston: Houghton Mifflin.

Fruhan, W. (1979). *Financial strategy*. Homewood, Ill.: Richard D. Irwin.

Keeney, R., and Raiffa, H. (1976). *Decisions with multiple objectives*. New York: John Wiley & Sons.

Lax, D. A. (1985). "Optimal search in negotiation analysis." Journal of Conflict Resolution, 29(3): 456-472.

Lax, D. A., and Sebenius, J. (1981). "Insecure contracts and resource development." *Public Policy* 29: 419-36.

Luce, R. D., and Raiffa, H. (1957). *Games and decisions*. New York: John Wiley & Sons.

MacMillan, I.C. (1978). *Strategy formulation: Political concepts*. St. Paul: West.

Pen, J. (1952). "A general theory of bargaining." *The American Economic Review* 42: 24-42.

Raiffa, H. (1968). *Decision analysis: Introductory lectures on decisions under uncertainty*. Reading, Mass.: Addison-Wesley.

———. *The art and science of negotiation*. Cambridge, Mass.: Harvard University Press, 1982.

Roth, A. E. (1979). *Axiomatic models of bargaining*. New York: Springer-Verlag.

Schelling, T. C. (1960). *The strategy of conflict*. New York: Oxford University Press.

Smith, D., and Wells, L. (1975). *Negotiating Third World mineral agreements*. Cambridge, Mass.: Ballinger.

Wriggens, W. (1976). "Up for auction: malta bargains with Great Britain, 1971." In *The 50% Solution*, edited by I. William Zartman. New York: Anchor-Doubleday.

The Role of Power and Principle in *Getting to YES*

William McCarthy

Editor's note: Lord McCarthy's article is a discussion of Getting to YES *by Roger Fisher and William L. Ury (Boston: Houghton Mifflin, 1981). Roger Fisher's reply follows.*

Getting to YES is a fascinating work, designed as a primer for bargainers of all kinds. It urges the adoption of what is termed "principled negotiation," in the form of a series of maxims or principles. As an academic student of industrial relations who has been much involved in the process of mediation and arbitration in labor disputes in the United Kingdom since 1968, my task is to say how far I agree with the ideas expressed and the assumptions that lie behind them. I can best do this by considering first those maxims with which I am in general agreement. I next discuss others about which I have reservations. I end with a number of more substantial criticisms and doubts.

Areas of Agreement
Getting to YES puts forth at least eight propositions which I would recommend without reservation to bargainers on both sides of industry. These do not include all the things I like about *Getting to YES*, but they cover the most important and are indicative of its general approach.

The first is that one should try to put oneself in the position of the person on the other side of the bargaining table. This must be right. Much time is wasted in mediation inducing people to listen to the argument of the other side, so that the area to be bridged can at least be objectively assessed.

Second is the stress on the need to move away from "position bargaining" so that bargainers can focus on interests rather than positions. Mediators and arbitrators are often required simply because the parties have been unable to do this for themselves.

Third is the suggestion that one should seek to generate as many options as possible so that the parties are not hemmed in by a particular alternative adopted early in the negotiation. One of the main tasks of third parties is to generate options, which is why it is essential to take the parties through all that has been discussed before, even though this can be mutually exhausting. Often one side or another is overly concerned to justify some position it

Lord William McCarthy, a Fellow of Nuffield College and the Oxford Management Centre, has served as an industrial relations adviser to secretaries of state for Employment and Social Security.

adopted in the past and which has contributed to the present impasse. Once this has been set aside, it may be possible to open up new prospects or return to discarded solutions.

This maxim is related to another I agree with, which is that the parties should look forward rather than look back. All collective agreements have implications for future behavior, so that it is essential to try, where possible, to improve future relationships, and not only those between the spokespersons themselves. The impact of a proposed agreement on constituents, and whether or not it will help them to solve future disputes, is also a critical issue. Looking to the future in this way is the best safeguard I know against Carthaginian solutions, that is, those which impose defeats on one side and which both sides live to regret.

The fifth point of agreement with *Getting to YES* is the injunction that one should never begin by assuming that all that is available is a "fixed pie." The fact that this so often turns out to be the case is the best possible reason for not making this assumption. For unless one is always trying to find ways of enlarging the pie, future relations between the parties will probably deteriorate. It is also the case that exploring the conditions under which the pie might be enlarged is usually educational. Both sides come to realize more clearly how the other is hemmed in by existing circumstances. Since this is usually the result of external factors, such as the state of the competition in the product market or the level of relevant pay settlements in other parts of the labor market, the parties come to appreciate the boundaries of their discretion and choice in a more relaxed and realistic mood.

Then there is the admirable concept of the BATNA (Best Alternative to a Negotiated Agreement). I find this an improvement on the conventional notion of a "bottom line," for the reasons stated in *Getting to YES*. It focuses attention on the fact that if the parties fail to agree, they must decide what to do next. This is often given insufficient attention by those who are overly concerned with proving that their original position was justified or right. BATNA is also a more flexible notion than bottom line and can be changed without invoking the same feelings of guilt. It is also true that the alternative to disagreement is often indeterminate and difficult to quantify. The sooner both sides start thinking about their BATNAs, the better.

So I come to my seventh maxim, which is that one should not reveal one's BATNA unless it is better than the other side thinks it is. An evidently true proposition, although in collective bargaining the other side may not provide a frank assessment of their view of your BATNA. Still, this is an option to consider: Do we have reason to believe that our opponents underestimate the consequences of disagreement? And, most important of all, will they believe us if we tell them what we intend to do if they refuse to move?

A large part of the mediator's job consists of getting the parties to accept the truth about the other side's intentions. So much that is said is part bluff, part bravado, and part propaganda for constituents. Once again, the sooner the parties' spokespersons consider issues of this kind, the better.

Finally, I come to my eighth and final maxim: "Separate the people from the problem." Fisher and Ury offer an excellent compression of the principles which third parties involved in the settlement of labor disputes practice all the time. What they propose, as I see it, goes beyond putting yourself in the other person's shoes. They emphasize instead the importance of moving from "points of view" in order to focus on the "problem in its own right," which those around the table are asked to address in an "objective" way. Of course, the parties will remain aware of personal and partisan concerns, for these are part of the problem, but it can help to get to yes if these can be looked at from a common viewpoint.

The most obvious way in which a mediator seeks to induce such an atmosphere is by asking the other party, "What would you do now if you were me?" This is really just an invitation to objectify the problem, and it often produces a helpful suggestion if asked at the right moment.

All these maxims in *Getting to YES* I see as part of a useful drill or model which would-be bargainers should practice and commit to memory. Like all drills, they look obvious enough, but unless they are fully understood and accepted they will be forgotten in the heat of the moment. To some extent, natural bargainers will observe such maxims without training or experience, but even they may lapse from time to time and develop bad habits. It helps to objectify and describe bad habits in the way that Fisher and Ury do in their book, which offers those of us who teach and practice in this area a useful primer that is easy to understand and refreshingly free from jargon.

Some Reservations

Unfortunately, I am unable to accept other suggestions in *Getting to YES* without qualification. The first is the suggestion that negotiators should always seek to maintain or improve long-term relationships between the parties. There are several problems here. First, union members, for example, may be relatively unconcerned with the long term; they may be demanding the best that can be obtained now. Leaders may think it unwise to press home short-run advantages, if only because this will encourage "hawks" on the management side and lead to long-term reprisals, but they may not be in a position to give their reasons for counseling caution. Similarly, on the employer's side, the "doves" may feel that if good relations are to be preserved, one more attempt to settle should be made by improving on the existing offer. Yet their superiors may decide, quite rightly from their tougher point of view, that short-run financial and market constraints rule this option out.

Even mediators and arbitrators can make mistakes if they believe that part of their task is to concern themselves with a long-run improvement in relationships. Often what the parties want is a way out of an immediate impasse, and long-term considerations may make this more difficult. Of course a mediator can always point out the long-term dangers of what appears to be an acceptable compromise; but it does not follow from this that those most immediately affected will be thankful for this advice.

Thus while I am only too willing to admit that all agreements are attempts to regulate the future and that the best agreements have in them an element of long-term reform, it seems to me that Fisher and Ury's model of negotiation gives too much emphasis to the importance of the long run. I know of many disputes which, unfortunately, were dominated by the need to avoid or terminate immediate conflict, even at the cost of worsening long-term relations.

Second we come to the maxim that one should set aside trust. This is a wise counsel insofar as it warns the would-be negotiator against those who constantly ask you to trust them. As an experienced union leader once told me, "A man who says 'trust me' is a man who cannot be trusted." The appeal to trust is no substitute for an argument, or for the specifications of areas of mutual interest.

But I suspect that Fisher and Ury mean more than this. They seem to offer a model of the bargaining process where trust has no significant role to play. I find this difficult to accept. There is a sense in which trust is essential if the chances of agreement are to be maximized. As Willy Loman said of optimism, "it comes with the territory." Once trust is totally lost between two bargainers, one of them should be replaced.

What I mean by "trust" is that the other parties have given you reason to believe that they will do their best to guard your back and will also respect confidences and seek to persuade their own sides to accept alternatives that have been jointly agreed upon. Trust is fostered among bargainers when these and related norms are observed. It probably begins with an appreciation that the other person understands your role and admires your skill. Where trust is sufficiently strong, it even survives the odd stab in the back. Yet it can be destroyed by a single act of betrayal, such as using confidences as a reason for going back on an agreement, or feeding wrong information with intent to deceive disguised as advice to a "friend."

Trust is important partly because it fosters informal contacts and a readiness to expose one's hand. To gain trust a mediator may have no alternative but to offer confidences — although only personal thoughts should be offered, and then in a way that is fair to both sides. Because of considerations of this kind, I would argue that the role of trust is underestimated in the Fisher-Ury model.

But I have even stronger reservations about their reference to the need for a "wise agreement" that "takes community interests into account." Once again constituents are not always prepared to limit their options in this way. Of course, the spokesperson realizes that in the long run those who are thought to ignore community interests too blatantly will lose public support and may find themselves in trouble with the government of the day. But this is not really the business of the mediators or arbitrators, unless they operate within a framework fixed by government which instructs them to take these things into account (for example, as interpreters of the norms of statutory incomes policy).

In any case, in collective bargaining both sides habitually argue that their demands are compatible with community interests; it is the other side which is being narrow or selfish. To attempt to decide how far either side is right in relation to questions of this kind is to import into the dispute an imponderable which will never be agreed upon (for example, the effect of a particular wage settlement on the general level of wage movements; or the consequences of a strike on public welfare). It may be easier to gain agreement if matters of this kind are not raised and parties concentrate instead on reaching a settlement which "balances" the felt interests of those immediately involved in the narrowest possible way.

I also doubt the general applicability of the maxim, "Whenever you can, avoid starting from extremes." It is certainly not usually observed as a rule in collective bargaining. This is partly because of the way in which unions formulate claims. These are based on grievances arising out of the administration of the existing contract, plus expectations and fears about future developments and recent settlements. As a result, each group insists on including in a claim items which are of particular importance to it. Nobody sees the need to argue in terms of priorities, or overall costs, since this might well diminish overall solidarity. The result is a total claim that few people take quite seriously, but this is seen as a part of the essential ritual of collective bargaining.

Similar pressures operate on the management side, where resistance to particular items in the claim varies from one part of management to another. Once again it is widely appreciated that many of these extreme positions will subsequently need to be modified.

All this is not to deny that overly ambitious claims and unrealistic offers can generate misunderstanding among those who accept them at face value. But it does not follow that such difficulties can best be avoided by opting for "moderation" or "realism" from the outset. This can lead to even more confusion.

What really matters is that there be a link between opening positions and the real power situation — as conceived by both sides. What is disastrous is a situation in which claims become more ambitious as the power to achieve them erodes.

Finally, I have doubts about the general advantages of what are termed "brainstorming sessions" as a way of "inventing options." I have found procedures of this kind of limited use. The problem is that they are often embraced as a way of avoiding hard decisions. In labor relations, especially on the management side, there is a tendency to believe that unpalatable courses of action can be avoided, "if only we think around them for long enough." By the time third parties become involved, the need often is for a rather different initiative. Two or three options, long known and debated, need to be costed out in great detail, and their likely consequences for other groups carefully considered. It is the grisly business of getting down to this kind of work that leads some bright spark to suggest another spot of brainstorming. The good bargainer is the one who knows when this has become a substitute for action.

Disagreements

So far I have been arguing that ways could be found to modify the maxims discussed above so that their application would be limited to particular situations. I turn now to a number of others where the differences between the authors and myself may not be so easily resolved. It is as well to begin with a relatively minor point, since it helps to illustrate one of my underlying doubts. This concerns the advocacy of what is termed "negotiation jujitsu."

I think this is based on a false analogy. In negotiation you cannot turn power on its originator, which I take to be the essence of the reference to jujitsu. The examples Fisher and Ury offer are not really examples of this process, deriving as they do from attempts to deal with bad manners, or attempts to undermine personal confidence. For the most part, the most effective ploy in these cases is to ignore them — to pretend one has not noticed. Take the man who has coffee spilled over him, or the woman who is seated facing the sun. What is the point of suggesting that these things have been done deliberately? What happens if the perpetrator denies this and decides to take offense? You have produced another dispute, which is about personal relations rather than the problem which needs to be solved. I suspect that the notion of negotiation jujitsu, like the related concept of "dirty tricks," derives from a desire to admit that negotiation is not quite as rational and high-minded as certain parts of the book assume it is, without facing the main reason why this is so.

I can best raise what I believe to be the main problem by suggesting that parts of *Getting to YES* seem to be directed at the unaggressive or "not natural" bargainer, especially one who is in a relatively weak position. It aims to raise such bargainers' confidence by providing a suitable drill or discipline to follow. I am not certain how far the authors had in mind the problems of naturally aggressive and self-confident negotiators, especially those who believe they hold relatively strong positions.

Consider the bargainer who has clearly absorbed the main thrust of the argument and replies to a somewhat unprincipled opponent in the following way:

> I don't respond to pressure, I just respond to principle. If I responded to pressure, I would lose my reputation as a negotiator. I must insist on deciding by objective standards.

I have to say that I find this individual a somewhat unrealistic and unrepresentative figure. I do not think that many people would find themselves thinking or acting in this way, unless they had very little power and nothing but an obstinate belief in the merit of their own case. Yet in collective bargaining, it is often clear enough that one side or the other is in the stronger position, which is not the same as having the best of the argument. In circumstances of this kind, both sides realize that if agreement is to be reached a way must be found of coming to terms with this fact. Bargaining is seen as not just a matter of logic and argument. As it has been put to me, "The name of this game is poker, not chess."

Part of the problem is that *Getting to YES* offers no direct analysis of the role of power — or the way the cards are dealt. I take it that this is because the authors prefer to deal with this aspect of negotiation via their notion of the BATNA. A party, or player, is powerful if he or she has a strong BATNA. Those who feel themselves to be in a weak position are advised: "develop your BATNA." I can see that this is good advice, but it does not take us very far. One wants to know more about the factors which affect the relative strength of rival BATNAs and how to decide between them. One looks in vain for an analysis of power and how to maximize it.

Here it may help if I give a short illustration drawn from collective bargaining. Where unions claim an increase in pay which management refuses to concede, they face a choice of either lowering their sights or giving notice of their intention to take some form of industrial action. In the words of Fisher and Ury, they consider their BATNA.

But often the problem is that it is impossible to say what the effect of a particular form of action will be, on either management or union members. Much may depend on the reaction of customers, competitors, suppliers, and other groups of employees. Still more may turn on the effect a prolonged withdrawal of labor has on the determination and morale of strikers and their families.

Sometimes the sum total of all these factors combines to convince one side or the other that "time is on our side." If this is the case, that side will not favor an early settlement, since it will feel that the longer the dispute lasts, the more it may be able to impose its will on the other side. At other times, the balance of power will not at first be clear to either side, or it may shift during the course of a struggle. As a result, it may be necessary to endure long periods of conflict, inflicting a great deal of damage on both sides, until the power position emerges.

The point here is that however long this process takes, the outlines of an acceptable settlement, in the end, will turn on the development of a shared view about the outcome of what can only be termed a "power struggle" — that is, the ability of one side to inflict more damage on the other than it receives in return. This struggle has its own logic and rationale, and the job of the good negotiator is to anticipate its outcome and secure the best deal possible when the power position of his or her own side is at its height. But this entails a willingness to recognize and respond to pressure, or the awareness of its existence, rather than an insistence on principle. It also has very little to do with objective standards, yet those who can do it best have the highest reputation among bargainers.

What books like *Getting to YES* can do is to help bargainers limit the need for what might be termed "ordeal by power." By observing the book's maxims, they can come to understand more clearly their true differences, the size of the gap that must be bridged, where possible by recourse to argument and persuasion. They can learn how to move from a wasteful discussion of past positions to a fruitful consideration of future interests. They can explore possible alternatives, within limits set by a mutual appreciation of external constraints. As a result, they may be less likely to begin by making vague and unconvincing threats, followed by unnecessary and damaging concessions.

But in the area of collective bargaining, at least, I know of no set of maxims or principles which will enable any of us to escape from the limits set by a given power situation. And sometimes there may be no other way of establishing these limits other than by conflict. Even where this situation is avoided, it will usually be because those involved are skilled at reading the signs: that is, they are able to assess the likely consequences of an ordeal by power, so that this can be taken into account in arriving at a settlement. Consequently, another and equally important primer needs to be written about what to look for in attempting such an assessment, for matters of this kind are not discussed in *Getting to YES*.

Which brings me to my final doubt. One of the attractions of the study is that the authors import their examples from a bewildering variety of dispute situations: the buying of books, family quarrels and neighborhood squabbles, corporate and governmental disagreement, collective bargaining, and international conferences — everything from haggling in street markets to the roots of East-West conflict. Yet they assume, rather than argue, that the factors which make for effective negotiation in all these circumstances are the same. Consequently, a common set of maxims, based on a common model, can be developed. I find this a fascinating notion, but I am not certain how far it is feasible.

Here I can only speak with any authority on labor disputes, but they seem to me to exhibit certain features which are not equally present in many other kinds of disagreement. To begin with, ours is undoubtedly a game which continues: There is a sense in which the terms of the bargain are renewed every day, so that it is unwise to exploit the passing advantage of a short-term power position. It is also a representative activity, where power structures and responsibilities differ on each side in a way that conditions the freedom of the spokespersons to commit their constituents to the agreement. When agreement is not possible, the alternatives available, at least on the union side, are also rather special, involving an attempt to deny supply, rather than sale, to another bidder. When sanctions are involved, they are difficult to determine in advance and apt to change through time. The process is also "political" in a rather special sense, since the union's aim is to narrow management's area of discretion, substituting predictability and "joint regulation" for what employers usually term their "right to manage." In addition, the underlying relationship between the parties is seen by many participants as essentially ideological or class-based.

This is not the place to say how, and to what extent, features of this kind create the need for a more tailor-made model of how to get to yes in collective bargaining. My point is simply that the factors to bear in mind are not necessarily the same, or of equal weight, as those involved in haggling over carpets in Quincy Market or deciding the Law of the Sea.

All of which is to suggest that the authors of *Getting to YES* have raised more questions than they have settled, most notably in relation to the role of power as principle and the differences between them in various kinds of dispute. What is needed now is further investigation and research to throw light on two related questions: (1) the factors influencing the generation and optimization of power in different bargaining situations; and (2) the relative importance of power and principle in determining the outcome of different areas of dispute. Meanwhile we look forward to the second edition.

Beyond *YES*

Roger Fisher

An author is naturally pleased to have as experienced and distinguished a labor relations professional as Lord William McCarthy find that *Getting to YES* contains useful ideas. His generous comments are deeply appreciated.

But even more valuable are his criticisms and questions. For as useful as *Getting to YES* may be, it falls far short of what is needed. Improving the theory and practice of negotiation and mediation will require an unending openness to both skepticism and new ideas. Let me skip all the nice things Lord McCarthy said and try to build on some of his qualifications and questions. Rather than defend what William Ury and I wrote, I will try to spell out what — stimulated by Lord McCarthy — I now think.

1. **". . .Negotiators should always seek to maintain or improve long-term relationships between the parties."** If that is what we said, it is certainly wrong. As Thomas Schelling has pointed out to me, when I negotiate with a panhandler, my primary objective may be to avoid any future relationship whatsoever.

Relationship issues, however, do constitute an important part of any negotiation. Negotiators benefit from consciously considering them.

It helps to recognize that there is a significant difference between relationship issues such as communication, mutual understanding, respect, acceptance, approval, trust, anger, fear, and affection on the one hand, and on the other, substantive issues such as price, delivery dates, conditions, specifications, and terms. The fact that the two sets of issues are likely to have an impact on each other just as reptiles and mammals interact, does not refute the validity or utility of the distinction.

Most negotiators would be well advised to consider whether their interest in a short-term, substantive outcome is in fact greater than their interest in good long-term relations. Sometimes a one-time sale to a stranger for a high price will be more valuable than an ongoing relationship. But for bankers, governments, trade unions, businesses, families, and many others, the ability to engage easily in future transactions is usually far more important than the substantive result of any one deal. Lord McCarthy has had far more experience with labor negotiations than I, but my own experience suggests that the danger that participants will pay too much attention to short-term considerations is greater than that they will over-assess the value of a long-term relationship.

Roger Fisher is Williston Professor of Law, *emeritus*, at the Harvard Law School and Director of the Harvard Negotiation Project. He and William Ury with Bruce M. Patton are the authors of the tenth anniversary second edition of *Getting to YES*, published in 1991 by Penguin Books.

At the Harvard Negotiation Project, we have developed two rules of thumb designed to avoid two common negotiating errors that mingle substantive and relationship issues: (1) Don't threaten a relationship as a means of trying to coerce a substantive concession. To do so will not work against a wise negotiator and damages the relationship whatever the outcome. (2) Don't try to buy a good relationship by making concessions that are unjustified on their merits. (Appeasement rarely works. You are likely to get more of any bad behavior you reward.)

2. ". . .We come to the maxim that one should set aside trust." Lord McCarthy is obviously right in emphasizing the important role which trust can play in a negotiation. To the extent that I am trusted, I am more powerful; others will be influenced by what I say. And in deciding whether or not to enter into a particular agreement, I will be influenced by the extent to which I can rely on the statements and promises of those on the other side.

Trust, however, should not be overloaded. Other things being equal, the less that an agreement depends on trust, the more likely it is to be implemented. That it is convenient to trust someone is no reason to do so. Behaving in a way that makes oneself worthy of trust is highly useful and likely to be well rewarded. But the more one trusts the other side, the greater the incentive one provides for behavior that will prove such trust to have been misplaced.

3. Must a "wise settlement" respect community interests? Lord McCarthy is no doubt right that it will sometimes be easier for a mediator to reach agreement if no attention is given to the interests of the community. But wouldn't a mediated agreement be better if it did? By what standards should we judge agreements that have been reached "voluntarily," that is, with no illegal coercion? Statutes that set minimum wages, safe working conditions, maximum hours, and limit child labor — to name but a few instances in which the community imposes limits on freedom of contract — demonstrate that society has an interest in the content of agreements as well as in settling disputes.

We members of the community would like negotiators and mediators to pay some attention to community interests even where their failure to do so is not illegal. Other things being equal, the more an agreement takes into account the legitimate concerns of others, the better it is for all of us.

4. Should one negotiate by starting with an extreme position? There is little doubt that if both parties are playing the haggling game of positional bargaining, the best position to start with is often an extreme one. Rather than denying that statement, we question whether haggling is the best game to play.

Getting to YES probably overstates the case against positional bargaining. The New York Stock Exchange demonstrates that thousands of transactions a day can successfully be concluded without discussing interests and with little concern for ongoing relationships. Yet most cases of what we all think of as negotiations involve more than one issue and also involve ongoing matters of implementation or future dealing. In such cases, I would suggest that taking an extreme position is rarely the best first move. Coming up with an extreme and unilaterally determined answer before understanding the other side's perception of the problem involves risks to one's credibility, to a cooperative problem-solving relationship, and to the efficient reaching of an agreement.

5. Brainstorming. Creative thinking is no substitute for the hard work of selecting among various options. That is certainly true, yet wise decision-making between adversaries, within a group, or by a single individual involves both generating possibilities and judging among them. Early judgment inhibits creativity. Of course, any valuable activity can be pursued too far. Nothing exceeds like excess. Yet I remain convinced that most negotiators will benefit from the maxim: Invent first; decide later.

6. "One looks in vain for an analysis of power and how to maximize it." Lord McCarthy correctly points out that the discussion of power in *Getting to YES* falls short of what is needed. A first attempt toward remedying that situation has already been undertaken (see my "Negotiating Power: Getting and Using Influence," which is also printed in this book.) Let me comment here more briefly.

Power — the ability to influence the decisions of others — is important in every negotiation. And negotiators need help in understanding how to optimize their power and how best to use it. Yet I do not agree with Lord McCarthy's proposition that the outcome of a power struggle will depend upon "the ability of one side to inflict more damage on the other than it receives in return." An openness to reason, combined with a principled refusal to yield to blackmail, can change the game. If, for example, a future U.S. president were to seek Vatican support for contraception as a means of limiting world population, would the outcome of a power struggle reflect the superior ability of the United States to destroy the Vatican with nuclear weapons? I doubt it. A papal refusal to listen to such threats would be convincing.

Negotiators, like other people, are influenced by more than risk of damage. Negotiators, like others, respond to logic, facts, friends, ideals, law, precedent, and persuasive rhetoric. It would be a mistake to assume that the final and decisive ingredient of negotiating power is either fear or a nice calculation of the relative costs of not reaching agreement.

7. Are all negotiations the same? Lord McCarthy questions the extent to which one can safely generalize about the negotiation process, advancing hypotheses that are supposed to apply to "family quarrels and neighborhood squabbles, corporate and governmental disagreement, collective bargaining, and international conferences."

Of course there are differences, and important ones, depending upon the subject under negotiation. Yet what Bill Ury and I were seeking — and often continue to seek — is the power that comes from general theory. A physicist advancing hypotheses about a general theory of matter does not deny differences among the elements. Like such a physicist, we have been looking for common concepts and a common structure that apply across the board. The assumption has been that those of us who focus our attention on one particular area, such as diplomacy, can learn much from those who work primarily in other areas.

Lord McCarthy's review of *Getting to YES* demonstrates the soundness of that approach. Not that our general ideas will provide the right answer for each of his labor disputes. Rather, his review demonstrates how much we can learn from the experience and insight of those who deal with different substantive problems.

Negotiating Power: Getting and Using Influence

Roger Fisher

Getting to YES (Fisher and Ury, 1981) has been justly criticized as devoting insufficient attention to the issue of power. It is all very well, it is said, to tell people how they might jointly produce wise outcomes efficiently and amicably, but in the real world people don't behave that way; results are determined by power — by who is holding the cards, by who has more clout.

At the international level, negotiating power is typically equated with military power. The United States is urged to develop and deploy more nuclear missiles so that it can negotiate from a position of strength. Threats and warnings also play an important role in the popular concept of power, as do resolve and commitment. In the game of chicken, victory goes to the side that more successfully demonstrates that it will not yield.

There is obviously some merit in the notion that physical force, and an apparent willingness to use it, can affect the outcome of a negotiation. How does that square with the suggestion that negotiators ought to focus on the interests of the parties, on the generating of alternatives, and on objective standards to which both sides might defer?

This article is a brief report on the present status of some thinking about negotiating power. It represents work in progress. After briefly suggesting a definition of negotiating power, and the kind of theory for which we should be looking, I set up two straw men — that are perhaps not made wholly of straw: (1) the basic way to acquire real power in a negotiation is to acquire the capacity to impose unpleasant physical results on the other side; and (2) an effective way to exercise negotiating power is to start off by letting the other side know of your capacity to hurt them and of your willingness to do so. Both propositions seem wrong. In the central body of the article, I discuss six elements of negotiating power that can be acquired before and during negotiation, only one of which is the capacity to make a credible threat. Finally, I consider the sequence in which those different elements of power are best used to maximize their cumulative impact, and explore the debilitating effect of making threats at an early stage.

How Should We Define Negotiating Power?

It seems best to define "negotiation" as including all cases in which two or more parties are communicating, each for the purpose of influencing the other's decision. Nothing seems to be gained by limiting the concept to formal negotiations taking place at a table, and much to be gained by defining the

---

Roger Fisher is the Williston Professor of Law, *emeritus*, at Harvard Law School, Cambridge, Mass. 02138, and Director of the Harvard Negotiation Project.

subject broadly. Many actions taken away from a table — ranging from making political speeches to building nuclear missiles — are taken for the purpose of "sending a message" to affect decisions of the other side.

The concept of "negotiating power" is more difficult. If I have negotiating power, I have the ability to affect favorably someone else's decision. This being so, one can argue that my power depends upon someone else's perception of my strength, so it is what they *think* that matters, not what I actually have. The other side may be as much influenced by a row of cardboard tanks as by a battalion of real tanks. One can thus say that negotiating power is all a matter of perception.

A general who commands a real tank battalion, however, is in a far stronger position than one in charge of a row of cardboard tanks. A false impression of power is extremely vulnerable, capable of being destroyed by a word. In order to avoid focusing our attention on how to deceive other people, it seems best at the outset to identify what constitutes "real" negotiating power — an ability to influence the decisions of others assuming they know the truth. We can then go on to recognize that, in addition, it will be possible at times to influence others through deception, through creating an illusion of power. Even for that purpose, we will need to know what illusion we wish to create. If we are bluffing, what are we bluffing about?

What Kind of Theory Are We Looking For?

An infinite number of truths exist about the negotiation process, just as an infinite number of maps can be drawn of a city. It is easy to conclude that negotiators who are more powerful fare better in negotiations. By and large, negotiators who have more wealth, more friends and connections, good jobs, and more time will fare better in negotiations than will those who are penniless, friendless, unemployed, and in a hurry. Such statements, like the statement that women live longer than men, are true — but they are of little help to someone who wants to negotiate, or to someone who wants to live longer. Similarly, the statement that power plays an important role in negotiation is true — but irrelevant.

As negotiators we want to understand power in some way that helps us. We want diagnostic truths that point toward prescriptive action. The statement that women live longer than men points toward no remedial action. I am unable to live longer by choosing to become a woman. On the other hand, the statement that people who don't smoke live longer than people who do smoke is no truer, but it is far more helpful since I can decide not to smoke.

Thus a lively interplay exists between descriptive and prescriptive theory. The pure scientist may not care whether his truths have any relevance to the world of action; he leaves that to others. But those of us who are primarily concerned with change (one hopes for the better) are searching for descriptive categories that have prescriptive significance. We are looking for ideas that will help us make better choices. We are not simply trying to describe accurately what happens in a negotiation; we are trying to produce advice of use to negotiators, advice that will help them negotiate better. We need to say something other than that powerful princes tend to dominate less powerful princes, as true as that may be. We are looking for the kind of theory that will help a prince. He, presumably, has two key questions with respect to negotiating power: how to enhance negotiating power and how to use such power as he may have.

Mistaken Views of Negotiating Power

(1) "Physical Force = Negotiating Power"

It is widely believed that in order to enhance our negotiating power we should acquire such assets as a strike-fund, a band of terrorists, or 100 MX missiles, which convey an implicit or explicit threat to harm the other side physically if it fails to agree with us. This belief is based on the assumption that, since threats of physical force undoubtedly exert influence, the ability to make such threats is the essence of negotiating power. Force is seen as the necessary and sufficient element of negotiating power.

Negotiating power is the ability to influence others. The pain that we threaten to inflict if the other side does not decide as we like is simply one factor among many. And as I have written elsewhere, making threats is a particularly expensive and dangerous way of trying to exert influence.[1]

Total negotiating power depends upon many factors. Enhancing negotiating power means building up the combined potential of them all. Exercising negotiating power effectively means orchestrating them in a way that maximizes their cumulative impact. And this is where a second, widely held assumption about negotiating power appears to be mistaken and dangerous.

(2) "Start tough, you can always get soft later."

There is a widespread belief that the best way to start a negotiation is with a hard line. "Let them know early who's in charge." The thought is that since, in the last analysis, physical power may be the decisive factor, the entire negotiation should take place governed by its shadow. Conventional wisdom insists that it is easier to soften one's position than to harden it. A negotiator is encouraged to start off flexing his muscles.

Alan Berger, reviewing Seymour Hersch's *Kissinger in the White House*, emphasizes this feature of Nixon's foreign policy. "Nixon's first impulse was to attempt to intimidate his adversaries." He was anxious to "get tough," to "seem tough," to "be tough." "The nuclear option was not an ultimate recourse to be considered only *in extremis*; it was, as Hersch persuasively demonstrates, the point of departure..." (*Boston Globe* 19 June 1983).

President Reagan appears to be operating on a similar assumption with respect to negotiating power. We begin with a threat. We seek to influence the Soviet Union with respect to intermediate-range nuclear missiles in Europe by starting off with a public commitment that U.S. Pershing II missiles will be deployed in Europe before the end of 1983 unless by that time the Soviet Union has agreed to withdraw all its missiles from Europe, on terms acceptable to us.

The notion that it is best to start off a negotiation with a warning or threat of the consequences of nonagreement may result from a false analogy. Other things being equal, it is true that, in purely positional bargaining, the more extreme one's initial position (the higher a price one demands or the lower a price one offers), the more favorable an agreed result is likely to be. But opening with a very low substantive offer is quite different from opening with a threat of painful consequences if that offer is not accepted. The more firmly one is committed at an early stage to carrying out a threat, the more damaging that threat is to one's negotiating power.

If these two propositions are wrong, how should someone enhance and exercise negotiating power?

Categories of Power

My ability to exert influence depends upon the combined total of a number of different factors. As a first approximation, the following six kinds of power appear to provide useful categories for generating prescriptive advice:

(1) The power of skill and knowledge

(2) The power of a good relationship

(3) The power of a good alternative to negotiating

(4) The power of an elegant solution

(5) The power of legitimacy

(6) The power of commitment

Here is a checklist for would-be negotiators of what they can do in advance of any particular negotiation to enhance their negotiating power. The sequence in which these elements of power are listed is also important.

1. The Power of Skill and Knowledge

All things being equal, a skilled negotiator is better able to influence the decision of others than is an unskilled negotiator. Strong evidence suggests that negotiating skills can be both learned and taught. One way to become a more powerful negotiator is to become a more skillful one. Some of these skills are those of dealing with people: the ability to listen, to become aware of the emotions and psychological concerns of others, to empathize, to be sensitive to their feelings and one's own, to speak different languages, to communicate clearly and effectively, to become integrated so that one's words and nonverbal behavior are congruent and reenforce each other, and so forth.

Other skills are those of analysis, logic, quantitative assessment, and the organization of ideas. The more skill one acquires, the more power one will have as a negotiator. These skills can be acquired at any time, often far in advance of any particular negotiation.

Knowledge is also power. Some knowledge is general and of use in many negotiations, such as familiarity with a wide range of procedural options and awareness of national negotiating styles and cultural differences. A repertoire of examples, precedents, and illustrations can also add to one's persuasive abilities.

Knowledge relevant to a particular negotiation in which one is about to engage is even more powerful. The more information one can gather about the parties and issues in an upcoming negotiation, the stronger one's entering posture. The following categories of knowledge, for example are likely to strengthen one's ability to exert influence:

Knowledge about the people involved. What are the other negotiators' personal concerns, backgrounds, interests, prejudices, values, habits, career hopes, and so forth? How would we answer the same questions with respect to those on our side?

Knowledge about the interests involved. In addition to the personal concerns of the negotiators, what additional interests are involved on the other side? what are their hopes, their fears, their needs? And what are the interests on our side?

Knowledge about the facts. It is impossible to appreciate the importance of unknown facts. Time permitting, it is usually worthwhile to gather a great deal of unnecessary information about the subject under negotiation in order to gather a few highly relevant facts. The more one knows about the history, geography, economics, and scientific background of a problem, as well as its legal, social, and political implications, the more likely it is that one can invent creative solutions.

It takes time and resources to acquire skill and knowledge; it also takes initiative and hard work. Lawyers who would never think of walking into a trial without weeks of preparation will walk into a negotiation with almost none: "Let's see what they have to say." Yet the lawyer would help his client more in persuading the other side next week than in persuading a judge next year. The first way to enhance one's negotiating power is to acquire in advance all the skill and knowledge that one reasonably can.

2. The Power of a Good Relationship

The better a working relationship I establish in advance with those with whom I will be negotiating, the more powerful I am. A good working relationship does not necessarily imply approval of each other's conduct, though mutual respect and even mutual affection — when it exists — may help. The two most critical elements of a working relationship are, first, trust, and second, the ability to communicate easily and effectively.

Trust. Although I am likely to focus my attention in a given negotiation on the question of whether or not I can trust those on the other side, my power depends upon whether they can trust me. If over time I have been able to establish a well-deserved reputation for candor, honesty, integrity, and commitment to any promise I make, my capacity to exert influence is significantly enhanced.

Communication. The negotiation process is one of communication. If I am trying to persuade some people to change their minds, I want to know where their minds are; otherwise, I am shooting in the dark. If my messages are going to have their intended impact, they need to be understood as I would have them understood. At best, interpersonal communication is difficult and often generates misunderstanding. When the parties see each other as adversaries, the risk of miscommunication and misunderstanding is greatly increased. The longer two people have known each other, and the more broadly and deeply each understands the point of view and context from which the other is operating, the more likely they can communicate with each other easily and with a minimum of misunderstanding.

Each side benefits from this ability to communicate. We may have interests that conflict, but our ability to deal with those conflicting interests at minimum risk and minimum cost is enhanced by a good working relationship. Two men in a lifeboat at sea quarrelling over limited rations have sharply conflicting interests. But the longer they have known each other, the more dealings they have had, and the more they speak the same language, the more likely they are to be able to divide the rations without tipping over the boat. The ability of each to affect favorably the other's decision is enhanced by an ability to communicate. More power for one is consistent with more power for the other.

A good working relationship is so helpful to the negotiation of satisfactory outcomes that it is often more important than any particular outcome itself. A banker, for example, is often like a person courting. The prospect of a satisfactory relationship is far more important than the terms of a particular loan or a particular date. A relationship which provides a means for happily resolving one transaction after another becomes an end in itself. Particular substantive negotiations become opportunities for cooperative activity that builds the relationship.

The same is true internationally. A better working relationship between the Soviet Union and the United States would facilitate the negotiation of particular arms control agreements. Even more important, having a better working relationship would enhance the security of each country more than would the outcome of any particular treaty. The better the working relationship we develop with the Soviet Union, the more likely they are to heed what we have to say.

3. The Power of a Good Alternative to Negotiation

To a significant extent, my power in a negotiation depends upon how well I can do for myself if I walk away. In *Getting to YES*, we urge a negotiator to develop and improve his "BATNA" — his Best Alternative To a Negotiated Agreement. One kind of preparation for negotiation that enhances one's negotiating power is to consider the alternatives to reaching agreement with this particular negotiating partner, to select the most promising, and to improve it to the extent possible. This alternative sets a floor. If I follow this practice, every negotiation will lead to a successful outcome in the sense that any result I accept is bound to be better than anything else I could do.

In the case of buying or selling, my best alternative is likely to result from dealing with a competitor. Obtaining a firm offer from such a competitor in advance of a proposed negotiation strengthens my hand in that negotiation. The better the competing offer, the more my hand is strengthened.

In other cases, my best alternative may be self-help. What is the best I can do on my own? If the two boys offering to shovel the snow off the front walk are asking an exorbitant price, my best alternative may be to shovel the walk myself. To think about that option, and to have a snow shovel in the basement, strengthens my hand in trying to negotiate a fair price with the boys.

The less attractive the other side's BATNA is to them, the stronger my negotiating position. In negotiation with my son to cut the lawn, I may discover that he lacks interest in earning a little pocket money: "Dad," he says, "you leave your wallet on your bureau and if I need a little money I always borrow some." My son's best alternative to a negotiated agreement to cut the lawn is to get the same amount or even more for doing nothing. To enhance my negotiating power, I will want to make his BATNA less attractive by removing that alternative. With my wallet elsewhere, he may be induced to earn some money by cutting the lawn.

Conventional military weapons typically enhance a country's negotiating power by making a nonnegotiated solution less attractive to a hostile neighbor. With adequate defense forces, Country A can say to Country B: "Let's settle our boundary dispute by negotiation; if you try to settle it by military force, you will fail." With sufficient military force, Country A may be able to improve its alternative to negotiation enough that it will be in an extremely strong negotiating position: "We hope you will agree through negotiation to withdraw your forces to the boundary which has been recommended by impartial experts; if you do not agree to withdraw your forces voluntarily, we may force them to withdraw."

The better an alternative one can develop outside the negotiation, the greater one's power to affect favorably a negotiated outcome.

4. The Power of an Elegant Solution

In any negotiation, there is a melange of shared and conflicting interests. The parties face a problem. One way to influence the other side in a negotiation is to invent a good solution to that problem. The more complex the problem, the more influential an elegant answer. Too often, negotiators battle like litigators in court. Each side advances arguments for a result that would take care of its interests but would do nothing for the other side. The power of a mediator often comes from working out an ingenious solution that reconciles reasonably well the legitimate interests of both sides. Either negotiator has similar power to effect an agreement that takes care of his or her interests by generating an option that also takes care of some or most of the interests on the other side.

A wise negotiator includes in his or her preparatory work the generation of many options designed to meet as well as possible the legitimate interests of both sides. Brainstorming enhances my negotiating power by enhancing the chance that I will be able to devise a solution that amply satisfies my interests and also meets enough of your interests to be acceptable to you.

In complicated negotiations, and even in some fairly simple ones, there is usually a shortage of options on the table. The United States and the Soviet Union would presumably welcome a plan that left them at the same level of insecurity at substantially less cost, but no one has yet been able to devise one. In any negotiation, generating a range of options in advance, some of which may later be put on the table, is another way to increase the chance that I will affect the outcome favorably.

5. The Power of Legitimacy

Each of us is subject to being persuaded by becoming convinced that a particular result *ought* to be accepted because it is fair; because the law requires it; because it is consistent with precedent, industry practice, or sound policy considerations; or because it is legitimate as measured by some other objective standard. I can substantially enhance my negotiating power by searching for and developing various objective criteria and potential standards of legitimacy, and by shaping proposed solutions so that they are legitimate in the eyes of the other side.

Every negotiator is both a partisan and one of those who must be persuaded if any agreement is to be reached. To be persuasive, a good negotiator should speak like an advocate who is seeking to convince an able and honest arbitrator, and should listen like such an arbitrator, always open to being persuaded by reason. Being open to persuasion is itself persuasive.

Like a lawyer preparing a case, a negotiator will discover quite a few different principles of fairness for which plausible arguments can be advanced, and often quite a few different ways of interpreting or applying each principle. A tension exists between advancing a highly favorable principle that appears less legitimate to the other side and a less favorable principle that appears more legitimate. Typically, there is a range within which reasonable people could differ. To retain his power, a wise negotiator avoids advancing a proposition that is so extreme that it damages his credibility. He also avoids so locking himself into the first principle he advances that he will lose face in disentangling himself from that principle and moving on to one that has a greater chance of persuading the other side. In advance of this process, a negotiator will want to have researched precedents, expert opinion, and other objective criteria, and to have worked on various theories of what ought to be done, so as to harness the power of legitimacy — a power to which each of us is vulnerable.

6. *The Power of Commitment*

The five kinds of power previously mentioned can each be enhanced by work undertaken in advance of formal negotiations. The planning of commitments and making arrangements for them can also be undertaken in advance, but making commitments takes place only during what everyone thinks of as negotiation itself.

There are two quite different kinds of commitments — affirmative and negative:

(a) Affirmative commitments

   (1) An offer of what I am willing to agree to.

   (2) An offer of what, failing agreement, I am willing to do under certain conditions.

(b) Negative commitments

   (1) A commitment that I am unwilling to make certain agreements (even though they would be better for me than no agreement).

   (2) A commitment or threat that, failing agreement, I will engage in certain negative conduct (even though to do so would be worse for me than a simple absence of agreement).

Every commitment involves a decision. Let's first look at affirmative commitments. An affirmative commitment is a decision about what one is willing to do. It is an offer. Every offer ties the negotiator's hands to some extent. It says, "This, I am willing to do." The offer may expire or later be withdrawn, but while open it carries some persuasive power. It is no longer just an idea or a possibility that the parties are discussing. Like a proposal of marriage or a job offer, it is operational. It says, "I am willing to do this. If you agree, we have a deal."

We have all felt the power of a positive commitment — the power of an invitation. (We are not here concerned with the degree of commitment, or with various techniques for making a constraint more binding, but only with the content of the commitment itself. Advance planning can enhance my power by enabling me to demonstrate convincingly that a commitment is unbreakable. (This subject, like all of those concerned with the difference between appearance and reality, is left for another day.) The one who makes the offer takes a risk. If he had waited, he might have gotten better terms. But in exchange for taking that risk, he has increased his chance of affecting the outcome.

A wise negotiator will formulate an offer in ways that maximize the cumulative impact of the different categories of negotiating power. The terms of an affirmative commitment will benefit from all the skill and knowledge that has been developed; the commitment benefits from the relationship and is consistent with it; it takes into account the walk-away alternatives each side has; the other will constitute a reasonably elegant solution to the problem of reconciling conflicting interests; and the offer will be legitimate — it will take into account considerations of legitimacy.

With all this power in its favor, there is a chance the offer will be accepted. No other form of negotiating power may be needed. But as a last resort, the negotiator has one other form of power: a negative commitment, or threat.

A negative commitment is the most controversial and troublesome element of negotiating power. No doubt, by tying my own hands I may be able to influence you to accept something more favorable to me than you otherwise would. The theory is simple. For almost every potential agreement, there is a range within which each of us is better off having an agreement than walking away. Suppose that you would be willing to pay $75,000 for my house if you had to; but for a price above that figure you would rather buy a different house. The best offer I have received from someone else is $62,000, and I will accept that offer unless you give me a better one. At any price between $62,000 and $75,000 we are both better of than if no agreement is reached. If you offer me $62,100, and so tie your hands by a negative commitment that you cannot raise your offer, presumably, I will accept it since it is better than $62,000. On the other hand, if I can commit myself not to drop the price below $75,000, you presumably will buy the house at that price. This logic may lead us to engage in a battle of negative commitments. Logic suggests that "victory" goes to the one who first and most convincingly ties his own hands at an appropriate figure. Other things being equal, an early and rigid negative commitment at the right point should prove persuasive.

Other things, however, are not likely to be equal.

The earlier I make a negative commitment — the earlier I announce a take-it-or-leave-it position — the less likely I am to have maximized the cumulative total of the various elements of my negotiating power.

The power of knowledge. I probably acted before knowing as much as I could have learned. The longer I postpone making a negative commitment, the more likely I am to know the best proposition to which to commit myself.

The power of a good relationship. Being quick to advance a take-it-or-leave-it position is likely to prejudice a good working relationship and to damage the trust you might otherwise place in what I say. The more quickly I confront you with a rigid position on my part, the more likely I am to make you so angry that you will refuse an agreement you might otherwise accept.

The power of a good alternative. There is a subtle but significant difference between communicating a warning of the course of action that I believe it will be in my interest to take should we fail to reach agreement (my BATNA), and locking myself in to precise terms that you must accept in order to avoid my taking that course of action. Extending a warning is not the same as making a negative commitment. If the United States honestly believes that deploying one hundred MX missiles is a vital part of its national security, then letting the Soviet Union know that in the absence of a negotiated agreement we intend to deploy them would appear a sound way of exerting influence. In these circumstances, the United States remains open to considering any negotiated agreement that would be better for us than the MX deployment. We are not trying to influence the Soviet Union by committing ourselves to refuse to accept an agreement that would in fact be in our interest (in hopes of getting one even more favorable to us). We are simply trying to influence them with the objective reality that deployment seems to be our best option in the absence of agreement.

Two kinds of negative commitments are illustrated by the MX case. One is the example of Mr. Adelman's letter, which apparently described the only possible agreement that the United States was willing to accept. His letter appeared to commit the United States to refusing to agree to any treaty that did not commit the Soviet Union "to forego their heavy and medium ICBMs" (*New York Times*, 26 June 1983). This was an apparent attempt to influence the Soviet Union by making a public commitment about what the United States would not do — we would not take anything less than a Soviet agreement to dismantle all its heavy and medium missiles in exchange for a United States promise not to add 100 MX missiles to our arsenal.

The second kind of negative commitment is illustrated by the MX case if one assumes, as many of us believe, that deploying 100 MX missiles does not really enhance U.S. security but rather damages it. The proposed deployment is bad for us; perhaps worse for the Soviet Union. On this assumption, the threat to deploy the MX missiles is like my trying to influence a fellow passenger by threatening to tip over a boat whether or not I am the better swimmer. Tipping over the boat will be bad for both of us, perhaps worse for him. I am committing myself to do something negative to both of us in the hope of exerting influence. If I make such a commitment, it is because I hope that by precluding myself from acting in some ways that would be in my interest, I will be able to achieve a result that is even more favorable.

To make either kind of negative commitment at an early stage of the negotiation is likely to reduce the negotiating power of a good BATNA. It shifts the other side's attention from the objective reality of my most attractive alternative to a subjective statement that I won't do things that (except for my having made the commitment) would be in my interest to do. Such negative commitments invite the other side to engage in a contest of will by making commitments that are even more negative, and even more difficult to get out of. Whatever negotiating impact my BATNA may have, it is likely to be lessened by clouding it with negative commitments. This is demonstrated by Deputy Secretary of State Kenneth Dam's insistence (following Mr. Adelman's ill-fated letter) that the MX "is not a bargaining chip in the sense that we are just deploying it for purposes of negotiation. It is a vital part of our national security." That statement implicitly recognizes that a statement made for negotiating reasons is likely to exert less influence at the negotiating table than would a good alternative away from the table. Mr. Dam's statement also reflects recognition on the part of the United States that a premature negative commitment weakens rather than strengthens our negotiating power.

The power of an elegant solution. The early use of a negative commitment reduces the likelihood that the choice being considered by the other side is one that best meets its interests consistent with any given degree of meeting our interests. If we announce early in the negotiation process that we will accept no agreement other than Plan X, Plan X probably takes care of most of our interests. But it is quite likely that Plan X could be improved. With further study and time, it may be possible to modify Plan X so that it serves our interests even better at little or no cost to the interests of the other side.

Second, it may be possible to modify Plan X in ways that make it more attractive to the other side without in any way making it less attractive to us. To do so would not serve merely the other side but would serve us also by making it more likely that the other side will accept a plan that so well serves our interests.

Third, it may be possible to modify Plan X in ways that make it much more attractive to the other side at a cost of making it only slightly less attractive to us. The increase in total benefits and the increased likelihood of quickly reaching agreement may outweigh the modest cost involved.

Premature closure on an option is almost certain to reduce our ability to exert the influence that comes from having an option well crafted to reconcile, to the extent possible, the conflicting interests of the two sides. In multilateral negotiations it is even less likely that an early option will be well designed to take into account the plurality of divergent interests involved.

The power of legitimacy. The most serious damage to negotiating power that results from an early negative commitment is likely to result from its damage to the influence that comes from legitimacy. Legitimacy depends upon both process and substance. As with an arbitrator, the legitimacy of a negotiator's decision depends upon having accorded the other side "due process." The persuasive power of my decision depends in part on my having fully heard your views, your suggestions, and your notions of what is fair before committing myself. And my decision will have increased persuasiveness for you to the extent that I am able to justify it by reference to objective standards of fairness that you have indicated you consider appropriate. That factor, again, urges me to withhold making any negative commitment until I fully understand your views on fairness.

The power of an affirmative commitment. Negative commitments are often made when no affirmative commitment is on the table. The Iranian holders of the hostages in Tehran said for months that they would not release the hostages until the United States had adequately atoned for its sins and had met an unambiguous set of additional demands. No clear offer was given by Iran, and the United States, accordingly, was under no great pressure to do any particular thing. During the Vietnam War, the United States similarly failed to offer those on the other side any clear proposition. We would not leave, we said, until North Vietnam agreed "to leave its neighbors alone" — but no terms were on the table; no offer, no affirmative commitment was given.

Once an affirmative commitment is on the table, the negotiator must make sure that the varied elements of the communication are consistent with each other. No matter what the magnitude of a threat, it will have little effect unless it is constructed so that the sum total of the consequences of acceptance are more beneficial to the other side than is the sum total of the consequences of rejection. While negotiators frequently try to increase power by increasing the magnitude of a threat, they often overlook the fact that increasing the favorable consequences of acceptance can be equally important.

But no matter how favorable the consequences of acceptance are to the other side, and how distasteful the consequences of rejection, the proposition will carry little impact if the various implications of timing have not been thought through as well. Just as my son will look at me askance if I tell him that unless he behaves next week he will not be permitted to watch television tonight, so the North Vietnamese were unable to comply when the United States said, in effect, "If over the next few weeks you haven't reduced support for opponents of South Vietnam, we will bomb you tomorrow." The grammar must parse. (See Fisher, 1969.)

To make a negative commitment either as to what we will not do or as to what harsh consequences we will impose unless the other side reaches agreement with us, without having previously made a firm and clear offer, substantially lessens our ability to exert influence. An offer may not be enough, but a threat is almost certainly not enough unless there is a 'yesable' proposition on the table — a clear statement of the action desired and a commitment as to the favorable consequences which would follow.

Conclusion

This analysis of negotiating power suggests that in most cases it is a mistake to attempt to influence the other side by making a negative commitment of any kind[2] at the outset of the negotiations, and that it is a mistake to do so until one has first made the most of every other element of negotiating power.

This analysis also suggests that when as a last resort threats or other negative commitments are used, they should be so formulated as to complement and reinforce other elements of negotiating power, not undercut them. In particular, any statement to the effect that we have finally reached a take-it-or-leave-it position should be made in a way that is consistent with maintaining a good working relationship, and consistent with the concepts of legitimacy with which we are trying to persuade the other side. For example, I might say:

> "Bill, I appreciate your patience. We have been a long time discussing the sale of my house, and I believe that we each fully understand each other's concerns. We have devised a draft contract which elegantly reconciles my interest in a firm deal, adequate security, and reasonable restrictions to protect the neighbors, with your interest in being able to move in early, to stretch out the payments,

and to have your professional office in the house. The only open issue is price. On that we have discussed various criteria, such as market value based on recent sales, providing me a fair return on my investment, and value based on professional estimates of replacement cost depreciated for wear and tear. These criteria produce figures ranging from $73,000 down to $68,000. I have offered to sell you the house for $70,000.

"Your response, as I understand it, is to say that you will pay no more than $100 above the best written offer I have from another potential buyer, now $62,000. Knowing that you would pay $75,000 if you had to, I am unable to understand why you should get all but $100 of the advantage of our shared interest in my selling and your buying the house. Nor, as we have discussed, do I think it a wise practice for me to defer to what looks to me like an arbitrary commitment.

"The transaction costs of further discussion would appear to outweigh any potential advantage. Unless you have something further you would like to say now, or unless you would like to try to convince me that this procedure is unfair, I hereby make a final offer of $68,000, the lowest figure I believe justified by objective criteria. Let me confirm that offer now in writing and commit myself to leaving that offer open for three days. Unless something wholly unexpected comes up, I will not sell the house to you for less. Please think it over.

"In any event, let's plan to play golf on Saturday afternoon if you are free."

A great deal of work remains to be done toward formulating the best general advice that can be given to help a negotiator increase his or her ability to influence others. Some of that work relates to what can be done to acquire power in advance of a negotiation; much relates to how best to use such power as one has. No attempt has been made to advance propositions that will be true in every case, only to advance rules of thumb that should be helpful in many cases. So far, I have been unable to come up with any better rules of thumb covering the same ground.

As indicated at the outset, this article does not cover the kind of negotiating power that comes from creating in the mind of others an impression that is false — from bluffing, deceit, misrepresentation, or other such act or omission. For the moment, I remain unconvinced that the best advice for a negotiator would include suggestions of how to create a false impression in the mind of the other side, any more than I would advise young lawyers on how best to create a false impression in the mind of a judge or arbitrator. But that is a subject for another day.

NOTES

1. See "Making Threats Is Not Enough," Chapter Three in *International Conflict for Beginners* (Fisher, 1969).

2. On reading this article, Douglas Stone of the Harvard Law School suggested that there may be one kind of negative commitment that could be made at the outset of negotiations without damage to the relationship, to legitimacy, or to other elements of one's total power. This might be done by establishing an early commitment never to yield to unprincipled threats. I might, for example, make a negative commitment that I would not respond to negative commitments but only to facts, objective criteria, offers, and reasoned argument. Like an advance commitment not to pay blackmail, such a negative commitment is consistent with legitimacy. In fact, one might propose that both sides make mutual commitments not to respond to threats. An early commitment not to respond to threats might, if convincingly made, preemptively foreclose threats from the other side.

REFERENCES

Fisher, R. (1969). *International conflict for beginners*. New York: Harper & Row.

——— and Ury, W. L. (1981). *Getting to YES*. Boston: Houghton-Mifflin.

Berger, A. (1983). "Hersch probes Nixon years relentlessly." *Boston Globe* (June 19): B-10, B-12.

Freudenheim, M. and Giniger, H. (1983). "Adelman gets a lesson in letter writing." *New York Times* (June 26): 2E.

Saying You're Sorry[1]

Stephen B. Goldberg, Eric D. Green,
and Frank E.A. Sander

As children, perhaps the first dispute resolution lesson that many of us learn is the importance of apologizing. This is, however, a lesson that is soon forgotten, or at least, little used, in American dispute resolution. Hegland (1982: 69) makes this point nicely:

> In my first-year Contracts class, I wished to review various doctrines we had recently studied. I put the following:
> In a long-term installment contract, seller promises buyer to deliver widgets at rate of 1,000 a month. The first two deliveries are perfect. However, in the third month seller delivers only 990 widgets. Buyer becomes so incensed that he rejects deliveries and refuses to pay for widgets already delivered.
> After stating the problem, I asked, "If you were Seller, what would you say?" What I was looking for was a discussion of the various common law theories which would force the buyer to pay for the widgets delivered and those which would throw buyer into breach for cancelling the remaining deliveries. In short, I wanted the class to come up with the legal doctrines which would allow Seller to crush Buyer.
> After asking the question, I looked around the room for a volunteer. As is so often the case with first-year students, I found that they were all either writing in their notebooks or inspecting their shoes. There was, however, one eager face, that of the eight-year-old son of one of my students. It seems that he was suffering through Contracts due to his mother's sin of failing to find a sitter. Suddenly he raised his hand. Such behavior, even from an eight-year-old, must be rewarded.
> "OK," I said, "What would you say if you were the seller?"
> "I'd say, 'I'm sorry.'"

Many mediators have had one or more experiences in which an apology was the key to a settlement that might otherwise not have been attainable. At times, all the injured party wants is an admission by the other party that he or she did wrong; no more is necessary to achieve a settlement. At other times, an apology alone is insufficient to resolve a dispute, but will so reduce tension and ease the relationship between the parties that the issues separating them are resolved with dispatch.

Steven B. Goldberg, Eric D. Green, and **Frank E.A. Sander** are the authors of *Dispute Resolution* (Boston: Little, Brown 1985). Goldberg is Professor of Law at Northwestern University School of Law, Chicago, Ill. 60611. Green is Professor of Law at Boston University School of Law, Boston, Mass. 02215. Sander is the Bussey Professor of Law at Harvard Law School, Cambridge, Mass. 02138.

Furthermore, to the extent that the dispute has occurred in the context of an ongoing relationship, the apology is valuable in repairing whatever harm to the relationship has resulted from the dispute. In this respect, the apology serves one of the goals of mediation — the repair of frayed relationships.

With the increasing role of mediation and other non-adjudicative dispute resolution techniques, one would expect the use of the apology to become more commonplace. Indeed, in Japan, where rights-based dispute resolution is less well entrenched, apology plays a central role in the resolution of disputes (Wagatsuma and Rosett, 1986). For example, following the 1982 Japan Air Lines crash in Tokyo Bay, the airline's president promptly visited all the families of the crash victims to offer apologies and compensation. Formal apologies of this nature are common in Japan, and often result in dispute resolution without recourse to litigation. In the 1982 case, in fact, no lawsuits were filed.

Obstacles to the Apology

There are several obstacles to the greater use of apology as a dispute resolution technique in the United States. Chief among these is the fact that, while in Japan filing a lawsuit is accompanied by shame, in the United States it is the apology that is often seen as demeaning. Hence apologies are hard to extract — often harder than money. (Sometimes in a neighborhood dispute, mediators manage to get the respondent to apologize as part of the final rapprochement but usually only after the parties' claims and counterclaims have been heard and resolved.)

Reluctance to apologize may also be the product of formal rules of evidence which treat an apology as an admission of fault that can be used to prove wrongdoing. Thus it is commonplace for insurance companies and attorneys to advise policyholders against expressing sympathy for a person injured by the policyholder, for fear such an expression will be treated as an admission of guilt.

It is possible that, with an increased emphasis on accommodative dispute settlement, the view that an apology is demeaning to the person who delivers it will diminish. Perhaps state legislatures, motivated by a desire to encourage settlement, and so decrease court congestion, will also take steps to eliminate the use of an apology or an expression of sympathy as an admission of wrongdoing in subsequent litigation.

For instance, in December of 1986, Massachusetts enacted a law (Chapter 652) providing that "gestures expressing sympathy or a general sense of benevolence relating to the pain, suffering or death of a person involved in an accident" would not be admissible into evidence as an admission of liability. Although this provision does not encompass apologies, one can readily envision an extension in that direction. Additionally, if an apology is offered as part of the settlement process, it would be inadmissable under common law rules excluding from evidence even admissions of liability made during settlement negotiations.

Friendly, but then . . .

One American corporation is said to have coupled an initially supportive approach with hard-nosed litigation tactics in a novel effort to reduce claims. According to the 7 November 1986 *Wall Street Journal*, following a 1985 airport crash that killed 137 people, Delta Airlines dispatched employees to be with every victimized family. The Delta employees helped with little things, such as looking for a briefcase lost in the crash, and with big things — such as funerals. If someone just wanted to talk, a Delta employee was there as a friend.

Subsequently, according to the *Journal*, many victims found it difficult to sue their "friend." Far fewer suits were filed against Delta than might have been expected based on the results of other accidents — only 65 out of a possible 152.

For those who filed suit, however, the *Journal* reports that Delta's attorneys showed them "just how painful a lawsuit can be." According to the attorney for one plaintiff, Delta and its insurance carriers used information that they had obtained from grieving family members against them in subsequent settlement negotiations. Thus, the attorney alleges, a distraught family member had told a sympathetic adjuster that one victim, a married man, had been having an extramarital affair. "They threw it back at us in settlement talks and really took us by surprise," said the lawyer, adding that victims should be cautioned that anything they say may be used against them in a suit. One may hope that this peculiarly American twist on a well-entrenched Japanese practice will not become commonplace.

Compensation and Timing

Although apology seems to be greatly underutilized in American dispute settlement, we should not expect it to be a panacea for resolving disputes. It would seem to hold particular promise where parties stand in a close personal relationship.

But as the 1982 Japan Airlines example illustrates, such a relationship can be created even where impersonal entities are involved. The Japanese experience also teaches us that, where substantial economic injury has been done, the apology is not an adequate substitute for compensation; the two must be effectively coupled.

Timing is a critical element. The expression of regret must come soon after the injury, or at least soon after the injured person voices his or her grievance. Once the respondent has taken the alternative path of denying responsibility (and perhaps even hurling countercharges), an apology is much more difficult to elicit, or even if given, to be accepted.

Hence the good news is that apology may be an important tool for professional dispute resolvers; the bad news is that, by the time they become involved, it may often be too late.

But if there will be some lost opportunities for us as dispute resolvers, there will be ample opportunities for us as disputants to make use of this powerful device. Recently a friend who had acted highhandedly toward a colleague received an angry and vituperative response. Instead of responding in kind, he expressed regret for his action and indicated (as was true) how much he valued his colleague's opinions and friendship. The effect on the colleague was remarkable; the apology totally took the sting out of a potentially poisoned relationship.

Indeed the potency of an apology is not limited to dispute settlement. Imagine, for example, how differently things might have gone if, as soon as the diversion of arms sales funds to the Contras had been revealed, President Reagan had gone on national television and said something like this:

"Although meaning well, I made a serious mistake in approving the sale of arms to Iran. I also should have monitored more carefully the path of the resulting funds. I regret that these funds were diverted to the Contras in violation of Congressional restrictions and have taken all necessary steps to see that the perpetrators will be punished and that such mistakes will not occur again. I hope and pray that these measures will help to restore the faith and trust that the American people have reposed in me."

NOTE

1. This column was adapted from the supplement to *Dispute Resolution*, written by the same authors and published in 1987 in Boston by Little, Brown and Co.

REFERENCES

Hegland, K. (1982). "Why teach trial advocacy? An essay on never ask why." In *Humanistic education in law*, Monograph III, edited by J. Himmelstein and H. Lesnick. New York: Columbia University School of Law.
Wagatsuma, H. and Rosett, A. (1986). "The implications of apology: Law and culture in Japan and the United States." *Law & Society Review* 20: 461-498.

Section IV

The Negotiations Proper

A pivotal element in preparation for negotiation away from the table is assessing one's alternatives (and the other side's), as well as understanding the kinds of power that each side may be able to exercise in the upcoming exchange. Once the negotiations proper begin, however, the parties' attention rightfully turns away from matters of dependence to some analysis of the factors that will contribute to negotiating effectiveness. Obviously, a vast array of considerations plays a part in the tactical choices and strategic decisions of the negotiators; this section highlights some of the most important of these considerations.

I. William Zartman's essay ("Common Elements in the Analysis of the Negotiation Process") provides a simple but useful framework for organizing various ways of thinking about the moves that take place during negotiation. Using the metaphor of the proverbial blind men and the elephant — each describing the beast on the basis of the part of the elephant he happens to take hold of — Zartman describes five "families" of negotiation analysis: structural analysis, which focuses on the distribution of various elements and the effects of such distribution on negotiation; strategic analysis, which involves the kinds of movement that are possible within the negotiations as a result of a series of interdependent choices made by the disputants; process analysis, which analyzes negotiating behavior as the result of some assessment by each side of the relative benefits and costs associated with reaching agreement; behavioral analysis, which uses the personalities of the negotiators as the point of departure; and integrative analysis, which ". . .stresses the need to manipulate conceptualizations of the problem into mutually satisfying positive-sum outcomes before proceeding to an elaboration of a detailed division of the spoils." Although all five of these general approaches to understanding what transpires in negotiation can coexist, says Zartman, there is a tendency for analysts (and, by implication, practitioners) to differ in their respective reliance on one of these perspectives over the others.

If the Zartman piece provides an overview of possible approaches to the analysis of any negotiation, then the second article, by David A. Lax and James K. Sebenius ("Interests: The Measure of Negotiation"), addresses one of the single most important issues in negotiation. As Fisher and Ury (1981) observed, negotiators too often base their exchange on "positions" (assertions about the reasons or needs that underlie statements of position). By focusing on interests, not positions, they write, it is often possible to devise agreements that would otherwise be overlooked or deemed impossible. Expanding on the view expounded by Fisher and Ury, they can then consider the circumstances where it may, in fact, be wiser *not* to move from positions to interests. Lax and Sebenius also distinguish between different kinds of interests in negotiation, and develop a series of prescriptive suggestions for assessing interests as well as possible tradeoffs among various interests.

A number of scholars over the years have advocated the use of a "single negotiating text" as a tool in effective negotiation. This is a draft that is typically developed by one side (or by a third party), then circulated to the other side for criticism and emendation. In the third article of this section ("Your Draft or Mine?"), Jeswald W. Salacuse explores the various uses and possible misuses of the single negotiating text in negotiation. While a draft text may have a number of important virtues and advantages in terms of identifying issues and moving toward a negotiated settlement, there are also some offsetting disadvantages — including the use of a draft in order to obtain a tactical advantage in the exchange. Salacuse suggests three ways of coping with a negotiator who is using a draft text as a way of controlling or manipulating the negotiation environment to his or her personal advantage: First, prepare a counterdraft of one's own; second, push for a discussion of principles first, before any draft is developed; and third, make use of the draft, but not in the order in which the other side has proposed various solutions.

The fourth article of this section ("Ten Commandments for a Negotiator") was written by Janos Nyerges, former director general of the Hungarian Ministry of Foreign Trade. Nyerges, a practitioner with extensive negotiating experience, outlines the ten principles of negotiation that he has found most valuable over the years. The reader will, we believe, find these various bits of "practitioner folk wisdom" reminiscent of many standard tenets of effective negotiation, although Nyerges clearly has his own distinctive point of view.

Common Elements in the Analysis of the Negotiation Process

I. William Zartman

Like the proverbial blind men who confronted the elephant and brought back conflicting accounts of its salient characteristics, contemporary analysts of negotiation appear to be talking about different things under the name of the same phenomenon. Some have even called for a search for a common understanding of the subject so that so that analysis can proceed on the same epistemological track.

This article, however, suggests that a common understanding of the negotiation process has already developed and analysts are using it. The diversity that can be found in a number of approaches — five of which are identified — merely displays different ways of talking about the same phenomenon, and in fact even involves the same questions and parameters presented from different angles and under different names. There is more unity than some have suspected, and more complementarity too, as different approaches reenforce and build on each other's analysis. However, many aspects of the process still elude this common but multifaceted analysis. The common notion of the process has led analysts to confront these continuing problems, but there is of course no certainty that further answers to obdurate problems will not produce new terms of analysis and even new notions of the whole process.

It is paradoxical and perhaps confusing that there is no single dominant analytical approach to negotiation. The confusion arises from the present of many different attempts at analysis, sometimes inventing their own wheels to carry forward their insights and sometimes cross-referencing from a number of different analytical approaches (e.g., see cases in Zartman, 1987a and 1987b; and Davidow, 1984). The fact that all of these are studies of great value only confirms the analytical confusion. The paradox arises because behind this analytical diversity lies a single phenomenon to be analyzed. Although some authors have a hard time seeing the essential identity of the negotiation process (Young, 1975), most others (including those who then focus on different subtypes for analytical purposes) start with a common definition of the phenomenon (Pruitt, 1981; Raiffa, 1982; Walton and McKersie, 1965; Iklé, 1964).

In simple terms, negotiation is a process of combining conflicting positions into a common position, under a decision rule of unanimity, a phenomenon in which the outcome is determined by the process (Kissinger, 1969, p. 212). The essential element of process is important because it posits a determining dynamic, not just an assortment of scattered actions or tactics.

I. William Zartman is Professor of International Politics at the Johns Hopkins University School of Advanced International Studies, Washington, D.C.

The challenge then becomes one of finding the nature of that dynamic and its parameters. It is because this challenge has not been met to universal satisfaction that there are still a number of contending approaches to the study of the process. The same reason also explains, in part, why there is such resistance among practitioners of the process to adopting and applying the work of analysts to their practice.

The question still remains: If there is a single recognized phenomenon, and if the various approaches that are employed to analyze that phenomenon are all insightful, why is there not greater consensus on how to explain negotiation? This article will propose some answers to that question, but in the process it will heighten — but also seek to remove — the paradox. The answer proposed is that each of the analytical approaches puts forward a deterministic analysis in its most rigorous form, but it is only useful insights, not whole theories, that are gained when the unreal conditions of determinism are dropped. The class between deterministic integrity and realistic looseness keeps each analytic approach separate from the others in trying to overcome its internal problems of analysis rather than facing external problems of coordination. The fact that many of the separate approaches are supported by a disciplinary basis also keeps them locked in their internal analytical problems.

The underlying paradox is that the approaches are really more similar than has been recognized, not only in their study of the same phenomenon but also in their answers to the same or similar questions in the same or similar ways, albeit under different disciplinary labels. Exorcising these differences may permit an economy of side movement and an increase of forward movement in the analysis of the negotiation process.

The basic analytical question for all approaches to answer is: How are negotiated outcomes explained? To give generalized answers and to get away from the idiosyncrasies of history, the analyst must find dominant variables which can be understood in operational terms. These, in turn, should be able to provide useful insights — indeed, even strategies for behavioral rules — for practitioners seeking to obtain the best possible outcomes for themselves. Thus, practical forms of the same question are: How can each party deploy its efforts to obtain an outcome favorable enough to be acceptable to itself but attractive enough to the other party to draw it away from its own attempts at a unilateral solution and win its acceptance of an agreement? Or (in the terms of the classic "Toughness Dilemma") when should a party be tough and when should it be soft, knowing that conceding little will mean holding to its position but decrease the chances of an agreement while conceding a lot will increase the chances of an agreement but move it away from the positions it values? (Bartos, 1987; Lax and Sebenius, 1986; Zartman and Berman, 1982) Five different "families" of analysis will be examined to see how these questions are handled, and where the differences and similarities of the approaches lie. (For attempts to show the differences in some or all of these schools, see Walton and McKersie, 1965; Young, 1975, Zartman, 1978 and 1987b.)

Structural Analysis
Structural analysis is based on a distribution of elements, in this case of instrumental elements or power, defined either as parties' relative positions (resource possessions) or as the relative ability to make their options prevail (or to counter the other's efforts to make its options prevail [see Schelling,

1960; Wriggins, 1987; Bacharach and Lawler, 1981; Habeeb, 1987]). Structural analysis is the most commonplace approach, and its deterministic statement that "the strongest side wins" is usually tautological and post hoc. To avoid the tautology, the definitional identity between power structure and winning must be broken both by using an independent measure of power and by focusing on the way in which parties with different relative strengths achieve their outcomes. The latter approach has received some attention in the analysis of situations of asymmetry, where the better performance of the weaker of the two sides provides an interesting challenge for explanation. The explanation most often given can be called "tactics." Tactics generally serve to restore the structural equality of power between the two parties (Snyder and Diesing, 1977, pp. 118-24; Hopmann, 1978; Deutsch, 1973; Zartman, 1985; Wriggins, 1987). Various tactics provide various prescriptions for overcoming asymmetry.

Another body of literature associated with the same approach starts with a different structural assumption, of symmetry rather than asymmetry. This is based on the finding that parties do best in negotiation when they are or feel equal (Rubin and Brown, 1975, pp. 199 and 214-21) and that negotiation takes place when parties' unilateral achievement of their goals is blocked either by the other's veto or by their own incapabilities. Thus, some analysis has used structures of symmetry to identify situations most propitious for negotiation, using *when* to negotiate as a key to *how* to negotiate (Saunders, 1985; Zartman, 1985).

By these paths, by the time that structural analysis has moved away from its initial post hoc formulation that outcomes are determined by the power positions of the parties, it has shifted toward simply tactical analysis based on a different definition of power. Power becomes no longer a position or a possession —something a party "has" — but a way of exercising a causal relation — something one "does" — to bring about an outcome and not just the ability to do so (Habeeb, 1987; see also Lasswell and Kaplan, 1950, p. 75; Simon, 1957, p. 5).

While such studies may be termed structural because they deal with power, that element is treated as a responsive, incidental, and situational characteristic rather than as an element of theory in conceptualization of the negotiation process. This is a common problem with studies of power, and in the case of negotiations it has produced an array of insightful, if idiosyncratic, books of proverbs on how parties can be brought to agreement. (Karrass, 1970; Nierenberg, 1973; Fisher and Ury, 1981) Their emphasis is on various angles of insight into the negotiation process.

Despite a lack of theoretical focus or coherence, these studies do propose ways to make a given offer appear more attractive, to induce the other party to accept the first party's current offer, or to induce it to improve its own offer. Whether stated or not, these tactics operate on either current offers, expectations, or outcomes to be obtained without negotiation (security points). They do so in one of only two ways — either by altering the contingent value of current offers relative to the other two points of comparison (expectations and security points) or by identifying certain procedures ("fractionate" or "trade off") or atmospherics ("trust" or "confidence") that facilitate the basic process. All these tactics are acts of (attempted) power, and all of them are ways to bring about acceptance of a given offer. Furthermore, they all focus on a part of a common and general process of replacing unilateral and conflicting positions with a common position or outcome, whether that process is explicitly stated as such or not. Explicit statements about the nature of the process should be useful and would facilitate links between approaches; but even in the absence of such statements, it is clear that the process is the same.

Strategic Analysis

Strategic analysis is also based on an array of elements, but its structure is one of ends, not means. Strategic analysis, as portrayed in game theoretic matrices, begins with the assumption that outcomes are determined by the relative array of their values to the parties, under conditions of rational (i.e., preferred) choice. The standard strategic models — Prisoner's Dilemma Game and Chicken Dilemma Game — are symmetrical, and therefore incorporate the same assumption of equality as often found in structural analysis. It has frequently been noted that game theory excludes any use of power as a result of its rigorous analytical forms and its clear logic of determinism: rather, it records values as given and shows the strategies that will be chosen and the consequences of doing so (Young, 1975; Axelrod, 1984).

As a result, some observers assert that strategic analysis is of real value only in comparing the decision to negotiate with the decision to hold out, a comparison parallel to the insights gained from an analysis of symmetrical structures. Since game theory values are given (and indeed, at worst, sometimes inferred from the strategies adopted), there is no way to fractionate or trade off; all that can be done is to enter the value of any such external operations into the appropriate box in the matrix. Likewise, there is no way to change any of those values within the matrix; the only option is to record any changes from one matrix to another.

Yet when the rigorous assumptions that provide the basis for determinism are relaxed and game theory presentations are used heuristically as the starting point for analysis, a number of the associated limitations fall away and new possibilities appear. Strategic analysis shows that the only way to break out of deadlock is through asymmetry. Therefore, instead of working to improve offers of cooperation (CC) — absolutely or in relation to expectations which cannot be shown on a matrix — parties are best advised to alter the payoffs or perceptions of payoffs associated with non-negotiated or unilateral outcomes (DD). This, in turn, brings in new understandings of power, seen as the use of security points to induce or resist changes in bargaining positions (Snyder and Diesing, 1977; Zagare, 1978; Brams, 1985).

Movement is the essence of the negotiation process, and movement cannot be shown on a matrix. But the conditions that produce movement — again, different evaluations of outcomes as the source of power — can be shown on a matrix and analysis drawn from it, just as movies result from a succession of stills. The result is the same process as indicated in the relaxation and refinement of structural analysis, in which parties move from their unilateral options to a common cooperative decision so shaped as to be more attractive than their security points.

The problem with strategic analysis at present is not its rigidity but its limited scope. Many of the important and more detailed questions on how to move parties toward a common solution lie outside the analysis; even such important insights as the ways to reenforce commitment (Schelling, 1960; Baldwin, 1987) are triggered by a need to consider security points, but are outside game theoretic analysis. An effort to render more precise the importance of the security point in comparison to unilateral demands and multilateral compromise is an important new advance of the strategic approach, but the calculation to Critical Risk depends on the difficult shift from ordinal to cardinal values in the matrix (Ellsberg, 1975; Snyder and Diesing, 1977).

On the other hand, strategic categories of encounters can help answer some of the puzzling analytical questions of negotiations. For example, the Toughness Dilemma may be resolved by use of the two game theory dilemmas: Whereas parties who see their situation as a Prisoner's Dilemma Game may do best by playing soft to open and tough to punish (Axelrod, 1984), parties who see themselves in a Chicken Dilemma Game do better by playing tough to demand and soft to reward (Nyerges, 1987). This, in turn, confirms an answer from structural analysis to the Toughness Dilemma, based on appropriate tactics for strong and weak powers, respectively. Further examples could be produced where strategic analysis, despite apparent limitations, ends up discussing elements of the same process, and often the same process problems, as other approaches, but in different terms.

Process Analysis

Process analysis has the common feature of explaining outcomes through a series of concessions determined by some element inherent in each party's position. The particular element varies slightly according to the particular version of the theory; most process analysis is based on a security point theory in some form, although a few other variations are also used. Process analysis indicates that the party will concede on the basis of a comparative calculation of its own versus its opponent's costs or of its own costs versus some acceptability level (Zeuthen, 1975; Cross, 1969, Pen, 1975, Hicks, 1932; Snyder and Diesing, 1977). On this basis, one can determine which party will concede how much until the final point of convergence is reached. This is, of course, a way of diagramming a negotiation process that is the same as that discussed by other approaches.

Other variations are end point theories and concession rate theories, both of which are parts of the same process. The first determines the parties' movement so as to assure a mutually fair and maximizing outcome; the second — concession rate theories —determines the parties' movement on the basis of reactions to each other's degree of concession (Bartos, 1978; Zeuthen, 1975; Nash, 1975; Cross, 1969, 1978; cf., Pruitt, 1981). These latter variations (endpoint and concession-rate theories of process) are only prescriptively deterministic; that is, they indicate how parties will act and where they will end up if they want to reach a mutually fair and maximizing outcome, and thus they are not good descriptions of the process. But they do serve the useful function of providing a baseline against which unfairness and power can be measured; hence, they are relevant to some understanding of the process (Pillar, 1983).

Process theories, which originate in economics, are in fact structural theories which indicate that the weaker party will concede until the tables are turned, at which point the other party will concede in its turn, and so on to agreement. Hence, they are theories of power, with power measured in terms of a comparison between offers and security points or, in other words, in terms of critical risk factors. Although this is never done in these theories, to the extent that parties can alter each other's or their own security points, they can exercise power as well as simply possess it; this therefore reduces the deterministic possibilities of the theory but increases its reality. The similarity between process and strategic theories has long been recognized (Harsanyi, 1956 and 1977; Wagner, 1975), although their mechanisms are indeed different. The similarity with structural theories should also be registered; although many structuralists would probably not "read" game theory or "talk" bilateral monopoly, their analyses are complementary, covering the same phenomena within the same process.

The neatness of processes theory only works in idealized situations, and then only with idiosyncracies (Khury, 1968; Bartos, 1974, 1987; Hamermesch, 1987). Concession behavior does not always match; often it mismatches or non-matches or tracks (Pruitt, 1981), and parties do not even concede responsively. Rather, they try to teach and learn, respond and elicit responses, all at the same time, combining several types of behavior that make theoretically neat patterns unrealistic (Coddington, 1968; Cross, 1969; Bartos, 1987). The point here is that in the process, analysts are discerning both involuntary and voluntary, mechanical and manipulative, process and power elements that make up negotiation, all of them clustered about a similarly understood effort to combine conflicting positions into a common one. As the references in this review are beginning to show, analysts do not even belong exclusively to one school or another but sometimes borrow naturally from different approaches. Yet the fact that the field is seen as pluralistic as it is, or that bibliographies remain largely in the author's discipline (Rubin and Brown, 1975) means that there is not enough natural borrowing and cross-referencing.

Behavioral Analysis
Behavioral analysis provides an obviously different explanation of negotiated outcomes by using the negotiators themselves as the focus of analysis (Jonsson, 1978). The terms of analysis used are the personalities of the negotiators, either directly or in interaction. Personality social psychology can be used to refer to personal predispositions that exist at a number of different levels, from biologically-ingrained needs to attitudes more capable of being influenced. At whatever level, this school of analysis responds to a common belief about negotiation — that "it all depends on the personalities of the negotiators." The challenge then becomes to translate that popular perception into identifiable and nontautological variables that can be used for analysis.

A more literary and intuitive basis for behavioral analysis began with Nicholson's (1939) distinction between Shopkeepers and Warriors. It has been extended and developed through a number of forms into Snyder and Diesing's (1977) Softliners and Hardliners. There are many characterizations possible for these basic types, but some can be given in terms already used by other schools: The Hardline Warrior sees situations as a Prisoner's Dilemma Game and acts as a mismatcher, expecting toughness to lead to softness (and his victory) and softness to lead to toughness (and his defeat); on the other hand, the Softline Shopkeeper sees situations as a Chicken Dilemma Game and follows matching behavior, expecting toughness to lead to toughness (and deadlock) and softness to lead to softness (and agreement). Thus, behavioral analyses take up the same parameters as elements in the same process as other approaches, combining them into typologies equated with the behaver rather than leaving them independent as behaviors.

A more developed approach involves categorizing personality types according to their Interpersonal Orientation (IO), an approach that is both more insightful and more complex because it is not merely dichotomous and because its effects depend on interaction rather than on simple or direct taxonomic associations. Opposed to a Low IO type are two types of High IOs — Cooperators and Competitors. Either produces a positive result when negotiating with the same type of personality, but, when cross-paired, the match is unproductive because the two types grate on each other. Rather than explaining an outcome in its own terms, as the previous typologies tend to do, IO analysis operates on the basis of a causal interaction (Rubin and Brown, 1975). It also identifies different types of outcomes, depending on joint or comparative maximization, a point also developed in studies of Motivational Orientations (Rubin and Brown, 1975; Filley, 1975). But this approach too deals with such elements as the propensity to compromise, to construct positive- or divide zero-sum outcomes, or to adopt a tough or soft fine (i.e., a flatter or steeper concession rate) during the process of combining conflicting positions into a joint decision.

Integrative Analysis

Integrative analysis, like behavioral analysis, would seem to constitute an exception to the general understanding of a negotiation process. Although it too conceives of negotiation as a process, its process runs through stages, in which the outcome is explained by the performance of behaviors identified as specifically appropriate to each successive stage (Gulliver, 1979; Saunders, 1985; Zartman and Berman, 1982; Zartman, 1987a, Druckman, 1986).

Rather than seeing a process that works from fixed points of discord to a common point of convergence, integrative analysis emphasizes the imprecision of parties' interests in their own minds. Integrative analysis stresses the need to manipulate conceptualizations of the problem into mutually satisfying positive-sum outcomes before proceeding to an elaboration of a detailed division of the spoils. By extending its concept of the negotiation process back before the time when positions appear as fixed points, integrative analysis not only allows for greater and more positive manipulation of those positions (Fisher and Ury, 1981) but also meets practitioners' understanding of negotiation by drawing attention to the prenegotiated part of the process (Bendahmane and McDonald, 1984 and 1986; Zartman, 1987b).

But again, these positive aspects of the approach should not obscure the fact that the subject is the same process analyzed elsewhere. The integrative analyst's emphasis on opening options is preliminary to a focus on closure, using expanded possibilities of mutual benefit to buy agreement to an outcome that is less than — or at least different from — what the original demands. The same process can be described as giving something to get something, a process of establishing terms of trade for an exchange of items in the absence of fixed prices and even of fixed monetary units. Using terms mentioned earlier, integrative analysis explores the mechanics of the Shopkeeper confronted with Warrior aspects of the problem and with the need to get around those Warrior aspects. Negotiators — at least diplomatic negotiators and probably most others — are not merely Shopkeepers who can make a deal on any issue. There are, after all, items that are better postponed, interests that are properly nonnegotiable, and limits to acceptable deals that are imposed by security points. If finding a common agreement through this maze is more than a matter of convergence, it is a matter of convergence as well.

A growing branch of this analysis focuses on precise mechanisms for identifying the best possible deal that each party can obtain, given the differences in the nature of their interests. While this is a complex extension of the Nash (1975) solution that occupies a basic position in the strategic and process approaches, the complexity of stakes makes a simple positive-sum outcome too schematic to be useful (Valavanis, 1958; Iklé and Leites, 1962; Barclay and Peterson, 1976, Raiffa, 1982; Sebenius, 1984). The process involves finding as many dimensions of components to the parties' interests as possible in order to provide the best tradeoffs, and thereby insure the greatest durability to the outcome. In addition to finding how much of a conflicting position a party must give up to gain assent, the process also involves finding how much of a non- (or less-) valued position a party can trade to gain a more valued position (Homans, 1961, p. 62). But the element of conflict is never absent, and the process of shaping a single multilateral decision out of conflicting unilateral claims remains.

An Agenda of Unanswered Questions
It should be clear that the study of negotiation has come a considerable way in the past two decades in building and expanding on a common concept of a process. The study today involves far more than the rather loose characterization given in the *International Encyclopedia of the Social Sciences* (Iklé, 1968) that negotiation was a "form of interaction through which (parties). . .try to arrange...a new combination of some of their common and conflicting interests." The "form of interaction" has taken a shape as a process of combining conflicting positions into a common outcome by joint decision, allowing more specific focus of attention on how this is done, whether by power, by patterns of movement, by restructuring stakes and values, by interacting personality types, or by a series of steps. Yet, just as clearly, there is much more to do to know the process, although many of those further directions are indicated by using the common concept of process as a starting point.

One problem raised by the notion of negotiation as a process is that of measuring success, an answer to which is necessary to an evaluation of behavior and prescriptions for its improvement. The question of success is more complex than it may appear (Zartman, 1987a). The nature of negotiation is to arrive at the largest mutually satisfactory agreement with any one (and therefore, each) getting at least enough to make it want to keep the agreement. By that very nature, negotiation is not a process of winning and losing, so success must be evaluated against the problem, not against the adversary. (However, there is a subcategory of negotiations in which one party's aims are to deny the adversary a particular payoff rather than to get as much as possible for itself, making a positive-sum evaluation more complex). Numerous criteria are potentially relevant for the evaluation of success, none of which gives a completely satisfactory answer.

First, *signature* of an agreement is a prima facie or nominal sign of success because it indicates a judgment by the parties that they expect to be better off with the agreement than without it, and that they can do no better by either continuing negotiations or choosing an alternative outcome. Second, this perception can be verified empirically to see if the parties are indeed *better off*, either by comparing their condition before and after the agreement or by comparing their position after the agreement with their presumed position at the same time in the absence of an agreement (a more relevant comparison, but a counterfactual one that involves some judgment [Sebenius, 1984, pp. 72-73]). While nothing says that the parties must be equally well off or even equally better off, further evaluations could also investigate how unequally better off the agreement made them and also whether they were Pareto-optimally better off — that is, whether they had missed opportunities to improve the condition of either of them without making the other less well off. Since some negotiations may be designed to redress power inequities while others may reflect power inequities, the criteria of success based on the relative improvement of the parties' positions will vary. Third, the results can be evaluated against the parties' *opening positions*, with all the caveats about the initial vagueness and inflation of demands that is inherent in the process. Nash solutions and Bartos solutions — discussed under end-point determinism — are a function of opening positions, and can serve as a baseline to evaluate actual outcomes. Despite the fact that they are commonly used, all three of these criteria for evaluation have flaws and complexities that call for further work — there is presently very little — on systems of evaluation.

Another topic of concern is the analysis of negotiations in the case of the three very different types of stakes — those solvable by division, those by creation, and those by exchange. Although much of the earlier literature on negotiation focused on the more obvious topic of division (Schopenhauer, 1896; Nicholson, 1939; Schelling, 1960), with its notion of negotiation as winning or losing, much more attention lately has been drawn to the improvement of exchanges (Homans, 1961; Axelrod, 1970; Nash, 1975; Sebenius, 1984; Zartman, 1987a), with its notion of mutual satisfactions.

The importance of resolving problems by exchange bears much emphasis because parties in conflict often forget that resolution by multilateral decisions means "buying" the other party's agreement through inducements in terms of items that party values, in order to make agreement attractive to itself. At the same time, emphasis on exchange carries a different image of negotiation from an encounter of conceding and winning, portraying instead a positive-sum process where "everyone wins" (something). Unfortunately, this is not the whole picture. Just as there must be a little Warrior in every successful Shopkeeper, so there is inevitably some zero-sum aspect to every positive-sum. Once parties have created a greater good, there is some need to decide how to divide and share it. Furthermore, there are some stakes that are indivisible and others that are unexchangeable. These aspects of negotiation are still not the subject of exhaustive or definitive treatment, and they are somewhat different from the earlier, insightful analysis of redistributive bargaining (Walton and McKersie, 1965).

To date, there are three ways of thinking about the problem of division. First is to replace it in the context of exchange by means of *compensation*. By determining what the item is worth, the other party can counterbalance it through compensatory concessions. Unfortunately, some stakes have an absolute or infinite worth, so that no compensation is possible. Second is to *restructure* perceptions of the stakes so that things are seen differently and the zero-sum nature of the outcomes is removed. Again, some stakes escape such creative reformulation or, even when subject of an attractive formula, they prove intractable in detail. Third is to manipulate notions of *justice* which can then be translated to the specific, an idea akin to the previous notion of a creative formula. But that merely intellectualizes the problem without solving it in many cases, since it is the conflicting notions of justice that make the problems of divisions so intractable in the first place. Obviously, practitioners need more help in ways of dealing with the zero-sum aspects of negotiation — the "Jerusalem Problems" — that lie beyond positive-sum creativity.

A third topic of continuing inquiry highlighted by the generally accepted notion of the negotiation process is the Toughness Dilemma. The question of when to be tough and when to be soft, and the paradox on which it is based, has already been identified as the major tactical question for analysts and practitioners alike. By now, it is plain that there is no way out of the dilemma as presented, and that correct and insightful answers depend on some intermediate variable, such as personality, timing, phase, power, etc. But there is still no sense of any hierarchy among these intermediate variables — other than the eternal debates among disciplines as to which gives the best analysis — and no notions as to which are trumps. Somewhere between the anecdotal proverbs and the unoperationalizable theory lies a not-yet-fully mined terrain of inquiry which may require new parameters.

Finally, an area of negotiation that falls outside the current paradigm is multilateral bargaining. The current process notion has thus far worked to exclude effective consideration of multilateral negotiation, and those that have been treated well tend to be reduced to bilateral analysis (Lipson, 1985, p. 220). When not reduced to dyads, multilateral negotiation tends to be treated merely descriptively even if insightfully, a problem that has posed particular challenges in regard to the successive GATT rounds (Preeg, 1970; Evans, 1971; Cline et al., 1978; Winham, 1987). There have been many excellent attempts to devise an approach to multilateral negotiations (that is, a large number of participants, not merely more than two, as in Raiffa [1982] and Zagare [1978], which indicate some promising directions [Zartman, 1987c]).

One set of approaches treats multilateral negotiations as a problem in *coalition*-formation (Rubin and Brown, 1975, pp. 64 ff.; Snyder and Diesing, 1977, pp. 349 ff.; Raiffa, 1982). However, coalition is a very different process from negotiation. And, to the extent that coalition covers the shaping of outcomes to be decided up or down by some sort of weighted decision rule, it hides a separate negotiation process. There is something going on in the interstices of coalition that needs a separate analysis that is not yet available. Like the strategic approach to bilateral negotiations, to which it is related, coalition analyzes what happens between negotiations and impinges on them but does not capture them.

Secondly, *preferences and scaling* have been used in some different and imaginative ways (Sebenius, 1984; Friedheim, 1987; Hipel and Fraser, 1984). But they too indicate ingredients to an agreement rather than the process by which it is obtained, as in coalition, negotiation becomes voting or at least approaches it. Other approaches are conceivable but have not been used — small group dynamics might provide a new analytical context, as might a conceptual examination of the construction of an agreement out of individual pieces.

In multilateral negotiation, as in the predominant bilateral mode, the two categories of ingredients are parties and stakes. Negotiated agreements are made of stakes by parties. Bilateral negotiation has its general process model as a basis for analysis that permits many approaches to coexist and reenforce each other. Multilateral negotiation needs either to fit into that concept of process or invent its own basic model to enjoy the same benefits. In any case, in regard to bilateral negotiation, there are many blind men but only one elephant, and the two should not be confused with each other.

NOTE

The original version of this paper was presented at a conference on negotiation organized by the Project on the Processes on International Negotiation (PIN) of the International Institute of Applied Systems Analysis, 18-22 May 1987, Laxenburg, Austria.

REFERENCES

Axelrod, R. (1970). *The conflict of interest*. Chicago: Markham.
———. (1984). The evolution of cooperation. New York: Basic.
Bacharach, S. and Lawler, E. (1981). *Bargaining: Power, tactic, and outcomes*. San Francisco: Jossey-Bass.
Baldwin, D. A. (1987). "Bargaining with airline hijackers." In Zartman, 1987b.
Barclay, S. and Peterson, C. (1976). *Multi-attribute utility models*. McLean, Va.: Designs and Decisions, Technical Report 76-1.
Bartos, O. (1974). *Process and outcome of negotiations*. New York: Columbia University Press.
———. (1978). "Simple model of negotiation." In Zartman, 1978.
———. (1987). "How predictable are negotiations?" In Zartman, 1987b.
Bendahmane, D. and McDonald, J., eds. (1984). *International negotiation*. Washington: State Department Foreign Service Institute.
———. and McDonald, J., eds. (1986). *Perspectives on negotiation*. Washington: State Department Foreign Service Institute.
Brams, S. (1985). *Superpower games*. New Haven: Yale University Press.
Cline, W. R. et al. (1978). *Trade negotiations in the Tokyo Round*. Washington: The Brookings Institution.
Coddington, A. (1968). *Theories of the bargaining process*. Chicago: Aldine.
Cross, J. (1969). *The economics of bargaining*. New York: Basic Books.
Davidow, J. (1984). *A peace in Southern Africa*. Boulder, Colo.: Westview.
Deutsch, M. (1973). *Resolution of conflict*. New Haven: Yale University Press.
Druckman, D. (1986). "Stages, turning points, and crises." *Journal of Conflict Resolution* 30: 327-360.
Ellsberg, D. (1975). "Theory and practice of blackmail." In Young, 1975.
Evans, J. W. (1971). *The Kennedy Round in American trade policy*. Cambridge, Mass.: Harvard University Press.
Filley, A. C. (1975). *International conflict resolution*. Glenview, Ill.: Scott Foresman.
Fisher, R. and Ury, W. L. (1981). *Getting to YES*. Boston: Houghton Mifflin.
Friedheim, R. (1987). "The third United Nations conference on the Law of the Sea." In Zartman, 1987.
Gulliver, P. H. (1979). *Disputes and negotiations*. New York: Academic Press.
Habeeb, W. M. (1987). *Asymmetrical negotiations: Panama, Spain, Iceland*. Baltimore: Johns Hopkins.
Hamermesch, J. (1987). "Who 'wins' in wage bargaining?" In Zartman, 1987b.
Harsanyi, J. (1956). "Approaches to the bargaining problem before and after the theory of games." In Young, 1975.
Harsanyi, J. (1977). *Rational behavior and bargaining equilibrium in games and social situations*. New York: Cambridge.
Hicks, J. (1932). *The theory of wages*. London: Macmillan.
Hipel, K. and Fraser, N. (1984). *Conflict analysis*. New York: Elsevier.
Homans, G. (1961). *Social behavior*. New York: Harcourt Brace.
Hopmann, P. T. (1978). "An application of the Richardson Process Model." In Zartman, 1978.
Iklé, F. C. (1968). "Negotiation." In *International Encyclopedia of the social sciences*, vol. 2, p. 117. New York: Macmillan.
———. (1964). *How nations negotiate*. New York: Harper & Row.
——— and Leites, N. (1962). "Political negotiation as a process of modifying utilities." *Journal of Conflict Resolution* 6:19-28.
Jonsson, C. (1978). "Situation-specific vs. actor-specific approaches to international bargaining." *European Journal of Political Research* 6:381-398.
Karrass, C. (1970). *The negotiation game*. New York: World.
Kissinger, H. (1969). "The Vietnam negotiations." *Foreign Affairs* 47:211-234.
Khury, F. (1968). "The etiquette of bargaining in the Middle East." *American Anthropologist* 70:698-706.
Lasswell, H. and Kaplan, A. (1950). *Power and society*. New Haven: Yale University Press.
Lax, D. and Sebenius, J. (1986). *The manager as negotiator*. New York: The Free Press.
Lipson, C. (1985). "Banker's dilemma." *World Politics* 38 (October): 200-255.
Nash, J. (1950). "The bargaining problem." In Young, 1975.

Nicholson, H. (1939). *Diplomacy*. New York: Oxford.

Nierrenberg, G. (1973). *Fundamentals of negotiating*. New York: Hawthorn.

Nyerges, J. (1987). "Ten commandments for a negotiator." *Negotiation Journal* 3:21-27.

Pen, J. (1952). "A general theory of bargaining." In Young, 1975.

Pillar, P. (1983). *Negotiation peace*. Princeton: Princeton University Press.

Preeg, E. (1970). *Traders and diplomats*. Washington: The Brookings Institution.

Pruitt, D. (1981). *Negotiation behavior*. New York: Academic Press.

Raiffa, H. (1982). *The art and science of negotiation*. Cambridge, Mass.: Harvard University Press.

Rubin, J. and Brown, B. (1975). *The social psychology of bargaining and negotiation*. New York: Academic Press.

Saunders, H. (1985). *The other walls*. Washington: American Enterprise Institute.

Schelling, T. (1960). *The strategy of conflict*. Cambridge, Mass.: Harvard University Press.

Schopenhauer, A. (1896). *The art of controversy*. London: Allen & Unwin.

Sebenius, J. K. (1984). *Negotiating the Law of the Sea*. Cambridge, Mass.: Harvard University Press.

Simon, H. (1957). *Models of man*. New York: Wiley.

Snyder, G. and Diesing, P. (1977). *Conflict among nations*. Princeton: Princeton University Press.

Valavanis, S. (1958). "Resolution of conflict when utilities interact." *Journal of Conflict Resolution* 2:156-169.

Wagner, H. (1957). "A unified treatment of bargaining theory." In Young, 1975.

Walton, R. and McKersie, R. (1965). *A behavioral theory of labor negotiations*. New York: McGraw Hill.

Winham, G. (1987). *International trade and the Tokyo Round negotiation*. Princeton: Princeton University Press.

Wriggins, H. (1987). "Up for auction." In Zartman, 1987b.

Young, O., ed. (1975). *Bargaining*. Urbana, Ill.: University of Illinois.

Zartman, I. W., ed. (1978). *The negotiation process*. Newbury Park, Calif.: Sage.

———, ed. (1983). *Ripe for resolution*. New York: Oxford University Press.

———, ed. (1985). "negotiating from asymmetry: The North-South Stalemate" *Negotiation Journal* 1:121-138.

———, ed. (1987a). *Positive sum: Improving North-South negotiations*. New Brunswick, N. J. : Transaction.

———, ed. (1987b). *The 50% solution*, 2nd ed. New Haven: Yale University Press.

———, (1987c). "Managing multilateral complexity: Many are called but few chose." Paper presented to the American Political Science Association, Chicago, September 1987.

——— and Berman, M. (1982). *The practical negotiator*. New Haven: Yale University Press.

Zeuthen, F. (1930). "Economic warfare." In Young, 1975.

Interests: The Measure of Negotiation

David A. Lax and James K. Sebenius

People negotiate to further their interests. And negotiation advisers urge attention to interests — often solemnly, as if the suggestion were original and surprising. Yet Socrates' admonition to "Know Thyself" surely scoops any late twentieth century advice of this sort. So, academic compulsiveness aside, why write an article on interests or, more to the point, why read one?

The answer, in part, is that negotiators often focus on interests, but conceive of them too narrowly. We will argue for a more expansive conception of negotiators' interests. Moreover, interests often conflict, and simply listing them without understanding the tradeoffs among them is a bit like writing out a recipe without including the proportions. In addition to determining interests, negotiators need ways to assess the relative importance of those various interests. We will try to clarify the logic of assessing tradeoffs.

As hard as it may be to sort out one's own interests, understanding how others see theirs — *their* subjective scheme of values as perceived through their peculiar psychological filters — can be extraordinarily difficult. Obviously, suggesting a stretch "in the other person's shoes" is good advice; equally obviously, it is only a starting point. In this article we will try to go further.

An Expansive Conception of a Negotiator's Interests

In evaluating the interests at stake, a typical negotiator might focus on commodities that can be bought and sold or on concrete terms that can be written into a contract or treaty. And negotiators definitely have such interests: the crippled plaintiff desperately wants compensation; a sales manager cares intensely about prices, profit margins, return on investment, and personal compensation; managers may derive value from seeing their particular product sweep the market or furthering some vision of the public interest.

Throughout this article, we assume that negotiators want to do well for themselves. Of course, "doing well" is only measured with respect to the things they care about, whether out of direct self-interest or concern for the welfare of others. Thus, doing "better" in a negotiation need not imply pressing for more money or a bigger share; rather, it means advancing the totality of one's interests, which may include money and other tangibles as well as fairness, the well-being of one's counterparts, and the collegiality of the process. For instance, furthering Robert's interests may mean taking less money to obtain a fair settlement by a friendly process; by the same token,

David A. Lax is managing director and general partner in ECO Management, New York City. **James K. Sebenius** is Professor of Management at the Harvard Business School, Boston, Mass. 02163.

Helen may want only to publicly humiliate her counterpart and extract from him the very biggest check.

It is especially common in business negotiations, however, to assume that interests extend only to the bottom line. Yet imagine holding rigidly to this assumption when negotiating with the number two executive of a technical products company from the upper half of the Fortune 500. He echoed his firm's philosophy when he stated:

> Our most important goal is to do a good job. We don't have a specific growth target, but what we want to do is make a contribution. Not just a "me too" thing, but to develop technically superior products. Another goal is to earn our way, to grow from our own resources. A third goal is to make this an interesting and satisfactory place to work. The fourth goal. . .there must be a fourth goal. I mentioned it also in a speech at [a nearby university]. Oh yes, the fourth goal is to make a profit. (Donaldson and Lorsch, 1984, p. 85)

Negotiators' interests can go beyond the obvious and tangible. Take for example the almost universal quest for social approval or the simple pleasure one derives from being treated with respect, even in a one-time encounter. A stockbroker may want to build a relationship with a customer because of the future business it may bring; or a plaintiff, anxious at the thought of a trial, may be willing to take a reduced settlement to avoid courtroom trauma. Negotiators have good reasons to be concerned with their reputations. A person who is widely known never to recede from a position may rarely be called on for concessions. Fisher and Ury (1981) argue that a negotiator should seek to be known for reaching agreements only by means of "objective" principles; once achieved, among other effects, such a "principled" reputation may reduce the need to haggle.

Beyond concern about reputation, relationship, and process, negotiators often care about subtle aspects of precedent. For example, Luther — a product manager in a fast-growing medical devices firm — confronted his colleague Francoise for the second time with a vigorous demand for priority use of the firm's advertising department — even though Francoise had informally "reserved" this block of the ad department's time for her people. After analyzing her interests in this unexpected negotiation, Francoise balked at a few seemingly reasonable settlements that Luther suggested. Why? Francoise sought to avoid two undesirable precedents: first, in the *substance* of the issue (*her* division needed to count absolutely on future ad department reservations); and second, in the *procedure* set for raising a whole range of similar matters (she wanted to bolster the use of established policies). Concern with both types of precedent abounds in organizations and elsewhere.

Strategic interests are often at stake for managers. By this, we refer to the alignment of a particular decision with the manager's long-term personal or institutional strategy. Suppose that a prompt investment in the capacity to manage mutual funds appears likely to have high short-term potential for a firm whose long-term plan has been to develop expertise in real estate investments. Would a key manager's proposal now to devote substantial energy to mutual funds research and investment be wise? Recourse to strategic rather than short-term financial analysis may unravel the firm's best interests in this case.

Through actions in one negotiation, a manager may have an interest in reducing the cost of later encounters and in affecting their outcomes. A manager may thus strive to create in subordinates the impression that explicit bargaining is impossible and that commands must be obeyed. Perhaps the back-and-forth process has become too costly and inefficient for the task at hand. In such cases, paradoxically, a prime managerial interest in routine dealings may actually be to drive out future overt bargaining. It is exceedingly ironic that a powerful interest to be achieved through a determined pattern of negotiation may be to establish an impregnable image of rigid hierarchy, potent command, and iron control — that brooks *no* conscious negotiation. Especially in early encounters, say, between a freshly hired vice president and others in the firm, the new officer may regard the establishment of a favorable pattern of others' automatic deference to "suggestions" as of central interest. Or the new officer may strongly weigh the effects on his or her perceived track record or esteem as an expert so that others may be more likely to show deference in the future.

Comparing obvious, "bottom line" interests with "others" — reputation, precedent, relationships and the like — a very detailed study of corporate resource allocation in a multidivisional chemical company noted:

> These are the dimensions a manager takes into account when he makes his decisions. In some instances they far outweigh the importance of the substantive issues in his assessment of decision-making priorities.
>
> It is worth pausing to emphasize this point. There is a very strong tendency in financial or decision-making treatments of capital budgeting to regard the personal status of managers as noise, "a source of bias." . . .Theoreticians do not consider the problem a rational manager faces as he considers committing himself to a project over time. He has made other commitments in the past, other projects are competing for funds and engineering at the division level, and other managers are competing for the jobs he seeks. At the same time those same managers are his peers and friends. Whatever he does, he is more than likely going to have to live with those same men for a decade or more. While only some projects are technically or economically independent, all are organizationally interdependent. (Bower, 1972, p. 302)

It is not always easy to know how to evaluate interests; sometimes they may derive from interactions too complex to understand directly. In such cases, carefully chosen *proxy interests* may help. For example, the President of the United States cannot possibly predict the effects of any particular negotiated outcome on all of his substantive interests over the course of his term or beyond. Taking account of this, Richard Neustadt, in his classic bargaining manual, *Presidential Power* (1980), counsels him to evaluate his dealings in terms of three particular interests. The first is obvious: his interests in the *substance* of the immediate issue.

Second, however, the president's *professional reputation* can heavily affect the reactions of important Washingtonians to his later concerns and actions. The president needs the resources and cooperation of these Washingtonians to carry out his programs. Thus, beyond the substance of the issue, Neustadt suggests, the effect of the current negotiation on the president's professional reputation among Washingtonians should be a proxy interest reflecting, in part, his ability to get the Washingtonians to act in accord with his subsequent desires.

Third, Neustadt argues that the president should evaluate the effect of his actions on his *popular prestige*. High prestige reflects the strength of his mandate and influences Washingtonians. It is, in part, a proxy interest; actions that enhance his public prestige improve his chances favorably to influence subsequent outcomes of direct concern. A president may also value popular prestige for its own sake. As negotiator, the president may well have to trade these interests off against each other; for example, he may yield somewhat on his substantive interest in the immediate issue to enhance his reputation and prestige elsewhere. In many positions less complex than that of the president, negotiators' interests are difficult to enumerate because the link between actions and eventual outcomes is hazy. In such cases, a negotiator may benefit by finding simplified proxy interests that predict outcomes either directly or indirectly, by predicting the negotiator's subsequent influence on outcomes of concern.

In short, interests include anything that the negotiator cares about, any concerns that are evoked by the issues discussed. Clarifying interests, however, can sometimes be difficult. We have often found that two distinctions can help.

Two Helpful Distinctions

Interests, Issues and Positions

Negotiators seek to reach agreement on specific *positions* on a specific set of *issues*. For example, a potential employee may initially demand $36,000 (the position) for salary (the issue). The job seeker's underlying *interests* may be in financial security, enhanced lifestyle, organizational status, and advanced career prospects. Or, the desire of a Midwestern utility company to build a dam may collide with farmers' needs for water and environmentalists' concern for the downstream habitat of endangered whooping cranes. Increased economic return, irrigated crops, and preserved species are the relevant *interests*; they conflict over the *issue* of the dam's construction, *positions* on which are pro and con.

Negotiation often assume that issues directly express underlying interests. Of course, many different sets of issues may reflect the same interests: a country might seek to serve its interest in mineral development through negotiations over *issues* as varied as simple royalty concessions, joint ventures, or service contracts. Conceivably, the country's interest could be equally satisfied by different terms on each of these alternative issues. The issue at hand, however, may by only a proxy for imperfectly related interests. For example, the United States in the Paris Peace Talks may have insisted on a round table and the North Vietnamese a rectangular one. The relevant compromise would hardly have been oval. The real interests were far from the rectangular versus round issue.

Many negotiators retard creativity by failing to distinguish the issues under discussion from their underlying interests. When the issues under discussion match the interests at stake, modifications of the issues sometimes enable all parties to satisfy their interests better. For example, recall the conflict between the Midwestern utility company, the farmers, and the environmentalists. After several years of costly and embittering litigation, the parties came to a resolution by a shift to issues that matched their underlying interests in a more fruitful manner. By moving from positions ("yes" and "no") on the issue of the dam's construction of discussions about the nature of downstream water guarantees, the amount of a trust fund to protect the whooping crane habitat, and the size of the dam, the parties reached an agreement that left all of them better off.

Negotiators who mistakenly see their interests as perfectly aligned with their positions on issues may be less likely to shift issues creatively. They might even suspiciously oppose proposals to modify the issues. Indeed, in attempting to protect their perceived interests, such negotiators may dig their heels in hard to avoid budging from their desired positions. In the "dam versus no dam" conflict, positions could have hardened to a point where the grim determination of each side to prevail over the other — whatever the cost — would have ruled out any real search for preferable options. At a minimum, such rigid dealings can be frustrating and time-consuming: impasses or poor agreements often result.

The prevalence of hard-fought, time-consuming, unimaginative "positional" negotiations led Fisher and Ury (1981, p. 11) to propose a general rule: "Focus on interests, not positions." While we think that negotiators should always keep the distinction clearly in mind, focusing exclusively on interests may not always be wise. When parties have deep and conflicting ideological differences, for example, satisfactory agreements on "smaller" issues may only be possible if ideological concerns do not arise. In such cases, the negotiations should focus on the issues or on a much narrower set of interests — not the full set of underlying interests. Two hostile but neighboring countries embroiled in tribal, religious, or ideological conflict may be best off handling a sewage problem on their common border by only dealing with this more limited issue. Or leftist guerilla leaders, each with an underlying interest in ruling the country, might unite on the issue of overthrowing the rightist dictator; an agreement that attempted to reconcile their underlying interests would likely be more difficult to achieve. Moreover, a negotiator may choose to focus on an issue that, for legal or other reasons, provides greater leverage than do discussions of underlying interests. The nature-loving group that has an abiding interest in preventing development may develop a sudden attachment to the issue of wetlands protection if the Wetlands Preservation Act provides the strongest grounds for negotiating with and deterring developers.

At times, a tenacious focus on positions may yield desirable results. With a group of landowners, the CEO of a major mining company had negotiated the general outlines of a contract along with a few critical particulars. Then the CEO turned the rest of the negotiations over to a company lawyer to finish in short order — before a hard-to-obtain environmental permit expired. One provision that the second group of negotiators inherited had not been extensively debated before. Yet its tentative resolution, while barely acceptable to the landowners, clearly would confer great benefits on the company. Though the landowners' representatives sought to focus on "interests" and "fairness" in order to undo the provision, the company's lawyer made a powerful commitment to it and turned a completely deaf ear to all argument, urging instead that they get on with "unresolved" matters. Though this tactic risked negative repercussions on the other issues, the lawyer's firm commitment to a position was an effective means of claiming value in this instance.

Thus interests should be distinguished from issues and positions.[1] Focusing on interests can help one develop a better understanding of mutual problems and invent creative solutions. But such a focus may not always be desirable when, for example, underlying interests are diametrically opposed or when a focus on particular issues or positions provides leverage. Whatever the focus, however, interests measure the value of any position or agreement.

Intrinsic and Instrumental Interests

It should be clear that negotiators may have many kinds of interests: money and financial security, a particular conception of the public interest, the quality of products, enhancing a reputation as a skilled bargainer, maintaining a working relationship, precedents, and so on. However, one distinction —between intrinsic and instrumental interests — can provide an economical way to capture some important qualities of interests, call negotiators' attention to often-overlooked, sometimes subtle interests, and lead to improved agreements.

One's interests in an issue is *instrumental* if favorable terms on the issue are valued because of their effect on subsequent dealings. One's interest in an issue is *intrinsic* if one values favorable terms of settlement on the issue independent of any subsequent dealings. Thus, a divorcing parent's interest in gaining custody of his or her child, the farmer's interest in water rights, or a country's interest in secure borders can usefully be thought of as intrinsic interests. Such interests need not have any obvious or agreed-upon economic value. For example, Charles, a 60-year-old venture capitalist, was negotiating the dissolution of a strikingly successful technology partnership with Marie, a young, somewhat standoffish woman whom he had brought on as a partner two years before. At first Charles bargained very hard over the financial terms because he viewed them as indicating who had really contributed important ideas and skills to the venture's success. When Marie belatedly acknowledged her genuine respect for his ideas and contributions, Charles became much less demanding on the financial issues. In this instance, it happened that the venture capitalist also had a strong intrinsic interest in psychic gratification from acknowledgement of his role as mentor and father-figure.

Most issues affect both intrinsic and instrumental interests. Dealings with a subordinate who wants to hire an assistant can arouse an intrinsic interest in the overall size of the budget as well as a concern with the perceived precedent the hiring will set in the eyes of the subordinate's peers — an instrumental interest. Recognizing the distinction may lead to improved agreements; the subordinate who can create a justifiable device to prevent decisions about his or her staff support from setting precedents may well receive authorization to hire a new assistant.

One of the main reasons we focus on the intrinsic-instrumental distinction is for the light it sheds on three often-misunderstood aspects of negotiation: interests in the process, in relationships, and in principles.

"Process" Interests — Intrinsic and Instrumental. Analysts often assume that negotiators evaluate agreements by measuring the value obtained from the outcome. Yet, negotiators may care about the process of bargaining as well. Even with no prospect of further interaction, some would prefer a negotiated outcome reached by pleasant, cooperative discussion to the same

outcome reached by abusive, threat-filled dealings. Others might even derive value from a strident process that gives them the satisfied feeling of having extracted something from their opponents. Either way, negotiators can have intrinsic interests in the character of the negotiation process itself.

Beyond such intrinsic valuation, an unpleasant process can dramatically affect future dealings; the supplier who is berated and threatened may be unresponsive when cooperation at a later point would help. Indeed, negotiators often have strong instrumental interests in building trust and confidence early in the negotiation process in order to facilitate jointly beneficial agreements.

"Relationship" Interests — Intrinsic and Instrumental. Negotiators often stress the value of their relationships; this interest sometimes achieves an almost transcendent status. For example, Fisher and Ury (1981, p. 20) say that "every negotiator has two kinds of interests: in the substance and in the relationship." Many negotiators derive intrinsic value from developing or furthering a pleasant relationship. Moreover, when repeated dealings are likely, most negotiators perceive the instrumental value of developing an effective working relationship. After studying hundreds of managers in many settings, John Kotter (1985, p. 40) sensibly concluded:

> Good working relationships based on some combination of respect, admiration, perceived need, obligation, and friendship are a critical source of power in helping to get things done. Without these relationships, even the best possible idea could be rejected or resisted in an environment where diversity breeds suspicion and interdependence precludes giving orders to most of the relevant players. Furthermore, since these relationships serve as important information channels, without them one may never be able to establish the information one needs to operate effectively.

Of course, the dissolution of a partnership or the divorce of a childless couple with few assets, the parties may find no instrumental value in furthering their relationship; that is, the parties would not be willing to trade substantive gains on, say, financial terms, to enhance their future dealings. In fact, a bitter divorcing couple may actually prefer a financial outcome that requires absolutely no future contact over another that is better for both in tax terms but requires them to deal with each other in the future. Similarly, a division head with two valuable but constantly warring employees may have a keen interest in separating them organizationally to prevent *any* active relationship between them. And, when dealing with an obnoxious salesperson who has come to the door or by the office, one's interest in the "relationship" may mainly be to terminate it.

Interest in "Principles" — Intrinsic and Instrumental. Negotiators may discover shared norms or principles relevant to their bargaining problem. Such norms may include equal division, more complex distributive judgments, historical or ethical rationales, objective or accepted standards, as well as notions that simply seem fair or are represented as such. (Gulliver, 1979; Fisher and Ury, 1981). Acting in accord with such a norm or principle may be of intrinsic interest to one or more of the parties; for example, a settlement of $532 — arrived at in accord with the mutually acknowledged principle that each party should be paid in proportion to time worked — may be valued quite differently than the same dollar figure reached by haggling. Of course, an acknowledged norm need not be an absolute value in a negotiation: it may be partly or fully traded off against interests.

Even when none of the parties derive intrinsic value from acting in accord with a particular principle, it may still guide agreement. Principles and simple notions often serve as naturally prominent focal points for choosing one settlement within the range of possible outcomes (Schelling, 1960). For example, equal division of a windfall may seem so irresistibly natural to the partners in a small firm that they would scarcely consider negotiation over who should get more.

The principles that guide agreement in the first of many related disputes may set a powerful precedent. Thus, negotiators may work hard to settle the first dispute on the basis of principles that they believe will yield favorable outcomes in subsequent disputes. They may take a loss with respect to intrinsic interests in the first negotiation in order to satisfy their instrumental interests in the principles used to guide the agreement.

In short, with many less tangible interests — such as process, relationships, or fairness — a negotiator should ask why they are valued. Distinguishing between their instrumental and intrinsic components can help. But even with these components sorted out, how can a negotiator go about assessing their "relative importance?" More generally, what logic guides setting priorities among conflicting interests?

Thinking About Tradeoffs

Listing one's own interests as well as a best guess at those of other parties is certainly useful. But difficult questions tend to arise in negotiations that force one to make sacrifices on some interests in order to gain on others: How much of a trade is desirable? In buying a seller-financed house, how should Ralph evaluate higher purchase prices compared to lower mortgage interest rates? How much more should a manufacturer be willing to pay for the next quality grade of components? How much should a sales manager trade on price for the prospects of a better relationship? How much should a manager be willing to give up on substance to secure a favorable precedent?

Thinking about tradeoffs is often excruciatingly difficult and badly done. Yet, whether or not negotiators choose to ponder priorities, they effectively make tradeoffs by their choices and agreements in negotiation. Because we believe that negotiators benefit by being self-conscious and reflective about their interests and the tradeoffs they are willing to make, we propose several methods to illuminate tradeoffs. These methods draw primarily on judgment about interests, not about negotiating. The methods we consider help to convert developed substance judgments into forms useful for analysis and practice (e.g., Raiffa, 1982; Keeney and Raiffa, 1976; Barclay and Peterson, 1976; or Greenhalgh and Neslin, 1981). Finally, although these techniques have formal origins rooted in management science and technical economics, we find that their prime value comes in their contribution to clear thinking rather than from their potential for quantification. While negotiators may often choose not to quantify their tradeoffs, they may benefit greatly by employing the same style of thought in comparing interests.

Certain tradeoffs are easy to specify. The present value or total cost of a loan is a well-known mathematical function of the amount and duration of the loan and the interest rate. Thus, beginning with a given price and interest rate for the seller-financed home, Ralph can calculate precisely the benefit of a one percent decrease in interest rate and how much of a price increase would be willing to accept before he became indifferent to the original price and interest rate. Yet other tradeoffs may seem much harder to think about, especially ones that involve "intangibles" like principles, anxiety about a process, or the relationship.

Assembling Tradeoffs Among Seemingly Intangible Interests. Seemingly intangible tradeoffs can also be deal with in analogous ways. For instance, consider Joan, a plaintiff crippled in a car accident who wishes to negotiate an out-of-court settlement with an insurance company that is better than her alternative of a full court trial. Suppose that, only taking trial uncertainties and legal fees into account, Joan would be willing to accept a settlement of $300,000. But this analysis leaves her uncomfortable. The trial would cause her great anxiety, and her analysis so far does not take this anxiety into account. How should she consider the anxiety factor in her preparation for negotiation? Perhaps she should lower her minimum requirements, but by how much? How can she even think about this?

After several anxious, inconclusive struggles with this assessment, a friend asks Joan to imagine the anxiety she would feel during a trial. The friend then asks her to imagine that a pharmacist offered to *sell* her a magic potion that would completely eliminate the feeling of anxiety from court proceedings. What would be the most she would pay for the potion before the trial? Would she pay $10? "That's silly. Of course." Would she pay $100? "Sure." $100,000? "Certainly not, that's one-third of my minimum settlement!" What about $50,000? "Probably not." $1,000? "I think so." $10,000? "Well, that's a tough one. But, if push came to shove, the trial would be an awful experience. So probably yes." $25,000? "Maybe not, but I'm not sure." . . .And so on.

We want to stress our opinion that the important point in making such assessments is not quantitative precision. An absolutely precise cutoff would seem artificial. What is important is to get a sense of the order of magnitude of the value Joan places on avoiding anxiety. Here we see that she would pay between $10,000 and $25,000 or a little more to eliminate the anxiety. Thus, she should be willing to reduce her minimum settlement requirements by that amount because a negotiated settlement would avoid the anxiety. She should, of course, strive for more, but she can feel more comfortable knowing that her minimum requirements now roughly reflect her interest in avoiding trial anxiety.

Similarly, Mr. Acton, the insurance company executive, may feel that going to trial against a plaintiff who evokes such sympathy will harm his firm's reputation. How should he value this reputation damage and how should it affect his approach to the negotiation? As described in this thumbnail sketch, in comparing the court alternative to possible negotiated agreements, the executive sees two interests at stake: money and reputation. Acton could try to value the reputation damage directly by estimating the number of present and future customers he would lose and the financial loss this would create. If he finds such direct assessment difficult, he could attempt, like the plaintiff, to place a monetary value on the "intangible" interest. What is the most he would be willing to pay a public relations firm to completely undo the reputation damage? If the most he would be willing to pay is $20,000, Acton could modify his maximum acceptable settlement and take this into account when negotiating with the plaintiff.

In some instances, concerns with precedent, prestige, anxiety, reputation, and similar interests loom large; negotiators focus on them and, because such interests are difficult to weigh, feel paralyzed with respect to their choices as a negotiator. After fretting inconclusively, the negotiators may ask themselves how much they would be willing to pay to have the prestige conferred upon them by other means. They might discover that they value the prestige possibilities little relative to possible substantive gains. Or, by similar analytical introspection, they might discover that they would be willing to pay only a small sum to avoid an undesirable precedent. In such cases, the negotiators would have learned a great deal. First, the intangible interest is a second or third order concern rather than a first order one as they originally feared; they can now feel freer to make concessions on the less important interest if necessary. Second, unless the choice between packages becomes close, they may need to pay little attention to this interest. In short, much of the purpose of such assessments is more to discover the relative importance of different interests rather than to be painstakingly precise about monetary or other valuations.

In other instances, interests in precedent or reputation overwhelm the possible improvements in substantive outcome. Suppose that Jeff, a lawyer working on a highly publicized class action suit against a corporation, has an interest in his financial compensation and in the reputation he might develop by exceeding expectations for how favorable a settlement he can get for his clients. Even if Jeff finds the range of possible financial compensation paltry, he may see that his interest in enhancing his reputation and political ambitions is extremely well-served by every increment he can obtain in the settlement. Thus, he may bargain tenaciously on his client's behalf. In this case, the nonmonetary interest was the first order concern. In other instances, simple self-assessment may suggest that the monetary and nonmonetary issues are roughly comparable concerns or that the monetary aspects predominate.

A More General Approach for Assessing Tradeoffs. The judgment that one "cares more about quality than price" cannot be made independently of the *range* of possible values of quality and price. That is, in the abstract, a manufacturer may say that it cares more about quality than about price. However, while the total increment in technologically feasible quality may be small, the price differential necessary to achieve it may be undesirably high. Relative to the feasible range of qualities, the manufacturer actually places greater weight on price. Similarly, the management negotiator who professes to care more about obtaining productivity-enhancing changes in work rules than about wages must analyze the ranges of work rules and wages that are possible outcomes from this negotiation. Wages might range from a minimum of $10 an hour to a maximum of $13 an hour — and this increment would have a significant impact on the competitiveness of the negotiator's firm. Yet if the increment from the worst to best possible work rules was small and would only marginally affect the firm's competitiveness, the negotiator should give greater weight or importance to wages. The tradeoff rate should result from comparing the valuation of the wage increment between $10 and $13 with the valuation of the benefit of moving from the worst to best work rules

— not on the judgment that the negotiator "cares more" about one or the other issue in general.

This leads to a straightforward method for such assessments. Like the preceding examples, the purpose of this method is to help organize one's subjective judgments to get a clearer sense of the relative importance of various interests. Again, we are concerned with orders of magnitude rather than precise quantification. To illustrate the central elements of this approach, we shall work through the thought process in a highly stylized, simplified example and then discuss the more general lessons for thinking about tradeoffs.

Assessing Lisa's Interests

Consider Lisa, a 34-year-old second level manager who has been offered a position in another division of her firm as the supervisor of a soon-to-be created department. She must soon negotiate with William, a long-time engineer who moved into senior management ranks seven years ago and has cautiously but steadily improved his division's results. Lisa has narrowed the issues she will have to negotiate to three: the salary, vacation time, and the number of staff for the new department. We will ask her to analyze her interests and then draw on her subjective judgment to assign 100 points to the issues in a way that reflects their relative importance to her. To begin, she should assess the range of possibilities for each issue. Based on a variety of discussions with William, with others in the firm, and on the results of numerous feelers, Lisa has concluded that the salary could plausibly run from $32,000 to $40,000, the vacation from two to four weeks, and the staff size from 10 to 20. Suppose that her current job pays her $32,000, gives her four weeks of vacation, and assigns her a staff of 10 (See Table 1).

TABLE 1
LISA'S NEGOTIATION: ISSUES AND RANGES

Issues	Range
Salary	$32 — 40,000
Vacation	2-4 Weeks
Staff	10-20 people

Lisa should start by imagining the least appealing scenario: $32,000, two weeks of vacation, and a staff of 10. Her next task is to assess her relative preferences on each issue. To do this, she must decide which one of the three incremental improvements she values most. That is, would she feel best with (a) $40,000 salary but only two weeks vacation and 10 subordinates; (b) four weeks vacation but only $32,000 salary and 10 subordinates; or (c) 20 subordinates but only $32,000 salary and two weeks of vacation? In making this evaluation, she examines her interests in money and the effects of a higher salary on her satisfaction, as well as the peace of mind and pleasure from longer vacations. On further reflection, Lisa realizes that she must also consider her ability to do her job effectively and thus to improve her subsequent career prospects. A bigger staff could help her effectiveness directly; enhanced organizational status from a big staff and high salary may independently bolster her job prospects as well as add to her effectiveness. Suppose that after contemplating her interests in this way, Lisa decides that she prefers the salary increment to the other two increments, and, of the other two, she prefers the staff increment to the vacation possibilities.

Now comes a harder part. She must allocate 100 points — importance weights — among the three increments in a way that reflects her underlying subjective feelings. Would she prefer the package with the largest salary increment but minimum vacation and staff to the package with the lowest salary but maximum staff and vacation? If so, she should allocate more than 50 points to the salary increment. If she is indifferent between the two packages, she should allocate exactly 50 points to the salary increment.

Lisa decides that she slightly prefers the salary increment and assigns an importance weight of 60 points to the salary increment. Now, she can either assign importance weights to the staff and vacation increments or she can think about the relative value she places on each of the possible salaries. She begins with the latter and again compares ranges. How does she compare the salary increment from $32,000 to $35,000 with the increment between $35,000 and $40,000? The first increment would improve her housing and thus enhance her life in direct and important ways; the second increment although larger, would go toward luxuries and saving. She thus feels indifferent between the first, smaller increment and the second, larger increment. In other words, she gives 30 of the 60 importance points to the increment between $32,000 and $35,000 and 30 to the remaining increment.

Table 2 presents importance scores that reflect Lisa's preferences for salary; Figure 1 shows a plot of them. Interpreting this assessment, Lisa would get 0 points if she receives a salary of $32,000, 30 points if she manages to receive $35,000, 60 points if she is able to get a salary of $40,000. She must now assign points reflecting her comparative valuations of the vacation and staff increments. Naturally, making an assessment like this can feel like comparing apples and oranges — but Lisa will end up doing it either explicitly or implicitly.

TABLE 2
LISA'S ASSESSMENT OF THE VALUE OF DIFFERENT SALARIES

Salary	Importance Points Assigned
$32,000	0
$33,000	10
$34,000	20
$35,000	30
$36,000	36
$37,000	42
$38,000	48
$39,000	54
$40,000	60

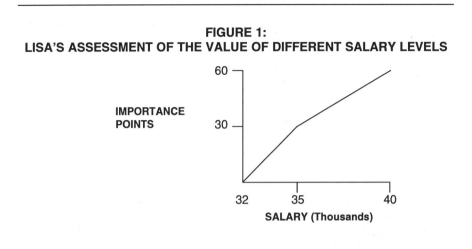

FIGURE 1:
LISA'S ASSESSMENT OF THE VALUE OF DIFFERENT SALARY LEVELS

She can assess her valuations of the other two issues by comparing their increments directly, or by comparing one of the increments with her salary assessments. For example, how does the increment from 10 to 20 subordinates compare with the salary increment from $32,000 to $35,000? If Lisa is indifferent, she should assign 30 importance points to the staff increment and, thus, the remaining 10 points to the vacation increment. She decides and continues in this manner, finishing the assessment by assigning 20 of the 30 importance points to the increment between 10 and 15 subordinates and 10 points to the remaining increment. Lastly, she assigns eight of the 10 vacation points to getting the third week of vacation and two points to the remaining week.

Table 3 shows a scoring system that reflects this assessment. From the table, a $35,000 salary, three weeks of vacation, and 15 subordinates would be valued at 58 points (30 + 8 + 20) whereas a salary of $37,500, two weeks of vacation and 16 subordinates would be valued at 67 points (45 + 0 + 22).

TABLE 3
LISA'S ASSESSMENT OF THE IMPORTANCE OF
SALARY, VACATION, AND STAFF SIZE

Salary (Thousands)	Importance Points	Weeks of Vacation	Importance Points	Staff Size	Importance Points
32	0	2	0	10	0
33	10	3	8	15	20
34	20	4	10	20	30
35	30				
36	36				
37	42				
38	48				
39	54				
40	60				

It is worth noting that all the scoring is relative to an arbitrarily chosen zero point. That is, the "worst" agreement — $32,000, two weeks of vacation and 10 subordinates, the bottom of the range for each issue — receives a score of zero. All other possible agreements are scored relative to this "worst" agreement. The important comparison, though, is with Lisa's current job which, at a salary of $32,000, four weeks of vacation, and 10 subordinates is valued at 10 points. Although any such scoring system is necessarily rough, Lisa can use it to evaluate possible agreements and to understand the tradeoffs she may have to make.

Comparing different increments can be difficult, but a few tricks can sometimes facilitate the process. For example, Lisa might construct one package of $32,000, two weeks of vacation, and 20 subordinates and another of $32,000, four weeks of vacation, and 10 subordinates. But, to compare them? Lisa might imagine that the phone rings and the call eliminates one of the options. Which option would feel worse to lose? Or, suppose that a coin flip will determine the choice of packages. Is a fifty-fifty chance of losing each appropriate? Or, would she prefer sixty-forty chances favoring one of the packages?

In helping Lisa construct this scoring system, we assumed that the value of an increment on one issue did not depend on how other issues were resolved; thus, scoring a package simply involves adding the points obtained on each issue. In some situations, though, the value of the outcome on one issue depends on how other issues are resolved.[2] For example, suppose that with a high salary Lisa would like a larger number of subordinates. With a low salary, however, she might feel aggrieved; a larger staff would mean more responsibility for which she was not compensated. Thus, how she values staff size could depend on her salary level. Such interdependent preferences could be assessed using more elaborate techniques, but the general logic of defining and comparing increments would remain roughly analogous.

Assessing William's Interests

Lisa, in addition to assessing her own interests, must also do the same for her negotiating counterpart and potential supervisor, William. Her preliminary investigations had fairly confidently bounded the ranges of the issues, but now the question becomes how *he* sees *his* real interests in them. Tentative discussions with William left Lisa little doubt that he would prefer to pay less, allow shorter vacations, and get by with as few new staff as possible. In fact, during a meeting in which he enthusiastically offered her the job "in principle," William sketched the terms he felt were appropriate: "a bit over $30,000, a few weeks vacation, and only the staff you really need." More than a little daunted by this less than forthcoming stance, Lisa feels a strong need to develop a much deeper understanding of William's interests.

Asking around, she discovers that William is generally not at ease with "personnel" matters and that he tends to seek out whatever firm "policy" he can find for guidance. Fortunately for Lisa, little in the firm would be directly comparable to the new department she would head. But a few discreet inquiries turn up the fact that the supervisor of the firm's largest department makes around $39,000. Since the new department is an important endeavor, Lisa feels fairly certain that salary money will not be too tight, but that the other supervisor's compensation will make any salary above $39,000 very uncomfortable for William to consider.

In trying to ferret out William's feelings about vacation, Lisa discovers that he has been a hard worker, seldom taking more than a few days or a week each year. Also he has mentioned the extreme importance of dedication and long hours during the uncertain start-up of this new organization unit. Lisa infers that the prospect of her taking extended vacations early on, while not at all uncommon elsewhere in the firm, would not sit at all well with William.

Finally, on the matter of staffing, Lisa recalls some comments William made during a long lunch they had together to explore the possibilities of her heading the new department. In the course of their conversation, he had mentioned two significant incidents from his career. First, he recalled extreme pressure on the engineering group some years ago to come up with a new design. The group was simply too small to produce the needed result in time. Quality of work and quality of life "needlessly suffered" and, to William's mind, that kind of "economizing" makes no business or personal sense. Yet William also recounted an agonizing experience some years later when the engineering group had greatly expanded. A mild economic downturn and the loss of a major customer had forced him to lay off nearly a quarter of the group's engineers. Recalling the pain of that experience, he noted that things would have been much better if most of those let go had never been hired in the first place; instead, others already in the department should have worked somewhat longer hours. To Lisa, the implications of these incidents seemed obvious: William would have little problem giving her the staff that he believed she really needed, but would be allergic to any perceived excess.

Lisa could then make this assessment much more precise, estimating importance weights for William. Already, however, the contours of a possible approach have begun to emerge as she considers her interests (recall Table 3) together with her insights into William's concerns. Lisa expects to press fairly hard for a salary in the $39,000 range, perhaps conceding a few weeks of vacation time for the last few thousand dollars. Money, she reasons, is most valuable to her and relatively "cheap" to William; in addition, he cares a great deal about avoiding too much time off and two extra weeks of vacation are not crucial to her. From her analysis of the new department's mission so far, Lisa has become increasingly sure that the job can be done with 15 people, though 20 would certainly be nice. She plans to devote a great deal of time to developing and presenting justification of the need for 15.

We will not go further in exploring how William's interests might be more formally assessed or how his and Lisa's preferences could be better dovetailed.[3] And, of course, this rough assessment of an artificially simplified set of issues only starts the process. As Lisa learns more, relative valuations may be revised, issues may be reformulated, and new options invented. For example, her interests in "salary" could be expanded to include stock options, bonuses, fringe and in-kind benefits. "Vacation" might encompass time to be taken in later years, a generous policy of accumulating unused vacation or turning it into salary, or leaves for various purposes like education. "Staff" may mean direct employees of various backgrounds and levels, "loans" from other departments, consultants, temporary help, or equipment to enhance the productivity of a given number of staff. But throughout, constant probing of each party's interests is the sine qua non of creating value by designing good negotiated agreements.

General Lessons for Assessing Interests

The most important lessons from this kind of assessment are those that help one think more clearly about the qualitative judgments that negotiators implicitly make all the time. Such evaluations are often made with respect to nominal issues rather than directly on underlying interests. Lisa's interests in money, lifestyle, peace of mind, career prospects, and organizational status are not perfectly aligned with the issues of salary, vacation limits, and staff size. When thinking about how well different packages satisfy her interests, the negotiator may discover reformulations that align more closely with her interests. If some of these "new" issues are easier to grant, they may form the basis for a better agreement.

During the process, the negotiator may learn about and change her perceptions about how well different positions on the issues serve her interests. As she learns, the relative importance of the increments on the issues may shift. If so, she should modify her assessments.

In contrast to the apparent crispness of the issues, interests are often vaguer. There may be no apparent scale with which to measure, for example, precedent or organizational status. Yet, the same logic that is useful for making issue tradeoffs can apply to assuring the relative impact of interests. The generic steps are as follows:

- Identify the interests that may be at stake.

- For each interest, imagine the possible packages that serve it best and worst; for example, imagine the range of precedents that might follow from the negotiation. This roughly defines the *increment*.

- As with Lisa's job negotiations, the importance of each interest depends on the relative importance of its *increment* compared to those of the other interests; how does the gain from the worst to the best possible precedent compare with the gain from the worst to the best possible monetary outcome?

The currency of negotiation generally involves *positions* on *issues* but the results are measured by how well underlying interests are furthered. As such, it is helpful to shuttle constantly between often abstract interests and more specific issues, both to check for consistency and to keep real concerns uppermost in mind.

Assessing the Interests of Others

Finally, it goes almost without saying that negotiators should constantly assess their counterparts' interests and preferences. Obviously, careful listening and clear communication help this process. Uninvolved third parties can render insights not suspected by partisans wrapped up in the negotiation. And some negotiators find that, as part of preparing for the process, actually playing the other party's role can offer deepened perspectives. In various management programs at Harvard, for example, senior industrialists have been assigned the parts of environmentalists and vice versa. To simulate arms talks, high-level U.S. military officers and diplomats have been assigned to play Russian negotiators in intensive simulations. Palestinians and Israelis have had to swap places. After some initial discomfort and reluctance, the most common reaction of participants in these exercises is surprise at how greatly such role-playing enhances their understanding of each side's interests, of why others may seem intransigent, and of unexpected possibilities for agreement.

Beyond various ways of trying to put oneself in the other's shoes, assessment of another's interests may be improved by investigating:

- Their past behavior in related settings, both in style and substance.

- Their training and professional affiliation: engineers and financial analysts will often have quite different modes of perception and approaches to potential conflict from, say lawyers and insurance adjusters.

- Their organizational position and affiliation. Those in the production department will often see long, predictable manufacturing runs as the company's dominant interest while marketers will opt for individual tailoring to customer specs and deep inventories for rapid deliveries. This is but one example of the old and wise expression "where you stand depends on where you sit."

- Whom they admire, whose advice carries weight, and to whom they tend to defer on the kind of issues at stake.

In the end, interests are bound up with psychology and culture. Some settings breed rivalry; others esteem the group. Some people are altruists; others sociopaths. To some, ego looms large; to others, substance is all. Airport bookstore wisdom names Jungle Fighters, Appeasers, Win-Winners, and Win-Losers. Professionals diagnose personality Types A and B and victims of cathected libido. Others have developed such classes, sometimes wisely, but for now we stress that *perceived* interests matter, that perceptions are subjective. Thus, to assess interests is to probe psyches.

Interests and Issues are Variable
Many academic treatments of negotiation take the issues and interests at stake as unchanging over the course of the negotiation. Yet both the issues under discussion and the interests perceived to be at stake can change.

The link between issues and interests is often unclear; the negotiator faced with a set of issues must figure out which of his or her interests are at stake. For example, getting a corner office might enhance prestige and status, but how much would this affect various dealings and decisions?

Because these links are often vague and complex, perceptions of the links can be influenced or manipulated. One may shape the "face" that an issue wears (Neustadt, 1980); presenting Food Stamps as a means to increase demand for agricultural products rather than as a welfare program may win agricultural state representatives' support for the program. Similarly, by portraying a new project that in reality departs sharply from a firm's past strategy as a direct extension of current projects, a subordinate may both obtain funding and avoid a review of the project's fit with broader strategic goals.

One may attempt less drastic changes in an individual's perception of the relationship between the issue at hand and the underlying interest. Thus, the mining company negotiator may attempt to persuade a small country's finance minister that high royalty rates, although they appear to further the country's interest in revenues, will actually be worse than lower royalty rates. The mining company might argue, "once rates reach a certain level, we will invest less, other companies will be scared off, and you will end up losing in terms of your monetary interests." If persuaded, the country's evaluation of how its interests would be satisfied by different potential agreements would change.

Certain other tactics may effectively expand or contract the interests evoked, often in ways not intended by the negotiator. "Take-it-or-leave-it" offers, forced linkages, commitment moves, threats, and preemptive actions all have potential to elicit strong negative reactions that may overwhelm the original issues at stake. Concern for one's reputation or self-esteem may predominate. A trade union's motivation for strikes, for instance, may shift over time from the strictly economic to a desire for revenge. Likewise, wars can escalate out of all proportion to the possible substantive gains for either side. The sudden Argentine occupation of the Falkland Islands in 1982 and the British response quickly came to involve weighty, irreconcilable interests such as "national honor" and the "right" response to aggression.

In many circumstances, threats, commitments, and deterrent moves are effective and can be analyzed in terms of values for the immediate issues involved (Tedeschi, Schlenker, and Bonoma, 1973). In other cases, such tactics can induce anger, loss of "face," and aggression (Deutsch and Kraus, 1962; Rubin and Brown, 1975). That is, the tactics bring new and often unhelpful interests into the negotiation. Countertactics may well bring in additional interests and a spiral begins. Conflicts are more likely to escalate when disputants attribute their concessions to their own weakness; similarly, escalation is less likely when concessions can be attributed to something impersonal, such as budgeting system, a formal procedure, or a widely accepted norm (Bacharach and Lawler, 1981).

The essence of some tactics is to add new interests. For example, one may make a commitment to a position by invoking an interest that the other negotiator cannot satisfy and that would not otherwise be part of the process; in holding to a position, the insurance claims adjuster may invoke a strong interest in maintaining a reputation as a tough bargainer for subsequent claims negotiations. The potential house buyer who announces that one's spouse would be tremendously angry if the purchase price were to exceed $150,000 adds a new interest to the negotiation: the relationship between husband and wife.

Other tactics, in contrast, may eliminate interests. Flipping a coin or submitting a dispute to arbitration may remove implications of weakness, strength, coercion, or tactical advantage.

Thus, interests can change even when issues remain fixed. The reverse is also true. Because the relation between issues and interests may be unclear, negotiators may reformulate the issues. During negotiations over deep seabed mining in the Law of the Sea negotiations, for example, many of the different nations' underlying interests remained fairly constant. However, as the negotiations evolved, the issues changed dramatically — from whether mining should be done by private firms at all or by an international mining entity to the nitty-gritty aspects of mining contracts for private firms and the financing mechanism for the first operation of a new international mining entity. Trying to pin down the precise nature of the final issues at stake occupied a great deal of the negotiators' time, perhaps more than it took ultimately to resolve the issues (Sebenius, 1984).

Prescriptive Summary

As a summary for analysts and practitioners, we have converted the main observations of this paper into the following prescriptive checklist:

Assessing Which Interests Are at Stake

- Beyond the obvious tangible interests that may be affected by issues to be discussed, consider subtler interests in reputation, precedent, relationships, strategy, fairness, and the like.

- Distinguish underlying interests from the issues under discussion and the positions taken on them.

- Distinguish between intrinsic and instrumental reasons for valuing interests, especially some of the subtler ones.

- In seeking to understand other's interests, remember that interests depend on perceptions, that perceptions are subjective, and thus that to assess interests is to probe psyches. This process can be aided by clear communication, the advice of third parties, role-playing, and taking into account past behavior, training, professional affiliation, and organizational position, as well as those to whom the other defers.

- Keep in mind that interests and issues can change on purpose or accidentally as the parties learn, events occur, or certain tactics are employed.

Assessing Tradeoffs

- Tradeoffs are as important to interests as proportions are to recipes.

- To assess tradeoffs among intangible interests, it is sometimes helpful to imagine services one could buy otherwise to satisfy the same interests.

- To assess tradeoffs among issues:

  — Specify the worst and best possible outcomes on each issue to define the possible increments.

  — Compare the increments by thinking hard about underlying interests and which increments are most valued.

  — Break the increments into smaller pieces and similarly compare their relative evaluation.

  — Change assessments with learning about how different positions on the issues affect interests.

  — Assess interest tradeoffs using the same logic.

When to Focus on Interests and When on Issues

- Focus the negotiation on interests to enhance creativity and break impasses by reformulating issues to align better with underlying interests.

- Focus the negotiation on positions, issues, or a narrower set of interests when underlying conflicts of ideology make agreement difficult or when a restricted focus is more advantageous for claiming value.

Negotiation is a process of potentially opportunistic interaction in which two or more parties with some conflicting interests seek to do better by jointly decided action than they could otherwise. The alternatives to negotiated agreement or what the parties could do alone define the threshold of value that any agreement must exceed. The potential of negotiation is bounded only by the quality of agreement that can be devised. But, for evaluating alternatives and creating agreements, interests are the measure and raw material of negotiation.

NOTES

We would like to thank Arthur Applbaum, Mark Moore, Howard Raiffa, Lawrence Susskind, and Thomas Weeks for helpful and friendly comments. A number of the ideas in this paper have been stimulated by the work of, and discussions with, Roger Fisher and William Ury, whom we also thank. Support from the Division of Research at the Harvard Business School and the Sloan Foundation Program of Research in Public Management is gratefully acknowledged. Much of this article is drawn from material prepared for a chapter of our book, *The Manager as Negotiator* (New York: The Free Press, forthcoming).

1. More technically-minded readers may find the following formulation helpful: Let us represent a negotiator's multi-attribute utility function; the attributes of u are the negotiator's interests. Let p be a vector of positions taken on the issue vector (i). Let f be a vector-valued function that reflects the negotiator's beliefs about how well an agreement with position p on issues i advances his interests. Thus, an agreement p gives the negotiator utility $u(f(i(p)))$. Typically, of course, the negotiator will be uncertain about the relationship between issues and interests, which we might model by letting w represent the random variable reflecting relevant uncertain events and letting $f(i(p),w)$ reflect the negotiator's beliefs about the relationship between issues and interests conditional on w. Thus, we might say that the negotiator wants to choose p to maximize $Ew[u(f(i(p),w))]$, where Ew is the expectation over the negotiator's subjective beliefs about w.

2. The "additive scoring rule" constructed in this example is a simple case of a multi-attribute value or utility function. When interdependencies exist, non-additive, multi-attribute utility functions (see Keeney and Raiffa, 1976) can be used in this assessment.

3. Or for that matter, how to take the twin scoring systems for Lisa's and William's values to produce a Pareto frontier. For a discussion of how to do this, see Raiffa (1982) or Barclay and Peterson (1976).

REFERENCES

Barclay, S. B. and Peterson, C. (1976). "Multi-attribute utility models for negotiators." *Technical Report* 76-1, McLean, Virginia: Decisions and Designs, Inc.

Bower, J. L. (1972). *Managing the resource allocation process*. Homewood, Ill.: Irwin.

Deutsch, M. and Kraus, R. M. (1962). "Studies of interpersonal bargaining," *Journal of Conflict Resolution* 6: 52-76.

Donaldson, G. and Lorsch, J. W. (1984). *Decision making at the top*. New York: Basic Books.

Fisher R. and Ury, W. L. (1981). *Getting to YES: Negotiating agreement without giving in*. Boston: Houghton Mifflin.

Greenhalgh, L. and Neslin, S. A. (1981). "Conjoint analysis of negotiator preferences." *Journal of Conflict Resolution* 25: 301-327.

Gulliver, P. H. (1979). *Disputes and negotiations: A cross cultural perspective*. New York: Academic Press.

Keeney, R. and Raiffa, H. (1976). *Decisions with multiple objectives*. New York: Wiley.

Kotter, J. (1985). *Power and influence*. New York: Free Press.

Neustadt, R. E. (1980). *Presidential power*, 4th ed. New York: Wiley.

Raiffa, H. (1982). *The art and science of negotiation*. Cambridge, Mass.: Harvard University Press.

Rubin, J. Z. and Brown, B. R. (1975). *The social psychology of bargaining and negotiation*. New York: Academic Press.

Schelling, T. C. (1960). *The strategy of conflict*. Cambridge, Mass.: Harvard University Press.

Sebenius, J. K. (1984). *Negotiating the law of the sea*. Cambridge, Mass.: Harvard University Press.

Tedeschi, J. T., Schlenker, B. R. and Bonoma, T. V. (1973). *Conflict, power, and games*. Chicago: Aldine.

Your Draft or Mine?

Jeswald W. Salacuse

For many persons, the word "negotiation" evokes images of a process that proceeds through a fixed sequence of phases: The parties first state their positions and interests, then make concessions and adjustments, eventually reach an understanding if all goes well, and finally write their agreement on paper. According to this view, the parties talk first and write last.

In many negotiations, however, the sequence of events is just the reverse. A common opening gambit in negotiations is for one party to present the other with a detailed document, known variously as a "draft," "model," "prototype," or "standard form agreement," to serve as a basis for their discussions. Thus, in practice, negotiators often write first and then talk.

The presentation of a comprehensive draft agreement as a first step is a frequent practice in both business and diplomatic negotiations. Multinational corporations use draft contracts to sell jet aircraft, form joint ventures, and lend Eurodollars (e.g., Wellons, 1977). Governments seeking bilateral relationships of varying sorts with foreign countries often launch negotiations by asking the other side to comment on their draft treaty. The United States and European countries, for example, have followed precisely this tactic in their current efforts to negotiate bilateral investment treaties with developing countries (Salacuse, 1985, p. 992; Vandevelde, 1988, pp. 209-211).

Because so many negotiations are launched with a previously prepared draft agreement, it is worth considering the reasons for this practice, the advantages and disadvantages, and ways that the other side should respond.

Purposes of the Draft

The draft or model agreement serves many purposes for the side presenting it. First, its preparation is an opportunity for negotiators representing an organization to consult with important internal and external constituencies and to formulate an acceptable negotiating position on the matter to be discussed. This preliminary consultation is not only important preparation for the negotiations themselves, but it also gives the negotiators some assurance that any negotiated agreement that closely follows the draft will be ratified by the home government or home office. Second, since the government or corporation often contemplates negotiating similar arrangements with many different parties, the model or draft agreement is an efficient means of informing potential negotiating partners about the type of contract or treaty that the propos-

Jeswald W. Salacuse is Dean and Professor of International Law at the Fletcher School of Law and Diplomacy, Tufts University, Medford, Mass. 02155.

ing party favors. Uniformity of contract language simplifies administration of numerous agreements or treaties, and also can avoid subsequent charges of discrimination and resulting demands for renegotiation by countries or corporations who believe that others have received better treatment than they have. Beginning all negotiations with the same basic draft is generally perceived as a cost-effective, efficient practice.

But perhaps the main reason for submitting a draft agreement at the beginning of negotiations is that it gives the proposing party a significant tactical advantage (e.g., Smith and Wells, 1975, p. 157). Many experienced negotiators believe that "the one who controls the draft controls the negotiations" (e.g., Pengilley, 1985, p. 194). If the other side accepts the draft as the basis for discussions, the presenter has in effect set the agenda of the negotiation and, more important, established the conceptual framework within which negotiations will take place. To a large extent, the party submitting the draft fixes the terms of reference, while the other side (at least at the outset) is merely reacting to the draft's language, rather than advancing specific proposals of its own. Indeed, the party that receives the draft may become so preoccupied with its analysis and reactions to various provisions that it neglects its own negotiating objectives and interests.

Disadvantages of the Draft

Although the side who controls the draft may indeed control the negotiation, wise negotiators should be careful about applying this bit of conventional wisdom indiscriminately. Insistence on your own draft may allow you to dominate the negotiation at the outset, but it may also impede reaching an agreement in the long run. Scholars of negotiation theory urge negotiators to focus on interests, not positions, and to search for creative options for mutual gain (e.g., Fisher and Ury, 1981). They also stress the importance of finding a "formula" to accommodate competing goals (e.g., Zartman and Berman, 1982, pp. 87-146).

Insisting on one's own draft in a negotiation may frustrate this useful advice. For one thing, submission of a prepared draft at an early stage in the negotiations may lock the parties into bargaining positions, thereby obstructing a search for common interests and creative formulas. A draft or model agreement is, after all, nothing more than a detailed statement of a position. Then, too, if one of the functions of the early phase of a negotiation is to allow both sides to gather and share as much information as possible about one another, focusing at the outset on the drafts is likely to hamper this vital process.

Although corporations and governments may believe that their model agreements have universal application, they may in fact be inapplicable to particular local conditions or the specific situation under discussion; consequently, unyielding insistence on their terms may sometimes lead to results that are unsatisfactory for both sides. For example, the refusal by an American fast food company to modify its master construct language was one cause of its failure to negotiate a franchise agreement in Australia. The final contract retained the franchisor's standard provision requiring the construction of top quality, snowproof buildings. Since Melbourne does not have heavy snowfalls, the resulting construction costs to the franchisee placed an unnecessary and, ultimately, a fatal burden on the Australian operation (Pengilley, 1985, p. 196).

Finally, since the party introducing the draft is usually in a superior bargaining position, the other side may view the presentation of the draft as an act of arrogance and a not-too-subtle signal or affirmation of the unequal relationship between the parties. Consequently, placing a detailed draft on the table at the very beginning of the negotiation may instill suspicion and hostility in the other side, factors which, at the very least, will slow the process of reaching an agreement.

All of the above suggests that negotiators should not automatically introduce a prepared draft as an opening gambit in all negotiations. Instead, they should carefully analyze each situation to determine the appropriate time to present their draft in the negotiation process, if at all. They should also recognize that an inflexible insistence on the draft's terms is likely to prolong negotiations, and may even derail any chance of agreement.

Coping With the Other Side's Draft
If one side does use the draft as a tactic aimed at dominating the negotiation, what can the other side do? Three approaches suggest themselves:

1. *Prepare a Counter Draft*
The obvious approach for the other side is to counter the proposed draft with a draft of its own. The counter draft may be one specifically prepared for the negotiation in question or one drawn from a completed agreement in another transaction. For example, in a bilateral investment treaty negotiation between the Federal Republic of Germany and Jamaica, Jamaica countered Germany's model treaty with an earlier advantageous treaty that Jamaica had signed with the United Kingdom.

Introducing a counter draft is an effort both to share control of the negotiations and to create an alternate conceptual framework. The preparation of a counter draft also has the benefit of forcing the party to think through its interests and to develop its own position on the issues under discussion. In addition, a party who objects strongly to the original draft may feel that submission of a counter draft is a positive, constructive way of making its concerns known to the other side.

Although the counter draft tactic may seem obvious, negotiators often fail to use it. Preparation of a counter draft, especially on highly technical matters, requires a level of expertise that a party simply may not have. Developing countries negotiating with multinational corporations often find themselves in this position. The preparation of a counter draft without adequate knowledge of the subject could result in a text that puts the developing country at a greater negotiating disadvantage than if it had chosen to base discussion on the original draft prepared by the multinational firm. Even if a country has the expertise, it may not be in a position to devote sufficient personnel and time to preparing a counter draft for a single transaction, unlike a multinational corporation or developed nation's government, which can afford to assign a team of experts for an extended period of time to devise such drafts.

Countering one draft with another may introduce an added element of disharmony into negotiations, and a party in a weak position may therefore hesitate to adopt this approach. The introduction of a counter draft will almost always result in a "duel of drafts," with each side insisting that *its* text be made the basis for discussion. The side offering the first draft will invariably argue that any changes will make subsequent ratification by the home office or home government uncertain, if not impossible, since all necessary constituencies at home have approved it. The party submitting the counter draft can make the same argument to support its own text. How can a potential stalemate be avoided?

One solution may be for the negotiators to accept both drafts for discussion and to adopt a version of the "one-text procedure" suggested by Fisher and Ury (1981, p. 118). This process involves the parties in working together to prepare a single text that incorporates common principles emerging from the two texts and their discussions. To accomplish this task, the parties will have to look beyond stated positions in order to determine underlying interests, and ultimately, develop creative, mutually satisfactory solutions.

2. Discuss Principles First
When confronted with a draft early in the negotiation, a party may counter it by politely requesting that it be put aside temporarily while the two sides discuss basic principles and concepts to govern their relationship. For example, in a joint venture negotiation, rather than discuss provisions of the draft agreement article-by-article, the negotiators should first outline the major elements of their venture, such as allocation of risk, distribution of profits, duration, and control. After consensus is reached, the parties might write their general understanding in the form of simple statements. These agreements would then serve as the framework for the details of their contract, thus supplanting the first draft originally proposed by one side.

3. Use the Draft but Not Its Order
In many circumstances, a party may have no choice but to accept the other side's draft as the basis for negotiation. In such situations, one may be well advised not to proceed to discuss the draft provision-by-provision, beginning with the first article and proceeding in order to the last.

Rather, the receiving party should determine the principal issues to be discussed and present them for consideration in the order it judges appropriate. This approach will, at the very least, enable it to shape the order of the agenda and perhaps avoid being locked into the conceptual framework that the other side seeks to impose through its draft.

REFERENCES

Fisher, R. and **Ury, W. L.** (1981). *Getting to YES: Negotiating agreement without giving in.* Boston: Houghton Mifflin.

Pengilley, W. (1985). "International franchising arrangements and problems in their negotiation." *Northwestern Journal of International Law and Business* 7: 185-207.

Salacuse, J. W. (1985). "Toward a new treaty framework for direct foreign investment." *Journal of Air Law and Commerce* 50: 969-1010.

Smith, D. N. and **Wells, L. T.** (1975). *Negotiating Third World mineral agreements.* Cambridge, Mass.: Ballinger.

Vandevelde, K. J. (1988). "The bilateral investment treaty program of the United States." *Cornell International Law Journal* 21: 201-276.

Wellons, P. A. (1977). *Borrowing by developing countries on the Euro-currency market.* Paris: OECD.

Zartman, I. W. and **Berman, M. R.** (1982). *The practical negotiator.* New Haven: Yale University Press.

Ten Commandments for a Negotiator

Janos Nyerges

Toward the end of my professional career — I was Special Representative of the Hungarian Government to International Economic Organizations — I was asked by my younger colleagues about the "secret" of my negotiation ability. This question, though flattering, took me by surprise because, as a matter of fact, I never gave much thought to how I did what I did.

As a very young man, I was almost literally pushed into the deep and troubled waters of economic negotiations. And representing Hungary in a not always friendly world — to put things mildly —was not a very easy task. When I began, my only assets were an interrupted academic education, a few foreign languages, and an unconditional identification with the country I was privileged to represent. I had no teachers, no systematic preparation for this job — other than experience I was soon to gain from experienced diplomats, businessmen, and other shrewd negotiators. As the result of dealing with these "teachers," I discovered the truth of a well-known saying in the prewar business community of Budapest: "The best professor of a businessman is his customer."

The question about my "secret" intrigues me, simply because I was not aware that I had any "secret" or that negotiations have some "secret" to be discovered at all. I've spent hours and hours of time with colleagues discussing what makes a successful negotiator. A large amount of reading was also necessary so that, at the end of my negotiating career, I became a student of negotiation. And being a student has eventually enabled me to teach.

The question of what makes a good negotiator continues to intrigue me. Based on my experience, observation, and study, I've developed my own "Ten Commandments for a Negotiator." Here they are:

1. You shall love and cherish your trade.

2. Be courageous. Accept your responsibilities gladly.

3. The eagle's eye must be yours: Assess situations quickly.

4. Remember, there are no problems, only opportunities.

5. Be honest under all circumstances.

6. Love your opponent even if you receive something less than that in return.

7. Put yourself in the shoes of your opponent, but do not remain there too long.

Janos Nyerges, former Director General of the Hungarian Ministry of Foreign Trade, has served as a Special Representative of the Hungarian Government at numerous international economic negotiations. Though "retired" since 1984, he remains a consultant to the Economic Commission of Europe, and is an adviser to the president of the Hungarian Chamber of Commerce. His address is 1146 Budapest, Abonyi u. 14, Hungary.

8. Convert your opponent into your partner.

9. Do not act before you have found out your partner's aims.

10. Your partner is at least as intelligent as you are; but, you must have more will.

Now, since nothing is ever quite as simple and straightforward as this little list of commandments, please indulge me while I offer some thoughts on the meaning of each of them.

1. *You shall love and cherish your trade.*
Regarding this admonition, an anecdote comes to my mind told to me by a close friend of Henri Spaak, the Belgian leader during World War II. Mr. Spaak was visiting Winston Churchill in London, and complimented him on his admirable conduct of war. To this, Churchill replied in French with a heavy English accent: "Pour bien faire la guerre, Monsieur le President, il fait l'aimer." (In order to make war well, Mr. President, one must love it.) Likewise, in order to negotiate well, one must love it. A good negotiator enjoys the negotiation process in the first place, is thoroughly involved in it, and strongly identifies with the issues at stake.

It is obvious that involvement and dedication to a cause are not enough; in fact, without a strong sense of professionalism, this type of adherence can be a liability. Professionalism, to my mind, is not simply the fact that a good negotiator has a high professional standing. I view professionalism as an intellectual and emotional involvement and commitment to the profession itself. True negotiators are enthusiastic about negotiation, just as good lawyers, doctors, engineers, and teachers are in love with their trades.

In international negotiations, true professional negotiators are quick to recognize each other. The true professional can recognize other professionals very soon, not in a formal way but through the mutual sympathy among people who worship the same goddess. This is a great asset, for such acceptance confers additional weight to anything the professional negotiator has to say. This bond of recognition sometimes crosses boundaries of countries and even ideologies without ever putting in question one's loyalty to his or her own constituency. An invitation to an informal dinner of fellow professionals some twenty years ago was my debut in these ranks; it showed that I was accepted not only as "the distinguished delegate of Hungary," but as one of them.

2. *Be courageous.*
A good negotiator must command respect. Respect cannot be conferred by rank or functions; it is due to character. Nothing confers respect more than courage, which is the readiness to accept responsibilities and make decisions.

In German terms, there are two different qualifications: *Entschlussähig* (i.e., capable to make decisions) and *Entshlussfreudig* (i.e., enjoys making decisions). Being capable of making decisions seems obvious. In reality, however, many negotiators are not born to negotiate, nor even trained to do so. They simply find themselves in the role of negotiator because they hold a corresponding rank in the bureaucracy. As well-trained and well-advised bureaucrats, they need orders from higher echelons of the hierarchy. To negotiate, to decide what positions to take, is a risky business for them. Bureaucrats prefer to accept decisions and not to make them. They are bad negotiators.

One of my former ministers was once negotiating with his colleague in a foreign country. As he made a proposal that was a bit unusual, his partner picked up the phone on his desk and, after a quick exchange with the person at the other end of the line, turned to my minister and said: "I am sorry, I cannot accept." Throughout the long discussions, this little scene was repeated several times, with different answers. Finally, my minister had had enough. He turned to his colleague and said, "Couldn't you give me, dear colleague, that phone number?" Enjoying decision making is a quality that's rarely found. It is a sign of a sovereign will, of self-confidence.

While a professor at the French War Academy, General Charles DeGaulle exalted the moral qualities of the military leader, noting that a strong character was the main ingredient for success. In his remarkable book *Le fil d'epee* (*The Sword's Edge*), DeGaulle (1962) wrote:

> The difficulty attracts the man of character, because embracing it, he becomes himself. Had he overcome it or not, it is an affair between them. Like a jealous lover he does not share what it gives him or what it costs to him. He seeks in it, whatever the outcome may be, the *bitter joy to be responsible*. (emphasis added).

3. *The eagle's eye must be yours.*
Needless to say, courage and acceptance of the challenges are not enough. Good judgment, quick assessment of the situation — "the eagle's eye" of my third commandment — is also necessary. Without it, courage remains blind. For a negotiator, quick assessment of the situation is what a targeting device is to a guided missile.

I would like to emphasize that good judgment, the correct assessment being a precondition for making an appropriate decision, has a specific importance in the context of the negotiation. More often than not in negotiation, the real situation is far from clear. Among the factors that obscure the truth are inconsistent behavior on the other side, the irresistible impact of one's own patterns of thinking, the smokescreen of purposely created impressions by the other side, and lack of information. There frequently are few "redcoats" on this battlefield that reveal the positions of the other party.

Speed of assessment is vital because time is the eternal enemy of the negotiator. Sometimes one can buy time, but such a purchase often involves a price that may later turn out to be too high. Instead of buying time, speed in recognizing the real situation *gains* time.

Computers nowadays are touted as the ultimate tool to use in assessing situations quickly. Computers are certainly useful, but they have two great shortcomings: Unlike people, computers do not have fears, nor do they entertain hopes. Computers merely reflect experience gained from situations and judgments. An anecdote might illustrate my point. During a maneuver, the general asks the computer, "Should I retreat or advance?" The answer comes quickly: "Yes."

One word of warning: Quick assessment does not always mean a quick answer. The answer of the good negotiator, once the assessment is quickly made, must be subordinated to tactical considerations.

4. *There are no problems, only opportunities.*

This very wise advice was quoted to me as having originally been said by a former president of Trans World Airlines. Problems often hypnotize the negotiator, just as the cold eyes of the snake immobilize the little rabbit. However, I believe there are no situations, no problems that do not offer opportunities — if you look for them. By viewing a problem as an opportunity, you often discover new, sometimes surprising proposals. Last but not least, this kind of opportunity can help you convert a seemingly zero sum situation into a non-zero sum situation. The only thing that a good negotiator must do is *look* for these opportunities. If this is how you view "problems," you will find opportunities.

5. *Be honest under all circumstances.*

The "commandments" described thus far apply not only to negotiators, but also to the military and to the boxing champion. These are rules for fighting persons.

Negotiation is a fight — I have no doubt about this — but not a fight alone. It is a fight with a specific character. The good negotiator is not simply a fighter for victory, but a fighter who seeks to win the mind, the sympathy, and the cooperation of his or her opposite number.

Therefore, the most needed quality — without which a negotiator is doomed to fail — is honesty, both intellectual and moral. Honesty has many manifestations and it's a quality that a good negotiator displays on each and every occasion. Negotiators should never have to say "Look how honest I am!" Such a protestation, in fact, places in question the honesty of the person speaking. Instead, honesty should be manifested by faithful observance of the rules of the game, loyalty shown in the way arguments are put forward, and giving the benefit of the doubt to the other party. Honesty is unconditional. A good negotiator should resist the temptation to be dishonest when dealing with a partner whose honesty is questionable. A good negotiator is a lady or a gentleman who assumes that the opponent is also a lady or gentleman. A good negotiator never qualifies the behavior of his or her opponent.

Because negotiation is an interaction between persons, the personal element is of great importance. Empathy is required to get a good relationship that, in turn, leads to the successful conduct of a negotiation. This in itself is not enough. A good negotiator must also develop an understanding of the needs of the negotiating partner — an impossible task if it is not accompanied and supported by one negotiator's friendly feelings toward the other. The basis of this mutual sympathy lies deep in the common "destiny" of the negotiators: Both are under the same stress, and both have the same problems with their respective constituencies, their own delegations, and their own public opinions. The same problems cause their sleepless nights. Even their personal problems are the same. Both of them often happen to be far away from their homes, families and friends, alone in a foreign city, in a lonely hotel room.

Interaction cannot be regarded only as the development of mutual sympathy based on personal understanding and esteem. It is an intellectual process as well. In addition, the presentation of facts in negotiation should be handled in a way that strengthens the feeling that the negotiators are *partners* rather than *opponents*.

6. *Love your opponent even if you receive something less in return.*

Negotiators are in a contradictory situation: Each wants the problem resolved in a self-interested way. This separates them. On the other hand, each of them has to resolve the same problem, and this unites them. Negotiators are like two workers carrying the same burden: Whether they like it or not, they are part of the same "chain-gang." The negotiator who dislikes or is rude to the other side adds to the mutual burden instead of alleviating it. The better negotiator, on the other hand, respects the other side.

7. *Put yourself in the shoes of your opponent, but do not remain there too long.*

The good negotiator feels the necessity to put himself or herself into the situation of the other side. This feeling is a natural byproduct of the negotiating process itself. Negotiation involves personal contact, communication, and interaction. The two parties are watching each other like two boxing champions in the ring. They continually watch for signs that give insight into the other champion's mind. Very often, one negotiator openly invites the other to understand his or her situation. Many times in my career, I heard something like this from my partners: "Look, if I accept your proposal, I would be killed at home." Once, when my partner thought my proposal was totally unacceptable, I was asked, "What would you do in my place?" My answer was "I would negotiate," to which my partner, with satisfied, good-humored laughter, made a new offer. You cannot reach an agreement without knowing as the Germans say, *wo die Schuh drückt* — where the shoe hurts.

Knowing it is one thing. Reacting to it is another. An inexperienced negotiator is sometimes tempted to use the internal difficulty of the negotiating partner as a welcome occasion to exert pressure. A good negotiator knows that this attitude is more often than not counter-productive. Instead, the good negotiator will try to understand and to alleviate this embarrassing situation. This attitude is sometimes mingled with a kind of sympathy and compassion.

Here lies the danger: Having put oneself in the shoes of the other fellow can lead to the road on which those shoes were marching — that is, seeking solutions which risk being beneficial to the other party alone. The right attitude in such a situation is to find answers that alleviate the burden of the other party while also providing satisfaction for yourself. Therefore, the more willing a negotiator is to assimilate, to feel the problems of the other side, the more that negotiator has to bear in mind the self-interested goals.

8. *Convert your opponent into your partner.*

Every negotiator needs help, and the person who is in the best position to give this help is the opponent. Hence, the importance of the conversion of the opponent into a negotiating *partner*. This comes almost automatically, if the previous three commandments were successfully observed. Combined, these precepts yield the indispensable element in any negotiation: trust. Even in extreme cases where the partners are known to each other as criminals or outlaws, they must trust each other, to a minimal extent at least, if the negotiations are to succeed.

9. *Do not act before you find out what your partner's aims are.*
In my mind, bargaining in negotiation begins when substantial discussion occurs, offers are made, positions are taken. But — and this mistake occurs very often — what happens if your partner's position is not what you believed it was? You made your overtures, your promises, and your threats all in vain. The harm is greater in such cases than to lose time and opportunity. By revealing your ignorance, you cease to be a competent negotiator.

Therefore, the first stage of the negotiations has to be to find out, to the greatest extent possible, what the partner really wants to achieve. Once you know it, start the bargaining.

10. *Your partner is at least as intelligent as you are; but you must have more will.*
The good negotiator never underestimates the intellectual capacity of any opponent. Rather, a good negotiator closely observes every move of a partner, giving very serious attention to each action. Soon a good negotiator will realize that negotiation is not a contest of intelligence but a contest of will.

In every negotiation, there is at least one critical moment when the other partner finally feels that he or she must say yes. Crises are certainly inevitable in negotiation, and there is tremendous tension in these last minutes. Not only are these minutes preceding the final solution, but they are also occasions when deadlock often occurs. At such times the negotiator must be persistent, even at the risk of losing.

The good negotiator sees such crises coming, and is prepared to meet them. The better negotiator prepares for such crises, taking good care that the stakes and risks on the other side are greater than his or her own.

Conclusion
Presenting my views in the form of "Ten Commandments" might convey the image of a rather romantic, nonrealistic person. This is partly due to my own cultural and educational background, and to my socio-political environment. In my country, personality and moral and intellectual qualities are highly valued; in addition, after forty years of negotiating experience, I have come to the conclusion that the negotiator's personality is a crucial negotiating tool.

In most cases, the negotiator is an educated person with high professional standing. The negotiator probably also underwent some training program, and is familiar with the relevant theories. I could go on to enumerate all the characteristics of a good negotiator, but all these characteristics boil down to a personality — i.e., being a person, having a distinctive personal character. In my opinion, a negotiator's impact and success will depend more on personal style than on erudition.

During my teaching and research work, I was interested in finding out what my students regarded as personal qualities that are essential to a good negotiator. Do qualities of personal character or intellect prevail in the image represented by students, researchers, and other competent observers?

At the end of my training courses, I often asked my students to draft their own "Ten Commandments of Negotiation." This test served two purposes: I tried to know to what extent they were able to penetrate the conceptual side of negotiation and, on the other hand, I wanted to see their perception of what a negotiator is, or should be.

Two broad divisions were used — personal character and intellectual qualities. It turned out that out of 340 specific "commandments," 185 were of an intellectual nature and 156 related to personal character (54 percent intellectual and 46 percent personal character).

I made another experiment. A high-ranking U.N. official, who had been involved as a mediator in numerous international negotiations, decided to retire. In appreciation of his truly outstanding service, the organization published a volume of letters from colleagues. I picked out the qualifications mentioned in these letters. It was not important to know to what extent these kind words were sincere. Even if one could assume that courtesy was perhaps the motivation, in many cases I thought that projection of various qualities onto the person was just as important as the perception of the real qualities.

So, using the descriptive language of those letters, I composed a "ghost picture" of the qualities that make a good international negotiator. Here are the results: 92 qualifications were talked about, of which 45 were intellectual and 47 related to personal character (roughly 50-50 percent).

Intellectual abilities that were cited included wisdom, deep insight, etc. in fourteen cases. Lucidity was mentioned in thirteen cases, creativity in seven cases, and intellectual leadership in five cases. Brilliance and experience were each cited three times. Of the moral qualifications, twenty-two described in various terms the harmony, patience, and objectivity of the person; eleven referred to dedication and commitment; seven cited courage, both intellectual and moral; six praised honesty; and four each mentioned perseverance and courtesy.

I do not draw any conclusion from these figures; they seem to confirm my own observation, however, that a good negotiator's personality should contain a roughly equal proportion of moral and intellectual qualities.

REFERENCE

de Gaulle, C. (1962). *Le fil de l'epee*. Paris: Union Generale d'Editions.

Section V

The Negotiation Context

Negotiations of any kind take place within a context. The negotiators themselves may be constrained in certain ways by this context, by virtue of the informational uncertainty of the negotiation problem at hand, the need or tendency of individual negotiators to make commitments that may subsequently become overdetermining in their effects, or the sense that there is a single "best" or "right" moment for making concessions. Section V samples some of the many considerations that can reasonably be described as negotiation "context," and indicates how these may have an important impact on the negotiations that occur.

Max H. Bazerman's article ("Negotiator Judgment: A Critical Look at the Rationality Assumption") takes into account the consequences for negotiating effectiveness of limitations in the judgments made by individual decision makers. As described by the author, this kind of contextual constraint plays out in terms of five kinds of "deviation from rationality": first, the framing of negotiator judgment, such that a "half-full cup" is sometimes regarded as half-empty, and vice versa; second, the "mythical fixed-pie of negotiations," by which negotiators are typically biased in the direction of assuming that negotiated solutions can only be zero-sum in nature; third, the nonrational escalation of conflict, by which negotiators become so invested in their pursuit of some objective in negotiation that they soon come to feel that they have "too much invested to quit," and find themselves trapped in a course of action from which they believe escape is impossible; fourth, negotiator overconfidence, the tendency for individual negotiators to be overly and inappropriately confident that their views or positions in negotiation will eventually prevail; and finally, the so-called "winner's curse," according to which negotiators may be so eager to reach agreement that they make a reasonable initial offer that is *accepted* — leading them to wonder what more they might have obtained had they not been cursed by "winning" so soon.

A good illustration of Bazerman's analysis of nonrational escalation of conflict can be seen in the second selection, by Robert B. McKersie ("The Eastern Airlines Saga: Grounded by a Contest of Wills"). Using the protracted conflict between Eastern Airlines owner Frank Lorenzo and the Machinists Union as a case in point, McKersie describes the contextual conditions that forced conflict to escalate, hardened positions on both sides, and caused the antagonists to believe that each had too much invested in defeating the other side to quit.

Thomas C. Schelling's essay ("Strategy and Self-Command: A Commencement Address to the RAND Graduate School of Policy Studies") traces this distinguished analyst's interest in "self-command": the development of commitments to some regimen of self-improvement or self-modification. Schelling implies that if one wishes to change the way one negotiates (e.g., to move away from a style that has proven ineffectual) it may be possible to do so through the "technology" of self-command. A series of small commitments, he argues, followed by other such small commitments, can create an environment of "over-commitment" in which a negotiator embarks on a course of self-command that — in keeping with the Bazerman and McKersie selections — can "bind the decision maker" to a new course of action. To state this in another way, if a negotiator feels that he or she is constrained by the personal context of a decision-making style that has limited one's effectiveness thus far, then this article describes a process that can be used to overcome such constraints.

Louis Kriesberg ("Timing and the Initiation of De-Escalation Moves") considers the view that there is a single right or "ripe" moment for conflicts to de-escalate. Thus, it is not enough that the parties be prepared, both internally and externally, for negotiation, or that they have an appropriate sense of their respective power, dependence, or interests in the negotiation. No, it is also necessary that they negotiate in a context that supports the possibility of moving toward agreement. In this article, Kriesberg explores the variety of conditions that may contribute to effective de-escalation efforts through the establishment of proper timing.

Negotiator Judgment: A Critical Look at the Rationality Assumption

Max H. Bazerman

There is growing evidence of increased attention to the scientific study of negotiation. Most of this effort has been devoted to specifying prescriptive principles negotiators can use to be more effective (e.g., Fisher and Ury, 1981; Raiffa, 1982). Prescriptive strategies focus on how negotiators should behave to maximize their utility. If followed, prescriptive approaches should increase the performance of negotiators. However, it is argued here that a number of systematic judgmental deficiencies impede individuals from implementing prescriptive strategies optimally. Specifically, the behavioral decision theory literature has proposed a number of cognitive limitations that inhibit our ability to follow prescriptive advice.

Negotiator judgment can be improved first by describing the ways in which negotiators deviate from rationality, and then by prescribing a strategy for eliminating these deficiencies from the negotiator's cognitive repertoire. Eliminating these deficiencies from the negotiator judgment allows the negotiator to come closer to following the prescriptive research. Thus the two approaches are complementary rather than competing.

The core of this article describes five specific deviations from rationality that affect negotiator judgment. It then specifies how biased decision processes differ from prescriptive analyses of negotiator behavior, prescribes how negotiators can be trained to eliminate deviations from rationality, and shows how this research can be integrated with prescriptive research.

The Framing of Negotiator Judgment

Consider the following two scenarios:

> You are a wholesaler of refrigerators. Corporate policy does not allow any flexibility in pricing. However, flexibility does exist in the expenses you can incur (shipping, financing terms, etc.), which have a direct effect on the profitability of the transaction. These expenses can all be costed out in dollar-value terms. You are negotiating a $10,000 sale. The buyer wants you to pay $2,000 in expenses. You want to pay less. When you negotiate the transaction, do you try to minimize your expenses (reduce the losses from the $2,000 figure) or maximize net price — price less expenses (increase the net price from the $8,000 figure)?

> You bought your house in 1977 for $60,000. You currently have the house on the market for $109,900, with a real target of $100,000 (your estimation

Max H. Bazerman is Professor of Organization Behavior and member of the executive committee of the Dispute Resolution Research Center at the Kellogg Graduate School of Management, Northwestern University, Evanston, Illinois 60201.

of the true market value). An offer comes in for $90,000. Does this offer represent a $30,000 gain in comparison with the original purchase price, or a $10,000 loss in comparison with your current target?

The answer to the question posed in each scenario is "both." Each is a "Is the cup half-full or half-empty?" situation. From a normative perspective, and based on our intuition, the difference in the two points of view is irrelevant. Recently, however, Kahneman and Tversky (1979, 1982; Tversky and Kahneman, 1981) have suggested that important differences exist in how individuals respond to questions framed in terms of losses versus gains. This difference is critical in describing negotiator behavior.

Tversky and Kahneman (1981) presented the following problem to a group of subjects:

> The U.S. is preparing for the outbreak of an unusual Asian disease which is expected to kill 600 people. Two alternative programs are being considered. Which would you favor?
>
> 1. If Program A is adopted, 200 will be saved.
> 2. If Program B is adopted, there is a one-third probability that all will be saved and a two-thirds probability that none will be saved.

Of 158 respondents, 76% chose Program A, while only 24% chose Program B. The prospect of being able to save 200 lives for certain was valued more highly by most of the subjects than a risky prospect of equal expected value. Thus, most subjects were risk-averse.

A second group of subjects received the same cover story and the following two choices:

> 1. If Program A is adopted, 400 people will die.
> 2. If Program B is adopted, there is a one-third probability that no one will die and a two-thirds probability that 600 people will die.

Out of the 169 respondents in the second group, only 13% chose Program A, while 87% chose Program B. The prospects of 400 people dying was less acceptable to most of the subjects than a two-thirds probability that 600 would die. Thus, most subjects given these alternatives were risk-seeking.

Careful examination of the two problems finds them to be *objectively* identical. However, changing the description of outcomes from lives saved (gains) to lives lost (losses) was sufficient to shift the majority of subjects from a risk-averse to a risk-seeking orientation. This result is inconsistent with utility theory, which predicts the same response when objectively identical problems are presented. These well-replicated findings, however, are consistent with Kahneman and Tversky's (1979) prospect theory, which predicts risk-averse behavior when individuals are evaluating gains and risk-seeking behavior when individuals are evaluating losses.

To exemplify the importance of "framing" to negotiation, consider the following labor-management situation suggested by Bazerman and Neale (1983): The union claims it needs a raise to $12 per hour, and that anything less would represent a loss given current inflation. Management argues that it cannot pay more than $10 per hour, and that anything more would impose an unacceptable loss. What if each side had the choice of settling for $11 per hour (a certain settlement) or going to binding arbitration (a risky settlement)? Since each side is viewing the conflict in terms of what it has to lose, following Tversky and Kahneman's (1981) findings, each side is predicted to be risk-seeking and unwilling to take the certain settlement. Changing the frame of the situation to a positive one, however, results in a very different predicted outcome: If the union views anything above $10 per hour as a gain, and management views anything under $12 per hour as a gain, then risk-aversion will dominate and a negotiated settlement will be likely. Using an example conceptually similar to the above scenario, Neale and Bazerman (1983a) found that negotiators with positive frames are significantly more concessionary and successful than their negative counterparts.

In a related study, Bazerman, Magliozzi, and Neale (1983) found that the frame of buyers and sellers in an open market simulation systematically affected their negotiation behavior. This simulation allowed buyers and sellers to complete transactions on a three-issue integrative bargaining problem with as many opponents as possible in a fixed amount of time — with total profit the goal. In this study, negotiators were led to view a transaction in terms of either (1) net profit (gains) or (2) expenses (losses) away from the gross profit of the transaction. While net profit was equal to gross profit less expenses, positivity (gain)-framed negotiators experienced the risk-aversion necessary to have an incentive to compromise. This incentive to compromise led negotiators with a positive frame to (1) complete a larger number of transactions and (2) obtain greater overall profitability than negotiators with a negative frame.

Many prescriptive approaches to negotiation (Raiffa, 1982) lead negotiators to evaluate their risk preferences as part of their prescriptive analysis. However, a negotiator's strategic choice is likely to be affected inappropriately by the negotiator's frame — nominal dollar gain versus real dollar loss, net profit or expenses away from gross profit, and so on. In evaluating their risk preferences, negotiators need to be aware of the influence of positive versus negative frames; otherwise, their decisions may reflect this cognitive distortion more than their actual preferences.

What determines whether a negotiator will have a positive or negative frame? The answer lies in the selection of a perceptual anchor. Consider the anchors available to a union negotiator in simply negotiating a wage: (1) last year's wage, (2) management's initial offer, (3) the union's estimate of management's resistance point, (4) the union's resistance point, or (5) your bargaining position, which has been announced publicly to your constituency. As the anchor moves from 1 to 5, what is a modest *gain* in comparison to last year's wage is a *loss* in comparison to the publicly specified goals. As the anchor changes from 1 to 5, the union negotiator moves from a positive frame to a negative frame. For example, if workers are currently making $10 per hour and demanding an increase of $2 per hour, a proposed increase of $1 per hour can be viewed as a $1 per hour gain in comparison to last year's wage (Anchor 1) or a loss of $1 per hour in comparison to the goals of the union's constituency (Anchor 5). In order to avoid the adverse effects of framing, the negotiator should be aware of his or her frame and examine the context from alternative frames.

In addition to thinking about how frames affect the primary negotiator, framing has important implications for the tactics negotiators can use. The framing effect suggests that in order to induce concessionary behavior from an opponent, a negotiator should always create anchors that lead the opposition to a positive frame and negotiate in terms of what the other side has to gain. In addition, the negotiator should make it salient to the opposition that it is a risky situation where a sure gain is possible.

Finally, the impact of framing has important implications for mediators. To the extent that the goal is compromise, a mediator should strive to have both parties view the negotiation in a positive frame. This is tricky, however, since the anchor that will lead to a positive frame for one negotiator is likely to lead to a negative frame for the other negotiator. This suggests that when the mediator meets with each party separately, he or she needs to create differing anchors to create risk-aversion in both parties. Again, if the mediator is to affect the frame, he or she also wants to emphasize the risk of the situation and create uncertainty, leading both sides to prefer the sure settlement.

Changing negotiator intuition requires that the negotiator find fault with current procedures. Negotiators can be trained by demonstrating how they behave differently with identical objective information, depending on their frame. Ideally, it is useful to have individuals exposed to both positive and negative frames in alternative simulations. Prescriptively, before a negotiator makes a decision, he or she should first explore whether other perspectives on the problem result in different decisions.

The Mythical Fixed-Pie of Negotiations

Integrative agreements are nonobvious solutions to conflict that reconcile the parties' interests and yield a higher joint benefit than a simple compromise could create. To illustrate, consider the compromise between two sisters who fought over an orange (Follett, 1940). The two sisters agreed to split the orange in half, allowing one sister to use her portion for juice and the other sister to use the peel of her half for a cake. The two parties in this conflict overlooked the *integrative* agreement of giving one sister all the juice and the other sister all the peel.

Walton and McKersie (1965) suggested two directly opposing models of the bargaining process. The distributive model views negotiation as a procedure for dividing a fixed-pie of resources, or, "How much of the orange does each sister receive?" According to this model, what one side gains, the other side loses. A number of situations are accurately depicted by the distributive model. If you were to purchase a commodity in a resort location with cash (with no other purchases from the seller possible), the negotiation for the amount of cash that you pay would be depicted by the distributive model. In contrast, Walton and McKersie's integrative bargaining model views negotiation as a means by which parties can make trade-offs or jointly solve problems to the mutual benefit of both parties, or, "How can the orange be divided to maximize the joint benefit to the two sisters?" According to this model, the two parties' success at joint problem-solving will determine the size of the pie of resources to be distributed. As we describe below, the integrative model describes far more negotiations than most people realize.

The fixed-pie assumption of the distributive model represents a fundamental bias in human judgment.[1] That is, negotiators have a systematic intuitive bias that distorts their behavior: They assume that their interests directly conflict with the other party's interests. The fundamental assumption of a fixed-pie probably results from a competitive society that creates the belief in a win-lose situation. This win-lose orientation is manifested objectively in our society in athletic competition, admission to academic programs, industrial promotion systems, and so on. Individuals tend to generalize from these objective win-lose situations and apply their experience to situations that are not objectively fixed-pies. Faced with a mixed-motive situation requiring both cooperation and competition, it is the competitive aspect that becomes salient — resulting in a win-lose orientation and a distributive approach to bargaining. This in turn results in the development of a strategy for obtaining the largest share possible of the perceived fixed-pie. Such a focus inhibits the creativity and problem-solving necessary for the development of integrative solutions.

The pervasiveness of the fixed-pie perception, as well as the importance of integrative bargaining, can be seen in the recent housing market. When interest rates first shot above 12% in 1979, the housing market came to a dead stop. Sellers continued to expect the value of their property to increase. Buyers, however, could not afford the monthly payments on houses they aspired to own, due to the drastically higher interest rates. Viewing the problem as a distributive one, buyers could not afford the prices sellers were demanding. This fixed-pie assumption (which was prevalent throughout the industry) led to the conclusion that transactions would not occur until seller resistance points decreased, buyer resistance points increased, and/or interest rates came down. However, once the industry began to view real estate transaction integratively, some relief was provided. Specifically, sellers cared a great deal about price — partly to justify their past investment. Buyers cared about finding some way to afford a house they aspired to own — perhaps their first house. The integrative solutions were the wide variety of creative financing developments (e.g., seller financing) of the early 1980s, which allowed sellers an artificially high price in exchange for favorable financing assistance to the buyer. Creative financing integrated the interests of buyers and sellers, rescuing an entire industry from our common fixed-pie assumptions.

The above arguments suggest that while some fixed-pies exist objectively, most resolutions depend on finding favorable trade-offs between negotiators, trade-offs that necessitate eliminating our intuitive fixed-pie assumptions. Winkelgren (1974) suggests that we often limit our finding creative solutions by making false assumptions. The fixed-pie perception is a fundamentally false assumption that hinders finding creative (integrative) solutions. A fundamental task in training negotiators lies in identifying and eliminating this false assumption, and institutionalizing the creative process of integrative bargaining.

The analytical development of integrative solutions is central to most prescriptive frameworks. However, most prescriptive approaches assume a negotiator will follow the prescription, unaffected by his or her intuitive strategies for negotiation. In contrast, this article argues that an individual fully versed in the prescriptive writing on negotiation may fall back on past intuitive fixed-pie strategies when faced with a potentially integrative problem. Why? The fixed-pie assumption is an institutionalized part of most nego-tiators' intuitive repertoire. Until this fundamental aspect of the negotiator's cognitive repertoire is altered, the bias will impede the individual's ability to implement the prescriptive recommendations.

One proven strategy for unfreezing (attacking) the fixed-pie assumption has been developed through the use of the open market simulation described earlier. In that integrative bargaining task, subjects were told to try to maxi-mize their profit in each transaction. The market lasted for 30 minutes. The negotiators tended toward their fixed-pie assumptions early in the exercise, then became significantly more integrative and successful as the exercise pro-gressed. Following the exercise, the negotiators were given feedback demon-strating their early failures at obtaining optimal resolutions, while emphasiz-ing the new behaviors they found to be effective as the exercise developed. The combination of identifying their early negotiation failures (unfreezing) and reinforcing integrative behaviors has a powerful effect on the way indi-viduals approach additional simulations.

The Nonrational Escalation of Conflict

Consider the following situation:

> It is 1981. PATCO (The Professional Air Traffic Controllers Organization) decides to strike to obtain a set of concessions from the U.S. government. It is willing to "invest" the temporary loss of pay during the strike in order to obtain concessions. No government concessions result or appear to be forthcoming. PATCO is faced with the option of backing off and returning to work under the former arrangement or increasing the commitment to the strike to try to force the concessions it desires.

In this example, PATCO has committed resources to a course of action. It is then faced with escalating that commitment or backing out of the conflict. This example illustrates a decision problem that occurs in a variety of con-flicts in which an actor can become trapped into a costly course of action. The escalation of commitment to a failing course of action has become a topic of interest among decision researchers (Rubin and Brockner, 1975; Rubin, 1980; Staw, 1976, 1981; Bazerman et al., forthcoming). Their studies indicate that individuals, groups, and organizations who make decisions that do not lead to expected positive results tend nonrationally to commit added resources to a previously chosen course of action. These researchers would have predicted that PATCO was far more likely to persist in its course of action than a rational analysis would have dictated.

It is easy to see the process of nonrational escalation of commitment unfold in a number of actual conflict situations. The negotiation process com-monly leads both sides initially to make extreme demands. The escalation lit-erature predicts that if negotiators become committed to their initial public statements, they will nonrationally adopt a nonconcessionary stance. Further, if both sides incur losses as a result of a lack of agreement (e.g., a strike), their commitment to their positions is expected to increase, and their willingness to change to a different course of action (i.e., compromise) is expected to decrease. The more a negotiator believes there is "too much invested to quit," the more likely he or she is to be intransigent.

An understanding of escalation can be very helpful to a negotiator in understanding the behavior of the opponent. When will the other party really hold out? The escalation literature predicts that the other side will really hold out when it has "too much invested" in its position to give in.

This suggests that there are systematic clues as to when you can threaten your opponent and win, and when the threat will receive an active response, due to your opponent's prior public commitment to a course of action. Strategically, then, a negotiator should avoid inducing the opponent to make statements or to behave in any way that would create the illusion of having invested too much to quit.

Descriptive research on the nonrational escalation of commitment can be integrated with prescriptive approaches to negotiation. Prescriptive approaches provide strategies for deciding whether or not to continue a conflict. The escalation literature, however, suggests that many of the inputs required by the prescriptive approach (e.g., What is the likelihood that the other side will give in? What are the costs of continuing the conflict?) are likely to be biased in favor of escalating the conflict. In order to use a prescriptive approach optimally, we need to understand and change the nonrational tendency of negotiators to escalate commitment to an existing conflict.

A number of principles have been identified by Bazerman, Beekun, and Schoorman (1982) and by Rubin (1980) concerning the avoidance of escalation in general. Many of these can be applied to negotiators:

Continually evaluate the cost and benefits of maintaining a conflict in its current form. When competition exists, we often lose perspective on our goals and instead seek victory over the opponent. Forced consideration of the costs and benefits of escalating the conflict encourages rationality — that is, following the course of action that will best achieve the objectives.

Be aware of the nonrational tendency to escalate commitment to a previous course of action. Escalation often takes the form of creeping incrementalism — "We need to strike for only one more week to get the company to give in." The strongest safeguard against this pattern of escalation is awareness. People who are trained to recognize escalatory situations are less likely to become entrapped.

Recognize sunk costs. Accountants and economics teach the principle that irrelevant historical costs should not be considered in a decision. Most of us, however, intuitively and inappropriately include sunk costs in evaluating courses of action. Instead, alternative courses of action should be evaluated in terms of *future* costs and benefits.

Be aware of the tendency to try to justify past actions. A primary explanation for why people escalate commitment to a course of action involves our need cognitively to justify past actions. That is, escalation of commitment to a strike can be seen as a psychological attempt to make the original decision to strike appear rational. The importance of this principle is strengthened when the constituency is monitoring the negotiator's success.

Negotiator Overconfidence

Consider the following scenario:

> You are an adviser to a major-league baseball player. In baseball, a system exists for the resolution of compensation conflicts that calls for a player and a team who do not agree to submit final offers to an arbitrator. Using final offer arbitration, the arbitrator must accept one position or the other, not a compromise. Thus, the challenge for each side is to come just a little closer to the arbitrator's perception of the appropriate compensation package than the opposition. In this case, your best intuitive estimate of the final offer that the team will submit is a package worth $200,000 per year. You believe that an appropriate wage is $400,000 per year, but estimate the arbitrator's opinion to be $300,000 per year. What final offer do you propose?

This scenario represents a common cognitive trap for negotiators. Individuals are systematically overconfident in estimating the position of a neutral third party and in estimating the likelihood that a third party will accept their position. In the baseball example, if the arbitrator's true assessment of the appropriate wage is $250,000, and you believe it to be $300,000, you are likely to submit an inappropriately high offer and overestimate the likelihood that the offer will be accepted. Consequently, the overconfidence bias is likely to lead the adviser to believe that less compromise is necessary than a more objective analysis would suggest.

The research discussed above demonstrates the frequency of systematic deviations from rationality in human judgment. Yet evidence also shows that individuals have unwarranted confidence in their truly fallible judgments (Einhorn and Hogarth, 1978; Fischoff, 1981; Lichtenstein et al., 1977). Individuals are overconfident in their assessment of the probability (confidence judgment) that their judgment will be accurate. Farber (1981) discusses this problem in terms of negotiators' divergent expectations. That is, each side is optimistic that the neutral third party will adjudicate in its favor. Assume that (1) the union is demanding $8.75 per hour, (2) management is offering $8.25 per hour, and (3) the "appropriate" wage is $8.50 per hour. Farber (1981) suggests that the union will typically expect the neutral third party to adjudicate at a wage somewhat over $8.50, while management will expect a wage somewhat under $8.50. Given these divergent expectations, neither side is willing to compromise at $8.50. Both sides will incur the costs of impasse and aggregately do no better through the use of a third party. In the baseball scenario, if one side had a more objective assessment of the opponent's offer and the position of the arbitrator, it could use this information strategically to its advantage in final offer arbitration.

Research demonstrates that negotiators tend to be overconfident that their positions will prevail if they do not "give in." Neale and Bazerman (1983b; Bazerman and Neale, 1982) show that negotiators consistently overestimate the probability, under final offer arbitration, that their final offer will be accepted. That is, while only 50% of all final offers can be accepted, the average subject estimated that there was a much higher probability that his or her offer would be accepted. If we consider a final offer as a judgment as to how much compromise is necessary to win the arbitration, it is easy to argue that when a negotiator is overconfident that a particular position will be accepted, the incentive to compromise is reduced. If a more accurate assessment is made, the negotiator is likely to be more uncertain and uncomfortable about the probability of success. One strategy to reduce this uncertainty is to compromise further.

Interestingly, individuals and organizations become aware of their overconfidence over time. When final offer arbitration was first introduced into baseball, the final offers of the two parties involved in any arbitration were drastically disparate, largely due to their overconfidence. Baseball negotiators have since learned that they fare better by coming closer to an objective analysis of the arbitrator's position. This is demonstrated by the fact that over the years final offers of competing parties converged dramatically.

Again, this descriptive research can be integrated with prescriptive approaches to negotiation. Prescriptive analyses necessitate the assessment of the positions of the other party and the arbitrator (when this third party is involved). The overconfidence finding suggests that these assessments are likely to bias negotiators away from compromise. In order to benefit from prescriptive approaches most profitably, we need to eliminate, or at least reduce, the overconfidence that mars the quality of the inputs required for prescriptive analyses.

Training negotiators to recognize the cognitive patterns of overconfidence should include the realization that overconfidence is most likely to occur when a party's knowledge is limited. Most of us follow the intuitive cognitive rule: "When in doubt, be overconfident." This suggests that negotiators should be aware of the benefits of obtaining objective assessments of worth from a neutral party, realizing that this neutral assessment is likely to be systematically closer to the other party's position than the negotiator would have predicted intuitively.

The Winner's Curse

Imagine that you are in a foreign country. You meet a merchant who is selling a very attractive gem. You have bought a few gems in your life but are far from being an expert. After some discussion, you make the merchant an offer that you believe (but are uncertain) is on the low side. He quickly accepts, and the transaction is completed. How do you feel? Most people would feel uneasy with the purchase after the quick acceptance. Yet, why would you voluntarily make an offer that you would not want accepted?

To understand this quandary, consider the experimental work of Bazerman and Samuelson (1983). The problem we posed to Boston University M.B.A. students can be summarized as follows:

> The subject is to play the role of the acquirer in a potential corporate takeover. The subject's firm (the acquirer) is considering making an offer to buy out another firm (the target). However, the acquirer is uncertain about the ultimate value of the target firm. It only knows that its value under current management is between $0 and $100 per share, with all values equally likely. Since the firm is expected to be worth 50% more under the acquirer's management than under the current ownership, it appears to make sense for a transaction to take place. While the acquirer does not know the actual value of the firm, the target knows its current worth exactly. The target can be expected to accept any offer that is profitable to its sharehold-

ers. In this exercise, what price per share should the acquirer offer for the target?

The problem is analytically simple (as will be demonstrated shortly) yet intuitively perplexing. The dominant response was between $50 and $75 (90 of 123 responses). How is this $50 to $75 decision reached? One common, naive explanation is that, on average, the firm will be worth $50 to the target and $75 to the acquirer; consequently, a transaction in this range will, on average, be profitable to both parties.

Now consider the logical process that a normative response would generate in evaluating the decision to make an offer of $60 per share (a value suggested naively to be "mutually acceptable.")

> If I offer $60 per share, the offer will be accepted 60% of the time — whenever the firm is worth between $0 and $60 to the target. Since all values are equally likely, the firm will, on average, be worth $30 per share to the target when the target accepts the offer. Since the value of the firm is worth 50% more to the acquirer, the average value of the firm to the acquirer when the target accepts a $60 per share offer will be $45 per share, resulting in a loss of $15 per share ($45-$60).

Consequently, a $60 per share offer is ill-considered. It is easy to see that the same kind of reasoning applies to any positive offer. On the average, the acquirer obtains a company worth 25% less than the price it pays. Thus, the best the acquirer can do is not to make an offer ($0 per share). Even though in all circumstances the firm is worth more to the acquirer than to the target, any offer leads to a negative expected return to the acquirer. The source of this paradox lies in the target's accepting the acquirer's offer when the acquirer least wants the firm — when it is a "lemon." Unfortunately, only 9 of 123 subjects correctly offered $0 per share.

Most individuals have the analytical ability to follow the logic that the optimal offer is $0 per share (no offer). Yet without assistance, most individuals would make a positive offer (typically between $50 and $75 per share). Thus, individuals systematically exclude information from their decision processes that they have the ability to include. They fail to realize that their expected return is *conditional* on an acceptance by the other party, and that an acceptance is most likely to occur when it is least desirable to the negotiator making the offer.

The key feature of the "winner's curse" in the bargaining context is that one side has much better information than the other side. Though we are all familiar with the slogan "buyer beware," our intuition seems to have difficulty putting this idea into practice when asymmetric information exists. Most people realize that when they buy a commodity they know little about, their uncertainty increases. The evidence presented here indicates that against an informed opponent, their expected return from the transaction may decrease dramatically. Practically, the evidence suggests that people undervalue the importance of accurate information in making transactions. They undervalue a mechanic's evaluation of a used car, a house inspector's assessment of a house, or an independent jeweler's assessment of a coveted gem. Thus, the knowledgeable gem merchant will accept your offer selectively, taking the offer when the gem is probably worth less than your estimate. To protect yourself, you need to develop or borrow the expertise to balance the quality of information.

Prescriptive approaches lead individuals to consider their opponent's decisions in their analysis. Although the naive analysis discussed earlier included an assessment of the opponent's decision processes, the logic was still deficient. While individuals should make their bid based on the expected value of the offer *conditional on the bid being accepted*, they often fail to include the selective acceptance of the opponent in their offer behavior. That is, individuals systematically fail to realize that the opponent's willingness to accept an offer provides relevant information. This critical inference must be made before the offer is made, not in a regretful manner afterwards.

To get individuals to incorporate this lesson in their decision processes requires that they see something wrong with the way they currently make inferences about an opponent's behavior. This provides the shock necessary for change. Anecdotal experience suggests that exposure to failure creates the shock necessary for future immunization against the winner's curse. In a somewhat looser form, before you make an offer, you should first ask: "Will I be happy if the offer is accepted quickly?"

Conclusion

This article demonstrates the powerful negative effects of limitations in judgment on the performance of negotiators. Five unique systematic biases have been identified that create cognitive limitations that reduce the negotiator's success: (1) the impact of the negotiator's frame, (2) the mythical fixed-pie, (3) the nonrational escalation of conflict, (4) negotiator overconfidence, and (5) the winner's curse. Future research is needed to provide empirical support for the existence of these biases in actual negotiation contexts. Further, the biases identified in this article are a mere sampling of the many biases relevant to negotiator judgment. For example, I have not dealt with the variety of ways in which negotiators tend to think of themselves as being superior to their opponents (more resourceful, brighter, more ethical, etc.). While the identification of systematic biases that affect negotiators is a critical step in the development of the conflict literature, research needs to provide prescriptive recommendations for improving negotiator judgment.

Extensive research (Lewin, 1947; Schein, 1980; Goodman et al., 1980) has demonstrated that creating *sustained* change in individuals, groups, or organizations is very difficult. Two major problems are resistance to change and the tendency to revert to comfortable methods of operation. Given the extensive institutionalization of our judgmental strategies, changes in this domain are likely to be particularly difficult. Consequently, the current research must be embedded in an explicit change program.

Lewin's suggested steps for creating change and making it last over time are useful in this regard. First, it is necessary to get the existing system (i.e., the negotiator's decision processes) to "unfreeze"; that is, the individual must be receptive to change. This frequently requires demonstrating to the individual that something is wrong with his or her intuition. Second, once the individual's current strategy is unfrozen, the content must be provided to direct the negotiator to the appropriate change. Third, the change must be "refrozen," making the change part of the negotiator's standard repertoire. If the change is not institutionalized, the negotiator is likely to revert to past, comfortable cognitive strategies. The explicit development of a planned change effort that incorporates these three steps is central to the improvement of negotiator judgment.

In conclusion, this article has identified a new direction for increasing negotiators' success by improving the quality of their decision-making processes. This area of research complements prescriptive approaches to negotiation by specifying cognitive limitations that inhibit the optimal implementation of prescriptive recommendations. Future research and training programs need to pursue the potential of improving judgment as a step in providing better prescriptions to negotiators.

NOTES

This research was funded by National Science Foundation Grant BNS8107331.

1. Pruitt (1983) has conducted extensive experimentation on the determinants of integrative behavior by negotiators. He found that negotiators who had an incentive to cooperate and high aspiration levels were far more likely to behave integratively than were negotiators without an incentive to compromise and with low aspiration levels. In addition, he found that when negotiators had a positive relationship with the other party and were highly accountable to a constituency, integrative bargaining was more likely. Finally, Pruitt provides an interesting taxonomy of five strategies for identifying integrative solutions: (1) increasing the resources the two parties have to divide, (2) having one party compensate the other party for concessions, (3) trading off issues of differing importance to the two parties, (4) reducing the costs of one party for giving in to the position of the other party, and (5) finding novel solutions that incorporate the underlying interests of both parties.

REFERENCES

Bazerman, M. H. and Neale, M. A. (1983). "Heuristics in negotiation: limitations to dispute resolution effectiveness." In *Negotiating in organizations*, edited by M. H. Bazerman and R. J. Lewicki. Beverly Hills, Calif.: Sage.
——— and Neale, M. A. (1982). "Improving negotiation effectiveness under final offer arbitration: the role of selection and training." *Journal of Applied Psychology* 67: 543-548.
———, Beekun, R. I. and Schoorman, F. D. (1982). "Performance evaluation in a dynamic context: a laboratory study of the impact of a prior commitment to the ratee." *Journal of Applied Psychology* 67: 873-876.
———, Guiliano, T. and Appelman, A. (forthcoming). "Escalation in individual and group decision making." In *Organizational Behavior and Human Performance*.
———, Magliozzi, T. and Neale, M. A. (1983). "The acquisition of an integrative response in a competitive market." Presented at the Academy of Management annual meeting, Dallas, Texas, August.
——— and Samuelson, W. F. (1983). "The winner's curse: an empirical investigation." In *Aspiration Oriented Decision Making*, edited by R. Tietz. New York: Springer-Verlag.
Einhorn, H. J. and Hogarth, R. M. (1978). "Confidence in judgment: persistence of the illusion of validity." *Psychology Review*. 85: 395-416.
Farber, H. S. (1981). "Divergent expectations, threat strategies, and bargaining under arbitration." Presented to the Econometric Society, San Diego, June.
Fischoff, B. (1981). "Debiasing." In *Judgment under uncertainty: heuristics and biases*, edited by D. Kahneman, P. Slovic, and A. Tversky. New York: Cambridge University Press.
Fisher, R. and Ury, W. (1981). *Getting to YES*. Boston: Houghton Mifflin.

Follett, M. P. (1940). "Constructive conflict." In *Dynamic administration: The collected papers of Mary Parker Follett*, edited by H. C. Metcalf and L. Urwick. New York: Harper & Row.

Goodman, P. S., Bazerman, M. H. and Conlon, E. J. (1980). "Institutionalization processes in organizational change." In *Research in organizational behavior*, vol. 2, edited by B. M. Staw and L. L. Cummings. Greenwich, Conn.: JAI Press.

Kahneman, D. and Tversky, A. (1982)."Psychology of preferences." *Scientific American* 247: 161-173.

——— and Tversky, A. (1979). "Prospect theory: an analysis of decision under risk." *Econometrica* 47: 263-291.

Lewin, K. (1947). "Group decision and social change." In *Readings in social psychology*, edited by T. M. Newcomb and E. L. Hartley. New York: Holt, Rinehart & Winston.

Lichtenstein, S., Fischoff, B. and Phillips, L. D. (1977). "Calibration of probabilities: The state of the art." In *Decision making and change in human affairs*, edited by H. Jungermann and G. de Zeeuw. Amsterdam: D. Reidel.

Neale, M. A. and Bazerman, M. H. (1983a). "Systematic deviations from rationality in negotiation behavior: the framing of conflict and negotiator overconfidence." MIT Working Paper.

——— and Bazerman, M. H. (1983b). "The effect of perspective taking ability on the negotiation process under different forms of arbitration." *Industrial and Labor Relations Review* 36 (April): 378-388.

Pruitt, D. (1983). "Integrative agreements: Nature and antecedents." In *Negotiating in organizations*, edited by M. H. Bazerman and R. J. Lewicki. Beverly Hills, Calif.: Sage.

Raiffa, H. (1982). *The art and science of negotiation*. Cambridge, Mass.: Harvard University Press.

Rubin, J. Z. (1980). "Psychological traps." *Psychology Today*, March: 52-63.

——— and Brockner, J. (1975). "Factors affecting entrapment in waiting situations: The Rosencrantz and Guildenstern effect." *Journal of Personality and Social Psychology* 31: 1054-1063.

Schein, E. H. (1980). *Organizational psychology*. Englewood Cliffs, N. J.: Prentice-Hall.

Staw, B. M. (1981). "The escalation of commitment to a course of action." *Academy of Management Review* 6: 577-587.

———. (1976). "Knee-deep in the big muddy: A study of escalating commitment to a chosen course of action." *Organizational Behavior and Human Performance* 16: 27-44.

Tversky, A. and Kahneman, D. (1981). "The framing of decisions and the psychology of choice." *Science* 211: 453-458.

Walton, R. E. and McKersie, R. B. (1965). *A behavioral theory of labor negotiations: An analysis of a social interaction system*. New York: McGraw-Hill.

Winkelgren, W. A. (1974). *How to solve problems*. San Francisco: Freeman.

The Eastern Air Lines Saga: Grounded by a Contest of Wills

Robert B. McKersie

Editor's Note: This essay was written in early June, 1989.

For months now, the saga of Eastern Airlines has been front-page news. The story has all the elements of a tabloid potboiler — a corporate raider genius or villain (depending on your point of view) in the person of Frank Lorenzo; high-salaried or victimized blue collar workers (again depending on your point of view); heroic or foolishly stubborn airline pilots (ditto); thousands of travelers inconvenienced; millions of dollars at stake; a new U. S. President who, despite some harsh criticism, refuses to get involved; and such "star" quality figures as ex-Baseball Commissioner Peter Ueberroth, ex-Astronaut Frank Borman, and capitalist supreme Donald Trump. There are, indeed, many stakeholders in this dramatic labor dispute, the rancor and personal animosity of which rival the fiercest of divorce cases. Eastern Airlines is locked in what appears to be a contest of personal wills, and custody of the business itself is the sought-after prize.

The first point to be made about the Eastern Airlines story is that the protagonists have obviously not read *Getting to YES* (Fisher and Ury, 1981) or other contemporary books on negotiation that posit that it is important to "separate the people from the problem." Clearly, Charles Bryant (president of the Machinists Union), Frank Borman (ex-CEO) and Frank Lorenzo (the current CEO) all have been singled out by the opposite side as the reason for the impasse. In effect, personalities have become the problem.

Perhaps it is useful to review some of the history of this imbroglio to understand better how everything became so personal. One place to begin would be to analyze the contest of wills that developed between Frank Borman and Charles Bryant. The relevant period to examine is 1983-85, when the parties engaged in a much-heralded "partnership" that placed union representatives on the company's Board of Directors; gave employees a substantial share of stock in exchange for major financial concessions; created a system of joint committees to improve productivity (with the inducement of enabling workers to earn back their wage cuts); and fostered an unprecedented sharing of information between labor and management.

The labor-management cooperation was genuine. I visited the Eastern offices at Logan Airport in Boston during that time period, and talked with both management and union officials. The delegation of responsibility to the working level had taken place to such an extent that, for many operations, no

Robert B. McKersie is Professor of Industrial Relations at the Sloan School of Management, the Massachusetts Institute of Technology, Cambridge, Mass. 02139.

supervisors were assigned. The workers had even formed task forces on various company projects, one of which recommended a plan for using idle planes during the night to handle major shipments of U. S. mail in and out of Logan Airport. Another example of the cooperative spirit at Eastern in those days was the establishment of a new hub at Kansas City. To undertake this project, labor and management signed a pioneering agreement that reduced the number of classifications, established teams, and created the kind of model, high commitment system that has been publicized in a number of manufacturing industries.

Bryant and Borman went around the country talking about the new era that had arrived, and the company appeared to be thriving — at least, until another round of fare cuts occurred in late 1985, resulting in a quick and disastrous nosedive for Eastern's profits.

The cooperative spirit unravelled further when management approached the unions in late 1985 asking for additional reductions in compensation costs, amounting to approximately 20 percent of salaries. Despite the fact that other Eastern unions grudgingly agreed, the Machinists firmly said "no," and an impasse developed. Ultimately, negotiations proceeded to the make-or-break point, with management maintaining it needed a minimum package of 15 percent concessions from the Machinists, without which it would have to file for bankruptcy or seek another buyer.

The union's response was that it would only go along with the concessions if the board voted to remove Frank Borman. From the union's point of view, Borman was responsible for the economic woes. Specifically, he had made several poor strategic decisions. First, he bought a fleet of fuel-efficient planes that added approximately $2 billion in debt to the balance sheet. The decision, made at a time when fuel prices were high and were thought by many to be going even higher, proved not to be a wise one. When fuel prices dropped, Eastern was left with a large load of debt at high interest rates. Second, when he expanded routes to the West Coast and offered low fares, the move proved unprofitable.

The Eastern Board called the union's hand and voted to continue Borman and, at the same time, to sell the company to Frank Lorenzo of Texas Air. How could a relationship that appeared to be so constructive sour to the point that the union was demanding the departure of the CEO as a price for its concessions? What are the dynamics by which a good relationship can deteriorate so quickly?

There is no single answer to these questions, but a number of factors can provide some explanation. First, the workers, particularly the machinists, developed expectations that labor-management cooperation was going to solve all their problems. They were not ready for the eventuality of further losses and the necessity of additional financial sacrifices. During the two-year period of the partnership, considerable information about "upside" activities was shared, such as suggestions and productivity improvements, but it is not clear that the workers were conditioned to the possibility of another downturn.

At the same time, on the other side of the fence, management was losing a good deal of its enthusiasm for the process of labor-management cooperation. At one point, an Eastern vice-president commented to me that, "With this employee ownership arrangement, every day is a stockholder's meeting."

Thus, from management's point of view, the downside of employee involvement was that all decisions needed union approval, creating an organizational gridlock that slowed things down considerably.

Some members of management also believed that many of the productivity savings that were being accumulated to justify restoration of concessions (for example, changing a supplier to reduce costs) were not due to joint accomplishments but reflected initiatives of management. Frank Borman in a recent TV interview summed up the Eastern management attitude with this comment: "We probably paid too high a price with the partnership."

The literature on conflict resolution makes the important point that a natural sequence is to move from conflict (what Pruitt [1981] calls contending) to cooperation. This is indeed what happened at Eastern Airlines in 1983 — since the relationship prior to that point had been characterized by considerable turmoil. However, our knowledge about how cooperation can be sustained and how to deal with the bitterness and disillusionment that inevitably accompany the breakdown of a positive relationship is much less developed.

Moving along with the story, Texas Air acquired Eastern Airlines in early 1986 and, for the past three years, everything has been down, down, down. Again, personalities appear on center stage. Shortly after Lorenzo bought Eastern Airlines, Bryant offered to sit down and have an amicable discussion with Lorenzo. His overture was refused.

From Lorenzo's viewpoint, the task has been to return Eastern to profitability by reducing its labor costs. Despite great controversy, he accomplished this goal at Continental Airlines by dropping labor costs from approximately 40 percent of the operating budget to approximately 25 to 30 percent. Cutting wage scales and improving productivity via the elimination of various work rule restrictions were the primary means of accomplishing this task.

From the union's side, the Lorenzo strategy appeared to be a steady plundering of the assets in favor of the parent company, specifically, the sale (at a low price) of the Eastern reservation system; the sale of jets and landing slots at favorable prices; and a shift of assets to the parent company via loan agreements — all under the newly-coined term of "upstreaming."

By 1988, matters reached the point where Lorenzo was insisting on yet another package of concessions from the Machinists' union which they refused to grant. Eastern Airlines was then taken on strike by the unions[1] and into bankruptcy by Lorenzo.

The Eastern strike is far more than a dispute over wages and resources — it is a power struggle for virtual control of the airline. The union in its commentary hearkens back to the two years of labor-management cooperation and the positive benefits to be derived from ownership and a leadership role for the unions. The importance to the unions of getting Lorenzo out of the picture was underscored by the unions' refusal to go along with a deal that would have put former Baseball Commissioner Peter Ueberroth in control but left Lorenzo in charge for an interim period. Lorenzo had become so much of an anathema to the unions that they were not willing to have him remain on the property for even a transition period, if they were going to agree to accept major concessions.

So what are the major themes and lessons? Certainly, a strike that seeks to change the ownership and the control of a company is a new development in labor-management relations.[2] Given trends in the corporate restructuring and the high stakes that are involved for union and management, we will probably see substantially more of these types of conflicts.

This sad saga vividly calls to mind many of the well-known dynamics of how conflict can escalate (see, for example, Pruitt and Rubin, 1986). Once matters become so personalized, positions harden, new areas of dispute can develop, and the parties lose respect for one another. The lack of trust — indeed, the lack of any kind of communication — is so severe that no common ground exists. The battle at Eastern is not about reaching agreement within some established framework; it is about changing the players and the basic relationship itself.

Another important point is that unions are very adept at distributive bargaining when the pie is growing larger, but they have great difficulty in managing the internal dynamics when the pie is shrinking and a type of reverse bargaining is required.

On the management side, it would appear that it is difficult to strike the right balance between joint consultation and taking the initiative within a framework of labor-management cooperation. Management tends to commit two types of errors. First, it overlooks the potential of employee involvement for enhancing commitment and organizational performance. Eastern Airlines missed this opportunity for most of its history. The second error occurs when management assumes that labor-management cooperation will bring about substantial benefits and the new "team spirit" will eliminate all conflicts in the relationship. Such a perspective often overlooks both the need for managerial initiative and a specific structure for participation. To sustain cooperation requires that all stakeholders be kept aware of the dangers that lurk around the corner, and that avenues must be found for the partnership to confront differences and bad news as well as celebrating the joint potential for improving productivity.

The problem with the complete breakdown of trust is that it becomes impossible to agree upon any type of armistice, even though safeguards may be available. For example, given the union's concern about the "upstreaming" of Eastern's assets that Lorenzo has allegedly been engaging in, it should have been possible (either through Ueberroth's purchase agreement or the surveillance of the court) to protect the well-being of Eastern during the interim period before new management actually assumed control. But given the estrangement that has occurred, even this potentially "win-win" possibility was never explored and as a result matters have gotten worse with the prospect of a vastly scaled-down Eastern Airlines within the Texas Air corporation.

We may never know exactly what happened during the crucial period when the Ueberroth offer was on the table and the union leadership and Lorenzo came to an impasse over just how Eastern Airlines would be controlled while the separation of the Eastern assets was being finalized. The unions insisted that, during this interim period, Eastern Airlines be run by a trustee and it was reported that a person of the caliber of Frank Carlucci, former Secretary of Defense, was in the court ready to step forward. Lorenzo, for his part, insisted on maintaining control until the sale was consummated. The unions saw a potential trap: Under the proposed sale, they would go back to work and with lower wages and benefits (part of the deal that they were willing to give to Ueberroth); but, if the deal eventually fell through, they would find themselves in the worst of all possible worlds (from their point of view) — back at work for Lorenzo with major concessions in place.

Of course, hindsight suggests that the unions did not have any BATNA[3] of consequence, given the fact that, after the Ueberroth deal did not go forward, the sale of the shuttle to Trump was approved. And as of the time of this writing (early June, 1989), it looks like the only course of action for the remaining parts of Eastern Airlines is a down-sizing that will leave it at less than half of its original scale.

So what is one to make of all of these high stakes negotiations? I am reminded of the apt phrase that Franklin Delano Roosevelt used when asked for his reaction to a major confrontation between the United Mineworkers and the coal owners: "A plague on both your houses." However, given my desire to maintain neutrality and remembering the quick response of union president John L. Lewis to the President's criticism, I will refrain from such summary judgments. By the way, Lewis' response to the President was: "It ill behooves one who has supped at Labor's table to curse with equal fervor the adversaries when they become locked in deadly embrace." (Where have all the labor leaders with such Shakespearean grace gone?)

Clearly, the dominance of personalities and an absence of trust have contributed to a process that has strayed far from "win-win" negotiations. Perhaps this is an instance where no accommodation is possible. The interests of the protagonists are so diametrically opposed that even the most imaginative problem solving and the most effective process would not overcome what may be an inherent negative range. Lorenzo has been heard to say in other settings that he does not "sit down with unions" and for their part the unions have decided that there is no way that any arrangement can be worked out for a continuing relationship with Lorenzo. In this sense negotiations are only possible if both sides accept the legitimacy of the other side and see as part of their interest the preservation and continuation of the relationship.

While Lorenzo can be faulted for an approach to people relations that is quite unenlightened, the Machinists' union can be faulted for having set the stage for the current predicament by demanding the ouster of Frank Borman in exchange for concessions to keep the airline going in late 1985. The type of relationship that appears to be viable in a setting of adversity is one of "tough trust," wherein the parties cooperate but with full realization of the realities and down-side consequences. The union gambled that the Board of Directors would not sell Eastern Airlines to Lorenzo and unfortunately they lost the high stakes game.

Once matters become so embroiled and personalities and pride assume undue importance, it is difficult for rationality to play its proper role. I would like to think that a solution of some sort could have been found and Eastern Airlines as a distinct entity could survive and regain its reputation as one of the top airlines in the United States. No doubt it would have taken intervention by some very high-level official to urge the parties in the direction of a solution that would leave all sides better off. But we appear to be in a period of history where market forces are the preferred mode for resolving important issues in product and labor markets.

NOTES

The author would like to thank Thomas Kochan and Robert Harris for their helpful comments on an earlier draft.

1. The refusal of the Airline Pilots to cross the picket line of the Machinists became the critical factor in forcing Eastern into bankruptcy.

2. Actually, such a strike would likely be declared illegal in the courts under the provisions of the National Labor Relations Act. However, airlines are governed by the Railway Labor Act, and it is not clear that bringing such an agenda item into the picture represents unfair bargaining.

3. BATNA — Best Alternative To a Negotiated Agreement — is a term popularized by Fisher and Ury (1981) to indicate the maximum a party can obtain without negotiating.

REFERENCES

Fisher, R. and Ury, W. L. (1981). *Getting to YES: Negotiating agreement without giving in.* Boston: Houghton Mifflin.

Pruitt, D. G. and Rubin, J. Z. (1986). *Social conflict: Escalation, stalemate, and settlement.* New York: Random House.

Pruitt, D. G. (1981). *Negotiation behavior.* New York: Academic Press.

Strategy and Self-Command

A commencement address to the RAND Graduate School of Policy Studies

Thomas C. Schelling

I spent a "graduate" year at the RAND Corporation, an applied research center, more than 25 years ago. How I felt about that experience is recorded in the preface to a book I published a year later:

> During the year before this book went to press, I was uniquely located to receive stimulation, provocation, advice, comment, disagreement, encouragement, and education. I spent the year with The RAND Corporation in Santa Monica. As a collection of people, RAND is superb, and I have mentioned above only the few whose intellectual impact on me was powerful and persistent; many others, truly too numerous to list here, have as individuals affected the final shape of this book. But RAND is more than a collection of people; it is a social organism characterized by intellect, imagination, and good humor (Schelling, 1960, p. vi).

Not a bad place for a graduate school. So when the president surprised me with an invitation to speak at RAND's commencement in 1985, I did not hesitate.

I should have. It was one of those weeks when Garry Trudeau, creator of *Doonesbury*, ran out of material and, as he had done before, took a few days' time out to make fun of commencement speakers. It was clear to me that the commencement address was an art form better suited to cartoonists than to aging academics. As if that were not enough discouragement, I came across six rules for giving advice to people a generation younger than oneself. The first was "Don't." Intimidated, I decided the best I could do was to talk about something that interests me in the hope that it would also interest you.

Those who know that I direct an Institute for the Study of Smoking Behavior often wonder how someone could jump from nuclear command and control to self-command and control in 25 years. Actually, it is not much of a jump. Even while I was working at RAND, I noticed that if I were designing safeguards against firing a weapon in panic, or falling asleep on watch, it didn't matter much whether it was I or somebody else who might fire a weapon or fall asleep.

Arranging not to lose one's temper, not to drive after too many drinks, or not to scratch an infected wound while asleep calls for the same kinds of tactics whether we do it for ourselves or for someone else. In strategic inter-

Thomas C. Schelling is Professor of Economics at the University of Maryland, College Park, Md. 20742. He is the Lucius N. Littauer Professor of Political Economy, *emeritus*, at the John F. Kennedy School of Government, Harvard University.

action with another person, we often try to commit ourselves to an action — carrying out a threat or fulfilling a promise — and the ways that we can commit our behavior for strategic advantage are not altogether different from the ways that we may commit our behavior for self-discipline.

There is a cocaine addiction clinic in Denver that uses "self-blackmail" as therapy. The patient is offered an opportunity to write a self-incriminating letter that will be delivered if — and only if — the patient, who is tested on a random schedule, is found to have used cocaine. A physician, for example, writes to the State Board of Medical Examiners confessing that he has violated state law and professional ethics by administering cocaine to himself and deserves to lose his license. That is a powerful deterrent.

But notice that if I worked for that physician, and I had evidence of his cocaine abuse and wanted to help him, I could write such a letter myself and threaten to mail it unless the physician stayed clean. Alternatively, I could threaten to mail it unless the physician doubled my salary. It is the same tactic, whether I use it to extort tribute, to coerce someone for his own good, or to allow someone to incur voluntarily a drastic change in his own incentives.

Obstetricians are increasingly being asked by patients to withhold anesthesia. The physician often proposes that a face mask be put beside the patient, who may inhale nitrous oxide as needed, but some determined patients ask that no such opportunity be provided. If gas is available they will use it, and they want not to be able to. This example nicely illustrates that there are ethical, legal, and policy issues in the practice of self-denial, self-restraint, and self-command. The Constitution of the United States does not permit me to be voluntarily incarcerated in a sanitarium that will not let me out until I have lost 30 pounds or gone 30 days without smoking. No matter what the contract says and how badly I want it enforced when I entered, when my appetite for food or cigarettes overwhelms me and I ask to be let out, the law requires that I be let out.

When self-command is discussed at all, it is usually in relation to appetites and temptations — food, sex, tobacco, gambling, alcohol, and addictive drugs. But the subject also includes one's own behavior in response to rage, panic, and pain. Consider the first paragraph of the first chapter of my favorite book on baseball, which reads as follows:

"Fear."

That's it.

The second paragraph says, "Fear is the fundamental factor in hitting, and hitting the ball with the bat is the fundamental act of baseball. This fact is the starting point for the game of baseball, and yet it is the fact least often mentioned by those who write about baseball" (Koppett, 1967, p. 13).

A book on military tactics might well begin with the same first paragraph. "Fear," it might continue, "is the fundamental factor in exposing oneself to enemy fire, and exposing oneself to enemy fire is the fundamental act of combat." I believe we could also add the next statement: This fact is the starting point for military combat, and yet it is the fact least often mentioned by those who write about combat.[1] Field Marshal Rommel understood this. He advised his World War II panzer divisions always to open fire *before* they were within range of the enemy: If the enemy could be frightened enough before Rommel's tanks came within range, they would be hiding, and therefore as ineffectual as they would be dead.

Fear can be a collective as well an individual problem in self-command. In Caesar's army, for instance, any advancing legionnaire who held back was to be killed instantly by the comrades on either side of him, who, if they failed to kill the soldier who held back, were themselves to be killed instantly by the legionnaires next to them. New legionnaires quickly learned, of course, that the rule actually enhanced their security, especially when the enemy learned that advancing legionnaires could never be intimidated.

The need for anticipatory self-command arises not only for the individual or the squad, but for government itself. The statutory debt ceiling, a proposed balanced budget amendment, and statutory efforts to make budget balancing automatic are well understood by families whose own efforts to live within their means leave behind a trail of good intentions and broken resolutions. Parents need, as the founding fathers needed, inhibition on cruel and unusual punishment when they lose their tempers; in fact, the entire Bill of Rights could be described as an effort of legislators to put some restraints on legislation beyond the reach of ordinary majority vote.

Albert Hirschman observed some years ago that technically backward countries are better at maintaining airlines than roadbeds. It is a matter of incentives: You can patch the road surface cheaply while letting the roadbed invisibly go to ruin over the years, but airplanes don't go to ruin invisibly! Had Hirschman been observing advanced countries, he might have made the same point about fire engines and sewers. Individuals display similar behavior: In a hurry, I shave rather than brush my teeth.

Many joggers have discovered the buddy system: Four people jogging together three times a week at the lunch hour may go on for years as a team; but if they jogged separately on different days, they might all be early dropouts. S. L. A. Marshall observed that most soldiers in World War II never fired their rifles — no matter how brave they were, how long a battle lasted, or what targets presented themselves. However, weapons that required joint action by two or three soldiers, like feeding a belt of ammunition, were regularly fired as intended (Marshall, 1947, pp. 50-84).

As long ago as 1957, in a classic work on game theory, Duncan Luce and Howard Raiffa pointed out that a person who wants to go on a diet but does not trust himself "announces his intention, or accepts a wager that he will not break his diet, so that later he will *not* be free to change his mind and to optimize his actions according to his tastes at *that* time" (Luce and Raiffa, 1957, p. 75). The same thing is accomplished by maneuver rather than by commitment when a smoker who wants to stop deliberately embarks on a vacation deep in the wilds without cigarettes.

We all know how to put the alarm clock across the room so that we cannot turn it off without getting out of bed; and executives in some corporations may join a voluntary arrangement in the corporate dining room: They will be served at lunch only what they ordered by phone at 9:30 that morning. And I have often wished that hotels would, for a small extra fee, disable the television in my room before I arrive.

Sometimes the problem is action, not abstention. I sometimes wonder whether I would enjoy skydiving as a hobby, and I wonder even more whether I would ever be able to initiate it. I recently saw an old friend, an Army general, and recalled that the last time I had seen him he was getting ready to command airborne troops. I had asked whether he would have to jump, and he said yes; I asked whether he anticipated any difficulty in actually leaping out of an airplane, and he said he understood that the Army had a man who took care of that.

I do not know how they do it at civilian skydiving resorts. No doubt our constitutionally inalienable rights might get in the way there, too, of any voluntary contract that would permit the skydiving crew to propel me out when I grab the door jamb and scream that I've changed my mind. Technology would probably help: A trap door and no communication between pilot and passenger might be legal, but would probably not pass safety inspection. A trap door that I could operate with my eyes shut might be easier to manage than diving head first with eyes open. Not only children but even adults find that they can better command their response to a four-inch needle inserted in the knee to draw out fluid if they turn their heads so they can't see it.

High technology has potential in helping us get ourselves under control. There is currently a device by which a prisoner, who might not otherwise be paroled, can be cheaply and remotely monitored outside of prison. Curfews are enforced by a transmitter that emits an encrypted signal that is picked up by a device attached to the parolee's telephone, and that can be interrogated at random from the local police station. The signal will be picked up only if the parolee is within 100 feet of the telephone. This electronic device is attached to the parolee's ankle; it cannot be removed and left by the phone because removing it makes it inoperable; and the parolee cannot buy a copy to leave by the telephone because the codes wouldn't match. Wearing the device could be a *condition* of parole; but a prisoner who didn't altogether trust himself and desperately wanted to succeed on parole (avoiding being sent back to prison), might assume it *voluntarily*. Likewise, a person might someday implant a device to measure blood alcohol that would emit a signal, render a painful shock, or even electronically disable an auto ignition when a certain danger point was reached.

The most controversial technology of all may ultimately be a diagnostic device that could be implanted in the brain to measure the extent of damage caused by a nonfatal stroke; the device would be programmed, above a certain threshold of damage, to make the stroke fatal. This would be the technological embodiment of the "living will." It would also be a technological alternative to the suicide that one might have hoped to commit in such circumstances but be unable to perform.

Technology can also be used to discipline speakers when a program must continue on schedule. It can even be used by a speaker to discipline himself. Some of you probably noticed that I set a timer and placed it on the podium in full view when I began this talk.

Twenty-five years ago, I attended an annual meeting of the Institute for Strategic Studies at Oxford, where the subject of discussion was nuclear deterrence. The chairman of the first morning's session grandly announced that he would hold all speakers to three minutes; and, just in case some speakers might think they could intimidate the chairman into relaxing the limit, he had brought to the occasion what he called "The Great Deterrent." This was a timer that would show a red light at two minutes, and sound a harsh noise at three. He demonstrated the noise — it was indeed a noise to deflate any speaker's dignity, truly a Great Deterrent.

It worked — for a while. The first dozen speakers stayed well within the limit, hastening to conclude when they saw the red light. But eventually a most distinguished member of Parliament, a former cabinet minister, rose to take the floor, walked to the front of the hall near the chairman's table (which was raised on a dais) and began an unhurried disquisition that could not possibly fit within the three minutes.

When he saw the red light, he strolled to where the Great Deterrent rested about shoulder high on the raised table, disdainfully rested his elbow on the table and turned his back on both chairman and timer, continuing his talk without interruption. The chairman squirmed more and more nervously as the minute went by. Then, perfectly visible to most of the audience, the chairman's hand snaked out over the table top and turned off the timer.

Most of us learned more about the credibility of deterrent threats from that one talk than from all the rest of the conference. And that is why, when I set my timer 19 minutes ago, I made myself place it where you could see it.

NOTES

This column is an adaptation of the address presented by the author at the 1985 commencement of the RAND Graduate Institute in Santa Monica, Calif.

    1. An exception that makes the point stunningly is John Keegan's (1976) work, *The Face of Battle*.

REFERENCES

Keegan, J. (1976). *The face of battle*. New York: Viking Press.
Koppett, L. (1967). *A thinking man's guide to baseball*. New York: E. P. Dutton.
Luce, R. D. and **Raiffa, H.** (1957). *Games and decisions*. New York: John Wiley & Sons.
Marshall, S. L. A. (1947). *Men against fire*. Washington: Combat Forces Press.
Schelling, T. C. (1960). *The strategy of conflict*. Cambridge, Mass.: Harvard University Press.

Timing and the Initiation of De-Escalation Moves

Louis Kriesberg

It is a matter of conventional wisdom that successful de-escalation efforts must depend upon the time being right for such efforts. Skilled mediators who want to be successful may refuse to attempt mediation if the situation is not "ripe." But what does ripe mean in this context? Is a situation ripe for settlement when any conflict resolution procedure will work and is it not when every procedure will fail? Furthermore, how would we know when a situation is ripe independent of successful de-escalation? Difficult as it may be to answer such questions, we must address them.

This article consists of five parts. First, I will discuss the concept of timing and the ambiguities of assessing when the time is ripe for effective de-escalating efforts. Second, I will review specific de-escalating efforts in the context of the U.S.-Soviet and Arab-Israeli conflicts. This will provide illustrative cases of efforts that did and did not lead to de-escalating moves. Third, I will discuss the major background conditions that have been said to be necessary for de-escalation to occur. Fourth, I will discuss major conflict resolution strategies that may be appropriate at different conflict stages. Finally, I will consider the implications of this analysis for conflict resolution applications.

The Concept of Timing

My interest here is on initiating moves toward de-escalating international conflicts. Therefore, timing refers to recognizing whether or not the adversaries are ready to move away from escalation or down from stalemate. The recognition may be by a possible intermediary considering mediation or by one of the protagonists considering a conciliatory gesture. The issue of timing is important since interventions or conciliatory gestures made at inappropriate times may be counterproductive. The efforts might be rejected and consequently hamper new efforts in the near future.

Ripe, in this context, means that the time is right for de-escalation. The time is right when the necessary, but not sufficient, circumstances for de-escalation exist. What must be added lies within the capability of the actor or actors who may be undertaking the de-escalating effort. What conditions are necessary, then, depends upon which actors we are considering as initiators of de-escalation. The metaphor of fertile may be particularly suitable because it suggests that something must be added for birth.

Louis Kriesberg is Director of the Program on the Analysis and Resolution of Conflicts at Syracuse University's Maxwell School of Citizenship and Public Affairs, 712 Ostrom Ave., Syracuse, N.Y. 13244. He is professor of sociology at Syracuse.

Many conceptual and empirical difficulties arise in assessing the role of timing in de-escalating efforts (Zartman, 1985; Saunders, 1985). Conditions would seem not to be ready for such efforts when, no matter what is done, the adversaries will not move toward de-escalation. That may appear tautological, but in a sense, every situation could be ready for de-escalating efforts. Consider even the Iran-Iraq war. All mediator efforts have failed thus far, suggesting that the parties are not yet ready to move toward peace. But that depends upon the terms of peace. Certain actors could take initiatives which would lead to a de-escalation of the conflict: in this case, Saddam Hussein could resign as President of Iraq.

This example suggests that we should restrict our analysis to a limited set of conflicts and possible kinds of de-escalations. I will focus on de-escalations which do not entail the surrender of one party to its adversary, but which involve a substantial degree of mutual concession and/or satisfaction.

Ripeness, therefore, must entail some readiness on the part of the primary adversaries to de-escalate their conflict with each other. We must specify timing relative to a particular phase of de-escalation. Are we considering when one party effectively signals another that it is willing to consider de-escalation; are we considering when adversaries come together to negotiate; or are we discussing when slow moving ongoing negotiations are hastened?

We must also specify timing relative to the kind of outcome that is likely to occur from the de-escalation. There is much room between one-sided surrender and mutual concessions and/or gains. Furthermore, there may be considerable disagreement about where in that space the outcome is likely to fall. In addition, different evaluations of possible outcomes are made. Groups within every adversary party generally differ about whether the expected outcome is a surrender, a great achievement for their side, a poor and yet necessary deal, or an unnecessarily poor deal.

Finally, we must specify the nature of the timing for different possible actors. The right time for the head of government of one of the primary adversaries may not be right for a rival leader, a subordinate official, or a possible mediator. The time is right for successful de-escalating efforts when the actor who wants the de-escalation has control over resources which, if added to the circumstances, could bring about a de-escalation movement. The addition may be indirect, that is, two or more steps away from the primary antagonists. Or, the addition may change some circumstances which then helps create the necessary ripe conditions. For example, President Anwar Sadat thought the participation of the U.S. government as a "full partner" in Egyptian-Israeli de-escalation efforts was necessary for peacemaking. He worked to bring that about in order to create the conditions needed for Egyptian-Israeli peace moves.

These observations lead to an important inference: There is no one right time for de-escalation efforts. Whether or not the time is right for a de-escalating effort depends on more than a certain set of conditions and the adversaries' expectations of future conditions. It also depends on:
1. the would-be de-escalators' judgment about the stage of conflict de-escalation (they seek);
2. their preferred outcome; and
3. the roles of the would-be de-escalating actors.

It is probably true that every time period is right for de-escalation for some actors, on some terms, for some aspect of a conflict. For purposes of this paper, I have made a few judgments that I can make explicit. I focus on initiating negotiations that might lead to agreements. The preferred outcome is one in which the basic interests of the antagonists are likely to be satisfied to such an extent that the outcome is relatively stable. The vantage point of government heads of the primary adversaries will be assumed.

Having specified that, I can return to the questions posed at the outset and restate them so that empirical evidence could help answer them. What conditions set limits and provide opportunities for effective de-escalating efforts? What kinds of efforts are likely to be effective under varying conditions? How important are the efforts made by government heads for initiating de-escalation relative to the background conditions?

Illustrative Cases

To select illustrative cases of effective de-escalating efforts, we must decide what changes were de-escalation movements. Movement is indicated by negotiations which resulted in agreements. Reaching an agreement through negotiations will be used as an indicator that the negotiations were conducted in good faith. It is one way of deciding that the negotiations were serious and not conducted merely for the sake of appearances. I will cite cases of de-escalating efforts which did and did not lead to explicit negotiations, especially ones resulting in agreements. (See Table 1.)

TABLE 1
De-Escalating Efforts and Moves

Efforts But No De-Escalating Movement	De-Escalating Movement
U.S.-Soviet Cases:	
Rapacki Plan, 1957	Austrian State Treaty, 1954-55
Berlin status, 1958, 1962	Antarctica Treaty, 1959
Comprehensive Nuclear Test Ban, 1958-61	Partial Nuclear Test Ban Treaty, 1963
Discussions about Middle East, 1969	Seabed Arms Treaty, 1971
START, INF, 1981-1983	ABM, SALT 1, Basic Principles, 1972
	Geneva Summit, 1985
Israeli-Arab Cases	
Egyptian-Israeli Indirect Discussions, 1953-1955	Jordan Valley Authority Negotiations, 1955
Jarring Mission, Rogers Plan, 1969	Egypt-Israel and Partial Withdrawal, Sinai, 1974-75
Suggestions for Partial Israeli Withdrawal, 1971	Syrian-Israeli Disengagement, 1974
Fez Plan, Reagan Plan, 1982	Egyptian-Israeli Peace Treaty, 1977-79
Israel-Jordan-PLO Preparations, 1985	

In the Israeli-Arab conflict, many efforts have been made and even negotiations often have been conducted. Since few of these have ever resulted in any explicit de-escalating agreements, it is easy to dismiss them as not being serious efforts. But for our purposes we want to consider whether they failed because the times were not ripe for significant moves or because the opportunities were missed by the inadequate application of conflict resolution methods or by the wrong selection of methods. To help make such determinations, I will consider these failures and compare them with the cases in which de-escalating initiatives led to negotiations that resulted in agreements.

Among the major efforts that failed to lead to de-escalating negotiations, the following deserve noting. In 1953-1955, several missions were conducted to initiate negotiations between the Egyptian and Israeli governments. These missions were carried out by officials from the U.S. government and by private persons and groups (Khouri, 1985; Touval, 1982). In 1969, there were several other mediating efforts, aimed particularly at Israeli-Egyptian relations, but striving for a comprehensive settlement. These efforts included the missions of Gunnar Jarring, the special representative of the U.N. Secretary General, the consultations between the U.S. and Soviet governments about the Middle East, and the Plan proposed by Secretary of State William Rogers (Touval, 1982; Kissinger, 1979).

At the end of 1970 and the beginning of 1971, proposals for a partial Israeli withdrawal from the Sinai were made informally by Minister of Defense Moshe Dayan and formally by President Anwar Sadat (Gazit, 1983).

In 1982, President Ronald Reagan proposed a general plan for a resolution of the Israeli-Arab conflict and U.S. State Department representatives undertook some mediating efforts.

In 1985, there were extensive and complex preliminary negotiations involving King Hussein of Jordan, Chairman Yasir Arafat of the PLO, Prime Minister Shimon Peres of Israel, President Hosni Mubarak of Egypt, and Assistant Secretary of State Richard W. Murphy.

The list of failed efforts could easily be extended. The list of effective de-escalating initiatives is much shorter. I include the 1955 negotiations involving the governments of Israel, Jordan, Syria, and Lebanon, mediated by the U.S. representative Eric Johnston. These negotiations led to an understanding about the construction of dams and allocation of water in the Jordan Valley; but the agreement was never ratified.

In 1974 and 1975, there were the agreements between the Israeli and Egyptian governments, mediated by Secretary of State Henry Kissinger, to disengage military forces and later for the partial withdrawal of Israeli military forces from a portion of the Sinai. Kissinger also mediated a Syrian-Israeli agreement in 1974 about the disengagement of forces on the Golan Heights.

Of course, the most noteworthy de-escalating moves followed President Sadat's trip to Jerusalem in November, 1977. These included the Camp David Agreements and the Egyptian-Israeli Peace Treaty, both mediated by President Jimmy Carter (Carter, 1982; Quandt, 1986).

The U.S.-Soviet conflict is likewise marked by very many de-escalating efforts, many of which have been effective, resulting in formal agreements. The efforts which proved to be ineffective, at least at the time, include many proposals for disarmament, made in the 1950s and 1960s (Ulam, 1974; Garthoff, 1985).

Other ineffective initiatives include the Rapacki Plan, proposed in 1957 to create a "nuclear free" zone that included the two Germanies, Poland, and Czechoslovakia. In 1961, Nikita Khruschev attempted to initiate discussions to "normalize" the status of Berlin.

The 1962 negotiations for a Comprehensive Nuclear Test Ban came close enough to an agreement that we probably should not regard the initiatives leading up to them as ineffective. In 1967, the summit meeting between President Lyndon B. Johnson and Prime Minister Aleksei N. Kosygin failed to produce negotiations on the ABM and SALT treaties immediately; but significant negotiations did occur later between the Nixon and Brezhnev administrations.

The START and INF negotiations in Geneva during President Ronald Reagan's first term probably should be regarded as including proposals that did not lead to serious negotiations (Talbott, 1984).

Effective initiatives may be regarded as ones that preceded the negotiations which led to the agreements such as the following: the 1955 Austrian State Treaty; the 1959 Antarctica Treaty; the 1963 Partial Nuclear Test Ban; the 1968 Nonproliferation Treaty; the 1971 Seabed Arms Agreement; and the ABM, SALT, and Basic Principles Agreement of 1972.

Theoretical Explanations

Reviewing explanations for effective de-escalation initiatives is a necessary step in deciding what the role of timing is. If we knew what conditions determined significant de-escalation, we could assess the appropriate and skillful application of various conflict resolution methods.

Three kinds of conditions are frequently discussed as the determinants of conflict de-escalation or of peacemaking (Kriesberg, 1982): domestic pressures, the relations between the adversaries, and the international context. I will discuss each, illustrating them by reference to the illustrative cases previously listed.

Domestic pressures certainly are likely sources of de-escalating efforts. The domestic pressure may be large-scale peace movements demanding accommodation with an enemy. The pressures may be direct or indirect, as when the demands are for resources which compete with the requirements for external conflict. For example, the anti-Vietnam War peace movement in the U.S. contributed to the pressure and the decision of the Nixon administration to seek detente with the Soviet Union (Kissinger, 1979; Garthoff, 1985). The lack of peace movement pressure in Arab countries helps account for the almost total absence of effective de-escalating initiatives by Arab governments toward Israel.

The orientation of a government toward accommodation is certainly important, but it alone does not determine when de-escalation occurs. Thus, a government headed by relative soft liners might be expected to take de-escalating initiatives (Snyder and Diesing, 1977). But many cases of effective de-escalating efforts can be seen to have been undertaken or pursued by relatively hard line government heads. It may be that a government leader who has demonstrated toughness against the adversary is able, *later*, to act accommodatingly without risking great domestic challenge from the hard line flank. This seems to have contributed to the success of President John F. Kennedy's initiative leading to the Partial Nuclear Test Ban, to the initiating of detente by

President Richard Nixon, and to President Anwar Sadat's and Prime Minister Menachem Begin's actions resulting finally in an Egyptian-Israeli Peace Treaty (Kriesberg, 1981; Kriesberg, 1984).

Whether or not hard liners actually undertake effective de-escalating efforts depends on many conditions relating to the adversary and to the international context. It also depends on the nature of the domestic pressure and the source of challenges to their leadership. For example, Chairman Arafat may be viewed as a hard liner in the international context but as a moderate by important segments of his constituency.

The adversary relations should be expected to set the basic conditions for de-escalating moves. They include the power balance, mutual acceptance, and shared understandings about the conflict. There is disagreement about what kind of balance of power is conducive to de-escalation. Often, government heads say they must bargain from a position of strength, meaning greater strength than that of the adversary. Other partisans and observers argue for parity. The argument is also made that stability and little prospect of change in the power balance is the prerequisite for de-escalation. Finally, it is argued that de-escalation occurs when the relatively weaker party is approaching parity with the stronger (Zartman, 1985).

Cases can be found to support each argument. Soviet leaders have argued that detente emerged when the correlation of forces had shifted so that the Soviet Union had reached parity with the U.S. But some U.S.-Soviet de-escalating moves certainly preceded detente. The greater effectiveness of peacemaking initiatives in Israeli-Egyptian relations after 1973 (compared to the prior years) might be interpreted as resulting from recognition of a fundamental power balance stalemate, of a gradually encroaching parity by the weaker party, or of a stable imbalance of power.

In addition to the balance of power is the probably related matter of mutual acceptance. This has been an obstacle early on in the Arab governments' relations with Israel. There have also been conceptual differences in the way in which the conflict was envisaged by antagonists in the Middle East. At times this has been true in U.S.-Soviet relations as well.

For conditions to be ripe for effective de-escalating moves, the adversaries must anticipate an acceptable possible outcome to those moves. Each party must believe that there is a high probability that its adversaries are ready and able to agree to an outcome that both regard as acceptable.

The international context is a major, and often neglected, aspect of the conditions determining the possibility of de-escalation. The international context includes the possible roles of intervenors, whether as allies or as mediators; it also includes shifts in the relative salience of other conflicts. Intervenors who may become allies of one side in a struggle obviously affect the balance of power between the adversaries. The introduction of the U.S.-Soviet Cold War into the Middle East in the mid-1950s probably interfered with de-escalating efforts by the primary adversaries because it seemed to hold out the promise of better terms in the future with the aid of external allies. It also gave the external allies grounds for supporting the local fight if it served their interests in the larger struggle in which they were engaged themselves.

At other times, intervenors can contribute to the conditions which underlie de-escalation. For example, note that in the early U.S.-Soviet successful de-escalations, other parties were active participants. This was certainly true of the Austrian State Treaty, the Antarctica Treaty, the Partial Nuclear Test Ban Agreement, and the Nonproliferation Treaty (Kriesberg, 1981; Seaborg, 1981). Once Egypt as well as Israel was significantly tied to the U.S., the U.S. government played a major role in creating conditions conducive to de-escalation.

This very brief discussion indicates that a variety of conditions may contribute to effective de-escalation efforts. This very variety, however, suggests that no particular set of conditions determines that de-escalation will or will not occur. Rather, it indicates there is room for strategic conflict resolution interventions. There are many times that are ripe for moves toward conflict reduction for at least some parties on some issues. But the terms of that conflict reduction can — and do — vary greatly. We should recognize that whether or not the conditions are ripe for a settlement depends upon the terms of the acceptable settlement.

Conflict Resolution Strategies

Much of the literature about conflict resolution approaches concerns particular techniques that mediators and negotiators might use. In this article, I am concerned with general approaches or strategies that may be pursued in conflict resolution. I will discuss them in terms of choices about issues, adversaries, and inducements.

In order to initiate effective de-escalating efforts, is it better to choose contentious issues that are central to the conflict or ones that are peripheral? Is it better to deal with the conflict in its entirety or to break it up into discrete issues (Fisher, 1964)? Is it better to keep issues isolated or to link several together (Kissinger, 1979)?

The evidence from the cases cited earlier strongly supports the effectiveness of starting with peripheral rather than central issues, and moving piece by piece toward a comprehensive settlement. This seems to be true of U.S.-Soviet as well as Egyptian-Israeli relations. The evidence about linkage is less clear. Linkage can be another way of breaking up a conflict into many issues and trading off gains on one for losses on another, facilitating reaching an agreement. But linkage can also be used as leverage, trying to gain large gains on one issue by holding out on another. That can appear to the adversary not as the use of tradeoffs but as the use of coercion in bargaining.

Strategic choices must also be made about who the adversaries are in the de-escalating effort. Every government in a conflict is part of a variegated coalition, consisting of many constituencies, foreign governments, and government agencies. A de-escalating initiative may be directed at the widest adversary coalition or at selected segments of it. It may be based on consultation and negotiation with a diverse representation of its own coalition or it may be undertaken after only a very circumscribed consultation. President Sadat, in deciding to visit Jerusalem in November 1977, clearly did not consult widely with his coalition, but made his approach to the Israeli government and its widest coalition. The Soviet government has often made overtures to portions of the Western alliance, while putting aside major efforts at reaching other parts of the coalition.

The parties selected must not only be willing to make significant de-escalating moves; they must also be able to make decisions that are binding on their constituencies. The problem resulting from having one of these conditions without the other is illustrated in the Israeli-Palestinian conflict. At times, the Israeli government has sought Palestinian representatives with whom Israel might negotiate what it regarded as a significant de-escalating agreement. Generally, the Palestinians who would be ready to do that are not able to ensure that a significant group of Palestinians would follow them.

A review of the cases listed earlier does not indicate that any one strategic choice is highly related to effective de-escalating moves. In the Arab-Israeli conflict, comprehensive participation has generally not been successful in initiating effective moves. But, for the U.S.-Soviet cases, the results are mixed; different strategies have been effective, depending on the issues and background conditions.

Finally, the inducements used in the de-escalating efforts are matters of strategic choice. Adversaries and mediators may try to gain their goals by coercion, persuasion, or reward. They may warn, threaten, or harm the interests of the adversary to force the movement they desire. They may promise, offer, or commit actions that are desired by the adversary. They may seek to persuade the adversary that what they seek is in the adversary's own best interests or helps meet the adversary's own principles. These inducements may be mixed in various combinations at the same time or over an extended period.

Again, no unambiguous formula for success can be found on the basis of the cases previously listed. The cases do indicate, however, that recently exercised coercion may contribute to effective de-escalating efforts, The 1962 Cuban Missile Crisis and the 1973 Egyptian, Syrian, Israeli war are examples. But coercion mixed with persuasion and reward at the same time has generally not been effective (e.g., note Khruschev's initiatives in the late 1950s and early 1960s). Mediation in the Middle East conflicts has been effective when it has included added benefits, usually provided by the U.S. government.

In short, there does not appear to be a clear formula for effective de-escalating strategies. No strategy is effective for all kinds of disputes and contexts. But some strategies do appear to be effective for many de-escalation movements. For a given set of conditions, often an appropriate strategy can be found to de-escalate the conflict. A window of opportunity is often open. But the de-escalation opportunity may be evaluated quite differently by different actors. The de-escalation may be regarded by many partisans as a sellout or sign of weakness.

Conclusions

Conflict resolution theory often appears to separate process from substance. It is a way to facilitate all the adversaries getting at least some of what they want at an acceptable cost. An important implication of this discussion is that process cannot be separated from content and outcome.

Conflict resolution approaches can be applied effectively under many conditions. The time is often ripe for one kind of settlement or another. The question then becomes what kind of settlement is acceptable to which parties under a given set of conditions? The many failures of efforts indicate that the terms of the settlements being sought were too far apart at the time or that the de-escalating strategies pursued were not suitable to the circumstances. Nevertheless, some parties can often discover a mutually acceptable de-escalating move, if only a partial one.

Those striving for a settlement must seek it within arenas that they can affect. For example, nongovernmental actors or a governmental leader may settle domestic disputes and build political support for international de-escalating efforts (Saunders, 1985). De-escalating movements that are only partial can be steps toward a broader settlement. For instance, the disengagement agreements between Egypt and Israel in 1974 and 1975 were steps toward the writing and ratification of the Israeli-Egyptian Peace Treaty.

We should recognize that every settlement is partial. There will always be some disgruntled parties on one or more sides of the conflict. No settlement will produce true and everlasting peace and harmony. Undue expectations of a settlement may even damage its survival and undermine the base it might otherwise provide for future settlements (Kriesberg, 1986).

In practice, one can never know that the conditions are ripe for a particular de-escalating initiation. One discovers whether or not that is the case by trying. Furthermore, the effort may help create the necessary conditions.

Nevertheless, studying the possible conduciveness of the circumstances for de-escalation is useful. It can indicate when some kinds of efforts may be counterproductive. It can also indicate which strategy is most likely to be appropriate. And it can indicate what kind of outcome is likely to be possible.

REFERENCES

Carter, J. (1982). *Keeping faith*. New York: Bantam Books.
Fisher, R. (1964). "Fractionating conflict." In *International conflict and behavioral sciences: The Craigville papers*, ed. R. Fisher. New York: Basic Books.
Garthoff, R. L. (1985). *Détente and confrontation*. Washington: The Brookings Institution.
Gazit, M. (1983). *The peace process 1969-1973: Efforts and contacts*. Jerusalem Papers on Peace Problems 35. Jerusalem: The Magnes Press.
Khouri, F. J. (1985). *The Arab-Israeli dilemma*, 3rd ed. Syracuse, N.Y.: Syracuse University Press.
Kissinger, H. (1979). *White House years*. Boston: Little, Brown and Co.
Kriesberg, L. (1981). "Noncoercive inducements in US-Soviet conflicts: Ending the occupation of Austria and nuclear weapons tests." *Journal of Political and Military Sociology* 9:1-16.
———. (1982). *Social conflicts*, 2nd ed. Englewood Cliffs, N.J.: Prentice Hall.
———. (1984). "Social theory and the de-escalation of international conflict." *Sociological Review* 32:471-491.
———. (1986). "Consequences of efforts at de-escalating the American-Soviet conflict." *Journal of Political and Military Sociology* 14: 215-234.
Peri. J. (1983). *Between battles and ballots: Israeli military in politics*. Cambridge: Cambridge University Press.
Quandt, W. B. (1986). *Camp David*. Washington: The Brookings Institution.
Saunders, H. H. (1985). *The other walls: The politics of the Arab-Israeli peace process*. Washington: American Enterprise Institute.
Seaborg, G. T. (1981). *Kennedy, Khruschev and the Test Ban*. Berkeley: University of California Press.
Snyder, G. H. and Diesing, P. (1977). *Conflict among nations: Bargaining, decision making, and system structure in international crises*. Princeton: Princeton University Press.
Talbott, S. (1984). *Deadly gambits*. New York: Alfred A. Knopf.
Touval, S. (1982), *The peace brokers*. Princeton: Princeton University Press.
Ulam, A. B. (1974). *Expansion and coexistence: Soviet Foreign Policy, 1917-73*, 2nd ed. New York: Praeger.
Zartman, I. W. (1977). "Negotiations as a joint decision-making process." In *The negotiation process*, ed. I.W. Zartman. Beverly Hills: Sage Publications.
———. (1985). *Ripe for resolution: Conflict and intervention in Africa*. New York: Oxford University Press.

Section VI

Culture, Race, Gender, and Style

We have already seen that effective negotiation requires adequate preparation, in the form of organizing one's own team properly, then coming the table prepared in a variety of ways. In addition, effective negotiation can only occur if each side attempts to evaluate the possible use of various tactics and strategies during the negotiations proper, while also taking into account various contextual factors and constraints within which decision making must occur. Section VI explores the important contribution to effective negotiation of yet another class of considerations: the ways in which individual negotiators may differ from one another as the result of their culture, race, gender, or individual personality.

Robert J. Janosik's essay ("Rethinking the Culture-Negotiation Link") identifies four distinct approaches to the analysis of links between culture and negotiation. The first evaluates culture as "learned behavior" — the kinds of things that negotiators *do* rather than what they *think* about. A second approach regards culture as "shared value" — looking for those attributes that distinguish the shared values of negotiators from one culture to another. Yet another approach takes a "dialectical" view of culture and negotiation, arguing that all cultures contain sets of opposites or polarities, and these affect the range of negotiations that result. Finally, the "culture-in-context" approach argues that negotiating behavior within a culture is the result of a complex amalgam of considerations — all of which affect the "context" in which negotiations occur.

The second article ("Breaking Away from Subtle Biases"), by J. William Breslin, describes the effect of cultural stereotypes and labels on the kinds of perceptions that negotiators bring with them to the proceedings. Using a cross-cultural teaching exercise as a case in point, Breslin indicates some of the ways in which stereotypes (about what negotiators from different cultures or nationalities are like) may overdetermine the kind of negotiating opportunities that result.

A third article on the general topic of culture and negotiation ("Making Deals in Strange Places: A Beginner's Guide to International Business Negotiations") outlines six common factors that should be taken into account in preparing to negotiate at the international level with business interests. Author Jeswald W. Salacuse describes these six factors, or constraints, as follows: first, "political and legal pluralism," namely, the fact that the political and legal constraints that operate in one's own culture may be very different from those that prevail in other cultures; second, international monetary factors must be taken into account, since the relative value of (often fluctuating) world currencies may change the dependence of each side on a negotiated settlement; third, the role of foreign governments and bureaucracies, in non-governmental negotiation, a role that may well vary from one country or culture to the next; fourth, the possibility of instability and sudden change; fifth, problems of ideology, that require the "wrapping" of proposals in ideological packages that are acceptable to the other side; and finally, culture itself — those differences that cross not only political, ideological, and bureaucratic lines, but also cultural ones.

Deborah M. Kolb and Gloria G. Coolidge's contribution ("Her Place at the Table: A Consideration of Gender Issues in Negotiation") offers a trenchant look at the role of gender in negotiation. Based on a series of interviews with three successful women negotiators, each operating in a different domain, the authors identify what they consider to be the distinguishing attributes of a "feminine" negotiating agenda. At another level, the analysis by Kolb and Coolidge can be regarded as concerning differences of style (from one woman negotiator to the next) as well as differences of gender (comparing the three successful women negotiators with their more common male counterparts).

Finally, the article by Roderick W. Gilkey and Leonard Greenhalgh ("The Role of Personality in Successful Negotiating") provides a glimpse at the complex contribution of personality differences. Based on a "personality assessment and feedback program," the authors describe a method for examining the effects of differences in personality on performance in negotiations throughout a semester-long course. As they observe, in keeping with the observations with other scholars over the years, differences in personality can and do have an effect on the kind of negotiating style one adopts, and the effects such stylistic differences have, in turn, on the results of negotiation.

Rethinking the Culture-Negotiation Link

Robert J. Janosik

Practicing negotiators have tended to rely on the concept "culture," or on related notions like national style, to explain behavior encountered at the international bargaining table. Scholars, too, have on occasion investigated the relationship of culture to negotiation, but with less vigor, perhaps because of the methodological problems inherent in such studies.[1]

Since the notion of culture as an explanatory tool holds such allure for negotiation analysts, this paper will examine the treatment of "culture" in the anecdotal and scholarly literature. It will soon become apparent that the concept has been used in a number of ways. Perhaps such an examination can sharpen the clarity of the discussion, since many analysts seem to agree that culture does have an impact on behavior, at least to some extent. But without a general working understanding of the various approaches to culture currently in use, practitioners and academics may use the concept in different ways without sufficient analysis of the possibilities and limits of these various approaches to culture and its impact upon negotiating behavior.

I have identified four distinct approaches in the negotiation literature which imply a connection between culture and behavior: culture as learned behavior; culture as shared value; culture as dialectic; and culture-in-context. Each approach differs from the others conceptually in significant ways with important consequences for the understanding of the culture-negotiation connection. Illustrations, drawn primarily from writings about Japanese, Russian, Chinese, and American negotiating practices will serve to illustrate the four approaches since the investigation of these four national groups has drawn the bulk of the attention given to this question.

Culture as Learned Behavior

The variety of human experience has daunted even the most persistent analyst. This variety has led observers to search for organizing principles that allow for valid generalizations which hold true despite "incidental" variations from overall patterns. The notion of culture has proven to be one such basis for generalization. Much of the literature on diplomacy resorts to generalizations based on the observed typical characteristics and behaviors of the inhabitants of a particular geographic entity.

The focus of the literature produced by such writers is often primarily on what negotiators *do*, rather than what they *think*. It is quintessentially pragmatic. There is little felt need for detailed analysis of when, why, and how a pattern of behavior occurs; rather, the primary consideration has to do with

Robert J. Janosik is Assistant Professor of Political Science at Occidental College, 1600 Campus Road, Los Angeles, Ca. 90041.

the reliability and sensitivity of the observer. For the practitioner in the audience, little more is thought to be necessary than an accurate and comprehensive catalogue of what to expect. It makes little difference why negotiators from a particular culture resist negotiations over dinner; what is important that one can always expect such behavior.

As early as 1716, de Callieres devoted sections of his classic, *On the Manner* of *Negotiating With Princes*, to the question of national "styles." At several points in the essay, he attributed certain favorable negotiating traits to the diplomats of specific nations, and hypothesized that there is a direct relationship between negotiating behavior and place of birth (de Callieres, 1963, p. 36):

> ...patience is one of the advantages which the Spanish nation has over our own; for we are naturally lively, and have hardly embarked on one affair before we desire the end in order to embark on another... Whereas it has been remarked that a Spanish diplomatist never acts with haste, that he never thinks of bringing a negotiation to an end simply from *ennui*, but to finish it with advantage...

Another classic, Harold Nicholson's *Diplomacy* (1963, p. 68) also suggests that the style of the diplomats of a nation is a function of that society's norms and values:

> ...there are marked differences in the theory and practice of the several Great Powers. These differences are caused by variation in national character, traditions, and requirements...

The long line of diplomatic diarists who have represented the United States and Great Britain in Japan since the first modern contacts in the 19th century similarly reflect an assumption about birthplace and negotiation. Townsend Harris, America's first Consul General to Japan, though unusually sympathetic to the Japanese he encountered, nonetheless commented on certain unsavory attributes of the Japanese style of dealing with foreign envoys to their nation. As his dealings in Japan dragged on, frustration increased, and he remarked (Harris, 1930, p. 366):

> They (the Japanese) do not regard the promise they gave me last August as worth the breath it cost them to utter it. However, to *lie* is, for a Japanese, simply to speak.

It should be noted that this approach can include observations about various levels of the process of negotiation. Learned behaviors may touch upon notions of reciprocity and justice, attitudes about acceptable outcomes, or concepts about the appropriate timing for certain bargaining behaviors. However, it is my sense that most of the observations derived from this approach involve comments on negotiating "etiquette," — on matters dealing with proper social customs and usages that surface in the typical bargaining encounter.

Many of the "how to" manuals about negotiating abroad focus on negotiating etiquette. Howard F. Van Zandt's much read "How to Negotiate in Japan" (1970) is a good example. In that article he notes 13 "distinctive behavioral characteristics" which are commonly encountered by Americans in talks with the Japanese, including the "avoidance of no," the "reluctance to enter into arguments" and gift-giving. Although admittedly important to good relations, such customs do not really go to the heart of the matter: whether participants have fundamentally different perspectives on the process of negotiation.

A second example can be located in Flora Lewis's astute observations in a brief analysis of U.S.-Saudi Arabian relations that appeared in the 27 February 1979 edition of the *New York Times*:

> ...As a sign of politeness and hospitality, the Arabs tend to listen and nod when high-level Americans talk with them. But this does not mean that they agree.

This approach to negotiation analysis, which involves the search patterns for patterns of behavior in groups of individuals, is akin to early 20th century "culture studies" in psychology, anthropology, and sociology. It is often typical of the writing of practicing negotiators who, not surprisingly, base their observations on experience at the negotiating table, and who view their task primarily in terms of making it possible for others in the same position to successfully manage for others in the same or similar situations in the future. Such experientially-based advice is, of course, invaluable to those facing comparable situations; however, the approach carries important limitations, as I hope to demonstrate.

Culture as Shared Value

A second commonly employed approach shifts the focus of investigation in an important way. Using this approach, the analyst begins with a description of a controlling concept or value assumed to be embedded in the culture and derives from that observation a series of predictions about how a participant in that culture will behave in negotiation. The assumption, simply put, is that thinking precedes doing, and that one's thinking patterns derive from one's cultural context.

For the purposes of comparison across cultures or groups, the analyst will search for a *central* cultural value or norm that distinguishes each of the groups being compared. From the practitioner's point of view, this approach — culture as shared value — like the first approach — culture as learned behavior — is appealing because it suggests an almost inevitable, and therefore entirely predictable, pattern of negotiating behavior.

Mushakoji Kinhide, for example, uses this approach to contrast American and Japanese understandings of the process of negotiation. Mushakoji (1976, p. 40) proposes that the Japanese negotiator represents an *awase* culture, while the United States is an *erabi* culture. The American *erabi* view implies "a behavioral sequence whereby a person sets his objective, develops a plan designed to reach that objective, and then acts to change the environment in accordance with that plan." Environments are perceived as offering dichotomies for choice. By contrast, the Japanese *awasi* view assumes that the environment must be adjusted to, not changed, and "the environment consists of a constantly changing continuum of find gradations."

According to Mushakoji, these cultural differences have profound implications for the American and Japanese perspectives on the process. Americans, for example, present a clear statement of their position and expect the same of others. The Japanese, on the other hand, would rather infer the other's position and avoid early commitment to stated objectives. Other, comparable cultural typologies are legion.[2]

There are several common variants of the "culture as shared value" approach to negotiation. One example, also drawn from the literature concerning the Japanese approach to negotiation, can be found in *Smart Bargaining: Doing Business with the Japanese*. After summarizing relevant factors in Japanese history and geography, Graham and Sano (1984) trace the "typical" Japanese bargaining style to a *cluster* of values implicit in Japanese culture that are said to generate the observed Japanese style. Like Mushakoji, Graham and Sano derive a predicted set of behaviors from certain postulated values in Japanese culture. Graham and Sano differ, however, in that they do not attempt to isolate one key aspect of culture; rather, they point to a set of cultural norms and values that contribute to the Japanese style. For example, Graham and Sano point to "amae," which they translate as "indulgent dependency," "wa (the maintenance of harmony), and "shinyo" (gut feeling), as some of the components of the Japanese value set. As regards "shinyo," the authors argue that this value encourages Japanese negotiators to spend a great deal of time at activities not directly related to the negotiation, including gift-giving.

The same authors sketch an American style of bargaining which they refer to as the "John Wayne Style." Pointing to the American frontier experience, Graham and Sano note a tendency on the part of American negotiators to prefer short, informal negotiations that emphasize the equality of the participants.

Yet another variant of this approach to the question of the nexus between culture and negotiation attributes aspects of a nation's negotiation style to ideology rather than culture. Political scientists define ideology as a tight-knit system of ideas which constitutes a full world view. Three modern systems — Liberalism, Fascism and Communism — are typically cited as examples of ideologies. Although no extended study linking negotiation behavior to Fascism or Liberalism has, to my knowledge, been attempted, Kenneth T. Young's *Negotiating With the Chinese Communists* (1968) does just that as regards to Communism. Young examines the history of American-Chinese negotiating encounters for the period between 1953 and 1967 for patterns in Chinese behavior. Chinese behavior in these negotiations featured a high degree of antagonism toward American counterparts and a casualness about reaching agreement which contrasted to the American desire to come to agreement quickly. Young attributes these patterns to the fact that "A Chinese Communist negotiator is an ideologist more than anything else." The result, he argues is that:

> ...the United States Government and the American negotiators are dealing with a closed mind in which conceptual thinking and logical analysis have not developed or matured for over a generation. The world has changed but Maoist ideology has enclosed China within a new ideological wall. (Young, 1968, p. 364)

Chinese negotiating behavior during this period, then, followed certain predictable patterns:

> Tactically, this kind of negotiator tried to outflank his opponent, demoralize and weaken him by every conceivable means at every possible point, take over his strategic position, separate him from allies, leave him no exit, and give him no quarter. (Young, 1968, p. 363)

Studies of Soviet negotiating patterns have also been done. An early example of the genre can be found in the essays contained in Dennett and Johnson's *Negotiating With the Russians* (1951). More recent examples are summarized by Louis J. Samelson (1976), who finds that Western observers typically ascribe deception, dissimulation, rigidity, non-accommodation, hostility, and harassment to both Soviet and Chinese Communist diplomatic representatives.

Despite the variants, all proponents of this approach assume that either a single shared value, a commonly-held cluster of values, or an ideology produce a typical bargaining style. Here, the attempt is to create a cultural explanation for behavior rather than a mere description of a pattern of negotiating behavior. This viewpoint represents a higher level of abstraction than the first approach — culture as learned behavior — since implicit in it is a causal relationship between the values of a cultural group and bargaining behavior.

It should also be noted that the "shared value" approach appears to minimize the role of individual choice for the bargaining actor. In other words, because a negotiator belongs to a culture or adheres to an ideology, he or she necessarily behaves in particular ways. As with the first approach, there seems to be a suggestion that culture largely predetermines negotiating behavior.

Culture as Dialectic

Analysts who favor the "shared value" approach typically assume a homogeneity in the culture's dominant value or value set. Graham and Sano, for example, appear to be suggesting that though a "bundle" of Japanese and American and cultural norms guide the negotiating behavior of those groups respectively, there is nothing inconsistent in the units that comprise the bundle of cultural norms. "Amae" and "shinyo" are presented as different but mutually reinforcing norms which lead to regularized Japanese negotiating patterns.

A quite different model of the make-up of culture is also available. Erik H. Erikson in *Childhood and Society* proposed a model of personal identity which is based on sets of opposites, or "polarities":

> ...the functioning American, as the heir of a history of extreme contrasts and abrupt changes, bases his final ego identity on some tentative combination of dynamic polarities such as migratory and sedentary, individualistic and standardized, competitive and co-operative, pious and freethinking, responsible and cynical, etc. (Erikson, 1963, p. 286)

Erikson was interested in explaining child development; a similar model of culture, explicitly derived from Erikson, was used by Michael Kammen (1972) to interpret the American historical experience. Kammen asserts that sets of "biformities," or values which are in dialectic tension, pervade the American national experience: "Collective individualism," "conservative liberalism," "pragmatic idealism," and "godly materialism" are a few examples of such pairs.

Proponents of this approach to culture suggest, at least implicitly, a criticism of the single value or "homogenous bundle" notion of culture discussed above. A culture, for an analyst of this approach, is defined by the tensions, the dialectics, which exist among values embedded in a particular culture. Tension, not consistency, typifies the component parts of any given culture.

Analysts of the culture-as-shared-value approach may find it difficult to come to grips with two problems: the problem of individual variations in a culture and changes over periods of time. If a culture is entirely homogenous, it is difficult to explain discrepancies from the modal pattern when they occur since all participants in the culture are thought to subscribe to the dominant value or value bundle. Similarly, change over time can only be explained by the complete rejection of whatever the dominant value or value bundle is in a particular culture under certain historical circumstances. The "culture as shared value" approach is static; it does not comfortably allow for the analysis of change or variation. By contrast, the third approach — culture as dialectic — can easily accommodate the study of both individual variation and changes over time.

An interesting use of the culture-as-dialectic approach can be found in Michael Blaker's *Japanese International Negotiating Style*, Blaker posits a dialectic in Japanese culture which parallels, but does not duplicate, the dualities Kammen and Erikson noted in the American case. Blaker notes two quite different "domestic ideals of conflict resolution," which he calls "harmonious cooperation" and "the warrior ethic." (Blaker, 1977, p. 4) The first, which often seems to take prominence in western commentaries on Japanese negotiation, involves an extended effort to avoid discord at all costs within the elaborately constructed social matrix that has characterized Japan historically. Such conflict is avoided through narrowly-defined obligations which are understood to operate between Japanese at different levels of society. The "warrior ethic," by contrast, encourages risktaking in dogged pursuit of a cause, even at the cost of social turmoil. Obviously, these two ideals are in some real sense incompatible. But the point Blaker underscores is that *both* ideals have a strong grounding in Japanese history and tradition; both are seen to be legitimate in certain circumstances.

From these general conflict resolution ideals in Japanese culture, Blaker derives five "norms of Japanese bargaining action": overcoming domestic opposition; dispelling western resistance; secrecy; careful deliberations; and situational adaptation. He also derives three "norms of Japanese negotiating tactics" (Blaker, 1977, p. 23): optimism; fatalism; and nonmoral pragmatism. Given this understanding of Japanese culture, Blaker then examines Japanese behavior in a variety of international negotiations in the latter part of the 19th century and the early 20th century, and in light of Japan's ongoing sense of itself as a beleaguered country. Through his analysis of these cultural premises, then, Blaker finds a distinctive Japanese negotiation style, which in another context (Blaker, 1977*a*), he dubbed the Japanese "probe/push/panic" tactical style of negotiation.

The "culture as dialectic" approach does not present the intellectual difficulties regarding change and choice that were noted in connection with "culture as shared value." Indeed, since both value sets within a culture are seen as legitimate, a negotiator must somehow reconcile them in light of the individual's perceptions of the demands of a situation. Reconciliation of two or more competing value sets is a continuing task for each culture-participant in all situations, including negotiation. This tension between competing "cultural commands" can lead the individual participant to paralysis since the choice may seem difficult; or, one or the other of the other of these values may be chosen; or, finally, the tension may encourage the participant to attempt some synthesis of the competing values. Indeed, the latter possibility is precisely the kind of fusion Blaker seems to be suggesting in the Japanese case. "Optimism" and "fatalism" seem hardly coherent to the outside observer; but to the Japanese negotiator faced with competing cultural demands, both attitudes may somehow "make sense."

This third model becomes increasingly interesting to the academic observer of the process of negotiation since it allows for the resolution of several persistent questions concerning the observed lack of uniformity in the negotiating behavior among the participants of a particular culture. On the other hand, to the practitioner who must know how to prepare for and react to negotiating strategies and tactics from foreign actors, this model may appear problematic. Since the "culture as dialectic" approach is not deterministic in the same sense as the first two approaches (because, theoretically, one could equally expect quite contrary behaviors from participants in such a dialectic culture), practitioners may wonder about the utility of the third approach for their purposes.

Culture-in-Context

A fourth approach to the question of impact of culture on negotiating behavior is even more complex than the approach just discussed. It reflects the dominant current understanding of the relationship between behavior and ideas among social scientists, and takes its cue from Max Weber, Talcott Parsons, Gabriel Almond and other modern scholars.

In attempting to understand the relationship between ideas and action, Parsons (1936) elaborated a complex model of human behavior. For Parsons, the notion of culture was critical to the endeavor. He understood culture in terms of its ability to generate certain values which, in turn, predispose individuals to prefer certain goals or choices (interests). A culture, in other words, generates values or human wants which individuals then act to fulfill. But Parsons and others went further — well beyond a single factor understanding of the sources of human behavior. This group of social scientists, often referred to as "systems theorists," suggests that an understanding of human behavior cannot rest on single cause explanations. Several interdependent sources must be accounted for prior to achieving a relatively complete understanding of human behavior. Though a complete exegesis of these ideas would go well beyond the confines of this essay, the basic insight is that analysis must encompass many factors, must be multicausal.

More specifically, the individual's personality, cultural values, and the social context in which the individual operates are three of the primary components which account for human behavior. Such a multicausal approach, in short, suggests that any attempt to understand negotiation behavior as a genre of human action which attends only to the culturally-defined values of the negotiator will, ultimately, be inadequate. The constraints of the social context or situation and the role of the individual personality must also be taken into account.

Such complex, multicausal models of negotiating behavior are typical of many academic analyses of negotiating behavior. Sawyer and Guetzkow's early monograph (1965) on negotiation is a notable and still useful effort in this direction. They create a "social-psychological model" of the process of negotiation in which situation-specific goals, conditions which structure the specific negotiation (including the negotiation's setting, and the number of parties), and a series of "background factors" (including "cultural variation," the negotiator's personality, status and background) have an impact upon the events which unfold in a particular negotiation and its outcome.

The efforts of many scholars at negotiation model-building are deeply indebted to this multicausal mode of thinking about the nature of negotiation. Though some analysts give more prominence to the culture factor than others, it seems clear from the evidence in the textbooks being written on the subject[3] that the multicausal approach is now greatly favored by academic analysts. All of these writers hold in common the assumption that though culture is important, it is not the only contributor to an individual's negotiating behavior. Rather, culture is interdependent, interactive.

A few examples of the application of this approach will serve to illustrate the distinctive features of it. A monograph by Druckman et al. (1976) examined the bargaining behavior of children from India, Argentina and the United States. The authors collected and compared data concerning the subject-negotiator (age, gender and nationality) and the negotiating context (the existence or absence of an audience). While the investigators found evidence to support the proposition that culture matters in determining behavior (Indian bargainers were more competitive than Argentinians and Americans), the study also underscores the important contributory effects that *all* of these factors have in determining bargaining behavior. For example, the Druckman investigators noted male bargainers were more competitive than females in the U.S. and India, while the opposite was the case in terms of Argentinian subjects. In other words, nationality/culture does have an important role to play, but any generalizations about the nationality/culture nexus might require modification to account for age, gender and the negotiating environment.

In another study, Mushakoji (1972), whose thoughts in another context were noted earlier, compared Japanese and American negotiators using a negotiation game and found that any comparisons between the two groups had to be qualified by an analysis of the specific negotiating conditions faced by the subject in the simulation. Similarly, Janosik (1983) observed that though cultural differences could be observed when Americans and Japanese were asked to perform the same negotiating tasks, the occupations of the negotiators as well as the bargaining situation (the "toughness" of the simulated negotiating adversary) made absolute cross-cultural comparisons difficult. For example, Americans initially tended to make more counter-responses to an opponent than Japanese negotiators did under all conditions of opponent toughness; however, this phenomenon became less noticeable as the negotiating opponent became tougher, more unyielding.

Each of these examples of multicausal modelling attempts to put the cultural factor into perspective with other factors that are thought to be operative in negotiation. Particularly important are the factors which define the individual negotiator (age, gender, religion, and personality, for example) as well as those factors which define the context of the negotiation. These latter situational factors can encompass the presence or absence of an audience, the nature of the bureaucratic controls on a negotiator, and the observed patterns of an opponent's conduct, to name a few.

But as the complexity of the model increases, its utility for the practitioner seems to decrease. And there's the rub. The beauty of the first two approaches to culture and negotiation discussed here is that they yield readily useable lists of do's and don'ts, of straightforward characterizations of the bargaining styles of individuals from other cultures. The third and fourth approaches, by contrast, involve increasing degrees of indeterminacy. The insights gained from laboratory experiments rather than on-site observation, come laden with qualifiers that make them difficult to utilize efficiently at the bargaining table.

Observations

The question of the relationship of culture to negotiating style is an important one since it points to a view of negotiation which differs considerably from that advanced by early negotiation theorists. These early students of negotiation theory were frequently economists who developed process models that considered various concession patterns and optimal solutions for various negotiating problems. Oran Young's anthology (1975) brings together many of these early essays. Often the authors assume a "rational" actor/negotiator who was engaged in maximizing his or her own outcome in a negotiating encounter. Such "rational" calculations were directed to the subject matter being negotiated. However, these models left little room for unconscious factors in the process of negotiation.

Although I do not wish to understate the importance of the rational actor model of the negotiation process, since it has yielded important insights about the nature of the phenomenon, I do feel that an alternative (rather, complementary) view must also be elaborated before our understanding of negotiation truly matures. This second perspective on negotiation, represented by scholars whose work has been briefly described in this article, attempts to account for situational and individual factors, including culture, in the process of negotiation.

These two views — one based in economics, the other in social psychology — have created one divide in the literature about negotiation. Another gap exists between practitioners and academics, but for different reasons. Since the goals of the scholar and the participant-observer of negotiation differ somewhat, there has at times been a tendency to dismiss or downplay the problems of definition and conceptualization in the examination of the various "contributory" factors to the phenomenon of negotiation, including the question of the impact of culture on the process. Yet, since the consideration of national styles and cultural differences appears to be essential to the practitioner's interest in behavior at the international bargaining table, the failure to establish a fruitful dialogue on the subject may have inhibited the development of a truly comparative perspective.

This survey of discussions of culture and negotiation indicates that practitioners prefer to employ the "culture as learned behavior" or the "culture as shared value" approaches; the academics more frequently use the "culture as dialectic" or "culture in context" approaches. The reason seems clear. The first two approaches allow a high degree of predictability concerning the negotiating behavior of the culture group being analyzed. The third and fourth approaches are rather less deterministic. The "culture as dialectic" and "culture in context" approaches make prediction a more complex and risky enterprise.

The insights garnered from all are important. But it should be remembered that observations tied to the first and second approaches are likely to yield a particular type of prediction — one that has more to do with what has been called negotiating "etiquette" than with descriptions of what Zartman and Berman (1982, p. 229) have called the "deeper 'causes'" of negotiating behavior.

A real dialogue between academics and practitioners would consider matters of negotiating "etiquette" — whether business may be discussed over dinner, whether business cards should be exchanged, how to use interpreters, and the like. Clearly, the failure to observe good manners in negotiation can reduce the likelihood of agreement. But such a dialogue must ultimately move on to more complex matters, matters that lie at the heart of the question of whether there is some trans-national, trans-cultural understanding of the fundamental nature of negotiation itself.

A sophisticated understanding of the "culture" concept in the negotiation process may present difficult methodological problems. Nevertheless, grappling with these problems can lead, in the end, to more reliable diagnoses of negotiation and a product that is useful to the practitioner and satisfying to the scholar.

NOTES

1. Rubin and Brown (1975) suggest this hypothesis to explain the scarcity of such studies.
2. See, for example, Okabe (1983), which contains an extensive list of such dualities.
3. See, for example, Wall (1985). Wall includes "cultural norms" as one of a number of "environmental factors" which can affect the negotiation process.

REFERENCES

Blaker, M. (1977). *Japanese international negotiating style*. New York: Columbia University Press.
———. (1977*a*) "Probe, push, and panic: The Japanese tactical style in international negotiations." In *The foreign policy of modern Japan*, ed. R. A. Scalapino. Berkeley: University of California Press.
De Callieres, F. (1716). *On the manner of negotiating with princes*, trans. A. F. Whyte. Notre Dame, Ind.: University of Notre Dame Press, 1963.
Dennett, R. and **Johnson, J. E.**, eds. (1951). *Negotiating with the Russians*. New York: World Peace Foundation.
Druckman, D., et al. (1976). "Cultural differences in bargaining behavior: India, Argentina, and the U.S." *Journal of Conflict Resolution*. 20: 413-52.
Erikson, E. H. (1963). *Childhood and society*, 2nd ed. New York: W. W. Norton & Co.
Graham, J. L. and **Sano, Y.** (1984). *Smart bargaining: Doing business with the Japanese*. Cambridge, Mass.: Ballinger.
Harris, T. (1930). *The complete journal of Townsend Harris, first American consul general and minister to Japan*. Garden City, N. Y.: Doubleday, Doran & Co.
Janosik, R. (1983). "Negotiation theory: Considering the cultural variable in the Japanese and American cases." Ph.D. dissertation, New York University.
Kammen, M. (1973). *People of paradox: An inquiry concerning the origins of American civilization*. New York: Vintage Books.

Mushakoji, K. (1972). "The strategies of negotiation: An American-Japanese comparison." In *Experimentation and simulation in political science*, ed. J. A. Laponce and P. Smoker. Toronto: University of Toronto Press.

———. (1976). "The cultural premises of Japanese diplomacy." In *The silent power: Japan's identity and world role*, ed. Japan Center for International Exchange. Tokyo: The Simul Press.

Nicholson, H. (1939). *Diplomacy*, 3rd ed. Oxford: Oxford University Press, 1963.

Okabe, R. (1983). "Cultural assumptions of East and West: Japan and the United States." In *Intercultural communication theory: Current perspectives*, ed. W. B. Gudykunst. Beverly Hills: Sage.

Parsons, T. (1937). *The structure of social action*. New York: Free Press.

Rubin, J. Z. and Brown, B. R. (1975). *The social psychology of bargaining and negotiation*. New York: Academic Press.

Samelson, L. J. (1976). *Soviet and Chinese negotiating behavior: The Western view*. Sage Professional Paper in International Studies, no. 02-048. Beverly Hills, Calif.: Sage Publications.

Sawyer, J. and Guetzkow, H. (1965). "Bargaining and negotiation in international relations. In *International Behavior*, ed. H. Kelman, New York: Holt, Rinehart and Winston.

Van Zandt, H. E. (1970). "How to negotiate in Japan." *Harvard Business Review* 48: 45-56.

Wall, J. A. Jr. (1985). *Negotiation: Theory and practice*. Glenview, Ill.: Scott, Foresman and Co.

Young, K. T. (1968). *Negotiating with the Chinese Communists*. New York: McGraw-Hill.

Young, O., ed. (1975). *Bargaining: Formal theories of negotiation*. Urbana, Ill.: University of Illinois Press.

Zartman, I. W. and Berman, M. R. (1982). *The practical negotiator*. New Haven: Yale University Press.

Breaking Away from Subtle Biases

J. William Breslin

I have a bias which leads me to believe in the essential goodness of my fellow man, which leads me to believe that no problem of human relations is ever unsolvable.

— Ralph Bunche
From remarks made at a May 9, 1949 testimonial in honor of Mr. Bunche, held in New York City and sponsored by the American Association for the United Nations.

*   *   *

Few people would question the wisdom of the particular kind of bias advocated by Ralph Bunche, whose determined humanism was one of the hallmarks of a life of accomplishment. Some might carp that there are individuals, nations, and organizations which are not essentially good, and that any attempt at interaction with them is fruitless. That would miss the point of Mr. Bunche's eloquent advice, for it assumes failure even before any kind of human interaction is attempted. If one has complete contempt for the other side, denying them any shred of humanity, then there really isn't much point in even attempting communication. The optimist — and the practical negotiator — rejects that stance, recognizing that solutions to conflict begin with talking, an acknowledgment of the common humanity we all share. That simple nonprejudicial act, which is surely not easy to achieve in all circumstances, is a prerequisite for negotiation to occur.

In addition to dealing with our perceptions about others, negotiators must also be concerned about the prejudices others have for or against us when they come to the table. For example, any Iranian-American negotiating relationship in 1989 is certainly colored by the very public fear and loathing the governments of both nations have displayed toward one another in recent years. Millions of Iranians view the United States as the "Great Satan," while Americans perceive Iran as a bloodthirsty outlaw nation. Each nation has occasionally succeeded in humiliating the other on the world stage, and such insults are difficult both to forgive and forget. Thus, any sort of dealings between Americans and Iranians are likely to be strongly influenced by the

---

J. William Breslin is Director of Publications for the Program on Negotiation at Harvard Law School, 513 Pound Hall, Harvard Law School, Cambridge, Mass. 02138.

excess baggage of prejudice each side currently bears for the other. The same could be said for a couple in the throes of a bitter divorce or for the main actors in a strife-filled labor and management negotiation.

Past histories of anger and dissension result in clearcut "us. vs. them" and "them vs. us" prejudices that are generally easy to identify in a negotiating relationship. Because this form of prejudice is a known factor in a relationship, dealing with it is relatively simple. However, there are other, more subtle forms of bias that often cloud negotiations, potentially posing an even greater threat to the chances of a good settlement than those caused by "upfront" prejudice. One such type of prejudice was explored during an exercise at the 1988 Salzburg (Austria) Seminar on the theory and practice of the international negotiation process.[1] The exercise, although it was only a small component of the curriculum for the full two-week session in Salzburg, provided a dramatic jumping-off point for a discussion of the unconscious biases negotiators bring with them to the table.

Briefly, the fifty Salzburg Fellows were divided into small groups of roughly similar (in some cases, very roughly similar) national and-or ethnic backgrounds. Since the number of Fellows was limited and time likewise was in short supply, some decisions on group formation were arbitrary — e. g., a Sudanese and a Ugandan composed a group representing all Sub-Saharan nations; an American of Chinese descent, a Thai, a Malaysian, and a Singapore national represented "Asians."

Perceptions

The small groups were then asked to meet for about fifteen minutes and develop a list of several stereotypic characteristics that people from other nations and cultures have about them. The lists would not be descriptions of legitimate difference in national negotiation styles; rather, they were to be an assessment of how others perceived them simply because they belonged to that particular grouping. In most cases, the assumptions included negative characteristics. Following is a sampling of the lists of stereotypes drawn up by the various groups:

Austrians: Friendly, sloppy, conservative, stubborn, culture-loving.

Mediterraneans: Warm-hearted, "Latin lovers," emotional, tendency toward procrastination, not punctual, disorganized, individualists, good businesspeople.

Sub-Saharan Africans: Mediocre and second-rate, emotional, irrational, easy-going and lazy, possessing more physical abilities than mental.

Central Americans: Idealistic, impractical, disorganized, unprepared, stubborn in arguments, flowery in style.

British: Old-fashioned, arrogant, reserved, eccentric, self-deprecating, fair, "generally British, really."

Irish: Fast-talking, good for a laugh but not reliable, simple but shrewd, quarrelsome and argumentative, good "social grease" (though not with each other) but not to be taken seriously.

Levantine (Lebanon, Syria, and Palestine): Violent — they're all terrorists; racist, aggressive, indecisive, irrational and temperamental; emotional, impulsive, and romantic; traditional and backward, illiterate, and primitive in social relations; hospitable "to the point of insanity" and naive.

Americans: Arrogant, impatient, direct and blunt, naive, generous, friendly and tolerant; self-critical; individualistic; risk-takers; idealistic; materialistic; domineering and aggressive.

Asians: Reserved, not verbose; careful; less open than others; mandate is limited by a hierarchical seniority system; conflict-avoiding; stress importance of personal relationships; shrewd and alert.

Israelis: Tough, single-minded, and well-connected; clever; self-righteous; cunning; ostracized; paranoid.

Germans: Disciplined and hard-working; rigid; well-organized but fanatic at times; keen to learn others' opinions of them; dominating and imposing; adhere to principles; stubborn.

Dutch: Reliable, thorough, and direct; too serious; inflexible; not very creative; tolerant.

A Fact of Life

When the "Sub-Saharan African" group reported that the stereotypic perception of their group was as "mediocre and second-rate. . . . easy-going and lazy," there were several gasps from the other Salzburg Fellows. "That is definitely *not* the case," one of the Fellows remarked a bit angrily. "We are all internationalists here — there's no place for that kind of prejudice in international relations."

At the Salzburg Seminar, that is certainly true. However, the exercise — which was not intended as a scientific study of perceived biases — did effectively make the point that negotiators believe such biases do exist in some negotiating forums. Whether we like it or not, prejudicial stereotyping, on the basis of national origin, gender, occupation, or some other characteristic, is a fact of life. So too is the perception of such prejudice, an assumption most negotiators bring with them to the table. Such an assumption itself is a form of bias — "They won't listen to me because of what I represent." That perception is likewise damaging, and can be self-defeating as well.

In the discussion that followed the exercise, several practical suggestions were made to help negotiators break away from prejudicial stereotyping. Much of the advice centered on focusing always on the individual, not the group he or she may represent by virtue of ethnic background, race, or gender. It was pointed out that differences within particular groups are often far greater than differences between groups; thus, an individual may or may not exhibit behavior that fulfills the perceived stereotype of his or her group. Increased, productive contact among different groups was another means suggested to combat stereotyping. If representatives of various groups learn more about one another, assumptions — particularly negative ones — will have less of an influence.

Perhaps the most valuable advice given was to urge individuals to be aware of the fact that they may be guilty of stereotyping or victimized by it. Stereotyping is often done unconsciously, and becomes an ingrained, unnoticed practice. Such biases are particularly deadly because they predispose a negotiator to view people as the problem, not as colleagues who work together to resolve a problem.

NOTES

1. The Salzburg Seminar is an independent, nonprofit educational organization that annually offers a series of seminars on topics of world significance at the Schloss Leopoldskron in Salzburg, Austria. Fellows invited to participate in these seminars are generally midcareer professionals who are already prominent or display promise in their respective fields.

"Negotiation Theory and Practice: Political Differences" took place May 22-June 4, 1988 in Salzburg with a faculty that included Jeffrey Z. Rubin of Tufts University, chair; Victor Kremenyuk of the Institute of USA and Canada Studies, Moscow; Roger Fisher and Bruce M. Patton of Harvard Law School; Louis Sohn of the University of Georgia; Pauline Neville-Jones, Britain's economic minister in Bonn, Federal Republic of Germany; and Howard Raiffa of the Harvard Business School. Fifty diplomats, educators, and business executives participated as Fellows in this seminar, which was the first in a three-year sequence of negotiation studies that was jointly sponsored by the Program on Negotiation at Harvard Law School and the Salzburg Seminars. Howard Raiffa served as chair of the 1989 seminar, focused on international business disputes, and Lawrence Susskind of the Massachusetts Institute of Technology was chair of the 1990 seminar, focused on the negotiation of international environmental conflicts.

The author (J. William Breslin) served as rapporteur for the 1988 Salzburg Seminar on negotiation; his report, entitled "Negotiation Theory and Practice: Political Differences," is available as Working Paper no. 89-3 of the Program on Negotiation at Harvard Law School. To obtain a copy, contact the Clearinghouse of the Program on Negotiation, 518 Pound Hall, Harvard Law School, Cambridge, Mass. 02138.

Making Deals in Strange Places
A Beginner's Guide to International Business Negotiation

Jeswald W. Salacuse

The decline in U.S. business competitiveness abroad has led policymakers and scholars to point to many causes: protectionism in foreign markets, unfair trade practices by other nations, failures in international economic cooperation, and inadequacies in our own educational system. While these institutional and policy factors certainly influence global trade and capital flows, and therefore deserve careful study, discussions about competitiveness have generally neglected the basic molecule of those flows — the international business deal.

Most economic commentators take international deal-making for granted, apparently on the assumption that if the right policies and structures are in place, business among nations will automatically follow. Experience clearly shows, however, that negotiating an international business transaction is a difficult, painstaking process that can fail even in the presence of the most favorable policies and institutions.

A second unstated assumption underlies much of the current talk about competitiveness and the need to "go international" as a solution to U.S. economic problems — that American corporations, so skillful at what they do domestically, only have to do the same things outside our borders to succeed internationally. For many government officials and corporate leaders, international business is really just an extension of domestic business. They seem to believe that the attitudes, skills, and knowledge that have served American companies in Akron and Kansas City will, with some adjustment to the local climate, almost certainly work just as well in Accra and Kuala Lumpur. After all, business is business, products are products, and, when you come right down to it, international business is really nothing more than making deals in strange places.

Both of these assumptions are false, and both are damaging to U.S. international competitiveness. First, success in international business will require U.S. executives to know much more about and to become more expert in negotiating international transactions, regardless of the policies and institutions that emerge to foster global trade and investment. Second, negotiating international business transactions must be seen as fundamentally different from making domestic deals, and not merely an extension of domestic activity.

Indeed, international business may be as much an extension of international relations as it is of domestic business. With only slight exaggeration, one might say that domestic business dealings probably have about the same rela-

Jeswald W. Salacuse is Dean and Professor of International Law at the Fletcher School of Law and Diplomacy, Tufts University, Medford, Mass. 02155.

tionship to international business as domestic politics do to international diplomacy. Just as we have come to realize that the craft of the diplomat is different from that of the politician, we must also recognize that the knowledge, skills and attitudes necessary for international business negotiation are not those ordinarily found in the average U.S. executive whose work is essentially local.

To become more competitive internationally, the United States must develop international negotiation as a distinct body of knowledge and expertise that can be taught in our schools, discussed in our management seminars, and analyzed in our journals. Certainly, the literature on the subject of negotiation is vast, but much of it is anecdotal, unsystematic, and limited to a specific country or region. It may tell us when to cross our legs in Saudi Arabia or how to drink our tea in Singapore, but it does not often provide a basic approach to international negotiations as a fundamental task in international business. My purpose in this brief article is to offer one such general approach — a beginner's guide, if you will — to thinking about international deal-making.

Six Common Factors in International Deals

International business transactions are extremely diverse. At first glance, it is difficult to see many similarities among a Eurodollar loan by a group of London banks, a manufacturing joint venture with a rural commune in China, a technology licensing agreement with a Japanese multinational, and a barter deal with a state trading organization in the Soviet Union. Nonetheless, the basic argument of this article is: 1. that international business transactions, *as a group*, are shaped by certain basic common factors that are not present in the ordinary domestic business deal; and 2. that these factors both give international transactions, of whatever type, a conceptual unity, while at the same time differentiating them sharply from ordinary U.S. domestic dealings. Equally important, these factors fundamentally shape the process of negotiating international business deals of all sorts, and they must therefore be studied and mastered.

In general terms, international business negotiations are conditioned by six fundamental constraints: 1. political and legal pluralism; 2. international monetary factors; 3. the role of governments and bureaucracies; 4. instability and sudden change; 5. ideological diversity; and 6. cultural differences. Together these six factors constitute a framework for analyzing the negotiation of international business transactions and perhaps eventually for building a general theory of international deal-making.

1. *Political and Legal Pluralism*

By engaging in international business, a company enters into an arena of intense legal and political pluralism. An export sale, a direct foreign investment, or a technology transfer brings at least one of the parties to the deal into contact with the laws and political authority of more than one country. As a result, a transaction may be taxed by two or more governments, a contract may be subject to two or more legal systems, and a dispute may be decided by two or more courts.

A notorious example of the kind of political and legal pluralism that a business deal may face is the construction of the Trans-Siberian pipeline in the early 1980s. American companies and their European subsidiaries were caught between the law and political power of the United States and the law and political authority of our European allies. In that case, the U.S. government ordered the European subsidiaries of American companies not to supply equipment and technology for the Trans-Siberian pipeline, while the European governments demanded that they respect their supply contracts. Only diplomacy at the highest level finally resolved the problem.

Although the Soviet pipeline case attracted considerable attention, it is certainly not a unique example of legal and political pluralism in international business. The practice of negotiating international business transactions is always a matter of complying with or avoiding a multiplicity of different national rules, laws and policies — of weaving between overlapping legislation and political decisions of numerous governments.

Although this problem is hardly ever a consideration in a domestic deal, it is constantly present in any international business negotiation, and clearly conditions the thinking of international business negotiators. As a result, international business transactions always include special measures, including provisions for international commercial arbitration, specific choice of governing law, and the use of tax havens.

2. *International Monetary Factors*
Monetary problems are a second set of special constraints to be faced in international business negotiations. Unlike purely domestic deals, international business transactions take place in a world of many currencies and monetary systems. Transactions cross monetary as well as political boundaries and there is no single world currency for making payment. The existence of so many different monetary systems creates two fundamental problems in negotiating any international business transaction.

First, the relative values of the world's currencies constantly fluctuate, and that factor creates special risks for the party who is to be paid in a currency that is not its own. Between the time an agreement is signed and the time that payment is actually received, the value of the payment currency may either increase or decrease, thereby creating an unexpected loss for one side and an undeserved gain for the other.

The rapid rise in the value of the yen in recent months, for example, has certainly affected Japanese negotiators in structuring new transactions. To cope with this problem, negotiators may seek to use various complicated devices whose function is basically to reallocate currency risk between the two sides or to shift it to a third party such as a bank.

The second major monetary problem that conditions international business negotiations derives from the fact that most governments to try to control the entry to, possession in, and exit from their territories of both foreign and local currencies. These regulations, known as exchange controls, may be imposed virtually without warning, and they can seriously affect the profitability of a transaction.

In many countries, a company's ability to pay for imported raw materials, to service foreign loans or to repatriate profits depends on the ability and the willingness of the host government to make convertible foreign currency available. In structuring direct foreign investments and joint ventures, one of the principal preoccupations of the negotiator is to find means to avoid or blunt the effect of these controls.

In purely domestic transactions, currency questions are hardly ever of concern; however, they are pervasive in negotiating any international business transaction. In long-term contracts, the parties often have to devise complicated mechanisms to protect themselves from currency fluctuations. Special arrangements and guarantees may have to be negotiated with local governments to assure the availability of foreign exchange. The lack of convertible currency has led to the growth of sophisticated types of barter transactions known as "counter trade," in which payment is made in goods, rather than cash. The possibility of countertrade is always present in business negotiation with many nations, including China and the Soviet Union.

3. *The Role of Foreign Governments and Bureaucracies*

Americans are often unprepared for the extensive — indeed pervasive — the role played by foreign governments in international business. Governments not only regulate economic activities and organize public utilities, as is fairly common in the United States, but they are also active as participants through governmental ministries, corporations and agencies in all sorts of business activities from trading and insurance to manufacturing and agriculture.

In many nations, government corporations have an exclusive monopoly over all imports entering the country and all exports leaving it. Indeed for American corporations seeking major customers or joint-venture partners in many parts of the world, governmental entities are the only realistic possibilities. As a result, transactions that in the U.S. are conducted between private parties are accomplished abroad with governments.

Does that fact make a difference in negotiating international transactions? Absolutely. Negotiations with government corporations and enterprises involve a host of different considerations from those with private firms. For example, freedom of negotiation may be limited. State corporations, like those in the Soviet Union, may be required to use standard form contracts that include mandatory clauses on payment terms, insurance, and guarantees, to mention just a few. They may also be tied by the rigid rules and regulations controlling government departments. The attitudes, work habits, and styles of operation of their officials often resemble those of a government bureaucracy, rather than of private enterprise, and their goals may conflict with those of a private company.

And, since they are subsidized by the state treasury, the principal goal of these state entities may not be the maximization of profit, but rather social and political ends. For example, if a manufacturing joint venture between a U.S. company and a state-owned foreign corporation were to be faced by a decline in product demand, the reaction of the U.S. partner might be to layoff workers while the foreign government corporation, despite reduced profitability, might reject that solution so as not to increase unemployment.

Foreign government officials bring to the negotiating table bureaucratic attitudes and approaches that introduce rigidity into the negotiating process. Moreover, negotiations with foreign state enterprises raise special legal problems including sovereign immunity and their authority to act without specific government approval.

4. *Instability and Sudden Change*

Change, of course, is a fact of life, and change in circumstances is to be found in both domestic and international business. Nevertheless, the nature and magnitude of the risk of change in the international arena appear to be far greater than in a purely domestic setting. The outbreak of war and revolution, the closing of international trade routes, the devaluation of currencies, *coups d'états*, and sudden shifts in government policies are just a few examples of events that have severe and widespread consequences for any international transaction. Within the past few years, we need only cite the closing of the Suez Canal as a result of the Arab-Israeli conflict, the fall of the Shah of Iran, and most recently the Iran/Iraq War as examples of sudden changes that have affected international business transactions in the Middle East alone.

To cope with these risks, business negotiators use a variety of mechanisms and strategies that they would not ordinarily employ in purely domestic transactions, including political risk analysis, force majeure clauses that allow cancellation of the contract upon the happening of specified events, the purchase of foreign investment insurance, and the provision of international arbitration in a neutral third country.

The risk of instability places strong pressure on international business negotiators to anticipate change, and, in this sense, negotiating an international deal is very much a predictive process. How does a negotiator anticipate change? How does he or she plan for it? Predictions, of course, are always difficult; they are especially difficult, it has been said, when they concern the future.

But surely the wise negotiator must begin with a thorough knowledge of the country and the region concerned, and of the political, economic and social forces at work. Consequently, these factors require the international business negotiator to have a breadth of knowledge and social insight that would not ordinarily be necessary in negotiating a U.S. business arrangement.

5. *Problems of Ideology*

Whether they are Republicans or Democrats, American business negotiators generally share a common ideology, but in the international arena business negotiators normally encounter — and must be prepared to deal with — ideologies vastly different from their own. Three areas of ideological difference often faced by U.S. negotiators are private investment, profit, and individual rights.

Americans tend to view private investment as a positive good, a force to create wealth, jobs, useful products, and income; however, many foreign countries look at it more circumspectly. For them, foreign investment has its benefits and its costs, and they seek to maximize the benefits and minimize the costs through governmental regulation. The subject of profit is also viewed differently. For Americans, profit results from growth and is good because it can be reinvested to yield further benefits; however, in some countries the profit one party gains is seen as value taken away from someone else. Similarly, Americans tend to stress the rights of the individual, but other nations emphasize the rights of the group.

The existence of a conflict in ideologies often requires the negotiator to find ways of wrapping proposals in ideological packages that are acceptable to the other party, and to find neutral means of communicating with negotiators on the other side.

6. *Cultural Differences*

International business transactions not only cross political and ideological boundaries, they also cross cultures. As a powerful factor shaping thought, communication, and behavior, culture conditions the negotiating process in some fundamental ways. Negotiators from different cultures may have quite distinct approaches to negotiations, and their styles of negotiating may be markedly different. Numerous books and articles have stressed the differences in negotiating styles of such diverse cultural groups as the Japanese (e.g., Tung, 1984); the Soviets (e.g., Vlachoutsicos, 1986); the Chinese (e.g., Pye, 1982); and the Americans (e.g., Graham and Herberger, 1983). While this literature is useful, some works are overly anecdotal and tend to create cultural stereotypes.

Persons of different cultures often speak different languages, a factor that certainly complicates the negotiating process, requiring interpreters and translators or forcing one side to negotiate in a foreign language. But communicating with another culture is not just a matter of learning the other side's vocabulary; it also requires an understanding of its values, perceptions, and philosophies. Different cultures operate on the basis of different unspoken assumptions, and each may interpret the same phenomenon in very different ways.

For example, it is possible for negotiators from different cultures to interpret the very purpose of their negotiation differently. For most Americans, the purpose of the negotiations, first and foremost, is to arrive at a signed contract between the parties. Americans view a signed contract as a definitive set of rights and obligations that strictly binds the two sides, an attitude succinctly summed up in the declaration that "a deal is a deal."

Japanese and Chinese, on the other hand, view the signed contract in a very different light. For them, the "deal" being negotiated is not the contract, but the relationship between the parties. Although the written contract expresses that relationship, the essence of the deal is the relationship, and it is understood that the relationship may be subject to reasonable changes over time. For the American, signing a contract is "closing a deal"; for the Japanese, signing the contract might more appropriately be called "opening a relationship."

Since the Japanese and the American view the end product of negotiations differently, perhaps one can say that, from an intercultural perspective, "a deal is not always a deal." The consequences of this difference in perception is important. For example, if a Japanese joint-venture partner seeks to modify the terms of the contract because of a change in business conditions, the American participant may view these efforts as an outrageous attempt to renege on a deal. The Japanese participants, on the other hand, may consider the American reaction to be unreasonable rigidity and a refusal to allow the contract to conform to the underlying relationship.

A reflection of this dichotomy is also found in differing approaches to writing a contract. Generally, Americans prefer very detailed contracts that attempt to foresee and anticipate all possible circumstances, no matter how unlikely. Why? Because the "deal" is the contract itself, and one must go to the contract to determine how to handle a new circumstance that may arise.

Other cultures, such as China, prefer a contract in the form of general principles, rather than detailed rules. Why? Because the essence of the deal is the relationship of trust that exists between the parties. If unexpected circumstances arise, the parties should look to their relationship, not the written contract, to solve the problem.

So in some cases, the American drive at the negotiating table to foresee all possible contingencies may be seen by another culture as evidence of mistrust in the stability of the underlying relationship.

Related to this issue is the question of whether negotiating a business deal is an *indicative* or *deductive* process. Does it start from agreement on general principles and then proceed to specific items, or does it begin with agreements on specifics (e.g., price, delivery date, product quality), the sum total of which becomes the contract?

One observer (Pye, 1982, p. 95) believes that the Chinese prefer to begin with agreement on general principles, while Americans seek first to agree on specifics. For Americans, negotiating a deal is basically making a whole series of compromises and tradeoffs on a long list of particulars. For Chinese, the essence is to agree on basic general principles which will guide and indeed determine the negotiation process afterwards.

A further difference in negotiating style is the dichotomy between the "building-down approach," where the negotiator begins by presenting the maximum deal if the other side accepts all the stated conditions, and the "building-up approach," where one side starts by proposing a minimal deal that can be broadened and increased as the other party accepts further conditions. According to many observers, Americans tend to favor the building-down approach, while the Japanese prefer the building-up style of negotiating a contract.

The purpose of any negotiation is not merely to reach an agreement, but to reach an agreement that will regulate the parties' behavior. For the Westerner, this necessary element raises the question of contract enforcement, of creating mechanisms to impose the agreement on one of the parties who at some later time may refuse to respect its provisions.

For Westerners, enforcement means the use of the courts, compulsory arbitration, and, ultimately, state power in some form. Many countries in Asia resist this tendency. China, for example, has opposed the use of Western courts and even international arbitration, preferring instead to resort to friendly negotiations, conciliation, and mediation in the event of a dispute.

As many authors have pointed out, culture also influences the organization of the negotiators. Here, the American approach to organization is sometimes characterized as "John Wayne" style of negotiations: one person has all the authority and plunges ahead to do the job, and to do the job as quickly as possible (Graham and Herberger, 1983, p. 162). Other cultures, notably the Japanese and the Soviets, stress team negotiations and collective decision making. Indeed, it may not be fully apparent who has the authority to bind the side.

In East-West deals, the American style of one-person management often collides with the collective decision-making approach found in the Soviet Union. In negotiating with the Soviets, decision-making authority may not always rest with the most visible member of the negotiating team and one must not overlook the power of lesser officials on the negotiating team (Vlachoutsicos, 1986, p. 83). In any international business negotiation, it is therefore important for each side to determine how the other side is organized, who has the authority, and how decisions on each side are made.

The various methods of organization, the varying degrees of authority given to the negotiators, and the differing needs to foster mutual trust and to build relationships all may significantly affect the pace of the negotiation process. Americans are often accused of wanting to go too fast in negotiations, of pushing to close the deal in the quickest time possible. On the other hand, one of the commonest complaints from American negotiators about any given international business negotiation — with virtually any foreign enterprise — is that the negotiations are proceeding too slowly. Rarely does one hear an American complain that negotiations are going too quickly.

Whether a negotiation is proceeding too quickly or too slowly may be less a function of some objective universal criteria than of the cultural perspective of the individual negotiators. Nonetheless, the pace of negotiations is an important factor and the party who is able to control the pace generally has an advantage, particularly in international transactions where one side is required to negotiate at a great distance (and therefore usually at great expense) from its home base.

Although cultural differences may create difficulties in international business negotiations, they are not insuperable obstacles. Through experience, negotiators begin to understand each other's perspectives and develop effective ways of cross-cultural communication.

Contrary to what some of the literature on international negotiations would lead us to believe, all negotiators from a particular culture are not cut from a uniform mold and do not represent a single stereotype. China, Japan, the United States, and the Soviet Union each are blessed with experienced negotiators capable of dealing effectively with foreigners, and they also have numerous parochial novices for whom cultural and other negotiating constraints may be nearly insurmountable.

This phenomenon would seem to argue for specialized formal training in international business negotiation. Such education would develop business negotiators in a systematic way rather than leave the process to costly on-the-job training, which all too often assumes that international business negotiation is merely making deals in strange places.

Conclusion

Any business negotiation, whether domestic or international, must treat a host of difficult commercial issues — price, product quality, size of capital contribution, delivery dates —depending on the nature of the transaction in question.

In failing to discuss these issues in this article, I do not mean to suggest that they are unimportant or are somehow easy to solve in the international setting. On the contrary, they go to the essence of the transaction, and are always subject to hard bargaining.

But in addition to the strictly commercial issues, an international business negotiation is profoundly influenced by the six special factors outlined in this article. The primary effect of these factors is that they increase the risks of the negotiation process — the risk that the parties will not reach agreement, the risk that their agreement may prove to be more apparent than real, the risk that any agreement reached will not, in fact, regulate their future behavior. The challenge for international negotiators is to find ways to reduce these risks. Certainly, the first step in this direction is to recognize the existence of these six constraints, and to understand their implications.

REFERENCES

Graham, J. and Herberger, R. (1983). "Negotiation abroad — Don't shoot from the hip." *Harvard Business Review* 61 (July-August): 160-183.
Pye, L. (1982). *Chinese negotiating style*. Cambridge, Mass.: Oelgeschlager, Gunn & Hain.
Tung, R. (1984). *Business negotiations with the Japanese*. Lexington, Mass.: Lexington Books.
Vlachoutsicos, C. A. (1986). "Where the ruble stops in Soviet Trade." *Harvard Business Review* 64 (September-October): 82-86.

Her Place at the Table: A Consideration of Gender Issues in Negotiation

Deborah M. Kolb and Gloria G. Coolidge

A central agenda of recent feminist studies across the social sciences has been to heed the often "unheard" voices of women. Rather than treat women's experience as a variant, typically an inferior variant, of a dominant male model (whether of personality, organizations, or research), recent scholarship has tried to right the record and include women.[1] In history and anthropology, this has meant documenting the experiences of women in their spheres of activity which are usually private (Collier, 1974; Lerner, 1974); in sociology, some of the attention has shifted from considering women in male-dominated organizations or activities to female-dominated structures (Kanter, 1977; Krieger, 1987; Keller, 1985). These structures, created by women for women, tend to be organized in webs or networks and run along different conceptions of management (Krieger, 1987; Menkel-Meadow, 1985). Several works associated with this feminist approach are those that document how traditional developmental theory excludes women's experience (Gilligan, 1982; Chodorow, 1978; Miller, 1976). What emerges from inquiry across these domains is a conception of an alternative way of making sense of the world and acting within it.

The alternative voice[2] starts with the notion that women's social development occurs in the context of relationships (Gilligan, 1982; Chodorow 1978; Miller, 1984), and that this fact affects significant aspects of their social lives. Oriented toward nurturance and affiliation, women make meaning through a screen of interconnection. Never having to repudiate identification with a caretaking mother to define her own sexual identity in adolescence, the developing woman need not rupture connection for her own growth (Chodorow, 1978). Instead of separation and individuation as a primary motive for action, women conceive of action within the context of affiliation and relatedness to others. What this means in the area of moral reasoning, for example, is that dilemmas can be resolved with reference either to abstract principles of justice or guided by grounded considerations of the ways decisions affect the people involved (Gilligan, 1982). While mature adults manifest both considerations in their decision making, there is a noticeable proclivity for one dimension to become prominent and this orientation tends to be associated with gender.[3]

Our purpose here is to explore the ramifications of feminist theories of development and social organization to the exercise of power and the resolu-

Deborah M. Kolb is Professor of Management at the Simmons College Graduate School of Management and Executive Director of the Program on Negotiation at Harvard Law School. **Gloria G. Coolidge** is Planning Coordinator for the Boston Children's Service Association and a Research Associate at the Simmons College Graduate School of Management.

tion of conflict in negotiated settings. Based on a review of some of the leading works, we suggest that there are four themes that are most relevant to an understanding of some of the ways that women frame and conduct negotiations. These are:

- a relational view of others;
- an embedded view of agency;
- an understanding of control through empowerment; and
- problem-solving through dialogue.

While these themes suggest some of the ways women may define their place in negotiated settings, we do not mean to suggest that all women would necessarily view themselves in this way. Clearly variations in class, race, culture, family constellation, and social setting certainly affect the meaning ascribed to gender differences and color the ways in which they are enacted (Krieger, 1987). Existing research and our own experience suggest that this voice, or the multiple voices of women, while real and distinct, is often hushed in formal negotiation. What may be occurring is that formal negotiation, conceived as a context in which conflict and competition are important, may not be a comfortable place for many women. In coping with what she might experience as an unnatural place, some women may try to emulate a culturally dominant style (and do so quite successfully), while others may find their accustomed strengths and skills impaired when placed in conflictual situations. What we try to do in the second part of this article, therefore, is to explore the ways in which women experience conflict and how this may impact their behavior and the perceptions others have of them in negotiation. In examining these themes, we draw on both anecdotal data from novice women negotiators as well as existing research in negotiations and related fields.

Her Voice in Negotiation

There is a certain irony about trying to articulate a woman's voice in negotiation. Negotiation is often put forth as an alternative to violence and adversarial proceedings; it is an alternative that some argue reflects a feminine view of interaction. That is, it is better to talk than fight, and to consider everybody's needs rather than pitting one party against the other in a win-lose contest (Menkel-Meadow, 1983; Northrup, 1987; Rothchild, 1988; Silbey and Sarat, 1988). Further, advocates of negotiation and alternative forms of dispute resolution often espouse a model of negotiation that is based on problem-solving principles presumably designed to create outcomes that meet the interests and needs of all those involved, again a presumed feminine principle (Fisher and Ury, 1981; Menkel-Meadow, 1983; Susskind and Cruikshank, 1987; Fisher and Brown, 1988). If this is so, why should we care about articulating another voice? Presumably, if these authors are correct, that voice is already being heard and dominates much of the current prescriptive thinking about negotiation.

There are at least three reasons why the subject of an alternative voice in negotiation is not closed. First, our experience and those of others suggest that there are significant differences in the ways men and women are likely to approach negotiation and the styles they use in a search for agreement.

Although the research often yields contradictory conclusions (Rubin and Brown, 1975; Deux, 1984; Eagly, 1987; Linn, 1986), in every training situation in which we have been engaged, women come up and ask us to talk about the gender issues. The inference we draw from these interactions is that at least some women experience their gender as a factor in negotiation. The fact that research may not capture this experience may derive from the settings of research (usually the laboratory) and the questions the research poses (which are usually aggregate behavioral indicators).[4] Secondly, there is evidence that in real negotiations (as opposed to simulations), women do not fare that well. In divorce mediation, for example, the settlements women received are inferior economically to those awarded in adjudication (Rifkin, 1984; Pearson and Thoennes, 1988). In queries about salary negotiations, men report higher raises than women (Womack, 1987). If negotiation is a woman's place, we would expect women to excel, not be disadvantaged. There is a third reason why we need to focus on a woman's voice in negotiation: The prescriptions to get to win-win outcomes in negotiation offer ambiguous advice to the negotiator, whether male or female.[5] The advice to focus on interests, not positions and invent options for mutual gain (Fisher and Ury, 1981) emphasizes the relational dimension of negotiation. There are indications, however, that this advice is quite difficult for many to heed because it runs counter to prevailing cultural norms about the competitive and gaming aspect of negotiation (McCarthy, 1985).

On the other hand, advice to separate people from problems and focus on objective criteria, gives a rationalized and objective cast to negotiation that may be quite different from the subjective and embedded forms of feminine understanding. Further, in the press to provide prescription, it is the technical and rationalized analysis that increasingly dominates. Integrative bargaining, or joint-gain negotiation, while acknowledging the importance of empathetic relationships, suggests that the critical skills necessary to implement win-win outcomes are primarily technical and analytic. Negotiators are advised to become more rational in their thinking and analysis (Bazerman, 1983). Even analysis of interests, presumably the ability to empathize with the other party, has become in the language of modern negotiation theory a technical problem:

> Identify the interests that may be at stake. For each interest, imagine the possible packages that serve it best and worst; for example imagine the range of precedents that might follow from the negotiation. This roughly defines the increment of value associated with each interest. . .the importance of each interest depends on the relative importance of its increment compared to those of the other interest; for example, how does the gain from the worst to the best possible precedent compare with the gain from the worst to the best possible monetary outcome? (Lax and Sebenius, 1986: 184-85).

Articulating an alternative voice (or voices) becomes increasingly important in an emerging field in which the driving force is to prescription. These popular theories of negotiation imply that all conflicts are susceptible to similar formulations and that all parties, despite differences in experience and status, can become equally proficient at and achieve the same results, in its application (Northrup and Segall, 1988). The prescriptive voice of principled or joint-gain negotiation, while there is much to applaud in its perspective, has a tendency to drown out alternative ways of seeing and doing things. We need to consider the structures and contexts in more nuanced ways. From our perspective we begin with gender and the themes that might comprise an alternative voice.[6]

Relational View of Others

Research pioneered by Miller (1976), Chodorow (1978) and Gilligan (1982) suggests that girls differ from boys in that they come to define themselves through their relationships. When asked to describe their resolution of moral dilemmas, girls' narratives consistently show a sensitivity to others' needs and an inclusion of others' points of view in their judgments (Gilligan, 1982). Keller (1986) describes women as living "in a domain between one and two" where self and other are not cast in opposition but rather in terms of mutual aid and support. In interactions, this translates for women into an interest in and attention to the other as a grounding for emotional connection, an expectation of a process of empathy and shared experiences, and an expectation of mutual sensitivity and responsibility (Surrey, 1985). In this two-way interactional model, to understand is as important as to be understood; empowering as important as being empowered.

There seem to be two major ways that a relational view of self is potentially manifest in negotiation. The first is the conception a woman has of herself as a party negotiating. She conceives of her interests within a constellation of responsibilities and commitments already made. That is, she is always aware of how her actions in one context impact on other parts of her life and on other people significant to her. Constraints from greater personal responsibilities for day-to-day management of private life and the impact those obligations have in limiting a woman's flexibility within working roles make it difficult to consider and separate interests in any single negotiation from the life context of which it is a part.

The second implication is that relational ordering in negotiation may be a prerequisite for interaction. Relational ordering means creating a climate in which people can come to know each other, share (or do not share) values, and learn of each others' modes of interacting. Expressions of emotion and feeling and learning how the other experiences the situation are as important, if not more important, than the substance of the discourse (Hochshild, 1983; Northrup and Seagall, 1988). In other words, separating the people from the problem is the problem. Negotiation conducted in a woman's voice would, we predict, start from a different point and run a different course than either a purely principled or purely positional model.

Embedded View of Agency

Women understand events contextually both in terms of their impact on important ongoing relationships and as passing frames in evolving situations which grow out of a past and are still to be shaped in the future. The male imagination stereotypically focuses on individual achievement and is sparked by opportunities for distinctive activity that are bounded by task and structure. This exemplifies a self-contained concept of agency (Bakan, 1966; Sampson, 1988). An embedded form of agency emphasizes the fluidity between the boundaries of self and other (Sampson, 1988). Thus, women are energized by their connections and so interpret and locate activities in a spatial and temporal context in which boundaries between self and others and between the task and its surroundings are overlapping and blurred (Keller, 1985; Sampson, 1988).

If one operates from an embedded view of agency, any negotiation must be understood against the background from which it emerges.[7] That means that there is the expectation that people in negotiation will act in a way that is consistent with their past and future behavior in other contexts. Negotiation is not, therefore, experienced as a separate game with its own set of rules but as part of the extended organization context in which it occurs (Greenhalgh and Gilkey, 1985). Further, in order to appreciate negotiating positions or the interests that underlie them, we need to understand their context and their historical evolution. Indeed, several of our students have commented that they rarely separated negotiation from other facets of their work. One student, for instance, noted:

> I worked in real estate. I remember an occasion where I had given a listing to an associate without a prior agreement as to the split arrangement. I trusted my associate. We had worked together for a long time and I assumed that he would realize my previous input and include me in the split. He did not and I had to go to management to get my share.

Operating from an embedded sense of agency, it is possible that women may be slow to recognize that negotiations are occurring unless they are specifically demarcated from the background against which they occur. At the same time, background understandings are likely to be imported into the negotiated setting and to shape what happens there. In a prisoner's dilemma type game that we ran with our students (all women in a woman's organization), the relationships the women had with each other spilled over into the game such that cooperative outcomes marked the behavior of all the groups.

Control Through Empowerment

Power is often conceived as the exertion of control over others through the use of strength, authority or expertise. It is usually defined as the ability to exert influence in order to obtain an outcome on one's own terms (Emerson, 1962). Conceiving of power in this way leads to a dichotomous division between those who are powerful and those who are powerless (Miller, 1982).[8] A model in which power is accrued for oneself at the expense of others may feel alien to some women and/or be seen by others as somehow incongruent with female roles. Anticipating that assertiveness may lead away from connection, women tend to emphasize the needs of the other person so as to allow that other to feel powerful. Her behavior may thus appear to be passive, inactive or depressed.

Instead of accepting the notion of power as dominion, mastery or "power over," feminist researchers propose an alternative model of interaction stressing "power with" or "power from emerging interaction" (Surrey, 1987). Through mutual empowerment rather than competition, a context is created and sustained which increases understanding and moves participants to joint action. This model overrides the active/passive dichotomy and calls for interaction among all participants in the relationship to build connection and enhance everyone's power.

There is a continuing debate about the place of power in negotiation. Some (e.g., Fisher, 1983) argue that it is possible to mobilize power in ways that contribute to better outcomes, while others suggest such a view denies the economic and political context in which negotiation occurs (McCarthy, 1985; Bazerman, 1987). An empowerment view which allows all parties to speak their interests and incorporates these into agreements that transcend the individualized and personalized notion of acquiring, using, and benefiting from the exercise of power is often dismissed as hopelessly naive. However, it is clear that there are situations (particularly those that involve ongoing and valued relationships) in which mutual empowerment is a much desired end.

Problem Solving Through Dialogue

Dialogue is central to a woman's model of problem solving. It is through communication and interaction with others that problems are framed, considered, and resolved. This kind of communication has specific characteristics that differentiate it from persuasion, argument, and debate. According to Surrey (1985), women seek to engage the other in a joint exploration of ideas whereby understanding is progressively clarified through interaction. There is the expectation that the other will play a part of active listener and contribute to the developing movement of ideas. Women come to distinguish between "really talking," which requires careful listening and shared interactions so that emergent ideas can grow as both participants draw deeply from their experiences and analytic abilities, and "didactic talk," where people hold forth without sharing ideas (Belenky et al., 1986). Studies of women in management roles suggest that women reveal more about their attitudes, beliefs, and concerns than men in similar positions and that this contributes to productive dialogue in certain situations (Baird and Bradley, 1979).

Women perceive problem-solving to be an interactive process. Just as conflicts build up over time as individuals or groups struggle for future resources or valued positions, women see conflict resolution as evolutionary and collaborative. While it is possible to plan and strategize about one's role prior to an interaction, a woman's strength may be in her ability to adapt and grow as she learns more about situations from involvement (Warren, 1988; Rosaldo, 1974). Women's well-honed problem-solving skills, which create interactive engagement and foster growth in the private sphere, are often not given free expression in public dispute resolution (Collier, 1974).

Problem solving through dialogue in negotiation suggests a special kind of joining and openness in negotiation. In place of a strategic planning model of negotiation, in which considerable effort is devoted to analyzing and second-guessing the possible interests and positions of the other, problem solving through dialogue involves the weaving of collective narratives that reflect newly-emerging understanding. There exists through this kind of interaction the potential for transformed understanding and outcomes. It is a stance of learning about the problem together and is built on the premise that you have a high regard for the other's interest and she has a high regard for yours. Such a framework suggests a rather different structure of negotiation than the "dance" of positions (Raiffa, 1982).

It also suggests a different process from that which is often described as the essence of joint-gain negotiation (Fisher and Ury, 1981; Raiffa, 1982; Lax and Sebenius, 1986; Susskind and Cruikshank, 1987). The essence of negotiating for joint gains involves a search for those sets of agreements that satisfy interests which the parties are seen to value differently. The tactics entail the logical identification of these differences and the creative exploration of options which will satisfy them. Implied in this model is a view that goals and interests are relatively fixed and potentially known by the parties. The secret to making agreement lies in designing a process where goals and interests can be discovered and incorporated into an agreement. In problem solving through dialogue, the process is less structured and becomes the vehicle through which goals can emerge from mutual inquiry. The stance of those involved is one of flexibility and adaptiveness (distinguished from control) in response to potential uncertainty (Marshall, 1984). This kind of sensing may lead to transformed understandings of problems and possible solutions.

Her Place at the Table

We rarely hear the woman's voice in formal, public negotiation and, when it is there, it tends to be muted and easily overwhelmed. This may occur because the formal negotiating table may be an alien place for a woman.[10] Negotiations are settings for conflict resolution and conflict itself may be uncomfortable for women, because it locates her in opposition to others and is hostile to her qualities and values (Marshall, 1984; Keller, 1985). Conflict is associated with aggressiveness, a stereotypical masculine attribute (Northrup and Segall, 1988). When women or girls act aggressively, their behavior is interpreted differently from aggressive actions of boys or men (Van Wagner and Swanson, 1979; Hennig and Jardim, 1976). Attitude studies consistently show that women are more peaceful and rejecting of violence than men (Northrup, 1987). Women are socialized to believe that conflict with men or others in authority is wrong and feel vulnerable in the face of it (Miller, 1984; Northrup and Segall, 1988). In their private sphere of influence, conflict more often takes on personal and emotional overtones that is quite different from the structured disputing in public settings (Collier, 1974). In common with others who are subordinate, women's conflict is traditionally suppressed and so they may lack experience in dealing openly with it (MacKinnon, 1982; Miller, 1984).

For all these reasons, many women may experience conflict situations as ones in which they have few options and limited ability to affect outcomes. It is not surprising, therefore, that in bargaining situations many women may find what natural problem-solving skills they might bring to the table are mitigated by their feelings about place.[11] These feelings may be expressed in a variety of ways. Some, fearing possible hostility or acrimonious relations, emphasize harmony over other interests including their own. Others, anxious about a situation, find that their presentation style and their ability to communicate impaired. For other women, whose socialization and professional experience lead them to cultivate a style that is congruent with dominant modes of negotiating, they often find that conventional stereotypes and perceptions of them may undermine their behavior and performance.

Preserving Harmony

In a recent class, one of the female students raised her hand and described herself as "incorrigibly integrative." Upon further discussion, it turned out that her definition of integrative, in contrast to others (See Raiffa, 1982; Lax and Sebenius, 1986), was one in which all parties were happy even if it meant that she downplayed her own interests. Studies of negotiation suggest that this preference for harmony may dominate other possible interests. Watson and Kasten (1988) observed experimentally that female negotiating pairs can avoid discussing the main point of a conflict and yet still believe they have negotiated effectively if their interaction with the other party has been pleasant. In studies of managers, it is clear that women relative to men have lower tolerance for antagonistic situations and do what they can to smooth over differences even when it means they are the ones to do the sacrificing (Hennig and Jardim, 1976; Champion, 1979; Loden, 1985).

There is evidence that empathy, considered to be a particular strength of women, leads them to behavior that promotes harmony (Ford, 1982). Empathy should be an advantage in ferreting out a negotiating partner's interests and intentions, and research has generally supported the assumption that women are more empathetic than males (Ford, 1982). Studies of empathy (Jordan, 1984) suggest that while males and females tend to be equal in their cognitive awareness, or ability to recognize and label other peoples' feelings, women generally are more personally responsive on an affective level and know how it feels.

However, there is some indication that when they get into negotiating situations, women may find their ability to empathize impaired (Womack, 1986). There are several possible explanations why women may not be as empathetic in negotiation, as able to take the role of the other, as we might predict. One is that empathy may lead to exploitation. In negotiation, learning of another's interests is carried out to benefit one's own position, sometimes although not always, at the expense of the other. If women are highly responsive to how what they do might impact their relationships, they may be reluctant to exploit what information they might acquire.

Secondly, since a negotiating table is not a "natural" place for a woman, the natural tendency to empathize may be suppressed. We have some evidence from our students (all of whom are women) that in bilateral negotiating situations, where the structure of the game is such that parties are pitted against each other, that they had difficulty placing themselves in the role of the other. In other classroom contexts where the situations involved group decision making, women distinguished themselves in listening to, understanding, and responding to each other. Yet when active listening was required for successful performance in the bilateral negotiation role plays, the students said that anxiety interfered with their ability to listen. Concern over their own next response led them to miss clues revealing unexplored issues of importance to their opponents. They experienced difficulty in eliciting information as they were reluctant to probe, persuade, influence or elicit alternatives. They assessed their opponents' interests based only on the information that was volunteered.

Third, it has been suggested that, in empathizing with others, women may undervalue their own interests and not develop self-empathy (Surrey, 1985; Greenhalgh and Gilkey, 1985). Studies suggest that in a variety of group settings, women listen more and speak less, perhaps limiting their opportunities to satisfy their own interests (Robb, 1988) The dilemma for women is to resolve the conflict between compassion for others and their own autonomy (Gilligan, 1982) and overcome a tendency only to be responsive. Comments from our students support these findings; typical are the remarks of the following student:

> In real life I find it easier to negotiate for others. While supervising two editors this fall, I fought tooth and nail for reasonable schedules, appropriate workloads, and fair performance evaluations. Interestingly enough, I fared better when I represented their interests than when I represented my own!

The ability to take the role of the other in negotiation, to ascertain interests and needs, is an important skill in negotiation (Bazerman, 1983). What the research suggests, however, is that it may be a double-edged sword for women.

Styles of Talk

The essence of negotiation is strategic communication. Parties want to learn about the alternatives available and the priority of interests of the other. At the same time, they want to communicate in ways that further their own aims, whether it is to elucidate their interests or obfuscate them depending on strategy (Lax and Sebenius, 1986). Research on gender in communications suggests that women's distinctive communication style which serves them well in other contexts may be a liability in negotiation (Smeltzer and Watson, 1986).

Women speak differently. Their assertions are qualified through the use of tag questions and modifiers (Lakoff, 1975; Nadler and Nadler, 1984; Womack, 1986). Krieger (1987) notes that the female pattern of communication involves deference, relational thinking in argument, and indirection. The male pattern typically involves linear or legalistic argument, depersonalization and a more directional style. While women speak with many qualifiers to show flexibility and an opportunity for discussion, men use confident, self-enhancing terms. In negotiation, these forms of communication may be read as weakness or lack of clarity and may get in the way of focusing on the real issues in conflict (Watson and Kasten, 1988). Indeed, the women in our class had difficulty putting their wants into words and tended instead to wait for information that was volunteered.

Similarly, women's modes of discourse do not signal influence. Women's speech is more conforming and less powerful (Rosaldo, 1974; Lakoff, 1975; Eagly, 1987). Women talk less and are easily interrupted while they, in turn, are less likely to interrupt (Zimmerman and West, 1979). In mixed groups, they adopt a deferential posture and are less likely to openly advocate their positions (Krieger, 1987). At the same time, there is a proclivity to be too revealing, to talk too much about their attitudes, beliefs, and concerns (Baird and Bradley, 1979). One of our students described her deferential efforts to negotiate with the mayor on the subject of AIDS resources:

> My strategy was to seek incremental progress to ensure that appropriate steps were taken to address the educational and service needs presented by the AIDS epidemic, and to eliminate discrimination against gay people. Given the environment of the mayor's office, I believe now that I weakened my position by being too reasonable for

too long. My strategy initially had been to demonstrate that I would not waste the mayor's time with trivialities, thereby establishing the understanding that when I pressured him, he should understand that it was a serious issue. I look back now on how polite, calm and respectful I was with him in communicating the urgency of the AIDS epidemic and in pushing funding and program proposals. It is a horrible and laughable memory, for I failed to make him uncomfortable enough to warrant his attention. My subtlety was a liability when it came to "persuading" the mayor to take action where he was resistant.

My negotiation style didn't change, even though I watched the mayor for two years and seldom saw him take action on anything unless he was pinned to the wall. I should have been far less deferential. . .I made it too easy for him to dismiss me. I was liked and relatively well respected, but as a negotiator these qualities don't go far. To risk being more of a kick-ass would have served me better, and the mayor as well, by getting things attended to *before* they reached crisis proportions.

Given that the process of negotiation as it is customarily enacted calls for parties to be clear and communicate directly and authoritatively about their goals, feelings, interests, and problems, a deferential, self-effacing, and qualified style may be a significant detriment. It is also possible that such a stance can also be an asset in projecting a caring and understanding posture (Nadler and Nadler, 1984). The choice for women is to learn to become more conversant with negotiation skills but also adept in an alternative style of communication at the negotiating table, one that is more congruent with the task.

Expectations at the Table
When men and women come to the table to negotiate, they bring with them expectations and ways of seeing the other that shape how each is seen and the credibility and legitimacy accorded to their actions. When women come to the table to negotiate they often evoke certain stereotypes about feminine behavior that can affect how they are seen by their negotiating partners. The stereotypes are familiar: Women are expected to act passive, compliant, nonaggressive, noncompetitive, accommodating and attend to the socio-emotional needs of those present (Eisenstein, 1984). If she displays these characteristics through her behavior, then she reinforces some of these stereotypes and, as suggested above, may find her efficacy impaired. However (and this is often the situation with professional women), she may act in ways that contradict these stereotypes. That is, she is aggressive and competitive in pursuing her interests; indeed, she may be quite distributive in the tactics she uses. The question is, can she pull it off?

Existing research is not encouraging. Evidence from research on women in organizations, particularly in management, suggest that it is not so easy for women to act forcefully and competitively without inviting criticism and questions about both her femininity and ability and threatening something of the accustomed social order (Kanter, 1977; Bradley, 1981; Harlan and Weiss, 1982; Marshall, 1984). When performance in decision-making and negotiating tasks are judged equivalent by objective measures, men and women are rated differently, to the detriment of women by those involved to the detriment of women (Deux, 1987). They are seen as less influential and receive less credit for what influence they may have exerted (Devanna, 1987; Harmon et al., 1988; Hoffman and Day, 1988). As mediators they are judged less effective, even when the outcomes they achieved are superior (Burrell, 1988).

At the same time, women are expected to do the emotional work in a group (Hochschild, 1983). In negotiation contexts, they often carry the burden for attending to relationships and the emotional needs of those involved. While such a burden might be consistent with a voice she might like to speak in, for a woman who has trained herself to negotiate from a different premise, these expectations frequently constrain her ability to maneuver for herself or those she represents. Learning how to use her strengths and manage the dual impressions of femininity and strategic resolve are important aspects of negotiating tactics for women.

Conclusions

We have tried to develop two themes in this article which in some respects stand in contradiction to each other. The first, arguing from existing feminist literature, describes what a woman's voice in negotiation might sound like. Here we are suggesting that women, if given the opportunity and setting, might create an alternative structure and process in public negotiation. We do not mean to imply that women would always speak in such a voice. Variations in class, race, culture, and social setting certainly affect the meaning ascribed to negotiated situations and so color the ways in which the process and women's roles within it are enacted. It may be more accurate to speak of alternative voices. However, an alternative voice, to the degree it exists in relatively coherent form, opens up possibilities in certain kinds of negotiations, not just to change the kinds of strategies we employ, but to transform our understanding of process. In situations where trust, openness, and long-term relationships are critical, this voice is likely to be heard and be influential. There are many other situations (indeed, the prototypical negotiated scene), in which the voice is not only hushed but may put its speaker in a situation in which she is open to compromise or exploitation. This is the theme we speak to in the second part of this article.

Gender has been a variable in hundreds of negotiating experiments and yields a picture that is contradictory at best (Rubin and Brown, 1976). A focus on central behavioral tendencies of either the cooperative, competitive, or enlightened self-interest sort may obscure some of the interesting ways that gender is important in negotiation. How an individual acts in a setting has to do with her sense of place and how she defines the situation in which she finds herself (McHugh, 1968). To the degree that negotiation signals conflict and competing interests, a situation often at odds with the voice in which they speak, women may experience anxiety and fraudulence in that place. These feelings compounded by her demeanor and style of communication may impact and sometimes impair her efficacy at the bargaining table. From experienced and professional women, we may learn about the specific tactics and strategies they use to manage a place at the table.

Our dual focus on voice and place suggests some new ways to pursue the "gender issue" in negotiation as a topic of research and training. First, there is the matter of voice. We speculate that an alternative voice, one based on a relational view of others, an embedded view of agency, a focus on empowerment, and problem solving through dialogue, can be deciphered. How can we document this? Comparative study of homogenous gender groups may not provide a reliable context. First, study suggests that in the laboratory women may be especially susceptible to cues in the experimental situation (Greenhalgh and Gilkey, 1985). Further, most comparisons would take place in a cultural context (professional schools, business and legal negotiations) where *the* voice dominates. What is required is a context in which another voice can be potentially heard (such as all female organizations, e.g., law firms, consulting practices [Krieger, 1987]). We need to learn more about how negotiation in these settings is conducted.

Inquiry about her place at the table, however, is a facet of understanding that we can study in more traditional settings. What we are after here is not simple descriptions of behavior, but rather interpretive understandings about how men and women experience the process of negotiation. We want to know not just what they do, but how they think and *feel* about what they do; how this is related to outcomes; and how those involved think about and feel about the outcomes and the process they used to get there. Inquiry of this sort will enhance our understanding about the phenomenon of place at the table that will form the basis for studying variations among men and women (Bailyn, 1988).

Education and training are quite complicated. On the one hand, we believe that it is important to know and articulate the voice women tend to bring to negotiation. It is part of the interpretive lens through which we understand what will happen at the table. What it is and how it is likely to be heard should become part of any analysis we carry out in preparation for negotiation. It is obviously important to realize that speaking the voice has its time and place. We need to help people become better at recognizing it and planning with such contingencies in mind. At the same time, we must be realistic about expectations that are placed on us as women at the table and develop ways to anticipate and manage these expectations. Appreciating some of the ways our style might impede our success, we need to experiment with a variety of presentation modes. There is much we can learn from experience and from those who have successfully managed to find a place at the table and come to speak with a voice that is their own.

NOTES

An earlier version of this paper was presented at a symposium on "Gender, Power, and Conflict" at Annual Meeting of the Academy of Management, Anaheim, Calif. 8 August 1988.

1. Some argue that this distinction is more apparent than real. If women are evaluated relative to men either as deviating from a male standard or representing a different perspective entirely, the comparison with the dominant male model still grounds the observations (Marcus et al., 1984).

2. Significant works in the field of psychology describe moral, cognitive, and affective development as the evolution of identity through a process of separation and differentiation. Self-reliant adults grow beyond the dependence of childhood to define their individual goals, to enter contractual relationships for the achievement of their ends, to apply laws justly in the settlement of their disputes, and, when mature, to join with partners in mutually beneficial relationships and in procreation. The claim is made that each of these thinkers derives his theory primarily from the study of male subjects and that these chronicles of growth may not capture women's experience.

3. In recent studies of adolescents and young adults, Gilligan and her colleagues found that "there is an overwhelming tendency in men to focus on justice and only minimally to represent caring. Only three men from a total of 60 demonstrated a care focus." Sixty percent of a sample of 140 women focused on care. (Marcus et al., 1984: 48)

4. Gender is one of the most studied variables in negotiation simulations in the laboratory, in part, because of the ease of measurement. Despite these prolific efforts, the question of how gender might matter in negotiations is still very much a matter of debate. There are several reasons why these matters are still unsettled.

The first relates to the conception of gender that informs much of the laboratory study. Gender is usually conceived as a stable set of behavioral attributes, the result of biology, sociology, and social role (Eagly, 1987; Hanisch and Carnevale, 1988). Aggregate comparisons of men and women in negotiation situations emphasize gender-based differences along the following:

(1)   dimensions of cooperative-competitive moves (Maccoby and Jacklin, 1974; Amidjaja and Vinacke, 1965; Bond and Vinacke, 1961; Fisher and Smith, 1969; Grant and Sermat, 1969; Greenhalgh and Gilkey, 1984; Miller and Pyke, 1973; Rubin and Brown, 1975; Rapoport and Chammah, 1965; Sampson and Kardush, 1965; Nadler and Nadler, 1984; Wall and Virtue, 1976; Putnam and Jones, 1982; Loden, 1985);

(2)   assertive v. expressive styles of negotiation (Kimmel et al., 1980; Yamada et al., 1983; Hanisch and Carnevale, 1988; Harmon et al., 1988); and

(3)   forms of communication (Nadler and Nadler, 1984; Womack, 1986; Greenhalgh and Gilkey, 1984; Kimmel et al., 1980; Semltzer, and Watson, 1986).

The findings of these studies are equivocal. Although we have not counted directly, at least as many studies conclude that men are cooperative as find that it is women who are so (Greenhalgh and Gilkey, 1984). Whether a man or women adopts an assertive or expressive style is also highly variable and seems to depend on such factors as the sex of the negotiating partner, the role called upon to play, experience with the process, time horizon, and goals to achieve (Putnam and Jones, 1982; Womack, 1986; Greenhalgh and Gilkey, 1984; Rubin and Brown, 1976; Wall and Virtue, 1976; Krieger, 1987). Communication styles that are predicted to detract from a woman's efficacy, the use of apology, equivocal language, and reluctance to press for information (Lakoff, 1973) are not uniformly supported in more recent studies (Nadler and Nadler, 1984; Womack, 1986).

One problem with much of this research is its very conception of gender as a stable set of characteristics that describe all women (or men) in negotiation situations. The characteristics describe central tendencies and tell us very little about variation within each gender group (Bailyn, 1988). It is clear that context matters in terms of the degree to which gender-related characteristics are observed (Deux, 1984). For example, there is evidence that when women negotiate with other women, they tend to be more cooperative and use different forms of argument than they do in mixed groups (Wall and Virtue, 1976; Putnam and Jones, 1982). Our own experience of women in a women's organization reinforces these perceptions (see Krieger, 1987).

Another issue is the focus on behavior. Negotiation tactics are likely to be highly variable dependent upon a host of individual and situational factors. To trace behavior back to gender is to ignore the multiple influences on tactical choice (Neale and Northcraft, 1988). However, there is some evidence that the way negotiators interpret and experience negotiation contexts may have some basis in gender. For example, Rubin and Brown (1976) conclude that women may be more responsive to interpersonal and situational cues and so conceive their strategic choices differently. Similarly, Greenhalgh and Gilkey (1984) demonstrate that women apply a longer time frame to negotiation and so interpret isolated negotiation events in the context of longer-term relationships. Research must attend more to the ways that different groups experience negotiation situations and see what aspects of these differences may be traced to gender and variations within groups.

5. Some suggest that a woman's voice resembles the kinds of tactics associated with integrative (as opposed to distributive) bargaining. The difficulty with this formulation is that it equates voice with behavior. Voice refers not just to what people do, but to how they understand what they are doing. It is a way that individuals define situations so that they can act in them. The particular tactics, whether they are distributive or integrative, are likely to be quite variable as individual negotiators respond to the particular situations they face.

6. While gender has cultural and psychological dimensions like other social variables, gender identity has its roots in biology. Research on parent-infant interaction shows that, from birth, girls are handled with less horseplay and their cries are interpreted to signal different needs and evoke different parental responses than the cries of male infants. By the age of three, most children identify themselves as male or female (Marcus et al., 1984), and that dimension of identity remains constant until death for all but a very few. Perceptions of appropriate action for "a young lady" or the admonition for boys not to "act like a girl" or praise for a professional woman's ability to "think like a man" color each person's understanding of how to act in the world. Particularly in this time of re-examination of the roles women and men ought to play in both public and private spheres, the implications of gender merit careful study. At the same time it is quite clear that it would be a mistake to lump all women into one category and men into another. A focus on women provides the source of ideas about alternative voices. These then become the bases for studies of how these characteristics of voice vary among both men and women (see Bailyn, 1988).

7. Obviously, considerations of ongoing relationships are not relevant to all negotiated settings. In short-term, distributive bargaining situations like automobile or real estate purchases, negotiators bring no common background or relational history to their dealings. Women's reported discomfort with such transactions may be attributable to their lack of familiarity with the snapshot nature of such an interaction (Greenhalgh and Gilkey, 1985).

8. Radical feminists take the position that in legal, political, economic and private spheres, in fact, women are a subordinate group. MacKinnon (Marcus et al., 1984: 27) asserts, "Dominance and submission made into sex, made into the gender difference, constitute the suppressed social content of the gender definitions of men and women." The "feminine" voice is actually the voice of the victim, they argue, and speaks in the only way differential status allows it to be heard by a dominant group bent on suppressing conflicts which challenge the established male-dominated hierarchy.

Our culture socializes men and women into different roles as a result of their status differences, some theorists argue (Northrup, 1987; Miller, 1976). While men are brought up to be achievers and winners in highly-valued, public roles, women are primarily trained to be caretakers and nurturers with responsibility for maintenance and support activities. When women are dependent on men both economically and psychologically, they find initiating open conflict practically impossible (Collier, 1974). In situations of inequality, women lose conflicts. Urging values of care makes sense for women, MacKinnon argues, because that is what women have been valued for and because they have been given little choice to be valued for anything else (Marcus et al., 1984).

9. Gilligan (Marcus et al., 1984: 45) relates the interaction of a pair of four-year-olds who were playing together as an example of reaching an inclusive solution through transformational thinking. The girl suggested they play next-door neighbors. The boy wanted to play pirates instead. "Okay," said the girl, "then you can be the pirate who lives next door." Rather than coming to a "fair" solution where each child would have an equal turn to play a favored game, in her inclusive solution, both the pirate and neighbor game changed into a combined pirate-neighbor game that neither child had separately imagined. This new game arose because a dialogue was established about what to play.

10. Research and experience in training situations demonstrate that mastery of negotiating skills and their practiced application will diminish women's sense of alienation. As women become more used to negotiating, their outcomes improve (Raiffa, 1982; Schenkel, 1984). However, some evidence suggests that women for whom considerations of relationship guide moral reasoning will continue to experience a sense of alienation even from their own words and actions as they reason from principles of justice at the negotiating table. Gilligan illustrates this tension with a girl named Amy to whom she twice poses the Heinz dilemma, a moral reasoning problem about whether a husband should steal a drug he cannot afford in order to save his wife's life. At age 15, Amy gives the "right" answer that he should steal the drug because life comes before property. She explains, though, that she "really thinks" just as she did at age 11 that "It all depends. What if the husband got caught? It would not help his wife. And anyway, from everything I know about cancer, it cannot be cured in a single treatment. . ." (Marcus et al., 1984: 41). By 15, Amy has learned not to voice her contextual and relationship-based frame for judgment.

This feeling of being out of place was also confirmed by Isabel Marcus, Associate Professor of Law at the State University of New York at Buffalo, who responded to a lecture by Gilligan with the insight, "Now I understand at a new level why I felt so uncomfortable in law school" (Marcus et al., 1984: 11).

11. McIntosh (1985) has found feelings of fraudulence to be especially severe in women and to arise in acute forms in particular situations. Training experiences indicate that negotiated settings trigger feelings of fraudulence in inexperienced women. McIntosh describes fraudulence as feeling illegitimate in doing or appearing as something unfamiliar; as feeling anxious,

uncomfortable, incompetent, undeserving, tenuous and guilty. She contends that women are taught to feel like frauds and that the teaching is no accident but is designed to perpetuate existing hierarchies.

REFERENCES

Amidjaja, I. R. and Vinacke, W. E. (1965). "Achievement, nurturance, and competition in male and female triads." *Journal of Personality and Social Psychology* 2: 447-451.

Bailyn, L. (1988). "Issues of gender in technical work." Paper presented at the Tokyo Symposium on Women, August 25-27.

Baird, J. E. and Bradley, P. H. (1979). "Styles of management and communication: A comparative study of men and women." *Communications Monographs* 46: 101-111.

Bakan, D. (1966). *The duality of human existence*. Chicago: Rand McNally.

Bazerman, M. H. (1987). "*Getting to YES* six years later." *Dispute Resolution Forum*, May. Washington, D.C.: National Institute for Dispute Resolution.

———. (1983). "Negotiator judgment: A critical look at the rationality assumption." *American Behavioral Scientist* 27: 211-228.

Belenky, M. F., Clinchy, B. M., Goldberger, N. R. and Tarule, J. M. (1986). *Women's ways of knowing: The development of self, voice and mind*. New York: Basic Books.

Bond, J. R. and Vinacke, W. E. (1961). "Coalitions in mixed-sex triads." *Sociometry* 24: 61-75.

Bradley, P. (1981). "The folk linguistics of women's sphere: An empirical examination." *Communication Monographs* 48: 73-90.

Burrell, N. (1988). "Training Mediators as Interests Mergers: The Impact of Gender Stereotype on Roommate Disputes." *Communication Research*.

Champion, D. L. (1979). "A comparison of men and women managers on preference for organizational conflict management." DBA, Florida State University.

Chodorow, N. (1978). *The reproduction of mothering*. Berkeley: University of California Press.

Collier, J. F. (1974). "Women in politics." In *Women, culture and society*, edited by M.Z. Rosaldo and L. Lamphere. Stanford: Stanford University Press.

Conrath, D. W. (1960). "Sex roles and 'cooperation' in the game of chicken." *Journal of Conflict Resolution* 60: 265-277.

Devanna, M. A. (1987). "Women in management: Progress and promise." *Human Resource Management* 26 (4): 469-481.

Deux, K. K. (1984). "From individual differences to social categories: Analysis of a decade's research on gender." *American Psychologist* 39: 105-116.

Eagly, A. (1987). *Sex differences in social behavior: A social-role interpretation*. Hillsdale, N.J.: Lawrence Erlbaum.

Eisenstein, H. (1984). *Contemporary feminist thought*. London: Unwin Paperbacks.

Emerson, R. A. (1962). "Power-dependence relations." *American Sociological Review* 27: 31-40.

Fisher, R. (1983). "Negotiating power." *American Behavioral Scientist* 27: 149-166.

———. and Brown, S. (1988). *Getting together: Building a relationship that gets to YES*. Boston: Houghton Mifflin Company.

———. and Smith, W. P. (1969). "Conflict of interest and attraction in the development of cooperation." *Psychonomic Science* 14: 154-155.

———. and Ury, W. (1981). *Getting to YES: Negotiating agreement without giving in*. Boston: Houghton Mifflin Company.

Ford, M. E. (1982). "Social cognition and social competence in adolescence." *Developmental Psychology* 18 (3): 323-340.

Gilligan, C. (1982). *In a different voice: Psychological theory and women's development*. Cambridge, Mass.: Harvard University Press.

Greenhalgh, L. and Gilkey, R. W. (1985). "Our game, your rules: Developing effective negotiating approaches." In *Not as far as you think*, edited by L. Moore. Lexington, Mass.: Lexington Books.

———. (1984). "Effects of Sex-Role Differences on Approaches to Interpersonal and Interorganizational Negotiations" Paper presented at the Academy of Management Annual Meeting, Boston, Mass., August.

Grant, M. J. and Sermat, V. (1969). "Status and sex of other as determinants of behavior in a mixed-motive game." *Journal of Personality and Social Psychology* 12: 151-157.

Hanisch, K. A. and **Carnevale, P.** (1988). "Gender differences in mediation and negotiation: General effects and situation specific effects." Unpublished paper.

Harlan, A. and **Weiss, C.** (1982). "Sex differences in factors affecting managerial career advancement." In *Women in the Workplace*, edited by P. Wallace. Boston: Arbor House.

Harmon, J., Schneer, J. A., and **Hoffman, L. R.** (1988). "Power, influence, and conflict-handling behavior in established groups: Gender differences and medium of communication." Paper presented at the Academy of Management, Anaheim, Calif., August.

Hennig, M. and **Jardim, A.** (1976). *The managerial woman*. Garden City, N.Y.: Anchor Press/Doubleday.

Hochschild, A. (1983). *The managed heart*. Berkeley: University of California Press.

Hoffman, L. R. and **Day, A.** (1988). "Gender and influence in the problem-solving process in groups." Paper presented at the Academy of Management, Anaheim, Calif., August 8.

Jordan, J.V. (1984). "Empathy and self boundaries." *Work in Progress* No. 84-05. Wellesley, Mass.: Stone Center Working Paper Series.

Kanter, R. M. (1977). *Men and women of the corporation*. New York: Basic Books.

Keller, E. F. (1986). "How gender matters, or, why it's so hard for us to count past two." *New Ideas in Psychology*.

————. (1985). *Reflections on gender and science*. New Haven: Yale University Press.

Kimmel, M. J., Pruitt, D. G., Magenau, J. M, Konar-Goldband, E., and **Carnevale, P. J.** (1980). "Effects of trust, aspiration, and gender on negotiation tactics." *Journal of Personality and Social Psychology* 38: 9-22.

Krieger, S. (1987). "Organizational theory: Implications of recent feminist research (ways women organize)." Talk presented at the Organizational Behavior and Industrial Relations Colloquium, School of Business Administration, University of California, Berkeley, 29 October 1987.

Lakoff, R. (1975). *Language and women's place*. New York: Harper and Colopher.

Lax, D. A. and **Sebenius, J. K.** (1986). "Interests: The measure of negotiation." *Negotiation Journal* 2: 73-92.

Lerner, G. (1979). *The majority finds its past: Placing women in history*. New York: Oxford University Press.

Linn, M. (1986). "Meta-analysis of studies of gender differences: Implications and future directions." *The Psychology of gender, advances through meta-analysis*. London: Johns Hopkins University Press.

Loden, M. (1985). *Feminine leadership, or, how to succeed in business without being one of the boys*. New York: Time Books.

Maccoby, E. E. and **Jacklin, C. N.** (1974). *The psychology of sex differences*. Stanford: Stanford University Press.

MacKinnon, C. (1982). "Feminism, Marxism, method and the state: An agenda for theory." *Signs* 7: 515-544.

Marcus, I., Spiegelman, P. J., DuBois, E. C., Dunlap, M. C., Gilligan, C. J., MacKinnon, C. A., and **Menkel-Meadow, C. J.** (1985). "Feminist discourse, moral values, and the law — A conversation." Edited transcript of the 1984 James McCormick Mitchell Lecture at the Law School of the State University of New York at Buffalo. *Buffalo Law Review* 35: 11-87.

Marshall, J. (1984). *Women managers: Travelling in a male world*. Chichester, England: Wiley.

McCarthy, W. (1985). "The role of power and politics in Getting to YES." *Negotiation Journal* 1: 59-66.

McHugh, P. (1968). *Defining the situation: The organization of meaning in social interaction*. New York: Bobbs-Merrill.

McIntosh, P. (1985). "Feeling like a fraud." *Work in Progress* No. 18. Wellesley, Mass.: Stone Center Working Paper Series.

Menkel-Meadow, C. (1985). "Portia in a different voice: Speculating on a women's lawyering process." *Berkeley Women's Law Journal* 1: 39-63.

Miller, G. H. and **Pyke, S. G.** (1973). "Sex, matrix variations, and perceived personality effects in mixed-motive games." *Journal of Conflict Resolution* 17: 335-349.

Miller, J. B. (1984). "The development of women's sense of self." *Work in Progress* No. 84-01. Wellesley, Mass.: Stone Center Working Paper Series.

————. (1982). "Women and power: Some psychological dimensions." *Work in Progress* No. 82-01. Wellesley, Mass.: Stone Center Working Paper Series.

————. (1976). *Toward a new psychology of women*. Boston: Beacon Press.

Nadler, L. B. and **Nadler, M. K.** (1984). "Communication, gender, and negotiation: Theory and findings." Eastern Communication Association Convention, Philadelphia, 9 March 1984.

Neale, M. and Northcraft, G. (1988). "Experience, expertise and decision bias in negotiation." In *Research in Bargaining and Negotiating in Organizations*, vol II. edited by B. Sheppard, M. H. Bazerman, and R. Lewicki. Greenwich, Conn.: JAI Press, in press.

Northrup, T. A. and Segall, M. H. (1988). " 'Subjective vulnerability': The role of disempowerment in the utilization of mediation services by women." Proposal submitted to The Fund for Research on Dispute Resolution, June.

Northrup, T. A. (1987). "Women's and men's conceptualizations of war, peace, and security: Two realities." Working Paper No. 3. Syracuse, N.Y.: Maxwell School of Citizenship and Public Affairs.

Pearson, J. and Thoennes, N. (1988). "An empirical study of child support mediation." Unpublished paper.

Putnam, L. L. and Jones, T. S. (1982). "Reciprocity in negotiations: An analysis of bargaining interaction." *Communication Monographs* 49: 171-191.

Raiffa, H. (1982). *The art and science of negotiation*. Cambridge, Mass.: Harvard University Press.

Rappoport, A. and Chammah, A.M. (1965). "Sex differences in factors contributing to the level of cooperation in the prisoner's dilemma game." *Journal of Personality and Social Psychology* 2: 831-838.

Rifkin, J. (1984). "Mediation from a feminist perspective: Problems and promise." *Law and Inequality*, 21: 2.

Robb, C. (1988). "What did you say?" *The Boston Globe Magazine*, 30 March 1988.

Rothschild, J. (1988). "The feminization of conflict resolution: The influence of gender on the ideology, language, and practice of mediation." Paper presented at the Annual Meeting of the Law and Society Association, Chicago, Ill., June.

Rosaldo, M. Z. (1974). "Women, culture, and society: A theoretical overview." In *Women, culture and society*, edited by M. Z. Rosaldo and L. Lamphere. Stanford: Stanford University Press.

Rubin, J. Z. and Brown, B. R. (1975). *The psychology of bargaining and negotiation*. New York: Academic Press.

Sampson, E. E. and Kardush, M. (1965). "Age, sex, class, and race differences in response to a two person non-zero sum game." *Journal of Conflict Resolution* 9: 212-220.

———. (1988). "The debate on individualism: Indigenous psychologies of the individual and their role in personal and societal functioning." *American Psychologist*, January.

Schenkel, S. (1984). *Giving away success: Why women get stuck and what to do about it.* New York: McGraw-Hill.

Segall, M. (1988). "Psychocultural antecedents of male aggression: Some implications involving gender, parenting, and adolescence." In *Psychological implications for human development*, edited by M. Sartorium, P. Dasen and J.W. Berry. Newbury Park: Sage.

Silbey, S. and Sarat, A. (1988). "Dispute processing in law and legal scholarship." Paper prepared for the Institute for Legal Studies, University of Wisconsin School of Law.

Smeltzer, L. and Watson, K.W. (1986). "Gender differences in verbal communication during negotiations." *Communication Research Reports* 3: 74-79.

Surrey, J. L. (1987). "Relationship and empowerment." *Work in Progress* No. 30. Wellesley, Mass.: Stone Center Working Paper Series.

———. (1985). "Self-in-relation: A theory of women's development." *Work in Progress* No. 13. Wellesley, Mass.: Stone Center Working Paper Series.

Susskind, L. and Cruikshank, J. (1987). *Breaking the impasse: Consensual approaches to resolving public disputes*. New York: Basic Books.

Van Wagner, K. and Swanson, C. (1979). "From Machiavelli to Ms.: Differences in male-female power styles." *Public Administration Review* 39: 66-72.

Wall, J. A. and Virtue, R. (1976). "Women as negotiators." *Business Horizons* 19: 67-68.

Warren, C. A. B. (1988). *Gender issues in field research*. Beverly Hills: Sage.

Watson, C. and Kasten, B. (1988). "Separate strengths? How women and men negotiate." Newark, N.J.: Center for Negotiation and Conflict Resolution at Rutgers University.

Womack, D. F. (1987). "Implications for women in organizational negotiations." Presented at the Speech Communication Association Convention.

Yamada, E. M., Tjosvold, D., and Draguns, J. G. (1983). "Effects of sex-linked situations and sex composition on cooperation and style of interaction." *Sex Roles* 9: 541-553.

Zimmerman, D. and West, C. (1979). "Sex roles, interruptions and silence in conversations." In *Language and sex*, edited by B. Thorne and N. Henley. Rowley, Mass.: Newbury House.

The Role of Personality in Successful Negotiating

Roderick W. Gilkey and Leonard Greenhalgh

Anyone who has negotiated with people who are stubborn, short-tempered, shy, Machiavellian, or risk-averse will attest to how important negotiators' personalities can be in determining how negotiations unfold. These traits are a small sample of the wide range of personality factors that can make negotiations productive or unproductive. Traits are stable and enduring characteristics of individuals that predispose negotiators to react situations in particular ways. Negotiators who are aware of their own traits can adjust the strategies and tactics their personalities induce them to adopt; negotiators who are keen observers of others' personality characteristics know what to expect and can make strategic adjustments in dealing with others. Thus every negotiator should be a student of how individuals differ from each other and how such differences affect negotiating behavior.

Despite the importance of this topic, almost no comprehensive attention has been given to how personality affects negotiation (a notable exception is Rubin and Brown, 1975). This neglect is occurring at a time when there is a welcome, sudden growth in the number of books and articles about negotiation. Most of this emerging literature focuses on either the decision making of negotiators (e.g., Raiffa, 1982) or the approaches and tactics negotiators use (e.g., Walton and McKersie, 1965; Fisher and Ury, 1981; Lewicki and Litterer, 1985). Personality, which is more difficult to study, tends not to receive the attention it deserves.

Before looking more specifically at how personalities affect negotiations and what can be done to develop negotiators' self-understanding and awareness of others, it is useful to pause and consider what, exactly, is meant by the term "personality."

Personality concerns patterns in individuals' behavior that reappear in various situations. Personality *traits* are labels that summarize those patterns. For example, "conservatism" is an example of a trait that reappears in such diverse areas as political views, style of dress, child-rearing practices, and negotiated business decisions. Similarly, an "aggressive" person is likely to be aggressive on dates, behind the wheel of a car, in business meetings, and in sports activities, as well as in conflict situations. Such patterns exist because traits are *predispositions* to respond in characteristic ways: situations simply trigger what "comes naturally" to each individual.

Roderick Gilkey is Associate Professor of Management at the School of Business Administration, Emory University, Atlanta, Georgia 30322. **Leonard Greenhalgh** is Associate Professor at the Amos Tuck School of Business Administration, Dartmouth College, Hanover, N.H. 03755.

Conflict situations trigger the participants' characteristic styles of dealing with conflict (see, e.g., Thomas, 1975). To illustrate the importance of personality in conflict situations, consider how different personality types might approach the negotiation of a divorce settlement. If the husband tends to be highly *competitive*, he is likely to define the situation as one in which he must win as much as possible in the settlement. If the wife tends to be highly *accommodating*, she might submit to his exploitive demands and not strive to preserve her own interests. She might even let his lawyer handle the whole thing.

Consider instead the case in which both parties are *compromisers*. They would be likely to seek outcomes that split the difference between his interests and her interests. The result might be a solution that is not optimal for either party. Suppose, for example, that the couple had a breeding pair of championship Siamese cats. A simple middle-of-the-road settlement would be that the wife take one cat and the husband take the other; but, since the value of the cats in their being a breeding *pair*, both husband and wife would lose some value in this settlement. If instead of being compromisers, the couple both tended to be *collaborators*, they would search for solutions to the problem that would benefit them both. Perhaps one party could keep the breeding pair and the other could keep all the kittens in the next litter.

Even worse than the situation in which both parties are compromisers is the situation in which both parties are conflict *avoiders*. Here the couple may let the marriage drag on after it should have been ended. This may place the children in a situation that is worse than living with one or the other divorced parent.

These enduring personality traits may well have evolved before the individuals reached grade school. The traits are likely to have developed as a result of the individuals' relationships with their parents and siblings. For example, if children find that they usually get their way by being intransigent, then intransigence will have been reinforced and is likely to emerge when the individual is involved in a disagreement. If ingratiation or passive-aggressiveness works better, then those traits will endure instead. Other children will learn to compromise or to stand up and fight for what they want, or perhaps to smooth out conflicts whenever these arise between their siblings or even their parents. These early lessons often are the foundation for adults' negotiating styles.

It is therefore important for negotiators to learn to recognize their own tendencies and make adjustments in their negotiating behavior if these tendencies prove to be more of an impediment than a help. Likewise, capable and alert negotiators should be able to identify accurately such tendencies in those with whom they negotiate — and again, compensate as necessary. Thus, personality assessment and feedback, along with individualized development of compensatory mechanisms, should be an important component of programs to develop negotiators.

The Tuck Personality Assessment and Feedback Program

A course in power and negotiation has been under development for many years at The Amos Tuck School of Business Administration at Dartmouth College. Four years ago, with the addition of a clinical psychologist to the faculty, it became possible to explore in depth the influence of personality on negotiating behavior and to determine how negotiators can build on their strengths and compensate for their weaknesses.

The course is designed to develop students' abilities to negotiate and does so primarily through the use of simulations based on actual business negotiations. The students write a comprehensive analysis of their performance in each negotiation as a part of a continuous journal. The instructors provide confidential feedback on each entry. In addition, selected simulations are videotaped and further feedback is given.

Specific feedback concerning students' personality traits and how these affect negotiating performance is provided as a result of a personality appraisal program. The program is conducted by a clinical psychologist and is highly confidential. Although participation in this aspect of the course is voluntary, all of the 64 students in the course take advantage of this opportunity.

Data are gathered by means of an in-depth personality assessment, and a summary of the results is presented to each student. This information becomes the basis for an ongoing working relationship between the individual students and the course instructors. Once student know their basic predispositions, they become keen observers of how their personality affects their performance in negotiations and the instructors help them build on their strengths and either compensate for or hold in check the traits that get in their way.

The comprehensive assessment program provides an in-depth profile of each individual. The clinician needs this information to fully understand the basic psychodynamic features of each individual, particularly central conflicts and ego defenses. To achieve this depth, participants spend two hours of their own time filling out test batteries, another two hours doing group-administered projective tests, and at least one more hour in a face-to-face meeting with the clinician. The set of tests used is explained in Appendix 1; further information can be obtained by contacting the authors.

Some of the results are fed back to students in written form, but the major vehicle for feedback is interaction with the clinician. In many cases the students initiate a series of follow-up meetings in which there is extended exploration of the issues addressed in the initial feedback session. The agenda for such discussions is set by the individual students, usually as a part of a general effort to change particular aspects of their negotiating style. The findings from the personality assessment provide a focus for the discussions that follow, in which the student supplements his or her self-observations with the results of the tests. In this way, the objective of the program is to facilitate self-improvement rather than change students' behavior.

The emphasis of these sessions is on trying to help students identify their own particular strengths as managers who need to be effective in achieving negotiated agreements, and to refine their approaches to fully capitalize on these strengths. Liabilities are addressed as "areas to work on," and the discussions focus only on those conflicts and defenses that are close to the individual's consciousness — in other words, there is no attempt to engage in in-depth psychotherapy.

In those few instances where there is clear evidence of serious pathology, the scope and depth of the feedback is carefully limited so as not to disrupt the individual's already fragile psychological defenses. Of course, students have in some cases used the personality assessment experience as an opportunity to explore some of their general psychological adjustment difficulties. These cases demonstrate the necessity for only the most experienced and well-trained clinicians to be involved in such efforts.

Personality Profiles of Negotiators: Some Examples

The examples presented earlier were oversimplified in that we discussed only one personality attribute, such as conflict-avoidance. In practice, the personality assessment process is quite comprehensive and yields a complex profile of each individual. In this section, we present three such profiles to illustrate how personality can affect performance in negotiations.

The case examples chosen illustrate some of the diversity in the personalities we have encountered. Of course, participants in the program spanned the range from those having personality characteristics that were virtually debilitating in negotiation to those who were well-adjusted to interpersonal interactions. For the individuals who were well-adjusted, much of the assessment and feedback process involved sensitizing them to realize how others might have different personalities that would predispose them to react in different ways. Additional attention was given to helping these high-functioning negotiators experiment with and refine their negotiating styles — for example, by going over their videotapes — to make sure these individuals were capitalizing on their strengths. The three cases presented next depict individuals whose personalities were posing some disadvantages in negotiations.

Case Example: Paul

Like most students who come to the Tuck School, Paul had considerable previous work experience. He had been a product manager for the marketing division of a consumer goods company, where he was described as a solid performer. However, his employer believed that Paul had not fully realized his leadership potential, and Paul agreed with this assessment. He was friendly with members of his product management team, had demonstrated sound decision-making skills, and had the capacity to generate good marketing concepts. However, he had not "made things happen": his good ideas were often overlooked, even though he was respected by everyone.

In the negotiation course, Paul quickly emerged as an articulate and often forceful mediator. However, it was not long before his impact on others began to diminish, and Paul sensed that his peers no longer gave him or his ideas the consideration they once had. He also noticed a similarity between the way his classmates responded to him and the way his former co-workers responded to him.

Data from the testing program showed that Paul was a bright, energetic young man with strong affiliative needs and a high degree of interpersonal sensitivity (for example, both his Interpersonal Orientation and Empathic Concern scores were high). While he was capable of being very focused and decisive, his apprehension about hurting or alienating others led him to withdraw from interpersonal conflict situations. His anxiety about displaying his aggression led him to quickly give in whenever it became clear to him that he was not going to achieve his objectives immediately. Consequently, he began to feel rather powerless in situations where he should have been quite capable of influencing important outcomes. Despite his general effectiveness,

Paul's high score on external locus of control evidenced his experience of losing control when his anxiety level was high.

Consistent with these tendencies, Paul's highest score on the Thomas-Killman Conflict Mode Instrument was Competing (that is, forcefully pursuing his interests in a directive manner). His second highest score, however, was being Accommodating, reflecting his tendency to sacrifice his own interests in favor of the other person's. He scored low on Collaborating and Compromising — traits that measure an individual's tendency to participate in give-and-take bargaining to resolve differences.

As a result of the feedback program, Paul became more aware of these features of his personality and the effect they had on his negotiating performance, and he began to alter his style. He began to demonstrate more patience when his point of view was not immediately accepted, and learned to persist quietly rather than give way to the other party. This tolerance allowed him to participate in a collaborative process of negotiating so that his ideas began to receive more consideration and were more frequently adopted.

At times, Paul complained that his negotiating sessions had become "more of a hassle than before." But, he also observed, "I know at the same time that more of my ideas are being used and implemented, especially in a group situation." This, of course, is an important managerial lesson: It always seems more expedient for a manager to make decisions without consulting those affected by them; however, decisions are easier to implement if the others are drawn into the decision process, and thereby become committed to making the agreed-upon course of action successful.

While Paul's discomfort in bargaining situations was noticeable, he had learned to discipline himself so that he would continue to engage himself in the process, and he became more consistently effective. He was able to build on his ability to establish rapport with others and engage them in mutually productive exchanges. These relationship-building abilities, which had always been present, had been underutilized particularly when Paul was called upon to exert his leadership in more formal or stressful circumstances. Paul is, therefore, a good example of someone who learned to mobilize existing strengths and overcome limitations of his negotiating style.

Case Example: Bruce

As an "idea man" in an advertising agency, Bruce had advanced very rapidly because of his creative and innovative ideas. He had worked with a small group of people with whom he had been closely associated for a number of years. "We all liked each other — we understood each other, we thought the same way, and so we didn't have to explain ourselves to each other," he noted. Bruce had returned to school for an MBA degree so that he might more easily move into a general management position in marketing.

While he was successful in the creative, collaborative environment of the ad agency, Bruce's style did not appear to serve him well in other settings. He was characterized as being a "flighty" individual who jumped to conclusions and was unable to explain the logic of his position. At worst, he was described as being a "flake" whose impressionistic approach to problem solving left others confused and frustrated. Bruce was very aware that if he was to achieve his next career goal, he would have to change his interpersonal style, and he had enrolled in the negotiating course to help achieve this change.

The personality assessment revealed that Bruce was a very intuitive individual who made full use of his rich inner resources. His Rorschach responses were highly elaborated and creative. He took great pleasure in the process of arriving at original responses to the ink blots; however, he seemed to be unaware of the difficulties he was causing the clinician who was trying to record his numerous responses. This insensitivity to others was consistent with his low scores on Interpersonal Orientation and on the Collaboration index of the Thomas-Killman Conflict Mode Instrument.

In contrast, Bruce was measured as having a high tolerance of ambiguity which was consistent with his general relaxed and creative style. Though Bruce reported that he had been interpersonally attuned in the environment of the ad agency, in general he appeared to be more absorbed by his inner life than by the presence of those around him. Despite these tendencies toward introversion, Bruce was very concerned about his impact on others and the difficulty he was having "constructively connecting with other people to get things done."

When the results of the personality assessment and the observations cited above were shared with him over the course of a number of discussions, Bruce began to work on changing his approach to negotiating. He quickly recognized, for example, that he was going to have to spend more time preparing for his negotiating sessions so that he could clearly spell out the logic of his position for others. He also learned to elaborate his points to increase the clarity of the way he expressed himself and thereby enhance his general credibility. He worked hard to listen better to others so that he could gain a clearer understanding of their positions and reasoning.

Bruce's efforts to alter his style were largely successful. Based on the journal entries of his fellow students, it was clear that he was able to gain a great deal of credibility. People began to recognize Bruce's ability to provide new insights in problem-solving situations as he learned to explain his ideas in a more focused, detailed manner. His ability to contribute also increased as he made efforts to gain more information and ideas from others by actively probing and listening.

Bruce reported greater satisfaction and pleasure in his negotiations as he saw himself as a more collaborative participant. Though he still reported being concerned about losing some of his creative ability by "over-planning" and "over-involving myself in too much group stuff," Bruce recognized that this was a necessary risk if he was going to make the transition from being an idea man to a manager. While it is too soon to know whether Bruce will succeed in his career objective, he did make definite progress as a negotiator and greatly enhanced his prospects for managerial success.

Case Example: Wendy

Working as a commodities trader, Wendy had distinguished herself as an intense, competitive and effective trader. She elected to pursue an MBA degree to expand her career options. In the negotiation course, she quickly emerged as a hard bargainer who was tough, resourceful, and determined to be a "winner." One of her male peers described her in a journal entry as "an attractive lady, but I wouldn't want to meet her in a dark alley." During the initial phases of the course, she clung to her win/lose approach to negotiating. However, her competitiveness often led her to become combative and abrasive, and her peers soon brought these tendencies to her attention. The initial impetus for change thus came from other people; she found it painful to be criticized by those whom she liked and respected.

The personality tests yielded data that were generally consistent with Wendy's self-assessment, but some had the benefit of being quite specific in pointing out her exact strengths and weaknesses as a negotiator. Her responses on the Thematic Apperception Test (TAT) exhibited a high need for power. She apparently learned how to satisfy this need, according to her high score on Internal Locus of Control: that is, she had discovered how to become generally successful at making things happen the way she wanted them to turn out. Her forceful style was diagnosed in her scores on the Thomas-Conflict Mode Instrument. Her tendency was to ruthlessly pursue her own interests, as evidenced by her high score on Competing and low scores on Compromising and Avoiding. Consistent with this urge to dominate others was her high score on the Masculinity scale of the Bem Sex Role Inventory.

There were, however, tendencies that counterbalanced these more competitive and authoritarian traits. For example, she received a relatively high score on Interpersonal Orientation and similarly high scores on Empathic Concern and Perspective-Taking Ability.

With her customary energy and intensity, Wendy worked hard to alter her perspective and behavior in dealing with others. She made lists of objectives for herself which included both attitudinal changes ("try to be more receptive and open, think about mutual opportunities for gain and joint solutions") and behavioral ones ("don't interrupt, ask more questions, take more time"). She was critical of her efforts and impatient with herself, and needed occasional support and encouragement so that she created realistic expectations about how soon she could expect to change things for herself. Her capacity for self-observation was excellent, and she was able to note that she would fall back into "the old style" when she felt pressured or fatigued. This self-monitoring ability helped her to continue to alter and refine her negotiating style. She finally emerged with a much more cooperative style for dealing with conflict. While she was jokingly able to say that her desire to "always get my way" was still at the core of her personality, she succeeded in altering her tactics for dealing with others, a change that was obvious both to herself and to her fellow students.

Learning from Personality Assessment

Personality assessment can be a valuable teaching tool in expanding negotiators' awareness of the way they think and act. In addition to mobilizing their capacities for self-awareness, negotiators also learn to benefit from the feedback of peers and clinically-trained observers. In addition, as they become more aware of their particular assets, they can make more explicit and effective use of them. Such self-awareness can often create the desire for change as the students become aware of alternative approaches to dealing with conflict that can allow them to use their individual strengths more fully.

The program has evolved beyond its developmental phase and is now being used in executive programs that specialize in negotiation. Because the executive programs run for only three to five days, the personality assessment component is condensed. Selected tests and measures that can be self-administered are mailed out to the executives in advance of the seminar (particularly the Bem Sex Role Inventory, the Perspective-Taking Ability and Empathic Concern scales, the Interpersonal Orientation Scale, the Conflict Mode Instrument, and the psychological history questionnaire). Projective tests (Rorschach and Thematic Apperception Test) are administered in a group session during the early part of the program. Following this, one-hour private feedback sessions are scheduled. These highly interactive discussions focus on the identification of key strengths that are fundamental in negotiation and on the exploration of abilities that the individual may be underutilizing (for example, the capacity for empathy and collaboration that can easily be overlooked as a key strength to be used in negotiation).

Individual feedback is also provided during a videotaped negotiation session in which pairs of negotiators are taped doing one of the negotiations, and then provided with an appraisal of their performance. In addition, a certain amount of unscheduled time is built into these programs to allow for informal private exchanges between executives and the clinician. When combined with the simulated negotiations and group debriefing sessions, participants are provided with multiple opportunities to learn more about their personality and its effects on their negotiating style. Because executives are more experienced in handling organizational conflicts and therefore are much more aware of their dominant approaches, the learning process seems more efficient and the discussions much richer. Personality assessment and feedback has therefore been a well-received addition to executive programs on negotiation.

Our experience suggests that some knowledge of the underlying dynamics of personality (such as the individual's motives, needs, and fears) is necessary to produce lasting change in an individual's negotiating style. This does not mean probing into their core conflicts or interpreting major ego defenses; rather, it means providing a supportive, confidential environment so students can engage in self-exploration. In that environment, those dynamics that are closest to consciousness and most amenable to change can emerge and be freely discussed. While the permanence of any change effort can never be taken for granted, it seems probable that some of the major changes in perspective and attitude toward negotiation are likely to be enduring.

For example, we had an opportunity to work with Wendy one year after graduation; when she returned to the Tuck School for a visit. Her behavior displayed a significant change from what we had encountered at the beginning of the assessment and feedback process. Instead of the tough, competitive demeanor that predominated during her early days in the MBA program, we were impressed with the warmth and personableness that was showing through. She was receptive and accommodating and conveyed a sense of interpersonal concern and sensitivity that earlier had been masked by her dominating tendencies.

Our clinical impression was that some of her tests (interpersonal orientation, perspective-taking ability, and empathetic concern) had successfully identified latent traits in Wendy's personality that were becoming manifest as she continued to evolve her approach to interacting with others. While some progress is attributable to the maturing experience of a year of corporate life, it seems likely that the course and the assessment and feedback program had done much to accelerate her progress. Such progress would be accelerated because the program pinpointed aspects of her personality that might not serve her well in certain types of negotiations. Armed with this knowledge, she was given the opportunity to experiment with different approaches in simulated managerial situations in which she could get specific feedback as to how effective were her attempts to compensate for dysfunctional tendencies.

As we endeavor to understand more about the factors associated with successful negotiation, the importance of understanding the individuals involved must not be underestimated. Heretofore, the role of decision-making approaches and tactics has been given disproportionate consideration. However, a truly comprehensive understanding of how conflicts are handled through negotiation may not be possible without equal attention being given to understanding the negotiators themselves, especially their personal perspectives, motives, and aims. The Tuck Personality Assessment and Feedback Program is a step toward this objective.

Career Assessment

The addition of the Assessment and Feedback component to the negotiation course was viewed by students as a great success. They did indeed learn that what made them different as individuals made them different as negotiators. They also learned that this new knowledge was directly relevant to the job choices they were making. In fact, many of them wished they had had the information earlier in the Tuck MBA program, before they had chosen summer jobs, and certainly before they had chosen courses in the second year.

As a result of this demand, we designed a more general Career Assessment and Feedback program for entering MBA students. Ninety percent of the first-year class chose to participate. They filled out several questionnaires on their personal history and job preferences. They also took a number of personality tests to help them assess such diverse qualities as their motivation, general style of coping with pressure, interpersonal behavior, and capacity to deal with stress. After this information had been collected, a trained psychologist gave each person a clinical interview. At that time, students were given feedback from the various personality assessment instruments and had the opportunity to discuss the implications of these psychological findings as they related to job selection and performance. Students were then given recommendations to help them capitalize on their strengths and deal with their weaknesses. In some cases, follow-up programs were developed to help students improve their listening skills, their ability to make presentations, or their ability to cope with pressure.

While the short-term goal of the project was to help students make realistic and appropriate choices for summer jobs, the long-term goal was to help them gain a self-awareness that would allow them to develop and use their full potential in whatever jobs they chose after graduation. The objective was to help students gain sufficient self-understanding so they could mobilize their strengths to deal with both problems and people in their organizations; at the same time, we wanted them to be aware of their weaknesses.

The importance of being aware of weaknesses is illustrated in the case of a young manager in strategic planning who tended to lose his long-range perspective whenever he was under pressure. Why this happened to him and what he could do to overcome the problem was the central focus of his feedback interview. Such problems are often the result of subtle features of the individual's personality of which he or she is unaware. As in the case of negotiators, once people become aware of some of the unconscious causes of their problems, they are more likely to be able to handle them constructively.

APPENDIX I
Summary of the Tests Used in Assessment

1. *Thematic Apperception Test*. Participants study a series of pictures and comment on what images the pictures evoke for them. Such imagery reflects underlying needs. Of particular interest in the context of negotiation are the need for power (the need to feel in control of relationships and not feel dominated by others) and the need for affiliation (the extent to which the individual will sacrifice immediate gain in order to preserve and improve the relationship with others.)

2. *Rorschach Test*. The clinician observes how participants respond to the classic inkblots. Responses to these ambiguous stimuli reflect how participants characteristically perform in conceptual problem-solving situations. The test is therefore obviously relevant to the problem-solving aspect of the negotiation process.

   Participants' interpretations of the inkblots provide insights about whether they tend to focus on "the big picture" or on small detail. Those who rely on their intuitive sense of the whole must become aware of the dangers of overlooking vital components of a negotiated agreement. Opposite types must be wary of becoming hung up on small details of the agreement at some sacrifice to the total package.

   The Rorschach test also measures creativity. People who provide novel responses are likely to be innovative in the search for clever integrative solutions; those who are not particularly creative may be well-advised to involve others in brainstorming ideas for solutions.

   Finally, the Rorschach can even provide insights as to how emotions — such as anger and anxiety — evoke defenses that in turn affect problem-solving ability. For example, anxiety gives some people "tunnel vision" in which anxious negotiators fail to see the rich array of alternatives available to them. Individuals who become aware of this tendency can make a point of "thinking out loud" in the presences of colleagues, friends, or consultants, to help them overcome tunnel vision.

3. *Bem Sex-Role Inventory*. This test shows whether participants have predominantly masculine or feminine tendencies. Our own research (Greenhalgh and Gilkey, 1986) shows these tendencies to be related to fundamentally different approaches to negotiating. Masculine negotiators tend

to have a short-term, winner-takes-all, dominating approach, whereas feminine negotiators tend to have a long-term, relationship preserving, nurturing approach. It is obviously crucial for negotiators to be aware of their own tendencies and to make adaptations to others having opposite tendencies.

4. *Empathy Measures*. Two tests were used to determine the extent to which participants are attuned to the people with whom they are dealing. The first, Perspective Taking Ability, measures the cognitive dimension of empathy — the extent to which the participant takes into account the other negotiator's point of view. The second, Empathic Concern, measures the emotional dimension — the extent to which the participant identifies with the other negotiator's feelings. Because a central aspect of negotiation is responding to the other person's needs, empathic tendencies are vitally important.

5. *Interpersonal Orientation*. Less specific but closely related to the empathy measures is interpersonal orientation. People who score high on this dimension are interested in and reactive to other people. They tend to take others' behavior very personally. They are highly sensitive to others' cooperativeness and competitiveness, the relative power and dependencies in relationships, and the fairness of exchanges. By contrast, people who score low on this dimension tend to be unresponsive to interpersonal aspects of negotiations. They focus instead on their own gain with little concern for the other party's outcome, approach, or fairness. Participants scoring on either extreme need to be counseled as to the potential hazards of their predispositions. The high scorers' tendency to take the other negotiator's behavior very personally can get in the way of a productive, ongoing relationship, whereas the insensitivity of the low scores can impede the development of that relationship.

6. *Assertiveness*. Assertiveness is the ability to be firm in pursuing one's interests. People who score low on this dimension do not know how to insist that their interests be given adequate consideration without offending the other, and are consequently anxious and vulnerable to exploitation. This test is therefore a good diagnostic tool to identify those who need coaching in self-assertion tactics (such as avoiding the use of powerless speech, and facilitating face-saving when refusing to comply with another person's attempt to influence them).

7. *Leadership Opinion Questionnaire*. This test measures two orientations in a leader's relationship to others that are applicable to understanding negotiators' relationships to others. Someone whose focus is on "structure" gives attention to the task at hand, concentrating on the *content* of the negotiation; someone whose focus is on "consideration" gives attention to the relationship, concentrating on the *process* of the negotiation. It is important to know whether a negotiator has a tendency to focus on one at the expense of the other. An ideal negotiator is, perhaps, one who can give both dimensions equal emphasis.

8. *Locus of Control.* This test measures whether participants generally believe that their actions give them some control over what happens in their lives (internals) or believe that luck or other forces determine their fate (externals). As a measure of the general feeling of power versus powerlessness, one would expect an effect on people's attitudes toward negotiation. For example, internals might be likely to initiate solutions, to persist in pursuing their interests, and to display self-confidence and a positive outlook in negotiations. At the extreme, however, internals can be overly controlling and abrasive. They can even become overwhelmed with the burden of negotiations: Because they believe so strongly in their own efficacy, extreme internals feel singularly responsible for outcomes, and as a result, are unable to delegate responsibility to other members of the negotiating team. Others become discouraged at their lack of involvement and the extreme internals become frenzied because the entire burden rests on their shoulders. By contrast, extreme externals would be likely to react to others' initiatives, give in easily, and have a fatalistic outlook in negotiations. At the extreme, externals can be helpless and apathetic, and avoid conflict.

9. *Conflict Resolution Mode.* This self-appraisal measure provides an assessment of a person's approach to conflict on five different dimensions: Competing, Collaborating, Compromising, Accommodating, and Avoiding. The five separate scores can be used to create a profile that can help participants identify their dominant approaches to dealing with conflict and consider which particular modes they might be overutilizing or underutilizing.

REFERENCES

Fisher, R. and Ury, W. L. (1981). *Getting to YES: Negotiating agreement without giving in.* Boston: Houghton Mifflin.

Greenhalgh, L. and Gilkey, R. W. (1986). "Our game, your rules: Developing effective negotiating approaches." In *Not as far as you think: The realities of working women*, edited by L. Moore. Lexington, Mass.: Lexington Books.

Lewicki, R. L. and Litterer, J. L. (1985) *Negotiation.* Homewood, Ill.: Irwin.

Raiffa, H. (1982). *The art and science of negotiation.* Cambridge, Mass.: Harvard University Press.

Rubin, J. Z. and Brown, B. R. (1975). *The social psychology of bargaining and negotiation.* New York: Academic Press.

Thomas, K. (1975). "Conflict and Conflict Management." In *The handbook of industrial and organizational psychology*, edited by M. D. Dunnette. Chicago: Rand McNally.

Walton, R. E. and McKersie, R. B. (1965). *A behavioral theory of labor negotiations.* New York: McGraw-Hill.

Section VII

Follow-Up and Implementation

It is not enough to prepare wisely for negotiation, nor even to succeed in concluding an agreement at the table. Negotiators must also pay attention to the possible events that may transpire *after* a settlement has been reached. At least two important problems arise in this regard, both of which are addressed in Section VII: First, negotiators may reach agreements that are subsequently undermined or reversed either because the antagonists have "changed their minds" or because parties who were not included in the exchange try to "torpedo" the negotiated settlement. Second, negotiators may reach an agreement that endures, but it may be a suboptimal agreement — something far less attractive than the agreement that could have been reached had both sides been able to proceed from some understanding of underlying interests.

The first two selections of this section focus on the problems that arise when negotiators fail to adopt a sufficiently long-term perspective and, as a result, either do not settle their conflict or fail to reach agreements that endure. The article by William L. Ury, Jeanne M. Brett, and Stephen B. Goldberg ("Designing an Effective Dispute Resolution System") looks most generally at the conditions that are necessary in order to design a more effective system for settling disputes. These conditions, of course, apply quite appropriately to the problems of follow-up and implementation, and each of their six espoused principles — if followed — should make agreements more likely to endure. These principles are as follows: First, put the focus on interests, not positions; second, build in "feedback" loops to negotiation, transforming a linear process into a circular one; third, provide low-cost procedures for settling unresolved issues, making it more likely that these procedures will be chosen; fourth, build into the system, consultation arrangements before conflicts arise (making it less likely that they will do so), and feedback arrangements afterwards; fifth, arrange dispute settlement procedures in a low-to-high-cost sequence, thereby creating a "menu" of procedures that parties will find as appealing as possible; and finally, try to provide the parties with the necessary motivation, skills, and resources to design and abide by a dispute settlement system.

Deborah M. Kolb and Susan S. Silbey's contribution "Enhancing the Capacity of Organizations to Deal with Disputes" offers another view on the "dispute systems design" movement that has begun to emerge in the United States over the past several years. While agreeing with a number of ideas suggested by Ury, Brett, and Goldberg, the authors take issue with this approach on several grounds, including the possibility that there may well be disputes that *should* not be managed through such arrangements, and the possibility that some disputes *cannot* best be settled through better "design."

The next three articles focus on ways of improving upon agreements that have been reached through negotiation, thereby making it more likely that the wisest possible agreements are concluded. Howard Raiffa's brief essay ("Post-Settlement Settlements") describes a simple but important procedure that has received considerable attention since the article first appeared in 1985. Imagine, says Raiffa, that two (or more) parties have already concluded an agreement, but may not have extracted as much gain in this agreement as each might have — had they been aware of the other side's underlying concerns. Under such circumstances, a settlement "embellisher," after analyzing the information, could make a recommendation for a "post-settlement" settlement — in the form of an agreement that leaves each side better off (or at least no worse off) than he or she is already. Each side can exercise a unilateral veto if it is not satisfied with this new proposed agreement; and if this post-settlement is accepted, the intervenor is given a share of the increased value. The appeal of this arrangement is thus that *everyone* stands to do better.

Alvin E. Roth ("Some Additional Thoughts on Post-Settlement Settlements") concurs with Raiffa's earlier analysis, then describes the special circumstances where this innovative procedure is most likely to prove helpful. In particular, Roth observes that it is when a small number of negotiators are faced with a large number of possible settlements that the potential for post-settlement settlement may be greatest.

Max H. Bazerman, Lee E. Russ, and Elaine Yakura ("Post-Settlement Settlements in Two-Party Negotiations") also build on the earlier Raiffa contribution to turn the post-settlement settlement procedure in a slightly different direction. Using data from three distinct business cases to document their position, the authors develop the view that the disputants themselves may be able to manage the post-settlement settlement of their own disputes. That is, while an outside intervenor can certainly be helpful, it should be possible for the parties directly involved in the conflict to improve on the agreement reached without recourse to an "embellisher."

The final selection of this section is by Jeswald W. Salacuse ("Renegotiations in International Business"), and addresses the circumstances under which international business negotiators are likely to be able to develop agreements that endure. How can one proceed to "renegotiate" a deal, he asks, once an agreement has already been struck? Three types of renegotiation exist, observes Salacuse, each with its own special characteristics and opportunities: post-deal renegotiations (e.g., the negotiations that may take place at the expiration of a contract); intra-deal renegotiations (e.g., when the negotiated agreement itself calls for review of its contractual provisions at specified times); and extra-deal renegotiations (e.g., those undertaken in response to the apparent violation of an agreement). Approaches to renegotiation, Salacuse observes, independent of the type in question, should probably begin *before* (rather than after) an original deal has been reached; in this sense, the spirit of this concluding article is very much consistent with the view espoused by Ury, Brett, and Goldberg on dispute systems design.

Designing an Effective Dispute Resolution System

William L. Ury, Jeanne M. Brett,
and Stephen B. Goldberg

How can you persuade people or organizations to talk more and fight less? If they regularly deal with their problems by going to court, striking, threatening to break off the relationship, or physically attacking each other, how can you encourage them instead to negotiate their differences? If the relationship or organization is new — a marriage, a corporate joint venture, a company — how can you help ensure that disputes are handled effectively and cooperatively?

You may be a manager faced with an ongoing series of disputes with your employees, with your customers or vendors, or with other departments. You may be a lawyer wondering how you can draw up a partnership contract to ensure that disputes will be negotiated not litigated. Or you may be a dispute resolution professional — a mediator, court administrator or family counselor working with people who are continually doing battle at high cost to themselves and to the community. You may be involved in the disputes yourself or you may be an outsider.

Whatever your situation, it is obvious that the costs of disputing lawyers' fees, lost wages and lost production, physical and emotional injuries are often too high. In addition,the outcomes of disputes are often unsatisfying:people do not get what they want or need, relationships are strained, agreements collapse, old disputes reemerge. The consequences of such disputing patterns may be severe: in a business, lowered productivity and profitability; in a marriage, unhappy children and divorce; among nations, bloodshed and war.

While some disputes can be prevented, many cannot. Disputes are inevitable when people with different interests deal with each other regularly. Those different interests will conflict from time to time, generating disputes. Those disputes can have constructive consequences if the parties air their different interests, make difficult tradeoffs, reach a settlement that satisfies the essential needs (if not aspirations) of each, and move on to cooperate in other realms. Such a process can help people and organizations grow and change.

If disputes are inevitable, what can you do to get them resolved satisfactorily? In a particular dispute, you might be able to step in and personally try to settle it. But even if you succeed, the underlying conflict of interests that generated the dispute will remain. New disputes will arise and the parties may go back to fighting. If you want to have an impact beyond a single dis-

William L. Ury is Associate Director of the Program on Negotiation at Harvard Law School, Cambridge, Mass. **Jeanne M. Brett** is J. L. Kellogg Professor of Dispute Resolution and Organizations at the Kellogg Graduate School of Management of Northwestern University. **Stephen B. Goldberg** is Professor of Law at the Northwestern University School of Law.

pute, the challenge is to develop procedures that the parties will use, even in your absence, to resolve their disputes more satisfactorily and at lower cost.

This was the challenge facing IBM and Fujitsu in the 1980s. The two computer giants had wrangled for years over hundreds of disputes in which IBM charged that Fujitsu had stolen IBM software. At an impasse, IBM and Fujitsu, with the help of arbitrators Robert Mnookin and John Jones, negotiated a set of procedures allowing Fujitsu to examine and use IBM software in exchange for adequate compensation. The result: future disputes about use are to be resolved by a neutral technical expert; future disputes about compensation are to be resolved by the arbitrators.[1]

A similar challenge arose at Bryant High School in New York (see Davis, 1986). Troubled by tensions and violence, the school instituted a mediation program in the early 1980s. Dozens of students, teachers, administrators, and parents were intensively trained in mediation skills. These new mediators resolved disputes ranging from student-teacher and student-parent problems to student fistfights. The number of suspensions for fighting dropped drastically, and the school's overall climate improved. The successful program was extended to other high schools and has since been used nationwide.

In many families, conflicts between parents and their rebellious teenagers are handled through confrontation and fighting, often ending up in court. Even if the particular problem that brought the family to court is resolved, the underlying conflicts are not, so the cycle of confrontation, fighting and litigation continues. In an effort to break this cycle, the Children's Hearings Project in Massachusetts taught families to use negotiation and avoidance to deal with their problems rather than confrontation and fighting. Six to nine months after the hearing, two-thirds of the participating families reported less arguing and fighting, and almost half said they handled conflict by talking things over (Merry, 1987).

Each of these examples illustrate how changing the procedures for dispute resolution can reduce the costs of disputing. Changing procedures alone, however, is not enough; disputants must have the motivation, skills, and resources to use the new procedures. The challenge is to change the dispute resolution system — the set of procedures used and the factors affecting their use — in order to encourage people and organizations to talk instead of fight about their differences.

Designing a dispute resolution system is somewhat like designing a flood control system. Like rainfall, conflict is inevitable. Properly controlled, it can be a boon; too much in the wrong place can create a problem. The challenge is to build a structure that will direct disputes along a low-cost path to resolution.

In the design of any dispute system, whether it be to handle international relations or neighborhood conflict, we believe six principles are crucial. They are:

1. Put the focus on interests;

2. Build in "loop-backs" to negotiation;

3. Provide low-cost rights and power back-ups;

4. Build in consultation before, feedback after;

5. Arrange procedures in a low-to-high cost sequence; and

6. Provide the necessary motivation, skills, and resources.

Principle 1: Put the Focus on Interests

Three major ways to resolve a dispute are to reconcile underlying interests, to determine who is right, and to determine who has more power. We argue elsewhere (Ury, Brett, and Goldberg, 1988) that, in general, it is less costly and more rewarding to focus on interests than to focus on rights, which in turn is less costly and more rewarding than to focus on power. The straightforward principle that follows is to encourage the parties to resolve disputes by reconciling their interests wherever it is possible through negotiation or mediation. We suggest four complementary ways to do this: design procedures, strengthen motivation, enhance skills, and provide resources.

Designing Procedures

Various design procedures can put the focus on interests:

Bringing About Negotiation as Early as Possible. At International Harvester during the 1950s and early 1960s, the number of grievances and arbitrations skyrocketed. In response, management and union introduced a new procedure:the oral handling of grievances at the lowest possible level. When an employee raised a complaint, every effort was made to resolve it on the spot that very day — even if it meant senior management and union officials coming down to the shop floor. As the manager of labor relations put it, "We don't want paper [written grievances] coming upin the organization, we want people going down; we want to avoid the litigation approach of the past and adopt a problem-solving attitude." (McKersie and Shropshire, 1962: 144). The results were impressive:the number of written grievances plummeted to almost zero; if anything, union and management officials spent less rather than more time handling disputes (McKersie and Shropshire, 1962: 146). The International Harvester example shows the value of applying problem-solving negotiation to disputes as early as possible.

Establishing a Negotiation Procedure. An established negotiation procedure becomes increasingly useful as the number of parties to the dispute grows, the complexity of the issues increases, and the parties grow larger and more bureaucratic. Such a procedure will designate, for example, who will participate in the negotiation, when it must begin and end, and what happens if it is unsuccessful. Such negotiation procedures exist in a variety of realms, from collective bargaining between labor and management to negotiation of federal environmental and safety regulations.

One example is mandatory negotiation about the location of hazardous waste treatment facilities. The siting of such facilities is a recurring problem in many states, often resulting in extensive litigation, legislative battles, and even power contests. When faced with the decision of a state agency to place unwanted waste facilities in their community, some local residents have obstructed highways, threatened to dynamite existing facilities, and taken public officials hostage — all to vent their anger about policy-making processes that failed to adequately address their concerns. Faced with this recurrent problem, one state has provided for compulsory negotiation between a prospective developer and representatives of the community. The goal of the negotiation is to minimize the detrimental effects of the facility and to compensate the community for whatever damage or risk remains. In the event that interests-based negotiations fail to result in agreement, the state may compel arbitration (Bacow and Mulkey, 1982). The goal of the legislation, however, is to create a negotiation procedure focused on interests and thus to avoid not only arbitration but also costly litigation and power contests.

Federal agencies looking for better ways to deal with conflict over proposed federal regulations have come up with another creative way to substitute interests-based negotiation for litigation. Typically, an agency publishes a proposed rule, interested parties comment on it, and the agency then issues a final rule. All too often, parties dissatisfied with the rule challenge it in the courts. In an effort to reduce litigation, some federal agencies have developed a new negotiated approach to making regulations (often referred to as "regneg") in which the agency and the affected parties participate in mediated negotiations designed to produce a consensus. The process, as described by Susskind and McMahon (1985: 137) works in the following manner:

> Together the parties explore their shared interests as well as differences of opinion, collaborate in gathering and analyzing technical information, generate options, and bargain and trade across these options according to their differing priorities. If a consensus is reached, it is published in the *Federal Register* as the agency's notice of proposed rulemaking, and then the conventional review and comment process takes over. Because most of the parties likely to comment have already agreed on the notice of proposed rulemaking, the review period should be uneventful. The prospects of subsequent litigation should be all but eliminated.

Agencies using this procedure typically provide resources to support it, primarily third parties who coordinate the negotiations and provide mediation services (Susskind and McMahon, 1985: 160-163).

Designing Multiple Step Negotiation. In multistep procedures, a dispute that is not resolved at one level of the organizational hierarchy moves to progressively higher levels, with different negotiators involved at each step. One example is the contractual grievance procedure used in the U. S. coal industry:Step 1 is negotiation between the miner and his foreman; Step 2 is negotiation between the mine committee and mine management; and Step 3 is negotiation between the district union representative and senior management.

Multistep negotiation procedures, common in the labor-management context, are increasingly being used by parties to long-term business contracts. One such procedure was described by an attorney who frequently uses it:

> Lower-level business people — such as project managers from each organization who relate to each other on a day-to-day basis — try to resolve (the dispute). If they can't, the dispute is passed up to their superiors. If the superiors can't resolve it, the dispute goes up to a vice-president, a senior vice-president, or the CEO, depending on the size of the company. The forces at work here are (1) You don't want your boss to know you failed to solve a problem, and (2) the people at the higher levels tend to have a broader perspective than the day-to-day operating people do.[2]

Another example of multistep negotiation is the "wise counselor" procedure used in the oil industry. If negotiation fails to resolve a dispute between partners in a joint venture, they will refer it to two senior executives, one from each company, both uninvolved in the joint venture. The executives' task is to study the problem and, in consultation with their respective companies, to negotiate a settlement. An even broader perspective is achieved because the two "wise counselors" are deliberately selected for their detachment from the particular dispute. Using "wise counsellors" is the closest one can come to involving a mediator without actually doing so.[3]

In adding negotiation steps, however, the designer needs to be careful. In some cases, the easy availability of a higher-level person will simply discourage people from reaching agreement at a lower level and will thus make lower-level negotiation a pro forma step.

Strengthening Motivation

Interests-based negotiation is inherently motivating. It tends to provide more satisfying outcomes, more voice, and more sense of control, and it does so at lower transaction costs than do procedures such as litigation or a power contest. However, there are frequently obstacles, specific to the situation, that discourage parties from using interests-based negotiation. These obstacles can often be surmounted with the appropriate design.

Creating Multiple Points of Entry. A person with a claim to make may not trust or feel a rapport with the person with whom she should raise the claim. This problem can be alleviated by providing multiple points of entry into the dispute resolution system. At the Massachusetts Institute of Technology, for instance, a student with a grievance can bring it up with the dean of students, the head of the academic department, a university administrator, or an ombudsman (see Rowe, 1984). At IBM, an employee can raise a problem with his manager, his manager's superior, or, for personnel decisions, even the president of the company (Kochan, Katz, and McKersie, 1986: 95).

Providing a Negotiator With Authority. At the Caney Creek coal mine in Kentucky (a pseudonym), a strike-ridden mine where the authors had been invited by union and management to consult, miners were lumping many of their complaints, storing them up until they would erupt in a strike. Miners told us that it was not worth raising a grievance with their foreman since he had no authority to resolve it. Two approaches to this problem are possible:Provide the foreman with the necessary authority, or offer the employee the opportunity to take his complaint to someone with authority. The first approach, decentralizing authority, is no small task; it may require significant organizational change. We suggested this approach at Caney Creek, but it was not carried out. At International Harvester, the second approach was taken:those with authority to settle the grievance came to the shop floor.

Stopping Retaliation. At Caney Creek, miners were reluctant to use the established negotiation procedure because it was generally perceived as an adversarial act, and many miners feared retaliation from their foremen. To allay this fear, management issued a call for miners to bring up their grievances and a public warning that any foreman found retaliating against an employee for filing a grievance would be discharged.

Providing Opportunities to Meet. Sometimes disputants fear that suggesting negotiations will convey an impression of weakness. One way to deal with this problem is to provide for mandatory negotiations. Judges do this when they schedule pretrial settlement conferences. Another way is to provide occasions to meet, not explicitly for negotiation but at which negotiations can easily take place. The United Nations serves this purpose for dozens of disputing nations and groups for whom the risks of a formal meeting are too high. The cloakroom in the United States Senate serves a similar purpose, providing informal and private opportunities for senators to resolve their legislative disagreements. The systems designer can provide such occasions for informal interaction by, for example, encouraging managers to wander around the plant, organizing meetings on a topic of mutual interest, or even a regular social gathering.

Providing Skills and Resources
In addition to strengthening the motivation to negotiate, a designer can encourage interests-based negotiation by providing for ongoing training and coaching in negotiation skills.

Negotiation Training. Successful training programs combine presentation, demonstration, and discussion of appropriate techniques with simulation exercises and feedback (Wexley and Latham, 1981). Training the parties together is valuable. Joint training gives participants a common vocabulary with which to discuss alternative approaches to resolving disputes; it instills common expectations about appropriate behavior in interests-based negotiation and provides a safe environment in which to try out new procedures. It also offers an opportunity to jointly set goals for using the new procedures.

The designer must decide whom to train and how intensely. Training large numbers of potential disputants can help, even if the training is brief. In the mediation project at Bryant High School, more than 3,000 students attended classroom seminars on mediation and nonviolent problem solving. As a result, almost any time a dispute arose, several students were present who knew how to use a problem-solving approach to resolve it (Davis, 1986).

Even some parties who seem personally unsuited for interests-based negotiation may benefit from training. Consider the story of a prison inmate called "Heavy," as told by one designer:

> The first prison we worked in in New York was a big maximum security place, a couple of thousand men locked up. And one of the men on the design committee who later became a committee member was a guy named Heavy. I don't remember what his first name was but they called him Heavy because he just sat there. I don't know how smart Heavy was, he was just a moose of a guy who apparently had a very quick temper, which we saw a little bit of, and who also in his earlier days had been very quick with his fists.
>
> When we got this thing going, Heavy got the training. Sometime after it started, a grievance clerk said, "I can't believe it. Yesterday Heavy got into an argument and I thought he was going to drop the sucker right in his tracks. Heavy just kept talking to him!" I don't know how much of this you can attribute to the training, but the guy who was talking to us was attributing all of it to the fact that Heavy had learned

that he didn't have to drop people in their tracks, he could just talk to them and get something out of that.[4]

The designer will also want to provide continuity by establishing an ongoing program for familiarizing and training new people to participate in the new procedures. Both school and neighborhood mediation programs have been successful in sustaining their dispute resolution procedures despite the turnover of mediators. They have done this primarily by periodically training large numbers of mediators so that newly-trained people can work side by side with more experienced mediators.

Ideally, the designer will coach the disputants through their initial disputes. He or she will encourage each participant to prepare by identifying interests, creating options, and considering tradeoffs. After the negotiations, the designer can debrief participants and give them feedback on their process skills.[5] Two risks are associated with coaching: creating the appearance of bias and succumbing to the temptation to mediate. These risks can be minimized if the designer makes his services available to all parties and avoids providing advice on the substantive aspects of the dispute.

Providing a Person to Turn to for Help. The designer can also ensure that people are available to assist disputants — to listen to grievances, to represent the disputants, and to manage the process. For example, IBM has a resident manager program in which a senior manager is given the responsibility for listening to the employees in a given area, hearing their complaints and discussing what to do about them (Kochan, Katz, and McKersie, 1986: 95).

A variant on this same idea is to hire an ombudsman. The role originated in Scandinavia to investigate the grievances of citizens against government bureaucracies. In the United States, ombudsmen deal primarily with complaints in institutions such as corporations, hospitals, prisons, and universities (Goldberg, Green, and Sander, 1985: 283-84). A central function of the ombudsman, who typically lacks decision-making power, is to be available to listen to grievances, to direct them to the appropriate person, and to see that they are dealt with expeditiously. Often the matter will be resolved if the ombudsman simply listens or provides objective information; if the complaint concerns salary, for instance, the ombudsman may provide information about average salary rates.

If disputants are unable to acquire the necessary negotiation skills, if the amount at stake is insufficient to warrant the cost of negotiation skills training, or if the emotional component of the disputes is great, the designer should consider providing representatives for the disputants. In informal negotiations, a colleague might play this role; in a more formal setting a lawyer might do so.

The greater the number of parties, the greater the necessity for people who can manage the dispute resolution process. In federal rule-making negotiations, the federal agencies typically provide facilitators to bring all the parties together and orchestrate the negotiations (Susskind and Cruikshank, 1987: 145). The more complex the issues, the more technical assistance is necessary, particularly for those without technical competence or the resources to acquire it.

Mediation

One resource, a mediator who helps the disputants reach agreement, deserves separate treatment. Mediation is negotiation assisted by a third party. Negotiations often run up against roadblocks that a mediator can help remove. A mediator may be able to move the negotiations beyond name-calling by encouraging the disputants to vent their emotions and acknowledge the other's perspective. A mediator can help parties move past a deadlock over positions by getting them to identify their underlying interests and develop creative solutions that satisfy those interests. Where each side is reluctant to propose a compromise out of fear of appearing weak, the mediator can make such a proposal. Mediators are thus well placed to shift the focus from rights or power to interests. Mediation can serve as a safety net to keep a dispute from escalating to a rights procedure, such as litigation, or to a power procedure, such as a strike.

Mediation is widely used in labor relations — in bargaining over contracts, as well as increasingly in resolving grievances. Environmental and community mediation programs are becoming increasingly common. Mediation is used in all kinds of disputes ranging from family quarrels to business problems to international conflicts.

Peer versus Expert Mediation. Mediation procedures come in many varieties. Perhaps the most significant factor affecting the cost of the procedure is whether the mediator is an expert from outside the organization or a peer of the disputants. Using peer mediators is not only less costly (unlike experts, they are typically unpaid) but often provides someone on the spot to intervene informally before the dispute has a chance to escalate. For example, in one San Francisco elementary school program, children are trained to mediate disputes they see brewing on the playground (see Davis, 1986).

One hospital in Texas provides several levels of mediation. A designer has trained large numbers of supervisors so that there is always some supervisor close to the disputants who can mediate. Key individuals in personnel, pastoral care, and social services have also been identified as expert providers of formal mediation services. In addition, the designer has agreed to provide professional mediators who can be called on for assistance in particularly difficult disputes. Thus, the hospital has three levels of mediation: informal on-the-spot problem-solving assistance from supervisors, experts from within the organization, and outside professionals.[6]

Enhancing Motivation. Establishing a mediation procedure is not enough. Disputants need to be motivated to use the procedure. The school mediation program at Bryant High School, for instance, began with classroom seminars in conflict resolution on the assumption that students familiar with mediation would be motivated to try it if they had a dispute. In another arena, people who go to court are encouraged by court officers or a judge to try mediation.[7]

Properly designed, mediation can meet some of the same needs for emotional venting served by fighting. Particularly in those interpersonal disputes where underlying emotions are a central element, disputants can be encouraged to express their concerns and to acknowledge the concerns of the other side. Consider the account of a Bryant High School girl who became involved in the school mediation program (Davis, 1986: 289):

All I ever wanted to do was fight. . .I came into a mediation session as a disputant with four girls on the other side. I thought, "Who needs this? What am I doing here?." I just wanted to punch these girls out. I figured that the mediator would tell me what I was going to have to do. But she didn't. Instead she drew me out, listened to me. It felt so good to let it all out: then I wasn't angry anymore. I thought, "Hey, if this can work for me, I want to learn how to do it." After my training, the atmosphere around me changed."

Enhancing Skills. Mediators often need training. The classroom seminars at Bryant High School were followed by intensive training for mediators. The training consisted of lectures, discussion, and mock mediation in which trainees played mediators as well as parties to the dispute. The designer can use mock mediation to introduce the parties as well as potential mediators to the procedure. Disputants and mediators learn what is expected of them and see people like themselves using the procedure to work out an agreement.

Providing Resources. Mediation programs require institutions to select, train, assign, and evaluate mediators. Neighborhood justice centers have been established to perform this function for community disputes. Such institutions can also support mediators, offering feedback on their performance as well as refresher courses. They provide continuity as mediators leave and they serve as a collective memory, able to evaluate the results of the program and make changes in the mediation procedure. Lastly, such institutions can serve to diffuse the program more widely within the organization or the larger community.

Principle 2:Build in "Loop-Backs" to Negotiation

Interests-based procedures will not always resolve disputes, yet a rights or power contest can be excessively costly. The wise designer will thus build in procedures that encourage the disputants to turn back from such contests to negotiation. Those are what we call "loop-back" procedures. It is useful to distinguish such procedures on the basis of whether they encourage disputants to "loop back" from a rights contest or from a power contest.

Looping Back from a Rights Contest

Some loop-back procedures provide information about the disputant's rights and the likely outcome of a rights contest. The disputants can then use this information to negotiate a resolution. Rights are thus determined at the lowest possible cost while the resolution remains consensual — usually enhancing the parties' satisfaction, the quality of the relationship, and the durability of the agreement. A brief description of some of those procedure follows:

Information Procedures. In recent years, thousands of claims against asbestos manufacturers have flooded the judicial system. Some innovative designers, working as agents of the court, have set up data bases containing information about the characteristics and results of asbestos claims that have been resolved either by trial or by settlement. When a new claim is filed, the designers identify similar claims in the data base and use the information about the outcomes of previously resolved cases to determine the range within which the new case is likely to be resolved. This information reduces uncertainty about the likely outcome of the case and provides an independent standard that can help the lawyers settle the case (see McGovern, 1986).

This procedure requires human resources: experts to design the data bank and an analytical procedure to extract information from it, experts to familiarize the lawyers with the methods, and experts to enter the data and run the analyses. The ultimate goal is to render the experts unnecessary. When a new case is filed, court clerks will be able to run a simple computer program to provide the information to the lawyers.

Advisory Arbitration. Another way to provide information about rights is advisory arbitration. While the arbitrator's decision is not binding, it provides the parties with information about the likely result if the dispute is taken to arbitration or court. This information encourages a negotiated resolution by reducing the parties' uncertainty about an adjudicated decision.

The transaction costs of advisory arbitration are typically lower than in binding arbitration or court because hearings are brief and predictions delivered orally. As a result, many courts compel the use of advisory arbitration in certain types of cases; they will decide only those cases not resolved in advisory arbitration (Goldberg, Green, and Sander, 1985: 225-243).

Mini-trials. One variant on advisory arbitration, also intended to encourage a negotiated settlement by providing information, is the mini-trial. In this procedure, lawyers representing each side present evidence and arguments to representatives of the parties who have settlement authority. Ideally, these representatives are high-level executives in their own organizations who have not previously been personally involved in the dispute. Typically, a neutral adviser, often a former judge, is also present. After hearing the presentations, the executives try to negotiate a resolution. If they have difficulty, they may ask the neutral adviser to predict the likely outcome in court. This procedure has several strengths. It puts negotiation in the hands of people who are not emotionally involved in the dispute, and who have the perspective to view it in the context of their organizations' broad interests. It gives these people information about rights and the likely court outcome which helps them negotiate a successful resolution (Goldberg, Green, and Sander, 1985: 271-280). It also provides lawyers with an opportunity to exercise their skills, thereby defusing their potential opposition to the procedure.

The summary jury trial is an adaptation of the mini-trial offering more direct information about likely juror reaction. The lawyers present short summaries of their cases to a mock jury selected from the court's regular jury pool. The jury deliberates and returns a verdict, typically without knowing that the verdict is only advisory. Then, as in the mini-trial, representatives of the disputing parties use the information to attempt to negotiate a settlement (Goldberg, Green, and Sander, 1985: 282-83).

Looping Back from a Power Contest
The designer can also build in ways to encourage disputants to turn back from power contests and to engage in negotiations instead.

Cooling-off Periods. Rarely does a negotiated agreement look so attractive as when the parties are on the verge of a costly power contest or are in the midst of one. One simple procedure designed to take advantage of this receptivity is a cooling-off period — a specified time during which the disputants refrain from a power contest. The Taft-Hartley Act and the Railway Labor Act both provide for cooling-off periods before strikes that threaten to cause a national emergency (Dunlop, 1984: 157). During the cooling-off period, negotiations, while not required, normally take place. Cooling-off periods are also useful in small-scale disputes. In the Noel Coward play *Private Lives*, a bickering couple agree that, whenever an argument threatens to get out of control, one person will shout "Solomon Isaacs," which will bring all conversation to a halt for five minutes while each tries to calm down.

Crisis Negotiation Procedures. At Caney Creek, the miners often struck without discussing their complaints with management. We recommended two additional steps to avert strikes. Before any strike, union officials would meet with management to consider the miners' concerns. The miners would then discuss management's response and vote on whether to strike.

Negotiation in times of crisis places special demands on negotiators. It may be useful therefore to provide crisis negotiation training—simulations, checklists, and standard operating procedures. It may also be helpful to establish a crisis communication mechanism. In disputes between the United States and the Soviet Union, the hotline serves this purpose. One of us has worked for the last five years with American and Soviet officials to establish "nuclear risk reduction centers" — crisis centers, staffed around the clock in Washington and Moscow, for emergency communications and negotiations aimed at preventing accidental nuclear war (see Ury, 1985). An agreement to set up such centers was reached in Washington on September 15, 1987, and they are now in operation.

Intervention by Third Parties. If violence breaks out during a strike or a family argument, the police intervene to stop the fighting. A form of third-party intervention is thus already built into many dispute resolution systems. In some cases, additional third-party intervention is useful. One example is the Conflict Managers Program in San Francisco schools, which trains children to intervene in playground disputes (Davis, 1986). Wearing bright orange T-shirts printed with the words "Conflict Manager," the children work in pairs during lunch and recess to spot and try to mediate emerging disputes. On the international scene, neutral United Nations peace-keeping forces separate hostile forces and buy time for negotiation and mediation. Such efforts require skills training as well as such resources as administrators and third-party intervenors.

Principle 3:
Provide Low-Cost Rights and Power Back-ups
A key part of an effective dispute resolution system is low-cost procedures for providing a final resolution based on rights or power. Such procedures serve as a back-up should interests-based negotiation fail to resolve the dispute.

Low-Cost Procedures to Determine Rights
Conventional Arbitration. A less costly alternative to court is arbitration — in other words, private adjudication. Like court, arbitration is a rights pro-

cedure in which the parties (or their representatives) present evidence and arguments to a neutral third party who makes a binding decision (Goldberg, Green, and Sander, 1985: 189). Arbitration procedures can be simpler, quicker, and less expensive than court procedures. Formal rules need not be followed, strict time limits can be agreed to, and restrictions can be placed on the use of lawyers and of expensive evidence discovery procedures.

Arbitration has long been used to settle a variety of disputes. Today, more than 95 percent of all collective bargaining contracts provide for arbitration of disputes arising under the contract (Goldberg, Green, and Sander, 1985: 189). It is also used to settle some international disputes. Using the term in its broadest sense, arbitration regularly takes place in most organizations. Disputing managers will turn to a superior for a decision.[8]

Arbitration comes in several forms. Where stakes are low or similar disputes arise regularly, the parties may choose a streamlined arbitration procedure that can handle many cases quickly; this is known as expedited arbitration. Two other types of arbitration are of particular interest because they encourage the parties to loop-back to negotiations: med-arb and final offer arbitration.

Med-Arb. The designer who is torn between mediation and arbitration may prescribe a hybrid, med-arb, in which the mediator serves as arbitrator if mediation fails. One advantage over mediation alone is efficiency. If mediation fails, there is no need to educate another neutral in the substance of the dispute. Another advantage is that the parties will know that the neutral will decide the dispute if they cannot, so they will pay greater attention to the neutral's suggestions, including the rights standards the neutral may advance. A further advantage over arbitration alone is that med-arb encourages a negotiated resolution instead of an imposed one. The procedure also gives the third party the flexibility to arbitrate only those issues that the parties cannot settle themselves, so it keeps the determination of rights to a minimum and provides a built-in "loop-back" to negotiation.

Med-arb has several disadvantages. What appears to be a negotiated resolution may be perceived by the parties as an imposed one, thus diminishing the degree of satisfaction and commitment. Moreover, because the parties know that the neutral may decide the dispute, they may withhold information that would be useful in reaching a mediated settlement but that would hurt them in arbitration. Alternatively, they may reveal information to the mediator that will have no bearing on a decision if the dispute ends in arbitration. If the dispute must be arbitrated, it may be difficult for the mediator to discount the information and even more difficult for the losing party to believe that such information was discounted (see McGillicuddy, Welton, and Pruitt, 1987).

Final-Offer Arbitration. Arbitration can encourage negotiated settlement in yet another way. In final offer arbitration, the arbitrator does not have the authority to compromise between the parties' positions but must accept one of their final offers as the arbitrated decision. Each is thus under pressure to make its final offer more reasonable than the other's, anticipating that the arbitrator will adopt the more reasonable final offer as the decision. In doing so, each party will move toward the position of the other—in many cases enough so that they will be able to bridge whatever gap remains by negotiation. This procedure is most attractive when there is no well-defined rights standard for arbitral decision, so that a compromise decision is likely. It has been used successfully to bring about the negotiated resolution of disputes about the salaries of major league baseball players as well as about the terms of public-sector collective bargaining contracts (Goldberg, Green, and Sander, 1985: 282).

Providing Motivation, Skills and Resources. How can one motivate parties to use arbitration if interests-based procedures have failed? If the likely alternative is court, the advantages of arbitration will supply some motivation. Still, some parties may prefer court, where an adverse decision can be far more easily appealed. Making the arbitration advisory may reassure them, especially if it is advisory for them but binding on the other side. For example, in an effort to persuade dissatisfied consumers to submit their grievances to arbitration, some business-consumer arbitration programs provide that the arbitrator's decision is binding on the business, but not on the consumer (McGillis, 1987).

Another means of encouraging arbitration is for the parties to make a commitment in advance of any dispute to use binding arbitration. It is often easier for disputants to agree in principle to arbitration than in the context of a specific dispute. Then, when a dispute does arise, a leader can tell his or her constituency that there is no choice; they are bound by contract or treaty to submit the dispute to arbitration.

If all else fails, arbitration can be made mandatory. As previously noted, some courts require disputants to submit their dispute to arbitration before they can take it to court. If negotiation fails to resolve disputes over the siting of hazardous waste facilities, the law mandates arbitration.

All these varieties of arbitration require arbitrators. The designer may need to help the parties select arbitrators. Arbitrators may need skills training; representatives of the parties may need advocacy training. Here an institution such as the American Arbitration Association can be helpful in providing training and arbitrators.

Low-Cost Procedures to Determine Power
Sometimes, even when interests and rights-based procedures are available, agreement is impossible because one or both parties believes it is more powerful than the other, and can obtain a more satisfactory resolution through a power contest. The designer, anticipating this situation, should consider building into the system a low-cost power procedure to be used as a back-up to all other procedures. Getting the parties to accept such a procedure may be difficult, since each party is likely to oppose any new procedure that appears to give an advantage to the other. As a result, such a design effort is likely to succeed only when the use of power procedures imposes high costs on all parties. There are a variety of relatively low-cost power contests including voting, limited strikes, and rules of prudence.

Voting. Before the National Labor Relations Act (NLRA) of 1935, disputes about workers' right to engage in collective bargaining were handled through bitter strikes and violence. Some workers were killed; many were seriously injured. The NLRA did a great deal to end the violence by setting up a low-cost power contest—the union election — and by requiring employers to bargain in good faith with a union elected by a majority of the employees.

Limited Strikes. One proposal would reduce the high costs of a strike by replacing it with a mock strike. Take, for example, the 1987 professional football players' strike. Under the proposal, the employees would continue to work instead of striking — the players would continue to play football. But, as in a strike, they would forego their regular salary, and management would forego its usual profits. These sums would be placed in escrow, and a portion, gradually increasing over time, would be given to jointly selected charities. In this fashion, the power contest would continue to take place, but it would not keep the parties from pursuing their mutual goal, promoting the game of football. In the end, the power contest would be less costly to the disputants than a conventional strike, because the money remaining in escrow would be returned to them when the dispute was resolved.[9]

This ingenious proposal for a lower-cost power contest has yet to be adopted, but other kinds of low-cost strikes are used occasionally. One example is the symbolic strike in which workers strike for an hour (or less) in order to demonstrate their power without incurring or inflicting high costs. In Japan, workers sometimes resort to a "stand-up" strike. Work continues as usual, but each worker wears a black armband to signal unhappiness and to keep grievances alive and visible to management.

One of our suggestions for reducing the costs of striking at Caney Creek was for the union to abandon the existing practice by which the first shift to go out on strike was the first shift to return to work, even if the dispute that led to the strike had been resolved in time for an earlier shift to return to work. The union adopted a new policy of returning to work as soon as the dispute was settled; that policy is still in effect eight years later.

As with all power contests, lower-cost contests carry the risk of unintended escalation. Skills training can sometimes help. For example, the leaders of the demonstrations at the Seabrook, New Hampshire nuclear power plant were worried that the confrontation might turn violent, so they organized extensive training in nonviolent action for would-be protesters (see Katz and Uhler, 1983).

Rules of Prudence. The parties may agree, tacitly or explicitly, to limit the destructiveness of tactics used in power contests. For example, youth gangs may agree to use only fists, not knives or guns in their fights. The United States and the Soviet Union observe certain rules of prudence — such as no use (explosion) of nuclear weapons, no direct use of force against the other side's troops, and no direct military action against the other's vital interests — in order to avert the highest-cost power contest, a thermonuclear war (see Allison, 1989).

What motivates disputants to refrain from exercising their power to its fullest extent? Almost always it is the fear that the other side will resort to similar unrestrained tactics and that both will end up incurring heavy losses. One simple rule of prudence is to stay away from the other side if contact is likely to produce a fight. That is why groups as large as nations and as small as youth gangs agree on boundaries and buffer zones.

Principle 4:
Build in Consultation Before, Feedback After

A fourth design principle is to prevent unnecessary conflict and head off future disputes. This may be done through notification and consultation, as well as through post-dispute analysis and feedback.

Notification and Consultation. At Caney Creek, we recommended that management notify and consult with the union before taking action affecting employees. Notification refers simply to an announcement in advance of the intended action; consultation goes further and offers an opportunity to discuss the proposed action before it takes place. Notification and consultation can prevent disputes that arise through sheer misunderstanding. They can also reduce the anger and knee-jerk opposition that often result when decisions are made unilaterally and abruptly. Finally, they serve to identify points of difference early on so that they may be negotiated.

Post-Dispute Analysis and Feedback. Another goal is to help parties to learn from their disputes in order to prevent similar disputes in the future. Some disputes are symptomatic of a broader problem that the disputants or their organizations need to learn about and deal with. The wise designer builds into the system procedures for post-dispute analysis and feedback. At some manufacturing companies, lawyers and managers regularly analyze consumer complaints to determine what changes in product design might reduce the likelihood of similar disputes in the future. At the Massachusetts Institute of Technology, ombudsmen identify university practices that are causing disputes and suggest changes in those practices (Rowe, 1984).

Where a broader community interest is at stake, the designer may include a different sort of feedback: a procedure for aggregating complaints and taking action to protect the community. For example, some consumer mediation agencies keep records of complaints against each merchant and alert the appropriate state authorities when repeated complaints are lodged against the same merchant (McGillis, 1985: 13-14).

Establishing a Forum. One means of institutionalizing consultation and post-dispute analysis is to establish a regular forum for discussion.[10] The parties may benefit from meeting regularly to discuss issues that arise in a dispute but whose causes and implications range far beyond the dispute. At Caney Creek, we revived the monthly meetings of the communications committee for this purpose. As Pacific Bell went through the wrenching transition of deregulation, the company and union formed "common interest forums" to discuss ways to work together and to prevent unnecessary disputes (Kanter and Morgan, 1987).

Principle 5:
Arrange Procedures in a Low-to-High-Cost Sequence

The initial four design principles suggest the creation of a sequence of procedures, from interests-based negotiation to loop-back procedures to back-up procedures. The sequence can be imagined as a series of steps up a "dispute resolution ladder." Table 1 shows a menu of procedures to draw on in designing such a sequence.

TABLE 1

Dispute Resolution Systems Design Procedures

Prevention procedures

    Notification and consultation
    Post-dispute analysis and feedback
    Forum

Interests-based procedures

    Negotiation
        Early handling of disputes
        Multiple points of entry
        Mandatory negotiation
        Multiple-step negotiation
        Wise counsellors
    Mediation
        Peer mediation
        Expert mediation

Loop-back procedures

    Rights
        Information procedures
        Advisory arbitration
        Mini-trial
        Summary jury trial
    Power
        Cooling-off periods
        Third-party intervention

Low cost back-up procedures

    Rights
        Conventional arbitration
        Expedited arbitration
        Med-arb
        Final-offer arbitration
    Power
        Voting
        Limited strikes
        Symbolic strikes
        Rules of prudence

In creating a sequence, the designer might begin with interests-based negotiation, move on to interests-based mediation, and proceed from there to a low-cost rights procedure. A sequence used successfully to resolve disputes between partners in a joint venture contains three successive steps:first, try to catch disputes early by resolving them in the partnership committee; if that fails, bring in two uninvolved senior executives to negotiate; and, if that fails, turn to low-cost arbitration rather than to expensive litigation.[11]

The sequence principle suggests filling in potential "gaps" in the system. If the parties regularly jump straight from negotiation to court, the designer will want to consider intervening steps such as mediation, advisory arbitration, and arbitration. In adding steps, however, it is important to think through the possible impact of the new procedures on others already used.Adding a procedure may lead disputants to treat earlier steps as pro forma. The attractiveness and accessibility of mediation may lead disputants to negotiate less. Arranging many procedures in a sequence, each only slightly more costly than the preceding one, may have the paradoxical effect of encouraging escalation. The closer the rungs on the ladder, the easier it is to climb up. This paradox of dispute systems design ought not to stop the designer from building progressive sequences, but it should alert him or her to possible unintended consequences.

Principle 6:
Provide the Necessary Motivation, Skills, and Resources

A final principle cuts across all others: Make sure the procedures work by providing the motivation to use them, the relevant skills, and the necessary resources. In designing a system, for example, to deal with disputes over the location of hazardous waste treatment facilities as described earlier, one state legislature makes negotiation mandatory and provides resources in the form of technical assistance to aid the negotiation process. Without the necessary motivation, skills, and resources, procedures might well fail.

Conclusion

Dispute systems design offers a practical method for achieving savings and gains. Any relationship or organization could benefit from a periodic dispute resolution diagnosis: a review of what kinds of disputes are occurring, how they are being resolved, and why these procedures are being used rather than others. Where the diagnosis indicates room for improvement, dispute systems design is in order:adding or altering procedures, strengthening motivation to use them, building skills, and adding resources. The great advantage of a systems approach is that it addresses not just a single dispute but the ongoing series of disputes that occur in any organization or relationship.

Such an exercise is best done even before the relationship or organization is formed. Anyone sitting down to work out a contract — lawyers with their clients, union representatives with management officials, diplomats negotiating a treaty — should consider establishing an interests-based system for resolving disputes.

Dispute systems design needs to be developed in both theory and practice. As a field, it is now in its infancy. In the future, dispute systems design may join the ranks of other well-known dispute resolution methods, such as mediation and arbitration. For some, it may one day become a profession. For many — managers, lawyers, diplomats and others — it should become, just as negotiation is now, an essential tool in their repertoire of skills.

NOTES

We are indebted to many dispute systems designers who spent many hours sharing their experiences and wisdom with us: Richard Chasin, John Dunlop, Mary Margaret Golten, Eric Green, Wiliam Hobgood, Deborah Kolb, Michael Lewis, Bernard Mayer, Marguerite Millhauser, Robert Mnookin, Christopher Moore, Richard Salem, Carl Schneider, Raymond Shonholtz, Sylvia Skratek, Linda Singer, Karl Slaikeu, Lawrence Susskind, Marty Van Parys, and Susan Wildau. For valuable comments, we are also indebted to: Graham Allison, James Anderson, Max Bazerman, Beth Cataldo, Phillip Cousins, Harry Edwards, Julius Getman, Thomas Kochan, Linda Lane, David Lax, Michael LeRoy, Roy Lewicki, Martin Linsky, Robert McKersie, Jeffrey Rubin, Marc Sarkady, Frank Sander, Elizabeth Sherwood, Mark Sommer, and Rolf Valtin.

1. See *International Business Machines Corporation v. Fujitsu Limited,* American Arbitration Association, Commercial Arbitration Tribunal, Case no. 13-I-117-0636-85 (September 15, 1987).
2. "CPR Legal Program Proceedings: VII. ADR Contract Clauses." *Alternatives to the High Cost of Litigation* 5 (1987): 101-103, quoting G. E. Moore: 101.
3. "The `Wise man' Procedure." *Alternatives to the High Cost of Litigation* 5 (1987): 105, 110-111.
4. Recorded conversation with Michael Lewis, May 14, 1987: 40-41.
5. Recorded conversation with Christopher Moore, May 18, 1987; letter from Karl Slaikeu to authors, November 5, 1987. See also Slaikeu and MacDonald, 1987.
6. Telephone interview with Karl Slaikeu. March 25, 1988.
7. Whether court officers, judges, or others with power over disputants should use that power to encourage mediation is a matter of considerable debate. Some commentators view such conduct as inappropriate coercion. Others, accepting the element of coercion, argue that a bit of a push toward mediation does not seem too serious as long as the disputants are free to choose any outcome in the mediation. See Goldberg, Green, and Sander (1985: 490).
8. This really is using arbitration in its broadest sense. Managers determining the resolution of a dispute will often have no rights standard against which to judge the claims of the parties and may not provide any structured procedure for the presentation of evidence and arguments. Research on managers acting as third parties in dispute resolution indicates that managers may do a number of things: restructure the organization so that disputants do not have to come into contact; fire or transfer one or both; act as inquisitor-judges, doing their own investigation and making a decision; throw resources at the problem. Cf., Kolb (1986); Kolb and Sheppard (1985); and Sheppard (1983).
9. Known as a "nonstoppage," strike, this procedure is discussed by Dunlop (1984: 165); and by Raiffa and Lax (1987: 7).
10. For an interesting discussion of forums, see Dunlop and Salter (1987).
11. "The 'Wise man' Procedure." *Alternatives to the High Cost of Litigation* 5 (1987): 105, 110-111.

REFERENCES

Allison, G. (1989). "Rules of prudence." In *Windows of opportunity: From Cold War to peaceful competition in U.S.-Soviet relations*, eds. G. Allison and W. L. Ury. Cambridge, Mass.: Ballinger.

Bacow, L. and **Mulkey, J.** (1982). "Overcoming local opposition to hazardous waste facilities: The Massachusetts experience." *Harvard Environmental Law Review* 6: 265-305.

Davis, A. M. (1986). "Dispute resolution at an early age." *Negotiation Journal* 2: 287-298.

Dunlop, J. T. (1984). *Dispute resolution, negotiation, and consensus building.* Dover, Mass.: Auburn House.

———. and **Salter, M. S.** (1987). "Note on forums and governance." Cambridge, Mass.: Harvard Business School Working Paper 0-388-046.

Goldberg, S. B., Green, E. D. and **Sander, F. E. A.** (1985). *Dispute resolution.* Boston: Little, Brown.

Kanter, R. and **Morgan, E.** (1987). "The new alliances: First report on the formation and significance of a labor-management 'business partnership'." Cambridge, Mass.: Harvard Business School Working Paper 87-042.

Katz, N. and **Uhler, K. L.** (1983). "An alternative to violence: Nonviolent struggle for change." In *Prevention and control of aggression.* New York: Pergamon.

Kochan, T. A., Katz, H. C. and **McKersie, R. B.** (1986). *The transformation of American industrial relations.* New York: Basic Books.

Kolb, D. M. (1986). "Who are organizational third parties and what do they do?" In *Research on Negotiations in Organizations*, ed. R. J. Lewicki, B. H. Sheppard, and M. H. Bazerman. Greenwich, Conn.: JAI Press.

———. and **Sheppard, B. H.** (1985). "Do managers mediate or even arbitrate?" *Negotiation Journal* 1: 379-388.

McGillicuddy, N. B., Welton, G. L. and **Pruitt, D. G.** (1987). "Third-party intervention: A field experiment comparing three different models." *Journal of Personality and Social Psychology* 53: 104-112.

McGillis, D. (1987). *Consumer dispute resolution: A survey of programs.* Washington: National Institute for Dispute Resolution.

McKersie, R. B. and **Shropshire, W. W.** (1962). "Avoiding written grievances: A successful program." *Journal of Business* 35: 135-152.

McGovern, F. E. (1986). "Toward a functional approach for managing complex litigation." *University of Chicago Law Review* 33: 440-493.

Merry, S. E. (1987). "The culture and practice of mediation in parent-child conflicts." *Negotiation Journal* 3: 411-422.

Raiffa, H. and **Lax, D. A.** (1987). "Touchdowns in the football impasse." *Los Angeles Times*, November 9 1987: 7.

Rowe, M. P. (1984). "The non-union complaint system at MIT: An upward-feedback mediation model." *Alternatives to the High Cost of Litigation* 2: 10-13.

Sheppard, B. H. (1983). "Managers as inquisitors: Some lessons from the law." In *Negotiating in Organizations*, ed. M. H. Bazerman and R. J. Lewicki. Newbury Park, Calif.: Sage.

Slaikeu. K. A. and **MacDonald, C. B.** (1987). *Conflict resolution in churches: A model for systems consultation.* Austin, Tex.: Center for Conflict Management.

Susskind, L. and **Cruikshank, J.** (1987). *Breaking the impasse: Consensual approaches to resolving public disputes.* New York: Basic Books.

———. and **McMahon, J.** (1985). "The theory and practice of negotiated rulemaking." *Yale Journal on Regulation* 3: 133-165.

Ury, W. L. (1985). *Beyond the hotline.* Boston: Houghton Mifflin.

———. **Brett, J. M.** and **Goldberg, S. B.** (1988). *Getting disputes resolved.* San Francisco: Jossey Bass.

Wexley, K. N. and **Latham, G. P.** (1981). *Developing and training human resources in organizations.* Glenview, Ill.: Scott, Foresma

Enhancing the Capacity of Organizations to Deal with Disputes

Deborah M. Kolb and Susan S. Silbey

Conflict is a dirty word in organizations. Managers invest considerable time and money on programs and policies that either contain conflict or that work to convert difference into consensus. The general aim is to make organizational functioning smoother and less contentious.

To accomplish these tasks, corporations purchase from an expanding market of service firms offering a wide array of programs designed to clean up the clutter of human conflict littering organizations. Among the current titles of such offerings are "dealing with diversity," "win-win negotiations," "interpersonal peacemaking," "mediation skills for managers," and "structuring for collaboration." The newest entry in the catalogue of conflict management services is dispute systems design. Dispute systems designers promise in-house, cost-efficient service, and consumer satisfaction for resolving conflicts. It sounds like dispute systems do it all. A question that remains, however, is: Do dispute systems designers "do" prevention?

Dispute systems design is an extension of such alternative dispute resolution processes as mediation and other forms of assisted negotiation into the instructional and programmatic realm. It is an intervention to help clients — families, organizations, communities, nations — deal systematically with a continuing stream of disputes rather than a single episode. The design of a dispute system is based on a diagnosis of the state of disputing in an organization or relationship, with an eye toward reducing the costs of conflict and enhancing the benefits to those involved. Costs are reduced and benefits realized by expanding the range of alternatives available while emphasizing interest-based dispute resolution methods rather than processes that rely primarily on rights (arbitration, litigation) or coercive power (war, strikes). (See Ury, Brett, Goldberg, 1988; cf. Silbey and Sarat, 1988.)

In this article, we consider whether dispute systems that are designed to alter conflict patterns in organizations directly can, or should, aim to prevent or reduce the frequency of conflict in an organization. Two primary issues are involved in the discussion of this question. The first relates to the notion of prevention itself and what it implies about the way organizations work. We want to suggest that the very notion of prevention is inconsistent with contemporary conceptions of effective process in organizations. A more useful way to view the issue is to consider not prevention, but enhanced capacity.

Deborah M. Kolb is Professor of Management at the Simmons College Graduate School of Management and Executive Director of the Program on Negotiation at Harvard Law School, 513 Pound Hall, Harvard Law School, Cambridge, Mass. 02138. **Susan S. Silbey** is Professor of Sociology at Wellesley College, Wellesley, Mass. 02181.

The second issue relates to the ways in which dispute systems designed by outsiders indirectly enhance or constrain the ability of members at all levels of hierarchy to deal with disputes and differences in more open and productive ways.

The Problem with Prevention

What does it mean to have a dispute design system that prevents conflict? As systems designers discuss it, prevention implies that the frequency of disputes in an organization is reduced, in part, because a dispute system encourages people to deal with the underlying or deeply rooted causes of conflict. There are several problems with this conception, however.

Dysfunctional?

First, it assumes that conflict is somehow detrimental to organizational functioning. Clearly, administrators and others in charge of organizations bemoan the existence and imputed inefficiency of conflict in their institutions and seek means of silencing it. But even observers who take a broader view that conflict is functional, that it mobilizes innovation, promotes flexibility and adaption, and builds group cohesion (Coser, 1956: Bacharach and Lawler, 1981) nonetheless also support this perspective. Debates about the functions or dysfunctions of social conflict actually reinforce the perception that the presence of conflict is evidence of organizational malfunctioning (Weick, 1979).

In contrast with these analyses of the positive and negative functions of conflict, recent scholarship on conflict in organizations is based on a different premise (Bacharach and Lawler, 1980; Kolb and Bartunek, 1992; Pfeffer and Salancik, 1978). Contemporary organization theory and research is marked by a shift away from consensual and rationalized models of organization process and toward ones that emphasize power and political struggle. Instead of viewing conflict as either detrimental to or facilitative of organizational functioning, this research defines conflict as the essence of organization. Conflict is central to what an organization is and contributes to its durability. Indeed, Pondy (1986) notes that the oldest organizations in the world, four parliaments and sixty-two universities, have conflict and diversity at their very foundations. To prevent conflict by dealing with its causes is incompatible with this view of organizations.

What is a Cause of Conflict?

Secondly, claims that one can prevent conflict by dealing with root causes confuse what we mean by cause. Conflict is foundational in organizations because it is built into the very structure and modes of operating. For instance, we know that when you create different departments and divisions in order to work more efficiently, conflict often arises over matters such as scheduling and responsibility. It has also been observed that, when a new layer of management is created in order to organize and rationalize work, others in the organization simultaneously lose some autonomy and control. Sometimes two or more groups in an organization, formerly separate with independent and different modes of operating, have to work closely in an integrated fashion to bring out a new product. Division of labor, the delegation of authority, the requirements for task interdependence, and more immediate issues such as sharing a common resource pool, all cause conflict in organizations.

These causes are not usually obvious. The reason is that conflict in organizations is typically embedded in the ongoing events and activities of members, and specific conflict episodes are not easily disentangled from other forms of interaction. What is a cause and, indeed, what is in dispute will be understood in different ways depending upon who gets involved, the interests they have to serve and protect, and the kinds of outcomes envisioned (Burroway, 1979). Ask the manager of an organization about the working relationship between two professionals, then ask the professionals, then ask the support staff. The stories each tells about that relationship — and particularly about conflict in that relationship — will be different, as will the attribution of cause.

Diagnosing cause is also complicated by the tendency of conflict "splitting" that occurs in organizations — that is, when conflict splits off and moves around an organization and gets expressed in locations quite different from its point of origin (Smith, 1989). For example, two male senior managers who act outwardly in a congenial and collaborative manner ship their disputes with each other to two female subordinates elsewhere in the organization. The women develop reputations as contentious and difficult to work with. Feeling that this relationship is having a detrimental effect on the organizations, the senior managers hire a consultant to help "fix the women," that is, to help them work out their difficulties (Smith and Berg, 1987; Weick, 1979). Over a period of several months, the consultants begin to trace the problem back to the senior managers who were not consciously aware of their own dispute.

There is also a consistent finding in the literature that those engaged in conflict tend to experience it in personal and immediate terms, and to attribute cause to the personality or behavior of the other — the "unreasonable" boss, the uncooperative person in sales, the ambitious colleague, the generic "difficult" person (Pettigrew, 1973; Kolb, 1989a). Determining whether the person is the problem, or whether it is the particular situation or the encompassing systemic structure, will always be both a methodological and theoretical judgment that has a major impact on the kinds of causal diagnoses a dispute system designer might make.

Too Many Disputes?

A third problem with the "dispute-systems-design-decreases-conflict" concept is that designers, in their desire to reduce the frequency of conflict, imply that a major problem in organizations is that there are just too many disputes. This judgment is challenged by numerous studies which suggest that most conflicts in organizations, as well as other settings such as families, communities, and informal groups, never get publicly expressed as disputes. When probed, people reveal all sorts of grievances, complaints, and differences that could be — but rarely are — voiced. Sometimes people fear retribution or loss of social acceptance, others avoid entrapment in complex processes, others believe that they lack sufficient resources to pursue their grievance, while yet others see complaining and confrontation as evidence of moral laxity or lack of independence (e.g., Miller and Sarat, 1980-81; Merry and Silbey, 1984; Bumiller, 1987; Greenhouse, 1986; Goodman, 1986). For example, in a study of professional accounting firms, Morrill (1992) reports that 73% of conflict episodes among partners are never expressed directly. Avoidance and toleration are the modal forms of conflict management rather than confrontation and negotiation. The consequences of avoidance are serious. Not only does the organization lose opportunities for innovation and change, but suppressed conflict also generates resistance to organizational goals.

In summary, we suggest that the notion of prevention is problematic because it is based on assumptions that conflict is dysfunctional for organizations; that its causes are accessible to objective diagnosis and remedy; and that there are too many disputes in an organization rather than too few. Recent scholarship challenges all of these assumptions. Further, prevention in the service of organizational agendas (lower costs and greater tranquility) inevitably leads to the preservation of the status quo to the detriment of those who may be disempowered or disadvantaged by current arrangements (see Martin, 1992).

However, there is another way to think about dealing with the clutter of conflict in organization, and that is in terms of enhancing capacity for the expression of differences.

Enhancing Capacity
Dispute system designers seek to improve the handling of conflict by directly addressing the organizational barriers that interfere with low-cost, interest-based resolution of persistent disputes. This approach tends to focus on proximate or presenting causes of conflict. If one accepts the notion that organizations are patterned systems of conflict, it is clear that the capacity of dispute systems designers to reduce the frequency of conflict by attending to underlying causes is severely limited.

Nonetheless, there may be other ways that dispute systems designers, like the wide range of currently available management consultants and interventionists, might have an impact on the capacity of an organization and its members to deal with conflict. Rather than directly prevent disputes (which we have argued is mistaken) they may indirectly reduce the frequency of disputes that are processed through formal systems. There are three ways that this might occur.

Alter Understandings of Conflict and Its Causes
Disputes can be read in many ways. One indirect effect of a dispute-focused intervention may be that new, and more complicated, ways of understanding conflict, its causes and possible outcomes, become possible. For example, when members of an organization view their disputes as ones based on personal differences, they are often reluctant to voice problems and work toward accommodating difference. A dispute interventionist working on this organization may enlarge members' understanding of causality (i.e., that conflict is in the structure and roles of the organization).

Another example of the enlarged understanding that can develop is the case of a vice president in an aerospace company, who insisted that the two people charged with planning and operations on a special project just could not get along with each other because their personalities were incompatible. After several reorganizations had failed to resolve matters, expert intervention helped the aerospace vice president to see that the problem was not in the personnel but in the organization's structure and goals. The tasks and responsibilities continually put the two managers at odds with each other while the vice president had failed to establish or assist in setting priorities for balancing long- and short-term milestones.

Similarly, people experience bias as an individual problem. Racist remarks and sexist treatment is typically viewed as conscious or unconscious mistreatment by particular persons (Silbey, 1989). Thus, a woman manager speaks of her sexist boss who refuses to allow her the visibility to attract clients necessary for her success. She complains through an ombudsman's office and, by exploring the problem, she and the ombudsman come to see the problem differently. They then recast the problem in terms of the institutional culture that legitimizes what appear to be individual actions. Changing this situation will require much more than dealing with the particular supervisor.

When dispute systems designers enlarge people's understandings of the causes of conflict, new outcomes are possible. Broader understanding may also produce greater tolerance for conflict. A culture of tolerance can lead to effective changes in informal arrangements as people feel able to communicate openly. Organizational creativity may also be enhanced as people feel empowered to confront those in positions of authority. Studies of organizations in which the capacity for the expression of conflict is high suggest that these cultures, which value difference and diversity, channel these differences into productive and imaginative, task-related endeavors (Kunda, 1992).

Enhanced capacity can result in significant structural change as well. When members' understandings about their disputes shift from isolated individual episodes to ones that question the entire system, the possibilities for emancipatory changes in organizations become possible.

Encourage Spillovers from the Formal Dispute System
When interventionists describe themselves as dispute systems designers, they typically emphasize deliberate and segregated mechanisms for monitoring, handling, and resolving conflicts. If conflict is the essence of organization, however, disputes should not be pigeonholed into specialized procedures. Acknowledging and embracing the intransigence of conflict, dispute interventionists and management consultants should attend to the informal, diffuse, routine interactions that may result from experiences with formalized procedures. There are two primary ways this may occur.

Experience in the legitimate expression of differences, collaborative and cooperative problem solving, as well as interest-based forms of conflict management (learned in the context of a formal disputing system) can spill over into other aspects of organizational life and impact earlier stages in a disputing process. Thus personnel who participate in dispute resolution procedures generally become more adept at dealing with their differences not only at the negotiating table but also when they appear in the workplace.

For example, in a dispute over who should get overtime, a machine operator with recent experience in mediation observed that the current practice of assigning overtime failed to take account of the family responsibilities of the women on the line, and so decides to use this mediation experience to engage her supervisor in a discussion of these assignments. For this kind of interaction to occur, however, employees must be able to express diverse interests and supervisors need to be tolerant of employees who challenge their decisions and authority. Those expressions of interest and challenge are not perceived as welcome nor legitimate if they are segregated and isolated in specialized procedures. Legitimacy and tolerance require taking the conflict out of the closet.

Secondly, dispute capacity can be enhanced as experience in a dispute system is generalized, and members come to see the consequences of their actions in new ways. In grievance mediation, for example, there is a practice in some organizations to invite an audience of managerial and union personnel to participate alongside the parties primarily involved in the grievance. This broad participation often encourages the immediate parties to the grievance to see their actions from the variety of perspectives presented in the process, an insight that may lead to new models of conflict management on the shop floor (Kolb, 1989b). In this way, conflict escalation — here defined as movement into specialized procedures — may be contained.

Learning from Dispute Systems Data
Dispute-processing mechanisms in organizations cover a wide range of formal procedures and informal processes (Ewing, 1989). These include grievance procedures, peer review boards, ombuds offices, speak-outs, open-doors, electronic bulletin boards, etc. The complaints that funnel through these systems are most often individual — that is, they are initiated by members based on a specific experience.

However, taken as a whole, these complaints provide data that can be analyzed as a means of diagnosing organizational well-being and identifying sources of stress. If dispute-processing data are to become a source of insight about organizational effectiveness, expressions of grievance, conflict, and difference must be solicited, respected, and prized rather than suppressed, contained, or prevented.

These data may be the basis for both narrow or broad-based change agendas in organizations. In one organization, for example, continual complaints about the provision of certain insurance benefits led to a change in procedures that eliminated this particular problem. In another organization, several complaints from women about their limited career options led to a wide-ranging analysis and subsequent intervention to effect changes in the organizational culture (Kolb, 1989a). Similarly, in yet another organization, persistent complaints by minority members about subtle forms of exclusion led to an in-depth analysis of the institutional culture and, ultimately, to the commitment of resources to effect significant change (Silbey, 1989).

For these kinds of action to occur, those charged with overseeing a dispute system need to encourage expressions of conflict and pay attention to patterns among individual cases, aggregating issues where appropriate. This would require that they define their roles as change agents and not simply dispute resolvers and preventers.

Barriers to Increased Capacity
It is clear that dispute systems designers can have both direct and indirect impacts on the capacity of organizations to deal with conflict. However, it is also good to consider the ways in which such systems designers may inter-

fere with some of the naturally occurring ways conflicts are handled in organizations.

Disputes arise in the context of relationships and within a structure of
everyday activities. While some differences may be publicly aired, field
research on conflict processes in organizations suggests that the vast majority occur out of sight (Kolb and Bartunek, 1992).

Some people in organizations emerge as mediators or peacemakers,
working behind-the-scenes to empower members in confronting disagreement and orchestrating the airing and resolution of disputes (Kolb, 1989a).
Peacemakers are sought out by their organizational colleagues for their position, their skills, the relationships they have with others, and often, their gender (cf. Merry, 1982). In conducting a peacemaking process, the locus of the
dispute and the intervention are closely entwined. There is also an emphasis
on preserving and enhancing relationships (Putnam, 1990).

Dispute systems design may work against these less public approaches.
The danger arises because conflicts are channeled into a system, often centralized and rationalized, that is removed from the work settings in which the
conflicts occur. Dispute processing comes to be seen as something external
to routine interactions, the province of experts or outsiders, rather than an
integral part of the organization's structure and culture. People need to bring
problems to the expert system rather than problem-solving indigenously.
What we know about expert-designed systems is that, over time, they create
a dependency among users, simplify and categorize people and problems,
routinize solutions, and mask power by claiming to be neutral (Silbey and
Sarat, 1988).

Ironically, while informal dispute resolution takes place with little or no
fanfare, the expert systems seem to require constant "selling" and negotiation
to attract users and to implement solutions (see Ury, Brett, and Goldberg,
1988, Chapter 6).

Conclusion

Conflict is a pervasive fact of organizational life. Enhancing members' capacities to understand their disputes in new ways, to feel free to express differences and know they will be heard, and to have multiple channels available,
makes for more humane and, perhaps, more productive organizations. While
unlikely to reduce the frequency of disputes in organizations, dispute systems,
if broadly construed, can contribute directly and indirectly to this end.

In designing these systems, however, we need to attend to the informal,
behind-the-scenes, interstitial and nourishing forms of disputing. These interactions are often unnoticed and devalued in organizations. However, from a
fuller appreciation of informal and formal modes of conflict management and
the interplay between them comes the potential for enhancing the capacity
of organizations to deal with differences and diversity. This — not prevention
— is the real service which dispute interventionists can offer.

REFERENCES

Bacharach, S. and Lawler, J. (1980). *Power and politics in organizations.* San Francisco: Jossey-Bass.

Bumiller, K. (1987). *The civil rights society.* Baltimore: Johns Hopkins University Press; "Victims in the Shadow of the Law," Signs, 12:421.

Burroway, M. (1979). *Manufacturing consent.* Chicago: University of Chicago Press.

Coser, L. (1956). *The functions of social conflict.* New York: Free Press

Ewing, D. (1989). *Justice on the job: Resolving grievances in the nonunion workplace.* Cambridge, Mass.: Harvard Business School Press.

Goodman, L. H. (with Sanborne, J.). (1986). "The legal needs of the poor in New Jersey: A preliminary report." Submitted to the Legal Services Program of New Jersey, National Social Science and Law Center, Washington, D.C.

Greenhouse, C. (1986). *Praying for justice.* Ithaca: Cornell University Press.

Kolb, D. M. (1989a). "Labor mediators, managers, and ombudsmen: Roles mediators play in different contexts." In *Mediation research,* edited by K. Kressel and D. Pruitt. San Francisco: Jossey-Bass.

———. (1989b). "How existing procedures shape alternatives: The case of grievance mediation." *Journal of Dispute Resolution* (1989): 59-87.

——— and Bartunek, J. (1992). *Hidden conflict in organizations: Uncovering behind-the-scenes disputes.* Newbury Park, Calif.: Sage.

Kunda, G. (1992). *Engineering culture: Culture and control in a high-tech organization.* Philadelphia: Temple University Press.

Martin, J. (1992). "Deconstructing organizational taboos: The suppression of gender conflict in organizations." *Organization Science* (4): 339-359.

Merry, S. E. (1982). "The social organization of mediation in nonindustrial societies: Implications for informal community justice in America." In *The politics of informal justice* (vol. 2), edited by R. Abel. New York: Academic Press.

——— and Silbey, S. S. (1984). "What do plaintiffs want: Reexamining the concept of dispute." *Justice System Journal* 9: 151-179.

Miller, R. and Sarat, A. (1980-1981). "Grievances, claims, and disputes: Assessing the adversary culture." *Law and Society Review* 24: 1-9.

Morrill, C. (1992). "Little conflicts: The dialectic of order and change in professional relations." In *Hidden conflict in organizations,* edited by D. Kolb and J. Bartunek. Newbury Park, Calif.: Sage.

Pettigrew, A. (1973). *The politics of organizational decision-making.* London: Tavistock.

Pfeffer, J. and Salancik, G. (1978). *The external control of organizations.* New York: Harper & Row.

Putnam, L. (1990). "Feminist theories, dispute processes, and organizational communication." Paper presented at Arizona State University Conference on Organizational Communication: Perspectives for the 90s.

Pondy, L. (1986). "Reflections on organizational conflict." Paper presented at the 25th Academy of Management Meeting, Chicago, Ill.

Silbey, S. (1989). *Report of the Task Force on Racism at Wellesley College.* Wellesley, Mass.: Wellesley College.

Silbey, S. and Sarat, A. (1988). "Dispute processing in law and legal scholarship: From institutional critiques to the reconstruction of the juridical subject." *Denver University Law Review* 66: 437-499.

Smith, K. (1989). "The movement of conflict in organizations: The joint dynamics of splitting and triangulation." *Administrative Science Quarterly* 34: 1-21.

Smith, K. K. and Berg, D. N. (1987). *Paradoxes of group life.* San Francisco: Jossey-Bass.

Ury, W. L., Brett, J. M., and Goldberg, S. B. (1988). *Getting disputes resolved.* San Francisco: Jossey-Bass.

Weick, K. (1979). *The social psychology of organizing.* Reading, Mass.: Addison Wesley.

Post-Settlement Settlements

Howard Raiffa

"It's all very well to talk about collegial, joint problem-solving negotiation processes, but my opponent has unreasonable aspirations and I'm not going to weaken my just claim by trying to be a nice guy. I'm going to bargain tough, for myself, by myself." No matter how much we might bemoan this state of affairs, we must recognize that a lot of disputes are settled by hard-nosed, positional bargaining. Settled, yes. But efficiently settled? Often not. Both sides are often so intent on justifying their individual claims that not much time is spent on creating gains to be shared. They quibble about sharing a small pie and often fail to realize that perhaps the pie can be jointly enlarged. Even where there is a modicum of civility and some cooperative behavior on the part of the negotiators, it is not easy to squeeze out joint gains.

Here's one suggestion for how such intransigent negotiators might be helped. Let them negotiate as they will. Let them arrive at a settlement, or let a judge or jury impose a settlement on them. Mr. Jones, one protagonist, might feel happy about the outcome — he got more than he expected — but Ms. Spencer, the other protagonist, is unhappy — she did not realize her just aspirations. But even in this case the negotiators might not have squeezed out the full potential gains. There may be another carefully crafted settlement that both Jones and Spencer might prefer to the settlement they actually achieved.

Now let's imagine that along comes an intervenor from the Contract Embellishment Service, and he asks Jones and Spencer after they have achieved their settlement if they would be willing to let him try to sweeten the contract for each. The intervenor carefully explains to Jones that he will have the security of the outcome level he has already achieved but that he (Jones) may have the opportunity to do still better. The intervenor proposes that after some analysis he will suggest an alternate settlement — a *post-settlement settlement*, if you will — that would replace the original settlement only on the condition that both parties agree to the change; and of course they would only do this if each prefers the new settlement proposal to the old one.

Is this pie in the sky? Can the intervenor deliver the goods? Not always, but then Spencer and Jones would not have lost anything in trying, except perhaps their time. But it is my contention that in really complex negotiations where a lot of issues are at stake, where uncertainties are involved, or where settlements could involve transaction and payments over time, jointly desir-

Howard Raiffa is Frank Plumpton Ramsey Professor of Managerial Economics at Harvard Business School and the John F. Kennedy School of Government, Harvard University, Cambridge, Mass. 02138.

able post-settlement settlements more often than not could be achieved by an analytical intervenor. If successful, the intervenor would add a surplus value to each side, and he might be recompensed for his effort by getting a small proportional slice of this surplus (if there is such a surplus) from each of the protagonists. So everybody would be happy.

Let's suppose that Spencer is eager to cooperate with the intervenor and that Jones also reluctantly agrees, but each side is not too happy about resuming face-to-face negotiations. The intervenor proceeds by meeting separately with each side and doing a careful, deep analysis of its interests and values, probing in particular values that may be quite sensitive. The intervenor promises each side not to reveal these confidentialities to the other (nor to anyone else), and his promise is credible because of his existing reputation and his desire to do business of a similar kind with others.

In the course of these separate meetings, Jones and Spencer might each give the intervenor information that was deliberately distorted or only partially revealed during the original negotiations. Also, the intervenor might help crystallize values that each protagonist might not have clearly articulated to himself or herself. It might be self-evident that Jones wants more of attribute X and less of Y, and vice versa for Spencer, but the critical ingredient might involve intricate quantitative tradeoffs between different incommensurable qualities.

By the end of these deep-mapping exercises, the intervenor would be privy to information that neither side had about the other. Now the analytical task is clear. Can the intervenor craft a new settlement that each party would prefer to the old one? Can he sweeten the old contract for Jones and Spencer simultaneously? There may be more than one new settlement that would be better for each than the old one, and then the intervenor would have a choice. Of course, he would then want to select a settlement that would squeeze out all potential joint gains. Several choices might still then remain, but that possibility should not detract from the scheme. How to find appropriate candidate settlements becomes a mathematical optimization problem, and a host of techniques can be employed to help the intervenor identify candidates and make his selection.

Let's push on and assume that, on the basis of the information the intervenor has elicited privately and confidentially from each of the parties, he designs a new settlement that he believes each party will prefer to the old negotiated (or imposed) settlement. He then proposes, in a take-it-or-leave-it way, the new post-settlement settlement. Each side has veto power. There's no bargaining. If both say yes, so be it. If one says no, the old settlement prevails. That's the scheme.

If you were a party to a dispute and had already negotiated a settlement or had a settlement imposed on you, would you, on a contingent fee basis, employ the services of the intervenor from the Contract Embellishment Service? Would you tell him the truth about your value tradeoffs and judgments about critical uncertainties?

I have never put this embellishment scheme into practice, but I do have some promising laboratory evidence. I and a host of others have shown that in two-party negotiations with several interacting issues to resolve, negotiated settlements in laboratory settings usually leave room for potential additional joint gains. Again in laboratory settings, I have asked many pairs of contending players (after each pair has negotiated a settlement) whether they would be willing to let a third party try to find a new settlement that would jointly be preferred to the old settlement. Practically all subjects say something to the effect of, "Why not? I have nothing to lose." A lot of them consider how they might distort their values and interests to the intervenor, but they then realize that it is not so clear how they should falsify information to their advantage, and they end up by saying that they would disclose their value tradeoffs as truthfully as possible. Let's suppose that Mr. A discloses his interests to the intervenor in a distorted fashion and that the intervenor then succeeds in finding a post-settlement settlement he believes A should prefer to the old settlement according to the values A has stated. If this post-settlement settlement is in reality worse for A than the old settlement, then A will reject the offer. On the other hand, A might get a better final settlement by providing the intervenor with false information, but, as I said, how to distort information to one's advantage is far from clear. It is simply prudent to tell the truth.

Thus far I have talked about suggesting this post-settlement embellishment scheme to the negotiating protagonists after they have already reached a settlement. What would happen to the first-stage negotiations if the parties were to know initially that their settlement yet-to-be-decided would be, or might be, subject to this post-settlement scrutiny? I suspect that it would not have much impact on the negotiators in really complicated negotiations. In the tension that exists in negotiations between creating joint value and claiming individual value, this post-settlement scheme might distort the initial negotiations unfortunately in favor of the claiming-value side. Certainly, we can concede that two very analytical protagonists in clearly structured games with clear payoffs would in a laboratory setting modify their initial negotiating behavior if they were certain that there would be post-settlement embellishments. But even in this extreme case, an astute game theorist would be in a quandary about how to behave if information about the preferences of the other protagonist was ambiguous, if it was not certain that post-settlement analysis would be forthcoming, and if it was not clear how the intervenor would in fact choose a post-settlement settlement from a myriad of possibilities. Indeed, I myself as a game theorist would be tempted to forget about this potential second-stage embellishment feature.

If it makes such good sense to engage in post-settlement embellishments, why not call in this analytical intervenor right from the start? Why not do pre-settlement embellishments? Of course this could be done, and is done, in the arbitration of disputes. But let's go back to Jones and Spencer. Jones feels that he has the real power, whatever that means, and he is not going to take chances with this outside intervenor. He might intuitively calculate that he could do better against Spencer in a rough-and-tumble bargaining joust than he could in a so-called fair settlement suggested by the intervenor. Stated alternatively, his certainty equivalent for the uncertain outcome of the negotiation alternative is higher than his certainty equivalent of the uncertain outcome he would achieve through the intervenor.

Furthermore, if he initially requests a suggested resolution by the intervenor and then does not like the suggestion and rejects the offer in favor of conventional negotiation, it will be hard to budge his adversary, Spencer, from the suggested agreement. She can be resolute in her demand for her just share because an astute and fair analytical intervenor has deemed her demand most reasonable. But this argument against intervention does not cut in a proposed post-settlement settlement!

A shift of attitude, from belligerent positional bargaining to constructive collaboration with an intervenor, might very well take place *after* each side has gained the security of some negotiated settlement.

Some Additional Thoughts on Post-Settlement Settlements

Alvin E. Roth

One use of mathematical models in the study of negotiation is to make certain kinds of insights precise, permitting a systematic exploration of their implications. An opportunity to see how such analysis can be used is provided by the comments of Howard Raiffa (1985) on the opportunities for intervenors to propose "post-settlement settlements" that may benefit all parties in a negotiation. I will briefly describe some results that add force to his contention about two-party negotiations that ". . . in really complex negotiations where a lot of issues are at stake . . . more often than not jointly desirable post-settlement settlements could be achieved by an analytical intervenor." These results show that the percentage of possible settlements that could be improved in this way grows very rapidly as the number of issues (and hence of possible settlements) increases. The same results will also show that the opportunities for successful post-settlement intervention decrease as we move from two-party to multi-party negotiations.

The particular results described here are drawn from a penetrating paper by Barry O'Neill (1981), who considered the simple case in which **n** negotiators must try to agree on one of **m** possible settlements, where **n** and **m** are positive integers. (When many issues are under discussion, each combination of ways the issues could be resolved constitutes a possible settlement.) Each negotiator has a rank-ordering over the **m** settlements and, for simplicity and specificity, all rank-orderings are assumed to be equally likely, independent and without ties. The numerical results depend on these assumptions which imply, for example, that any two negotiators are as likely to agree as to disagree on the relative desirability of any two randomly selected settlements but similar qualitative results could be obtained under other assumptions. (For our present purposes, no assumptions need be made about whether these rank-orderings are known, even to the negotiators themselves.)

In the terminology of economics, a settlement is called *Pareto-optimal* (after the Italian economist Vilfredo Pareto) if there is no other settlement that all of the negotiators prefer. If a settlement that is not Pareto-optimal is the outcome of negotiations, there is room for an intervenor to propose a post-settlement settlement that all parties would prefer; if the outcome of negotiations is Pareto-optimal, no possibility of successful intervention of this kind exists. The likelihood that such intervention can be useful is thus related to the percentage of possible settlements that are Pareto-optimal.

Alvin E. Roth is A. W. Mellon Professor of Economics, Department of Economics, University of Pittsburgh, Pittsburgh, Pa. 15260.

For example, in the case of two negotiators (**n** = 2), if by chance it happens that the rank-ordering of one is exactly the opposite of the other's rank ordering, then *all* settlements will be Pareto-optimal (since any change of settlement would help one negotiator and hurt the other). Therefore, in this case, any post-settlement settlement that would be accepted by one party would be rejected by the other. However if the rank-orderings of the two negotiators are independent, the probability that they will be exactly the opposite decreases quickly as the number of possible settlements (**m**) increases. The expected percentage of Pareto-optimal settlements also declines with surprising suddenness.

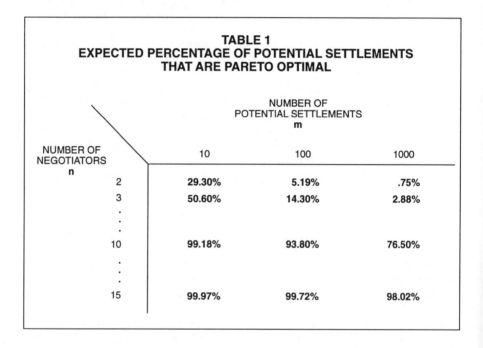

TABLE 1
EXPECTED PERCENTAGE OF POTENTIAL SETTLEMENTS THAT ARE PARETO OPTIMAL

NUMBER OF NEGOTIATORS n	NUMBER OF POTENTIAL SETTLEMENTS m		
	10	100	1000
2	29.30%	5.19%	.75%
3	50.60%	14.30%	2.88%
.			
.			
.			
10	99.18%	93.80%	76.50%
.			
.			
.			
15	99.97%	99.72%	98.02%

The first row of Table 1 (adapted from O'Neill, 1981) shows that, when there are only two parties to the negotiations (**n** = 2), the percentage of possible Pareto-optimal settlements on average will be less than 30 percent when there are 10 possible settlements (i.e., the expected number of Pareto-optimal settlements will be 2.93. This percentage will drop to less than 1 percent when there are 1000 possible settlements. If it is costly to evaluate possible settlements, and if strategic considerations prevent the negotiators from frankly revealing their preferences, then the possibility that the final outcome of negotiations will not be Pareto-optimal can be expected to increase as the percentage of Pareto-optimal settlements declines. Thus the probability that mutually profitable post-settlement settlements can be found is potentially very large when there are many possible settlements.

The situation is quite different as the number of negotiators grows. This can be understood by noting that, the larger the number of negotiators with independent interests, the harder it is to propose a change from one settlement to another that all regard as an improvement. The second row of the table shows that the case of three negotiators ($n = 3$) is already significantly different from the case $n = 2$. And by the time we reach the case $n = 15$, the expected percentage of Pareto-optimal settlements is over 98 percent, even when there are as many as 1000 possible settlements. Even if the negotiators choose a final outcome entirely at random, the likelihood of selecting one that could not be mutually improved upon by a post-settlement settlement would be overwhelming. This is, of course, in stark contrast to the situation that exists when there are only two negotiators.

In conclusion, this simple model shows clearly that the potential for successful post-settlement intervention of the kind discussed by Raiffa will be greatest when two negotiators are faced with a large number of possible settlements. In this case, the potential for this sort of intervention may be quite large. However when many negotiators with independent interests are involved, the probability that such post-settlement intervention can be successful will be small.

NOTE

This work has been supported by grants from the National Science Foundation and the Office of Naval Research, and by a Fellowship from the Alfred P. Sloan Foundation.

REFERENCES

O'Neill, B. (1981). "The Number of Outcomes In the Pareto-Optimal Set of Discrete Bargaining Games." *Mathematics of Operations Research* 6: 571-578.

Raiffa, H. (1985). "Post-settlement Settlements." *Negotiation Journal: On the Process of Dispute Settlement* 1: 9-12.

Post-Settlement Settlements
in Two-Party Negotiations

Max H. Bazerman, Lee E. Russ, and Elaine Yakura

> *... we must recognize that a lot of disputes are settled by hard-nosed, positional bargaining. Settled, yes. But efficiently settled? Often not...They quibble about sharing a small pie and often fail to realize that perhaps the pie can be jointly enlarged...There may be another carefully crafted settlement that both (parties) might prefer to the settlement they actually achieved.*
>
> — Howard Raiffa (1985)

Howard Raiffa's article in the premier issue of *Negotiation Journal* offered a promising new approach to minimizing limitations on rationality in negotiation. His basic idea is that players reaching a mutually acceptable agreement can later choose to allow a third party to help them search for a Pareto-superior agreement — one that is better for both parties. Raiffa suggests that the negotiators may be more willing to allow a third party to create a superior agreement after the initial pact is reached. In the end, each negotiator would reserve the right to veto the post-settlement settlement (PSS) proposed by the third party, and revert to the original agreement.

This article extends Raiffa's PSS concept by arguing that, in complex two-party relationships, the creation of PSSs (without the help of a third party) should be viewed as part of an effective working relationship. In many situations, the development of a Pareto-optimal agreement at a first or second meeting may not be feasible. After an initial agreement is reached, however, there may be ample opportunity for contract modification. In fact, the success of the ongoing two-party, or dyadic, relationship often depends largely on the propensity and ability of the negotiators to handle the PSS process. In our opinion, in fact, PSSs are more prevalent in complex dyadic agreements than Raiffa suggests, and should be part of our two-party training process — not a procedure reserved for third party experts.

Raiffa's use of a third party is based on their expertise in: (1) pooling the information already available to the negotiators, and (2) objectively analyzing the existence of mutually superior agreements based on that information. While helpful, this expertise need not be limited to third parties. *Skilled* nego-

Max Bazerman is Professor of Organization Behavior and member of the executive committee of the Dispute Resolution Research Center at the Kellogg Graduate School of Management, Northwestern University, Evanston, Illinois 60201. **Lee E. Russ** is Acquisitions Analyst with the Kohler Co., Kohler, Wisconsin 53044. And, **Elaine Yakura** is a doctoral student at the Sloan School of Management, Massachusetts Institute of Technology, Cambridge, Massachusetts 02139.

tiators can share information and make the appropriate analytical insights. In addition, skilled negotiators can capture the bulk of the benefits available through PSSs. We argue that PSS training for involved parties, rather than an outsider, offers the greatest opportunity to increase the frequency and success of negotiated agreements.

We also distinguish between Raiffa's view of PSSs as an outcome, and the notion of PSSs as a process. Raiffa views a PSS as a subsequent agreement improving on an initial arrangement from the perspective of both parties. We see the concept as being most useful if thought of in terms of a process culminating in that end. Parties must constantly be alert to improving on an initial agreement. An effective process might also include an institutionalized structure to encourage such agreements. Thus, we see the PSS process as a method by which parties reaching an initial agreement have the commitment to continue to search for a more integrative solution as more information is obtained and analyzed.

This study is based on complex negotiations involving the consulting divisions of three different offices of the same national Big Eight accounting firm. The authors selected these negotiations based on their access to detailed written and oral accounts from both the consulting firm *and* the clients involved. Two of the cases are viewed as successes, and one is viewed as a failure (for both parties). The ability to manage and/or facilitate the dyadic PSS process is considered a critical determinant of that success or failure.

The dyadic PSS between consulting firm and client can take a variety of forms. If both parties are better off expanding the initial scope of the project, an opportunity for a PSS exists. If both parties are better off with the consulting firm providing a different "package" of services, an opportunity for a PSS exists. In this article, we will explore the existence or lack of existence of PSSs when the potential for improving the initial agreement exists. Initially, we will briefly describe the nature of the consulting firm, the three negotiations, and the effectiveness of the PSS process in each. More general recommendations on the role of PSSs in complex two-party negotiations will then be offered. Finally, we will argue that the PSS concept is relevant to negotiating parties in a wide variety of complex settings, particularly in the service sector, and is not limited to the specific consulting environment documented in this paper.

The Consulting Firm and the Nature of its Business

The market for auditing large corporations is dominated by the Big Eight public accounting firms. These firms are generally organized into three divisions — auditing, tax, and consulting. While the auditing component is the largest group in all Big Eight firms, consulting is viewed as the area with the greatest potential for growth.

Our focus here is on three negotiations involving the consulting division of Jones Jenkins, or JJ. (All organizations and people in this paper are disguised.) JJ has been actively working to expand its consulting practice. Once an auxiliary service for their auditing clients, the consulting division now plans to build its own clientele. In addition, its services have moved from a focus on general consulting ("If it's broken, we'll fix it") to a specialized focus on systems consulting — primarily computer systems.

Case 1 — Client: Southern and Central States

Southern and Central States (SCS) is a public utility holding company with a number of subsidiaries. Prior to 1979, data processing was handled within each of those subsidiaries. The need for better control over operations and a response to mounting federal regulatory pressure (to justify its holding company structure) drove SCS to unify its data processing operations. Primary responsibility for this task was given to Mitchel Berardi, Director of Management Information Systems (MIS).

Berardi, who had recently been hired by SCS, had both his reputation and his future riding on the integration of the data processing function. The project was expected to cost millions of dollars, but the savings to the firm had the potential to be ten times the cost. Berardi, a former consultant in computer applications, an economics Ph.D., and a seasoned manager, commanded an unusually broad perspective on his new employer's strategic concerns. Importantly, he also spoke the consultant's technical language.

The need for consulting arose from both a resource shortage and a general reluctance to hire new people for a project as short-lived as the development of a strategic plan for an integrated data processing function. Berardi sent a "Request for Proposal" to 11 consulting firms, eight of which prepared preliminary evaluations of the work involved. At that point, Berardi told each firm what he wanted — at a level of detail well beyond that of the typical management information systems consulting client. Written proposals were due on a given date, and the number of contenders was trimmed to three. Berardi invited these three firms to make oral presentations. His final choice, he noted, would be based on the firm's response to the Request for Proposal and its ability to work with SCS's internal team.

Berardi believed that the SCS data processing project would eventually lead to a methodology that would have substantial strategic benefit later. Jones Jenkins — or JJ — committed three of its best management information systems people to the endeavor. The resulting proposal followed Berardi's outline without deviation. Berardi's suggested objectives were refined into specific tasks, and the scope of the project was outlined exactly as Berardi had requested. In addition, JJ's $175,000 price tag was well within SCS's upper limit. Price was not a major issue. Only $50,000 separated the highest from the lowest of the eight bidders, and the importance of the project to SCS made a $50,000 difference seem insignificant.

JJ won the bid. Both parties agree that this occurred because JJ promised Berardi exactly what he wanted, and guaranteed him that JJ's most desirable personnel would work on the project. The two other finalists presented their proposals in different ways. One focused on *its* assessment of what Berardi should want as the scope of the project — views that were interpreted as forcing a preexisting framework on SCS. The second unsuccessful bidder argued cogently for its plan, but refused to commit certain consultants to the project (as a matter of company policy). JJ won on the strength of its presentation team (led by John Cloutier) and its willingness to propose exactly what Berardi was seeking. JJ Management believed this was not the time for a creative examination of Berardi's underlying interests — after all, he had told each consulting firm exactly what he wanted!

A narrow view of negotiation would suggest that bargaining ended with the selection of JJ. While Cloutier, the JJ spokesman, had some idea that this project could develop into more business, neither JJ nor SCS knew that their relationship would extend beyond the initial planning project. JJ's work was impressive, and Cloutier earned the client's respect. SCS successfully obtained a viable plan for integrating a management information systems project, and JJ made a healthy profit.

A more complex view of negotiation would see this initial engagement as laying the groundwork for subsequent expansions of the contract. While it is reasonable to view additional work as part of a separate pact, Cloutier and Berardi viewed the future as a way to extend or change the initial scope of the project —an opportunity to increase the joint success of their interaction.

The initial project had been limited to the development of a strategic plan. That plan would have to be implemented, and who was more knowledgeable for the implementation than JJ? While the initial project cost a substantial sum of money, it was only a small component of their total interaction. Six years later, SCS had paid $4.2 million for JJ's services, and there is little reason to expect their relationship to lapse in the near future.

This interaction yielded enormous personal benefits as well. The cost reductions associated with the new system brought Berardi visibility, a promotion to vice president for Information Systems, and possibly an avenue for further advancement. For Cloutier, the on-site manager of the initial project, the SCS account brought firm-wide recognition and a promotion to national partner status in record time.

This case illustrates the most common form of post-settlement settlement (PSS). Satisfied with the initial outcome, two organizations expand the scope of the agreement. Could JJ and SCS have contracted for the entire six-year package in advance? Definitely not. SCS did not know what it needed in terms of implementation until the strategic plan was created. Even if SCS had the ability to create such a long-term contract, it did not have the confidence in JJ to commit $4.2 million. Once the initial project was completed, JJ had an advantage in the competition for the follow-up work.

To begin the interaction with SCS, JJ had to create an initial agreement that "beat" the competition on surface level issues — rather than a deep understanding of SCS's interests. Only after reaching this initial agreement could the relationship be redefined to the benefit of both parties. JJ was able to revise and expand Berardi's plans for the implementation work. In doing so, it provided SCS with an outcome that was better than anything obtainable from the initial agreement — and procured for itself a very large piece of business. The fact that both parties view the interaction so positively emphasizes the integrativeness of the PSS.

Case 2 — Client: General Produx

General Produx (GP) is an integrated manufacturer of paper goods. Having passed through a period of management information systems inactivity and a myriad of computer problems, the division gained sudden prominence under a new chief executive officer. With that thrust came both attention and pressure to perform. Unfortunately, the department had lost many of its best people under the former leadership.

The local office of JJ suffered from a similar pressure. A decision to redirect the practice to a focus on management information systems had produced wholesale changes in personnel. Ted Hibble, the managing partner of the GP account, was perhaps the most notable newcomer. His lofty position attracted a great deal of attention from his superiors. JJ had made a sizable investment in Hibble, and it expected a suitable return. Thus, both Hibble and the management information systems division at GP had something to prove.

Hibble held many strong opinions about the nature of the transaction process. He did not like the use of the term "negotiation" because he believed it had too much of a competitive connotation. He felt that the formation of the consultant-client relationship was not defined by their actual contract. Rather, he argued, the nature of consulting contracts is to provide boundaries for legal protection, but the nature of consulting work was a constantly evolving process — preferably growing in scope.

For a variety of political reasons, GP chose to sever its management information systems relationship with one of JJ's leading competitors. This was a major decision. GP desired a long-term relationship, and it planned to spend $2 million per year for external services in this field. Internal discussions narrowed the choice to two firms, and GP officials decided to try a "test": Each company was offered a small job to evaluate its performance. GP was not interested in extracting rate concessions. (GP officials apparently assumed that the industry had a fairly fixed standard — an assumption that the authors found not to be the case.) Rather, GP was concerned with which firm would best meet their needs.

Hibble suspected that the initial project was a test, and he wanted to do well. The project would require four days on-site at GP. JJ set the following four explicit goals:

- Giving GP officials more than their money's worth.

- Learning what GP liked and disliked in its former consulting firm.

- Doing everything possible to make JJ generally look attractive.

- Gaining insight into the motivations of the major players within GP.

The expenses for doing the project added up to $30,000, but the fees charged were held to $20,000. JJ was investing in the future.

During the on-site visit, Hibble learned about the projects on which GP would be working in the future. The largest, a manufacturing cost account system, would have a price tag of approximately $2 million. This was Hibble's target. After completing the initial project, Hibble met with GP officials, and proposed that JJ help them with the manufacturing cost account system. Before a decision was reached, Hibble and his associates provided a proposal that was of great value as a blueprint for developing the system. That proposal included two oral presentations. This initiative led GP to choose JJ over the competing firm.

Interestingly, JJ began the project (at standard rates) with only a working draft of the contract. Both sides felt that time was too important to waste while waiting for the attorneys to finish the details.

With the work thus initiated, GP concluded that, although the time frame established by the proposal was acceptable, the overall cost figure was too high. The firm also felt that there was a technical flaw in the proposal. Although the price (the maximum was $1.84 million) would remain the same, the scope had to be enlarged. GP agreed to do more of the work internally under JJ's direction, paying only for hours actually worked by JJ personnel. In addition, GP reserved the right to terminate the agreement at any point upon 15 days' notice. Thus, the project was respecified in its first week.

This fluid agreement process sowed the seeds of a PSS even before a final legal agreement was established. We consider this a PSS, rather than the creation of the initial agreement, because the work was started under a set of implicit agreements concerning what would be included in the eventual contract.

Another fascinating feature of this PSS process was the specification of a steering committee comprised of representatives of both organizations. This group was to redefine the project as necessary. As a result, a number of items continued to be renegotiated. While the agreement called for fees to be paid at the prevailing JJ rates, the steering committee agreed to accept payment under the old rates for quite some time after a broader increase.

Similarly, GP experienced a shortage of internal management information systems, and agreed to increase the scope of the consulting agreement — which was always an objective of JJ. The direction of the project remained under the constant review of the joint steering committee. While the contract specified the delivery of services that JJ would provide for a maximum fee, the steering committee continually revamped as needed the initial agreement.

This case again illustrates a PSS by expanding the scope of the initial agreement. In this instance, however, the PSS process was institutionalized in the steering committee. As the engagement unfolded, the steering committee made mutually desirable changes in direction and scheduling. Thus, the negotiation evolved over time through a learning and sharing process that produced greater joint benefit.

Case 3 — Client: Allied Health Plan

Allied Health Plan (AHP) is the largest health insurance provider in its state. It accounts for 47 percent of the state's health insurance subscriptions, for which it bills $750 million per year. Marc Morris, the president of AHP, decided to give top priority to achieving a unified computer system to handle the company's private sector business. The existing system consisted of eight overlapping and unconnected systems which AHP had unsuccessfully attempted to consolidate.

Morris commissioned JJ to review the existing system. The resulting report cited several serious deficiencies. Incompetence in the internal management of data processing activities was widely acknowledged. In response to this report, Morris disbanded the firm's management information systems division — turning the function over to Data Systems International (DSI).

Data Systems International specializes in replacing an organization's data processing function. (JJ does not do this type of work.) The normal arrangement calls for a ten-year, multimillion dollar agreement. Clients often develop negative feelings toward DSI, but most acknowledge that they get the job done. One drawback of the DSI system was that it did not include a financial reporting system. That responsibility fell to the Finance Division at Allied.

Unfortunately, the Finance Division did not have the talent to devise such a system, and — after six months — had not progressed very far in its task. Mike Baker, a JJ partner, was asked to review the project and determine the problem areas. Morris asked JJ to identify any "obstacles to progress," as well as any "reckless decisions" being made with regard to the financial system. At that time, Morris expected JJ's involvement to be of very short duration. He expected that JJ would be able to identify the problem quickly, recommend solutions to get the project back on schedule, and end its commitment.

Baker proposed a "top-down" approach in which the objectives and design of the system would be determined before specific pieces of programming were complete. Allied Health Plan rejected this approach largely because of its commitment to the completed work of DSI. Baker believes that the rejection of his strategy was due to the "bottom up" nature of the DSI effort. That is, they start writing pieces of programs without knowing how they will later be combined.

Despite that disagreement, Morris asked Baker whether or not he could "rent a manager," a senior JJ person who would oversee the creation of Allied's new financial system. As a rule, Big Eight firms are not interested in just selling their partners' time. While partner fees are high, the firm can gain greater benefits by having these senior people sell projects that include lower-level employees. Given the length of their audit relationship, however, JJ wanted to be responsive. The firm offered to assign Baker full-time to the project, which was expected to take four to six weeks. When asked by Morris to estimate how much his services for the project might cost, Baker suggested his hourly rate ($165 per hour) multiplied by the number of billable hours to be expected from a month of full-time work. This was satisfactory to Morris.

Baker's assignment required working with the existing Allied Health Plan staff to complete a plan for the financial system, thereby allowing Allied to complete its overall data processing systems. In essence, Baker was functioning as Allied's senior vice president for finance. The project was the principal activity of the division. As Baker became more involved with the project, he realized that there were more problems than he had expected. His "top-down" strategy, while logically superior, ran counter to the approach that dominated the organization. Nonetheless, Baker firmly believed in developing systems "the right way."

A month came and went, but Baker's task was not accomplished. Morris asked him to continue his work. Two months later, the end was still not in sight. At that point, Morris found an Allied employee who felt the project could be completed in a month if he were given control. Baker argued that this was unrealistic. Morris, looking for someone who said he could get the job done, moved Baker aside (into a full-time advisory role at $165 per hour) and replaced him with the optimistic in-house alternative.

A month later, an additional month had been wasted, and Baker was reinstalled as the leader of the project. Six months after the start of what initially was viewed as a four- to six-week engagement, Baker had completed between 80 and 90 percent of the specified work. Both Allied and JJ felt that this was good time to end his full-time involvement. For Allied, progress was slow and Baker's orientation continued to run against the grain of internal management information systems professionals. For JJ, too much partner time was being taken away from finding new clients.

Baker remained available to the project as a consultant "touching base" with Allied every three or four weeks. He believes that this project was an "unusual" engagement. He says he did "everything possible," but did not succeed: "We were in the position of trying to go to the moon in a model airplane," said Baker.

JJ was stuck with a technical approach which it opposed, and the firm was unable to get the job done properly. While JJ collected $165 an hour for Baker's time, it lost far more than it gained.

Baker left JJ soon after this project. Morris, on the other hand, was disappointed in the performance of JJ. He does, however, concede that he may have had unrealistic expectations. Morris was not perturbed by the fees paid to JJ, but he was offended by the opportunities lost to various delays. This project was a mutual failure in every respect.

Why?

Morris and Baker initiated their interaction without knowing the true extent of the project. This uncertainty should have served as a signal to later consider a PSS. In this case, however, no such awareness was created. Morris was looking for a quick solution. Baker hesitantly accepted the project as a service to a long-time audit client.

Both agreed, in retrospect, that there were many mutually better ways of specifying the project. Baker could have brought in a team of JJ consultants to develop a top-down system. Alternatively, Baker could have replaced himself with someone who would better fit the Data Systems International approach. Clearly, none of these alternatives could have been known at the point of the initial agreement. No one knew, or suspected, the true nature of the situation. Thus, Baker's assignment to the project was completely reasonable — he could objectively diagnose the problem.

Neither party considered the need to create a PSS. Instead, they nonrationally escalated their commitment to a previous course of action. This is a common and generally unproductive response to a negotiated agreement that is not working out for either party.

Creating the awareness and structure for a PSS process is a way to avoid the dysfunctional tendency to escalate to a prior course of action when rationality suggests that the time for reconsideration has arrived. What was needed in this case was a reassessment of the project after Baker's initial diagnosis. At that point, both firms were in a position to identify a viable PSS.

Conclusions

In each of the three cases, the complexity of the project combined with the limited information available at the time of the transaction, thereby forcing the creation of initial agreements that were less than Pareto-efficient. In two of the cases, PSSs evolved naturally as the result of both parties' negotiation skills and the existence of structures encouraging modifications to the initial agreement. In the failure situation, a PSS was needed but not initiated by either side.

A critical ingredient in these cases is complexity. All three cases describe situations in which the parties did not have the information necessary to create a more integrative agreement at the initial transaction point. The clients did not know enough about management information systems, and JJ did not know enough about the clients' problems. Further, part of the complexity was due to the fact that service sector agreements must often be based on trust. Trust is easier to develop after the relationship has begun to build.

The existence of this complexity is not limited to consulting contracts. Agreements from many different arenas may lend themselves to a dyadic PSS. There are, however, some reasons to expect agreements in a service sector economy to have greater complexity, and need for PSSs, than agreements in a manufacturing sector economy. As our economy grows increasingly service-oriented, the PSS process becomes essential to the national well-being.

Transactions in the service sector generally have more dimensions than their manufacturing counterpart. Among the characteristics of service sector transactions are the following:

1. Services typically require greater customization than hard goods.

2. Two firms are more likely to have an ongoing and highly interdependent relationship.

3. Ongoing support of an ambiguous nature will often be part of the contract.

The result of these differences is that negotiations in a service-sector economy will be more uncertain, more varied, and more novel than their counterparts in the earlier manufacturing-based economy.

Perhaps the most important difference is that the full nature of an agreement will often be unspecifiable until the work begins. The consultant, for example, can often be trapped by a Catch-22 since he or she cannot know the true problem without providing a great deal of service. In effect, a consultant cannot begin the project without knowing what the project is, and cannot know what the project is without beginning the project. PSSs provide an approach for resolving this Catch-22.

Many negotiations will lead the parties into the trap illustrated by the third case — escalating their commitment to a flawed initial agreement (see Rubin, 1981, for a discussion of escalation in entrapment situations). A number of solutions exist. *First*, managers, consultants, and other professionals must be trained to consider the possibility of PSSs. Consideration of the possibility of an alternate arrangement may have led JJ and Allied Health to a reasonable resolution. Training should include instruction in creativity-building processes in negotiation and an awareness of the tendency of people to escalate commitment to a previous course of action. *Second*, institutionalized structures can be created to monitor the viability of an initial agreement. JJ and GP created such an arrangement through the use of a steering committee. No such arrangement existed in the JJ/Allied Health project. *Third*, contracts should be written to be firm, yet flexible. They must provide parties with a variety of legal protections, yet they should not bind the parties into bad business decisions. Obviously, negotiators can always jointly decide to destroy one contract and write a new one. Nonetheless, writing contracts in a way that *explicitly* considers the possible need for renegotiation emphasizes to both parties the potential benefit of a PSS.

In arguing for a dyadic approach to PSS, we are *not* arguing against Raiffa's inclusion of a third party in the PSS process. In fact, we believe that third parties can generate benefits that too often escape the negotiators themselves. However, negotiators should also be trained to create opportunities for PSSs *without* the help of a third party. It should be understood that outsiders also have disadvantages, and they will not be available in most negotiation situations. PSSs should be part of the standard training in negotiation courses.

Students in courses taught by the first author are trained to use an agreement as an opportunity to be more open about their situation, allowing for better problem solving and the potential creation of a PSS. A general finding is that problem solving is easier once the two parties have a legally binding agreement to which they can retreat. We see ample opportunity to improve the quality of agreements through PSSs, even when a qualified third party is not involved in the process.

NOTE

This research was supported by the Management in the 1990s Project of the Sloan School of Management at the Massachusetts Institute of Technology. Part of the first author's contribution was completed while he was on the faculty at MIT and while he was a visiting faculty member of the Graduate Institute of Business Administration at Chulalongkorn University, Bangkok, Thailand. Part of the second author's contribution was completed while he was a graduate student at the Sloan School of Management at MIT. Part of the third author's contribution was supported by a grant from the National Institute for Dispute Resolution. The authors appreciate the comments made by Harris Sondak and Marla Felcher on a previous draft of this article, the data collection assistance of Craig Rosenkrantz, and the intellectual and organizational contributions made by John Sifonis.

REFERENCES

Raiffa, H. (1985). "Post-settlement settlements." *Negotiation Journal* 1:9-12.
Rubin, J. Z. (1981). "Some ins and outs of psychological traps." *Psychology Today*, March, 1981:52-63.

Renegotiations in International Business

Jeswald W. Salacuse

The challenge of international business negotiations is not just "getting to yes," but also staying there. International business agreements, solemnly signed and sealed after hard bargaining, seem to break down frequently, bringing the parties back to the negotiating table. Indeed, many international business negotiations are in reality negotiations of preexisting commitments.

In recent years we have seen many examples of the phenomenon of renegotiation. Since the outbreak of the international debt crisis in 1982, Western commercial banks and their Third World borrowers have been engaged in a constant process of renegotiating loans that developing countries have been unable to repay, an exercise commonly known as "debt rescheduling." The dramatic fall in the price of oil and gas from the heights of the early 1980s has forced purchasers to seek renegotiation of long-term supply agreements that once seemed profitable but have now become ruinous. And the rapid decline in the value of the dollar, particularly against the Japanese yen, has since 1986 prompted attempts to renegotiate other long-term contractual relationships.

Renegotiation in international business is by no means peculiar to the 1980s. For decades, host country governments, often with the threat of nationalization in the background, have periodically sought to revise investment arrangements which they had previously made with foreign corporations but later judged no longer advantageous (Vasts, 1978, p. 17). These examples illustrate a traditional theme in international business circles: the lament over the "unstable contract," the profitable agreement that the other party refuses to respect. One common response to contractual instability is renegotiation.

The heightened risk of contractual instability in the international business arena suggests that negotiators of an initial agreement must be acutely aware of the possibility of eventual renegotiation and must seek creative ways of dealing with that possibility. As the number of long-term international business arrangements increases, and particularly if their time-frames lengthen, considerations about the need for and timing of renegotiations will be ignored at one's peril. Moreover, international business executives need to recognize that the process of renegotiation raises special problems not ordinarily encountered in negotiating the first instance deal, and that it requires tech-

Jeswald W. Salacuse is Dean and Professor of International Law at the Fletcher School of Law and Diplomacy, Tufts University, Medford, Mass. 02155.

niques and approaches differing from those employed in ordinary international deal-making. The purpose of this column is to explore these issues.

Factors Contributing to Renegotiation

Although hard empirical data on the subject are lacking, anecdotal evidence suggests that renegotiation is more prevalent in international business than in the purely domestic setting. Certainly one can say that international business transactions involve special factors not present in domestic business deals and that these factors seem to heighten the risk of contractual instability thereby creating pressure for the renegotiation of existing arrangements. First, because the environment in which they take place has many sources of uncertainty, international business dealings seem particularly susceptible to sudden changes in circumstances. These may include currency devaluations, coups d'états, wars and radical shifts in governments and governmental policies (Salacuse, 1988, p. 9). Second, mechanisms for enforcing agreements are often less sure or more costly in the international arena than in a purely domestic setting. Without effective recourse to the courts to enforce a contract or to seize a debtor's assets, a party to a contract that it considers favorable may have no choice but to renegotiate the agreement's terms when faced with a threat, expressed or implied, of outright repudiation. Third, foreign governments and governmental corporations are often important participants in international business dealings, and they traditionally have reserved for themselves the right to repudiate onerous contractual commitments on grounds of protecting national sovereignty and public welfare.

Finally, the world's diverse cultures and legal systems attach differing degrees of binding force to a signed contract and recognize varying causes justifying avoidance of burdensome contractual obligations. Thus, for example, an American in a transaction with a Japanese may view their signed contract as the essence of the deal and the source of rules governing their relationship in its entirety; a Japanese, on the other hand, may tend to see the deal as a partnership that may be subject to reasonable changes over time, a partnership in which one party ought not to take unfair advantage of purely fortuitous happenings like radical and unexpected changes in the prices of raw materials or the values of currencies. It is interesting to note that, as a result of the recent rise in the value of the Japanese yen, certain American companies, tied to long-term supply agreements payable in yen for components and materials produced in Japan, relied upon this distinctly un-American approach to contracts to seek renegotiation of payment terms which unanticipated monetary changes had made unprofitable.

Three Types of Renegotiation

Discussions of "renegotiation" apply the term to three fundamentally different situations, and it is important to distinguish each of them at the outset. They may be referred to as post-deal, intradeal and extra-deal renegotiations.

(1) Post-Deal Renegotiations

In this context, negotiations may take place at the expiration of a contract, when the parties, though legally free to go their own ways, nonetheless seek to renew their previous relationship. For example, at the end of a five-year distribution contract between a U.S. manufacturer and its foreign distributor, the parties may discuss a second distribution contract, thereby "renegotiating" their original relationship. In this situation, the renegotiation process may be very much like the negotiation in first instance, but there are also some notable differences. First, unlike the situation prevailing in their original negotiation, the manufacturer and the distributor now have a shared experience of working together and a resulting knowledge of each other's goals, methods, intentions and reliability. Obviously the nature of that earlier experience will significantly affect the renegotiation. Thus, the problems of cross-cultural communication, which may have complicated the first negotiation, will probably be far less significant in the second, since the parties have learned a great deal about each other's culture during the previous five years. Similarly, many of the original questions about their venture —its risks and its opportunities — have now been answered, and bargaining positions in the negotiations will certainly be shaped by that information.

Then too, the willingness of the participants to reach agreement will be influenced by their tangible and intangible investments in their first relationship, to the extent that those investments may be used advantageously in their second contract. For example, the foreign distributor will have trained its employees and organized itself to handle the U.S. manufacturer's products. All other things being equal, it may therefore find it more advantageous to renegotiate a new agreement with the manufacturer than to make a contract with another producer, which would entail significant new training and organizational costs. Similarly, the U.S. manufacturer, having helped to develop the marketing organization and networks of the distributor, would prefer to avoid the added costs to be incurred in identifying and training a new distributor.

(2) Intra-Deal Renegotiations

A second type of renegotiation occurs when the agreement itself provides that, during its life at specified times, the parties may renegotiate or at least review certain of its provisions. Here, renegotiation is anticipated as a legitimate activity in which both parties are to engage in good faith. For example, in a long-term supply contract, the two sides may agree to meet periodically to determine raw material prices.

Because of the length of many international business arrangements and the wide variety of changing circumstances to which they are subject, the inclusion in the contract of some sort of periodic, intradeal renegotiation of key elements would appear to be a wise basis for establishing a long-term relationship. Although commentators have advocated specific renegotiation or revision clauses in long-term international agreements, these provisions are, in fact, relatively rare (See, e.g., Barrels, 1985, p. 65). Apparently, westerners view them with suspicion and consider them as increasing uncertainty in an already risky type of arrangement. Moreover, they offend western concepts of the sanctity of contract and the need by investors for certainty and predictability in business transactions (Stoever, 1981, p. 27). Then too, there is always the danger that one of the parties will use a renegotiation clause as a lever to force changes in terms that strictly speaking were not open to revision. On the other hand, some parties, such as many government officials in developing nations, consider provisions for renegotiation only at specified intervals as overly restrictive, particularly if they believe that review of contractual terms whenever necessary is an inherent condition of their bargain.

(3) Extra-Deal Renegotiations

The most difficult and emotional renegotiations are those undertaken in apparent violation of the agreement, or at least in the absence of a specific clause for redoing the deal. These renegotiations take place "extra-deal," for they occur outside the framework of the existing agreement. The renegotiations of the 1980s over Third World loans, petroleum prices, and currencies all fit within the category of extra-deal renegotiations, because in each case one of the participants was seeking relief from a legally binding obligation without any basis in the agreement itself for renegotiation.

Unlike negotiations in first instance, which are generally fueled by both participants' hopes for future profits, extra-deal renegotiations begin with both parties' disappointed expectations. One side has failed to achieve the profit expected from the transaction, and the other is being asked to give up something for which it bargained hard and which it expected to enjoy for the duration of their relationship. And whereas both parties to a proposed new venture participate willingly (if not eagerly) in negotiations, one party always participates reluctantly (if not downright unwillingly) in an extra-deal renegotiation.

Beyond mere disappointed expectations, extra-deal renegotiations, by their very nature, can create bad feeling and mistrust. One side sees itself as being asked to give up something to which it has a legal and moral right, and it views the other side as having gone back on its word, as having acted in bad faith by reneging on the deal. Indeed, the reluctant party may even feel it is being coerced into participating in extra-deal renegotiations, since a refusal to do so would result in losing the investment already made in the transaction or joint venture. Thus, it is very difficult for the parties to see renegotiations as any thing more than a "zero-sum game," where one side wins and the other side loses.

The extra-deal renegotiation of an established arrangement may also have significant implications beyond the transaction in question. The party being asked to give up a contractual right may feel obligated to show various political constituencies, both inside and outside its own organization, that it is not "weak," and cannot be taken advantage of. Moreover, a party will usually fear that yielding to a demand for the renegotiation of one contract may encourage other parties to seek renegotiation of their agreements as well. This concern for the potential "ripple" effect from renegotiations clearly contributed to the reluctance of the international commercial banks to yield to demands by individual developing countries for a revision of loan terms. Concessions to Mexico would inevitably lead Argentina to demand equal treatment in its own renegotiation.

The desire to protect one's image and other contracts may lead a party to take a position, at least at the outset, of rejecting all changes in the relationship, no matter how small or inexpensive. Similarly, the party seeking relief from an agreement that is no longer reasonable may feel it must link its demand to some higher, political principle, such as national sovereignty or the public welfare, in order to prevail. As a result, the national governments of the parties may intervene in the process, and various types of legal actions may be threatened or actually invoked. The political dimensions of renegotiations have been particularly present in transactions between developing country governments and foreign corporations, as for example those concerning international loans and mineral concessions.

Thoughtful commentators urge that negotiations be based on principle and that negotiators seek to found their agreements on objective criteria (e.g., Fisher and Ury, 1981, p. 86-98). Since respect for agreements is a basic norm in virtually every culture, how can an attempt to renegotiate a valid contract be anything more than an unprincipled power play? After all, a deal is a deal, isn't it?

While respect for agreements is indeed a norm in virtually all societies and may even rise to the level of a universal principle of law, most cultures also provide relief, in varying degrees, from the binding force of a contract in exceptional circumstances. "A deal is a deal" is certainly an expression of a fundamental rule of human relations, but then so is the statement, "Things have changed." In international business, the principle of changed circumstances underlies demands for renegotiations, but the nature of the change in circumstances is broadly and variously interpreted, and therein lies a source of conflict. While a request for extra-deal renegotiations may provoke bad feeling in one party, an outright refusal to renegotiate may also create ill will on the other side since it will be seen as an attempt to force adherence to a bargain that has become unreasonable.

Ultimately, the basic conflict between the parties in an extra-deal renegotiation will be over the type of changed circumstances justifying the negotiations. Such circumstances may cover a broad spectrum, ranging from sudden changes in objective conditions over which neither of the parties has control, such as rising exchange rates or closed trade routes, to conditions determined subjectively by one side alone. With regard to the latter, for example, host country governments often reassess their relations with foreign investors, based on the country's current need for the investor's capital and technology. Thus, at the time the investment is first offered, the host country may believe it has no other options to secure the capital and technology needed for development than to give the investor extremely favorable terms. Later, after the technology has been transferred and indigenous entrepreneurs become capable of undertaking production themselves, the government may seek to renegotiate the original agreement on grounds that its economic circumstances and developmental needs have changed (Vernon and Wells, 1981, pp. 145-148).

Approaches to Renegotiations

The side seeking to change an existing business relationship may be able to choose from among a variety of approaches to renegotiation. The first, and ostensibly least offensive tactic, is to cast the renegotiations as merely an effort to clarify ambiguities in the existing agreement, rather than to change its basic principles. This approach, at least formally, respects the sanctity of the contract and thereby may avoid the friction and hostility engendered by demanding outright extra-deal renegotiations. For example, a host country government finding that a foreign investment project granted an exemption from "all taxes and duties" is placing increasing demands on the economy, may seek to require the project to pay "user fees" for certain government services, on the grounds that they are not taxes or duty. Through this approach, the government hopes to attain its revenue goals while respecting the sanctity of its contract with the investor.

A second approach is to request reinterpretation of certain key terms on the ground of changes in circumstances, while still preserving the principles negotiated in the original agreement. For example, even if it were specifically agreed that the investment project is exempt from user fees, requiring it to pay the additional costs incurred by the government to supply power to the project during an energy crisis might be a principled basis for redefining the scope of the exemption without altering the fundamental principle agreed by the parties.

Waiver is yet another approach that respects the sanctity of the agreement yet enables the burdened party to obtain the relief it seeks. For example, a manufacturer in a distribution agreement may prefer to waive the specified sales quota required of its foreign distributor during periods of slack product demand, rather than to renegotiate and change the amount of the quota permanently.

In many cases, of course, the parties will have no choice but to confront the necessity of redoing the deal by entering into active and acknowledged extra-deal renegotiations to change the principles on which their relationship is based. These are precisely the situations that create sharp conflict between the sanctity of a contract on the one hand and the need to adapt the existing relationship to changing circumstances on the other.

But perhaps approaches to renegotiation should begin before, rather than after, the two sides make their original deal. Accordingly, both sides should recognize at the outset that, in any long-term relationship, there is high probability of eventual extra-deal renegotiations of the original terms of their agreement.

Today, most contracts explicitly or implicitly deny the possibility of change and therefore make no provision whatsoever for adjustments to meet changing circumstances. This assumption of contractual stability has proven false time and time again. For example, most mineral development agreements assume they will continue unchanged for periods of from 15 to 99 years, yet they rarely remain unmodified for more than a few years (Smith and Wells, 1975, p. 18). As Raymond Vernon (1971, p. 46) has argued, with reference to mineral investment agreements, a bargain, once struck, will inevitably become obsolete and issues once agreed upon will be reopened at a later time as circumstances change. Indeed, to borrow Vernon's phrase, international business negotiations should probably assume that most long-term deals are "obsolescing bargains."

How, then, are participants in a long-term international business arrangement to deal with the problem of change? If the risk of instability is inherent in long-term international business relationships, what is the appropriate approach to make toward the problem of renegotiation?

The traditional approach in international negotiations has been to assume stability of the contract and only grudgingly, if at all, to agree to changes as a result of hard, extra-deal renegotiations. Certain observers have suggested that this approach is unrealistic and in the long run leads to unnecessary conflict between the parties. Instead, they argue that the need to redo the contract is inherent and that a long-term arrangement, such as a mineral concession, should be seen as one in which bargaining powers and interest change over time (Smith and Wells, 1975, p. 23).

Beyond recognizing the inevitability of renegotiations of long-term agreements, how should the negotiators proceed in the first instance? Three approaches suggest themselves. The first is to continue the traditional approach of seeking a long-term unchanging contract, with detailed provisions and guarantees to assure adherence to the maximum extent possible. At the same time, the calculations on which the contract are based should take account of the realistic prospect of extra-deal renegotiations so that pricing, rates of return, and other essential terms used by one party reflect a realistic assessment of the duration of the initial agreement, rather than the duration specified in the contract.

A second approach is to create a more balanced agreement in the first instance. The assumption here is that, if the agreement is balanced and mutually beneficial, both sides will be less likely to seek renegotiations of its terms. A balanced agreement, for example, might be one which allocates specific risks in the venture to the party best able to bear that risk, rather than merely on the basis of raw bargaining power (e.g., see Blitzer, Lessard, and Paddock, 1984, p. 1).

And finally a third approach is to provide specifically in the agreement for intra-deal renegotiations at defined intervals on specific issues that are particularly susceptible to changing circumstances. A variation of this approach is to provide for a series of linked short-term contracts that together will extend over the life of the contemplated business relationship. Each of these agreements will be subject to negotiation as the relationship evolves.

These three approaches are by no means mutually exclusive; all three could be employed in shaping a long-term deal in the first instance so as to avoid the difficulties of unplanned extra-deal renegotiations later on.

NOTE

The author is grateful to Professor James L. Paddock of the Fletcher School of Law and Diplomacy, Tufts University, and Vice Dean David N. Smith of the Harvard Law School for their helpful comments on this article.

REFERENCES

Barrels, M. (1985). *Contractual adaptation and conflict resolution.* Deventer, The Netherlands: Kluwer.

Blitzer, C., Lessard, D. and **Paddock, J.** (1984). "Risk-bearing and the choice of contract forms for oil exploration and development." *The Energy Journal* 5: 1-28.

Fisher, R. and **Ury, W.** (1981). *Getting to YES: Negotiating agreement without giving in.* Boston: Houghton Mifflin.

Salacuse, J. W. (1988). "Making deals in strange places: A beginner's guide to international business negotiations." *Negotiation Journal* 4: 5-13.

Smith, D. N. and **Wells, L. T.** (1975). *Negotiating Third-World mineral agreements.* Cambridge, Mass.: Ballinger.

Stoever, W. A. (1981). *Renegotiations in international business transactions.* Lexington, Mass.: D.C. Heath

Vasts, D. F. (1978). "Coercion and foreign investment rearrangements." *American Journal of International Law* 72. 17-36.

Vernon, R. (1971). *Sovereignty at bay: The multinational spread of U.S. enterprises.* Cambridge, Mass.: Ballinger.

———— and **Wells, L.** (1981). *Economic environment of international business* (3rd ed.). Englewood Cliffs, N.J.: Prentice-Hall.

Section VIII

Multilateral Negotiation

A considerable amount of influential scholarship on negotiation proceeds from the assumption that negotiation involves *two* parties in conflict over a *single* issue. While this simplifying assumption has validity in the abstract and in some actual cases, it largely ignores the many situations in reality where there are multiple parties attempting to negotiate a settlement over multiple issues. This section offers a sampling of articles that highlight the host of variables that arise when one addresses the far more complex — and realistic — problems of multilateral negotiation.

Saadia Touval ("Multilateral Negotiation: An Analytical Approach") presents an overview of the kinds of issues that are apt to arise before, during, and after multilateral negotiations take place. The most important work, writes Touval, takes place *before* negotiations, and during this pre-negotiation phase, issues such as the following should be addressed: the identity and number of parties to be invited to the negotiations, possible coalitions among them, different possible roles and functions of these multiple parties, and the shaping of an acceptable negotiating agenda. The article closes by developing several general recommendations for increasing the likely effectiveness of multilateral negotiations.

Charles Heckscher ("Multilateral Negotiation and the Future of American Labor") takes a close and critical look at the changing shape of the American labor-management relationship, which, he argues, has changed dramatically over the last several decades. While labor-management relations once consisted of two sides locked in a purely adversarial (zero-sum) arrangement, the lines of division are now blurred. The assumption that there are only two parties, writes Heckscher, is no longer valid. For example, "management" now includes large categories of employees — data processors and various technicians, for example — who simply do not regard themselves either as management or as workers. Since the problem is no longer a bilateral one, but is truly multilateral, there may be new opportunities to settle labor disputes using ideas drawn from other arenas in which multilateral negotiation has been used.

There are many parallels between the changing nature of labor-management negotiations and negotiations in the domain of international relations. The contribution by Victor Kremenyuk ("The Emerging System of International Negotiations") analyzes the changing nature and increasingly interdependent environment of international relations. These changes highlight the importance of multilateral negotiation in reaching international accords. And finally, in the concluding article of this section, Klaus Aurisch ("The Art of Preparing a Multilateral Conference") offers a thorough description of the many factors involved in planning for an international conference. His "nuts-and-bolts" approach may also prove useful to planners of other multilateral negotiations in other settings.

Multilateral Negotiation: An Analytic Approach

Saadia Touval

The term *multilateral* literally means "many sided." Because multilateral negotiation generally calls for simultaneous negotiation by three or more parties over multiple issues, and aims at an agreement acceptable to all participants, it is often regarded as a complex and cumbersome process. Nevertheless, multilateral negotiation occurs in a wide variety of international settings, and it is considered to be an acceptable and effective means of reaching settlement.

The question I wish to address is *how*, given the complexity of multilateral negotiation, such agreements are actually arrived at. Although systems of three or more parties can logically be broken down into dyadic component sub-systems — and although multilateral negotiation often takes place through bilateral interactions — I believe that the dynamics of multilateral negotiation cannot adequately be described as a sequence of bilateral negotiations. Understanding multilateral negotiation requires explanation of the process by which the interests of all participants are adjusted and a *joint* decision is reached.

Even though the study of negotiation has benefited from considerable attention in the past three decades, most of this work has focused on bilateral negotiation. Trilateral negotiation, which is less extensively studied, has also received much attention, especially in studies of coalition formation and the intervention of third parties. Multilateral negotiation, however, has been the object of relatively little analytic consideration. There are numerous case studies of particular negotiations, but few theoretical analytic treatments explaining the process and the way it leads to agreement.[1]

This paucity of conceptual emphasis and research must be juxtaposed against the frequent use of multilateral negotiation as a tool of international diplomacy. As contemporary international problems have increasingly come to affect the interests of several states, governments have resorted to multilateral processes in their attempts to reach agreement among all the parties concerned. Multilateral negotiation has been used to establish new organizations (the United Nations, NATO, the European Economic Community, to mention a few prominent ones); negotiate arms control and other agreements for the reduction of international tensions (e. g., the Nuclear Non-Proliferation treaty, the 1975 Helsinki agreements of the Conference on Security and

Saadia Touval, Professor of Political Science at Tel Aviv University, is Visiting Professor, Department of Political Science, Tufts University, and Associate of the Center for International Affairs, Harvard University, 1737 Cambridge St., Cambridge, Mass. 02138. He would like to thank the Center for International Affairs for its generous support during the preparation of this article.

Cooperation in Europe); settle bitter conflicts (e. g., the 1954 Geneva accords to end the Indochina war, the 1979 Rhodesia/Zimbabwe settlement); and regulate economic relations among states (e. g., the various trade liberalization agreements, or concerted action for the adjustment of currency exchange rates). The trend toward seeking unanimous agreement is apparent even in international organizations that are authorized by their charters to decide issues by vote.[2]

Phases of Multilateral Negotiation: An Overview
All negotiations move through a series of stages or phases, and multilateral negotiations are no exception.[3] In examining each of these phases, I shall compare multilateral negotiation with its bilateral counterpart.

Pre-negotiation
This phase is characterized by informal contact among the parties. Several important aspects of the negotiation are typically addressed during this preliminary stage: A list of participants is agreed upon; initial coalitions emerge; role differentiation takes place among the participants; and substantive and procedural issues are addressed as the parties learn more about the problems, develop an agenda, and search for a formula or general framework within which an agreement can be reached.

1. *Participants.* In bilateral negotiation, by definition, the question of who should participate does not arise at all. In multilateral arrangements, this is a crucial — and at times highly controversial — question (except, of course, in negotiations within international organizations where participation is coterminous with membership). Without agreement on the list of participants, negotiations cannot take place.

Several considerations are likely to affect the actors' attitudes on the question of participation. First, who must be included if agreement is to be reached? The participation of some actors is necessary because their contribution is required for resolving the issue in question. Others must be invited simply because they may act as spoilers if excluded. Second, there are considerations of competitive advantage. All participants hope that the presence of certain other parties will improve their chances of attaining their own goals. By the same token, each expects that the inclusion of certain others stands to make the attainment of those goals more difficult. Third, there are considerations of status. When participation is believed to enhance a party's status, some states may seek to exclude others, while those who would be excluded, in turn, covet an invitation.

The discussions about who should participate in the 1954 Geneva Conference on Indochina brought all these considerations into play. The United States did not recognize the People's Republic of China at the time, yet realized that China's participation was necessary if any effective agreement was to be reached. The participation of the Vietminh, the Communist-backed movement that was fighting France, was also essential, although the movement was not recognized by any of the Western allies.

The newly independent states of Vietnam, Laos and Cambodia, which were just emerging from French rule, presented a different problem. Because these states were expected to take a strong anti-Communist stand, and because participation would strengthen their domestic and international legitimacy, their inclusion was favored by the United States. France, however, was hesitant, since to include them as full and equal participants would necessitate granting the same standing to the Vietminh. Furthermore, France may have been reluctant to accord the three states such status at that moment because the terms of their newly acquired independence were still being negotiated. The possibility that their strong anti-Communist stand might inhibit France's freedom of action, especially if French interests required granting concessions to the Communist side, appears to have been an additional reason for French hesitation. Proposals for the participation of additional Asian states were evaluated in light of the attitudes that each would likely adopt at the conference. In the end, it was agreed (in consultations among the Western allies and with the Communist side) that participation would be limited to nine parties: France, Britain, the United States, Vietnam, Cambodia, Laos, the Soviet Union, China, and the Democratic Republic of Vietnam (Vietminh).[4]

2. *Coalitions*. Usually coalitions antedate negotiations, especially in East-West and North-South discussions. When this is not the case, coalitions are often formed during the pre-negotiation phase. Needless to say, there are no coalitions in bilateral negotiations.

Why do coalitions form if multilateral decisions are not made by voting? States probably believe that being a member of a coalition improves their bargaining power. A coalition is better able to affect the interests of other actors than a state acting alone. The implicit threat to others that if they do not accept the terms proposed, their relationship with all members of the coalition will suffer is more impressive than a similar threat made by a single state. Threats to break off negotiations without reaching an agreement may also be more effective, for states will be perceived by their opponents as being better able to withstand the consequences of no agreement if they are members of a coalition.

3. *Role Differentiation*. Social psychologists have amply demonstrated that whenever a group of people proceed to work on a set of group tasks, members tend to differentiate themselves in various roles, serving a variety of functions. Such role differentiation also tends to take place within a group of states. Some states may assume leadership roles, persuading participants to take a common stand on an issue and to join a coalition. Leaders may also play a more active role than other members of the coalition in the negotiating process proper: shaping proposals, urging members of their coalition to assume certain positions, and seeking to influence members of other coalitions. Leaders often have greater resources at their disposal than other members of the coalition and may use them in their persuasive efforts.

An actor who takes on the role of mediator may plead with participants to change their positions. In contrast to leaders, who are advocates and encourage participants to rally to a cause, mediators search for a middle ground and seek compromise between conflicting points of view. Although leaders may sometimes act as mediators, there are important differences between the two roles. They differ both in style (compromise vs. rallying to a cause), and in the methods and resources used in the course of persuasion; leaders have greater recourse to sticks and carrots than mediators. While leadership is usually determined by the power and status of the actor, both inside and outside the negotiation, and is a relatively permanent role performed by few states, mediation can be assumed by almost any participant, and can be temporary — actors may move in and out of a mediator's role as the negotiation evolves.

Usually, some states will be more active in the negotiations than others. Such states likely have a greater stake in the issues being discussed; thus, their active cooperation may be more crucial for the implementation of any agreement reached than that of the other participants. Such activist states may sometimes act as representatives of a group even without being regarded as leaders.

Finally, chairing meetings constitutes a role in its own right. While this is primarily a formal-procedural role, it may also overlap with the roles of leader and mediator; for instance, the chair will usually perform some mediatory functions, leaders may serve as chairs, and they may sometimes perform all three functions simultaneously (Midgaard and Underdal, 1977, p. 335-336).

4. *Learning, Formula, Procedures, and Agenda.* In both bilateral and multilateral negotiation, much of the learning about issues takes place through informal discussion. In multilateral arrangements, because of the number of parties and issues, this learning process may be prolonged — as the parties seek to familiarize themselves with the positions of each participant on each of those issues. When issues are highly technical, such as in the Law of the Sea negotiation, learning through preliminary contacts may take years (Friedheim, 1987, p. 90).

Preparatory discussions among the parties often lead to an understanding on a formula or framework within which a detailed and formal agreement will be sought (Zartman, 1978, p. 67-86). Finally, the participants must agree on an agenda and on the rules of procedure; without such agreement the formal negotiation cannot open.

In both bilateral and multilateral negotiation, these pre-negotiation steps all have an important effect on formal negotiations. There is a difference, however, in the process by which these understandings are reached. Not surprisingly, the process is far more complex in multilateral arrangements.

The Formal Negotiation Phase

The exchange of information and the negotiation proper over the detailed terms of an agreement takes place during this phase. The actors explore various alternative packages, and may reach some tentative, conditional understandings.

The processes that take place in the formal negotiation phase in multilateral negotiation resemble those at this same phase in bilateral talks. Since these have received much attention in the literature, I shall not discuss them here.

The Agreement Phase

It is here that the parties translate tentative understandings into legally phrased agreements. The parties — in both bilateral and multilateral arrangements — often have second thoughts about the terms that they have agreed upon. Furthermore, their concerns over the implementation of the agreement tend to increase. Such misgivings may prompt efforts to obtain new assurances about compliance and implementation. These last-minute problems may prolong the agreement phase, the end of which is sometimes facilitated by deadlines. Because of the sheer number of participants, such reservations and the introduction of any new proposals at this stage are both likely to delay the conclusion of a multilateral negotiation.

In addition, some participants in a multilateral negotiation may be tempted to choose this concluding moment to press for the adoption of proposals that thus far were unacceptable. By simply withholding consent until the last possible moment — when an agreement is ready for signature — an actor exercises considerable leverage. For example, at the 1975 Conference on Security and Cooperation in Europe, when Romania, Malta and Turkey withheld their consent to the text of the Final Act, they delayed closure of the conference until their respective proposals were accepted (Maresca, 1985, p. 184-5, 187, 193).

Impediments to Effectiveness

There are elements in both the structure and process of multilateral negotiation that make it more difficult and cumbersome than bilateral negotiation.

Structure. Clearly the sheer *number* of participants in multilateral negotiation is a major problem. Each participant has interests that require accommodation. The larger the number of participants, the greater the likelihood of conflicting interests and positions, and the more complex the interconnections among the parties. Small wonder, then, that the process of reshaping the participants' positions and rendering them mutually compatible will be cumbersome.

The workings of coalitions may also hinder agreement. Because it is often difficult for coalitions to agree on a common negotiating stance, any consensus that a coalition does reach may well leave little room for flexibility; any change in position would require a difficult renegotiation, and perhaps generate tensions and disagreements that the members of the coalition prefer to avoid. An example of this problem is the rigid stance assumed by UNCTAD and the Group of 77 in the negotiations on commodity trade. According to Rothstein (1987, p. 33) they "had become prisoners of the bargaining structure in which they operated, for unity was the primary value; compromise threatened unity. . . and thus the only choice was to 'hang tough'. . ."

Process. Several processes are strongly affected by the structural features of multilateral negotiation. Communication and information processing, despite the multilateral setting, often takes place through bilateral contact. In addition, there are meetings of groups of states. The sheer quantity of communication, increasing as it does with the number of participants, is difficult to manage. Each participant is likely to experience difficulty orchestrating the different signals that are to be sent — sometimes simultaneously — to different audiences, and interpreting the statements and signals made by the other participants. In addition, inconsistent or contradictory messages, as well as errors in interpretation, may cause friction, generate distrust, and hinder the successful conclusion of negotiations.

Another impediment is the tendency of participants to engage in oratory and grandstanding. Even when the public and the press are excluded from the meeting, the presence of a sizable number of representatives — along with their attendant staff — often tempts participants to posturing (Nye, 1986, p. 90). Such behavior, in turn, may lead to the development of extreme positions from which the parties feel disinclined to budge.

A further obstacle to agreement stems from the complexity of trading concessions in a multilateral forum. In bilateral negotiation, the norm of reciprocity facilitates the exchange of concessions. But, the reciprocal exchange of concessions often loses its meaning in multilateral negotiation because a concession offered to one participant may have a differential effect upon the rest, and may even be considered by some as detrimental to their interests.[5] Another problem, described by Gilbert Winham (1977, p. 359), with reference to the Kennedy Round of trade negotiations, involves losing track of information: Because of the complexity of the issues, negotiators sometimes are unaware of a concession they may have received. Thus, granting concessions may not lead to reciprocity, nor will it necessarily bring the parties any nearer to agreement.

Finally, there is the potential problem of time. Since multilateral negotiation involves so many moving parts, it is reasonable to expect it will require a great deal of time. The analysis of issues, communication and information processing, decision making, and development of plans for implementation and monitoring the behavior of the parties to the agreement, all take time. Snags in the agreement phase of the talks compound the problem and add to the time required to reach agreement.

Facilitating Factors

Despite the hindrances discussed in the previous section, the fact remains that multilateral negotiation often leads to agreement. The question then is, how are these impediments overcome?

Coalitions and Groups. The almost chaotic structure suggested by large numbers of participants is, in practice, somewhat simplified by the coalescence of states into groups. These may endure through the entire negotiation, or may be ad hoc arrangements that form over specific issues. In either case, coalitions can simplify the process.

For instance, participants in the United Nations Law of the Sea conference, which involved more than 150 states, reorganized for negotiating purposes into a much smaller number of groups. These groups sometimes overlapped, as states chose to identify with different groups on different issues. The principal groups that emerged were the West European, the East European, and the "Group of 77." The last-mentioned coalition split on occasion into the Latin American, African, and Asian groups. In addition, some states joined to form a group identified as "Landlocked and Geographically Disadvantaged." Negotiations at the Conference on Security and Cooperation in Europe, with 35 participants, were also simplified by the emergence of three major groups — East, West, and neutrals. Similar processes take place in most other multilateral negotiations.[6]

The effective negotiating structure that emerges as a result of the coalescence of groups may be reduced to very few negotiators. However, bargaining among a small number of groups is still much more complex than in bilateral negotiation. Even when the structure is reduced to merely two coalitions, the complexities of intra-group negotiations and the problems of maintaining group cohesion and preventing defections to rival coalitions result in a process that is significantly different from — and far more difficult than — bilateral negotiation. Nevertheless, the coalescence of participants into groups greatly reduces the cognitive complexity discussed in the previous section and renders communication and information processing more manageable.

Negotiation by Representatives. Negotiation between coalitions is often conducted through representatives. These may be the leaders of coalitions or states that particularly care about the issue in question. Among the examples of negotiation by leaders are the roles of the U. S. and the USSR in several of the disarmament negotiations conducted within U. N. committees. On several occasions, draft agreements were concluded in American-Soviet bilateral negotiations that were subsequently adopted by the disarmament committee. This kind of procedure brought about the conclusion of the treaty banning nuclear testing in outer space; the Non-Proliferation Treaty; the agreement prohibiting the emplacement of nuclear weapons on the seabed and the ocean floor; and the Convention on Biological Weapons. Additional examples are the roles of Saudi Arabia and Iran in negotiating OPEC's oil production quota agreement in August 1986. There are numerous other examples of the roles of representatives, who are not leaders, in the Law of the Sea, General Agreement on Tariffs and Trade (GATT), and Conference on Security and Cooperation in Europe (CSCE) negotiations. In the latter case, during 1974 and 1975, it was Britain that negotiated for NATO, while the United States deliberately assumed a low profile.[7]

Putnam and Bayne (1984, p. 31-32) describe an interesting example of a simplifying restructuring of the negotiation that led to the adoption of the currency exchange rates regime at the Rambouillet summit, in November 1975, by the leaders of Britain, France, Italy, Japan, West Germany, and the United States. The agreement was actually prenegotiated by France and the U.S., two states that had sharply disagreed over the issue in the past. The understanding between these two states served as the basis for the Rambouillet agreement among all the participants.

Flexible Participants. The differentiation among participants is not limited to the roles that they assume as leaders, mediators, representatives and chair. Another important distinction is between active and passive participants. The more active participants usually have important interests at stake, while the passive ones may have joined the negotiation for reasons of status, rather than because of a strong concern about the substantive issues. This differentiation also helps to simplify the negotiation process, as the more passive states usually adopt a flexible stance and tend to go along with arrangements developed by the more active participants.

Asymmetries of Interest and Priority. The different parties to a negotiation are likely to have different interests, priorities, and resources. In multilateral as in bilateral negotiation, these asymmetries facilitate the creation of package agreements. The increased number of parties in multilateral negotiation enlarges the potential for "circular barter" and for linkages to issues that are of concern to some participants, but not to all, as well as to issues that may be extraneous to the negotiation. Linkage sometimes provides an opportunity for side payments that compensate parties for concessions, thus increasing the possibility of constructing package agreements. A circular barter can take place when a bilateral exchange of concessions is not possible. But, if party A desires something from party B, and B can be compensated by a resource that is possessed by C, and C can benefit from some action of D, and D can be paid off by A — a circular barter is possible (Touval, 1982, p. 327).

An example of potential linkage took place at the Geneva negotiations on Indochina in 1954. One of the proposed arrangements mentioned at the time would have linked the cessation of Communist pressure on France in Vietnam to French abandonment of the proposed establishment of the European Defense Community (EDC), to which the Soviet Union was strongly opposed. Another proposal, attributed to France, would have linked Communist concessions in Vietnam to American recognition of the People's Republic of China and its admission to membership in the United Nations (Randle, 1969, p. 42, 130).

Nothing came of either idea (the EDC project was defeated in the French National Assembly for reasons unrelated to the Indochina negotiation). But the floating of such ideas illustrates how the possibility of satisfying the needs of the various parties through creative packaging and circular barters tends to increase with the number of participants and the concomitant asymmetry of their interests and priorities. This is not to say that it is easier to reach a multilateral agreement than a bilateral one. Rather, the argument is that the complexity and difficulty of multilateral negotiation is offset to some extent by opportunities that are inherent in multilateral structures and do not exist in bilateral ones.

Power Asymmetry. The more powerful parties in a negotiation may possess resources that can be used as "sticks" and "carrots" to influence other participants and bring about agreement. "Power asymmetry" may actually refer to resource asymmetry — with some parties possessing greater capabilities on some issues and in some domains. Such asymmetries, like those in interests and priorities, tend to create opportunities for exchange and linkage, and thus carry the potential for constructing package agreements. The opposite condition of power symmetry would eliminate the possibility of using "sticks" and "carrots" in this way. Moreover, equality of resources would certainly offer fewer possibilities for creative linkages that can facilitate multilateral agreement.

Stable versus Changing Structures. The preceding discussion has implied that stable structures — coalitions and powerful actors who can serve as leaders — tend to facilitate the conclusion of agreements. Yet such stability also has a drawback: It inhibits the bridging effect of the cross-cutting interests that are likely to exist when several parties are present. For example, although the United States, Britain and France on the one hand, and the Soviet Union on the other, almost always find themselves in opposing camps, the four joined in a group at the CSCE in 1974-75 to press for protection of their status as occupying powers in Berlin. On this issue, the four took a common stand, in opposition to the formulation preferred by most other participants. The cross-cutting associations and communication that result from such a distribution of interests may help overall communication within the system, may reduce antagonisms, and facilitate the construction of creative linkage and package agreements (Zartman, 1987, p. 295-296; Maresca, 1985, p. 82-84, 183).

Problem Solving. States usually approach negotiation with a mixture of competitive, zero-sum perceptions and problem-solving, positive-sum dispositions. A multilateral forum tends to induce some restraint in competitive attitudes, since the presence of parties with whom no serious conflict exists requires that their interests be taken into account. The desire to win the support and cooperation of those other parties tends to moderate attitudes, and to stimulate the search for solutions that accommodate the interests of as large a number of participants as possible.

Trust and Risk. The absence of trust often hinders agreement in bilateral negotiation. It would seem to make sense that if this absence is an obstacle when only one other party is involved, it should be an even greater impediment when there are many others. Paradoxically, it is not; in fact the issue of trust may be even less of an impediment in multilateral than in bilateral arrangements.

The problem of trust arises because of the risk that the other party may seek to exploit the trusting negotiator. There is also the risk that the other will violate any agreement that has been concluded. These same risks exist, of course, in multilateral negotiation, and may even be multiplied by the number of participants. Yet the impact of any single negotiator is less in a multilateral structure than in a bilateral one. As a result, the harm caused to trusting negotiators by the exploitative behavior of a single participant is likely to be smaller in a multilateral structure than a bilateral one.

The same argument can be applied to the risk of violation of an agreement. Because of the aura of legitimacy that usually accompanies multilateral agreements, and because a violator would have to contend with the displeasure of all the parties to the agreement, violations of multilateral agreements may be less likely to occur than violations of bilateral ones. The enhanced ability to manage the risk of negotiation in multilateral settings will therefore facilitate negotiations and counterbalance some of the impediments.

Mediation

There are many similarities between mediation of bilateral and multilateral conflicts, perhaps because, even in multilateral negotiation, mediation is often between two sides. The functions of mediators are therefore basically the same in the two settings: Mediators help the parties to communicate, explain to each the interests and constraints of the other, invent and propose ideas, help the parties to reduce the risks of negotiation and agreement, and use incentives and pressures to persuade them to agree.[8]

Despite this functional similarity, there are several distinctive features of mediation in multilateral settings. Mediators in bilateral negotiation are typically external to the conflict, and often must use leverage to gain acceptance. Their intervention transforms the bargaining structure from a dyad to a triad. In multilateral settings, on the other hand, mediators are usually part of the negotiation; their intervention neither alters the structure of the situation, nor requires a difficult decision about acceptance. Furthermore, there are likely to be several mediators in multilateral negotiation, performing their role from several different vantage points. The chair of a negotiation inevitably combines mediation with the purely formal and technical functions of chairmanship. So do representatives and rapporteurs. Since all of them are also participants in the negotiations, their involvement is less likely to raise the usual questions of acceptability.

Another distinction concerns the leverage that the mediator exercises in trying to persuade parties to change their positions. The degree of leverage of the successful mediator seems to be greater in negotiations concerning political-security issues — when the conflict is between two cohesive and antagonistic coalitions, and the context is highly competitive — than in disputes over political-economic issues, where coalitions are not strongly cohesive and the parties approach the issues more in a problem-solving than competitive spirit.

Mediator leverage derives from three main sources: the parties' needs; the mediator's ability to manipulate the parties and their perceptions of need; and mediator ability to exert pressure, and offer inducements and side-payments in order to persuade the parties to agree (Zartman and Touval, 1985).

A mediator's use of leverage in multilateral negotiation over political-security issues resembles mediation in the same context in bilateral conflicts. An interesting example is Britain's mediation at the 1954 Geneva conference on Indochina. Britain was motivated to mediate by its concern that the French setbacks in the war might lead to American intervention, thereby drawing in Britain and leading to a major war, the outcome of which was highly uncertain. Although Britain was not an impartial third party, its mediation was readily accepted by the Communist side, which preferred to see Britain as a mediator at the conference rather than as an enemy on the battlefield. Britain's influence derived from its reluctance to support American military intervention in Indochina. The source of Britain's leverage is indicated in a reported conversation between Anthony Eden, the British Foreign Secretary, and Chou En-lai, his Chinese counterpart. In a private conversation on May 20, 1954,[9] Eden reportedly warned Chou that the "situation was dangerous and might lead to serious and unpredictable results." Chou replied that he "was counting on Britain to prevent this happening." In response, Eden "warned him not to do so," because in the event of a showdown "Britain would stand with the United States." Although Britain did not use its leverage very skillfully, it did play an important role in bringing about an agreed settlement to the war.

A mediator is likely to have far less sway in negotiations over political-economic issues, when alignments are not so sharply drawn, and when the parties approach the negotiation more in a problem-solving spirit. Two sources of mediator influence — the manipulation of the parties and the ability to punish and reward — appear less effective here than in negotiation over security issues. In the latter case, the mediator's position may have a significant effect on the balance of power. Furthermore, within such a context, the mediator may be the only source of possible side payments and "creative linkages." But in negotiation over economic issues, the effect of the mediator defecting from one coalition and joining a rival coalition is not likely to be as fateful. Side payments may be available from several other participants, thus diminishing the relative weight of the mediator's contribution. If the mediator is not the leader of a coalition, then the mediator's resources, either for pressure or inducement, are less significant than those of coalition leaders who, by definition, are endowed with considerable resources. The mediator is also not the only source for possible linkages. All participants in the negotiations are potential providers of linkage. All of the mediator's contributions can be diluted, even neutralized, by other participants. For all these reasons, mediators are likely to be less influential in this context.

Although a single mediator may not be as influential in negotiations over economic issues, the cumulative contribution of mediatory functions — often performed sequentially by several actors — can still be crucial in the successful conclusion of an agreement.

The work of mediators (as well as chairs) in multilateral negotiation can be greatly facilitated by the use of the "single negotiating text" technique. This technique is sometimes used in bilateral talks as well, but in multilateral negotiations, it is almost essential. As described by Fisher and Ury (1981) and by Friedheim (1987), the single negotiating text procedure allows a mediator to move back and forth between the principals, extracting from each a set of suggested requirements for inclusion in the single draft proposal that results. The mediator requests that each side criticize the single draft proposal developed, indicating what needs to be changed in order to produce an acceptable text. This technique assumes the acceptance by the parties of a basic framework for agreement, and allows for marginal changes. By moving from one party to the next and eliciting suggestions for improving the emerging draft agreement, it is possible for the mediator to construct a document that all sides can perhaps live with. This technique has been used with some success in a number of negotiations, most notably the Law of the Sea between 1975 and 1980, and the Camp David mediation between Egypt and Israel in 1978.[10]

Building Consensus

The principal challenge of multilateral negotiation is inherent in the requirement that agreements be unanimous. Examination of the nature of agreements, the meaning of unanimity, and the way in which such agreements are reached, all help to explain the ability of many multilateral gatherings to arrive at a successful conclusion.

Many agreements are reached by *consensus*. The term has come to mean that none of the participants opposes the agreement, although the degree of support for the agreement among them may vary. Decisions by consensus are quite common not only in ad hoc multilateral gatherings, but also in many negotiations conducted within the framework of those international organizations whose charters provide for decisions to be reached by voting.[11] The key to the adoption of consensus decisions in multilateral negotiation is the differentiation of interests and motives among the participants. As stated earlier, the parties rarely hold equally strong views on the issues discussed, and some may participate for reasons of status (or mere membership in the case of international organizations) rather than a substantive interest in the issue on the agenda. The building of consensus often begins from a small core of those who are most interested in a given issue, and are able to reach agreement on it, then proceeds to winning the adherence of the other participants who are less concerned with that issue.

Still, arrival at consensus requires that those opposed to the terms of an agreement drop their objections. This is accomplished in part by bilateral bargaining, mediation, and the construction of package agreements, and through compensation and side payments.

Several additional techniques facilitate consensus. A common practice involves narrowing the agreement to cover only those issues on which consensus is possible, while leaving other issues unresolved. Given the impediments to multilateral negotiation, however, reaching even partial agreement is usually a difficult process.

Another technique entails resorting deliberately to ambiguous and imprecise wording of agreements. By creating the possibility of different interpretations, it is often possible to win the assent of participants who would otherwise oppose the agreement. While this also holds true for bilateral agreements, it seems more prevalent in multilateral negotiation — where the consent of many parties is required. Prominent examples of ambiguous multilateral documents are the U. N. Security Council Resolution 242 on the Arab-Israeli conflict, and the Final Act of the 1975 Conference on Security and Cooperation in Europe.

The disadvantages of ambiguity are obvious. Ambiguity creates, in the words of Robert Rothstein (1987, p. 30), "counterfeit agreements." It produces the illusion of agreement where little agreement actually exists, and increases the risk of a bitter dispute developing over conflicting interpretations of the document. Yet ambiguity also confers important benefits; it is often better to arrive at an imprecise agreement (and thus establish a modicum of cooperation) than to use the continuing gap between existing positions to justify refraining from any cooperation. The balance of advantages and disadvantages will, of course, depend on the particular circumstances of the case. Important to note here, however, is simply that the technique of ambiguity greatly facilitates the conclusion of multilateral agreements.

Occasionally, the conclusion of agreements is facilitated because of the aversion that many states have to isolation. The prospect of finding oneself alone on an issue over which agreement exists among a large group of states can sometimes be uncomfortable for governments. To avoid isolation, states may withdraw their objections, enabling a consensus or unanimous decision to be adopted. According to Putnam and Bayne (1984, p. 49), this aversion to isolation was a significant factor facilitating agreement at the Seven Power Summit conferences.

One should not credit the aversion to isolation with too great a role in facilitating agreements. After all, it is from the ability to veto agreements that the participants derive their bargaining power in multilateral negotiations. This implies the necessity to stand alone sometimes, and even risk exclusion from the negotiating group. An extreme example of such behavior is provided by Malta's position at the CSCE gatherings, where even the threat of exclusion failed to deter it from pressing its position, and winning points in the compromise agreements to which Malta finally consented (see Maresca, 1985, p. 185-187; Sizoo and Jurrjens, 1984, p. 58-59 and 242-244).

The legal device of allowing participants to register reservations is another method that helps in the adoption of consensus decisions. To be sure, serious reservations among actors who are essential to the implementation of an accord can nullify an agreement; the views of such critical actors must therefore be accommodated. But the opposition of states whose cooperation is of lesser consequence can be addressed merely by allowing them to place their reservations on the record.

An interesting case, going beyond mere registration of reservation and falling short of a veto, was the American position with respect to the Final Declaration of the Geneva conference on Indochina in 1954. The United States refused to join in the Declaration as worded; instead, it made a formal statement "taking note" of the agreements concluded, declaring that the U. S. would view a violation of those agreements "with grave concern," and restating the American position on the reunification of Vietnam through free elections. This device enabled the Conference to end in agreement, while at the same time allowing the United States to demonstrate its dissociation from the outcome.[12]

Finally, the assent of wavering states is sometimes won by the aura of legitimacy that accompanies the pronouncements and actions of large groups of states. When a view is endorsed by many, it acquires a certain legitimacy that can be used by politicians to persuade domestic opponents of the agreement about the merits of joining in a consensus.

Conclusion

The complexity of multilateral negotiation is widely recognized. In the words of K. J. Holsti (1982, p. 160), "the problem with this kind of diplomacy. . . is that it is often a very messy affair, almost defying generalization." Part of the reason generalization appears difficult is that key concepts that are usually helpful in the analysis of bilateral negotiation — bargaining, information processing, decision making — are inadequate for describing and explaining multilateral negotiation. The employment of additional concepts is called for: coalition formation, differentiation of interests, and differentiation of roles. Furthermore, an understanding of multilateral negotiation requires a comprehensive systemic perspective, recognizing the variety of structures, sub-structures, and processes that are present. Thus, in addition to bilateral bargaining, one finds mediation within triangular structures, coalition formation, and the enactment of different roles by different actors.

The metaphor of the market perhaps comes closest to describing the apparent chaos of multilateral negotiation: it involves many traders exchanging a variety of goods. Bargaining takes place in this market. But it takes place among different kinds of actors (states as well as coalitions); in different contexts (within coalitions, as well as between them; among allies, as well as among rivals); and within a complex system, with many sensitive interrelationships among actors and issues.

Multilateral negotiation has become an important instrument for the management of international problems. It is therefore incumbent upon social scientists and practitioners alike to understand how it works. I hope that the ideas presented here will help advance this understanding, and suggest directions for further research.

NOTES

The author is grateful to Jeffrey Rubin for his contributions to an early draft of this article.

1. Among the analytic studies of multilateral negotiation, see Holsti (1982), Midgaard and Underdal (1977), Raiffa (1982), Sebenius (1984), Winham (1977 and 1987) and Zartman (1987).

2. According to a recent study, more than half of the U.N. General Assembly resolutions adopted since 1975 were adopted without a vote. In 1950, those adopted by vote constituted only 23.1 percent. See Marin-Bosch (1987, p.709).

3. For general models of negotiation phases, see Gulliver (1979) and Zartman and Berman (1982). For a discussion of phases in the Law of the Sea negotiations, see Friedheim (1987).

4. These various considerations are reflected in the diplomatic correspondence of the period. See *Foreign Relations of the United States*, 1952-1954, vol. XVI: *The Geneva Conference* (Washington, D.C.: U.S. Government Printing Office, 1981) passim, and especially pp.16-17, 415-417, 428-432, 481-483, 514-519, 591-592.

5. This is not to minimize the importance of reciprocal obligations, often formally institutionalized in international organizations. Robert Keohane's (1986, p. 4) distinction between specific and diffuse reciprocity is of relevance in this connection.

6. On the simplification of structures, see Midgaard and Underdal (1977, p. 343). On the Law of the Sea negotiations see Sebenius (1984); Friedheim (1987, 73-114); and Miles (1977, p.159-234). On the Conference on Security and Cooperation in Europe (CSCE), see Maresca (1985) and Sizoo and Jurrjens (1984).

7. On the disarmament negotiations see Thorsson (1985); on the OPEC example, see *New York Times*, August 7, 1986, p. D-3; on the Law of the Sea, see Sebenius (1984, p. 38); on GATT, see Patterson (1986, p. 186); on CSCE, see Maresca (1985, p. 89 and 102).

8. There is a vast literature on international mediation. For an elaboration of the mediator's functions listed here, see Rubin (1981, p. 3-43) and Zartman and Touval (1985).

9. *Foreign Relations of the United States*, 1952-1954, vol. XVI: *The Geneva Conference* (Washington, D.C.: U.S. Government Printing Office, 1981), p. 864.

10. In his analysis of the single negotiating text in the Law of the Sea negotiations, Friedheim (1987, p. 92-101) draws an interesting distinction between the tactics used by those who willingly accept the basic framework and those who accept it unwillingly. On the use of the technique in the Egyptian-Israeli negotiation, see Quandt (1986, p. 225-253).

11. For a review of the evolution of decision rules in international organizations, see Claude (1971, p. 118-140); see also Henrikson (1986, p. 241-243). On decisions by consensus in GATT, see Patterson (1986, p. 184). In the Law of the Sea Conference, see Koh (1986, p. 41-42) and Buzan (1981). On consensus decisions at the Conference on Security and Cooperation in Europe, see Sizoo and Jurrjens (1984). On decisions in the Commonwealth, see Smith (1985, p. 62-63).

12. Even stronger objections were expressed by the representative of the State of Vietnam (South Vietnam). For a description of the final session, and the texts of the various reservations, see Randle (1969, p. 341-346). For an account of the Rules of Procedure of the CSCE with respect to the registering of reservations, see Sizoo and Jurrjens (1984, p. 60-63).

REFERENCES

Buzan, B. (1981) "Negotiating by Consensus: Developments in technique at the United Nations Conference on the Law of the Sea." *American Journal of International Law* 75 (2): 324-348.

Claude, I. L. Jr. (1971). *Swords Into Plowshares*. 4th ed. New York: Random House.

Fisher, R. and **Ury, W. L.** (1981). *Getting to YES*. Boston: Houghton Mifflin.

Friedheim, R. L. (1987). "The third United Nations conference on the Law of the Sea: North-South bargaining on ocean issues." In *Positive sum*, ed. I. W. Zartman. New Brunswick, N.J.: Transaction Books.

Gulliver, P. H. (1979). *Disputes and negotiations*. New York: Academic Press.

Henrikson, A. K. (1986). "The global foundations for a diplomacy of consensus." In *Negotiating world order*, ed. Alan K. Henrikson. Wilmington, Del.: Scholarly Resources, Inc.

Holsti, K. J. (1982). "Bargaining theory and diplomatic reality: The CSCE negotiations." *Review of International Studies* 8 (3): 159-170.

Keohane, R. O. (1986). "Reciprocity in international relations." *International Organization* 40 (1): 1-27.

Koh, T. T. B. (1986). "Negotiating a new world order for the sea." In *Negotiating world order*, ed. Alan K. Henrikson. Wilmington, Del.: Scholarly Resources, Inc.

Maresca, J. J. (1985). *To Helsinki: The Conference on Security and Cooperation in Europe 1973-1975*. Durham N.C.: Duke University Press.

Marin-Bosch, M. (1987). "How nations vote in the General Assembly of the United Nations." *International Organization* 41 (2): 705-724.

Midgaard, K. and Underdal, A. (1977). "Multiparty conferences." In *Negotiation: Social-psychological perspectives*, ed. D. Druckman. Beverly Hills, Calif.: Sage.

Miles, E. (1977). "The structure and effects of the decision process in the Seabed Committee at the Third United Nations Conference on The Law of the Sea." *International Organization* 31 (2): 159-234.

Nye, J. S., Jr. (1986). "The diplomacy of nuclear proliferation." In *Negotiating world order*, ed. Alan K. Henrikson. Wilmington, Del.: Scholarly Resources, Inc.

Patterson, G. (1986). "The GATT and the negotiation of international trade rules." In *Negotiating world order*, ed. Alan K. Henrikson. Wilmington, Del.: Scholarly Resources, Inc.

Putnam, R. D. and Bayne, N. (1984). *Hanging together: the seven-power summits*. Cambridge, Mass.: Harvard University Press.

Quandt, W. B. (1986). *Camp David*. Washington, D.C.: The Brookings Institution.

Raiffa, H. (1982). *The art and science of negotiation*. Cambridge, Mass.: Harvard University Press.

Randle, R. F. (1969). *Geneva 1954*. Princeton: Princeton University Press.

Rothstein, R. L. (1987). "Commodity bargaining: The political economy of regime creation." In *Positive sum*, ed. I. W. Zartman. New Brunswick, N.J.: Transaction Books.

Rubin, J. Z., ed. (1981). *Dynamics of third party intervention*. New York: Praeger.

Sebenius, J. K. (1984). *Negotiating the Law of the Sea*. Cambridge, Mass.: Harvard University Press.

Sizoo, J. and Jurrjens, R. T. (1984). *CSCE decision-making: The Madrid experience*. The Hague: Martinus Nijhoff.

Smith, A. (1985). "Commonwealth cross sections: Prenegotiation to minimize conflict and to develop cooperation." In *Multilateral negotiation and mediation*, ed. Arthur S. Lall. New York: Pergamon Press.

Thorsson, I. (1985). "Multilateral forums." In *Multilateral negotiation and mediation*, ed. Arthur S. Lall. New York: Pergamon Press.

Touval, S. (1982). *The peace brokers: Mediators in the Arab-Israeli conflict, 1948-1979*. Princeton: Princeton University Press.

Winham, G. R. (1977). "Complexity in international negotiation." In *Negotiation: Social-psychological perspectives*, ed. D. Druckman. Beverly Hills, Calif.: Sage.

———. (1987). *International trade and the Tokyo Round negotiation*. Princeton: Princeton University Press.

Zartman, I. W. (1978). "Negotiation as a joint decision-making process." In *The negotiation process*, ed. I. W. Zartman. Beverly Hills, Calif.: Sage.

———. (1987). "Conclusion." in *Positive sum*, ed. I. W. Zartman. New Brunswick, N.J.: Transaction Books.

———. and Berman, M. R. (1982). *The practical negotiator*. New Haven: Yale University Press.

———. and Touval, S. (1985). "International mediation: Conflict resolution and power politics." *Journal of Social Issues* 41 (2): 27-45.

Multilateral Negotiation and the Future of American Labor

Charles Heckscher

The fact that the American labor movement is in crisis can no longer be denied. For thirty years, as organized labor's share of the work force has dropped steadily, those in and around unions have tended to downplay the problem. Noting that the history of the movement has always been one of ups and downs, they have predicted a rebound at any moment. But it has not come: Through recession and recovery, through Democratic and Republican administrations, the decline has continued unrelenting. During the last few years, as the Reagan administration has legitimized open anti-union efforts, it has even accelerated. Today the union share of the private sector work force stands at less than 16%, well below half its peak in 1954, and it seems likely to dwindle still further.

The questions I will take up in this article, though extremely briefly, are: What does this decline mean? And, what does it imply for future policies? Although the dismantling of organized labor has generated remarkably little public debate, it is not, from a historical perspective, a trivial event. For more than a century, unions have been the primary means of employee representation and a central pillar of the "New Deal" political coalition. The needs which generated them, I will argue, may have changed in form, but they have not disappeared. If that is true, then what we are seeing is not an end but a transition — a period in which unions are groping for a new form to meet the current reality.

Many employers would say the matter is more simple than this: There is, in their view, simply no more need for union representation. They will generally concede that fifty years ago the labor movement responded to legitimate grievances. Indeed, the history of corporate abuse — of child labor, of violent suppression of protest, of brutal supervision, of callous disregard for the life and health of workers — is a dark blot on our societal record. But these obvious abuses, though they have by no means disappeared, are certainly far less prevalent than they used to be. Relatively few are now driven to unions by intolerable conditions at work. Even labor leaders will often agree that in this sense their function has weakened: "We have done our job too well," they say. "Workers today don't remember the struggles we went through to make the gains we have."

Charles Heckscher, a sociologist by training, is chairman of the Department of Labor Studies at Rutgers University, New Brunswick, N.J. His publications include *The New Unionism: Employee Involvement in the Changing Corporation* (New York: Basic Books, 1988).

But, if the particular issues that gave birth to the labor movement have grown less intense, it does not follow that employee representation is no longer needed. On the contrary, even the most superficial study of workplaces uncovers significant discontent which has no channels of expression. The Opinion Research Corporation, which has surveyed attitudes in major corporations for three decades, traces a deep and pervasive slide over that period in employee perceptions of their companies. The majority has grown increasingly critical of decision-making processes, seeing them as hierarchical and controlling, and sharply questions the fairness of company policies and rules. Two figures should be enough to underline the problem:

- Among managers, the percentage who rate their companies good in terms of fairness has dropped from 80% in the 1950s to barely 40% in the early 1980s.

- Among clerical workers, over the same span, the drop has been from 70% to 20%.[1]

These are enormous shifts. They have not produced explosions or mass movements; yet their effects have nevertheless been felt profoundly in the economy. Daniel Yankelovich, who has also extensively surveyed attitudes at work, summarizes his evidence in this way:

> . . .Americans freely admit that they are holding back effort from their jobs — they are giving less than they are capable of giving to their jobs; precisely when, from a competitive point of view, there is the greatest need for American job holders to give higher levels of commitment and effort (quote in private company report).

The issues that generate this unease are generally not the classic stuff of collective bargaining. Certainly wage levels are important, as they have always been, but other concerns have also crowded onto center stage. The thematic complaints of employees today focus at several different levels. On the one hand are rather specific issues of "quality of work life" — job pressure, over-supervision, and lack of autonomy. These have given rise to the widespread movement for "employee involvement" which has touched most American corporations in one way or another during the past decade.

At the other end of the spectrum, there is growing concern among employees about the long-range impacts of the highest levels of management decision-making. The new buzzword in corporate suites is strategic planning, which enables companies to respond flexibly to change. A less beneficent result, however, is that it also creates new levels of uncertainty for those affected by corporate policies. While the norm used to be, by and large, for companies to stick with a stable location and product mix, these basic elements are becoming open to continuous questioning in the fast-moving game of competitive positioning. Employees and communities are just becoming aware that the decisions made by planners today will affect careers, industries, and regions for years to come. Unions are finding that strategic shifts — such as the automobile industry's experiments with "world production," to take one dramatic example — can quickly destroy them. Among the responses are efforts at legislated limits on plant closings and, in a few troubled industries such as airlines, representation of workers on company boards of directors.[2]

But these initial responses have been quite inadequate. Employee involvement efforts have had great success at a few — very few — companies; but for the most part they are bogged down in resistance. Employee attempts to gain access to the mysteries of corporate planning have run into long-standing barriers, legal and cultural, that guard the prerogatives of property. Most important, the labor movement has been confused and ineffective. The vast majority of American unions, for instance, have sat on the fence regarding employee involvement programs. They can't really oppose them, since participation is obviously a good thing; but they fear the encroachment on their representative functions. Similarly, most unions have resisted involvement in strategic planning, such as seats on corporate boards, because they do not want to give up their independence. Thus they have lost the position of leadership on many of the most important concerns of employees today.

In brief, the decline of the labor movement does not mean that workers' concerns are fully represented; it means that the existing system of representation is not filling the bill. For our current labor relations order is a strangely limited one. It is limited in the people it covers: generally only blue-collar workers or those who exercise no autonomy and independence at work. It is limited in the issues with which it deals: the legal phrase is "wages and working conditions," which has been interpreted to exclude most long-range planning. And, it is limited in its ways of resolving collective disputes: there are too few effective alternatives to the strike. These restrictions come in part from the law, and in part from long tradition and habit. They increasingly confine the labor movement to a corner, away from many of the significant concerns of employees and the public.

The Two-Party Assumption

One way of describing the limitations of the current system is to say that it assumes that all disputes must involve just two parties. During the 1930s, when the order was codified in the Wagner Act (NLRA), that assumption simply mirrored experience: The growth of large corporations had spawned, in reaction, equally massive movements of industrial workers, culminating in the violent pitched battles of 1933-34. Over time, however, the inevitability of a bilateral structure has become less obvious. Increasingly, the law has needed to *force* issues into the mold of adversarial confrontations.

Until World War II, for instance, there was little dispute about who should be in unions. The line between "workers" and "managers" was so evident that it was an obvious basis for organization. It was only when the war produced a small boom in organization among supervisors that legislators felt the need to draw the line more carefully, excluding them from coverage. But by the 1970s, "management" had become such a varied and complex category that this no longer sufficed: It included large categories of employees, such as technicians and data processors, who felt themselves a part neither of management nor of workers. Once again the law stepped in to draw a distinction which was no longer obvious. The Supreme Court, in a series of decisions, essentially ruled that only those with no managerial responsibilities of any sort qualify for protection under the Wagner Act.[3] The existence of "gray areas" between the traditional parties has, in effect, been denied.

The use of the strike is another example of this restrictive pattern. The struggles of the 1930s were, as I have said, pitched battles in which workers' power depended on massing together and totally shutting down their employers' operations. That is not, however, the only conceivable form of pressure; there are many more subtle forms of action, from publicity to partial stoppages, that are less damaging to the public and more suited to varied issues. As companies have become more dependent on "image" and more closely interdependent, they have in fact grown more vulnerable to such pressures. Yet over time most of these other options have been ruled out by the legal framework. The use of publicity has been curtailed by the ban on secondary boycotts in the Taft-Hartley law, and by the courts' tendency to see criticism of employers as violations of the duty of "loyalty."[4] Partial strikes, slowdowns, and other actions have been thrown in the same bin. Thus the law supports tradition in casting battles into an "all-or-nothing" format: The twin colossi, management and labor, must periodically threaten each other with destruction in order to exert effective pressure for their positions.

A key provision of the Wagner Act was the system of exclusive representation: It established in each bargaining unit a *single* representative, chosen by the majority and certified by the state. This provision was originally pushed by unions to reduce the risk of fragmentation; later, management also found that dealing with one party was easier than a multiplicity. The fact that there might be serious divisions among those represented was, once again, passed over. In recent years groupings of blacks, for example, have been told by the courts that they must go through their official union channels to obtain a voice. Such rulings mean minorities will necessarily have a hard time being heard. That is one reason why the growing self-consciousness of blacks and women at work has not been reflected in the composition of union leadership.

There is, of course, a strong logic to the two-party assumption. The labor movement arose, as it were, by the laws of action and reaction: The tremendous growth in corporate power around the turn of the century generated a balancing counter-movement. The entire thrust of the Wagner Act framework is to establish a *balance of power* — to support workers in forming organizations that can *match* the employer in battle. When the goal is cast in these terms, the need for a narrowing of parties and issues is obvious: a balance is a hard thing to sustain. Multiple parties and shifting issues would upset the carefully-established equilibrium.

Most of the limitations of the current system of representation, and the "crudeness" of which unions are so often accused, can be traced to the need to maintain the power balance. Unions *cannot* deal effectively with quality-of-worklife issues: These are so particular that they cannot form a base for mass pressure, and they tend to fragment the large-scale unity needed for strikes. Complex strategic issues, likewise, are too abstract to support collective action. In these domains management — with, generally speaking, the ability to command organizational resources far beyond those of any union — has all the advantages. A company can develop a strategic plan and command its employees to carry it out; but a union must wait for the effects to become evident before it can successfully mobilize a response. By that time it is usually too late.

The balance-of-power model also leads inevitably to other problems. One is *centralization*. It is up to the two parties to keep their troops in line so as to present an ordered front for the enemy. Public revelations of internal disagreements, or local attempts to allow for particular needs, bring weakness. No one really expects management to be democratic, of course; but unions, too, must be quite centralized in this framework. They are constantly caught in dilemmas between supporting the central contract, around which all energies can be focused, and allowing for local variations that might fragment the movement. It is one of the ironies of labor history that efforts to open, decentralize, and "democratize" labor unions have frequently been led by conservatives who were essentially seeking their destruction.

A second problem of the two-party structure is *exclusion*: Voices that cannot make themselves heard through the internal processes of labor and management are cut out of decision making altogether. This applies not only to internal groups of employees such as women and blacks, as mentioned before, but also to external groups — environmentalists, community activists, and so on — who are affected by corporate decisions. Their only recourse is to the regulatory power of the state.

Third, the system places a premium on *adversarial* relations: In a face-off, the easiest way to maintain discipline and unity is by focusing attention on the evils of the enemy. If there are many parties involved, it becomes harder to concentrate an attack, and therefore more necessary to build a positive position, but when there are only two, the political advantages of an adversarial stance are almost inescapable. Thus problem-solving approaches are dangerous for union leaders since they lead to fragmentation of the membership rather than unity. The United Auto Workers' attempt to find a "responsible" course to ensure the future health of their industry is a classic instance: Though cooperation with management may be good strategy in this instance, it has certainly generated more internal opposition to the union leadership than would ever have resulted from pure company-bashing.

Finally, a balance of power is relatively rigid. It tends to be established over time through a series of confrontations in which the principals explore each other's strengths and jockey for position. Once they become thoroughly familiar with each other's moves, they can settle into a reasonably stable and peaceful relationship. This has been the history, for instance, of labor-management relations in the auto and steel industries. But it also means that any significant change in the resources of either side is likely to open up the whole conflict again; peace depends on lack of change. That is not a condition which is often met today.

The essential structure I have described — the balancing of centralized organizations — is often referred to as "corporatism."[5] In outline, it is close to universal in the industrialized world. There are, naturally, some major variants: The Scandinavian labor movements, for example, have developed their political leverage to a degree inconceivable in this country, and so depend less on "whipping up the members" in adversarial actions. Nevertheless, the same pattern of centralized bilateral bargaining reappears throughout Europe.

The weaknesses of the structure have been mercilessly exposed by developments in the past twenty years. First came the growth of interest groups; rather suddenly, unions lost their position as leaders of the "liberal" coalition and became just one among a crowd of interests. Their failure to surrender their autonomy enough to establish effective alliances has had much to do with their decline. Later came the tidal wave of internal competition, smashing the foundations of bilateral relationships which had been stabilized within national borders; understandings resulting from long struggles between the parties were suddenly challenged by new entrants to the competitive scene. Finally, the accelerating pace of change, both in technology and markets, has produced an array of issues which simply cannot be encompassed in triennial contract negotiations. The whole picture has become too crowded and active to allow a balance to be sustained.

It is significant that, while unions are in worse shape in the United States than anywhere else, labor's sense of having lost the leadership position, of being pushed into the margins of social development, is common to other countries as well. And the reasons are basically the same. The established organizations are proving slow to adapt to the increased pace of change, and they have had difficulty in relating to newly vocal interests both inside and outside the firm. A leader of IG Metall, the powerful West German auto and steel union, offers a warning which could be applied almost anywhere:

> We trade unionists have got to be damned careful that we don't stand
> there as the people of yesterday, the backward ones, while the right
> wing and the greens (environmentalists) are considered the creators
> of the future. (*Spiegel* #12, 1985:96)

The problems, in other words, are deep. They go back well before the Reagan administration, and far beyond our borders. The pressure now is for a system of representation which will allow a far greater array of players, of tactics, and of issues than is possible within a bilateral balance of power.

Employee Rights

Readers of this journal, given how I have defined the problem, will already have a solution in mind: If two-party bargaining is too limited for the present situation, it should be possible to substitute broader forms of *multilateral* negotiation. Are these techniques, which have been applied successfully in other fields, applicable to the labor relations scene?

There are a few examples which indicate that they might be —instances in which unions play more of a coordinating role among multiple employee groups, rather than insisting strongly on their position as exclusive representative. There is a Shell chemical plant in Sarnia, Canada, for example — just down the river and across from Detroit — in which employees are organized into teams, any one of which can run the entire operation. It is possibly unique in that it has maintained this structure in a unionized setting, with extremely good operating results, for over eight years. The formal contract is extremely brief, covering only the most basic and objective issues of pay and benefits; all other matters are open to continuous negotiation. Decision making involves a complex mix of management, the union, the seven teams, and temporary task forces. A change in the shift schedule, to take one case, involved all these bodies in an extended back-and-forth discussion over many months; the outcome was an innovative schedule which meets both operational and employee needs better than the industry norms. In this system the union, as one of its officials puts it, is "just one party in a galaxy of parties." One might add that collective bargaining, in the traditional sense, is just one mechanism of dispute settlement in a galaxy of mechanisms.

Recently, a rather different example has emerged in our own country in the planning of the General Motors "Saturn Project." In response to the growing threat from imports, the company decided to produce a new car which could take on the foreign competition head-to-head. Management and the union agreed on the need for cooperation, which was not in itself surprising. The form of their cooperation, however, was unprecedented. Ninety-nine representatives of different segments of the company —union officials, operating managers, production workers, skilled crafts workers, and others — undertook a fundamental rethinking of the whole structure of management, including all aspects of workplace relationships. Their recommendations, reached by consensus after a year of work, were so dramatic that the company and the union are still trying to absorb the implications. They included autonomous operating teams, the virtual elimination of job classifications, very strong guarantees of job security, a pay system which is based on breadth of skill, and explicit contractual provisions for consensus decision making.[6] The formal bargaining which followed, according to the United Auto Workers' Don Ephlin, "just rounded off the edges" of this remarkable agreement.

There are a few other demonstrations of the possibility of multilateral negotiation in employee representation, but it must be admitted that they are rare. They occur almost exclusively under one infrequent condition: when the union is powerful enough that it can risk the fragmenting effects of these initiatives without fearing destruction. In other circumstances the risks are too great for sufficient trust to be maintained in the process.

The limitations on multilateral negotiations in labor relations are built into the foundations of the Wagner Act, but they are not inevitable. A system of negotiation depends on, and must be preceded by, some equalization of power. If one party holds all the cards, there is really no incentive to negotiate. The Wagner Act was designed to provide such a check on management by setting up countervailing organizations. That approach, I have argued, forces disputes into a bilateral structure. But there is also another way of limiting power, one with a long and honorable tradition, which is potentially less restrictive. I refer to systems of *rights*.

The development of rights enforceable against governments has, of course, been a central theme of our political history going back to the Magna Carta. Our Constitution contains guarantees, such as freedom of speech and religion, which are considered vital to our concept of a free citizenry. Yet these rights have traditionally been stopped at the door of the workplace by the common-law insistence on the private nature of corporations. Free speech, for example, is not applicable to employees; they can be fired or disciplined for criticizing management, or simply for espousing unpopular views. In fact, they can be fired for just about anything. Until very recently, courts held consistently that companies could discharge people even for refusing to carry out illegal acts. The law viewed firing simply as the dissolution of a private contract, which should not involve the state. Employees, on the other hand, tend to see it as a fearsome form of power. To avoid it they will, and often have, violated the law and their consciences so as not to displease their bosses.

The Wagner Act did pierce this "veil" (as the courts call it) protecting the private affairs of corporations, but it did so as minimally as possible. The only right provided to employees under the Act, in essence, is that of forming labor unions. Other forms of association remain largely unprotected.[7] And, as for things like free speech or due process, they have to be won by the union in the struggle of private parties, while the state remains a (theoretically) neutral onlooker. Thus respect for the corporate veil is a key reason for the limitations of the current framework of representation.

But the area of *employee* rights, as *distinct* from the rights of unions, has been the scene of some of the most important developments and struggles of the past twenty years. The erosion of public support for organized labor has not meant that management power has simply gone uncontested; rather, the focus of claims has shifted. If one asks, for example, what has forced the broadest change in personnel management since the 1950s, the answer would not involve contractual advances by unions. A prime candidate, instead, would be Title VII of the Civil Rights Act of 1964. By granting large categories of employees direct rights in relation to management, that Act essentially required corporations to establish standards of due process. For the first time,[8] claims of injustice could be taken directly to the courts. Many companies completely revamped their personnel policies to deal with the new requirements.

There have been many further developments since then. In terms of national legislation, we have seen further prohibitions of discrimination on the basis of age, and, in more limited areas, physical and mental handicap. At least 26 federal statutes have included provisions protecting employees who exercise particular rights: For example, employers are restricted from firing those who report health and safety violations. Many states, moreover, have gone much further. Various laws at this level prevent discrimination on the basis of sexual orientation, political activity, medical condition, and marital status. Some have begun to recognize an employee right to privacy by, for instance, forbidding the indiscriminate use of lie detectors by companies.

Equally important has been a major shift by the courts: The formerly impregnable wall protecting companies' common-law right to fire has rather suddenly been breached at several points. During the 1970s, several courts finally ruled that employees who refused to violate the law could receive protection through the legal system. Simple though that seems, this "public policy exception" to the employment-at-will doctrine shook the foundations of employment law. Since then, moreover, the exceptions have been considerably extended. A number of courts have read an "implied covenant of good faith and fair dealing" into employment contracts; in this view, any discharge "motivated by bad faith. . .or based on retaliation" is subject to judicial review. One recent decision went still further by applying the Constitutional guarantee of free speech as a "public policy" constraint on the corporation.[9]

These movements, both legislative and judicial, have so far been scattered and *ad hoc*, responding to particular abuses of interest-demands. The forces driving them have ebbed and flowed; no stable organization has yet pulled them together. The labor movement, concerned that such extensions of rights might encroach on its own functions, has generally been ambivalent about them, and so has failed to take a leadership role. Thus the current situation is very far from yielding a consistent system of voice based on employee rights. For the time being, different courts and states conflict with each other, and serious inconsistencies remain; the scene looks, from a slight distance, more like a lottery than a system of justice. The "corporate veil" has been so torn that it no longer clearly protects management authority, but it is still strong enough to impede the formation of an alternative system of employee representation.

But the forces driving the expansion of employee rights seem, once more, both deep and broad. Daniel Yankelovich has traced a profound shift in values — what he calls a "psychology of entitlement" — which has been gathering momentum in this country for more than two decades (Yankelovich et al., 1983, esp. pp. 113 ff.). This shift has already produced major eruptions such as the Civil Rights and women's movements; and, though its manifestations have been quieter in this conservative era, the pressure for workplace rights has shown no signs of slackening. In fact, some of the most important developments have occurred under the Reagan administration: *Fortune* recently noted with alarm that court decisions and state legislation since 1980 "impinge much more on day-to-day management than the myriad regulations heaped on corporations over the last six decades" (January 9, 1984, p. 92). Support comes not just from the narrow base of traditional unionism — the "blue-collar" production workers — but also from vast sectors of employees who are not covered by the traditional system: from white-collar workers, engineers and professionals, and the ranks of middle management.

This transformation, like others I have described, goes beyond our own borders. Indeed, many European nations have gone much further than we have in the extension of employee rights. The time period has been the same — a gradual increase in momentum since the 1960s — and the conflict with traditional unionism —the "blue-collar" production workers — but also from vast sectors of employees who are not covered by the traditional system: from white-collar workers, engineers and professionals, and the ranks of middle management.

This transformation, like others I have described, goes beyond our own borders. Indeed, many European nations have gone much further than we have in the extension of employee rights. The time period has been the same — a gradual increase in momentum since the 1960s — and the conflict with traditional systems of labor relations is also similar. One observer of the European scene writes:

> Although it takes somewhat different forms. . .the new industrial relations is fundamentally a single phenomenon: the fact that job rights
> . . .are being elevated to political and legal parity with property rights. (McIssac, 1977, pp. 22-23)

What these events offer, at least potentially, is a new route for making claims on employer power. The assertion of rights does not require the creation of large and powerful organizations to counterbalance management, nor does it depend on mobilizing large numbers of people for confrontation. It therefore breaks free —again, potentially — of the fundamental limitations of the "balance-of-power" model. Neither centralization nor exclusion are necessary for *this* kind of check on corporate power. A more open, pluralistic form of negotiation becomes at least conceivable.

Associational Unionism

Still, the rise of employee rights, even if we imagine a future in which they are far more highly developed than now, does not guarantee open negotiation. In fact, it seems far more likely to lead in quite a different direction: to the expansion of expert administrative regulation of industrial relations.

The reasons for this caution should be apparent. Employee rights could simply play right into the worst features of an already litigious society, flooding the courts with individual claims. There is already some evidence of such a trend. The reflex, built over at least the past fifty years, is simply to set up new agencies to handle the flood. For example, the State Bar of California has proposed legislation to codify limits on wrongful discharge; central to the proposal is an enormously expanded role for the State Mediation and Conciliation Service in establishing a system of arbitration to handle cases rapidly and impartially. In Europe, similarly, the new rights have generally been enforced by specialized systems of "labor courts."

These solutions, I believe, are wrong for the long run, because they substitute expert judgment for the negotitated agreement of the actual parties involved in disputes. They would simply exacerbate the already-severe crisis in the legitimacy of administrative rulemaking, which has much to do with the current disenchantment with the whole liberal agenda. Philip Harter (1983, p. 475) has described the weaknesses of expert regulation:

> (The) process does not allow actual participation, in the sense of sharing in the ultimate decision, that normally provides the legitimacy for political decisions. Nor is there a political consensus that would cause the body politic to have faith in the integrity of the agency decision. . .Thus there is a crisis of legitimation with regulation. . .This crisis is apparent in the frequency of judicial review, in the frequency of criticism in publications of virtually all the interest groups, and from a simple inquiry of any participant.

It is also worth recalling that the Wagner Act was originally offered as an alternative to direct government regulation of labor relations. President Franklin D. Roosevelt tended to favor the latter approach, as evidenced in his support of the Fair Labor Standards Act, but he was won over to the idea that disputes could best be handled by a healthy system of bargaining rather than by rulemaking. It has been one of the great successes of the Wagner Act that creative advances have been made by the parties themselves. It would be somewhat ironic if the inadequacies of collective bargaining were to produce a retreat to the ideas of a half-century ago.

The alternative, of course, would be to *expand* the system of collective bargaining to include the full variety of interests and issues which are central to employee relations today. But in order for that to happen, two major conditions would need to be met. The first of these would be the establishment of a coherent set of employee rights, as discussed above. The second would be a transformation of unions themselves to enable them to deal with the new conditions in the workplace.

The coordination of rights, if it is to avoid an individualistic free-for-all, requires some organization of people into groups. What is needed is a set of representative bodies which can organize and interpret claims to rights, transforming them from individual grievances into public claims and engaging in negotiations with employers over their implementation. These groups would be something like unions, but not exactly. Unlike industrial unions, their primary function would not be to weld their members into a powerful fighting force; the emphasis need not be on organizational strength. Instead a broadened system of negotiation needs groupings which can effectively wield *influence* — which can build consensus among their memberships and alliances with other interests.

Industrial unions in their present forms have shown themselves ill-suited to this task. Their response to employee participation efforts is symptomatic: local autonomy and decentralized decision-making are profoundly disturbing to them. They have also proved unable to build effective alliances with other types of groups which should be their friends. They are organizations that are built to maximize power, and they tend to lay stress on their autonomous resources.

Employee associations might be closer to the model I am imagining, since they are more nearly voluntary groupings of people with shared interests. Their weakness, however, is that they have historically avoided the function of negotiation and, in general, have shied away from any form of "pressure." The bodies needed for multilateral negotiation in industry would therefore need to *combine* qualities of unions and associations; they would be voluntary groupings geared to exerting pressure. Their primary weapons would be assertions of legal rights, publicity, and negotiation with employers. Such bodies might be called "associational unions."

In a certain sense, there has actually been a converging movement of associations and unions over the past two decades or so. In the public sector, many associations have nearly transformed themselves into industrial unions; yet they often retain important traces of their origins in a relatively decentralized structure and in a tactical emphasis on lobbying and publicity rather than strikes. Professional associations have rarely gone so far, but many of these have also moved, with great controversy, toward a more forceful role in asserting their members' interests with employers. From the other end, some unions have begun to look more like associations. This is most true of those which have gone furthest with joint efforts in worker participation. These unions — including the United Auto Workers, the Communications Workers, and, in Canada, the Energy and Chemical Workers — have begun to allow more variation from the central contract, to lay great stress on active member participation and education, and to reduce the traditional emphasis on enforcement of rules. Finally, certain interests which cut across the workplace have developed pressure groups that act in a quasi-union capacity for their members on the job: I am thinking especially of women's groups descended from 9 to 5.

Though none of these has yet perfected a new organizational form, they share certain qualities, including decentralization and a relatively high level of ongoing member involvement. It is also significant that they all tend to focus on the clarification of *principles* — in contrast to the usual union focus on elaboration of *rules*. Effective union-based worker participation efforts, for example, are grounded in agreement on a few clear principles that guide the local teams, allowing flexibility in implementation; in this setting, the union serves, in the words of leaders at Shell-Sarnia, as "the conscience of the company."

Likewise, professional associations and other interest groups tend to lay great stress on the development of consensus on values and ethical codes, which then become the basis for their pressure on the corporation. The parallels to other examples of multilateral negotiation, which often begin by clarifying agreement on principles, are striking. In these and other ways these varied organizations are exploring the nature of an associational form of industrial representation.

Since the functions of associational unions would not center on building adversarial positions, they could extend their scope of action well beyond that of industrial unions. There need be no sharp line between "management" and "workers"; these bodies could perfectly well represent, for example, middle managers in their capacity as employees. Since they are among the groups that are suffering most from the rapid organizational changes now under way in many corporations, and since their concerns are largely being ignored, they would be likely to be receptive to such a development. Furthermore, because the need for disciplined unity would be less, it would be possible to open the range of issues discussed far beyond the bounds practicable in periodic centralized bargaining. As in the Shell-Sarnia and GM-Saturn cases described earlier, associational unions would be involved in continuous negotiations at multiple levels, forming coalitions and task forces as needed.

The practicality of this model depends, of course, on the techniques of multilateral negotiation. That is a matter of considerable skepticism in labor relations; it seems hard to believe that more than two or three parties can be brought to consensus in a reasonable length of time.

Yet, there is *evidence*, such as that of Saturn and Sarnia, which at least puts in question the traditional assumptions. There is also growing experience in other realms. Indeed, business has in recent years begun to embrace the basic notion of multiple groupings in continuous negotiation as the most effective way to run an organization: stable centralized bureaucracy is out — except in labor relations. Finally, the need is pressing. The "two-party" system of industrial unionism is proving too exclusive, limited, and rigid for a situation of rapid change. "Single-party" organizations — those without independent employee representation — fall too easily into self-deception and manipulation to reliably meet the concerns of employees. A system that can directly involve multiple interests may be the only long-term alternative to adversarial bitterness.

Conclusion

This sketch has barely touched on many implications of the current crisis of unions, and of the emerging solution which I have outlined. The developments now under way will, I believe, take many years to work themselves out. For what I am suggesting is that the decline of labor is no temporary swing of the pendulum, nor a matter that can be dealt with through tactical shifts; rather, it signals a fundamental change in the nature of the movement. This is not unprecedented: Labor went through a similar transformation during the 1920s and 1930s. The analogies, in fact, are worth exploring as a way of clarifying the patterns of the present.

The labor movement before the Depression was quite different in form from today's. The central body was the American Federation of Labor, which was organized on the basis of craft groupings, and which had achieved on this basis rapid growth and considerable clout in industry by about 1920. But the decade of the 1920s was one of severe decline. The rapid growth of mass production industry, with concomitant changes in the labor force, left the craft organizations behind. Their inability to penetrate the new economic sectors was exacerbated by a conservative political climate; by the end of the decade, the movement was fragmented and ineffective. It was, in short, a period very like the present for the unions.

The eventual outcome was a revival of labor, but — this is the central point — not in the same form. John L. Lewis punched a leader of the AFL, "Big Bill" Hutcheson, in the jaw on the floor of the Federation convention and walked out to form a new organization. The revival was led by Lewis' Congress of Industrial Organizations, using quite different tactics, jurisdictions, organizing approaches, and internal structures. This transformation was a painful one in which much of the old leadership was left behind; but it produced a form of representation better suited to the needs of a changing economy.

We have not progressed that far in this cycle: We are still witnessing the agony of old structures, and the new has not taken clear form. This is again similar to the situation during the 1920s. At that time, many observers saw clearly the unmet needs of industrial workers which were to produce the CIO, and many movements had already erupted among these new groups. But they had as yet left no permanent organization in their wake; so, during the calm of the late 1920s, it was possible to believe that all concerns could be dealt with by employer benevolence. The outlines of a new system were seen but dimly until the cataclysmic conflicts of 1934-35 led to a more stable solution. Today, it is the unmet needs of white collar workers, of semi-professionals, and of middle managers that are becoming visible, though they are still formless; and it is pressure for employee rights that has burst out in many places, though without yet producing a coherent structure.

One can hope that we will learn from the transition of the 1930s and avoid such turmoil again; the demand for employee rights, constructively used, could become a basis for commitment at work which, the pollsters tell us, is sorely needed. But there is reason for concern. Battle lines are already being drawn: Management has generally reacted to proposed employee rights with fierce opposition. In this they may be repeating the mistakes of the 1930s, when they fought the rise of unions with every weapon at their disposal, contributing to a tone of bitterness that has soured labor relations down to the present. Unions today, moreover, rather than being the agents of change, are for the most part also resistant to it. Thus the pressure for a new form of representation, in the face of such obstacles, could well build up to an explosive point. The best signs of hope are the experiments in multilateral efforts that show the possibility of a more flexible system.

NOTES

1. These figures are pieced together from two sources: Schiemann, W. A. and Morgan, B. S. (1982), and Cooper, M. R. et al. (1979).
2. The analysis of issues "above" and "below" the collective bargaining sphere is carried much further by Kochan, T. A., McKersie, R. B., and Cappelli, P. (1984).

Plant-closing legislation of a limited sort has been passed in Massachusetts, Maine, and Michigan. In Europe, many countries have gone much further in requiring advance notice of corporate plans, and in placing employee representatives on boards of directors.

3. The two key decisions were NLRB v. Bell Aerospace, 416 US 267, which ruled that all managerial personnel were excluded from coverage by the NLRA; and NLRB v. Yeshiva University, 444 US 672 (1980), which significantly broadened the definition of "managerial." Some passages in the decision suggest that it includes virtually any employee who exercises substantial autonomy and discretion on the job.

4. The duty of "loyalty," derived from master-servant law, has continued to be enforced by many courts despite its clear conflict with the idea of an "impersonal" and limited employment contract. See Atleson, J. B. (1983), ch. 5.

5. "Corporatism" is a term used especially in European studies of labor relations; see, for example, Schmitter, P. C. and Lehmbruch, G. (1979); and Crouch, C. (1977).

6. The contract for the Saturn production plant has been agreed to by union and management, but it has not yet been officially released. My description is taken from discussions with knowledgeable sources.

7. Court rulings have been inconsistent on this, as on other topics in labor relations. The Wagner Act protects "concerted action" by employees; courts have sometimes taken this to protect from discharge workers who stage spontaneous protests. For the most part, however, they have excluded actions outside the union framework from such protection.

8. "For the first time" is, as usual, an exaggeration; there were many precedents for the Civil Rights Act's intrusion on management. It did, nevertheless, mark a sharply new phase.

9. For more complete discussions of recent trends in the doctrine of employment-at-will, see Kauff, J. B. and McClain, M. E. (1984), esp. chs. 1-4; Ewing, D. W. (1983); St. Antoine, T. J. (1985); Stiebert, J. (1985); and Heshizer, B. (1985). The first of these is extremely detailed, listing and describing all the relevant cases; the last is perhaps the best introduction to the subject.

REFERENCES

Atleson, J. B. *Values and Assumptions in American Labor Law.* Amherst, Mass.: University of Massachusetts Press, 1983.

Cooper, M. R. et al. "Changing Employee Values: Deepening Discontent?" *Harvard Business Review* 57 (Jan.-Feb., 1979): 117-125.

Crouch, C. *Class Conflict and the Industrial Relations Crisis.* Atlantic Highlands, N.J.: Humanities Press, 1977.

Ewing, D. W. *"Do It My Way Or You're Fired!"* New York: John Wiley & Sons, 1983.

Harter, Philip. "The Political Legitimacy and Judicial Review of Consensual Rules." *American University Law Review* 32 (1983):471-496.

Heshizer, B. "The New Common Law of Employment: Changes in Concept of Employment at Will." *Labor Law Journal* (February, 1985):95-107.

Kauff, J. B. and **McClain, M. E.** *Unjust Dismissal 1984: Evaluating Litigating, Settling, and Avoiding Claims.* New York: Practising Law Institute, 1984.

Kochan, T. A., McKersie, R. B., and **Cappelli, P.** "Strategic Choice and Industrial Relations Theory." *Industrial Relations* 23 (Winter 1984): 16-39.

McIssac, G. S.: "Thinking Ahead: What's Coming in Labor Relations?" *Harvard Business Review* (Sept.-Oct., 1977):22ff.

Schiemann, W. A., and **Morgan, B. S.** "Managing Human Resources: Employee Discontent and Declining Productivity." Paper presented at an Opinion Research Corp. strategy briefing for human resource executives, San Francisco, 26 October 1982.

Schmitter, P. C. and **Lehmbruch, G.,** eds. *Trends Toward Corporatist Intermediation.* Beverly Hills: Sage Publications, 1979.

St. Antoine, T. J. "The Revision of Employment-at-Will Enters a New Phase." *Labor Law Journal* (August 1985): 563-567.

Stieber, J. "Recent Developments in Employment-at-Will." *Labor Law Journal* (August 1985): 557-563.

Yankelovich, D. et al. "Work and Human Values." Queenstown, Md.: Aspen Institute for Humanistic Studies, 1983.

The Emerging System of International Negotiations

Victor A. Kremenyuk

International negotiation is subject to many influences. As a situation in which sovereign partners meet to find a joint and mutually acceptable solution to a disputable problem, international negotiation attracts the attention of many interested parties both at home and abroad. And, the more important the problem negotiated, the larger the scope of that attention, which is a significant factor in the conduct and outcome of international negotiations. This factor interacts with the dynamics of the process in a specific way: Sometimes it works to achieve a stable and desirable outcome, but sometimes it interferes with and destabilizes the successful conduct of international negotiation.

In assessing the role of this factor and its impact on the processes of international negotiations, it is important to understand the nature of its influence and the different ways in which can be brought to bear. There are purely domestic factors which may — and indeed do — have crucial impact on the processes of international negotiations. Among them are:

- directives from the government which regards the international negotiation as a continuation of its foreign policy and tends to adjust it to the interests of that policy;
- concern of the interested political groups, such as legislative bodies, political parties, major corporations, mass media, and the public.

All of these sources of influence do not necessarily work in the same direction. More than that, in the countries with multi- or bipartisan political systems, these sources may produce so controversial an impact on international negotiation that it becomes a real challenge for the negotiators of those countries to convey a consistent and logical behavior which, in turn, complicates the process and may cause its deadlock or failure.

There are also purely international factors that have a great impact on the international negotiation process. Allies of the negotiating parties, third countries, international organizations, world press — all of them may interfere, both positively and negatively, in the normal sequence of events in the negotiating forum and contribute to its success or failure.

Those engaged in negotiations, practitioners, are fully aware of this impact. While they sometimes actively use it in their own interests, gradually a common understanding has emerged that, for the sake of the stability of the process, makes it necessary to find ways to make international negotiations

Victor A. Kremenyuk is Deputy Director of the Institute of USA and Canada Studies, Academy of Sciences, Moscow, Russia.

more independent of this impact, and to reduce, to the extent possible, its interference in the way the sides in the negotiation handle their affairs. At least in some important cases, such as Soviet-U.S. disarmament talks, the sides agreed from the very beginning to reduce as much as possible the interference of the external factors in the process of the negotiation.

And still, it is absolutely impossible to eliminate completely the external influences on the process of international negotiations. In the contemporary world, every international negotiation is part of a much broader network of interests and negotiations and, explicitly or implicitly, it interacts with the network of which it is a part. Inherent ties among international negotiations have become a new phenomenon of the world of negotiations and, though many practitioners and researchers are aware of this, until recently it was not studied in depth, with all the possible conclusions that can be derived thereby.

The Problem

The problem here is as old as international negotiation itself. It is the problem of managing the negotiations to achieve two different, though overlapping, goals: to fulfill one's own purposes in the international negotiation and, at the same time, to contribute to the stability of the process and its successful outcomes (which is sometimes close to the former). The traditional way of achieving these goals — and hence, managing the processes of international negotiation — is to mobilize all possible factors to build up "bargaining power," and to use it to elaborate an efficient negotiating strategy and appropriate tactic. Essentially, this way is still relevant in most cases. So, what then is the problem?

The problem is that international negotiations, as an object of management, have become much more complex and elaborate. And, to cope with that growing complexity, successful negotiators must take into account not only what was traditionally regarded as an essence of "bargaining power" but also the fact that their options and constraints are limited by the changing nature of contemporary international negotiations. In other words, the correlation of the management procedures and of the subject of management has to be reassessed to strike the desirable balance between *what* is managed and *how* it can be managed.

For this purpose, it would be insufficient just to change the tactics or find new ways to outwit the partner. The situation is much more sophisticated: International negotiation is in the process of acquiring new and important functions and, without a proper assessment of those functions, it is impossible even to speak of a genuinely new approach to managing international negotiation. Sometimes these new functions are self-evident, as in the case of the United Nations Law of the Sea Conference; sometimes they are not that visible, but this does not significantly change the necessity to treat the whole problem of international negotiation as a new and important feature of the international environment which demands the restructuring and rethinking of the traditional approach.

The Analytical Approach

International negotiations grow in number and diversity. This is evidenced not only by the traditional issues, such as security, borders, trade, communications, etc., but also by various subjects from the sphere of scientific and cultural exchange, humanitarian problems, environment, outer space, and oceans.

The growing number of international negotiations is an indicator of a much more significant process which is taking place underneath — the process of formation of a certain system of international negotiations. So far, this is not a comprehensive, institutionalized system of international negotiations which incorporates talks between/among countries on all disputable and controversial issues. Many of these issues still are waiting to become the subject of talks. But, nevertheless, one can speak with full evidence of an emerging system that has already become an integral part of international reality and thus far has not yet been assessed in all aspects.

First of all, it is not the mere number of international negotiations that makes one draw a conclusion that there is a system, although the rapidly and even dramatically growing number of international negotiations has already drawn the attention of many analysts. There are attempts to make inventories on a country-by-country basis (e. g., USSR-U. S., as B. M. Blechman [1985] did in the area of prevention of the risk of nuclear war), or inventories for different problematiques: negotiations on arms control, trade, the environment, etc.

It is the growing interaction among international negotiation forms that deserves attention and leads one to suggest that the expanding number of international negotiations definitely is not developing sporadically (although sometimes it may seem so), but in some systematic way which reflects such crucial processes as the burgeoning interdependence of nations and of disputable issues among them, the increasing impotence of traditional ways of resolving conflicts (such as military), and the increasing need to turn negotiation into the only possible institutionalized and codified way to resolve international disputes in the absence of a real alternative. In other words, the changing international environment brought, as a result, the emerging importance of international negotiations. International negotiations have gone from a forum of sporadic international interaction to the sometimes only thinkable way of conflict resolution under conditions of growing interdependence, which has contributed to the formation of a certain system.

This means that any international negotiation now should be regarded not only within the framework of the foreign policy of the nations engaged in the negotiations, but also within the framework of a certain "microcosm" of international negotiations to which it belongs. In this case some new factors of the negotiation appear which greatly affect the processes and the management of international negotiations.

The Conceptual Approach
This conclusion is based on a solid foundation of analysis made in different countries of the main features of the contemporary international system. Taken together, the major three findings in this sphere are:

1. *Structural and functional features of the international system.* The whole world system is in a transitional stage. Structurally, it is shifting from the bipolar world of the 1950s to a much more diversified (sometimes called multipolar, although this may not be correct, since it bears no accurate descrip-

tion) world structure. The process is far from being completed. Decolonization turned huge and rather loose political entities called colonial empires into an array of newly independent states. The different results of economic development brought into play new political forces and centers of power and influence. New alignments and groupings appeared both in the political and economic areas, such as the nonaligned movement, European Economic Community and OPEC.

On the functional side, this process is accompanied by the changing nature of the traditional means of interaction among states: The value of military power has diminished because of the impossibility of nuclear war and the constraints produced by the rough parity between the major military blocks. The value of economic power has also changed, since the emphasis on it is shifting from the mere production of goods and commodities and finance, to technological innovation. The rising importance of humanitarian issues also brings a new dimension to traditional power alignments and interactions.

2. *Interdependence of state and issues.* Structural and functional processes overlap and interact with another important element of the emerging international system — the growing interdependence of nations in all spheres. This notion is much broader than the one used in the 1970s (especially after the oil crisis of 1973-74). The interdependence of nations, which has become an objective reality of the 1980s, has several dimensions, the most important and prominent being interdependence in matters of security: The national security of any country in the present situation is inalienable from the security of others — there can be no security for one country if it threatens the others' security. The only possible solution of the security problem is common security, which can be attained only through a comprehensive and logical system of international negotiation.

Another dimension is economic. The economic growth and development of nations has long ago ceased to be only their own concern. It is impossible to imagine now any country, large or small, which could cope with its development problems without cooperation with and from the outside world. And still another dimension is the environment, which only emphasizes to a large extent that all the nations of the world are interdependent and can only survive together.

The process of growing interdependence develops not only extensively (including new spheres in which nations become dependent on each other) but also intensively. This means that the spheres in which the countries find themselves dependent on each other also become interdependent. For example, the interdependence between security and economy, disarmament and development, which is a subject for numerous discussions at international conferences, and the interdependence between the economy and environment (or to be more exact, industry and environment).

3. *Complexity.* A number of controversial issues have appeared at the cross-section of these two spheres of interdependence. Sometimes these issues have a very traditional character: controversies and conflicts in security, trade, finance, environment, etc. But, if we look at them from the perspective of the environment in which they exist and of the complex network of interdependencies which produce them, it becomes clear that these con-

troversial issues form some interconnected and mutually dependent network. Such conflicts then have, as one of their main features, the ability to spill over to other spheres or to escalate, thus producing a "multi-layered" form of conflict in which the issues of an ideological, ethical or other nature are interconnected. The growing complexity of the international system in this way produces no less complex types of controversies and conflicts which should be adequately treated.

Main Features of the System

Now, what relation has all this to the processes of international negotiations? This is a problem to be studied in the remaining sections of this article with some suggestions which may be of interest to those engaged both in the theory and practice of negotiations. In the above-mentioned context, international negotiation is regarded as the main means of conflict resolution which, together with the unilateral actions of nations, can contribute in a significant manner to keeping the international system stable and predictable.

What are the main features that appear in international negotiations due to these processes?

First, the emerging system of international negotiations tends to reflect, both in its structure and essence, the existing system of conflicts and disputes. Hence, it becomes more and more universal, incorporating the formal negotiations and consultations, informal talks and meetings of government officials, experts, public figures and others engaged in the activities of exchanging views and ideas on the possible ways to find a resolution to disputable problems. The mere existence of this huge international structure should be regarded as a kind of specific environment within which some specific "rules of conduct" exist: nonviolence, adherence to joint problem-solving, cooperation, etc. This does not mean that even here there do not exist political and diplomatic struggle, coercion, threats and the like. But, nevertheless, this environment gives a maximum gain to those who adhere to the "rules of conduct," and is rather unfriendly to those who try to break them.

Second, this system tends to become more and more autonomous. It is self-evident that a negotiation may be created, as a situation, only due to the sovereign will of the parties; but once in existence, a negotiation becomes to an extent estranged from that will, since it becomes a part of the system and is plugged into it through the information flows, interplay of interests, influence of observing parties, and so on. Within the system a negotiation acquires a second dimension (the first is that it is a continuation of a foreign policy) and becomes a part of an international network which has its own rules and its own laws of dynamics.

Third, once it is a part of a system, a negotiation has to respond to the needs and elements of that system. The main demand is that it should contribute to the stability and growth (optimization) of the system. The entropy or disorder of the system can be prevented not through stagnation of an individual cell (part) but through its efficient operation, which means a successful and timely resolution of a conflict. Thus, the system and its basic parts have an interdependent relationship: The more efficient the functioning of each international negotiation, the more stable and durable is the whole system of international relations.

Fourth, the above factors all place an additional burden on the process of international negotiation. Thus far, a negotiation's main function has been to serve the interests of the parties engaged. It was their interest and their will which primarily dictated the whole process, while the accepted rules served a secondary role in establishing the procedure. Now, with the emergence of the system of negotiations, parties to any international negotiation have to take into consideration not only their interests at the given negotiation but also the whole array of their interests and positions at other negotiations and even the state of affairs at other negotiation forums. The decision-making process becomes magnified and complicated by several orders.

Changing Structure of the Process

Since international negotiation acquires a dual capability — as a function of a foreign policy and a basic part of the stability of the international system — it cannot help but experience some changes in its nature and process. As to changes in nature, partly they have already been described: The burden of conflict resolution gradually shifts from unilateral actions and decisions to joint problem-solving and agreed solutions. At this particular moment, this statement may sound premature, but the trend is evident. Even in the sphere of national security, there is no way to achieve durable solutions without taking into consideration the necessity to strike a balance of interest of all parties concerned.

As to the process, the change is not that evident, but gradually it is becoming more elucidated.

Roger Fisher (1986) summarized the changes of the structure of negotiations in two models — Model "T" (for "traditional") and Model "A" (for "alternative"). The gist of his conclusions is that gradually the structure of the process of international negotiation has changed from strictly formal, diplomats-to-diplomats "one-shot" conferences to a combination of governmental and nongovernmental experts' talks which become an indefinite, ongoing process working as a production line for producing a series of jointly agreed recommendations to governments on possible solutions of disputable problems.

To continue this trend, one can suggest that, in a period of time, these international negotiations will become a kind of permanent, continuous activity which would then suggest to the appropriate governments either to sign an agreement with the other side or to make unilateral decisions within an agreed framework to solve a dispute without having an agreement. In any case, the role of international negotiations is changing from a mere form of government-to-government activity to an international function of government, nongovernmental organizations (NGOs), public figures, and even children and youth (thus institutionalizing its autonomy), producing a conceptual framework of possible agreements for governmental deliberation and decision.

But, meanwhile, recognition of the fact of the changing nature of the process poses several problems both for practice and research.

In practice, this brings up several tasks:

1. To make an inventory of all contemporary negotiations with some definite and practicable classification along the following criteria:

- Bilateral and multilateral (with some additional criteria, such as whether or not they are institutionalized, i.e., within the framework of existing international organizations, or noninstitutionalized, etc.);
- Formal (official) and informal (nongovernmental);
- By subject of negotiation (political, security, economic, environmental, etc.)

This type of inventory will permit developing an adequate database, which could be used both by the government agencies and researchers to gain at least an idea of the scope and nature of the contemporary network of international negotiations.

2. To compare the existing network of international negotiations with the scope of the issues to be solved in international relations.

It is understandable that this task will demand the introduction of stricter approaches to the evaluation of the issues. But each side concerned may unilaterally decide whether or not the existing network of international negotiations matches the scope of the issues and whether it forms an international joint problem-solving system. It is very possible that such a tremendous job will produce another problem — that of "negotiation on negotiation," how to rearrange the contemporary network of international negotiations to bring it close to the needs of the international problem-solving process.

3. The solution of these practical aspects of the problem will demand at least two types of research. One of them is relatively simple — a program for computer database on international negotiations which would permit the collection of all the existing information on negotiations in some orderly manner, useable by negotiators of any country and international agency: when, where, who, what is negotiated, what is the result (or absence of result). The only necessary condition for such a program is that is should be universal and distributed through the existing international information services.

The other direction of research is more complicated and will demand much more time. It includes:

- The assessment of the type and nature of systemic changes that have already happened and will happen in the conduct of negotiation, because of the existence of the system;
- The elaboration of the necessary modifications which should be introduced into the conduct of the negotiations to bring it closer to the needs of the contemporary system; and
- As a final aim, the elaboration of a new code for negotiation, which can be undertaken on a genuinely international basis.

One of the major consequences of the emergence of the system of international negotiations is that the negotiation process which is largely organized along the traditional lines is becoming less and less effective. The negotiations, at least the most important among them, take more time and lag behind the evolution of the international environment. The most evident examples are issues concerning security, trade and finance and technology. The agreements achieved are very often regarded as inadequate and unjust, which make them vulnerable to criticism and attacks. If one compares the modest results of negotiations with the scope of the issues in security, economics, the environment, etc., it becomes clear that the process should be changed.

In sum, the state of affairs in the area of international negotiation is not satisfactory, and needs a substantive innovation. One of the most promising ways to do this is through an international effort to try to assess the changes in the process of negotiations from both methodological and multidisciplinary perspectives.

Among methodological perspectives one could suggest the following:

- the role of negotiations in the contemporary international system;
- the significance of the emerging system of negotiations;
- changes in the processes of negotiation;
- the internal debates and their impact on negotiating strategies; and
- a "new negotiator," and his or her psychology, training, and background.

All of these aspects of the problem could be assessed from different disciplinary approaches, including historical, international relations and law, organizational theory, cognitive studies, psychological and cross-cultural, decision support sciences and game theoretical approach. The combination of different approaches, along with the intensive study of specific national styles, could suggest a genuinely new idea of how the negotiation process should be reorganized to match the necessities of the new "era of negotiations."

NOTE

This paper was originally prepared under the auspices of the Processes of International Negotiation (PIN) Project at the International Institute for Applied Systems Analysis (IIASA) in Laxenburg, Austria, with support from the Carnegie Corporation of New York.

REFERENCES

Blechman, B. M., ed. (1985). *Preventing nuclear war*. Bloomington: Indiana University Press.
Fisher, R. (1986). "The structure of negotiation: An alternative model." *Negotiation Journal* 2: 233-235.

The Art of Preparing
a Multilateral Conference

Klaus L. Aurisch

A multilateral conference is a complex mechanism of group interaction. In order to be an effective diplomatic tool, such a meeting must be organized with tremendous forethought, for its design can contribute significantly to the outcome. Global problems, such as the preservation of world peace, disarmament, the world economy, and development; and environmental problems, such as the protection of the ozone layer, the preservation of forests, and the dangers of nuclear radiation; and other issues, such as drug abuse and excessive population growth, are all topics that are discussed among nations. Furthermore, in regional groups of states, such as the European Community, the North Atlantic Treaty Organization, or the Organization of African Unity, member states must agree, for instance, on measures to harmonize rules and standards for many economic questions, or on a defense strategy. Peacemaking efforts in the Middle East, in Central America, and in other war-torn regions also require multilateral talks.

No matter what problems are being addressed, the way a multilateral negotiation meeting is prepared is crucial to its success. Even within the framework of established international organizations — where most parameters are already set by statutes, established procedures, and practices — there is still room for creativity in the preparation of a multilateral conference. The following remarks, based on ten years of practical experience, focus on international conferences with large numbers of participating states mostly in the framework of the United Nations and environmental diplomacy. The most typical conferences today are the open-to-all conferences in the United Nations system, with global participation and a maximum of diverging interests; and members-only internal decision-making meetings of integration-oriented regional alliances. The following examples are mainly based on meetings of these types. In some instances, examples of bilateral or smaller multiparty meetings are cited when they seem to highlight a certain element of general value particularly well. Of course, there are many more examples in various fields, many of them known only to those involved.

Determining the Purpose and Anticipating the Outcome
Much will be accomplished by determining the purpose and the elements of a conference in advance. To make a conference a success, it is necessary to have a clear assessment of the situation or problem at the start, a vision of the

Klaus L. Aurisch is former Deputy Permanent Representative of the Federal Republic of Germany to International Organizations in Vienna. His mailing address is c/o Consulate General of the Federal Republic of Germany, 6222 Wilshire Boulevard, Suite 500, Los Angeles, Calif. 90048.

desired outcome and some ideas on how to get there. In working toward these goals, a variety of national interests, regional groups, cultural diversities, different mentalities, and value systems must be taken into account. A clear definition of the purpose should be established at the beginning. Is a firm commitment sought for directly implementable measures (e.g., to reduce emissions that pollute the air and produce acid rain, to limit commercial whaling, etc.), or is a process of international awareness to be started, for which the goal is just a declaration of political will? An ad hoc conference to achieve a worldwide declaration against drug abuse, like the one in Vienna in 1987, differs in character from a conference called to agree on a concrete convention containing legal measures, such as forfeiture of assets related to illicit drug trafficking, as was negotiated in Vienna in 1988. In the preparation of the meeting, every structural detail, organizational feature, procedural decision, and facilitating support must be conducive to the purpose.

Typically, the purpose of a multilateral conference is to agree on future action. Warring coalitions may negotiate among themselves and with the opponents in the course of wars about the war effort and, after victory, about the distribution of the booty and the future tasks to keep peace. Such well-known conferences as Versailles, Yalta, and Potsdam fall into this war-related category. Since World War II, conferences have been aimed primarily at peaceful international action, achieved through a formal agreement implemented by each participant or through the establishment of a permanent institution. In this period there have been many conferences designed to create regional institutions, such as the European Economic Community, and institutions with global membership, such as the United Nations and its specialized agencies. For decades, United Nations conferences gave birth to new institutions, to pursue such purposes as fighting drug abuse, resolving development matters, studying environmental issues, and so on. Arms control and disarmament conferences make up a special category, as do summit conferences of the "Group of Seven" nations. An evolutionary theory of conference types would have to start with an ad hoc meeting of an integration-oriented community.

Depending on their main purposes, several types of multilateral conferences may be distinguished. These include conferences dealing with:

- War-related issues (coalitions, ceasefires, armistice, peace, reparations, mediation of peace-making efforts);

- arms control and disarmament;

- trade;

- the establishment of an international organization;

- global cooperation (economic, development, environment);

- ad hoc meetings for special purposes;

- institutionalized decision making in an integration-oriented organization (European Community); and

- summit meetings (few participants, highest level, global priority issues).

The characteristics of each of these categories of conferences have been developed and repeated over years and decades. The type of meeting determines the way countries are selected to participate, the firmness of the required commitment or the vagueness of the result, the duration of the meeting (from a few days to a series of meetings over years), and potentially the frequency and institutionalization of future meetings. A particular conference may combine the features of more than one category. Planning a conference involves choosing the most appropriate format.

When determining the purpose and the desired result of a conference, one must also consider the form that the outcome should take. Will it be presented as a formal accord, a political declaration, or a public relations communique? The product of a modern international conference may take various guises, each different in status, quality, and consequences. The classic outcome may be a formal accord, an agreement binding under international law. The authority to sign usually lies with the foreign minister. Under most constitutions, such an agreement also needs subsequent consent by parliament and formal ratification by the head of state. It often takes years to obtain the number of ratifications necessary to put a multinational agreement leading to a formal accord into effect. For real-time, communication-age politics, the procedure associated with a formal accord may be much too slow. Therefore, politicians have come to prefer the form of a "declaration." It does not require ratification, is a political commitment but not a legal obligation, may sometimes be signed by a minister other than the foreign minister, does not have to be so scrupulously worded as a legal instrument, and politically it can have the desired effect. In the field of transboundary environmental cooperation, this form has been used successfully, for instance, in the 1984 Ottawa Declaration on Acid Rain, the 1984 Munich Declaration on Air Pollution, the 1985 Bucharest Declaration on Danube Water Pollution, and the 1989 Declaration of The Hague on environmental questions. The achievable result of some conferences may be no more than a joint communique which, since it is less binding and less substantive, may be easier to agree upon. In this case agreement need not be complete or perfect. Communique language permits almost any level of agreement to be expressed: complete, almost complete, partial, fractional, nonexistent, or even false. Any of those may be politically useful, although deliberately ambivalent agreements usually mean trouble in the future.

Participants, Host, and Location

Participants make or break a conference. The problem is how to persuade desirable participants to join in the proceedings and, conversely, to exclude undesirable participants. For example, the participation of the Soviet Union in the 1984 Munich Conference on Air Pollution was essential for a meaningful discussion of long-range air pollution in Europe. The Soviet Union, at that almost icy period of East-West relations following the deployment of missiles in Europe, was reluctant to come to any conference with the West. Careful preparation, bilaterally and in the United Nations Economic Commission for Europe in Geneva, was required to make participation acceptable to the Soviet Union at that time. We can assume that environmental considerations alone, as important as they may seem, would not have been sufficient. Political obstacles regarding East-West relations, and Soviet reservations about the participation of the West German Federal Environmental Agency (because of its location in Berlin), had to be overcome.

Inversely, there is an advantage in limiting participation to those governments that have a legitimate stake in the substance of the conference. The larger the number of participants, the more difficult it is to reach agreement. Countries that in a particular instance have little to contribute or that may pursue goals quite apart from the substance of the conference are likely to create additional problems. However, excluding certain states may appear to be politically unacceptable discrimination. It is almost impossible to choose at will the countries to be invited to a conference. The three organizing countries of the International Environmental Conference held in The Hague in March 1989 were criticized for allowing an over-representation of African and Arab countries while leaving Latin America and Eastern Europe underrepresented, and for not inviting the superpowers — the United States, the Soviet Union, and China —at all. It is helpful, when possible, to resort to an established formula, such as the member states of the United Nations. Participation in the 1984 Munich environmental conference was determined by a formula along the lines of the membership in the United Nations Economic Commission for Europe and adherence to the Convention on long-range air pollution.

Closely related to the selection of participants are the designation of the conference's host and its location. A respected, trusted, and legitimate host is vital to the success of a multilateral conference. At United Nations conferences that take place at established international headquarters, without any host country, the issue becomes the presidency of the conference. When a country or a political leader assumes the role of host, it is essential that the state or the leader be acceptable to all participants. The conference-host issues were satisfactorily resolved at the 1984 Munich Conference on air pollution: the German Federal Chancellor invited the participants, while the minister responsible for the environment presided at the session. Under a carefully balanced formula, the conference was organized in cooperation with the United Nations, and the representatives of the United Nations acted as co-hosts. Frequently, conferences take place under the auspices of the United Nations to ensure that no country will have difficulty in accepting the invitation. The host plays a vital role in making the convening of the conference possible. Later on, in a potential deadlock of the conference, the ranking representative of the host country might be called to bring his or her authority to bear on some parties in order to reconcile conflicting points of view and to remove obstacles to an agreement.

The conference location generally has both symbolic power and practical value. Symbolic power may derive, for example, from the tradition of victorious powers to schedule peace talks in geographically significant locations. At the end of World War II, the 1945 conference at Potsdam, outside Berlin, was seen as a gesture of victory. In recent times, a few neutral cities have successfully built reputations as international meeting places for certain categories of negotiations. Helsinki, for instance, has become synonymous with the confidence-building process between West and East, the Conference on Security and Cooperation in Europe. Geneva has become the venue for nuclear arms control meetings, while Vienna is the location for conventional arms control talks. Being linked in this way to an issue may occasionally be a disadvantage: France initially argued against Vienna as the site for new conventional arms control negotiations in 1987, which were to be distinct from the previous fruitless Mutual and Balanced Force Reduction talks, in which France had not participated. An extreme case of symbolism, combined with information purposes, may have been the convening of an expert meeting concerning the protection of Antarctica at the Chilean research station on the eternal ice in 1984. Locations for summit meetings are sometimes chosen for their historic value, as was Williamsburg, Virginia, in 1983.

Power value, i.e., bargaining leverage, is also attached to the choice of a meeting place, as examples in history reveal. The location could express the rank and prestige of participants, or it could mean an advantage or disadvantage in negotiating leverage. When the German Emperor Henry IV had to go to Canossa in 1077 to meet Pope Gregory VII, his bargaining power was visibly weakened from the outset. Monarchs and states therefore prefer to meet on neutral grounds at about equal distance. Napoleon and Czar Alexander I met on a raft in the Neman River in 1807. Ronald Reagan and Mikhail Gorbachev chose Reykjavik, Iceland, an island in the middle of the Atlantic Ocean, in 1987. Although those meetings were all bilateral, they are cited here as examples of the relationship between the venue and negotiating leverage. The rule was neglected by the western allies when they agreed to meet in Potsdam in 1945, in the middle of the Soviet occupation zone, where Stalin had full control of the negotiation environment and they had none. Stalin used this advantage to the full extent, with strong negative effects on the bargaining position of the western allies (Murphy, 1964, p. 265). Panmunjom, located in the no-man's-land between the Koreas, was chosen as neutral ground in 1953; Paris for the Vietnam talks of 1971; and Geneva for the Afghanistan talks of 1988. As things stand now, it would be inconceivable to hold a Middle East conference in Jerusalem, because the holy city itself is part of the conference issue.

With large numbers of participants, practical considerations play a decisive role in most modern multilateral conferences of a technical nature. A major international conference — with over 160 states participating, hundreds of delegates, representatives of nongovernmental organizations, and the media — requires a very complex infrastructure. This is why these large conferences tend to be held in a limited number of "conference service capitals" which offer the required resources and support facilities. A highly reliable and extensive communication system is vital, since everybody is on the telephone all the time for instructions. Qualified interpreters may be the most crucial resource of all. Sometimes a state will host an important conference because it adds to its international prestige, and the state will take on heavy financial burdens to make the required infrastructure available. In specialized United Nations conferences, the participation of developing countries is influenced by whether or not they have permanent missions in the particular city. Development considerations also come into play in choosing the site of an important international conference. Experts on environmental law gathered in Montevideo, Uruguay, for a 1983 United Nations conference. In 1984 the United Nations Commission on Human Settlements convened in Libreville, Gabon; the 1983 meeting of the signatories of the Washington Convention on Endangered Species took place in Gaborone, Botswana. There are many more examples of this kind in the history of the United Nations and its specialized agencies. Choosing meeting places on different continents in less well-known areas, even when tents have to serve as additional facilities, helps to enhance international understanding and may underscore and promote the purpose of the conference. Because the developing countries attach such great importance to serving as host nation, the United Nations, even during its worst financial crisis, decided to build a new conference center in Addis Ababa, Ethiopia.

Agenda and Rules of Procedure

When governments agree to attend a multilateral conference, they want to know what they are being asked to negotiate about. Surprises are not welcome. One of the first tasks of the organizers, therefore, should be to lay out the agenda itself. This means the organizers must agree on what topics to include, how to formulate them, and in what order they should be considered. The decisions about the agenda and the rules of procedure sometimes preempt important decisions on substance. Shaping the agenda in a nondiscriminating and fair way avoids concern about potential initial disadvantages for some parties and minimizes the danger of embarrassing surprises. Sometimes an attempt to introduce a new item in a late stage of conference preparation or in a critical stage of the ongoing conference may cause a crisis and necessitate a difficult negotiating process in itself. In East-West disarmament conferences, for instance, the parties have even gone so far as to work on a double, rotating agenda (Iklé, 1964, p. 97). Careful attention should also be given to the rules of procedure. Over the years, United Nations conferences have helped to develop a standard set of rules to which many subsequent conferences refer. However, individual modifications are significant.

Structure and Protocol

Multilateral negotiations involve a vast number of parties. On the global level of the United Nations, this number includes 160 full members (anticipating the accession of Namibia), as well as observers and international organizations. In such an environment, a variety of unpredictable moves and initiatives are possible that could have considerable impact on the mainstream of the conference. It is important, therefore, that all initiatives and proposals pass through several filters before they reach the formal conference level. Wide support may be gathered for a good idea, while, conversely, damage limitation may be possible off-stage in informal groups, with the help of respected leaders.

The United Nations has developed a very elaborate structural pattern over the past four decades. A conference meets in plenary sessions, the highest formal level, for the ceremonial acts, the basic procedural decisions, the formal political statements of the dignitaries, and the endorsement of the final agreement. The actual negotiating is done in committees, subcommittees, working groups, contact groups, and in many individual lobbying efforts in and around the conference room. If the matter cannot be entrusted to a committee because everybody wants to participate, but the formal level of the plenary is undesirable, the conference participants may sit as a Committee of the Whole. With a great number of parties, the negotiation process in multilateral conferences requires a clearinghouse for procedural moves that frequently are matters of substance in disguise. The so-called "bureau" (in the United Nations system this means the elected officers of the conference, representing the regional groups) exercises this function. Sometimes a steering committee which also includes conference officers of previous meetings is formed to broaden the basis and experience of this body. These persons can provide great negotiating help by improving communication, separating the problem from people or countries, calming emotions, and suggesting compromise options. This multilateral negotiating system is admirably flexible and open to creative procedural and operative ideas.

Another procedure for structuring a multilateral conference is to break the parties down into groups of common interests, which can then form common positions and negotiate through group chairpersons. In United Nations conferences, there are the established Regional Groups for the geographic-political regions of the globe. For matters of the North-South dialogue, there is the Group of 77, representing the developing countries. Increasingly, the twelve member states of the European Community negotiate as an entity. This is the case for matters of trade policy, for which the Community has the exclusive competence, but it also holds true in political matters. One example was the 1987 Montreal Conference of Plenipotentiaries on the Protocol on Chlorofluorocarbons, where intensive bargaining took place between the representative of the Commission of the European Community and the United States representative about a formula to reduce the production of ozone-depleting chemicals in a way that would not create unfair economic advantages or disadvantages for certain parties.

Organizers of a multilateral negotiation, therefore, should take great pains to assure that no participant finds reason to be offended. That includes attention to the correct spelling of names and titles, the right rank order in the listing of participants, the correct categories of participants, and sometimes creative imagination to invent ranks and categories in order to avoid conflict. For example, when there are elected Members of Parliament as members of delegations who outrank the heads of these delegations, where should they be put on the list? One solution is to invent a category of "special advisors," as was done for the special session of the Governing Council of the United Nations Environment Programme in Nairobi in 1982. Good protocol avoids unnecessary friction potentially detrimental to the negotiation effort. It creates a favorable disposition to do business.

Negotiating

What actually happens at the conference, of course, is a whole story in itself. Preparation is only an attempt to anticipate some of the typical difficulties and provide institutional tools for use in critical situations. A preparatory committee can try to bring positions as close together as possible without formal political decisions or concessions. However, the process has its limits. Sometimes states are reluctant to reveal their positions too early. For example, despite several preparatory expert meetings over the course of two years, there were still some unwelcome surprises for negotiators at the 1987 Montreal conference on a Protocol on Chlorofluorcarbons to the Vienna Convention for the Protection of the Ozone Layer. Several developing countries had not participated in the preparatory work and wanted to start the discussion of the problem from square one. One other country, instead of considering reducing production soon, wanted to build and operate a new plant first, in order to fulfill its economic plan. A complicated formula accommodating these interests, but softening the Protocol, was adopted.

In the course of a multilateral conference, it is usually necessary at pivotal points, or when the negotiation has run into a dead end, to use key persons or institutions to facilitate action. High-level efforts of the host or the conference president can often bring about a compromise agreement. When planning the conference, it is wise to provide facilities and allow time for such efforts. In United Nations meetings, there are innumerable examples of this kind of action. They frequently take the form of mediating third-party intervention of a different regional group. For instance, in the 1988 meeting of the United Nations Commission on Narcotic Drugs, the Latin American group wanted to include a paragraph directly offensive to the United States in a draft resolution. The chairmen of the Western European and Other Group and of the European Community, Spain and West Germany, negotiated with the Latin American group chairman to have the text withdrawn and the point reflected only in an oral statement.

Public Information

The plenary session of an international conference is not the place for secret diplomacy. There may be some confidential and effective diplomacy going on in the halls and corridors, but modern public opinion often requires transparent negotiation. This requirement has made the task of the negotiator much more difficult. Each move has to qualify both as a good move in the negotiating process and as a good public statement.

Organizers of multilateral conferences should consider this aspect of the process very seriously. The list of speakers for the main statements is very much aligned to the domestic prime-time television hours of the respective speakers' countries. Sometimes pressure for agreement is created by this very fact. It even happens that someone wants to be the first to announce a deal that is only expected to be made later that night. This method is not unusual in the practice of the European Community's Council of Ministers, where decisions are frequently made in the wee hours of the night.

A distinct identity for a multilateral conference enhances its impact on the public. In an age of "power through mass media," a negotiation effort has to be immediately justified before the public and any agreement reached has to be supported by it, if it is to be ratified and implemented. For that reason, a conference needs a "trademark," an identity that allows people to relate to it. Therefore, the core substance of the conference has to be crystallized into a name, an acronym, and a logo. As trivial as it may seem, this helps people to rally to the cause and to sympathize with the objectives of the conference. The identity also helps build continuity for extended negotiation efforts over time, which are necessary for many international problems that cannot be solved in a one-shot conference.

A conference title should be distinctive, accurate, and inoffensive. For example, when a 1984 conference on the environmental protection of the North Sea was planned, the name "North Sea Conference" was not distinctive enough, because there had been other conferences related to North Sea shipping and other matters. "North Sea Environmental Protection Conference" sounded rather clumsy; finally, "North Sea Protection Conference" was chosen. To find a title for the United Nations World Drug Conference in 1987, it was necessary to take into consideration the fact that several international conventions and institutions already existed. The correct title of "International Conference on Drug Abuse and Illicit Trafficking" was not really practical for everyday use. The acronym "ICDAIT" became the trademark. Since public awareness was one of the conference goals, much thought was given to the public dimension. It proved impossible to find a pictorial logo that would transmit the idea of fighting drug abuse. A verbal slogan, "No to drugs, Yes to life," was chosen, translated into all official and other languages, and distributed on posters, buttons, headbands, T-shirts, United Nations stamps, and works of art such as the design poster and a woven carpet displayed at the Vienna International Center. Logos for environmental conferences against air pollution, water and sea pollution, and acid rain were a little easier to design, depicting smokestacks, clouds, raindrops, waves, damaged trees and buildings. How do these details relate to the negotiating process? They create negotiating leverage in the sense that public pressure is put on the delegations to agree on something that helps solve a publicly perceived problem.

Relations with the public are not a one-way street. A modern multilateral conference draws great numbers of public and special interest groups as participants. For many matters, nongovernmental organizations have acquired an observer status with the United Nations and can participate with the right to speak. In other cases, they have organized parallel conferences or have tried to influence the negotiation by putting on demonstrations in front of the conference building. When the International Whaling Commission met in Brighton, England, in 1982, for example, the Greenpeace ship Rainbow Warrior was moored in front of the conference hotel and a life-size inflated plastic whale was beached on the sidewalk. Demonstrations sometimes cross the border into violence; as a consequence, security considerations have become an indispensable part of conference preparation.

Conclusion

Conference preparation can create a setting conducive to a good outcome. The chances for a bona fide implementation by the parties lie in the agreement itself. The likelihood of compliance is enhanced if the agreement:

- satisfies the different interests well enough to be durable;

- is legitimate for all;

- contains commitments that are well planned, realistic, and operational; in other words, if it meets the criteria of being a mutually satisfying, fair, and wise agreement (Fisher and Ury, 1981, p. 14).

What more can a conference do to ensure implementation? An agreement requiring ratification usually names a depositary —one or several governments or the Secretary General of the United Nations — that collects the instruments of ratification and announces the entering into force, a formal point. The agreement may also establish a mechanism for monitoring the implementation. The preferred method for several decades has been to create a permanent secretariat or an international organization. A crisis of multilateralism — considered to be expensive and inefficient — has slowed down this trend in the 1980s. Another method is to decide on and set a date for a follow-up conference, or event to institutionalize a series of follow-up conferences to be held at specific intervals. This tends to become a pattern for multilateral conferences on global issues that cannot be solved by a single conference. A five-year cycle was proposed, but not agreed to, in 1987 for the United Nations World Women's Conference. Only an interim compromise formula, deciding on the next conference but not on a mandatory cycle, was finally agreed upon. An example reflecting the vulnerability of an outcome, possibly lacking some of the mentioned criteria, is the history of agreement, subsequent non-implementation, renegotiation, ratification, and slow implementation of the multilateral accord of the states bordering the Rhine River to reduce the salt emissions, in particular those resulting from the production of potash fertilizer. A complicated agreement, involving technical and economic issues, was ratified and already partially implemented by all but one party. Eventually it had to be renegotiated. A skillfully worded, very sophisticated amendment was then signed in 1983, after a renewed bargaining process. The question of ratification developed into an important foreign policy issue, especially between the Netherlands and France. The accord — after top-level political intervention — was finally ratified by all parties in 1985, and its gradual implementation has started.

In the course of any multilateral conference, perceptions, attitudes, goals, and relationships are modified — first those of the acting individuals, then those of their constituencies —through subsequent inside negotiation. A conference generates a momentum of its own toward agreement, because nobody likes to declare failure. Creating a good negotiating relationship is a confidence-building measure and, as such, a joint gain in the long term, since multilateral conferences are repetitive games. Designing their constituent parts in such a way that the dynamics of the negotiating process lead to gradual progress and eventual success in spite of the foreseeable difficulties, may well be called an art. Perhaps it is even a survival technique in our increasingly interdependent environment on this planet earth.

REFERENCES

Fisher, R. and Ury, W. L. (1981). *Getting to YES*. Boston: Houghton Mifflin.
Iklé, F. C. (1964). *How nations negotiate*. New York: Harper & Row.
Murphy, R. (1964). *Diplomat among warriors*. Garden City, N.Y.: Doubleday.

Section IX

Third Party Intervention

Sometimes the best or only way of reaching negotiated settlement is for one or more of the parties involved to seek out the services of a third party. This individual or group, by definition, stands apart from the conflict in question, and may be able — by virtue of this perspective as well as substantive or process expertise — to intervene in ways that make agreement more likely. Third parties differ widely in the degree of control they may be able to exercise in a dispute, ranging from mediation (where advisory recommendations for dispute settlement are made) to arbitration (where the parties agree to accept a third party recommendation that is binding). While there is never any guarantee that third party intervention will lead to negotiated agreement — indeed, there may be circumstances where such intervention makes an already bad situation even worse — third parties can often help. In this closing section of the book, we present several articles that describe some of the many roles and functions of third parties.

The first contribution, by Lawrence Susskind and Connie Ozawa ("Mediated Negotiation in the Public Sector: Mediator Accountability and the Public Interest Problem"), summarizes three case studies of mediation in the "public sector" — where governmental officials, citizens, and others come together to settle a variety of complex disputes. While the article is particularly addressed to these public sector conflicts, the authors develop general principles that can reasonably be applied to *any* conflict in which a mediator is likely to become involved. Thus, in outlining the criteria for successful public sector mediation, Susskind and Ozawa develop six points that can be applied to *any* conflict involving mediators. First, they write, the agreement should be acceptable to all sides; second, the results must be fair; third, the agreement should maximize joint gains; fourth, it should take past precedents into consideration; fifth, the agreement should entail minimal expenditure of time and money; and finally, it should improve the relationship between disputants as much as possible.

William P. Smith ("Effectiveness of the Biased Mediator") looks at a commonly misunderstood assumption about mediation, namely that the third party must be unbiased in order to be effective. While true absence of bias, neutrality, or impartiality may be possible in some settings, bias is almost an inevitable implication of intervention in certain disputes. Intervention in international conflicts, in particular, invariably implies that the intervenor — who is, after all, a citizen of some nation, coming from a particular national or cultural background — *will* be biased in some way. The challenge is not to try to remove such bias, but to understand it and to use it as a lever in the service of increasing the chances of agreement.

Christopher Honeyman ("Bias and Mediators' Ethics") builds on Smith's earlier contribution to discuss some of the ethical implications of mediator bias. Honeyman argues, in effect, for the importance of "truth in advertising," providing the disputants with the equivalent of an informed consent arrangement, so that if they choose to invite a biased mediator to intervene, they do so with full awareness of the third party's inclinations and their possible consequences. "Fair notice of bias," he writes, "can serve as the unifying principle which will dispose of much of the confusion over a mediator's ethical obligations."

The final selection in this section, by Mary P. Rowe ("The Corporate Ombudsman: An Overview and Analysis"), broadens the spectrum of possible third party roles by introducing a form of intervention that has become increasingly important in the latter part of the twentieth century: the ombuds. An ombuds intervenes and/or provides guidance in disputes between individuals and institutions — that is, between an individual grievant and the institution of which the grievant is a part and to which the grievance is directed. As Rowe points out, ombuds roles are to be found increasingly throughout all sectors of American society, from colleges and universities, to newspapers, to hospitals, consumer complaint offices, prisons, governors' offices, and now in corporations as well. Her informative and comprehensive report describes the challenges and opportunities faced by the ombudsman in the organization.

Mediated Negotiation[1] in the Public Sector

Lawrence E. Susskind and Connie Ozawa

Elected officials and administrators in the public sector, confronted with increasingly complex choices, must make resource allocation decisions that take into account the competing claims of individuals and groups. In the search for more efficient and effective means of handling these adjudicatory responsibilities, mediated negotiation is being tried more and more frequently. While Americans are quite familiar with the way mediation has been used in collective bargaining and labor relations, for the most part they are unaware of the extent to which mediated negotiation is now being used to resolve family disputes, community disputes, environmental disputes, intergovernmental disputes, and, more recently, scientific controversies and state budget battles.

The list of cases in which mediated negotiation has been used to supplement traditional administrative, legislative, and judicial decision-making is growing steadily (Goldmann, 1980; Talbot, 1983; and Susskind et al., forthcoming). Mediated negotiation was used in Connecticut to decide on the distribution of federal block grant funds for social service programs (Watts, 1983). Several federal agencies, including the Environmental Protection Agency, have experimented with mediation in the rule-making process (Baldwin, 1983). Mediation was used to resolve a crisis in the funding of the state unemployment compensation fund in Wisconsin (Bellman and Sachs, 1983), to resolve water policy disputes in the Denver area and elsewhere (Kennedy and Lansford, 1983; Folk-Williams, 1982), and to handle a variety of complicated cases that the federal district court thought might be resolved more expeditiously by a court-appointed mediator (Goldberg, 1983). Dozens of land use and facility-siting disputes have been resolved through face-to-face negotiation assisted by a "neutral third party" (Susskind, 1981; Bacow and Wheeler, forthcoming). Indeed, several states have incorporated mediated negotiation into the process of siting hazardous waste treatment facilities (Bacow, 1982). These and other instances of mediated negotiation in the public sector go far beyond the processing of interpersonal disputes between neighbors (Alper and Nichols, 1981), husbands and wives (Haynes, 1981), and the more traditional mediation of disputes between labor and management (Simkin, 1971).

Mediated negotiation is attractive because it addresses many of the procedural weaknesses of conventional dispute resolution mechanisms; that is, it allows for more direct involvement of those most affected by decisions than

Lawrence E. Susskind is Professor Urban and Environmental Studies at the Massachusetts Institute of Technology, Cambridge, Mass. **Connie Ozawa** is an Associate of the Program on Negotiation at Harvard Law School, Cambridge, Mass.

do most administrative and legislative processes; it produces results more rapidly and at lower cost than do courts; and it is flexible and therefore more adaptable to the specific needs of the parties in a given situation.

Mediated negotiation depends on the assistance of a nonpartisan facilitator. In practice, the roles played by mediators vary tremendously from situation to situation. At a minimum, the prototype mediator arranges meetings, assists in the exchange of information, tenders proposals at the request of one party or another, and assists the parties in developing clearer statements of their interests. Mediators also can propose possible settlements that parties themselves would accept but not put forward for fear of appearing "soft." Mediators involved thus far in mediated negotiation in the public sector have come from various backgrounds and have very different operating styles. Most, however, look to collective bargaining (labor mediation) for their cues, although this well may be inappropriate, as we will explore further on.

Public sector disputes are special. They differ from conventional two-party private disputes in that they involve choices with substantial spillover effects or externalities that often fall most directly on diffuse, inarticulate, and hard-to-represent groups (such as future generations). It is our contention that mediators involved in resource allocation decisions in the public sector have responsibilities that transcend those facing mediators in more traditional situations. While the record thus far is impressive, it is important to ask whether mediation is as responsive to the broader public interest as are traditional dispute resolution and resource allocation mechanisms. The key question is whether mediators are as accountable to those most affected by their actions as are elected and appointed officials.

In this article we will (1) review some examples of mediated negotiation in the public sector; (2) analyze the process of mediation involved in these cases in an effort to draw some general conclusions; (3) examine measures of success appropriate to judge the outcome of mediated negotiation efforts; (4) analyze the responsibilities of the mediator in public sector resource allocation disputes; (5) assess the relative usefulness of various mediation models and strategies insofar as they apply to public sector mediation; and (6) specify the critical barriers to more widespread use of mediated negotiation in the public sector.

An Introduction to Mediated Negotiation in the Public Sector

We begin with a review of three cases involving the use of mediated negotiation. Each case summary includes a brief chronology of events, an analysis of the mediator's role, and an assessment of the outcome of the negotiation.

The Foothills Case

The Foothills case was sparked by a proposal in the 1970s to construct a water treatment facility, dam, and reservoir on the South Platte River near Denver, Colorado (Burgess, forthcoming). The U.S. Army Corps of Engineers, the Environmental Protection Agency (EPA), the Bureau of Land Management, the Denver Water Board, and numerous environmental action groups stubbornly debated the merits of the proposal, its projected impacts on urban sprawl, on air pollution, and on Waterton Canyon, a valuable wildlife and recreation area.

Congressional Representative Pat Schroeder offered to mediate the case but was rebuffed by the Denver Water Board, one of the project's supporters. When Congressmen Tim Wirth, however, a well-known environmental advocate who appeared to favor some version of the proposed facility, volunteered to serve as mediator, all the parties agreed to negotiate.

Wirth arranged a series of joint meetings with the Corps, EPA, and the Denver Water Board. As soon as these three groups agreed to the terms of a basic settlement, a coalition of environmentalists was consulted. They objected to only a few points in the proposed settlement, and a final agreement was reached with only minor alterations. Although construction of the dam constituted a major concession on the part of the environmentalists and EPA, the parties felt that sufficient compensation and steps to mitigate adverse impacts had been promised.

Congressman Wirth's acceptance as a mediator was particularly noteworthy because of his public stand on the issues in dispute. His position allowed him to bring both subtle and direct pressure to bear on the negotiating parties. He had enough political clout that the federal agencies involved felt he might "cause problems for them" if they did not make concessions. The local organizations and actors involved believed he represented their best interests, although, officially, Wirth was accountable only to the voters in his congressional district. From our standpoint, he appeared at times to demonstrate little concern for interest groups not represented directly at the bargaining table.

Although the participating parties supported the negotiated settlement, in retrospect the negotiation process appears flawed. First, Wirth's decision to bring local environmental groups into the dialogue only after the basic agreement had been drafted by the key governmental agencies caused difficulties in implementing the agreement. A discontented faction of the environmental coalition later contested the settlement in court. Second, the reduced capacity of the negotiated water facility could cause severe water shortages in the Denver area in the future. Ratepayers and future homeowners will be stuck with the costs of expanding the water system (probably at a higher price) sometime in the future. Their interests were not well represented in the negotiation.

In the eyes of the federal, state, and local agencies involved in the Foothills dispute, the mediation effort spearheaded by Wirth appeared to preempt some of their powers and duties. The court judge who presided over the Foothills case trial objected strenuously to the fact that the parties were engaged in an informal negotiation outside the courtroom. From the standpoint of the parties involved, however, an agreement was reached that exceeded what they thought they might achieve in court; or at least they achieved with certainty results that they had only a small chance of gaining in court.

Mediated negotiation does not, in fact preempt the statutory powers of elected and appointed officials. They can choose whether to participate in the negotiations. They can agree whether to be bound by the agreements reached. Eventually, they must grant the necessary permits, licenses, or permissions under the rules and procedures prescribed by law. Mediated negotiation does, however, create a clearly stated public consensus that is difficult for elected and appointed officials to ignore.

In the Foothills case, the key agencies and interest groups informally reached a negotiated settlement that was later ratified through the formal regulator (permitting) process. No group's legal rights were abridged. While there were legitimate stakeholding interests (albeit hard to represent), whose interests were probably not well served, the mediator used his elected position to force some of the reluctant parties to the negotiating table. He did not, however, use his position to ensure that all the stake holding interests were represented (nor did he claim to represent the public interest himself).

Brayton Point Case

Acting under authority granted by the Energy Supply and Environmental Coordination Act (ESECA) of 1974, the Department of Energy notified the New England Power Company (NEPCO) that it would be required to burn coal instead of oil in three units of its electricity generating plant in Somerset, Massachusetts (Smith, forthcoming). NEPCO contested EPA's estimates of the cost of conversion and the steps required to meet air pollution standards. It appeared that prospects for a conversion at the Brayton Point plant that would satisfy all affected parties (i.e., NEPCO, federal and state regulatory agencies, and energy consumers) were poor. Not only were the relationships among the parties uncertain, but the ESECA program itself was new and its policies ambiguous.

In April 1977, the Center for Energy Policy, a nonprofit organization, persuaded the principal parties to accept the services of a mediator and arranged a meeting attended by officials of NEPCO, DOE, EPA, and the Massachusetts Department of Environmental Quality Engineering (DEQE) to explore the possibilities for coal conversion. Although agreeing to participate in the mediated negotiation process, DOE continued to pursue the conversion through formal regulatory channels. (The formal conversion process entailed the issuance of a prohibition order, the preparation of an EIS, and cooperation with EPA in obtaining certification under the State Implementation Plan, as stipulated by the Clean Air Act.) Eleven months later, agreement was reached on all issues.

The final agreement allowed for a phased-in conversion plan at Brayton Point, set limits on the sulfur content of the coal to be burned, and indicated special particulate standards for the facility.

David O'Connor from the Center for Energy Policy served as mediator in the Brayton Point case. He assumed an active role in formulating and negotiating the settlement. His activities can be grouped under five headings.

O'Connor served first as an organizer of the negotiations. He sought approval of informal ground rules for setting the agenda, raising issues, making proposals, dealing with the press, documenting discussions, and formulating agreements. He chaired the meetings, kept written records of the discussions, and documented points of consensus.

Second, he served as an information resource. He helped to explain technical and legal matters to all the parties, ensuring that their understanding of the situation was accurate.

Third, he acted as a source of encouragement, emphasizing the progress being made by the group throughout the negotiations. This provided an important psychological boost and helped to sustain the momentum of the meetings.

Fourth, O'Connor played the role of confidential advisor. He held private meetings with individual parties to help them clarify their understanding of their own interests and allowed them to articulate new positions and proposals in a nonthreatening and risk-free environment.

Finally, through these private interactions, he sought to comprehend the groups' priorities and to understand the central technical factors on which positions turned. From this standpoint, he was able to develop and present composite ideas and options to the groups.

All participating parties expressed satisfaction with the negotiated agreement. DOE, in particular, saw great advantage in gaining voluntary conversion. Although the negotiation did not include representatives of consumer groups, environmentalists, or other public interest groups, additional procedures (i.e., public hearings) required under formal regulatory rules were used to supplement the negotiation process in order to obtain the concurrence and support of unrepresented parties.

While an attempt was made to ensure that the concerns of all affected groups would be heard and presumably incorporated into the ultimate conversion plan, the negotiated agreement could be criticized for neglecting to consider the interests of residents living in areas adjoining the plant. Moreover, while local residents might be satisfied with the phased-in conversion plan, distant portions of the Northeast, susceptible to increased sulfate effluents and acid rain, were offered no direct involvement in the negotiation.

In the eyes of the key participants in the Brayton Point case, the mediated negotiation effort was a success. The parties achieved a voluntary agreement that satisfied all their interests. Not unlike a labor mediator, O'Connor measured his success in terms of the satisfaction with the final agreement expressed by the parties at the negotiation table. While he ensured that all sides based their positions on scientifically accurate interpretations of the coal conversion process, he did not press the participants to address the broader representation issue. One could argue that the state and federal agency officials involved in the negotiation had an obligation to represent the interests of the broader public and that, through the elected officials to whom they reported, they were indirectly accountable to the public at large. This seems, though, to be a rather weak argument.

The Connecticut Negotiated Investment Strategy

The Connecticut Negotiated Investment Strategy (NIS) was aimed at developing a strategy for distributing $33 million of federal aid in the form of a Social Services Block Grant (SSBG) received by the state of Connecticut for fiscal year 1984. Initiated by the Governor's office, 18 state agencies, 114 municipalities, and numerous private service agencies participated in a mediation negotiation (Watts, 1983).

Three teams, representing the 18 state agencies, the municipalities, and the nonprofit public service providers, convened formally in five joint sessions held from October to December 1982. Prior to the negotiating sessions, representatives from the teams met to select a mediator. Training sessions were held to educate the participants about the NIS process and negotiating techniques. Ground rules for the negotiations were established by the participants.

The negotiating sessions involved debating and revising a written statement prepared ahead of time by the participants. They addressed an agenda of issues determined jointly at the first formal meeting. At the fourth full session (held on December 7, 1982), the mediator presented a draft agreement he had prepared by incorporating items of agreement generated during previous discussions. This helped the group narrow the discussion sufficiently to bring the process to a conclusion. A final agreement was reached in a specially scheduled session on December 23, 1982.

The final agreement outlined a process for distributing the SSBG funds and established a Tripartite Commission to monitor the implementation of the agreement, resolve outstanding issues, and serve as interpretor of the agreement in future disputes.

Josh Stulberg, a lawyer and trained mediator, was selected by the negotiating teams to serve as the mediator. The ground rules established by the teams specified a rather passive role for the mediator. His job was to facilitate the negotiating process by designating official observers for the joint sessions, preparing minutes of all joint sessions, coordinating meeting schedules, developing agendas, controlling the pace of the bargaining sessions, and assisting the teams in writing formal statements. Stulberg made little effort to rectify rather obvious power imbalances among the teams. Stulberg, furthermore, made no attempt to clarify technical issues, although the state agencies' representatives apparently had a much more thorough grasp than others of the complicated financial maneuverings that were being proposed.

The document produced through the NIS process and ultimately approved by the governor and the state legislature has been described as "a summary statement of all the teams' positions rather than a collaborative effort to maximize joint gains" (Watts, 1983: 39). The agreement was lacking, it seems, in several important respects: (1) The language of the agreement was ambiguous in numerous places, portending disputes involving interpretation of the document in the future. (2) Incentives and mechanisms to ensure compliance with the agreement were specifically neglected. (3) No timetable for implementation of the agreement was specified. (4) The mediator was not assigned (and did not independently assume) any responsibility for the monitoring of the final agreement.

The Connecticut SSBG allocation for FY 1984 represented a substantial reduction in the level of federal aid available to address crucial human service needs. The allocation criteria and plan developed through the NIS process clearly would affect the entire population of the state, since it stipulated how some of the state's own revenues would be spent to match the federal allocation. Should decisions like these be made through an informal negotiation process? While the governor and the legislature had to approve the NIS proposal, to fail to do so after such an elaborate effort had produced consensus would have thrown the entire budgetary process into turmoil.

A few key interest groups were not involved directly in the Connecticut negotiations, most notably certain human service consumers. Conceivably, the state agency administrators or local elected officials on the teams could have claimed to represent these groups, but they did not. The mediator in this case made no special effort to take account of the externalities, or the spillover effects, of the agreements reached. He did not raise the issue of representation with the teams once they had been selected. He made little or no effort to respond to obvious imbalances in the technical sophistication of the teams. In short, he behaved in a manner quite consistent with the traditional role of a labor mediator. He assumed a rather passive posture, let the parties at the table make the agreement their own, stayed out of the substance of the debate, and took no positions.

Measuring Success

Any evaluation of a dispute resolution effort must consider the fairness, efficiency, and stability of the *outcome* as well as the *process.* Moreover, an assessment of any method of dispute resolution would be incomplete without a comparison of the outcome to other possible outcomes likely to result from other available methods.

At least six criteria have been suggested by which to judge the success of mediation efforts in the public sector:

(1) The negotiated agreement should be readily acceptable to the parties involved.

(2) The results must appear fair to the community.

(3) The results should maximize joint gains (as judged by a disinterested observer).

(4) The results should take past precedents into consideration.

(5) An agreement should be reached with a minimal expenditure of time and money.

(6) The process should improve rather than aggravate the relationships between or among the disputing parties (Fisher, 1979).

In the Foothills case, while the agreement was acceptable to the parties directly involved, some groups affected but not involved directly in the negotiation were not pleased with either the outcome or the process. While the results appeared fair to the community *at large at the time of the agreement,* there is some question as to whether or not the consensus will hold as economic and ecological conditions change. The agreement took a great deal of time to hammer out, but the expenses were less than what it probably would have cost to pursue all the legal opportunities to appeal. Communications among the parties were improved somewhat — they learned how to talk to each other — but it is not clear whether underlying relationships improved at all. With regard to precedents, there were few to take into account. Whether or not joint gains were maximized is a matter of some dispute — some observers felt that the environmentalists gave away too much.

In the Brayton Point case, the agreement was acceptable to the key parties involved, although, again, some groups obviously affected had only the most indirect opportunity to shape the terms of agreement. No special attempt was made to publicize the terms of the settlement so it is hard to judge whether the results were deemed fair in the eyes of the community at large. The agreement was readily acceptable to the parties at the table. The way they dealt with their differences certainly improved relationships among the key actors. It is doubtful, though, that a precedent was established, since so many situational factors were crucial and probably will never occur that way again. Most observers feel that the agreement did maximize the possible joint gains to the parties at the table, but clearly some interests were not attended to in the negotiations.

The Connecticut NIS agreement was acceptable to the parties directly involved, although some concern was expressed by members of the Hispanic community who felt they were not adequately represented. Relationships otherwise were definitely improved. The time and money spent were, in total, probably more than what would have been consumed if the state agencies only were involved. However, a unilateral decision by the state probably would have created substantial political backlash and subsequent instability that would need to be calculated into the net costs. Some observers feel the NIS negotiators in Connecticut sidestepped some of the toughest allocation decisions by turning responsibility for detailed decisions over to the new Tripartite Committee.

If the mediated negotiation process undertaken in the three cases described here were compared with the typical administrative, judicial, or legislative processes used to resolve such conflicts (or competing claims), we would likely find that the outcome and the process of mediation appeared fairer and more efficient to most of the parties involved and produced more stable agreements. It is hard, though, to generate convincing comparative data without artificially created experiments. Moreover, it is important to point out that mediated negotiation is typically a *supplement* to rather than a replacement for the more traditional mechanisms for resolving resource allocation disputes. In this sense, an "either-or" comparison is not really appropriate.

In our American representative democracy, citizens are given the opportunity to affect the decisions of legislative bodies through lobbying and voting. Given the general level of (in)accessibility of most levels of government, lobbying is commonly an option reserved only for the most highly organized and (financially) resourceful groups.

The vote is the most dominant instrument by which individuals may register their concerns; however, it is inadequate in three significant ways. First, our system of "majority rule" in most instances allows little accommodation of minority views, even though the "minority" might comprise a sizable 49% of the enfranchised population. Second, public resource allocation disputes often involve concerns that are not reducible to a yes-or-no decision. Or, in referenda, an individual might wish to vote yes if certain future circumstances become true, and no otherwise. The vote precludes conditional decision-making. Elections limit the expression of opinion by forcing voters to cast their ballots for candidates who usually represent "packages" of positions on various issues. Again, the ultimate outcome of initiatives, referenda, and elections is unlikely to reflect the true wishes of the voting community on any particular public resource allocation dispute. Lastly, the chances of attaining pareto-optimal decisions are usually forfeited by the rigid yes-or-no structure of the ballot. Trades that might maximize joint gains are precluded.

Opportunities for concerned and affected parties to express their views on the judgments made by administrative agencies usually take the form of ad hoc participation in issue-specific public hearings, citizen advisory boards, and public opinion polls and surveys. These methods, too, are limited and fall short of the benefits of direct participation in mediated negotiation.

The outcome of disputes resolved administratively may not appear fair to the community since public input is seldom binding. Decisions are usually made behind closed doors and certain groups often feel frustrated about their inability to influence them. The long queue of legal suits before the courts provides an indication of the lack of success of most administrative dispute resolution efforts.

The judicial process is perhaps the most visible means of dispute resolution. It is not only a means of decision-making, but it is also a device for contesting resource allocation decisions made by legislative and administrative bodies. The adversarial character of legal proceedings, however, discourages joint problem solving and short circuits the search for mutual gain. Typically, the issue is whether a given administrative decision is legal, not whether it is wise. Judicial dispute resolution rarely leaves the disputants with a better working relationship than they had before the conflict erupted.

While mediated negotiation may raise serious questions about the accountability of mediators and the representation of all groups, when compared to traditional means of dispute resolution, mediated negotiation — as a *supplement* to conventional legislative, administrative, and judicial processes — is quite appealing.

Role and Responsibility of the Mediator in Public Resource Allocation Disputes

Public resource allocation disputes invariably involve the interests of parties not easily represented, as in the case of natural resource management decisions affecting future generations. Consideration of the interests of all affected parties, however, often is crucial for the successful implementation and stability of agreements. How can mediation in the public sector be structured to take account of externalities and to ensure appropriate representation of all interested parties?

In labor mediation, negotiating parties are expected to act in their own best interest. While the parties involved in public resource allocation disputes rarely consider the interests of unrepresented stakeholders voluntarily, especially if doing so would impinge on their own interests, a mediator might encourage active consideration of hard-to-represent interests. Such prodding might take the form of question asking. For example, the various proposals on other named (but nonparticipating) groups. In other words, the mediator might purposefully shape the mediation *process* in an effort to influence the *outcome*. This would help assure that mediated settlements serve unrepresented interests to the greatest extent possible.

How might mediators achieve such a result without jeopardizing their neutrality in the eyes of the parties actively involved, and without asserting personal power that nonelected individuals are not expected to have?

One step might be to imagine a credo for mediators to which all those practicing in the public sector would subscribe. Such a credo should include normative statements regarding the ethics of intervention in public sector conflicts, as well as the following:

(1)   Guidelines for defining stakeholding interests in ad hoc dispute resolution and methods of identifying their legitimate spokespersons.

(2)   A list of the objectives of ad hoc negotiation and standards for the conduct of negotiation.

(3)   A description of mechanisms for ensuring the protection of interests not present at the bargaining table and not directly involved in negotiation.

(4)   Prescriptions about the terms of final agreement and the monitoring and implementation of such agreements [Center for Environmental Problem Solving, 1982: 56-61].

We would urge that all potential stakeholding interests be informed that a mediation process is to occur and be given advice on how they can participate. Second, all stakeholding interests should be told how representatives will be selected, and again, how they might become involved. Third, those unable to represent themselves ought to be given the assistance necessary to present their views effectively. Fourth, private stakeholder representatives, who should be selected by those they represent, should be required to state clearly the extent to which they are authorized to speak on behalf of their constituents. Finally, all stakeholding interests, whether represented directly in the negotiations process or not, should be provided the opportunity to express their views on issues under consideration (through a public hearing, at special meetings of the negotiating parties, etc.)

We would further urge that the objectives of each mediated negotiation be stated explicitly and approved by the participating parties. Ground rules should be adopted by consensus to guide the pacing of the negotiation (with attention to time for thoughtful reflection and consultation with constituents), confidentiality, and communications with the public.

Procedures should be integrated into the negotiation process to ensure the protection of those interests not represented at the bargaining table but likely to be affected by the ultimate settlement. The responsibility for "second guessing" what views such interests might express in the negotiation should not rest with the mediator; rather, the mediator should be prepared to question the negotiating parties as to how they perceive the welfare of those unrepresented will be affected by proposed agreements. If the mediator believes that the interests of stakeholders not present at the negotiation would be adversely affected, he or she ought to point this out. Responsibility for such action derives from the mediator's obligation to help the parties develop a *stable* agreement, since disgruntled parties might seek to block implementation of the negotiated agreement. In a similar vein, agreements should not be finalized until all the steps necessary to ensure implementation have been clarified. This might require public review and comment on the proposed agreement, or consultation with administrative bodies with relevant jurisdiction. Ideally, mediated negotiation should be conducted so as to leave the disputing parties in the best possible working relationship in the future.

In our view, the language of agreements should meet certain minimum standards. First, agreements should be comprehensible to the lay public. Details such as contingencies, linkages to formal decisions by bodies with pertinent authority, and remediation procedures should be stated explicitly. All the negotiating parties should carefully review the terms of agreement to ensure that joint gains have been maximized and that the agreement is grounded on principles that they will be prepared to endorse in the future.

Finally, from our standpoint, the roles and responsibilities of each of the participating parties — and the mediator — with respect to implementation and monitoring of the agreement should be specified in the written document.

The mediator should be required at the outset of the negotiation to outline in writing how he or she will ensure consideration of the points mentioned above. Such a procedure might protect the mediator from subsequent charges of bias, prevent the incidence of a "mediator with a mission" from subverting the negotiations, and ensure the integrity and credibility of the mediation process in the eyes of the public-at-large.

It has been suggested by a number of observers that the impartiality of the mediator is one of the prominent and critical conditions that makes mediation attractive to disputants in the first place. Although the mediator is expected to maintain an interest in the mediation *process*, it has been argued that he or she must be neutral with regard to *outcome*. Based on the labor mediation model, mediators assume the roles of catalyst, educator, translator, seeker of additional resources, bearer of bad news, agent of reality, and scapegoat (Stulberg, 1980). Our proposal, that mediators might not be neutral with regard to the adequacy of representation, has been attacked as heresy in the mediation field (McCrory, 1980).

While it may be necessary for mediators to be perceived as nonpartisan, the claim of neutrality, in our view, is misleading. Mediators are rarely disinterested in the outcome of their efforts. Every mediator has a motive for engaging in dispute resolution. Whether that motive is primarily money, fame or public service, mediators have an interest in bringing parties not only to an agreement, but to an agreement that satisfies the disputants and "sits well" with their peers.

The growing popularity of alternative methods of dispute resolution (mediation, arbitration, etc.) has created an increasing willingness to experiment with mediation in public sector disputes. Because of the substantial and long-lasting impacts that public sector resource allocation decisions can have on the public welfare, those who play mediating roles in public sector disputes ought to reflect on the special responsibilities that face them.

Searching for an Appropriate Model of Practice

The Labor Model and its Shortcomings
Collective bargaining has provided the model of practice for most professionals interested in public sector dispute resolution. In at least one type of public dispute, involving environmental impacts, the labor model has been found inadequate (Susskind and Weinstein, 1980). There are strong indications that in the larger realm of public resource allocation disputes, the labor model may prove similarly inappropriate.

In collective bargaining situations, the mediator is assumed to be preoccupied primarily (if not exclusively) with *process*. In contrast, as suggested earlier, it may be preferable for the mediator in environmental and other public disputes to assume the additional responsibility of attending to certain key qualities of the *results* of the resolution process (i.e., fairness, efficiency, and stability).

Discrepancies between these two conceptions of the mediator's role and responsibilities may be accounted for by differences in the nature and context of the disputes and in the relationships among the disputing parties. Seven aspects of public sector disputes which call into question the applicability of the labor mediation model to public dispute mediation have been identified.

(1)   While the parties in labor disputes are easily identifiable and able to select spokespersons to participate in mediation, groups whose interests are likely to be affected by public resource allocation decisions often are not. Fifty years of experience in the labor relations field has helped to institutionalize both expectations and procedures for representation. Such institutionalization has not occurred in the public disputes field.

(2)   While the issues at stake in labor disputes are fairly well defined (wages, fringe benefits, working conditions), and the distribution of costs and benefits is more or less predictable, in public sector disputes the concerns are frequently amorphous and difficult to articulate (e.g., the risks involved with the siting of hazardous wastes), and the magnitude and distribution of impacts is not well understood.

(3)   In collective bargaining, the relationship between the disputing parties is ongoing, well established, and involves familiar strategies (strikes, lock-outs, etc.). In public sector disputes, the conflict may represent a one-time encounter between adversaries who have never negotiated with each other before.

(4)   The parties involved in labor disputes are relatively experienced in negotiating techniques. In public sector disputes, the experience of the parties in negotiation varies tremendously; often some parties may be completely new to the give-and-take of negotiation.

(5)   In labor disputes the parties' interests in settling are usually symmetrical (they both incur increasing costs the longer the dispute remains unresolved). This is not always the case in public sector disputes. In land use disputes, for example, environmental groups may come out ahead as long as no decision is reached.

(6)   Labor mediation usually entails bilateral negotiations; public sector disputes commonly involve numerous public agencies and several special interest groups. Multilateral disputes (and the attendant issues of coalition politics) make public disputes much more complicated and unpredictable.

(7)   In collective bargaining, potential "spillover effects" caused by excessive demands are minimized by standard references to inflation rates, government consumer price indices, and other indicators which guide the fairness of the settlement. In public sector disputes, similar constraints have not been developed to moderate the demands of individual negotiators (Susskind and Weinstein, 1980).

In summary, since the structure, context, and content of collective bargaining is well established, a mediator acting only as the guardian of the process might well be acceptable. Representation is rarely an issue, since the parties are readily identifiable and participate directly. There is less need for the mediator to serve as educator, since the parties are usually experienced in negotiation and well-informed about the issues. The bilateral nature of negotiations between parties accustomed to bargaining with one another reduces the pressure on the mediator to coordinate concessions and counterproposals actively. Also, the parties' continuing relationship tends to ensure their compliance with both procedural conventions and the terms of negotiated agreements. These assumptions, in our view, do not match the circumstances surrounding most public sector disputes.

The International Model
The role of mediators in international disputes contrasts sharply with the labor model of mediation. In international mediation, the mediator maintains overt control over the proceedings and plays a much more active part in the development of the terms of settlement. This, in our view, resembles more closely the appropriate role of mediators in public sector disputes.

Zartman and Berman point out that "nothing requires the third party itself to be subtle and indirect, except for the general requirements of effectiveness" (1982: 78). It is acceptable, according to Zartman and Berman, for the mediator to take an active posture. He or she can use tactics such as pointing out benefits that will flow from a solution or new possibilities for resolving the problem, showing harm that will occur if no solution is found, or even taking a more active stance and offering inducements for a negotiated outcome or threatening deprivations if one or both parties refuse to talk.

Although Henry Kissinger is generally considered exceptional among international mediators, Pruitt explains that Kissinger's intervention in the Middle East illustrates a number of traditional mediation strategies and techniques (Rubin, 1981). These extend beyond the role of "facilitator" or "catalyst." As mediator, Kissinger,

(1) directly controlled all communications between the disputing parties;

(2) actively persuaded the parties to make concessions;

(3) acted as a scapegoat and deflector of the parties' anger and frustration, rather than allowing the parties to express their emotions to one another;

(4) coordinated the exchange of concessions, and, by so doing, masked the bargaining strengths of the parties to one another;

(5) made his own proposals for possible resolution; and

(6) created and maintained the momentum of the talks.

Moreover, Kissinger's entry into the Israeli-Arab conflict was strongly motivated by the interest of the U.S. government. In *Dynamics of Third Party Intervention*, a collection of analyses of Kissinger's Middle East efforts, Rubin notes that "several contributors conclude that Kissinger was primarily interested in protecting or enhancing the power and reputation of the United States in the Middle East, particularly in relation to the perceived interests and objectives of the Soviet Union." (1981: 274). Kissinger's interest in bringing the two parties to a settlement was apparently strong enough to warrant exorbitant promises of U.S. military and economic assistance aimed at inducing the parties to make concessions.

How can a mediator have an agenda of his or her own and still retain the trust of the parties? Both Fisher and Zartman have commented on this issue. Zartman (1983) suggests that mediators are not indifferent to the prospect of reaching agreement, nor to the principles that are referenced in choosing among alternative solutions, nor to the ways they are perceived by the parties before, during, and after a dispute. He also suggests that mediators typically exert leverage by taking advantage of the parties' relative eagerness for a settlement, suggesting possible side payments, and allowing the parties to "be soft, but act tough" (by transmitting concessionary offers privately while the parties continue to posture in public). Such active involvement in negotiations suggests that mediators are far from neutral, although Zartman does emphasize that mediators manipulate the parties only with their tacit permission. Fisher (1984) suggests that mediators can exert influence in the same way any party can, by taking advantage of (1) the power of skill and knowledge, (2) the power of a good relationship, (3) the power of a good alternative to negotiating, (4) the power of a good option, (5) the power of legitimacy, and (6) the power of commitment. Mediators can and do exert influence. If mediators of international disputes can play such an active role and still retain the confidence of all the parties, why should mediators in public sector disputes adopt the more passive style of their labor counterparts?

Obstacles to More Widespread Use of Mediated Negotiation in the Public Sector
There are several obstacles to more widespread use of mediated negotiation in the public sector.

Representation
One of the first hurdles to overcome, as we have noted already, is the identification of all the parties likely to hold an interest in the outcome. In private disputes, the affected parties identify themselves. In public disputes, especially those with spillover effects, the definition of legitimate stakeholding interests can itself lead to conflict.

Assuming the problem of identifying interests can be overcome, the next obstacle is to ensure that appropriate spokespersons are selected. The lack of organization or structure of certain interests hinders the selection process. However, since the effectiveness of a negotiated agreement often depends on the ability of representatives to reflect accurately and respond effectively to the needs, priorities, values, and interests of the groups involved, the selection of spokespersons is critical. Difficulty in ensuring that spokespersons have the authority they need to commit their constituents may undermine an entire effort.

Finally, the ad hoc selection of a representative to participate in mediated negotiations may provoke opposition from true believers in "representative democracy." Our system of government was established on the premise of representation by elected officials. Beginning with the Interstate Commerce

Act of 1887, officials have delegated limited public policymaking authority to independent commissions and "New Deal"-type agencies. This has not, however, been achieved without criticism (Lowi, 1969). Mediated negotiation in the formulation of public policy and public resource allocation decisions may suggest to some yet another undesirable step away from representative democracy (Haefele, 1974).

Linking Informal Negotiation to Formal Regulatory and Adjudicatory Mechanisms

Elected decision-makers may hesitate to participate in a mediation effort. They may feel threatened by a process that forces them to surrender even a modicum of their authority. Government agencies may be unsure about the propriety of participating in ad hoc negotiation in light of their legislative mandates. Reporting on recent U.S. Geological Survey (USGS) and Council on Environmental Quality (CEQ) experiments with environmental mediation, Sachs found that "federal officials fear that mediated settlement might be challenged under the Administrative Procedures Act" (Sachs, 1982: 97).

Individuals and action groups participating in informal dispute resolution efforts may feel uncertain about the extent to which they relinquish their constitutional rights if they agree to participate. They may be concerned that statements made during informal negotiations will be used against them should negotiations fail and litigation follow. Sachs notes that "some attorneys feel the use of collaborative procedures in the early stages of a case might weaken their position in later court action" (1982: 97).

Insufficient Incentives to Bring All the Key Parties to the Bargaining Table

A significant hindrance to the more widespread use of mediated negotiation in public resource allocation disputes is the lack of sufficient incentives to bring all disputing parties, particularly the most powerful, to the bargaining table.

In disputes involving groups with unequal bargaining power, the party holding the advantage may not recognize the need for mediation. The more powerful group may believe that it can achieve its goals without making concessions. Negotiations are unlikely to attract all the parties to the bargaining table as long as one or more parties is convinced that it can "win it all."

Unfamiliarity with Mediation

Another obstacle to more frequent use of mediated negotiation is the sheer lack of information about the method and its advantages. Past experiments with mediated negotiation in the public sector have not received much attention in the press, government publications, or in the university programs that train administrators, planners, and lawyers. The concept of mediation remains tied, in the public's mind, to collective bargaining, divorce proceedings, and, more recently, community disputes (consumer complaints, disputes between neighbors, and other small-scale disagreements).

Availability of Trained Mediators

Even if an administrator or a private citizen involved in a public resource allocation dispute wishes to advocate a mediated approach, the lack of trained mediators acceptable to all the parties may impede the effort.

Disputants in search of a nonpartisan and qualified mediator are often at a loss as how to locate a suitable person. Referral services are not yet well established. Thus far, most mediators are volunteers. Prominent citizens, respected by all the parties in the dispute or identified through an ad hoc network of professionals in the field of dispute resolution, may be available. This is not a system that can work as the demand grows.

The payment of mediators is a sensitive matter. The parties to a dispute may question the nonpartisanship of a mediator paid by only one of the parties. Most of the experiments in public sector mediation have been financed by private foundations. These funds are limited. No equivalent to the Federal Mediation and Conciliation Service (one source of mediators in collective bargaining disputes) exists yet. Mechanisms for equitable sharing of the costs of mediation will be needed to overcome a critical barrier to the more widespread use of mediation in public disputes.

Conclusion

Some of the obstacles described above may dissolve as the field of public dispute resolution matures and existing institutional arrangements are adapted to accommodate the peculiarities of mediated negotiation. Other obstacles will give way only to further research and experimentation.

Our objective in this article has not been to advocate the use of mediated negotiation in public disputes, but rather to urge its proponents to consider seriously whether mediators can be held sufficiently accountable to the interests of the public at large. In our view, mediators *might* be sufficiently accountable, but only if (1) they choose an appropriately activist model to guide their practice (which in our view is definitely not the labor mediation model); (2) they adopt an appropriate credo that is known to all potential participants in each mediated negotiation effort; (3) they assume measures of success that emphasize the quality (but not the particular substance) of agreements; and (4) they continue to seek better ways of overcoming the obstacles to more widespread use of mediated negotiation in the public sector.

NOTE

1. The term "mediated negotiation" rather than "mediation" is used in order to emphasize the presence of a neutral intervenor and to distinguish mediated negotiation from other consensual approaches to dispute resolution that employ the assistance of a third party.

REFERENCES

Alper, B. S. and **Nichols, L. T.** (1981). *Beyond the Courtroom*. Lexington, Mass.: D. C. Heath.

Bacow, L. S. and **Milkey, J. R.** (1982). "Overcoming opposition to hazardous waste facilities: the Massachusetts approach." *Harvard Environmental Law Rev.* 6, 2: 265-305.

Bacow, L. S. and **Wheeler, M.** (forthcoming). *Environmental Dispute Resolution*. New York: Plenum.

Baldwin, N. J. (1983). "Negotiated rulemaking: a case study of administrative reform." Master's thesis, Department of Urban Studies and Planning, Massachusetts Institute of Technology (unpublished).

Bellman, H. and **Sachs, A.** (forthcoming). "Similarities in labor and environmental mediation." Public Disputes Program, Harvard Law School.

Burgess, H. (forthcoming). "The Foothills water project: a case study of environmental mediation." In L. Susskind et al., *Resolving Environmental Regulatory Disputes*. Cambridge, Mass.: Schenkman.

Center for Environmental Problem Solving [ROMCOE] (1982). Workshop Summary. Environmental Conflict Management Practitioners' Workshop, Florissant, Colorado, October 27-29.

Fisher, R. (1979). "Some notes on criteria for judging the negotiation process." Presented at the Negotiation Seminar of the Harvard Negotiation Project, Harvard Law School.

———. (1978). *International Mediation: A Working Guide*. Cambridge, Mass.: Harvard Negotiation Project, Harvard Law School.

———. (1984). "Negotiating power: Getting and using influence." *American Behavioral Scientist*.

——— and **Ury, W.** (1981). *Getting to YES: Negotiating Agreement Without Giving In*. Boston: Houghton Mifflin.

Folk-Williams, H. A. (1982). Water in the West. Santa Fe, N. M.: The Western Network.

Fuller (1979). "The forms and limits of adjudication." *Harvard Law Rev.* 92, 353: 294-404.

Goldberg, S. (1983). "Mediation in Civil Suits: Three Case Studies." Presented at the Harvard Negotiation Seminar, April 19.

Goldmann, R. B. (1980). *Roundtable Justice: Case Studies in Conflict Resolution*. Boulder, Colo.: Westview Press.

Haefele, E. (1974). *Representative Government and Environmental Management*. Baltimore, Md.: Johns Hopkins University Press.

Haynes, J. (1981). *Divorce Mediation: A Practical Guide for Therapists and Counselors*. New York: Springer.

Kennedy, W. J. D. and **Lansford, H.** (1983). "The metropolitan water round table: resource allocation through conflict management." *Environmental Impact Assessment Rev.* 4:1.

Lake, L. M. (1980). *Environmental Mediation: The Search for Consensus*. Boulder, Colo.: Westview Press.

Lowi, T. J. (1969). *The End of Liberalism: Ideology, Policy, an the Crisis of Public Authority*. New York: W. W. Norton.

McCrory, J. P. (1981). "Environmental mediation — another piece of the puzzle." *Vermont Law Rev.* 6, 1: 49-84.

Murray, F. [ed.] (1981). *Detailed Reports of the Task Forces: Two Volumes and a Summary*. National Coal Policy Project, Washington, D.C.: Center for Strategic and International Studies, Georgetown University.

O'Connor, D. (1978). "Environmental mediation: the state-of-the-art." *Environmental Impact Assessment Rev.* 2: 91-17.

Rubin, J.Z. [ed.] (1981) *Dynamics of Third Party Intervention: Kissinger in the Middle East*. New York: Praeger.

Sachs, A. (1982). "Nationwide study identifies barriers to environmental negotiation." *Environmental Impact Assessment Rev.* 3, 1: 95-100.

Simkin, W. E. (1971). *Mediation and the Dynamics of Collective Bargaining*. Washington, D. C.: Bureau of National Affairs.

Simkin, D. (forthcoming). "Brayton Point coal conversion." In L. Susskind et al., *Resolving Environmental Regulatory Disputes*. Cambridge, Mass.: Schenkman.

Stulberg, J. B. (1981). "The theory and practice of mediation: a reply to Professor Susskind." *Vermont Law Rev.* 6, 1: 85-117.

Sullivan, T. (forthcoming). *Resolving Development & Disputes Through Negotiations*. Environment Mediation: Channeling Conflict Into Compromise. New York: Plenum.

Susskind, L. (1981). "Environmental mediation and the accountability problem." *Vermont Law Rev.* 6, 1: 147.

——— and **Keefe, F.** (1980). "The negotiation process: negotiated investment strategy for Columbus, Ohio" (unpublished).

——— and **Weinstein, A.** (1980). "Towards a theory of environmental dispute resolution." *Boston College Environmental Affairs Law Rev.* 9, 2: 311-357.

———, **Bacow, L.** and **Wheeler, M.** (forthcoming). *Resolving Environmental Regulatory Disputes.* Cambridge, Mass.: Schenkman.

Talbot, A. R. (1983). *Settling Things: Six Case Studies in Environmental Mediation.* Washington, D. C.: Conservation Foundation.

Watts, S. (1983). "Description and assessment of the Connecticut negotiation investment strategy experiment." Prepared for the Program on Negotiation, Harvard Law School (unpublished).

Zartman, I. W. (1983). "Mediation in International Disputes." Presented at the Harvard Negotiation Seminar, May 17.

——— and **Berman, M. R.** (1982). *The Practical Negotiator.* New Haven, Conn.: Yale Univ. Press.

Effectiveness of the Biased Mediator

William P. Smith

Third-party mediation of social conflict has become an important element of conflict resolution, regardless of the particular setting: the family, industrial organizations, or international relations. The typical image people have of mediation is drawn largely from labor-management conflict and, to a lesser extent, from divorce mediation — what Pruitt (1981a) has called "traditional mediation." However, there is some question as to whether the principles of traditional mediation are general enough to permit their effective application to international mediation. My aim is to compare traditional mediation with international mediation, particularly with regard to the role of mediator bias, in an effort to broaden understanding of the mediation process. Examples are drawn from United States mediation in the Middle East and in the 1982 Falkland Island crisis.

Traditional Mediation

Parties with a conflict of interest often find it difficult to reach a mutually acceptable agreement, even when both favor negotiated settlement. They may become committed to particular negotiating positions even when they suspect that other, more viable settlement points are available. Such commitments result from fear of losing the confidence of allies or constituents, and of appearing weak in the eyes of the community and/or the opposing negotiator. Parties locked in conflict often develop highly competitive attitudes toward each other and may break off communication, or use it to denounce each other. The intervention of third parties as mediators in such conflict often proves helpful in moving the parties toward resolution.

Analyses of traditional mediation have led to the tentative identification of numerous characteristics of effective mediators and mediation. One requirement for successful mediation often stressed in such analyses is the mediator's impartiality to the adversaries and their positions. The underlying logic of this requirement is that a mediator with a significant bias toward one party will be perceived as its ally. The opposing party will then regard the mediator with the same suspicion and hostility that already characterizes its attitude toward the "favored" party. In addition, the favored party, feeling strengthened by the mediator's support, will find even less incentive to concede or seek new solutions than was the case prior to the third party's entry. In this way the entry of a biased mediator may make the original conflict even more intractable.

William P. Smith is a Professor of Psychology at Vanderbilt University, 134 Wesley Hall, Nashville, Tenn. 37240.

Traditional mediators are accepted by the adversaries and exert influence because they are seen as having no interest in the conflict beyond its peaceful resolution. Indifference toward the parties' positions permits the mediator to consider each in a detached fashion and to explore alternatives that the parties' own confrontational postures would not allow. It also permits the mediator to represent each party's interests to the other with greater credibility than either would have through direct contact since, of the three parties, only the mediator has no direct stake in the outcome. Hence when the mediator argues for the importance of concession making, the message is more likely to be taken seriously than are the adversary's protestations.

The impartiality of traditional mediators stems from the absence of any extended relationship between mediator and disputants. Mediators fill a societally defined role as facilitators; their economic and social outcomes derive from the successful performance of this role, which explicitly prohibits mediation in settings where they have some extended relationship with either of the parties in the dispute.

There are also institutional arrangements that protect the mediator from economic pressure applied by adversaries; for example, a divorce mediator typically requires payment in advance from the couple, or is paid by some third, institutional party such as a court of law. In the case of divorce mediation, the ultimate agreement is legally sanctioned; precluding any further mediator involvement. Similar arrangements exist for mediation in industrial relations. In short, the societally imposed role requirements for traditional mediators insulate them from any direct interests in the respective fates of the parties in dispute.

Even these institutional arrangements cannot be expected to render mediators wholly unbiased. Inasmuch as they are held to certain standards of fairness and stability of agreement, mediators are likely to have some preferences about the form an agreement ultimately takes (Susskind and Ozawa, 1983). Further, being human, mediators often come to like one party more than the other or view one as more reasonable than the other. Nonetheless, it is generally assumed that such biases are likely to undermine the effectiveness of mediation, and institutional arrangements are designed to minimize the potential interest that a mediator may have in the substance of an agreement.

International Mediation

The importance of mediator impartiality, or "even-handedness," has also been stressed in the context of international conflict. For instance, the United Nations, for some years after its establishment, was regarded as the major hope for peaceful resolution of international disputes; significantly, its Secretary-General, one of whose major roles was that of mediator in international conflicts, was (and is) typically drawn from small, relatively weak, and non-aligned nations. Representatives of such nations are regarded as having more limited interests than are characteristic of great powers. Moreover, even when great powers do become involved in the mediation of international conflict, they usually issue public avowals of impartiality. This has certainly been true for the United States in the Middle East and in the Falkland Islands Crisis of 1982.

When one considers the role of individual nations as mediators in international conflict, however, it is difficult to see how the criterion of impartiality can be met. In most cases, the mediating nation's interest in resolving the conflict stems from considerable interest in its own relationship with one or both of the adversaries. The mediator offers — or thrusts upon the adversaries — its services either out of fear that its own interests may be injured in the course of the conflict, or in the hope that it may gain something from the adversaries or their allies. Furthermore, the mediator may have a direct stake in the particulars of any agreement that the adversaries may reach, independent of either of the adversaries' positions. In the context of the Falkland Island crisis, it seems clear that the United States had a direct interest in discouraging armed takeovers in the Western Hemisphere, especially when done in the name of anticolonialism. We need only consider the difficulties that the Panama Canal Treaty posed for the United States in order to grasp the nature of these interests. Far from being the detached and disinterested broker that is evidenced in the traditional mediator, the international mediator is often a highly involved and interested party. This is so because there is little motivation for international mediation outside the mediating nation's interests in its relationship with the adversaries, and in the particulars of the agreement: in effect, there is no international society that can enforce role requirements.

Institutional arrangements insure that traditional mediators' payoffs are contingent simply on efforts to help the adversaries reach an agreement. Hence the relationship that motivates traditional mediators is one totally outside the ring of the conflict to be mediated. Despite similar efforts by regional and worldwide international organizations to establish disinterested mediation services (such as the Organization for African Unity, Organization of American States, and the United Nations), these services rarely assure the mediator's detachment from the conflict. These organizations function more like voluntary interest groups than like the legal and police systems of a society.

Furthermore, since the international community is small by the standards of modern human communities, each member state knows each of the others and has some interest in each of them. The result is that the organization sponsoring the mediator is likely to form a web of interests in any particular conflict, with member states pressuring the mediator and threatening to withdraw support from any mediated solution that does not please them. Instead of insulating a mediator from pressure, international organizations may simply complicate that pressure. Thus while an organization such as the United Nations may stimulate the process of mediation; pressures from within the organization's membership deprive the mediator of the insulated environment necessary for traditional mediation. In any case, my focus here is on the role of individual states, rather than international organizations as mediators.

Given that mediators on the international scene typically intervene because of interest in one or both of the adversaries, or in the particulars of any resolution itself, what place does unbiased mediation have in this context? One approach might be to define mediators as unbiased if their strong interest in each adversary would make it difficult to choose between them.

However, having an interest in one party does not ordinarily cancel the mediator's interest in the other. For one thing, the nature of the interests to be served may well differ with respect to each party. The mediator's ties with one side may stem from ideological affinity and economic cooperation, while those with the other may involve military alliances against parties outside the focal conflict. Mediators are motivated to serve all such interests, and enter the conflict out of a desire to avoid having to choose between the parties. In analyzing the role of a mediating nation in international conflict, it is important to identify the mediator interests in each of the adversaries, as well as its own direct interests in the particulars of any agreement.

Consider, for instance, the case of Kissinger's 1973-75 mediation in the Middle East. The United States certainly had an interest in the security of Israel; it also had vital interests in blunting Soviet influence in Egypt, as well as in convincing Arab nations to end the oil embargo. While the United States had interests on both sides of the conflict, could Kissinger be considered unbiased? It seems impossible to make such a calculation: as representative of the United States, Kissinger was biased in different respects toward all parties involved.

Or consider the interests of the United States in the Falkland Islands crisis. The U.S. had a strong relationship with the United Kingdom, including deep ideological ties, strategic ties through NATO, and numerous economic and cultural ties. On the other hand, the U.S. was also attempting to develop a relationship with Argentina designed to combat Communism in Latin America, an issue of great importance to the administration in power at the time. Further, as I noted earlier, there is good reason to believe that the U.S. had an interest in the particulars of any agreement between Britain and Argentina; specifically, it had a stake in Argentina withdrawing its troops from the Falklands in an effort to enforce provisions of the U.N. Charter. While it could be argued that when forced to choose, the U.S. clearly would side with Britain, and thus was a biased mediator, the aim of mediation is the avoidance of such a choice. In short, mediation in international conflict is probably always biased to some degree. Biased mediation, as shown by Kissinger in the Middle East, can sometimes work. The question is how it works.

I have noted that the mediating nation in an international conflict offers its services out of an interest in the adversaries, or in the specifics of the outcome of their negotiations. The question that obviously follows is why would the adversaries accept the services of a biased mediator? The answer appears to lie in the interdependence between the adversaries and the mediator. From the perspective of each adversary, the mediator's interest in a relationship with it gives it some leverage over the mediator. Even if a party to the conflict believes that the mediator has strong ties to its opponent, it will accept mediation to the extent that it feels it has something to offer or withhold in its relationship with the mediator.

On the other hand, the mediator also has something to offer the adversaries. In part, what it can offer each side derives from its relationship with the other. As Saadia Touval (1982) has commented in his analysis of mediation in the Arab-Israeli conflict, one party can expect the mediator's relationship with the other to offer leverage in the conflict — leverage not available to the one party alone. Indeed, in many cases, the stronger the mediator's relationship with the other party, the greater its leverage; hence, the more desirable it is as a mediator.

In addition, a powerful mediator may be able to hold out the promise of benefits independent of the adversary's concessions. One important benefit of mediation by the great powers is the promise to enforce an agreement the parties reach. Since there is no institutional guarantee of agreements in international relations, a mediator's offer to enforce an agreement is an important inducement to concessions. Other benefits may stem from the mediator's promise of economic and military support, unrelated to the conflict in question. In short, a mediator is accepted by each adversary because of the mediator's power over the opposing party, and the adversary's own power over the mediator.

The actual value of the mediating nation's services in resolving the conflict is directly related to the nature of its interdependent relationships with the adversaries; it is based on the same factors that lead to the mediator's acceptance by the parties in conflict. The biased mediator can be expected to use its relationship with each of the parties to gain concessions for the other. Further, it can be expected to heed each party's vital interests in pressing for concessions, and in helping to develop new alternatives because of its interests in the relationship with that party. As Touval (1982) has pointed out, mediation in the international setting becomes three-cornered bargaining in a very real sense. In contrast, the influence of traditional mediators is based on their lack of connection with the adversaries, and hence their lack of bias.

One implication of this analysis is that the mediating nation's power within the international community, as well as its power over each of the adversaries, will play an important part in its acceptability and success as a mediator. It's therefore logical to expect that great power mediation will be generally more successful than small power mediation. On the other hand, even great power mediation will not work unless the great power's own interests are in some measure held hostage by both adversaries.

Do the ingredients of traditional mediation — detachment and credibility — play any role in the international domain? It seems clear that they play critical roles, but their basis is different. Even biased mediators are likely to be less committed to, and more detached from, the particular positions the adversaries have put forward than are the adversaries themselves. To be sure, mediators have their own interests, but these are likely to parallel rather than be identical to those of either adversary. These differing interests themselves may unfreeze a deadlock between the adversaries — they may suggest new perspectives. With respect to credibility, biased mediators can be trusted not to advocate actions that would endanger their own interests in each of the parties. They are trusted not because they are disinterested, but because their joint interest in both parties keeps them from being the pawn of either. To put this point another way, mediators are unlikely to pursue settlements that are seen as threatening to either party's vital interests, as long as the mediator has some incentive to maintain a positive relationship with both parties. To be sure, where a mediator's interests in one party are much stronger than in the other, the party with the weaker relationship must be wary. But as Touval (1982) has noted, errors in communication can occur also in traditional mediation; if one knows the leanings of the mediator, attempts can be made to allow for bias in interpreting the mediator's actions.

One additional factor that the biased mediator brings to the conflict may also help in the search for resolution: the mediator's direct interest in the particulars of the agreement. Schelling (1963) has noted that a mediator's suggestion may form the basis for agreement in an otherwise intractable conflict simply because the suggestion is a prominent cue. The particular elements a mediator prefers to see in the agreement may then form part of what Zartman (1977) has called the formula around which the actual negotiations take place. In addition, in the case of an interested, biased mediator, the mediator's own preferences will also be seen as difficult to counteract, especially the preferences of a powerful mediator. This is all the more reason for those preferences to form a prominent focus for agreement.

Understanding Bias

I have argued here that mediators in international conflict typically are far from impartial because of interests in their relationship with one or both parties, and in the specifics of the agreement reached. Nevertheless, mediators who are biased in the sense of having a stake in the contents of the agreement can still be effective. Indeed, as Touval (1982) has pointed out, the mediator's relationship with one adversary may be seen by the other as representing possible leverage for wresting concessions. However, the concept of "relationship" typically denotes a potential for a two-way flow of influence. If the mediator has leverage with one party by virtue of a relationship with that party, that party by the same token, has some leverage with the mediator. An adversary must see at least some possibility of a relationship with the mediator as well as between the opponent and the mediator for the mediation to be accepted. The adversary can then use the leverage of his or her own relationship with the mediator to insure that the mediator's bias toward the opponent will not dominate the process. In short, mediator acceptability and effectiveness are determined by both the control each party believes the mediator exerts over the other, and the control each party believes it has over the mediator. Hence Touval's characterization of biased mediation as tripartite bargaining seems entirely apt.

Nonetheless, the fact that mediator effectiveness in international conflict is based on interests and control presents its own unique problems. For one, the mediator must credibly display an interest in both parties. This undoubtedly accounts for the proclamations of "even-handedness" in a would-be mediator's initial public statements of intent to mediate, as with Kissinger in the Middle East and Haig in the Falkland Islands crisis. Such statements are probably critical in circumstances where the potential mediator has clearly important ties to one party, but weaker or less proven ties to the other. The statements themselves commit the mediators publicly to some weakening of identity of interests with the favored party, and at least indicate the possibility of a stronger relationship with the less-favored party.

However, statements alone may be received as hollow rhetoric unless the less favored party can find more concrete evidence of the mediator's need or desire for a relationship. In the case of U.S. mediation in the Middle East, Egypt in particular had good reason to believe that Kissinger viewed Egypt as a key to influencing the supply of Middle East oil, as well as a possible bastion against Soviet influence in the area. In the Falkland Islands Crisis, the U.S. had already lifted the arms embargo on Argentina, and had made clear its view of

Argentina's role in a Latin American pact to oppose Communist influence in the Western Hemisphere.

Unfortunately, mediator efforts to assure the less-favored party of interest in that party's welfare can backfire. They can ultimately lead either or both parties to misinterpret the real interests of the mediator. For example, the adversaries may conclude that the more favored party's interests are truly no longer favored very strongly; the favored party may then balk at concessions requested by the mediator. Or, the less favored party may be misled into positions and actions that are in fact unacceptable to the mediator because of the mediator's relationship with the more favored party.

An effective mediator must be able to communicate just what settlements are unacceptable as a consequence of its own interests. However, just how and when to communicate such proscriptions is another matter. A mediator may be able to steer one of the adversaries away from the unacceptable demands without ever stating their unacceptability. Indeed, a blunt statement of the mediator's own interests at the outset of mediation may chill the process. Nonetheless, at some point a clear signal may be necessary, even at the expense of impeding agreement in order to forestall even more serious consequences.

Two examples from international mediation illustrate the problems of effectively communicating mediator interests. One case was largely successful: that of Kissinger in the Middle East in 1973-75. The U.S. commitment to Israel was clear not only from the context of the historical relationship of these countries, but also more immediately from the emergency military support the U.S. provided Israel after the Yom Kippur attack by Egypt and Syria. On the other hand, the U.S.-Egyptian relationship was far more tentative, and more a matter of potential than of fact. That each side of the U.S.-Egypt dyad saw potential benefits from a relationship is clear. Egypt sought economic and military assistance and leverage with Israel, while the U.S. sought leverage on the oil crisis, and a significant means of blocking Soviet influence in the area. Nonetheless, a war had just taken place between Egypt and Israel, with the U.S. a staunch ally of Israel.

In offering mediation, the Nixon administration promised an evenhanded approach, but U.S.-military support continued to flow to Israel. In effect, the statement of impartiality could not be viewed, at least initially, as a repudiation of the alliance with Israel, since concrete evidence of continuing U.S. support for Israel was obvious. The Kissinger efforts were initially highly successful, producing both troop disengagement agreements and territorial readjustments. However, as the U.S.-Egyptian relationship blossomed, more concessions from Israel were expected. Israeli leaders began to accuse Kissinger of strong pro-Arab sympathies and rejected further concessions. This resulted in the termination of Kissinger's effective mediation role (Kochan, 1981; Pruitt, 1981). Thus, although the Kissinger efforts were effective up to a point, it may be that continuing pressure from an ally for concession to an adversary inevitably erodes the relationship and the leverage of the ally as mediator.

The unsuccessful efforts of Alexander Haig as mediator in the 1981-82 Falkland Islands crisis illustrate a different aspect of the problem of biased mediation. In that case, there is reason to believe that the less-favored party (Argentina) interpreted statements of even-handedness as essentially a repudiation of support for the more favored adversary. Despite stronger ties to

Britain and interests in averting any precedent for armed intervention in the hemisphere (at least armed intervention for purely territorial motives), the United States proclaimed its even-handedness in approaching the conflict. This proclamation (along with contacts promoted with the Argentine delegation to the U.N.) pleased and emboldened Argentina. It implied that while the United States would not endorse forceful occupation of the Falklands by Argentina, neither would it necessarily support British efforts to dislodge Argentine forces. Given that the Argentine government appeared confident of the ultimate success of its unilateral action, such a position on the part of the United States may simply have strengthened Argentina's commitment to its position.

This U.S. stance did not alter Britain's view that its own vital interests were bound up in the Islands and the end of the Argentine occupation. Further, the U.S. position may have led the British to feel that U.S. mediation was likely to move the parties toward a settlement unacceptable to Britain, that is the continued presence of Argentine troops on the Islands. In short, by proclaiming its even-handedness, the United States may have heightened the probability of a military confrontation in the Falklands.

As Harold Kelley (1966) has noted, it is unwise for negotiators to conceal their vital interests in a conflict. The same holds true for a mediator in international conflict, whose own position is that of a negotiator rather than a disinterested broker. To be sure, the United States was concerned not to undermine its emerging Argentine relationship by stating its commitment to Britain, but such was the consequence of failing at mediation in any case. In fact, the United States managed to offend both parties to the conflict by its effort to offend neither.

Of course, the failure of mediation in the Falkland Islands crisis may have been due to factors beyond the control of any mediator. The issue was basically one of national identity on both sides; further, the Falklands crisis had already progressed beyond deadlock and had moved into a phase of commitment to the use of force. It may be that mediators can have little success at such a point. However, the professed impartiality of the U.S. may also have played an important role in the failure of mediation.

Bias in Traditional and International Mediation
In cases of intervention by an interested and powerful mediator — regardless of context — it is important that the mediator's vital interests be clearly communicated to the disputants, just as it is important that the disputants make the mediator aware of their vital interests. The pretense of impartiality in such cases may lure one or both disputants into strategic choices that are at the very least unproductive. It seems possible that the Argentine commitment to military force in the Falklands crisis was in some measure encouraged by the United States' unrealistic presentation of itself as an "even-handed" mediator.

The tactics of U.S. mediation, represented by Kissinger in the Middle East, stand in sharp contrast to the actions taken by the U.S. in the Falklands. While Kissinger made it clear that the U.S. had interests on both sides of the conflict, there was no concealment of the nature of those interests, nor of just how far the U.S. would go in support of either side's demands (Sheehan, 1981). It is also true that the interests and limits of the United States in the

Middle East would have been difficult to conceal: the historical relationship with Israel, and dependence on oil imports from Arab nations. In addition, the United States pursued a highly active role in the Middle East, to such an extent that Kissinger was accused of orchestrating the course of the conflict itself, especially through pressure on Israel. In the Falklands crisis, the United States appeared to take a far more uncertain and passive role. Conceivably, had the U.S. made the unacceptability of Argentine military occupation of the Falkland Islands clear to Argentina before the invasion occurred, the likelihood of military confrontation would have been reduced. The expression of concern over the possibility of such a confrontation is helpful in such cases, but a statement of just what kinds of outcome the mediator would find unacceptable, and what actions the mediator will take should those outcomes be pursued, is surely more effective.

In summary, I have argued that the assumption of mediator impartiality, drawn from analyses of traditional mediation, is unlikely to be met in the context of international conflict. Nonetheless, biased mediation can be effective when the mediator has at least some significant interests in the welfare of both parties and some power over each. In addition, the mediator must clearly acknowledge its own vital interests and their implications in terms of limits on the character of acceptable outcomes. A mediator who claims impartiality but in fact has interests that are clearly bound up in the outcome may do more harm than good.

The contrast I have presented between traditional and international mediation implies that the traditional mediator can and indeed must be identified as totally above the conflict and interested only in helping the parties reach a mutually-acceptable settlement, while the mediator in international conflict must communicate and pursue interests in the conflict in unequivocal fashion. The contrast is much too sharp. Traditional mediators, too, have their interests in the outcome of the conflict. For example, the traditional mediator, in keeping with community standards of justice, has a clear limit on what would be considered a reasonable settlement (Susskind and Ozawa, 1983).

I would suggest that in the traditional context, as well as in the international, such limits must be clearly communicated and pursued with the adversaries if mediation is to be effective. Divorce mediators, for instance, often present their concerns with the welfare of any children involved in a divorce as a focus for settlement (Haynes, 1983). While such concerns are presented as part of an effort to induce a problem-solving orientation (the children being a common concern of the parties), they also signal the mediator's own interests and minimal demands for a settlement. Other external standards may also be emphasized by a traditional mediator, e.g., the prohibition of punitive awards for spouse misbehavior in marriage, or of lopsided settlements that are likely to invite the scorn of the community (as well as grievances by the disadvantaged party) in divorce or labor-management agreements.

Nonetheless, these statements of mediator interest carry a risk. They may result in rejection of mediation when they counter deeply-felt emotion and demands of one of the adversaries, especially if presented early in mediation, when conflict is sharply felt. Delay in presenting these interests may, as in the case of the Falkland Islands crisis, encourage unacceptable positional commitments by one or both of the adversaries.

Traditional theories of mediation are correct in emphasizing the dangers of mediator interests in the conflict to be mediated. Yet such interests seem inevitable. The competent mediator knows when and how to signal such interests, rather than attempting to disavow them.

REFERENCES

Haynes, J. M. (1983). "The Process of Negotiations." *Mediation Quarterly* 1: 75-92.
Kelley, H. H. (1966). "A Classroom Study of the Dilemmas in Interpersonal Negotiations." In *Strategic Interaction and Conflict*, ed. K. Archibald. Berkeley: University of California Press.
Kochan, T. A. (1981). "Step-by-Step in the Middle East from the Perspective of the Labor Mediation Process." In *Dynamics of Third Party Intervention: Kissinger in the Middle East*, ed. J. Z. Rubin. New York: Praeger.
Pruitt, D. G. (1981). "Kissinger as a Traditional Mediator with Power." In *Dynamics of Third Party Intervention: Kissinger in the Middle East*, ed. J. Z. Rubin. New York: Praeger.
Pruitt, D. G. *Negotiation Behavior*. (1981a). New York: Academic Press.
Schelling, T. C. (1960). *The Strategy of Conflict*. Cambridge, Mass.: Harvard University Press.
Sheehan, E. R. F. (1981). "How Kissinger Did It: Step by Step in the Middle East." In *Dynamics of Third Party Intervention: Kissinger in the Middle East*, ed. J. Z. Rubin. New York: Praeger.
Susskind, L. and Ozawa, C. (1983). "Mediated Negotiation in the Public Sector." *American Behavioral Scientist* 27: 255-279.
Touval, S. (1982). *The Peacebrokers*. Princeton, N. J.: Princeton University Press.
Zartman, I. W. (1977). "Negotiation as a Joint Decision-Making Process." *Journal of Conflict Resolution* 21: 619-638.

Bias and Mediators' Ethics

Christopher Honeyman

A recent *Negotiation Journal* article by William Smith (1985) points the way toward a unifying statement of principle which resolves a knotty problem for mediators. Smith (with Saadia Touval and others) has established that, at least in international disputes, biased intervention can be both acceptable to the disputants and successful. This fits in with a trend toward acceptance, or even encouragement, of certain mediator conduct traditionally regarded as biased.

"Traditional" mediators in Smith's use (or "apolitical" in Touval's) have claimed freedom from bias as the cornerstone of their moral authority and even their existence. Perfect neutrality, however, is unobtainable even under the best circumstances. Smith notes the likelihood that a given mediator will acquire a degree of personal bias toward or against one of the parties during the course of a case, even if the mediator began the case personally neutral; and I have identified in another paper (Honeyman, 1985) several structural biases which operate regardless of the mediator's origin or intent.

Such biases as the preference of moderates over radicals, negotiators over principals, and weaker parties over stronger ones are well enough known to experienced parties (albeit perhaps at a "gut level") that such parties have always regarded mediators' protestations of utter neutrality with skepticism. The result is that the traditional theory of mediation is flawed by its failure to account for the inevitability of these biases in real life. It thus creates a false image of even the most neutral mediator obtainable.

At the same time, the current of thought exemplified by Lawrence Susskind (Susskind and Ozawa, 1983) tends to equate certain desirable social goals with responsibilities of the mediator. The perceived duties which result may have many elements, including a duty to inform parties of the "sufficiency" of a settlement, a duty to advance the general "public interest," and a duty to go and find parties of interest not already included in the negotiations. These have already been proposed as ethical requirements for members of the Society of Professionals in Dispute Resolution[1] or elsewhere, and are merely the beginning of what may be a long list.

To "traditional" mediators, these concerns are clear examples of a set of biases which might be called biases of social reform. Recognizing that many of the parties they deal with can be characterized as *opponents* of social reform (at least as to one or another of these issues at a time), these mediators

Christopher Honeyman is Coordinator of Arbitration Services for the State of Wisconsin employment Relations Commission, P.O. Box 7870, Madison, Wis. 53707. He has served as a mediator, arbitrator, and administrative-law judge in labor and environmental issues.

are likely to find such "duties" inconsistent with their perception of neutral status. A schism is thus probable.

Smith's discussion of the successes and failures of biased intervention in international disputes comes close to identifying the principle which resolves this problem. That principle is that parties be given fair notice of the mediator's biases.

The fact that biased intervention has been successful in international disputes can be explained in terms of such notice. Parties in international disputes, each equipped with a diplomatic service, are uniquely qualified to discern the intent of a mediator even when no explicit statement of the mediator's interests is made. In effect, for this reason and because of the "small size of the international community" cited by Smith, these parties are on permanent "constructive notice" of the biases of the intervenor, even when that "neutral" fails to make a fair disclosure. Consequently, such a biased intervention as Kissinger's Middle East effort was acceptable to the parties (and tolerated by hard-line Arab states) largely because no one involved expected him to do anything else. Smith's discussion of the Falklands crisis also supports this view, by saying that the war was likely the result of failure by Argentina to comprehend the U.S.'s true interests as well as failure by the U.S. to explain those interests: In other words, the system of "constructive notice" failed on this occasion.

Outside the "international" arena, such failure can reasonably be expected to be the norm. Even in complex business disputes, the battalions of outside counsel available to the parties are heavily loaded toward specialists in litigation rather than negotiation; and most other fields of dispute display less sophistication than that. We therefore cannot expect parties to allow for these biases unless we tell them, in one way or another.

The obligation of mediators to disclose their *personal* biases has been generally accepted. There is no persuasive reason to excuse the same obligation where it applies to those biases I describe as situational. (These are biases which stem from the intervenor's obligations to persons or parties other than those immediately involved in the dispute. See Honeyman, 1985.) The parties' right to know the institutional interests of an appointing agency, for example, cannot be denied either on ethical or pragmatic grounds. Smith's Falklands example will serve as well as any to show the practical need for this kind of understanding by both parties: If for any reason a party misunderstands the commitments of the intervenor, it is less likely to engage in "principled negotiations" based on a common set of criteria. Settlement is thus less likely, and the probability of a truly disastrous miscalculation of self-interest by that party is significantly increased. On an ethical plane, failure to identify such biases is equally indefensible. It amounts to a claim that "we know what's good for you" to the parties, and deliberately distorts the parties' perception of what they are getting. Mediators who act in this manner prevent the parties from making an informed choice of the type of intervention they want.

By careful analysis of personal interests and those of his or her appointing agency, an intervenor can identify those interests, be they political, social or other, that impinge on his or her function. In many contexts these interests have long been identified to parties, by statutory requirements, agency regulation, handbook, letter or oral explanation. While these "disclosures" are not often labeled as such, competent parties can read between the lines of, for example, an agency rule restricting the availability of mediators to testify in litigation. Such a rule is commonly established in order to protect the confidentiality of discussions; but its tendency to deprive a party seeking to prove bad faith of highly credible evidence is apparent. Its existence is therefore a reminder to parties that mediation can further bad-faith bargaining. This history is sufficient to show the practicality of a "fair notice" principle: It allows sufficient flexibility that different circumstances can be accommodated while we still get the message across.

Identification of those biases I describe as structural, however, is difficult to make on a case-by-case basis, and poses additional problems for a mediator. (Structural biases are those which are inherent in the mediation process. See Honeyman, 1985.) First, these biases, can combine in shifting and unpredictable ways as a case progresses, and their net effect is difficult to calculate. Second, mediators are likely to resist a "fair notice" requirement if it is taken so far as to threaten their effectiveness. A literal reading of the obligation to disclose all biases would imply a duty to point out to a radical faction that the mediator is about to undercut its position by structuring a deal designed to appeal to the majority interest on each side. But saying anything of this nature at the moment when it is most relevant is likely to queer the deal entirely. Yet no one who approves of the American Revolution can maintain that the radicals are always wrong, or that a mediator has an affirmative ethical duty to try to undercut them. It may be that no better warning to parties can be given of the "inherent biases" of mediation than by the "inherent disclosure" of academic publication.

In general, fair notice of bias can serve as the unifying principle which will dispose of much of the confusion over a mediator's ethical obligations. To the extent that some of the biases of mediation are not avoidable by any mediator, as previously noted, publication of their nature in some standardized manner to parties not so sophisticated as to fall under the "constructive notice" principle would do much to alleviate those parties' nagging fears. Notice of the biases described previously as personal and situational should be required on a case-by-case basis, where it is not obvious.[2]

No one is obliged to accept mediation (unlike other neutral functions such as arbitration), and a party confronted with a proposed intervenor known to be biased may choose to reject that intervenor. But I do not agree with Smith that this type of disclosure carries a serious risk of rejection of mediation as a process. Instead, it enables a party to make an informed decision. That decision may often be to accept the intervention and bear in mind the altered uses and interpretations to give to the relationship, for the reasons Smith has noted. The success of mediation attempts known to be biased by all parties shows that parties can be capable of recognizing their overall interest even in the heat of the moment. In the long run, the acceptability of mediation is better served by encouraging the sophistication which makes such choices fruitful than by permitting obfuscation.

NOTES

1. See *Draft Rules of Ethics*, Committee on Ethics, Society of Professionals in Dispute Resolution (1985).

2. The "acquired personal bias" noted by Smith seems to me an example of an obvious bias which requires no explanation to the parties. In my experience, parties who so irritate the mediator as to engender such a bias during the course of the dispute are well aware of that fact.

REFERENCES

Honeyman, C. (1985)."Patterns of Bias in Mediation." *Missouri Journal of Dispute Resolution*: 141-150.

Smith, W. (1985). "Effectiveness of the Biased Mediator." *Negotiation Journal* 1: 363-372.

Susskind L. and **Ozawa, C.** (1983). "Mediated Negotiation in the Public Sector." *American Behavioral Scientist* 27: 255-279.

The Corporate Ombudsman: An Overview and Analysis

Mary P. Rowe

In the past two years, at least fifty North American employers created ombuds offices; the total number of corporate ombuds offices has risen now to an estimated 200. This paper attempts to answer the questions most commonly asked by the CEOs and Human Resource managers exploring the concept. The paper is drawn from the author's 14 years of experience as an ombudsman; from several dozen interviews with corporate ombuds practitioners; and from several pilot surveys conducted from 1982 to 1986 among members of the Corporate Ombudsman Association, by members of the COA Research Committee.

There is no universally accepted definition of an intra-corporate ombudsman. And many companies that have an ombudsman structure call it something else (e.g., Liaison, Work Problems Counsellor, Personnel Communications). Nevertheless, the term "ombudsman" is now growing to be the generic word, amid many corporate "brand names." My definition is a neutral or impartial manager within a corporation, who may provide confidential and informal assistance to managers and employees in resolving work-related concerns, who may serve as a counsellor, go-between, mediator, fact-finder or upward-feedback mechanism, and whose office is located outside ordinary line management structures.

The term "ombudsman" causes discomfort to many who would prefer "ombudsperson." Corporations and practitioners, in fact, use many forms of the word. Some refer to the practitioner as an "ombud" or "ombuds." Many use the term as an adjective, as in "ombuds office" or "ombuds practitioner." Purists speak of an "ombudsman." If the word is to be contracted, neither "ombud" nor "ombuds" is technically more correct; the choice is, therefore, a matter of taste for those who use these terms. This author will use many variations in this paper.

Technically speaking, a pure or classic ombudsman is created by statute and reports (and is paid) *outside* the turf overseen by the office. All intra-institutional practitioners are then, by this definition, "quasi-ombuds." In common parlance in the United States, this distinction has been lost, but it is important to keep in mind when talking with lawyers, non-Americans, and academic specialists who are accustomed to the classical concept.

Mary P. Rowe, a founder of the Corporate Ombudsman Association, is an economist. She is Adjunct Professor at the Sloan School of Management and Special Assistant to the President of the Massachusetts Institute of Technology.

Is a Corporate Ombudsman Really a Neutral?

An ombudsman clearly is *not* an ordinary kind of advocate; this practitioner specifically is not a conventional "employee advocate." But the definitions of "neutrality" and "impartiality" adopted by practitioners vary from company to company.

About half the companies with ombuds offices have designated their practitioners as neutrals. Nearly all expect the practitioner to be at least impartial in all interpersonal interactions, including those with senior managers. (All expect the practitioner to uphold relevant laws, statutes and company policies; one is, in other words, not "neutral" with regard to the law or company policy.)

Practitioners tend to talk about these matters in company-specific terms, such as:

> "I am an advocate for fair *process*, not for any specific person or position."

> "I am impartial and neutral up to the point that I find a law or company policy being flouted."

> "My company believes the long-range interests of the company lie with anyone who has been unfairly treated. If two people have each treated the other unfairly, the company may have an interest on both sides."

Most practitioners simply say, "I have to find solutions that meet many sets of rights and interests," or "The ombudsman will take into account the rights of all employees and managers and the obligations of the company. . . and also the rights of the company and the obligations of employees and managers." In technical terminology, the ombudsman is committed to integrative solutions, and avoids distributive solutions both by the design of the office (an informal, nonadjudicatory structure) and by personal commitment.

In protecting their neutrality, most ombuds practitioners pay particular attention to the issue of recordkeeping. Most keep aggregate statistics, but maintain individual records only briefly or in obscure shorthand. Many would resist a subpoena by attempting in the public interest to have it quashed. About half say they would, if necessary, refuse a subpoena; some also have an agreement with their employers that they will not be called by the company in any court case. (To date, this author knows of no case of an ombudsman being called into a court case, let alone of a subpoena being sustained.) Since most ombuds practitioners are not usually a formal part of any formal grievance procedure and stay out of formal contractual matters, this possible threat to neutrality has not so far been a problem.

But How Can a Manager Inside the Company Really Be Neutral?

Most ombuds practitioners report to the CEO or someone close to the CEO. And most do not have oversight over others who report to that same senior officer. Most practitioners report themselves neutral or impartial with respect to everyone else in the company.

Although observers regularly presume that bosses put a lot of pressure on ombudspeople, in practice ombuds practitioners report relatively little stress over the issue of neutrality. Nearly all can remember one or two attempts to "lean" on them, but this experience is very rare. The ombudsman's neutrality is usually protected by the structure of the situation:

- the office reports to the top;
- most contacts to the office are brief; practitioners are not usually locked into long-term fights, or major battles over company strategy;
- many contacts to the office are inquiries, problems or suggestions rather than solely complaints;
- policy, company ethics, law, and "principle" are usually on the side of the ombudsman;
- practitioners typically avoid polarization and, instead, seek integrative solutions;
- practitioners typically avoid the appearance of close social relationships at work;
- most managers seem to respect and even at times to protect the impartiality of the ombuds office; and
- where there is tension, there are usually powerful forces on all sides that push the practitioner toward a neutral stance. (In fact, quite a number of practitioners report themselves to have become, if anything, far "more neutral" over time, as they continuously hear two or more sides of any given story.)

Confidentiality

All ombuds offices known to this author affirm that they will, if asked, keep the confidence of their visitors "under almost all circumstances." The definition of exempted circumstances varies by practitioner from "I would report illegal activities" to "I would report a situation threatening to life or safety." Most practitioners will not report minor infractions of company policy.

Most practitioners also report they have either never knowingly broken confidentiality, or if so, that this has happened only once or twice. The apparent bind between confidentiality and "duty to warn" is actually less troublesome in practice than in theory. The major reason is that an experienced ombudsman will nearly always find acceptable alternatives: that the ombudsman is given permission to report or investigate a problem using no names, that the client will report the problem directly to responsible managers, that a generic solution can be found which obviates the individual problem, or other responsible recourse.

The development of professional practice with respect to confidentiality will be particularly interesting with the recent advent of a few "ethics officers" or "ethics ombudsmen," among defense contractors. This narrowly-focused, new subgroup has developed in very specific response to concerns about waste, fraud and abuse. General ombuds practitioners hypothesize that this new group will find, as have the rest, that confidentiality is the cornerstone of the perceived trustworthiness of their structure.

Purposes and Functions of Ombuds Practitioners

One important difficulty people experience in thinking about ombudsmanry is that many North Americans view "work problems" as if they were all "complaints." And they associate the term "complaint-handling" with courts, with other formal grievance structures and procedures, and with a wide variety of ideas that have come collectively to carry the name of "due process." (For a list of ideas associated with "due process," please see Appendix One.)

One purpose of an ombudsman *is* clearly to foster and support fair and proper communications and processes. But, typically, the major purpose is to help with a very wide variety of problems and inquiries and concerns at work, in whatever ways are perceived as helpful by the employer and by the managers and employees of the company. For example, one ombudsman has two formal charges:

1. To help every individual manager and employee who comes in, as well as possible; and

2. To get needed information back to line managers (in ways consonant with the privacy and confidentiality of clients) so that the managers will be more effective.

It is obvious that ombuds work may differ a good deal, company by company, as the needs of the company and skills and interests of the practitioner may vary. But these characteristics are clear: An ombudsman is meant to deal with *people* as individuals, and with *problems* as systematically as possible.

The principal functions of an ombudsman are:

• *Dealing With Feelings*
On occasion, living and working bring rage, grief and bewilderment to everyone. Managers and employees often feel there has been "no one to listen." Possibly the most important function of a complaint handler (or complaint system) is to deal with feelings. If this function is not otherwise provided, by line and staff managers, it will fall to the ombudsman.

Sometimes this is in fact all that is needed. Every practitioner has the odd experience of having someone blow up and/or weep for hours in the office, only to report back on the morrow that "everything now seems much better."

At other times, it is critical to help someone with a problem express feelings (for days or weeks or months) before a responsible plan of action can be chosen and undertaken, or before the matter can be appropriately dropped and forgotten.

• *Giving and Receiving Information on a One-To-One Basis*
Many employees do not even know the name of their CEO, much less how the company determines promotions, transfers, or benefits, or how it deals with problems in the work place like harassment. It is therefore very important that line and staff managers be prepared to give out information, and make referrals to helping resources, on a one-to-one basis, at the time and in the fashion needed by an individual with a problem. This may again be all that is needed. If appropriate information and referrals are not made available by other managers, this function may fall to the ombudsman.

An ombudsman may also *receive* vital data. This may, for example, happen with a "whistleblower" who either does not know where to go, or is afraid to go to anyone but a confidential adviser. It is also likely to happen with new problems. That is, an ombudsman is likely to be the bellwether or early warning device for whatever problems the employer has not yet met, but will soon have to deal with. Examples of such problems include sexual harassment in the early 1970s, AIDS in the early 1980s, and now new kinds of drug problems.

- *Counselling and Problem-Solving to Help the Manager or Employee Help Himself or Herself*

Many employees and managers face tenacious problems with only three alternatives in mind: to quit, to put up with their problem, or to start some formal process of complaint, or suit or investigation.

These are not the only alternatives, nor are they always the best available. The skilled ombudsman will help a visitor develop and explore and role-play new options, then help the visitor choose an option, then follow-up to see that it worked. And in many cases, the best option may be for the person with a problem to seek to deal with it effectively on his or her own.

Many people would prefer to "own" their own concerns and, if possible, learn how to deal on their own with their difficulties, if effective options to do so can be developed and pursued. Thus, a critical function for the ombudsman is not only to "give a fish to the hungry person," but "to teach how to fish." Many senior ombuds practitioners therefore function frequently as in-house consultants, to employees and managers, rather than intervening directly in every case.

These first three functions are available on a confidential basis. (Ombuds practitioners report many discussions on the phone at night or at outside restaurants, or even occasionally with a person who wishes to remain anonymous, if the topic is particularly sensitive.)

- *Shuttle Diplomacy*

Sometimes a visitor will opt for a go-between. This is especially true where one or more parties need to save face or deal with emotions before a good solution can be found. This is much the most common type of intervention reported by ombuds practitioners, especially if the company is quite hierarchical in style and organization. In some companies, this function may also be pursued by the ombudsman — during or between the steps of a formal, complaint-and-appeal, grievance process — as an option for settling outside any adjudicatory process.

- *Mediation*

At other times, a visitor will choose the option of meeting *with* others, together with the ombudsman. Like shuttle diplomacy, this usually happens on an informal basis. However, the "settlements" of shuttle diplomacy and mediation may be made formal by the parties involved.

- *Investigation*

Investigation of a problem or a complaint can be formal or informal, with or without recommendations to an adjudicator — for example, to a grievance committee or to a line or senior manager. All four of these investigatory options are reported by ombuds practitioners, and are more or less common depending on the company and the ombudsman.

- *Adjudication or Arbitration*

This function is very rare for the ombudsman. Here, the classic phrase about ombuds practitioners is likely to obtain: "They may not make or change or set aside a management rule or decision; theirs is the power of reason and persuasion."

Even those few practitioners who do have arbitration power use it very rarely, for this is seen to be the province of line management. In some companies, however, the ombudsman may facilitate or chair formal grievance processes (as a nonvoting neutral).

• *Upward Feedback*

Possibly the most important function of the ombudsman is to receive, perhaps analyze, then pass along information that will foster timely change in a company. Where policies are outdated or unintelligible, or new problems have arisen, or a new diversity appears in the employee pool, an ombudsman may be a low-key, steady-state change agent at very low cost to the employer.

This function also provides a mechanism for dealing with some very difficult confidentiality problems. An ombudsman can, for example, suggest that a department head instigate an apparently "routine," department-wide discussion about safety or harassment or waste-management or theft, in response to an individual concern, at no cost to anyone's privacy or rights, in such a way as to eliminate an individual problem (if not necessarily the perpetrator).

Ombuds practitioners appear to vary a good deal as to how they spend their time. Some observers believe that the prior career of the ombudsman may influence ombuds practice. A former Employee Assistance practitioner may primarily listen, counsel, and help with transfers. A former engineer or top manager or group leader may spend more time helping the system to change.

It also may be that an ombudsman will "pick up" whatever functions other managers are performing least well, or that an ombuds office simply responds to varying company problems. And ombuds practice may change over the career of the practitioner. Several long-term practitioners report they now intervene less, and spend more time as in-house consultants, helping managers and employees deal directly with their concerns.

Pilot surveys among Corporate Ombudsman Association members indicate that ombudsmen spend about one-third of their time on upward feedback and systems change, with formal mediation the least common activity of ombuds practitioners.

Relationships Between Ombudsmen and Other Line and Staff Managers

Ombuds practitioners are often asked what other managers think of them: "Don't they hate you?" No one wants to answer "yes" to this question, and for a practitioner to answer at all may be disingenuous. However, some data suggest that 90-95 percent of all line and staff managers feel relatively comfortable about an ombuds office, at least after the second or third year of its existence.

For one thing, managers tend to seek out ombuds practitioners proportionately more often than do employees, at least by the ombudsman's second year. Experienced and self-confident managers, especially technical managers, seem especially likely to seek assistance. Managers tend to bring in new, usually painful, and sometimes bizarre management problems, or to come in with their own personal concerns. The general rule that most clients are most satisfied with mediation-oriented problem solving may also be partly responsible for the considerable acceptance of ombuds by other managers.

Moreover, most ombuds practitioners avoid any appearance of substantive decisionmaking, work hard to get line managers the data they need to manage better, and place great emphasis on the protection of everyone's privacy, including that of line managers. The typical ombudsman wants line managers to get the credit for any constructive changes that occur — and never, or almost never, uses the name of the boss to get something to happen. The role of the practitioner is support rather than competition. In addition, most ombuds practitioners take on themselves full responsibility for getting along with other managers, in the spirit of commitment to the employer and to the team.

It is quite common to find that the ombudsman conforms his or her working style considerably to the style of other senior managers. Thus, if a department head says, "Fix anything you can; the more time you save for me the better!" the ombudsman may scarcely see that department head, and will problem-solve at the lowest possible level. If a department head says, "Look, let me know if you can, when you're on my turf," the ombudsman is more likely to seek permission to do just that. To the employee in that area, the ombudsman may say, "Look, how do you feel if you or I let Sandy McHierarch know about this problem? You know old Mac really cares about knowing what's going on; would it make sense to touch base with Mac?"

Sometimes, the ombudsman has been asked to intervene and needs to decide whether to go first to the immediate supervisor (who will desperately want this to happen), or to go first to the department head. Much will depend on the facts of the case, on the known wishes of the department head, and on who first returns the ombuds' call. But most ombuds practitioners will start at the lowest relevant level, if only because that supervisor may prefer to be the one who goes to the department head. (The practitioner who plans generally to follow this approach is probably well-advised to discuss this contingency, early on, with the department heads.)

Another reason for the generally agreeable relations with line and staff managers is the constant cross-referral that occurs. Most ombuds practitioners consult with and refer continuously to helpful line managers; Employee Assistance; Equal Opportunity staff; relevant security/police officers; and especially, to every variety of Human Resource professional in the company. Referrals to health care practitioners, religious counsellors, marriage counsellors, divorce attorneys, and a wide variety of other professionals are also common. Frequent consultation with company counsel is typical for many ombuds practitioners.

The commonest source of referrals to an ombuds office are, likewise, line managers and staff professionals, as other colleagues seek to build a safety net for employees and managers with problems. The close interdependence of the ombudsman and other colleagues thus powerfully reinforces the sense of a team rather than of turf. Or, alternatively speaking, one may simply note that almost no one really wants to "own" the most serious people problems at work; most sensible managers are only too glad to "share" such problems.

Why Would a CEO Want an Ombuds Office in Addition to Employee Relations and Employee Assistance?[1]

This is a question best answered by current ombuds practitioners who once were Employee Relations and Employee Assistance professionals. They usually say, "Because more and different problems come to the ombuds office."

Those ombuds practitioners who have held both Employee Relations and ombuds jobs note that some people will choose an ombuds office for reasons that include:

- because it is seen as neutral;
- because someone they once knew did not trust the Employee Relations (or Personnel Office);

- because they do not like the specific Employee Relations or Personnel officer assigned to them, or think "their supervisor eats lunch with that person";
- because they do not want this problem in their (real or imaginary) personnel file;
- because some Employee Relations offices increasingly handle administrative matters like benefits, rather than listening to people;
- because the concerned person has no idea where to go or hates formal grievance procedures;
- because the problem is seen as bizarre or embarrassing or shameful;
- because there is a hidden agenda (for example, to seek referral to a counsellor or clergy), and they would rather get there via an ombudsman;
- because the ombudsman is seen as close to the CEO and they want to take an ethical or whistleblowing problem up higher. Ombuds practitioners who come out of Employee Assistance often note that the problems brought to the ombuds office are more directly work-related, including for example, safety and ethics issues, and require detailed knowledge of the individual company.

It seems also to be true that "more" problems will surface, or surface earlier, if any additional communications channel is added within a company. Some of these problems may never need to have surfaced, but it seems clear that a small, significant group of problems brought to an alternative channel either are extremely serious or would have become so. This certainly appears true in the experience of ombuds offices which regularly get a small number of new, or very peculiar problems of some gravity.

CEOs who have added an ombuds office usually justify its creation by one or more of these three statements:

- the office more than pays for itself — it is cost-effective;
- the rights and responsibilities of employees and of the company are well supported by such an office;
- it is humane and caring human resource policy to have such an office.

It should be noted that a number of companies with an in-house Employee Assistance program have decided to locate the Employee Assistance and ombuds offices in the same place. This is especially true where both functions are available to managers and employees via an 800 telephone line, as well as in person.

It may also be noted that this "Who needs it?" question parallels an older, similar question as to why one wants any Human Resource functions at all, when all the functions of the Human Resource Department also might lodge with line supervision. The practical answer to that question is, of course, that many line supervisors are promoted for technical skills, and that many do not have all the human resource management skills needed by the company. In addition, most employers wish to provide an option for managers and employees who want advice and data they do not get from line supervisors.

The parallel is an important one. As Human Resource managers are not there to replace line management, ombuds practitioners are not there to replace either Human Resource or line managers.

The purpose of an ombuds office, in particular, is continuously to put itself out of a job by supporting clients and regular line and staff offices so that they can deal effectively with each question and problem that arises. With respect to each concern brought to the office, the ombudsman's job is back-up, fail-safe, check and balance, rather than turf building. In this context, it is important to note that a high proportion of referrals to ombuds offices come from Human Resource Management, Employee Assistance, Equal Opportunity, Medical, line supervision and other colleagues.

What Kinds of Problems Does an Ombudsman Handle?

Many ombuds offices now keep careful statistics. Pilot surveys indicate that once an office is up and running, it appears to get calls from two to eight percent of the constituent community each year. Practitioners commonly report a considerable fraction of very brief contacts to the office (which may or may not be serious problems).

One practitioner estimates about one-tenth of the contacts to the office concern rather serious problems in terms of (potential) disruption to the individual and/or the company. Another practitioner estimates that, at any given time, the "open" office case load runs at about 12-15 percent of the yearly caseload, indicating that many problems can be resolved rather promptly.

Common topics include salary and benefits; promotion and demotion; performance appraisals; job security and retirement issues; company policies; discipline/termination; discrimination and harassment; safety, ethics and whistleblowing; transfers; personality conflicts/meanness; information/referral; suggestions; working conditions; personal health, mentoring, and counselling issues; management practices; bizarre behavior and problems. Established offices that are reasonably well-known in a sizable company will see all these kinds of contacts each year. The profile of concerns, however, varies somewhat from company to company.

A majority of ombuds practitioners in companies where at least some employees are unionized, do see bargaining unit employees. Union employees are however appropriately referred elsewhere if they bring up concerns that are covered by the union contract. Ombuds offices are typically very respectful of their local unions and practitioners commonly report good relations with bargaining unit officers. In fact, many an ombudsman has had union officers as clients in the office.

How Effective Are Ombuds Offices?

Most offices seem to be evaluated on the basis of intuition, word of mouth, "happy client" letters and the like. Some practitioners, in fact, believe their formal reports are not widely read.

Corporate Ombudsman Association practitioners have given this subject careful review and are pursuing cost-effectiveness analyses. Thus far their hypotheses focus on three main areas: client use, policy changes, and cost-savings.

• *Client Use*

To some extent, an office can be evaluated on the basis of its client use rate. Successful offices are seen to be those which are quite busy, with 2-8 percent of the community making contact each year. Possibly of equal importance, some offices appear to attract clients who mirror the company population by race, gender, pay classification, shift, etc. If the office attracts clients rather randomly from the total company community, one may hypothesize that the office is seen to be relatively fair in its service to managers, employees, women and men, minorities and nonminorities.

Several ombuds practitioners have attempted to estimate what proportion of their clients are "satisfied." Their estimates of the "satisfied" range from 50 to 90 percent. One practitioner reckoned in his first year that 55 percent of his visitors received positive help, and another 30 percent expressed appreciation, although no substantive change occurred in the situation they reported. Another practitioner also estimates that 10-20 percent of her case load feels that "nothing much was done," with about 50-60 percent receiving at least some immediate improvement with the problems reported. A number of practitioners have reported that they receive unusually favorable ratings in routine employee attitude surveys.

It should also perhaps be noted that it is common, both in research and anecdotally, to find that most people prefer problem solving to mediation, and prefer mediation to adjudication. Results of this sort are also relatively stable whether those queried feel they "won" or "lost" their original point of view. It would therefore be expected that employee and manager satisfaction would usually be higher where people perceive that their concerns are addressed in a problem-solving mode, and where their complaints are addressed if possible through mediation or shuttle diplomacy.

In my own experience, this common tilt toward informal, mediation-oriented problem solving is not universal. Some people, probably at least 10 percent of ordinary U.S. work populations, prefer adjudication of work problems. If this estimate is correct, it underscores the point that employers need to provide *both* well-understood, fair, formal grievance procedures and informal counselling and mediation processes. Further, it appears likely that morale will be higher if managers and employees feel they have some choice in what kind of procedures they will use.

• *Policy Changes*
Many ombuds practitioners report informally and constantly to line managers throughout the system, as they are given permission by clients to do so. As a result, the typical ombudsman can name a great many changes in policies and procedures and structures that resulted from information flowing through the ombuds office. (Most practitioners feel this steady-state, upward feedback is far more important than their formal annual reports.) No serious studies have yet been made of this low-key, change-agent phenomenon (nor estimates made of whether similar or better changes might not have occurred in the absence of the ombuds offices). Nevertheless, the change-agent role is widely perceived by practitioners to be valuable.

One important aspect of this role is when an ombudsman "picks up" a new problem that will prove to be very important to the company. This "early warning" has helped a number of companies prepare early for dealing with problems like the fear of AIDS.

• *Cost Savings*
Most practitioners have many examples of costs-savings attributable to their offices. Typical examples include: keeping very valuable employees who would otherwise have left; averting expensive litigation or damaging publici-

ty; preventing or averting theft or sabotage; timely apprehension of unsafe or unethical practices; timely intervention in cases of bizarre or psychotic behavior; introduction of cost-saving or damage-prevention or morale-enhancing suggestions from employees.

In addition, practitioners hypothesize some reductions in absenteeism, sick and disability leave, and turnover, as a result of their work. And many practitioners believe their work enhances the productivity of others, especially if some particularly good idea is adopted by a line manager.

No careful studies have yet been done on any one office, although any one of the cost-savings here attributed to ombuds offices might more than pay the annual cost of a given office. To date there is also no known case of major costs or damages attributed to a corporate ombudsman. Practitioners, as a profession, have a firm belief in the cost-effectiveness of their offices.

Who Becomes an Ombudsman? How Should an Employer Choose an Ombudsman?

Casual survey of about 50 U.S. ombuds practitioners reveals wide diversity of backgrounds. At least 90 percent worked for the present employer before being chosen as an ombudsman and were "picked from within," so most ombudspeople have in common the facts that they have previously known their companies and been personally trusted by their employers. But in most other respects, practitioners are diverse.

About half are women and a significant minority are black, Hispanic and Asian. Some came from Employee Assistance or Equal Opportunity offices; one or two were internal counsel. Many were line managers, and perhaps a quarter were quite senior line managers, deliberately taking on a "last career" within the company. Many knew the CEO or other very senior executives well. Some have developed the job from related Employee Relations or Human Resource Management positions. The college and graduate school majors of ombuds practitioners were diverse, including some with engineering, economics and management degrees. In addition, many have come from social work, counselling, liberal arts, divinity studies, and other disciplines.

When this author is asked about choosing an ombudsman, she usually recommends "finding a person to whom colleagues naturally turn," or "picking someone who may be doing the job anyway." "Natural mediators" in the company are actually quite easy to identify, and are usually well-known to their peers as effective troubleshooters and sympathetic listeners and counsellors. They typically have a reputation for dealing fairly and comfortably with both employees and managers, and with people of different races, religions, income and gender.

The typical ombudsman will comfortably take high emotional risks but is not an entrepreneurial risk taker. The effective practitioner will be seen as an excellent listener. This person likes almost everyone, finds it easy to imagine "the other side of the story," finds it easy to "separate the people from the problem," and may actually say how interesting it is that one can like someone whose behavior is inappropriate.

An ombudsman typically has no particular need to rush off to act in the face of a harrowing tale, and in fact finds a sense of accomplishment in helping other people help themselves. Nevertheless, the successful practitioner is capable of recognizing an emergency and prepared if necessary to take decisive, swift action. Most practitioners are very curious about other people and about management dilemmas, but seem to have a low need for power and public accolade; many in fact are somewhat shy.

The effective ombudsman appears comfortable as a neutral, and relatively comfortable with paradox, and may be known for not leaping quickly to conclusions. The practitioner is likely to be very sensitive to "data," to be somewhat analytic, and to be interested in problem solving and in puzzles for their own sake. Most are very independent people, who can either deal peacefully with high emotion from others, or who quickly learn how to give that impression. Most also are — or become — very circumspect at work, avoiding major social issues (like abortion or politics) where responsible people do not agree with each other.

An ombudsman must be able to speak well and succinctly, and to write constantly and comfortably. The practitioner should learn a considerable body of employment law, at least a little about common personality types and disorders, and a great deal about company goals, policies and customs. The practitioner must be willing to deal with anyone and with any kind of problem with consistent courtesy, and must be willing to try to work together with any colleague, no matter how difficult.

In some companies, the ombuds role is filled for two or three years at a time by managers on the way up. In other companies, the position is deliberately one's "last" career step, to guarantee an experienced manager and to underscore the protection of objectivity of the ombudsman. Sometimes, the job appears to be just another Human Resource Management option within the company. And in some companies, the original incumbent sees the ombuds job as a profession and will very likely continue. There are a number of cases of practitioners who have served successive CEOs, and a number of cases of original incumbents who have turned over the job to successors.

Part-Time and Multiple Ombudsman Options

Small companies and single plants often have one or more part-time ombuds practitioners. Typically where there is more than one part-time or full-time ombudsman, the different practitioners are chosen from different population groups: minority, nonminority; technical, nontechnical; male, female; Spanish-speaking, English-speaking; and so on.

Some employers have opted to employ several, part-time, "internal mediators." In their ombuds role, such practitioners closely resemble the ombudspeople described earlier, whatever their other job assignments. Practitioners in this role typically practice independently, but meet together regularly (discussing cases with strict guidelines for protecting the confidentiality of their clients). In some models, any employee or manager may approach any practitioner anywhere in the company. In other models, different employee groups have different practitioners. Despite the obvious potential for conflicts of interest, part-time ombudspeople report few difficulties with their (informal, nonadjudicatory) ombuds role.

In larger companies, an ombudsman will have assistants, often of different race and gender. In this model, the practitioners keep common records and may consult together, although typically any manager or employee may choose to consult anyone in the office.

In order to keep a practitioner "close" to the given population group, very large companies may designate one practitioner per plant. In other very large companies, most ombuds work is done via an 800 telephone line to a central, multi-practitioner office. In practice, each of these options appears to work well.

Is the Emphasis on Ombudsmanry Something New?

Ombudsmanry is a relatively old concept. People who served this kind of function appeared in rabbinical courts, as court jesters, as troubleshooters, etc., over the ages. The first classic ombudsman appeared in Sweden at the beginning of the 19th century. Classical ombuds offices now appear in many countries.

Designated neutrals within corporations are a relatively new concept. Managers with ombuds-like functions appeared here and there between the World Wars in a few companies. But serious interest in the United States began in the late 1960s and grew only slowly until the 1980s.

Increasing heterogeneity in the workforce, rapidly changing laws and statutes, an increasingly well-educated employee pool, and stresses associated with huge increases in government contracting, have all led to increased recent interest in ombudsmanry. Contributing to the sense of a zeitgeist is the fact that ombuds-like structures and offices have appeared spontaneously and independently in many different companies and also elsewhere in the economy.

In North America, there are about 100 ombuds offices in colleges and universities, an estimated 200 in corporations. Three dozen newspapers have an ombudsman. Nearly 4,000 hospitals have patient ombuds offices and a great many businesses have client or consumer complaint offices. Each state has a nursing home/long-term care ombuds structure, and there appear to be about 1,500 part-time and full-time ombudspeople attached to those offices. In addition, there are perhaps two dozen classical ombuds offices in states, provinces and cities, and scattered practitioners for prisons and other institutions. Some radio and television stations and newspapers also have citizen's complaint or citizen's service structures, as do also mayors' and governors' offices.

In sum, the ombudsman concept is very varied and currently very lively. There is almost no general rule about ombuds offices that holds true for all such offices. But the overall ideas of listening to people as individuals, and of trying to deal with problems at an early stage, are clearly ideas of current interest to a wide variety of employers.

NOTES

The National Institute for Dispute Resolution provided generous financial support for the research and writing of this article. The opinions expressed herein are solely those of the author.

1. See Appendix Two for a more detailed description of typical characteristics of persons who use a complaint system and relevant specifications for an effective complaint system.

APPENDIX ONE

ELEMENTS OF DUE PROCESS

(As commonly recognized in the United States)

I. Due process seen as a matter of specific elements of grievance procedure, for example:
• Notice to the defendant; right to know the charges. In some cases, right to know accuser;

- Timeliness of process and to each step of the process;
- Right to present own evidence;
- In some cases, right to question the evidence brought by the other side; and in some cases, right to face or meet with the accuser;
- Right to answer the concerns that are raised;
- Right to accompaniment and someone to advise; in some cases, right to legal counsel;
- A fair and impartial fact finding; a fair and impartial hearing;
- Right to a decision that is not capricious, arbitrary or unreasonable in nature;
- Notice of the decision; in some cases, right to a written decision with a statement of reasons for the decision;
- In some cases, right to an appeal process;
- Freedom from retaliation for raising a complaint in a responsible manner;
- In some cases, a regard for the privacy of all concerned.

II. Due process seen as "that which is due" under the circumstances. Sometimes people use the term loosely to mean just "the process that I deserve," whether as a matter of law, company policy, or just as a matter of what an individual perceives as "fair."

• • • •

Seen in the context of this list of specific elements of grievance procedure, it is evident that an ombuds office is not primarily a due process structure. Seen in the context of "fostering the process to which a person feels entitled," part of an ombudsman's work clearly relates to fair process, although the terms seem too ambiguous to be very useful.

APPENDIX TWO

TYPICAL CHARACTERSTICS OF PERSONS USING A COMPLAINT SYSTEM AND RELEVANT SPECIFICATIONS FOR AN EFFECTIVE COMPLAINT SYSTEM

I. Most people who use a complaint system:
- greatly fear retaliation;
- greatly fear loss of privacy; this concern may hold with respect to family members as well as with respect to those at the work place);
- fear they will be seen to be disloyal;
- have widely differing views of whom they will trust among complaint handlers;
- do not wish to lose control over their concern or complaint;
- feel they lack the skills they need effectively to change the situation;
- think it is probably pointless to try to complain;
- just want the problem to stop; (a desire for punishment or revenge against an alleged offender is relatively rare).

II. An effective complaint system must therefore:
- offer a chance to deal with feelings, learn appropriate information and seek counselling *on a confidential basis*;
- have redundant* channels and options, so people have a chance to choose among multiple modes and access points (for example, supervisors, and HRM, anonymous hot lines, ombuds offices, QWL groups, etc.);
- have at least one general channel that is used more or less proportionately by everyone in the company, managers and employees (for example, an ombuds office, hot line, etc.);
- have formal as well as informal complaint handling procedures open to the choice of the complainant; the formal process(es) must be perceived as fair;
- offer to most complainants the option to learn how to handle their concerns directly, on their own, or to ask for third party assistance (shuttle diplomacy, mediation or adjudication), or to seek a generic (systemic) approach;
- proscribe retaliation by supervisors and be known to take action against proven retaliation by supervisors, peers and subordinates;
- encourage responsible concerns by appropriate protection of the rights of complainants, the managers involved, and of all others involved in a complaint;
- be seen to produce some change in the treatment of individuals and with respect to policies and procedures and structures in the organization.

* "Redundant" here is used in the engineering sense of fail-safe, back-up checks and balances.

Subject Index

Accountability, 33, 35
Action, 30
Added value, 8
Agenda, setting of, 394
Agents, 81-88
  detachment of, 83
  effects of using in negotiation, 81
  effects on artifice and duplicity, 86-87
  expertise and, 81-83
  multilateral negotiation and, 357
  problems in using, 84-87
  reasons for using, 81-84
  tactical flexibility of, 83-84
Alternatives to negotiation, 97-113
  committing and, 107-108
  determination of, 97, 99
  evaluation of, 97, 99, 100-103
  improvement of, 98
  manipulation of, 111
  perceptions about the attractiveness of,
    103-105
  power of, 105-106, 132-133
  worsening over time of, 101-102
Analytical intervention, 89-93
Apologies
  obstacles to, 142
  timing of, 143-144
  use in negotiation, 141-144
Arab-Israeli negotiations, 60-69, 225-232
Arafat, Yasir, 62
Arbitration, 19, 20, 304, 305-307, 437
  as alternative to negotiation, 111
  conventional, 305-306
  final offer, 306-307
  med-arb, 306
Aspirations, 28
Associational unionism, 376-378
Bargaining
  collective, 100, 369-372
  positional, 29
  range, estimation of, 106
  "residue" effects of hard, 10-11
  tactics, experimenting with different
    styles of, 10
BATNA, 99, 112 (*n*), 116-117,

  defined, 116
  importance of not revealing, 116
  power of a good, 132-133
Begin, Menachem, 65
Behavioral analysis, 152-153
Berlin crisis, 42
Bias
  in mediation, 419-428, 429-432
Bilateral negotiation, 351, 369-371
Borman, Frank, 211-216
Bottom line, 7
Brayton Point (Mass.)
  mediation of, 404-405
Brainstorming, 125
Bunche, Ralph, 247
Bridging, 27
Camp David, 9, 57, 63, 226
Chicken, game of, 10
Coalitions
  analysis of, 99, 156-157
  as facilitating factor, 356-357
Coercion, 10
Commitment
  conflict escalation and, 202-203
  negative, 135-138
  power of, 134-135
  to negotiated settlement, 65-68,
    107-108
Concession making, importance of, 119,
    151-152
Concession rate, 32
Conflict
  analysis of, 5-6
  constructive uses of, 14, 17-18, 20-21
  costs of, 39
  cultural assumptions and, 6
  de-escalation of, 223-232
  definitions of, 3
  escalation of, 202-203, 211-216, 339
  fractionation of, 15-16
  history of interest in, 1, 2
  intractable, 58
  methods of dealing with, 14, 295-313
  nature of, 13-26
  "residues" and, 10-11

Kissinger, Henry
  mediation efforts of, 422, 425-426
  "shuttle diplomacy" and, 59, 66, 226
Khomeini, Ayatollah, 67
Legitimacy, power of, 133-134
Linkage, 357-358
Logrolling, 27, 34
Long-term relationships, importance of,
  123-124
"Loop-backs", 303-305
Mediation, 302-303, 359-361, 437
  ethics and, 429-432
  international, 413-414, 420-424, 430
  labor, 411-413
  measuring success of, 407-409
  models of, 411-414
  negotiation in relation to, 76
  obstacles to, 414-416
  public sector disputes and, 401-418
  role of apologies in, 141-142
  traditional, 419-420, 429
Mediator
  bias, 419-428
  responsibilities of, 409-411
Middle East
  1967 War in, 49, 59
  1973 War in, 49-51, 59, 226
  de-escalation and, 225-232
  "peace process" in, 59-69
"Mini-trials", 304
"Mock pseudo-negotiation", 89-93
  limitations of, 92
Multilateral negotiation, 156-157, 351-365
  agenda-setting and, 394
  in labor-management setting, 307-320
  participants in, 391-394
  structure of, 394-396
Mood, 34
Nasser, Gamel, 60
NATO, 351
Negotiated Investment Strategy,
  in Connecticut, 405-407
Negotiation
  agreement phase of, 354-355
  alternatives to, 10, 97-113
  "analytical intervention" into, 89-93
  anticipated future interaction and, 7, 34
  apologies and, 141-144
  approaches to, 147-159
  aspirations in, 28
  assumptions about, 8, 187-193

behavioral analysis and, 152-153
bilateral, 351
changing functions of, 75
common elements in, 147-159
conditions of uncertainty in, 50-51
context of, 195-225
crisis and, 47-54
culture and, 233-251
definition of, 147-148, 154
diagnostic phase of, 58
direct v. representative, 81-88
dual roles in, 76
economic v. relational focus and, 7
"firm flexibility" and, 28
"fixed pie" assumption and, 116
framing and, 197-200
gender and, 234, 261-277
high stakes and, 48-49
impediments to, 355-356
implementation and, 8, 291-348
importance of relationship in, 7
intangible interests and, 168-171
integrative approach to, 15, 16-17
integrative analysis and, 153-154
interests v. positions and, 9, 15, 63-64,
    115, 161-180, 200-202, 297-299
internal v. external, 71-79
judgment and, 197-209
limits to, 98-99
"loop-backs" and, 303-305
"mock pseudo", 89-93
motivation and, 299-300
multilateral, 156-157
mythical "fixed pie" of, 200-202
opening offers and, 8-9
options and, 115-116
outcomes in, 148
overconfidence and, 203-205
perceived feasibility and cost of, 35-40
personality and, 187-193, 234, 279-290
phases of, 7-8, 18-19, 352-356
"post-settlement settlement", 323-326,
    327-329, 331-340
power and, 119-122, 125, 127-140,
preparation and, 68-99,
process analysis and, 151-152, 355-356
psychological barriers to, 67
removing obstacles to, 61-68
renegotiation and, 341-348
"single-text" procedure and, 9, 91-92,
    181-185

Author Index

Page numbers listed in italic type include full references.